BARRON'S

LSAT®

12TH EDITION

JERRY BOBROW, PH.D.
Executive Director, Bobrow Test Preparation Services
Programs at major universities, colleges, and law schools throughout California
Lecturer, consultant, author of over 30 nationally known test preparation books
Dr. Bobrow personally instructs over 2,000 LSAT test takers each year

Contributing Authors and Consultants

William A. Covino, Ph.D.
Provost
California State University
Stanislaus, California

Brian N. Siegel, J.D.
Bar Review Specialist
Author/Legal Study Aids

Merritt L. Weisinger, J.D.
Attorney at Law, Lecturer
Weisinger and Associates

David A. Kay, M.S.
Chairman, Math Department
Moorpark College, California

Daniel C. Spencer, M.S.
Management Services Officer
University of California at
Los Angeles (UCLA)

Keith R. Strange, M.P.A.
Educational Administrator
Junipero Serra H.S., California

Bernard V. Zandy, M.S.
Professor, Math Department
Fullerton College, California

Allan Casson, Ph.D.
Former Chairman, Department
of English
University of Southern California
(USC)

Jean Eggenschwiler, M.A.
Writer, Author, Editor

BARRON'S

In Memory of

Dean Seymour Greitzer
May 21, 1924–March 3, 2000

Founder and Dean
Glendale University College of Law
Glendale, California

Dean Greitzer was devoted to his family and to his community. As one who touched many lives, he was a great humanitarian and a good friend.

All inquiries should be addressed to:
Barron's Educational Series, Inc.
250 Wireless Boulevard
Hauppauge, New York 11788
http://www.barronseduc.com

Paper Edition
ISBN-13 (book only): 978-0-7641-3638-2
ISBN-10 (book only): 0-7641-3638-0

ISBN-13 (with CD-ROM): 978-0-7641-9319-4
ISBN-10 (with CD-ROM): 0-7641-9319-8

International Standard Serial No. 1936-0185

PRINTED IN THE UNITED STATES OF AMERICA

9 8 7 6 5 4 3 2 1

Contents

Preface

The LSAT is a difficult exam and we want to give you every possible advantage!

In this book we have gathered the expertise and materials developed in over 30 years of successful LSAT, GMAT, GRE, CSET, NTE, CBEST, MSAT, RICA, ELM, and SAT preparation courses that are currently offered at over 25 universities, colleges, and law schools.

So how are we going to give you every possible advantage?

By thoroughly analyzing each of the sections of the LSAT and reviewing the thinking processes and the skills necessary for top performance, this text aims at complete preparation. It is up to date with the most recent forms of the latest test. The staff of writers and consultants includes specialists in problem solving, reading, writing, logic, law, and test psychology. All these authors and consultants have been teaching prelaw students in LSAT preparation programs for many, many years.

An introductory mini-exam will both acquaint you with the format of the LSAT and help you spot any of your test-taking weaknesses. Then, a series of insightful chapters on the most recent sections of the test will carefully analyze each question type, pinpoint specific test-taking strategies, and give additional practice. Six full-length practice tests will allow you to get the feel of the real thing while you begin applying new skills and techniques. Your answer sheet will resemble the machine-graded LSAT answer sheet, and an analysis chart will enable you to assess your strengths and weaknesses. The answers to each practice test are fully explained.

Will this be effective?

Complete analysis, thorough instruction, extensive practice, up-to-date examples, and the most successful overall systems of objective test taking are described in detail in this book to give you invaluable insight into the LSAT. The test-taking strategies and approaches we've included have been proven effective for over 2,000,000 graduate and undergraduate students and teachers whom we've assisted in preparing for these important exams.

All right, let's get down to business and start with a brief overview of how to prepare for the LSAT.

Preparing for the LSAT: A Five-Step Approach

Preparing to take the LSAT is no easy task; it takes a well thought-out, focused study plan. This plan should follow these five basic steps:

1. Awareness
2. Knowing the Basic Skills
3. Understanding the Thinking Processes
4. Applying Strategies and Techniques
5. Practice, Practice, Practice

AWARENESS

Before taking the LSAT, you should know everything possible about the test from the length of each section to the specific types of questions. Be an expert on the structure and construction of the exam.

The LSAT consists of five 35-minute multiple-choice sections. Four sections count toward your LSAT score; one experimental section is a repeat of the other sections and does not count toward your score. An unscored essay is also included. The types of questions are: Reading Comprehension (one section), Analytical Reasoning (one section), and Logical Reasoning (two sections).

Reading Comprehension—one section that includes four fairly sophisticated passages or passage sets, each ranging from about 400 to 600 words with 5 to 8 questions per passage for a total of about 26 to 28 questions. The passages can be from the fields of science, philosophy, economy, history, law, and so on, but the questions must be answered from the actual passages given, not from your general or specific knowledge of a subject.

Analytical Reasoning—one section that includes four sets of conditions, statements, or rules. You are required to see the relationships among the items being described and discussed. Constructing a simple display or diagram using the information given is an important part of attacking this question type. Each set is followed by 5 to 7 questions for a total of 22 to 24 questions. This section appears to be the most difficult for most test takers, but it also appears to be the most preparable.

Logical Reasoning—two sections that include short passages, statements, arguments, or discussions, each followed by usually 1 question (sometimes 2) asking about the reasoning involved. Each section contains between 24 and 26 questions. This question type requires good reading and reasoning skills and accounts for 50 percent of your LSAT score. You will have two sections of Logical Reasoning, about 50 of the 100 questions that count toward your score. A course in formal logic is not necessary but could be helpful, as would any course that requires critical reading and reasoning.

These sections total from 96 to 104 questions and are scaled to a scoring range of 120 to 180 with an average score about 150 or 151. Approximately 60 percent correct is necessary to obtain an average score. There is no penalty for guessing on the LSAT, so never leave a question without at least taking a guess.

Unscored Essay—the multiple-choice sections of the LSAT are followed by a 35-minute unscored essay. This essay is written on special lined sheets of paper. Scratch paper is given so that you can organize your essay before writing. A copy of your essay is sent to each law school to which you apply. The law schools may use the essay in a number of ways—as a tie-breaker between two applicants, as a measure for admittance, and so on. Test takers who have not seen a sample topic are often worried about the essay topic. You should review a few sample topics and try writing a few essays. The topics typically involve a selection that needs to be made between two people, items, techniques, or places, or an analysis of a given argument.

KNOWING THE BASIC SKILLS

You should know the basic skills necessary to do well on the LSAT. Because the LSAT is designed to measure skills necessary to do well your first year in law school (and not what kind of an attorney you are going to be), it is important to focus your study and some review on these skills. These skills include reading comprehension skills, critical reading skills, analytical skills, and reasoning skills. Notice that the test is reading and reasoning based.

UNDERSTANDING THE THINKING PROCESSES

The LSAT, unlike many other standardized exams, is not content oriented, but is reasoning oriented. Therefore, it is vital to understand the thinking processes involved in obtaining the correct/credited response. You should not memorize information, but focus your preparation on understanding the reasoning involved. Carefully analyzing each question type, the credited response, and the common mistakes will help you understand the thinking processes. You should understand that the correct answer to each question is facing you on the page and that the incorrect answers are called "distracters." An incorrect answer that looks good or is close is often called an "attractive distracter." Learn to avoid the attractive distracters by analyzing the choices and understanding the thinking processes.

APPLYING STRATEGIES AND TECHNIQUES

There are many strategies and techniques that you can and should learn before taking your LSAT. The general strategies include how and when to skip problems, eliminate answers, and circle important words. The specific strategies should include how to draw diagrams or simple displays for Analytical Reasoning, how to actively read Reading Comprehension passages and how to preread questions and focus on Logical Reasoning questions. You should also be very familiar with the many types of questions you could be asked in each section. You should take the test only after reviewing and practicing many specific strategies for the question types.

PRACTICE, PRACTICE, PRACTICE

As with other standardized exams, becoming a proficient LSAT test taker takes lots of practice. This practice helps you get acclimated to working under time pressure as well as dealing with the fatigue factor. When you practice, try to replicate testing conditions. Don't use scratch paper, do your work in the test booklet, and transfer your answers to an answer sheet. Don't practice on a large tabletop, as in most cases you will be taking your test in a classroom with fairly small desktops. When you practice, you should give yourself only 30 minutes to complete a section, even though the time allotted is actually 35 minutes. Shorting yourself on time will force you to work faster and should increase your speed. Another reason for extended practice is to identify the types of mistakes you make when you're tired, that is, dealing with the fatigue factor. Practice taking three 35-minute sections (giving yourself 30 minutes for each section) back to back to back with only about a five-second break between each one. Then, take a short break of about ten minutes and try another two sections. When you complete your practice tests, carefully analyze each section and watch for any consistent types of errors. On your next practice session, focus on eliminating those errors.

The LSAT is an important, difficult exam, but you can prepare for it, and you owe it to yourself to be prepared. Read and review this book carefully. You'll be glad you did.

Good Luck!!!
Jerry Bobrow, Ph.D.

Jerry Bobrow, Ph.D., author of *Barron's LSAT* and many other national best-selling preparation books, has been teaching and directing preparation programs for most of the California State universities for the past 30 years. He personally lectures and teaches over 2,000 LSAT test takers each year.

NOTE: If your book includes a CD-ROM, you'll find that the material on the CD-ROM contains two additional practice tests with complete explanations. The CD-ROM provides a study guide; using the book in conjunction with the CD will give you outstanding extra practice and review.

Acknowledgments

I gratefully acknowledge the following sources for granting permission to use materials from their publications:

Pages 319, 321, 324, 329, 447, 519, 579, 602, 604: Dean Seymour Greitzer, Law Reviews from Glendale University College of Law.

Pages 109, 117: Dr. Albert Upton, Design for Thinking, Stanford University Press, Stanford, Calif.

Pages 298, 303, 304: George E. Riggs, publisher; news articles and editorials from *The Herald News,* Fontana, California.

Page 324: Angela Roddey Holder and John Thomas Roddey Holder, *The Meaning of the Constitution*, 3rd Ed., Barron's Educational Series, Inc., Hauppauge, NY, 1997.

Page 338: John A. Garraty, *The Great Depression*, Harcourt Brace Jovanovich, 1986, pages 31–32.

Page 340: Edward W. Rosenheim, Jr., *Swift and the Satirist's Art*, the University of Chicago Press, 1963, pages 26–27.

Page 343: Fred Licht, *Goya: The Origins of the Modern Temper in Art*, Universe Books, New York, 1979, pages 14–15.

Page 335: From the Web (Federal Election Commission). "The Electoral College" by William C. Kimberling, Deputy Director, FEC Office of Election Administration, Revised 1992.

Page 346: C. Leland Rodgers, *Essentials of Biology*, © 1974 by Barron's Educational Series, Inc., Hauppauge, NY, pages 259–261.

Page 349: Erwin Rosenfeld and Harriet Geller, *Afro-Asian Cultural Studies*, 4th edition, © 1979 by Barron's Educational Series, Inc., Hauppauge, NY, pages 44–45.

Page 352: C. Leland Rodgers, *Essentials of Biology*, © 1974 by Barron's Educational Series, Inc., Hauppauge, NY, pages 65–66.

Page 451: C. Vann Woodward, *The Future of the Past.* New York: Oxford University Press, 1991.

Page 521: Roy Sieber and Arnold Rubin, *Sculpture of Black Africa: The Paul Tishman Collection.* Los Angeles: Los Angeles County Museum of Art, 1981. By permission of the copyright holder.

Page 524: John Kenneth Galbraith, *American Capitalism.* Sentry edition. Boston: Houghton Mifflin, 1962.

Page 544: Law Reviews from the University of California at Los Angeles (UCLA) Law School—Comment, "United States Tax Treaty Policy Toward Developing Countries: The China Example," 35 UCLA L. Rev. 369 (1987).

Page 546: Spiro Kostof, *A History of Architecture.* New York: Oxford University Press, 1995.

Page 548: Robert A. Nisbet, *The Present Age: Progress and Anarchy in Modern America.* New York: Harper & Row, 1988. Reprinted by permission of HarperCollins.

Page 551: Gabrielle I. Edwards, *Biology the Easy Way*, 3rd Ed., Barron's Educational Series, Inc., 2000.

Page 581: Fred Kaplan, *Dickens: A Biography.* New York: William Morrow & Company, 1988.

Page 606: Paul Veyne, ed., & Arthur Goldhammer, translator, *A History of Private Life: Volume I—From Pagan Rome to Byzantium.* Philippe Aries and Georges Duby, series general editors. Cambridge, Massachusetts: The Belknap Press of Harvard University Press, 1987. Copyright 1987 by the President and Fellows of Harvard College.

Page 608: Joachim Ekrutt, *Stars and Planets*, 2nd Ed. (Consulting Ed. Clint Hatchett), Barron's Educational Series, Inc., Hauppauge, NY, 2000.

Page 641: *Barron's Guide to Law Schools*, 17th Ed., © 2006 by Barron's Educational Series, Inc., Hauppauge, NY.

ON THE CD

Test One, Section 2, Questions 1–7: Ernst B. Schultz, *Democracy*, 2nd Ed., © 1977 by Barron's Educational Series, Inc., Hauppauge, NY.

Test One, Section 2, Questions 15–20: Adapted from Arthur Bell, Donald W. Heiney, and Lenthiel H. Downs, *English Literature: 1900 to the Present*, © 1994 by Barron's Educational Series, Inc., Hauppauge, NY.

Test Two, Section 2, Questions 1–6: Ann Fagan Ginger, *The Law, the Supreme Court and the People's Rights*, © 1977 by Barron's Educational Series, Inc., Hauppauge, NY.

Test Two, Section 2, Questions 8–14; 15–22: Dean Seymour Greitzer, Law Reviews from Glendale University College of Law.

Test Two, Section 5, Questions 8–14: Dean Seymour Greitzer, Law Reviews from Glendale University College of Law.

Test Two, Section 5, Questions 22–27: Mark Willner et al., *Let's Review: Global History and Geography*, 4th Ed., © 2006 by Barron's Educational Series, Inc., Hauppauge, NY.

(Note: Some of the Law Reviews have been edited, including changes in names, places, and dates.)

My thanks to James Zinger, President, Hypmovation, for the use of excerpts from his writings; to Jean Eggenschwiler, writer and editor, for her contributions; to Stacey Baum, Joy Mondragon, Kristen Fest-Tennison, and Deena Mondragon, for their assistance in assembling the manuscript; to Lynn Turner, Dana Lind, Brenda Clodfelter, and Jennifer Johnson for typing the manuscript; and to Linda Turner for manuscript editing and final preparation.

And finally, thanks to my wife, Susan Bobrow, for critical analysis and moral support; and to my three children, Jennifer, Adam, and Jonathan, for their many years of providing comic relief.

New Security Regulations

A complete list of test center regulations is available in the 2007–2008 *Information Book* and online. Below we highlight some of the most significant changes made:

- *Items permitted in the test room.* Tests takers may bring into the room **only** a clear plastic ziplock bag, maximum size one gallon (3.79 liter), which must be stored under the chair and may be accessed **only** during the break. The ziplock bag may contain only the following items: LSAT Admission Ticket stub; valid ID; wallet; keys; hygiene products; #2 or HB pencils, highlighter, erasers, pencil sharpener (**no mechanical pencils**); tissues; beverage in plastic container or juice box (20 oz./591 ml maximum size) and snack for break only.

- *Items permitted on the desktop.* Test takers may only have tissues, ID, pencils, erasers, a pencil sharpener, highlighter, and analog (nondigital) wristwatch. **No electronic timing devices are permitted.** This is a change from previous testing years.

- *Prohibited items.* Candidates are **not** permitted to bring into the testing room the following items: weapons or firearms, ear plugs, books, backpacks, handbags, papers of any kind, calculators, rulers, **timers**, listening devices, cellular phones, recording or photographic devices, pagers, beepers, headsets, and/or other electronic devices. Prohibited items may not be used during the break. **Bringing prohibited items into the test room may result in the confiscation of such items by the test supervisor, a warning, dismissal from the test center, and/or cancellation of a test score by LSAC. In addition, they may be referred to the LSAC Misconduct/Irregularities in the Admission Process Subcommittee or the Questioned Score Review Board.** LSAC and LSAT testing staff are not responsible for test takers' belongings.

- *Hats/hoods.* No hats or hoods are allowed (except items of religious apparel).

- *Handbags, backpacks, briefcases.* No handbags, backpacks, briefcases or other bags—except the ziplock bag described above—are allowed in the test room.

- *Cancellation/Complaint deadlines.* Test taker complaints and cancellation requests must be received at LSAC within six (6) days of the test date. (This is a change from previous years.)

If candidates need further clarification or information, please contact LSAC at 215.968.1001 or send an e-mail to *LSACINFO@LSAC.org.*

Introduction to the LSAT

Answers to Some Commonly Asked Questions

What does the LSAT measure?
The LSAT is designed to measure a range of mental abilities related to the study of law; therefore, most law schools use it to evaluate their applicants.

Will any special knowledge of the law raise my score on the LSAT?
The LSAT is designed so that candidates from a particular academic background are given no advantage. The questions measure reading comprehension, logical reasoning, and analytical reasoning, drawing from a variety of verbal and analytical material.

Does a high score on the LSAT predict success in law school or in the practice of law?
Success on the LSAT demonstrates your ability to read with understanding and to reason clearly under pressure; surely these strengths are important to both the study and the practice of law, as is the ability to write well, measured by the LSAT Writing Sample. To say that success on the LSAT *predicts* success in law school may overstate the case, however, because success in law school also involves skills that are not measured by the LSAT.

When is the LSAT administered?
The regular administration of the test occurs nationwide four times each year, around the beginning of the fall, winter, spring, and summer seasons. Except for the summer month, the test is usually administered on a Saturday morning from 8:30 A.M. to about 1:00 P.M. For the past few years, the *summer exam* has been given on a Monday afternoon. Dates are announced annually by the Law School Admission Council (LSAC) in Newtown, PA.

What if I cannot take the test on a Saturday?
Some special arrangements are possible: Check the Law School Admission Services (LSAS) General Information Booklet in your registration packet. Those who must take the exam at a time when the regular administration occurs on Saturday, but who cannot participate on Saturday for religious reasons, may arrange for a special Monday administration.

How early should I register?
Regular registration closes about one month before the exam date. Late registration is available up to about three weeks prior to the exam date. There is an additional fee for late registration.

How do I register for the LSAT?
You can register for the LSAT three different ways: online, by telephone, or by mail. **To register online**, use: www.LSAC.org. **To register by telephone**, call (215) 968-1001 (be sure to complete the worksheet in the *Registration/Information Book* before calling). **To register by mail**, complete the appropriate sections in the *LSAT & LSDAS Registration/Information Book* and mail with payment to Law Services in the preaddressed return envelope.

The Law School Admission Council encourages you to register online and take advantage of the benefits available. The benefits listed by the LSAC include:

"Faster test score delivery via e-mail
Access to real-time test center availability for LSAT registration
Fast, easy test date and center changes
Printable LSAT ticket
Electronic test disclosure material
Fast additional law school report orders
Up-to-date file status
Instantly accessible LSDAS documents
Faster processing for publication, video, and software orders
Forum preregistration—saves time at the forums
No snail-mail"

Is walk-in registration available?
No. The Law School Admission Council will not permit walk-ins on the day of the test. Be sure to read carefully the *LSAT & LSDAS Registration/Information Book* section on registering to take the LSAT.

What is the LSDAS?
The LSDAS (Law School Data Assembly Service) compiles a report about each subscribing applicant. The report contains LSAT results, a summary of the applicant's academic work, and copies of college transcripts. A report is sent to each law school that the applicant designates. Thus, if you register for the LSDAS, you will not need to mail a separate transcript to each of your prospective law schools. Reminder: You should review information regarding the Candidate Referral Service in your *LSAT & LSDAS Registration/Information Book.*

How is the LSAT used?
Your LSAT score is one common denominator by which a law school compares you to other applicants. Other factors also determine your acceptance to law school: A law school may consider your personal qualities, grade-point average, extracurricular achievements, and letters of recommendation. Requirements for admission vary widely from school to school, so you are wise to contact the law school of your choice for specific information.

How do I obtain registration forms and registration information?
The registration forms covering the LSAT and LSDAS are available in the *LSAT & LSDAS Registration/Information Book.* Copies of the book are available at the admissions offices of most law schools and testing offices at most undergraduate universities and colleges. You may also obtain the book and more information by writing to Law Services, Box 2000, 662 Penn Street, Newtown, PA 18940-0998; by Internet using *www.LSAC.org*; by fax at (215) 968-1119; by e-mail at *Lsacinfor@LSAC.org*; or by telephone at (215) 968-1001.

What is the structure of the LSAT?
The LSAT contains five 35-minute multiple-choice sections followed by a 35-minute Writing Sample. The Writing Sample does not count as part of your LSAT score. The common question types that do count toward your score are Logical Reasoning (two sections), Analytical Reasoning (one section), and Reading Comprehension (one section). In addition to these four sections, one experimental or pretest section will appear. This experimental or pretest section, which will probably be a repeat of one of the common question types, will not count in your score.

How is the LSAT scored?
The score for the objective portion of the test ranges from 120 to 180, and there is no penalty for wrong answers. The Writing Sample is unscored, but copies are sent to the law schools of your choice for evaluation.

What about question structure and value?
All LSAT questions, apart from the Writing Sample, are multiple-choice with five choices. All questions within a section are of equal value, regardless of difficulty.

Should I guess?
There is no penalty for guessing on the LSAT. Therefore, before you move on to the next question, at least take a guess. You should fill in guess answers for those you have left blank or did not get to, before time is called for that section. If you can eliminate one or more choices as incorrect, your chances for a correct guess increase.

How often may I take the LSAT?
You may take the LSAT more than once if you wish. But keep in mind that any report sent to you or to law schools will contain scores for any exams taken over about the past five years, along with an average score for those exams. The law school receiving your scores will decide which score is the best estimate of your ability; many law schools rely on the average score as a reliable figure. Normally, you may not take the test more than three times in a two-year period.

Is it possible to cancel my LSAT scores?
You may cancel your score at the test center or within six calendar days after taking the test.

How early should I arrive at the test center and what should I bring?
Arrive at the test center 20 to 30 minutes before the time designated on your admission ticket. Bring three or four sharpened No. 2 pencils, an eraser, and a noiseless watch (no alarm, calculator, or beeping), as well as your LSAT Admission Ticket and proper identification as described in the *LSAT & LSDAS Registration/ Information Book*. **Note:** You may use only a No. 2 pencil or highlighter pen to underline passages in the test book. Ink or ballpoint pens are not permitted.

Are there accommodations for persons with disabilities?
Persons with documented disabilities may have special accommodations available. Candidates who need accommodations are urged to register and submit all required documentation well in advance of the registration deadlines.

Can I prepare for the LSAT?
Yes. Reading skills and test-taking strategies should be the focus of your preparation for the test as a whole. Success on the more specialized analytical sections of the test depends on your thorough familiarity with the types of problems you are likely to encounter and the reasoning process involved. For maximum preparation, work through this book, and practice the strategies and techniques outlined in each section.

Basic Format of the LSAT and Scoring

THE *ORDER* OF THE FOLLOWING MULTIPLE-CHOICE SECTIONS *WILL* VARY. The Experimental Section is not necessarily the last section.

Section		Number of Questions	Minutes
I.	Logical Reasoning	24–26	35
II.	Analytical Reasoning	22–24 (4 sets)	35
III.	Reading Comprehension	26–28 (4 passages)	35
IV.	Logical Reasoning	24–26	35
V.	Experimental Section	varies	35
	Writing Sample	1 essay	35
TOTALS		118–132 questions (only 96–104 count toward your score)	210 minutes or 3 hours 30 minutes

NOTE: For your convenience, this Barron's text labels each section of the diagnostic test (e.g., Reading Comprehension, Logical Reasoning). In contrast, sections of the actual LSAT exam are not usually labeled.

The LSAT is scored on a 120 to 180 scale.

The following simple chart will give you a very general approximation of the LSAT scoring system. It shows the approximate percentage of right answers necessary on the LSAT to be in a certain score range.

Approximate % of Right Answers	Approximate Score Range
Between 75% and 100%	160–180
Between 50% and 75%	145–159
Between 25% and 50%	130–144
Between 0% and 25%	120–129

Note that this chart is meant to give you an *approximate* score range.

A CLOSER LOOK AT THE TIMING—WHAT IT REALLY MEANS

Although the LSAT comprises five 35-minute multiple-choice sections and a 35-minute unscored essay, it is important to understand the timing breakdown and what it means. The test is actually broken down as follows:

105 minutes	Section I 35 minutes Section II 35 minutes Section III 35 minutes
	Short break—usually 10–15 minutes
70 minutes	Section IV 35 minutes Section V 35 minutes
35 minutes	Writing Sample (Essay)—35 minutes

Notice that you are given three multiple-choice sections with no breaks in between. When they say "stop" at the end of 35 minutes, they will immediately say something like, "Turn to the next section, make sure that you are in the right section, ready, begin." So, in essence, you are working three sections back to back to back. This means that when you practice you should be sure to practice testing for 1 hour and 45 minutes without a break.

After the short break, when you may get up, get a drink, and go to the restroom, you are back for two more back-to-back multiple-choice sections.

For the final 35-minute writing sample, you will be given scratch paper to do your prewriting or outlining.

Keep in mind that there will be some time taken before the exam and after the exam for clerical-type paperwork—distributing and picking up paperwork, filling out test forms, and so on.

IMPORTANT REMINDERS

- At least half of your test will contain Logical Reasoning questions; prepare accordingly. Make sure that you are good at Logical Reasoning!
- The experimental or pretest section will usually repeat other sections and can appear in different places on the exam. At the time of the exam, you will not know which section is experimental. Take the test as if all of the sections count.
- Scoring will range from 120 to 180. This is the score, and the percentile rank that goes with it is what the law schools look at and are referring to in their discussions.
- All questions in a section are of equal value, so do not get stuck on any one question. The scores are determined by totaling all of your right answers on the test and then scaling.
- Answer all the easy questions first; then come back and answer the tougher questions. Don't be afraid to skip a question, but always at least take a guess.
- There is NO PENALTY for guessing, so at least take a guess before you move to the next question.
- The 35-minute Writing Sample will not be scored, but copies will be forwarded to the law schools to which you apply. Scratch paper will be provided for the Writing Sample only.
- Keep in mind that regardless of the format of your exam, two sections of Logical Reasoning, one section of Analytical Reasoning, and one section of Reading Comprehension always count toward your score.

Some Words to the Wise

ASK A FEW QUESTIONS

Before you actually start your study plan, there are four basic questions that you should ask the law schools to which you are applying:

1. Considering my GPA and other qualifications, what score do you think I need to get into your law school?
2. When do you need to get my score reports? Or, When should I take the test to meet your deadlines?
3. What do you do if I take the LSAT more than once? Remember that when the law school receives your score report it will see a score for each time you've taken the test and an average of the scores. It is up to the law schools and their governing bodies as to what score(s) they will consider. Try to do your best on the first try, and take the LSAT only once, if possible.
4. What do you do with my Writing Sample? Is it used as a tiebreaker? Do you score it yourself? Is it just another piece of the process?

Knowing the answers to most of these questions before you start your study will help you understand what is expected and will help you get mentally ready for the task ahead.

An Effective Study Program

A FIVE-WEEK LSAT STUDY PLAN

Many students don't even bother to read the LSAT bulletin, let alone do any thorough preparation for the test. You, however, should begin your LSAT preparation by reading the LSAT bulletin (book) carefully; information about how to obtain one is on page 3. The bulletin is filled with information about registration and score reporting. Also provided in the registration book is an "official" practice test. You should also send for copies of old exams (good practice) and check online for more materials and information.

With the preliminaries out of the way, begin working through this book. If you have the time, the following study plan is ideal and is used in many LSAT preparation programs at major universities and colleges. However, if you have a shorter time to prepare, simply adjust the following five-week plan to meet your needs (remember, lots of *practice* and *analysis*). You will find the techniques, strategies, practice, and analyses in this book invaluable to your preparation, either with the ideal five-week plan or with the shorter study plan.

Most people can keep up with the following study sequence by devoting about seven to ten hours a week. It is most important that you review and practice *daily*, for about an hour or two each day. Don't "save up" your practice for one long session each week. Shorter, regular practice sessions will allow you to assimilate skills and strategies more effectively and efficiently.

Always spend some extra time reviewing "why" you made your mistakes. Watch for repeated or consistent errors. These errors are often the easiest to correct. As you review, focus on the thinking process involved in reaching the credited response, and note specifically where you made the error.

If you have reviewed an explanation and still do not understand where you made an error, mark the problem in your book and go on. Return to review this problem later, after you have had an opportunity to review other problems that use similar thinking processes. Don't get stuck on reviewing one problem.

When reviewing answers, don't just look at the ones you got wrong. Instead, be aware of not only "what" questions you're getting right but also "how" you are getting them right. Positive habits need to be reinforced.

Week 1

- Read the section "Answers to Some Commonly Asked Questions" (p. 1).
- Complete, correct, and analyze the Diagnostic Exam (p. 15).
- Read carefully "Before You Begin" (p. 9), paying special attention to the "One-Check, Two-Check System" and the "Elimination Strategy." Applying these techniques confidently should make quite a difference in your test taking.
- Read carefully the chapters on Reading Comprehension, Logical Reasoning, Analytical Reasoning, and the Writing Sample.
- Spend some extra time reviewing the chapter on Logical Reasoning. Remember: Logical Reasoning will comprise two of the four scored sections of your exam.

Week 2

- Review the chapter on Reading Comprehension. Do the Reading Comprehension problems in the chapter, the ones in the LSAT sample test, and those in Model Test One (p. 393). Correct and analyze your performance.

  Note: Do not time yourself on these practice tests. Your task at present is to familiarize yourself with strategies and techniques, a task that is best done slowly, working back and forth between the introductory chapter and the practice problems. You may get an uncomfortable number of problems wrong at this stage, but, instead of being discouraged, you should attempt to understand clearly the reasons for your errors. Such understanding will become a plus in the future.
- Review the chapter on the Writing Sample, and write an essay about one of the given topics. Ask a friend with good writing skills to read your essay and offer constructive criticism.
- Review the chapter on Logical Reasoning. Do the Logical Reasoning problems in the chapter, those in the LSAT practice test, and those in Model Test One (pp. 397 and 404). Correct and analyze your performance.

Week 3

- Review the chapter on Analytical Reasoning. Do the Analytical Reasoning problems in the chapter, those in the LSAT practice test, and those in Model Test One (p. 393). Correct and analyze your performance.

  Note: At this point, you have introduced yourself to the whole test and have tried some effective strategies. Now you should begin timing each of your practice tests.
- Do the Reading Comprehension problems in Model Test Two (p. 447) and the Logical Reasoning problems in Model Test Two (pp. 462 and 476). Correct and analyze your performance.
- Do the Analytical Reasoning problems in Model Test Two (pp. 457 and 471). Correct and analyze your performance.
- Write another essay about one of the topics given in the Writing Sample chapter, and have a friend read and respond to your effort.

Week 4

- Do all of Model Test Three; practice and review two or three sections each day. For each section, time yourself (always short yourself on time during practice by about 10 to 15 percent), then correct and analyze your performance.
- Do all of Model Test Four in one sitting. Correct and analyze your performance. Have a friend read and respond to your Writing Sample.

  Note: This long practice testing will familiarize you with some of the difficulties you will encounter on the actual test—e.g., maintaining focus and concentration, dealing with fatigue, and pacing. It will also help you build your endurance. Remember, as you analyze your mistakes, to watch for repeated errors. Sometimes these are the easiest to eliminate.

Week 5

- If you have time early in the week or in the weeks before, and your book includes a CD-ROM, you may wish to do Model Tests One and Two on the CD for extra practice. You can follow the procedure used for Model Test Four or simply take and review individual sections as needed.
- For extra practice, you could use the full-length practice test offered by the Law Services at *www.LSAC.org.*
- A few days before your exam, review some of the problems you have already completed—focus on the thinking processes. You may wish to reread chapters that gave you the most difficulty.
- Finally, carefully read the review of test-taking strategies (Chapter 6). It will recap the highlights of the book and supply a variety of tips for putting yourself into an effective state of mind before the LSAT.

Before You Begin

THE MAIN FOCUS

Understanding the Thinking Processes

One of the key factors in your success on the LSAT is your mastery of the LSAT "thinking processes." There is no question that this will take lots of time working on practice problems, but it will also take a carefully focused analysis of that practice.

As you read each introductory chapter, keep in mind the thinking process involved as it is explained. You are not trying to learn or memorize any actual problem; rather, you are trying to learn the process behind solving each problem type so that you will be able to apply that process to new problems.

Notice that each section is designed to analyze this thinking process and to help you understand what the test maker had in mind when constructing the question. Learn to understand the reasoning behind the construction of each question.

If you focus on this reasoning as you prepare, the techniques carefully explained in each chapter will be easier to apply and will become even more effective. Remember that it is the mastery of this thinking process within the time constraints that will yield success on the LSAT.

SOME GENERAL STRATEGIES

The One-Check, Two-Check System

Many people score lower than they should on the LSAT simply because they do not get to many of the easier problems. They puzzle over difficult questions and use up the time that could be spent answering easy ones. In fact, the easy questions are worth exactly the same as the difficult ones, so it makes sense not to do the hard problems until you have answered all the easy ones.

To maximize your correct answers by focusing on the easier problems, use the following system:

1. Attempt the first question. If it is answerable quickly and easily, work the problem, circle the answer in the question booklet, and then mark that answer on the answer sheet. The mark on the answer sheet should be a complete mark, not merely a dot, because you may not be given time at the end of the test to darken marks.
2. If a question seems impossible, place two checks (✔✔) on or next to the question number in the question booklet and mark the answer you guess on the answer sheet. Again, the mark on the answer sheet should be a complete mark, not merely a dot.
3. If you're in the midst of a question that seems to be taking too much time, or if you immediately spot that a question is answerable but time-consuming (that is, it will require more than two minutes to answer), place one check (✔) next to the question number, mark an answer you guess on the answer sheet, and continue with the next question.
   NOTE THAT NO QUESTIONS ARE LEFT BLANK. AN ANSWER CHOICE IS *ALWAYS* FILLED IN BEFORE LEAVING THAT QUESTION.

STUDY TIP

All questions are of equal value. Don't get stuck!

4. When all the problems in a section have been attempted in this manner, there may still be time left. If so, return to the single-check (✔) questions, working as many as possible, changing each guessed answer to a worked-out answer, if necessary.
5. If time remains after all the single-check (✔) questions are completed, you can choose between

   a. attempting those "impossible" double-check (✔✔) questions (sometimes a question later on in the test may trigger one's memory to allow once-impossible questions to be solved);

   or

   b. spending time checking and reworking the easier questions to eliminate any careless errors.
6. Remember: Use *all* the allotted time as effectively as possible.

You should use this system as you work through the practice tests in this book; such practice will allow you to make "one-check, two-check" judgments quickly when you actually take the LSAT. As our extensive research has shown, use of this system results in less wasted time on the LSAT.

The Elimination Strategy

Faced with five answer choices, you will work more efficiently and effectively if you *eliminate unreasonable or irrelevant answers immediately.* In most cases, two or three choices in every set will stand out as obviously incorrect. Many test takers don't perceive this because they painstakingly analyze every choice, even the obviously ridiculous ones.

Consider the following Logical Reasoning problem:

EXAMPLE

According to the theory of aerodynamics, the bumblebee is unable to fly. This is because the size, weight, and shape of its body in relationship to the total wingspan make flying impossible. The bumblebee, being ignorant of this "scientific truth," flies anyway.

The author's statement would be strengthened by pointing out that

(A) the theory of aerodynamics may be readily tested
(B) the bumblebee does not actually fly but glides instead
(C) bumblebees cannot fly in strong winds
(D) bumblebees are ignorant of other things but can't do all of them
(E) nothing is impossible

A student who does not immediately eliminate the unreasonable choices here, and instead tries to analyze every choice, will find herself becoming confused and anxious as she tries to decide how even silly choices might be correct. Her thinking goes something like this: "I wonder whether bumblebees do glide; I've never looked that closely—maybe the test has me on this one . . . come to think of it, I've never seen a bumblebee in a strong wind; (C) is tricky, but it just might be right . . . I can't understand (D); it seems irrelevant but that just might be a trick . . ."

On and on she goes, becoming more and more uncertain.

STUDY TIP

Eliminating wrong answers is a terrific strategy! Learn to eliminate.

Using the elimination strategy, a confident test taker proceeds as follows:

?(A) Possible choice.
~~(B)~~ Ridiculous. Both false and irrelevant. Cross it out.
~~(C)~~ Another ridiculous, irrelevant one. Cross it out.
~~(D)~~ Incomprehensible! Eliminate it.
?(E) Too general to be the best choice.

This test taker, aware that most answer choices can be easily eliminated, does so without complicating the process by considering unreasonable possibilities.

To summarize the elimination strategy:

- Look for unreasonable or incorrect answer choices first. Expect to find at least two or three of these with every problem.
- When a choice seems wrong, cross it out in your test booklet *immediately*, so that you will not be tempted to reconsider it.

Eliminating choices in this fashion will lead you to correct answers more quickly, and will increase your overall confidence.

Anticipating an Answer

For some question types, it is helpful to have an idea about what a possible credited answer choice could look like. This is called "anticipating an answer," or "anticipation." For example, you may read a Logical Reasoning question and already have a good idea of what is being assumed before you read the choices. In this case, you could go in looking for "your" answer.

STUDY TIP

Mark items and draw diagrams efficiently and effectively! This takes lots of practice.

Marking in the Test Booklet

Many test takers don't take full advantage of opportunities to mark key words and draw diagrams in the test booklet. Remember that, in the Reading Comprehension and Logical Reasoning sections, *marking key words and phrases will significantly increase your comprehension and lead you to a correct answer.* Marking also helps to keep you focused and alert. In the Analytical Reasoning section, *drawing diagrams is absolutely essential.*

Further, more specific hints about marking are given in the introductory chapters that follow. The important general point to stress here is that active, successful test taking entails marking and drawing, and that passive, weak test takers make little use of this technique.

STUDY TIP

Never leave an answer choice blank! There is no penalty for guessing.

Guessing

Because there is no penalty for guessing, you should *never leave a question without taking a guess.* And because there is no penalty for guessing, when you have about 3 minutes left, place your finger on where you are on your answer sheet (or make a light mark in your question booklet); then take your favorite letter and fill in the remaining answers on your answer sheet for that section. That is, if there are 26 questions in a section, you should fill in 26 answers. Once you have taken your ending guesses, go back and continue working where you left off and change your answers on the answer sheet. That way, if the proctor says, "Stop, time is up!" you will at least have gotten all your guesses in.

PITFALLS—WHAT TO WATCH OUT FOR

The Common Mistake—The Misread

The most common mistake for many test takers is the MISREAD. The MISREAD occurs when you read the question incorrectly. For example, "Which of the following *must* be true?" is often read as "Which of the following *could* be true?" and "All of the following must be true EXCEPT" often loses the word "except."

If you MISREAD the question, you will be looking for the wrong answer.

To help eliminate the MISREAD, always underline or circle what you are looking for in the question. This will also help you focus on the main point of the question.

By the way, the MISREAD also occurs while reading answer choices. You may wish to underline or circle key words in the answers to help you avoid the MISREAD.

Distracters and "Attractive" Distracters

When the test makers put together the LSAT, they spend a great deal of time and effort not only making sure that "credited response" is the best answer given, but also that the wrong answer choices (distracters) are good possibilities.

Distracters, as the word indicates, are meant to distract you away from the right answer. Some distracters are easily eliminated as they are just "wrong"—they are irrelevant, contradict something, or bring in items that are not addressed. Some distracters are too general, too specific or narrow, or use a word or words that miss the mark or point of the question. Some distracters are very close to the best or right answer. We refer to the wrong answers that are close as "attractive distracters." The choice looked good but was wrong. When you have narrowed your choices down to two, let's say (A) or (B), keep in mind that one is probably an "attractive distracter."

STUDY TIP

Don't get caught by the second best answer! You are looking for the best answer.

As you prepare for the LSAT, it is important that you focus on the difference (in some cases a very fine difference) between the correct answer and the attractive distracter(s). When you analyze your practice tests, focus on what constitutes a right answer and on spotting the differences.

Analyzing Your LSAT Score: A Broad-Range Score Approximator

The chart that follows is designed to give you a general approximation of the number of questions you need to get right to fall into a general score range and percentile rank on your LSAT. It should help you see whether you are in the "ballpark" of the score you need. This range approximator is *not* designed to give you an exact score or to predict your LSAT score. The actual LSAT will have questions that are similar to the ones encountered in this book, but some questions may be either easier or more difficult. The variance in difficulty levels and testing conditions can affect your score range.

OBTAINING YOUR APPROXIMATE SCORE RANGE

Although the LSAT uses a very precise formula to convert raw scores to scaled scores, for the purpose of this broad-range approximation, simply total the number of questions you answered correctly. Next, divide the total number of correct answers by the total number of questions on the sample test. This will give you the percent correct. Now look at the following chart to see the approximate percent you need to get right to get into your score range. Remember, on the actual test, one of the sections is experimental and, therefore, doesn't count toward your score.

Approx. Scaled Score Range	Approx. % of Correct Answers Necessary	Approx. Score Percentile for 94–95 Test Takers (Est. % below)
171–180	95% and up	99–99.9%
161–170	80–94%	88–98%
151–160	65–79%	53–85%
141–150	45–64%	17–48%
131–140	30–44%	3–15%
121–130	20–29%	0–2%

On the actual LSAT, the percent of correct answers to get certain scores will vary slightly from test to test, depending on the number of problems and the level of difficulty of that particular exam.

An average score is approximately 151.

If you are not in the range that you wish to achieve, check the approximate percent of correct answers that you need to achieve that range. Carefully analyze the types of errors you are making, and continue practicing and analyzing. Remember, in trying to approximate a score range, you must take the complete sample test under strict time and test conditions.

Diagnostic Exam

The purpose of this exam is to familiarize you with the common areas on the LSAT. This is an actual exam, minus the experimental section. The chapters to follow on each exam area will broaden your understanding of the problem types and difficulties.

This exam should be taken under strict test conditions with each section timed as follows:

Diagnostic Exam

Section	Description	Number of Questions	Time Allowed
I.	Reading Comprehension	27	35 minutes
II.	Logical Reasoning	24	35 minutes
III.	Logical Reasoning	26	35 minutes
IV.	Analytical Reasoning	24	35 minutes
	Writing Sample		35 minutes
TOTALS:		101	175 minutes

The actual LSAT contains five 35-minute sections plus a 35-minute Writing Sample for a total of 3½ hours of testing. Note that one section will be experimental and will be a duplication of one of the above sections. Also note that it may appear anywhere in the test. Thus, only four sections will count toward your score—two Logical Reasonings, one Analytical Reasoning, and one Reading Comprehension.

After correcting this diagnostic exam and assessing your strengths and weaknesses, you should start your area analysis with Chapters 1 through 5.

Now tear out your answer sheet from this book, turn to the next page, and begin the exam.

Remove answer sheet by cutting on dotted line

Answer Sheet
DIAGNOSTIC EXAM

Section I Reading Comprehension	Section II Logical Reasoning	Section III Logical Reasoning	Section IV Analytical Reasoning
1 Ⓐ Ⓑ Ⓒ Ⓓ Ⓔ	1 Ⓐ Ⓑ Ⓒ Ⓓ Ⓔ	1 Ⓐ Ⓑ Ⓒ Ⓓ Ⓔ	1 Ⓐ Ⓑ Ⓒ Ⓓ Ⓔ
2 Ⓐ Ⓑ Ⓒ Ⓓ Ⓔ	2 Ⓐ Ⓑ Ⓒ Ⓓ Ⓔ	2 Ⓐ Ⓑ Ⓒ Ⓓ Ⓔ	2 Ⓐ Ⓑ Ⓒ Ⓓ Ⓔ
3 Ⓐ Ⓑ Ⓒ Ⓓ Ⓔ	3 Ⓐ Ⓑ Ⓒ Ⓓ Ⓔ	3 Ⓐ Ⓑ Ⓒ Ⓓ Ⓔ	3 Ⓐ Ⓑ Ⓒ Ⓓ Ⓔ
4 Ⓐ Ⓑ Ⓒ Ⓓ Ⓔ	4 Ⓐ Ⓑ Ⓒ Ⓓ Ⓔ	4 Ⓐ Ⓑ Ⓒ Ⓓ Ⓔ	4 Ⓐ Ⓑ Ⓒ Ⓓ Ⓔ
5 Ⓐ Ⓑ Ⓒ Ⓓ Ⓔ	5 Ⓐ Ⓑ Ⓒ Ⓓ Ⓔ	5 Ⓐ Ⓑ Ⓒ Ⓓ Ⓔ	5 Ⓐ Ⓑ Ⓒ Ⓓ Ⓔ
6 Ⓐ Ⓑ Ⓒ Ⓓ Ⓔ	6 Ⓐ Ⓑ Ⓒ Ⓓ Ⓔ	6 Ⓐ Ⓑ Ⓒ Ⓓ Ⓔ	6 Ⓐ Ⓑ Ⓒ Ⓓ Ⓔ
7 Ⓐ Ⓑ Ⓒ Ⓓ Ⓔ	7 Ⓐ Ⓑ Ⓒ Ⓓ Ⓔ	7 Ⓐ Ⓑ Ⓒ Ⓓ Ⓔ	7 Ⓐ Ⓑ Ⓒ Ⓓ Ⓔ
8 Ⓐ Ⓑ Ⓒ Ⓓ Ⓔ	8 Ⓐ Ⓑ Ⓒ Ⓓ Ⓔ	8 Ⓐ Ⓑ Ⓒ Ⓓ Ⓔ	8 Ⓐ Ⓑ Ⓒ Ⓓ Ⓔ
9 Ⓐ Ⓑ Ⓒ Ⓓ Ⓔ	9 Ⓐ Ⓑ Ⓒ Ⓓ Ⓔ	9 Ⓐ Ⓑ Ⓒ Ⓓ Ⓔ	9 Ⓐ Ⓑ Ⓒ Ⓓ Ⓔ
10 Ⓐ Ⓑ Ⓒ Ⓓ Ⓔ	10 Ⓐ Ⓑ Ⓒ Ⓓ Ⓔ	10 Ⓐ Ⓑ Ⓒ Ⓓ Ⓔ	10 Ⓐ Ⓑ Ⓒ Ⓓ Ⓔ
11 Ⓐ Ⓑ Ⓒ Ⓓ Ⓔ	11 Ⓐ Ⓑ Ⓒ Ⓓ Ⓔ	11 Ⓐ Ⓑ Ⓒ Ⓓ Ⓔ	11 Ⓐ Ⓑ Ⓒ Ⓓ Ⓔ
12 Ⓐ Ⓑ Ⓒ Ⓓ Ⓔ	12 Ⓐ Ⓑ Ⓒ Ⓓ Ⓔ	12 Ⓐ Ⓑ Ⓒ Ⓓ Ⓔ	12 Ⓐ Ⓑ Ⓒ Ⓓ Ⓔ
13 Ⓐ Ⓑ Ⓒ Ⓓ Ⓔ	13 Ⓐ Ⓑ Ⓒ Ⓓ Ⓔ	13 Ⓐ Ⓑ Ⓒ Ⓓ Ⓔ	13 Ⓐ Ⓑ Ⓒ Ⓓ Ⓔ
14 Ⓐ Ⓑ Ⓒ Ⓓ Ⓔ	14 Ⓐ Ⓑ Ⓒ Ⓓ Ⓔ	14 Ⓐ Ⓑ Ⓒ Ⓓ Ⓔ	14 Ⓐ Ⓑ Ⓒ Ⓓ Ⓔ
15 Ⓐ Ⓑ Ⓒ Ⓓ Ⓔ	15 Ⓐ Ⓑ Ⓒ Ⓓ Ⓔ	15 Ⓐ Ⓑ Ⓒ Ⓓ Ⓔ	15 Ⓐ Ⓑ Ⓒ Ⓓ Ⓔ
16 Ⓐ Ⓑ Ⓒ Ⓓ Ⓔ	16 Ⓐ Ⓑ Ⓒ Ⓓ Ⓔ	16 Ⓐ Ⓑ Ⓒ Ⓓ Ⓔ	16 Ⓐ Ⓑ Ⓒ Ⓓ Ⓔ
17 Ⓐ Ⓑ Ⓒ Ⓓ Ⓔ	17 Ⓐ Ⓑ Ⓒ Ⓓ Ⓔ	17 Ⓐ Ⓑ Ⓒ Ⓓ Ⓔ	17 Ⓐ Ⓑ Ⓒ Ⓓ Ⓔ
18 Ⓐ Ⓑ Ⓒ Ⓓ Ⓔ	18 Ⓐ Ⓑ Ⓒ Ⓓ Ⓔ	18 Ⓐ Ⓑ Ⓒ Ⓓ Ⓔ	18 Ⓐ Ⓑ Ⓒ Ⓓ Ⓔ
19 Ⓐ Ⓑ Ⓒ Ⓓ Ⓔ	19 Ⓐ Ⓑ Ⓒ Ⓓ Ⓔ	19 Ⓐ Ⓑ Ⓒ Ⓓ Ⓔ	19 Ⓐ Ⓑ Ⓒ Ⓓ Ⓔ
20 Ⓐ Ⓑ Ⓒ Ⓓ Ⓔ	20 Ⓐ Ⓑ Ⓒ Ⓓ Ⓔ	20 Ⓐ Ⓑ Ⓒ Ⓓ Ⓔ	20 Ⓐ Ⓑ Ⓒ Ⓓ Ⓔ
21 Ⓐ Ⓑ Ⓒ Ⓓ Ⓔ	21 Ⓐ Ⓑ Ⓒ Ⓓ Ⓔ	21 Ⓐ Ⓑ Ⓒ Ⓓ Ⓔ	21 Ⓐ Ⓑ Ⓒ Ⓓ Ⓔ
22 Ⓐ Ⓑ Ⓒ Ⓓ Ⓔ	22 Ⓐ Ⓑ Ⓒ Ⓓ Ⓔ	22 Ⓐ Ⓑ Ⓒ Ⓓ Ⓔ	22 Ⓐ Ⓑ Ⓒ Ⓓ Ⓔ
23 Ⓐ Ⓑ Ⓒ Ⓓ Ⓔ	23 Ⓐ Ⓑ Ⓒ Ⓓ Ⓔ	23 Ⓐ Ⓑ Ⓒ Ⓓ Ⓔ	23 Ⓐ Ⓑ Ⓒ Ⓓ Ⓔ
24 Ⓐ Ⓑ Ⓒ Ⓓ Ⓔ	24 Ⓐ Ⓑ Ⓒ Ⓓ Ⓔ	24 Ⓐ Ⓑ Ⓒ Ⓓ Ⓔ	24 Ⓐ Ⓑ Ⓒ Ⓓ Ⓔ
25 Ⓐ Ⓑ Ⓒ Ⓓ Ⓔ	25 Ⓐ Ⓑ Ⓒ Ⓓ Ⓔ	25 Ⓐ Ⓑ Ⓒ Ⓓ Ⓔ	25 Ⓐ Ⓑ Ⓒ Ⓓ Ⓔ
26 Ⓐ Ⓑ Ⓒ Ⓓ Ⓔ	26 Ⓐ Ⓑ Ⓒ Ⓓ Ⓔ	26 Ⓐ Ⓑ Ⓒ Ⓓ Ⓔ	26 Ⓐ Ⓑ Ⓒ Ⓓ Ⓔ
27 Ⓐ Ⓑ Ⓒ Ⓓ Ⓔ	27 Ⓐ Ⓑ Ⓒ Ⓓ Ⓔ	27 Ⓐ Ⓑ Ⓒ Ⓓ Ⓔ	27 Ⓐ Ⓑ Ⓒ Ⓓ Ⓔ
28 Ⓐ Ⓑ Ⓒ Ⓓ Ⓔ	28 Ⓐ Ⓑ Ⓒ Ⓓ Ⓔ	28 Ⓐ Ⓑ Ⓒ Ⓓ Ⓔ	28 Ⓐ Ⓑ Ⓒ Ⓓ Ⓔ
29 Ⓐ Ⓑ Ⓒ Ⓓ Ⓔ	29 Ⓐ Ⓑ Ⓒ Ⓓ Ⓔ	29 Ⓐ Ⓑ Ⓒ Ⓓ Ⓔ	29 Ⓐ Ⓑ Ⓒ Ⓓ Ⓔ
30 Ⓐ Ⓑ Ⓒ Ⓓ Ⓔ	30 Ⓐ Ⓑ Ⓒ Ⓓ Ⓔ	30 Ⓐ Ⓑ Ⓒ Ⓓ Ⓔ	30 Ⓐ Ⓑ Ⓒ Ⓓ Ⓔ

SECTION I

Time—35 minutes

27 Questions

Directions: Each passage in this section is followed by a group of questions to be answered on the basis of what is stated or implied in the passage. For some of the questions, more than one of the choices could conceivably answer the question. However, you are to choose the best answer; that is, the response that most accurately and completely answers the question, and blacken the corresponding space on your answer sheet.

Until the 1980s, most scientists believed that noncatastrophic geological processes caused the extinction of dinosaurs that occurred approximately 66 million years ago, at the end of the Cretaceous period. Geologists argued that a dramatic drop in sea level coincided with the extinction of the dinosaurs and could have caused the climatic changes that resulted in this extinction as well as the extinction of many ocean species.

This view was seriously challenged in the 1980s by the discovery of large amounts of iridium in a layer of clay deposited at the end of the Cretaceous period. Because iridium is extremely rare in rocks on the Earth's surface but common in meteorites, researchers theorized that it was the impact of a large meteorite that dramatically changed the Earth's climate and thus triggered the extinction of the dinosaurs.

Currently available evidence, however, offers more support for a new theory, the volcanic-eruption theory. A vast eruption of lava in India coincided with the extinctions that occurred at the end of the Cretaceous period, and the release of carbon dioxide from this episode of volcanism could have caused the climatic change responsible for the demise of the dinosaurs. Such outpourings of lava are caused by instability in the lowest layer of the Earth's mantle, located just above the Earth's core. As the rock that constitutes this layer is heated by the Earth's core, it becomes less dense and portions of it eventually escape upward as blobs of molten rock, called "diapirs," that can, under certain circumstances, erupt violently through the Earth's crust.

Moreover, the volcanic-eruption theory, like the impact theory, accounts for the presence of iridium in sedimentary deposits; it also explains matters that the meteorite-impact theory does not. Although iridium is extremely rare on the Earth's surface, the lower regions of the Earth's mantle have roughly the same composition as meteorites and contain large amounts of iridium, which in the case of a diapir eruption would probably be emitted as iridium hexafluoride, a gas that would disperse more uniformly in the atmosphere than the iridium-containing matter thrown out from a meteorite impact. In addition, the volcanic-eruption theory may explain why the end of the Cretaceous period was marked by a gradual change in sea level. Fossil records indicate that for several hundred thousand years prior to the relatively sudden disappearance of the dinosaurs, the level of the sea gradually fell, causing many marine organisms to die out. This change in sea level might well have been the result of a distortion in the Earth's surface that resulted from the movement of diapirs upward toward the Earth's crust, and the more cataclysmic extinction of the dinosaurs could have resulted from the explosive volcanism that occurred as material from the diapirs erupted onto the Earth's surface.

1. The passage suggests that during the 1980s researchers found meteorite impact a convincing explanation for the extinction of dinosaurs, in part because

   (A) earlier theories had failed to account for the gradual extinction of many ocean species at the end of the Cretaceous period
   (B) geologists had, up until that time, underestimated the amount of carbon dioxide that would be released during an episode of explosive volcanism
   (C) a meteorite could have served as a source of the iridium found in a layer of clay deposited at the end of the Cretaceous period
   (D) no theory relying on purely geological processes had, up until that time, explained the cause of the precipitous drop in sea level that occurred at the end of the Cretaceous period
   (E) the impact of a large meteorite could have resulted in the release of enough carbon dioxide to cause global climatic change

2. According to the passage, the lower regions of the Earth's mantle are characterized by

   (A) a composition similar to that of meteorites
   (B) the absence of elements found in rocks on the Earth's crust
   (C) a greater stability than that of the upper regions
   (D) the presence of large amounts of carbon dioxide
   (E) a uniformly lower density than that of the upper regions

GO ON TO THE NEXT PAGE.

3. It can be inferred from the passage that which one of the following was true of the lava that erupted in India at the end of the Cretaceous period?

(A) It contained less carbon dioxide than did the meteorites that were striking the Earth's surface during that period.
(B) It was more dense than the molten rock located just above the Earth's core.
(C) It released enough iridium hexafluoride into the atmosphere to change the Earth's climate dramatically.
(D) It was richer in iridium than rocks usually found on the Earth's surface.
(E) It was richer in iridium than were the meteorites that were striking the Earth's surface during that period.

4. In the passage, the author is primarily concerned with doing which one of the following?

(A) describing three theories and explaining why the latest of these appears to be the best of the three
(B) attacking the assumptions inherent in theories that until the 1980s had been largely accepted by geologists
(C) outlining the inadequacies of three different explanations of the same phenomenon
(D) providing concrete examples in support of the more general assertion that theories must often be revised in light of new evidence
(E) citing evidence that appears to confirm the skepticism of geologists regarding a view held prior to the 1980s

5. The author implies that if the theory described in the third paragraph is true, which one of the following would have been true of iridium in the atmosphere at the end of the Cretaceous period?

(A) Its level of concentration in the Earth's atmosphere would have been high due to a slow but steady increase in the atmospheric iridium that began in the early Cretaceous period.
(B) Its concentration in the Earth's atmosphere would have increased due to the dramatic decrease in sea level that occurred during the Cretaceous period.
(C) It would have been directly responsible for the extinction of many ocean species.
(D) It would have been more uniformly dispersed than iridium whose source had been the impact of a meteorite on the Earth's surface.
(E) It would have been more uniformly dispersed than iridium released into the atmosphere as a result of normal geological processes that occur on Earth.

6. The passage supports which one of the following claims about the volcanic-eruption theory?

(A) It does not rely on assumptions concerning the temperature of molten rock at the lowest part of the Earth's mantle.
(B) It may explain what caused the gradual fall in sea level that occurred for hundreds of thousands of years prior to the more sudden disappearance of the dinosaurs.
(C) It bases its explanation on the occurrence of periods of increased volcanic activity similar to those shown to have caused earlier mass extinctions.
(D) It may explain the relative scarcity of iridium in rocks on the Earth's surface, compared to its abundance in meteorites.
(E) It accounts for the relatively uneven distribution of iridium in the layer of clay deposited at the end of the Cretaceous period.

7. Which one of the following, if true, would cast the most doubt on the theory described in the last paragraph of the passage?

(A) Fragments of meteorites that have struck the Earth are examined and found to have only minuscule amounts of iridium hexafluoride trapped inside of them.
(B) Most diapir eruptions in the geological history of the Earth have been similar in size to the one that occurred in India at the end of the Cretaceous period and have not been succeeded by periods of climatic change.
(C) There have been several periods in the geological history of the Earth, before and after the Cretaceous period, during which large numbers of marine species have perished.
(D) The frequency with which meteorites struck the Earth was higher at the end of the Cretaceous period than at the beginning of the period.
(E) Marine species tend to be much more vulnerable to extinction when exposed to a dramatic and relatively sudden change in sea level than when they are exposed to a gradual change in sea level similar to the one that preceded the extinction of the dinosaurs.

GO ON TO THE NEXT PAGE.

It has become something of a truism in folklore studies that until recently the lore was more often studied than the folk. That is, folklorists concentrated on the folklore—the songs, tales, and proverbs themselves—and ignored the people who transmitted that lore as part of their oral culture. However, since the early 1970s, folklore studies have begun to regard folk performers as people of creativity who are as worthy of attention as are artists who transmit their ideas in writing. This shift of emphasis has also encouraged a growing interest in women folk performers.

Until recently, folklorists tended to collect folklore from women on only a few topics such as health and games. In other areas, as Weigle and Farrer have noted, if folklorists "had a choice between a story as told by a man or as told by a woman, the man's version was chosen." It is still too early to tell how profoundly this situation has changed, but one can point to several recent studies in which women performers play central roles. Perhaps more telling is the focus of the most recently published major folklore textbook, *The Dynamics of Folklore*. Whereas earlier textbooks gave little attention to women and their folklore, this book devotes many pages to women folk performers.

Recognition of women as important bearers of folklore is not entirely a recent phenomenon. As early as 1903, a few outstanding women folk performers were the focus of scholarly attention. But the scholarship devoted to these women tended to focus primarily on presenting the performer's repertoire. Recent works about women folk artists, however, have been more biographically oriented. Juha Pentikäinen's study of Marina Tokalo, a Finnish healer and narrator of folktales, is especially extensive and probing. Though interested in the problems of repertoire analysis, Pentikäinen gives considerable attention to the details of Tokalo's life and cultural background, so that a full picture of a woman and her folklore emerges. Another notable work is Roger Abraham's book, which presents a very clear picture of the significance of traditional singing in the life of noted ballad singer Almeda Riddle. Unfortunately, unlike Pentikäinen's study, Abraham's study contains little repertoire analysis.

These recent books reflect the current interest of folklorists in viewing folklore in context and thus answering questions about what folklore means to the people who use it. One unexpected result of this line of study has been the discovery that women may use the same folklore that men use, but for very different purposes. This realization has potential importance for future folklore studies in calling greater attention to the type of study required if a folklorist wants truly to understand the role folklore plays in a particular culture.

8. Which one of the following best describes the main point of the passage?

(A) It is only since the early 1970s that folklore studies have begun to recognize women as important bearers of folklore.
(B) A careful analysis of the repertoires of women folk performers has led to a new discovery with important implications for future folklore studies.
(C) Recent studies of women folk performers have focused primarily on the problems of repertoire analysis to the exclusion of a discussion of the culture within which the folklore was developed.
(D) The emphasis in folklore studies has shifted from a focus on the life and the cultural background of the folk performers themselves to a broader understanding of the role folklore plays in a culture.
(E) A change in the focus of folklore studies has led to increased interest in women folk performers and to a new understanding of the importance of the context in which folklore is produced.

9. The author of the passage refers to *The Dynamics of Folklore* primarily in order to

(A) support the idea that it is too soon to tell whether or not folklorists are giving greater attention to women's folklore
(B) refute Weigle and Farrer's contention that folklorists prefer to collect folklore from men rather than from women
(C) support the assertion that scholarship devoted to women folk performers tends to focus primarily on repertoire
(D) present an example of the new emphasis in folklore studies on the performer rather than on the folklore
(E) suggest that there are some signs that women folk performers are gaining increased critical attention in the field of folklore

GO ON TO THE NEXT PAGE.

10. The focus of which one of the following books would most clearly reflect the current interest of the folklorists mentioned in the last paragraph?
(A) an anthology of tales and songs collected exclusively from women in different cultures
(B) a compilation of tales and songs from both men and women covering a great variety of traditional and nontraditional topics
(C) a study of the purpose and meaning of a tale or song for the men and women in a particular culture
(D) an analysis of one particular tale or song that documents changes in the text of the folklore over a period of time
(E) a comparison of the creative process of performers who transmit folklore with that of artists who transmit their ideas in writing

11. According to the passage, which one of the following changes has occurred in the field of folklore since the early 1970s?
(A) increased recognition of the similar ways in which men and women use folklore
(B) increased recognition of folk performers as creative individuals
(C) increased emphasis on the need for repertoire analysis
(D) less emphasis on the relationship between cultural influences and folklore
(E) less emphasis on the individual performers and more emphasis on the meaning of folklore to a culture

12. It can be inferred from the passage that early folklorists assumed that which one of the following was true?
(A) The people who transmitted the folklore did not play a creative role in the development of that folklore.
(B) The people who transmitted the folklore were not consciously aware of the way in which they creatively shaped that folklore.
(C) The text of a song or tale did not change as the folklore was transmitted from one generation to another.
(D) Women were not involved in transmitting folklore except for songs or tales dealing with a few traditional topics.
(E) The meaning of a piece of folklore could differ depending on whether the tale or song was transmitted by a man or by a woman.

13. Based on the information in the passage, which one of the following is most closely analogous to the type of folklore studies produced before the early 1970s?
(A) An anthropologist studies the implements currently used by an isolated culture, but does not investigate how the people of that culture designed and used those implements.
(B) A manufacturer hires a consultant to determine how existing equipment in a plant might be modified to improve efficiency, but does not ask employees for their suggestions on how to improve efficiency.
(C) A historian studies different types of documents dealing with a particular historical event, but decides not to review newspaper accounts written by journalists who lived through that event.
(D) An archaeologist studies the artifacts of an ancient culture to reconstruct the life-style of that culture, but does not actually visit the site where those artifacts were unearthed.
(E) An architect designs a private home for a client, but ignores many of the client's suggestions concerning minor details about the final design of the home.

14. The author of the passage uses the term "context" (line 50) to refer to
(A) a holistic assessment of a piece of folklore rather than a critical analysis of its parts
(B) a study that examines a piece of folklore in light of earlier interpretations provided by other folklorists
(C) the parts of a piece of folklore that can shed light on the meaning of the entire piece
(D) the environment and circumstances in which a particular piece of folklore is used
(E) the location in which the story line of a piece of folklore is set

15. The author's attitude toward Roger Abraham's book can best be described as one of
(A) wholehearted approval
(B) qualified admiration
(C) uneasy ambivalence
(D) extreme skepticism
(E) trenchant criticism

GO ON TO THE NEXT PAGE.

J. G. A. Pocock's numerous investigations have all revolved around the fruitful assumption that a work of political thought can only be understood in light of the linguistic constraints to which its author was subject, for these prescribed both the choice of subject matter and the author's conceptualization of this subject matter. Only the occasional epic theorist, like Machiavelli or Hobbes, succeeded in breaking out of these bonds by redefining old terms and inventing new ones. The task of the modern commentator is to identify the "language" or "vocabulary" with and within which the author operated. While historians of literature have always been aware that writers work within particular traditions, the application of this notion to the history of political ideas forms a sharp contrast to the assumptions of the 1950s, when it was naïvely thought that the close reading of a text by an analytic philosopher was sufficient to establish its meaning, even if the philosopher had no knowledge of the period of the text's composition.

The language Pocock has most closely investigated is that of "civic humanism." For much of his career he has argued that eighteenth-century English political thought should be interpreted as a conflict between rival versions of the "virtue" central to civic humanism. On the one hand, he argues, this virtue is described by representatives of the Tory opposition using a vocabulary of public spirit and self-sufficiency. For these writers the societal ideal is the small, independent landowner in the countryside. On the other hand, Whig writers describe such virtue using a vocabulary of commerce and economic progress; for them the ideal is the merchant.

In making such linguistic discriminations Pocock has disassociated himself from historians like Namier, who deride all eighteenth-century English political language as "cant." But while Pocock's ideas have proved fertile when applied to England, they are more controversial when applied to the late-eighteenth-century United States. Pocock's assertion that Jefferson's attacks on the commercial policies of the Federalists simply echo the language of the Tory opposition in England is at odds with the fact that Jefferson rejected the elitist implications of that group's notion of virtue and asserted the right of all to participate in commercial society. Indeed, after promptings by Quentin Skinner, Pocock has admitted that a counterlanguage—one of rights and liberties—was probably as important in the political discourse of the late-eighteenth-century United States as the language of civic humanism. Fortunately, it is not necessary to rank the relative importance of all the different vocabularies in which eighteenth-century political argument was conducted. It is sufficient to recognize that any interesting text is probably a mixture of several of these vocabularies, and to applaud the historian who, though guilty of some exaggeration, has done the most to make us aware of their importance.

16. The main idea of the passage is that
    (A) civic humanism, in any of its manifestations, cannot entirely explain eighteenth-century political discourse
    (B) eighteenth-century political texts are less likely to reflect a single vocabulary than to combine several vocabularies
    (C) Pocock's linguistic approach, though not applicable to all eighteenth-century political texts, provides a useful model for historians of political theory
    (D) Pocock has more successfully accounted for the nature of political thought in eighteenth-century England than in the eighteenth-century United States
    (E) Pocock's notion of the importance of language in political texts is a logical extension of the insights of historians of literature

17. According to the passage, Pocock most clearly associates the use of a vocabulary of economic progress with
    (A) Jefferson
    (B) Federalists
    (C) English Whigs
    (D) English Tories
    (E) rural English landowners

18. The author's attitude toward Pocock is best revealed by which of the following pairs of words?
    (A) "fruitful" (line 2) and "cant" (line 39)
    (B) "sharp" (line 16) and "elitist" (line 46)
    (C) "naïvely" (line 17) and "controversial" (line 41)
    (D) "fertile" (line 40) and "applaud" (line 60)
    (E) "simply" (line 44) and "importance" (line 55)

19. The passage suggests that one of the "assumptions of the 1950s" (line 17) regarding the meaning of a political text was that this meaning
    (A) could be established using an approach similar to that used by literary historians
    (B) could be definitively established without reference to the text's historical background
    (C) could be closely read in several different ways depending on one's philosophic approach
    (D) was constrained by certain linguistic preconceptions held by the text's author
    (E) could be expressed most clearly by an analytic philosopher who had studied its historical context

GO ON TO THE NEXT PAGE.

20. The author of the passage would most likely agree that which one of the following is a weakness found in Pocock's work?
    (A) the use of the term "language" to describe the expressive features of several diverse kinds of discourse
    (B) the overemphatic denigration of the role of the analytic philosopher in establishing the meaning of a political, or indeed any, text
    (C) the emphasis on the overriding importance of civic humanism in eighteenth-century English political thought
    (D) the insistence on a single linguistic dichotomy to account for political thought in eighteenth-century England and the United States
    (E) the assignment of certain vocabularies to particular parties in eighteenth-century England without taking note of how these vocabularies overlapped

21. Which one of the following best describes the organization of the passage?
    (A) A description of a thesis is offered, specific cases are considered, and an evaluation is given.
    (B) A thesis is brought forward, the thesis is qualified, and evidence that calls the qualification into question is stated.
    (C) A hypothesis is described, examples that suggest it is incorrect are summarized, and supporting examples are offered.
    (D) A series of evaluations are given, concrete reasons are put forward, and a future direction for research is suggested.
    (E) Comparisons and contrasts are made, some categories of evaluation are suggested, and a framework for applying these categories is implied.

GO ON TO THE NEXT PAGE.

In 1964 the United States federal government began attempts to eliminate racial discrimination in employment and wages: the United States Congress enacted Title VII of the Civil Rights Act, prohibiting employers from making employment decisions on the basis of race. In 1965 President Johnson issued Executive Order 11,246, which prohibited discrimination by United States government contractors and emphasized direct monitoring of minority representation in contractors' work forces.

Nonetheless, proponents of the "continuous change" hypothesis believe that United States federal law had a marginal impact on the economic progress made by black people in the United States between 1940 and 1975. Instead they emphasize slowly evolving historical forces, such as long-term trends in education that improved segregated schools for black students during the 1940s and were operative during and after the 1960s. They argue that as the quality of black schools improved relative to that of white schools, the earning potential of those attending black schools increased relative to the earning potential of those attending white schools.

However, there is no direct evidence linking increased quality of underfunded segregated black schools to these improvements in earning potential. In fact, even the evidence on relative schooling quality is ambiguous. Although in the mid-1940s term length at black schools was approaching that in white schools, the rapid growth in another important measure of school quality, school expenditures, may be explained by increases in teachers' salaries, and, historically, such increases have not necessarily increased school quality. Finally, black individuals in all age groups, even those who had been educated at segregated schools before the 1940s, experienced post-1960 increases in their earning potential. If improvements in the quality of schooling were an important determinant of increased returns, only those workers who could have benefited from enhanced school quality should have received higher returns. The relative improvement in the earning potential of educated black people of all age groups in the United States is more consistent with a decline in employment discrimination.

An additional problem for continuity theorists is how to explain the rapid acceleration of black economic progress in the United States after 1964. Education alone cannot account for the rate of change. Rather, the coincidence of increased United States government antidiscrimination pressure in the mid-1960s with the acceleration in the rate of black economic progress beginning in 1965 argues against the continuity theorists' view. True, correlating federal intervention and the acceleration of black economic progress might be incorrect. One could argue that changing attitudes about employment discrimination sparked both the adoption of new federal policies and the rapid acceleration in black economic progress. Indeed, the shift in national attitude that made possible the enactment of Title VII was in part produced by the persistence of racial discrimination in the southern United States. However, the fact that the law had its greatest effect in the South, in spite of the vigorous resistance of many Southern leaders, suggests its importance for black economic progress.

22. According to the passage, Title VII of the 1964 Civil Rights Act differs from Executive Order 11,246 in that Title VII

(A) monitors employers to ensure minority representation
(B) assesses the work forces of government contractors
(C) eliminates discriminatory disparities in wages
(D) focuses on determining minority representation in government
(E) governs hiring practices in a wider variety of workplaces

23. Which one of the following statements about schooling in the United States during the mid-1940s can be inferred from the passage?

(A) School expenditures decreased for white schools.
(B) The teachers in white schools had more time to cover material during a school year than did teachers in black schools.
(C) The basic curriculum of white schools was similar to the curriculum at black schools.
(D) White schools did not change substantially in quality.
(E) Although the salaries of teachers in black schools increased, they did not keep pace with the salaries of teachers in white schools.

GO ON TO THE NEXT PAGE.

24. The primary purpose of the passage is to
    - (A) explain why an argument about black economic progress is incomplete
    - (B) describe the impact of education on black economic progress
    - (C) refute an argument about the factors influencing black economic progress
    - (D) describe black economic progress before and after the 1960s
    - (E) clarify the current view about the factors influencing black economic progress

25. Which one of the following best states the position of proponents of the "continuous change" hypothesis regarding the relationship between law and racial discrimination?
    - (A) Individuals cannot be forced by legal means to behave in nondiscriminatory ways.
    - (B) Discriminatory practices in education have been effectively altered by legal means.
    - (C) Legislation alone has had little effect on racially discriminatory behavior.
    - (D) Legislation is necessary, but not sufficient, to achieve changes in racial attitudes.
    - (E) Legislation can only exacerbate conflicts about racially discriminatory behavior.

26. The author concedes that "correlating federal intervention and the acceleration of black economic progress might be incorrect" (lines 58–60) primarily in order to
    - (A) strengthen the overall argument by anticipating an objection
    - (B) introduce another factor that may have influenced black economic progress
    - (C) concede a point to the continuity theorists
    - (D) change the overall argument in light of the views of the continuity theorists
    - (E) introduce a discussion about the impact of federal intervention on discrimination

27. The "continuous change" hypothesis, as it is presented in the passage, can best be applied to which one of the following situations?
    - (A) Homes are found for many low-income families because the government funds a project to build subsidized housing in an economically depressed area.
    - (B) A depressed economy does not cause the closing of small businesses in a local community because the government provides special grants to aid these businesses.
    - (C) Unemployed people are able to obtain jobs because private contractors receive tax incentives for constructing office buildings in an area with a high unemployment rate.
    - (D) A housing shortage is remedied because the changing state of the economy permits private investors to finance construction in a depressed area.
    - (E) A community's sanitation needs are met because neighborhood organizations lobby aggressively for government assistance.

S T O P

IF YOU FINISH BEFORE TIME IS CALLED, YOU MAY CHECK YOUR WORK ON THIS SECTION ONLY. DO NOT WORK ON ANY OTHER SECTION IN THE TEST.

SECTION II

Time—35 minutes

24 Questions

Directions: The questions in this section are based on the reasoning contained in brief statements or passages. For some questions, more than one of the choices could conceivably answer the question. However, you are to choose the best answer; that is, the response that most accurately and completely answers the question. You should not make assumptions that are by commonsense standards implausible, superfluous, or incompatible with the passage. After you have chosen the best answer, blacken the corresponding space on your answer sheet.

1. Walter: Although cigarette smoking is legal, it should be banned on all airline flights. Cigarette smoking in the confines of an aircraft exposes nonsmokers to harmful secondhand smoke that they cannot avoid.

   Which one of the following principles, if established, would justify the proposal put forth by Walter?

   (A) People should be prohibited from engaging in an otherwise legal activity in those situations in which that activity would unavoidably expose others to harm.
   (B) An activity should be banned only if most situations in which a person engages in that activity would inevitably expose others to harm.
   (C) A legal activity that has the potential for causing harm to others in certain situations should be modified in those situations to render it harmless.
   (D) People who regularly engage in an activity that has the potential for harming others when that activity takes place in certain situations should be excluded from those situations.
   (E) If an activity is legal in some situations in which a person's engaging in that activity could harm others, then that activity should be legal in all situations.

2. Physicist: The claim that low-temperature nuclear fusion can be achieved entirely by chemical means is based on chemical experiments in which the measurements and calculations are inaccurate.

   Chemist: But your challenge is ineffectual, since you are simply jealous at the thought that chemists might have solved a problem that physicists have been unable to solve.

   Which one of the following is the strongest criticism of the chemist's response to the physicist's challenge?

   (A) It restates a claim in different words instead of offering evidence for this claim.
   (B) It fails to establish that perfect accuracy of measurements and calculations is possible.
   (C) It confuses two different meanings of the word "solve."
   (D) It is directed against the proponent of a claim rather than against the claim itself.
   (E) It rests on a contradiction.

3. A certain strain of bacteria was found in the stomachs of ulcer patients. A medical researcher with no history of ulcers inadvertently ingested some of the bacteria and within weeks developed an ulcer. Therefore, it is highly likely that the bacteria strain induces ulcers.

   Which one of the following, if true, most supports the argument above?

   (A) People who have the bacteria strain in their stomachs have been found to have no greater incidence of kidney disease than do people who lack the bacteria strain.
   (B) The researcher did not develop any other serious health problems within a year after ingesting the bacteria strain.
   (C) There is no evidence that the bacteria strain induces ulcers in laboratory animals.
   (D) The researcher is a recognized expert in the treatment of diseases of the stomach.
   (E) A study of 2,000 people who do not have ulcers found that none of these people had the bacteria strain in their stomachs.

GO ON TO THE NEXT PAGE.

4. A recent study monitored the blood pressure of people petting domestic animals in the laboratory. The blood pressure of some of these people lowered while petting the animals. Therefore, for any one of the people so affected, owning a pet would result in that person having a lower average blood pressure.

The flawed pattern of reasoning in the argument above is most similar to that in which one of the following?

(A) Because a single dose of a drug acts as a remedy for a particular ailment, a healthy person can ward off that ailment by taking single doses regularly.
(B) Because buying an automobile is very expensive, people should hold on to an automobile, once bought, for as long as it can be maintained in running condition.
(C) Since pruning houseplants is enjoyable for some people, those people should get rid of houseplants that do not require frequent pruning.
(D) Since riding in a boat for a few minutes is relaxing for some people, those people would be more relaxed generally if those people owned boats.
(E) Since giving a fence one coat of white paint makes the fence white, giving it two coats of white paint would make it even whiter.

5. Of the five bill collectors at Apex Collection Agency, Mr. Young has the highest rate of unsuccessful collections. Yet Mr. Young is the best bill collector on the agency's staff.

Which one of the following, if true, most helps to resolve the apparent discrepancy?

(A) Mr. Young is assigned the majority of the most difficult cases at the agency.
(B) The other four bill collectors at the agency all consider Mr. Young to be a very capable bill collector.
(C) Mr. Young's rate of collections per year has remained fairly steady in the last few years.
(D) Before joining the agency, Mr. Young was affiliated with the credit department of a large department store.
(E) None of the bill collectors at the agency has been on the agency's staff longer than Mr. Young has.

6. A primate jawbone found in Namibia in southern Africa has been identified by anthropologists as that of an ape that lived between 10 million and 15 million years ago. Researchers generally agree that such ancient primates lived only in dense forests. Consequently, the dry, treeless expanses now dominating the landscape in and around Namibia must have replaced an earlier, heavily forested terrain.

The argument assumes which one of the following?

(A) Modern apes also tend to live only in heavily forested terrain.
(B) The ape whose jawbone was found lived in or near the area that is now Namibia.
(C) There were no apes living in the area that is now Namibia prior to 15 million years ago.
(D) The ape whose jawbone was found was adapted to a diet that was significantly different from that of any modern ape.
(E) The ancient primates were numerous enough to have caused severe damage to the ecology of the forests in which they lived.

GO ON TO THE NEXT PAGE.

7. Workers may complain about many things at work, but stress is not high on the list. In fact, in a recent survey a majority placed boredom at the top of their list of complaints. The assumption that job-related stress is the most serious problem for workers in the corporate world is thus simply not warranted.

Which one of the following, if true, most seriously weakens the argument?

(A) Those workers who are responsible for the planning and supervision of long-term projects are less likely to complain of either boredom or stress.
(B) Workers who complain of boredom exhibit more stress-related symptoms than do those who claim their work is interesting.
(C) Workers responding to opinion surveys tend to emphasize those experiences that have happened most recently.
(D) Workers who feel that their salaries are commensurate with the amount of work they do are less likely to complain of boredom.
(E) Workers are less likely to complain about work if they feel that their jobs are secure.

8. Would it be right for the government to abandon efforts to determine at what levels to allow toxic substances in our food supply? Only if it can reasonably be argued that the only acceptable level of toxic substances in food is zero. However, virtually all foods contain perfectly natural substances that are toxic but cause no harm because they do not occur in food in toxic concentrations. Furthermore, we can never be certain of having reduced the concentration of any substance to zero; all we can ever know is that it has been reduced to below the threshold of detection of current analytical methods.

The main conclusion of the argument is that

(A) the government should continue trying to determine acceptable levels for toxic substances in our food supply
(B) the only acceptable level of toxic substances in food is zero
(C) naturally occurring toxic substances in food present little danger because they rarely occur in toxic concentrations
(D) the government will never be able to determine with certainty that a food contains no toxic substances
(E) the government needs to refine its methods of detecting toxic substances in our food supply

9. Over the past twenty-five years the introduction of labor-saving technologies has greatly reduced the average amount of time a worker needs to produce a given output, potentially both reducing the number of hours each worker works each week and increasing workers' leisure time correspondingly. The average amount of leisure time per worker, however, has increased at only half the rate at which the average hourly output per worker has grown.

If the statements above are true, which one of the following is most strongly supported by them?

(A) Workers, on average, spend more money on leisure activities today than they did twenty-five years ago.
(B) Labor-saving technologies have created fewer jobs than they have eliminated.
(C) The percentage of the population that is in the work force has grown over the past twenty-five years.
(D) The average hourly output per worker has not risen as much as had been anticipated when modern labor-saving technologies were first introduced.
(E) Twenty-five years ago the average weekly output per worker was less than it is today.

GO ON TO THE NEXT PAGE.

10. Ten thousand years ago many communities in western Asia stopped procuring food by hunting and gathering and began instead to cultivate food. Archaeological evidence reveals that, compared to their hunter-gatherer forebears, the early agricultural peoples ate a poorly balanced diet and had diet-related health problems, yet these peoples never returned to hunting and gathering.

Which one of the following, if true, most helps to explain why the agricultural peoples of western Asia never returned to hunting and gathering?

(A) The plants and animals that the agricultural peoples began to cultivate continued to exist in the wild.
(B) Both hunter-gatherers and agriculturalists sometimes depended on stored and preserved foods instead of fresh foods.
(C) An increase in population density at the time required a higher food production rate than hunting and gathering could provide.
(D) Thousands of years ago similar shifts from hunting and gathering to agriculture occurred in many other parts of the world.
(E) The physical labor involved in agriculture burns more calories than does that needed for hunting and gathering.

11. Should a journalist's story begin with the set phrase "in a surprise development," as routinely happens? Well, not if the surprise was merely the journalist's, since journalists should not intrude themselves into their stories, and not if the surprise was someone else's, because if some person's surprise was worth mentioning at all, it should have been specifically attributed. The one possibility remaining is that lots of people were surprised; in that case, however, there is no point in belaboring the obvious.

Which one of the following most accurately states the conclusion of the argument above?

(A) Journalists should reserve use of the phrase "in a surprise development" for major developments that are truly unexpected.
(B) The phrase "in a surprise development" is appropriately used only where someone's being surprised is itself interesting.
(C) The phrase "in a surprise development" is used in three distinct sorts of circumstances.
(D) Journalists should make the point that a development comes as a surprise when summing up, not when introducing, a story.
(E) Introducing stories with the phrase "in a surprise development" is not good journalistic practice.

12. Individual pyrrole molecules readily join together into larger molecules called polypyrroles. If polypyrroles form from pyrrole in the presence of zeolites, they do so by attaching to the zeolite either in lumps on the outer surface of the zeolite or in delicate chains within the zeolite's inner channels. When zeolite changes color from yellow to black, it means that on or in that zeolite polypyrroles have formed from pyrrole. Yellow zeolite free of any pyrrole was submerged in dissolved pyrrole. The zeolite turned black even though no polypyrroles formed on its outer surface.

If the statements above are true, which one of the following must on the basis of them be true?

(A) Polypyrroles had already formed on or in the zeolite before it was submerged.
(B) Lumps of polypyrrole attached to the zeolite were responsible for its color change.
(C) At least some of the pyrrole in which the zeolite was submerged formed polypyrrole chains.
(D) None of the pyrrole in which the zeolite was submerged attached itself to the zeolite.
(E) Little, if any, of the pyrrole in which the zeolite was submerged reached the zeolite's inner channels.

GO ON TO THE NEXT PAGE.

Questions 13–14

Pedigreed dogs, including those officially classified as working dogs, must conform to standards set by organizations that issue pedigrees. Those standards generally specify the physical appearance necessary for a dog to be recognized as belonging to a breed but stipulate nothing about other genetic traits, such as those that enable breeds originally developed as working dogs to perform the work for which they were developed. Since dog breeders try to maintain only those traits specified by pedigree organizations, and traits that breeders do not try to maintain risk being lost, certain traits like herding ability risk being lost among pedigreed dogs. Therefore, pedigree organizations should set standards requiring working ability in pedigreed dogs classified as working dogs.

13. Which one of the following principles, if valid, justifies the argument's conclusion that pedigree organizations should set standards for working ability in dogs?

(A) Organizations that set standards for products or activities should not set standards calling for a particular characteristic if such standards increase the risk of some other characteristic being lost.

(B) Any standard currently in effect for a product or an activity should be rigorously enforced regardless of when the standard was first set.

(C) Organizations that set standards for products or activities should be responsible for seeing to it that those products or activities conform to all the specifications called for by those standards.

(D) Any standard that is set for a product or an activity should reflect the uses to which that product or activity will eventually be put.

(E) Organizations that set standards for products or activities should attempt to ensure that those products or activities can serve the purposes for which they were originally developed.

14. The phrase "certain traits like herding ability risk being lost among pedigreed dogs" serves which one of the following functions in the argument?

(A) It is a claim on which the argument depends but for which no support is given.

(B) It is a subsidiary conclusion used in support of the main conclusion.

(C) It acknowledges a possible objection to the proposal put forth in the argument.

(D) It summarizes the position that the argument as a whole is directed toward discrediting.

(E) It provides evidence necessary to support a claim stated earlier in the argument.

15. In rheumatoid arthritis, the body's immune system misfunctions by attacking healthy cells in the joints, causing the release of a hormone that in turn causes pain and swelling. This hormone is normally activated only in reaction to injury or infection. A new arthritis medication will contain a protein that inhibits the functioning of the hormone that causes pain and swelling in the joints.

The statements above, if true, most strongly support which one of the following conclusions?

(A) Unlike aspirin and other medications that reduce pain and swelling and that are currently available, the new medication would repair existing cell damage that had been caused by rheumatoid arthritis.

(B) The benefits to rheumatoid arthritis sufferers of the new medication would outweigh the medication's possible harmful side effects.

(C) A patient treated with the new medication for rheumatoid arthritis could sustain a joint injury without becoming aware of it.

(D) The new medication could be adapted for use against a variety of immune system disorders, such as diabetes and lupus.

(E) Joint diseases other than rheumatoid arthritis would not be affected by the new medication.

16. In their native habitat, amaryllis plants go dormant when the soil in which they are growing dries out during the dry season. Therefore, if amaryllis plants kept as houseplants are to thrive, water should be withheld from them during part of the year so that the plants go dormant.

Which one of the following is an assumption on which the argument depends?

(A) Most kinds of plants go dormant at some time or other during the year.

(B) Amaryllis are more difficult to keep as houseplants than other kinds of plants are.

(C) Water should be withheld from amaryllis plants kept as houseplants during the exact time of year that corresponds to the dry season in their native habitat.

(D) Any amaryllis plant that fails to thrive is likely to have been dormant for too short a time.

(E) Going dormant benefits amaryllis plants in their native habitat in some way other than simply preventing death during overly dry periods.

GO ON TO THE NEXT PAGE.

17. Most people believe that yawning is most powerfully triggered by seeing someone else yawn. This belief about yawning is widespread not only today, but also has been commonplace in many parts of the world in the past, if we are to believe historians of popular culture. Thus, seeing someone else yawn must be the most irresistible cause of yawning.

The argument is most vulnerable to which one of the following criticisms?

(A) It attempts to support its conclusion solely by restating that conclusion in other words.
(B) It cites the evidence of historians of popular culture in direct support of a claim that lies outside their area of expertise.
(C) It makes a sweeping generalization about yawning based on evidence drawn from a limited number of atypical cases.
(D) It supports its conclusion by appealing solely to opinion in a matter that is largely factual.
(E) It takes for granted that yawns have no cause other than the one it cites.

18. Everyone who is a gourmet cook enjoys a wide variety of foods and spices. Since no one who enjoys a wide variety of foods and spices prefers bland foods to all other foods, it follows that anyone who prefers bland foods to all other foods is not a gourmet cook.

The pattern of reasoning displayed in the argument above is most similar to that displayed in which one of the following?

(A) All of the paintings in the Huang Collection will be put up for auction next week. Since the paintings to be auctioned next week are by a wide variety of artists, it follows that the paintings in the Huang Collection are by a wide variety of artists.
(B) All of the paintings in the Huang Collection are abstract. Since no abstract painting will be included in next week's art auction, nothing to be included in next week's art auction is a painting in the Huang Collection.
(C) All of the paintings in the Huang Collection are superb works of art. Since none of the paintings in the Huang Collection is by Roué, it stands to reason that no painting by Roué is a superb work of art.
(D) Every postimpressionist painting from the Huang Collection will be auctioned off next week. No pop art paintings from the Huang Collection will be auctioned off next week. Hence none of the pop art paintings to be auctioned off next week will be from the Huang Collection.
(E) Every painting from the Huang Collection that is to be auctioned off next week is a major work of art. No price can adequately reflect the true value of a major work of art. Hence the prices that will be paid at next week's auction will not adequately reflect the true value of the paintings sold.

19. Without information that could only have come from someone present at the secret meeting between the finance minister and the leader of the opposition party, the newspaper story that forced the finance minister to resign could not have been written. No one witnessed the meeting, however, except the minister's aide. It is clear, therefore, that the finance minister was ultimately brought down, not by any of his powerful political enemies, but by his own trusted aide.

The argument commits which one of the following errors of reasoning?

(A) drawing a conclusion on the basis of evidence that provides equally strong support for a competing conclusion
(B) assuming without warrant that if one thing cannot occur without another thing's already having occurred, then the earlier thing cannot occur without bringing about the later thing
(C) confusing evidence that a given outcome on one occasion was brought about in a certain way with evidence that the same outcome on a different occasion was brought about in that way
(D) basing its conclusion on evidence that is almost entirely irrelevant to the point at issue
(E) treating evidence that a given action contributed to bringing about a certain effect as though that evidence established that the given action by itself was sufficient to bring about that effect

GO ON TO THE NEXT PAGE.

20. S. R. Evans: A few critics have dismissed my poems as not being poems and have dismissed me as not being a poet. But one principle of criticism has it that only true poets can recognize poetic creativity or function as critics of poetry—and that the only true poets are those whose work conveys genuine poetic creativity. But I have read the work of these critics; none of it demonstrated poetic creativity. These critics' judgments should be rejected, since these critics are not true poets.

The argument above is vulnerable to criticism on the grounds that it

(A) presupposes what it sets out to conclude, since the principle requires that only true poets can determine whether the critics' work demonstrates poetic creativity
(B) uses the distinction between poets and critics as though everyone fell into one category or the other
(C) gives no justification for the implicit claim that the standing of a poet can be judged independently of his or her poetry
(D) makes an unjustifiable distinction, since it is possible that some critics are also poets
(E) inevitably leads to the conclusion that poets can never learn to improve their poetry, since no poet is in a position to criticize his or her own work

21. Claim: Country X's government lowered tariff barriers because doing so served the interests of powerful foreign companies.

Principle: In order for a change to be explained by the advantage some person or group gained from it, it must be shown how the interests of the person or group played a role in bringing about the change.

Which one of the following, if true, can most logically serve as a premise for an argument that uses the principle to counter the claim?

(A) Foreign companies did benefit when Country X lowered tariff barriers, but consumers in Country X benefited just as much.
(B) In the period since tariff barriers were lowered, price competition among importers has severely limited importers' profits from selling foreign companies' products in Country X.
(C) It was impossible to predict how Country X's economic reforms, which included lowering tariff barriers, would affect the economy in the short term.
(D) Many of the foreign companies that benefited from Country X's lowering tariff barriers compete fiercely among themselves both in Country X and in other markets.
(E) Although foreign companies benefited when Country X lowered tariff barriers, there is no other evidence that these foreign companies induced the change.

22. A scientist made three observations: (1) in the world's temperate zones, food is more plentiful in the ocean than it is in fresh water; (2) migratory fish in temperate zones generally mature in the ocean and spawn in fresh water; and (3) migratory fish need much nourishment as they mature but little or none during the part of their lives when they spawn. On the basis of those observations, the scientist formulated the hypothesis that food availability is a determining factor in the migration of migratory fish. Subsequently the scientist learned that in the tropics migratory fish generally mature in fresh water and spawn in the ocean.

Which one of the following would it be most helpful to know in order to judge whether what the scientist subsequently learned calls into question the hypothesis?

(A) whether in the world's temperate zones, the temperatures of bodies of fresh water tend to be lower than those of the regions of the oceans into which they flow
(B) whether the types of foods that migratory fish eat while they inhabit the ocean are similar to those that they eat while they inhabit bodies of fresh water
(C) whether any species of fish with populations in temperate zones also have populations that live in the tropics
(D) whether there are more species of migratory fish in the tropics than there are in temperate zones
(E) whether in the tropics food is less plentiful in the ocean than in fresh water

GO ON TO THE NEXT PAGE.

23. No computer will ever be able to do everything that some human minds can do, for there are some problems that cannot be solved by following any set of mechanically applicable rules. Yet computers can only solve problems by following some set of mechanically applicable rules.

Which one of the following is an assumption on which the argument depends?

(A) At least one problem solvable by following some set of mechanically applicable rules is not solvable by any human mind.
(B) At least one problem not solvable by following any set of mechanically applicable rules is solvable by at least one human mind.
(C) At least one problem solvable by following some set of mechanically applicable rules is solvable by every human mind.
(D) Every problem that is solvable by following more than one set of mechanically applicable rules is solvable by almost every human mind.
(E) Every problem that is solvable by following at least one set of mechanically applicable rules is solvable by at least one human mind.

24. People were asked in a survey how old they felt. They replied, almost unanimously despite a great diversity of ages, with a number that was 75 percent of their real age. There is, however, a problem in understanding this sort of response. For example, suppose it meant that a 48-year-old man was claiming to feel as he felt at 36. But at age 36 he would have said he felt like a man of 27, and at 27 he would have said he felt just over 20, and so on into childhood. And surely, that 48-year-old man did not mean to suggest that he felt like a child!

Which one of the following techniques of reasoning is employed in the argument?

(A) projecting from responses collected at one time from many individuals of widely different ages to hypothetical earlier responses of a single individual at some of those ages
(B) reinterpreting what certain people actually said in the light of what would, in the circumstances, have been the most reasonable thing for them to say
(C) qualifying an overly sweeping generalization in light of a single, well chosen counterexample
(D) deriving a contradiction from a pair of statements in order to prove that at least one of those statements is false
(E) analyzing an unexpected unanimity among respondents as evidence, not of a great uniformity of opinion among those respondents, but of their successful manipulation by their questioners

S T O P

IF YOU FINISH BEFORE TIME IS CALLED, YOU MAY CHECK YOUR WORK ON THIS SECTION ONLY. DO NOT WORK ON ANY OTHER SECTION IN THE TEST.

SECTION III

Time—35 minutes

26 Questions

Directions: The questions in this section are based on the reasoning contained in brief statements or passages. For some questions, more than one of the choices could conceivably answer the question. However, you are to choose the best answer; that is, the response that most accurately and completely answers the question. You should not make assumptions that are by commonsense standards implausible, superfluous, or incompatible with the passage. After you have chosen the best answer, blacken the corresponding space on your answer sheet.

Questions 1–2

Those who support the continued reading and performance of Shakespeare's plays maintain that in England appreciation for his work has always extended beyond educated elites and that ever since Shakespeare's own time his plays have always been known and loved by comparatively uneducated people. Skepticism about this claim is borne out by examining early eighteenth-century editions of the plays. These books, with their fine paper and good bindings, must have been far beyond the reach of people of ordinary means.

1. The main point of the argument is to
   (A) suggest that knowledge of Shakespeare's plays is a suitable criterion for distinguishing the educated elite from other members of English society
   (B) provide evidence that at some time in the past appreciation for Shakespeare's plays was confined to educated elites
   (C) prove that early eighteenth-century appreciation for Shakespeare's works rested on aspects of the works that are less appreciated today
   (D) demonstrate that since Shakespeare's time the people who have known and loved his work have all been members of educated elites
   (E) confirm the skepticism of the educated elite concerning the worth of Shakespeare's plays

2. Which one of the following describes a reasoning error in the argument?
   (A) The argument uses the popularity of Shakespeare's plays as a measure of their literary quality.
   (B) The argument bases an aesthetic conclusion about Shakespeare's plays on purely economic evidence.
   (C) The argument anachronistically uses the standards of the twentieth century to judge events that occurred in the early eighteenth century.
   (D) The argument judges the literary quality of a book's text on the basis of the quality of the volume in which the text is printed.
   (E) The argument does not allow for the possibility that people might know Shakespeare's plays without having read them.

3. Organization president: The stationery and envelopes used in all of the mailings from our national headquarters are made from recycled paper, and we never put anything but letters in the envelopes. When the envelopes have windows, these windows are also made from recycled material. Therefore the envelopes, and thus these mailings, are completely recyclable.

   Which one of the following is an assumption on which the organization president's argument depends?
   (A) All the paper used by the organization for purposes other than mailings is recycled.
   (B) The mailings from the organization's national headquarters always use envelopes that have windows.
   (C) The envelope windows made from recycled material are recyclable.
   (D) The envelopes and stationery used in the organization's mailings are always recycled.
   (E) The organization sends mailings only from its national headquarters.

GO ON TO THE NEXT PAGE.

Questions 4–5

The frequently expressed view that written constitutions are inherently more liberal than unwritten ones is false. No written constitution is more than a paper with words on it until those words are both interpreted and applied. Properly understood, then, a constitution is the sum of those procedures through which the power of the state is legitimately exercised and limited. Therefore, even a written constitution becomes a liberal constitution only when it is interpreted and applied in a liberal way.

4. The main point of the argument above is that
   (A) written constitutions are no more inherently liberal than are unwritten constitutions
   (B) the idea of a written constitution, properly understood, is inherently self-contradictory
   (C) unwritten constitutions are less subject to misinterpretation than are constitutions that have been written down
   (D) liberal constitutions are extremely difficult to preserve
   (E) there are criteria for evaluating the interpretation and application of a constitution

5. If the statements in the argument are all true, which one of the following must also be true on the basis of them?
   (A) A careful analysis of the written text of a constitution can show that the constitution is not a liberal one.
   (B) It is impossible to determine that a written constitution is liberal merely through careful analysis of the written text.
   (C) There are no advantages to having a written rather than an unwritten constitution.
   (D) Constitutions that are not written are more likely to be liberal than are constitutions that are written.
   (E) A constitution is a liberal constitution if it is possible to interpret it in a liberal way.

6. As far as we know, Earth is the only planet on which life has evolved, and all known life forms are carbon-based. Therefore, although there might exist noncarbon-based life on planets very unlike Earth, our scientific estimates of the probability of extraterrestrial life should be generated from estimates of the number of planets like Earth and the likelihood of carbon-based life on those planets.

   Which one of the following general principles most strongly supports the recommendation?
   (A) There is no good reason to think that unobserved phenomena closely resemble those that have been observed.
   (B) A scientific theory that explains a broad range of phenomena is preferable to a competing theory that explains only some of those phenomena.
   (C) It is preferable for scientists to restrict their studies to phenomena that are observable and forego making estimates about unobservable things.
   (D) A scientific theory that explains observed phenomena on the basis of a few principles that are independent of each other is preferable to a theory that explains those same phenomena on the basis of many independent principles.
   (E) Estimations of probability that are more closely tied to what is known are preferable to those that are less closely tied to what is known.

7. Politician: Unless our nation redistributes wealth, we will be unable to alleviate economic injustice and our current system will lead inevitably to intolerable economic inequities. If the inequities become intolerable, those who suffer from the injustice will resort to violence to coerce social reform. It is our nation's responsibility to do whatever is necessary to alleviate conditions that would otherwise give rise to violent attempts at social reform.

   The statements above logically commit the politician to which one of the following conclusions?
   (A) The need for political reform never justifies a resort to violent remedies.
   (B) It is our nation's responsibility to redistribute wealth.
   (C) Politicians must base decisions on political expediency rather than on abstract moral principles.
   (D) Economic injustice need not be remedied unless it leads to intolerable social conditions.
   (E) All that is required to create conditions of economic justice is the redistribution of wealth.

GO ON TO THE NEXT PAGE.

8. Delta green ground beetles sometimes remain motionless for hours at a stretch, although they are more active in wet years than in dry years. In 1989 an observer spotted ten delta green ground beetles in nine hours; in 1985 the same observer at the same location had counted 38 in about two hours. This difference probably does not reflect a drop in the population of these rare beetles over this period, however, because 1985 was a wet year and 1989 was relatively dry.

Which one of the following, if true, most strongly supports the conclusion drawn above?

(A) Because of their excellent camouflage, delta green ground beetles are almost impossible to see if they are not moving.
(B) The only habitat of delta green ground beetles is around pools formed by the collection of winter rains in low-lying areas.
(C) Delta green ground beetles move about very little to get food; most of their moving from one place to another is related to their reproductive behavior.
(D) Delta green ground beetles are so rare that, although the first specimen was found in 1878, a second was not found until 1974.
(E) No predator relies on the delta green ground beetle for a major portion of its food supply.

9. Chronic fatigue syndrome, a condition that afflicts thousands of people, is invariably associated with lower-than-normal concentrations of magnesium in the blood. Further, malabsorption of magnesium from the digestive tract to the blood is also often associated with some types of fatigue. These facts in themselves demonstrate that treatments that raise the concentration of magnesium in the blood would provide an effective cure for the fatigue involved in the syndrome.

The argument is most vulnerable to which one of the following criticisms?

(A) It fails to establish that lower-than-normal concentrations of magnesium in the blood are invariably due to malabsorption of magnesium.
(B) It offers no evidence that fatigue itself does not induce lowered concentrations of magnesium in the blood.
(C) It ignores the possibility that, even in people who are not afflicted with chronic fatigue syndrome, concentration of magnesium in the blood fluctuates.
(D) It neglects to state the exact concentration of magnesium in the blood which is considered the normal concentration.
(E) It does not specify what methods would be most effective in raising the concentration of magnesium in the blood.

<u>Questions 10–11</u>

Consumer advocate: The toy-labeling law should require manufacturers to provide explicit safety labels on toys to indicate what hazards the toys pose. The only labels currently required by law are labels indicating the age range for which a toy is intended. For instance, a "three and up" label is required on toys that pose a choking hazard for children under three years of age. Although the current toy-labeling law has indeed reduced the incidence of injuries to children from toys, parents could prevent such injuries almost entirely if toy labels provided explicit safety information.

10. Which one of the following, if true, most strengthens the consumer advocate's argument?

(A) Certain types of toys have never been associated with injury to children.
(B) Most parents believe that the current labels are recommendations regarding level of cognitive skill.
(C) The majority of children injured by toys are under three years of age.
(D) Many parents do not pay attention to manufacturers' labels when they select toys for their children.
(E) Choking is the most serious hazard presented to children by toys.

11. The statement that the law should require explicit safety labels on toys serves which one of the following functions in the consumer advocate's argument?

(A) It is a general principle supporting the conclusion of the argument.
(B) It is a proposed compromise between two conflicting goals.
(C) It is the conclusion of the argument.
(D) It is evidence that must be refuted in order to establish the conclusion of the argument.
(E) It is a particular instance of the general position under discussion.

GO ON TO THE NEXT PAGE.

12. Proponents of organic farming claim that using chemical fertilizers and pesticides in farming is harmful to local wildlife. To produce the same amount of food, however, more land must be under cultivation when organic farming techniques are used than when chemicals are used. Therefore, organic farming leaves less land available as habitat for local wildlife.

Which one of the following is an assumption on which the author's argument depends?

(A) Chemical fertilizers and pesticides pose no health threat to wildlife.
(B) Wildlife living near farms where chemicals are used will not ingest any food or water containing those chemicals.
(C) The only disadvantage to using chemicals in farming is their potential effect on wildlife.
(D) The same crops are grown on organic farms as on farms where chemicals are used.
(E) Land cultivated by organic farming methods no longer constitutes a habitat for wildlife.

13. Reptiles are air-breathing vertebrates with completely ossified skeletons; so alligators must be air-breathing vertebrates with completely ossified skeletons.

In terms of its logical features, the argument above most resembles which one of the following?

(A) Green plants take in carbon dioxide and release oxygen back into the air; so it follows that grass takes in carbon dioxide and releases oxygen into the air.
(B) Some red butterflies are poisonous to birds that prey on them; so this particular red butterfly is poisonous to birds that prey on it.
(C) Knowledge about the empirical world can be gained from books; so Virginia Woolf's book *A Room of One's Own* must provide knowledge about the empirical world.
(D) Dierdre has seen every film directed by Rainer Werner Fassbinder; so Dierdre must have seen *Ali: Fear Eats the Soul*, a film directed by Fassbinder.
(E) Skiers run a high risk of bone fracture; so it is likely that Lindsey, who has been an avid skier for many years, has suffered a broken bone at some point.

14. Although inflated government spending for weapons research encourages waste at weapons research laboratories, weapons production plants must be viewed as equally wasteful of taxpayer dollars. After all, by the government's own admission, the weapons plant it plans to reopen will violate at least 69 environmental, health, and safety laws. The government has decided to reopen the plant and exempt it from compliance, even though the weapons to be produced there could be produced at the same cost at a safer facility.

The reasoning in the argument is most vulnerable to criticism on which one of the following grounds?

(A) It offers no evidence that the "safer" alternative production site actually complies with any of the laws mentioned.
(B) It concedes a point regarding weapons research laboratories that undermines its conclusion about weapons production plants.
(C) It relies on evidence that does not directly address the issue of wasteful spending.
(D) It confuses necessary expenditures for research with wasteful spending on weapons.
(E) It fails to establish that research laboratories and weapons production plants are similar enough to be meaningfully compared.

GO ON TO THE NEXT PAGE.

Questions 15–16

Dr. Godfrey: Now that high school students are allowed to work more than 15 hours per week at part-time jobs, those who actually do so show less interest in school and get lower grades than those who do not work as many hours at part-time jobs. Obviously, working long hours at part-time jobs during the school year contributes to the academic problems that many of our high school students experience.

Dr. Nash: That's not so. Many of our high school students set out to earn as much money as they can simply to compensate for their lack of academic success.

15. Dr. Nash responds to Dr. Godfrey's argument by doing which one of the following?
    (A) attempting to downplay the seriousness of the problems facing academically troubled high school students
    (B) offering an alternative interpretation of the evidence cited by Dr. Godfrey
    (C) questioning the accuracy of the evidence on which Dr. Godfrey bases his conclusion
    (D) proposing that the schools are not at fault for the academic problems facing many high school students
    (E) raising the possibility that there is no relationship between academic problems among high school students and part-time employment

16. The answer to which one of the following would be the most helpful in determining whether the conclusion that Dr. Godfrey draws could be logically defended against Dr. Nash's counterargument?
    (A) whether people who have had academic problems in high school are ultimately less successful in their careers than people who have not had such problems
    (B) whether students are allowed to spend more than 15 hours per week at school-sponsored nonacademic extracurricular activities such as team sports or clubs
    (C) whether the students who work more than 15 hours per week and have academic problems had such problems before they began to work that many hours
    (D) whether employers and high school students typically obey all the laws that regulate the conditions under which young people may legally be employed
    (E) whether high school students who have after-school jobs continue to work at those jobs after graduating from high school

17. X: Medical research on animals should not be reduced in response to a concern for animals, because results of such research serve to avert human suffering. In such research a trade-off between human and animal welfare is always inevitable, but we should give greater weight to human welfare.

    Y: With technology that is currently available, much of the research presently performed on animals could instead be done with computer modeling or human subjects without causing any suffering.

    The relationship of Y's response to X's argument is that Y's response
    (A) contradicts a premise on which X's argument relies
    (B) disagrees with X about the weight to be given to animal suffering as opposed to human suffering
    (C) presents a logical consequence of the premises of X's argument
    (D) strengthens X's argument by presenting evidence not mentioned by X
    (E) supplies a premise to X's argument that was not explicitly stated

18. In experiments in which certain kinds of bacteria were placed in a generous supply of nutrients, the populations of bacteria grew rapidly, and genetic mutations occurred at random in the populations. These experiments show that all genetic mutation is random.

    Which one of the following, if true, enables the conclusion to be properly drawn?
    (A) Either all genetic mutations are random or none are random.
    (B) The bacteria tested in the experiments were of extremely common forms.
    (C) If all genetic mutations in bacteria are random, then all genetic mutations in every other life form are random also.
    (D) The kind of environment in which genetic mutation takes place has no effect on the way genetic mutation occurs.
    (E) The nutrients used were the same as those that nourish the bacteria in nature.

GO ON TO THE NEXT PAGE.

19. Thomas: The club president had no right to disallow Jeffrey's vote. Club rules say that only members in good standing may vote. You've admitted that club rules also say that all members whose dues are fully paid are members in good standing. And since, as the records indicate, Jeffrey has always paid his dues on time, clearly the president acted in violation of club rules.

Althea: By that reasoning my two-year-old niece can legally vote in next month's national election since she is a citizen of this country, and only citizens can legally vote in national elections.

The reasoning in Thomas' argument is flawed because his argument

(A) fails to take into account the distinction between something not being prohibited and its being authorized
(B) offers evidence that casts doubt on the character of the club president and thereby ignores the question of voting eligibility
(C) wrongly assumes that if a statement is not actually denied by someone, that statement must be regarded as true
(D) does not specify the issue with respect to which the disputed vote was cast
(E) overlooks the possibility that Althea is not an authority on the club's rules

20. Calories consumed in excess of those with which the body needs to be provided to maintain its weight are normally stored as fat and the body gains weight. Alcoholic beverages are laden with calories. However, those people who regularly drink two or three alcoholic beverages a day and thereby exceed the caloric intake necessary to maintain their weight do not in general gain weight.

Which one of the following, if true, most helps to resolve the apparent discrepancy?

(A) Some people who regularly drink two or three alcoholic beverages a day avoid exceeding the caloric intake necessary to maintain their weight by decreasing caloric intake from other sources.
(B) Excess calories consumed by people who regularly drink two or three alcoholic beverages a day tend to be dissipated as heat.
(C) Some people who do not drink alcoholic beverages but who eat high-calorie foods do not gain weight.
(D) Many people who regularly drink more than three alcoholic beverages a day do not gain weight.
(E) Some people who take in fewer calories than are normally necessary to maintain their weight do not lose weight.

21. When a person with temporal lobe epilepsy is having an epileptic seizure, part of the brain's temporal lobe produces abnormal electrical impulses, which can often, but not always, be detected through a test called an electroencephalogram (EEG). Therefore, although a positive EEG reading—that is, evidence of abnormal electrical impulses—during an apparent seizure is a reasonably reliable indicator of temporal lobe epilepsy, ______

Of the following, which one logically completes the conclusion above?

(A) a positive reading is just as reliable an indicator of the absence of temporal lobe epilepsy
(B) a positive reading can also indicate the presence of other forms of epilepsy
(C) a positive reading is more frequently an erroneous reading than is a negative one
(D) a negative reading does not mean that temporal lobe epilepsy can be ruled out
(E) a negative reading is just as reliable an indicator of the presence of temporal lobe epilepsy

GO ON TO THE NEXT PAGE.

22. In Sheldon most bicyclists aged 18 and over have lights on their bicycles, whereas most bicyclists under the age of 18 do not. It follows that in Sheldon most bicyclists who have lights on their bicycles are at least 18 years old.

Which one of the following exhibits a pattern of flawed reasoning most similar to that in the argument above?

(A) Most of the people in Sheldon buy gasoline on Mondays only. But almost everyone in Sheldon buys groceries on Tuesdays only. It follows that fewer than half of the people in Sheldon buy gasoline on the same day on which they buy groceries.
(B) The Sheldon Library lent more books during the week after it began lending videos than it had in the entire preceding month. It follows that the availability of videos was responsible for the increase in the number of books lent.
(C) Most of the residents of Sheldon who voted in the last election are on the Conservative party's mailing list, whereas most of Sheldon's residents who did not vote are not on the list. It follows that most of the residents of Sheldon on the Conservative party's mailing list voted in the last election.
(D) In the county where Sheldon is located, every town that has two or more fire trucks has a town pool, whereas most towns that have fewer than two fire trucks do not have a town pool. It follows that Sheldon, which has a town pool, must have at least two fire trucks.
(E) In Sheldon everyone over the age of 60 who knits also sews, but not everyone over the age of 60 who sews also knits. It follows that among people over the age of 60 in Sheldon there are more who sew than there are who knit.

23. Asbestos, an almost indestructible mineral once installed as building insulation, poses no health risk unless the asbestos is disturbed and asbestos fibers are released into the environment. Since removing asbestos from buildings disturbs it, thereby releasing asbestos fibers, the government should not require removal of all asbestos insulation.

Which one of the following, if true, most strengthens the argument?

(A) Asbestos poses far less risk to health than does smoking, drug and alcohol abuse, improper diet, or lack of exercise.
(B) Asbestos can pose a health threat to workers who remove it without wearing required protective gear.
(C) Some kinds of asbestos, when disturbed, pose greater health risks than do other kinds.
(D) Asbestos is inevitably disturbed by building renovations or building demolition.
(E) Much of the time, removed asbestos is buried in landfills and forgotten, with no guarantee that it will not be disturbed again.

GO ON TO THE NEXT PAGE.

Questions 24–25

When volcanic lava solidifies, it becomes uniformly magnetized in the direction in which the Earth's magnetic field points. There are significant differences in the direction of magnetization among solidified lava flows from different volcanoes that erupted at different times over the past several million years. Therefore, it must be that the direction of the Earth's magnetic field has changed over time. Since lava flows differing by thousands of years in age often have very similar directions of magnetization, the change in the direction of the Earth's magnetic field must take place very gradually over hundreds of thousands of years.

24. The argument that the direction of the Earth's magnetic field has changed over time requires the assumption that
    (A) only lava can be used to measure the direction of the Earth's magnetic field as it existed in the distant past
    (B) a single volcano can produce lava of differing consistencies during different eruptions
    (C) not all solidified lava has changed the direction of its magnetization unpredictably
    (D) there are fewer volcanic eruptions now than there were millions of years ago
    (E) as lava flows down the side of a volcano, it picks up magnetized rocks

25. Which one of the following, if true, most seriously undermines the conclusion that the change in the direction of the Earth's magnetic field happened very slowly?
    (A) The changes in the direction of the Earth's magnetic field are determined by the chaotic movement of iron-containing liquids in the Earth's outer core.
    (B) There has not been a change in the direction of the Earth's magnetic field since scientists have begun measuring the direction of magnetization of lava flows.
    (C) The direction of the Earth's magnetic field has undergone a complete reversal several times over the past few million years.
    (D) A lava flow has been found in which the direction of magnetization in the center of the flow differs significantly from that on the surface, even though the flow took only two weeks to solidify completely.
    (E) Since the rate at which molten lava solidifies depends on the temperature and altitude of the environment, some lava flows from volcanoes in certain areas will take years to solidify completely.

26. When the manufacturers in a given country are slower to adopt new technologies than their foreign competitors are, their production costs will fall more slowly than their foreign competitors' costs will. But if manufacturers' production costs fall less rapidly than their foreign competitors' costs do, those manufacturers will be unable to lower their prices as rapidly as their foreign competitors can; and when a country's manufacturers cannot lower their prices as rapidly as their foreign competitors can, that country gets squeezed out of the global market.

    If the statements above are true, which one of the following must also be true on the basis of them?
    (A) If the manufacturers in one country raise their prices, it is because they have squeezed their foreign competitors out of the global market.
    (B) If manufacturers in one country have been squeezed out of the global market, this shows that their foreign competitors have adopted new technologies more rapidly than they have.
    (C) If a country's foreign competitors can lower their production costs more rapidly than the country's own manufacturers can, then their foreign competitors must have adopted new manufacturing techniques.
    (D) If a country's manufacturers adopt new technologies at the same rate as their foreign competitors, neither group will be able to squeeze the other out of the global market.
    (E) If a country's manufacturers can lower their prices as rapidly as their foreign competitors can, this shows that they adopt new technology at least as fast as their foreign competitors do.

S T O P

IF YOU FINISH BEFORE TIME IS CALLED, YOU MAY CHECK YOUR WORK ON THIS SECTION ONLY. DO NOT WORK ON ANY OTHER SECTION IN THE TEST.

SECTION IV

Time—35 minutes

24 Questions

Directions: Each group of questions in this section is based on a set of conditions. In answering some of the questions, it may be useful to draw a rough diagram. Choose the response that most accurately and completely answers each question and blacken the corresponding space on your answer sheet.

Questions 1–6

A professor will listen to exactly one speech from each of six students—H, J, K, R, S, and T. The six speeches will be delivered one at a time, consecutively, according to the following conditions:

The speeches delivered by H, J, and K, no matter what their order relative to each other, cannot form a sequence of three consecutive speeches.
The speeches delivered by R, S, and T, no matter what their order relative to each other, cannot form a sequence of three consecutive speeches.
H's speech must be earlier than S's speech.
J's speech can be neither first nor sixth.
T's speech can be neither immediately before nor immediately after J's speech.

1. **Which one of the following could be the order, from first to last, in which the students deliver their speeches?**
   - (A) H, J, R, S, T, K
   - (B) H, R, T, K, S, J
   - (C) K, J, T, H, S, R
   - (D) R, J, K, T, H, S
   - (E) T, R, J, S, K, H

2. **If T delivers the third speech, which one of the following must be true?**
   - (A) H delivers the first speech.
   - (B) J delivers the fifth speech.
   - (C) K delivers the fourth speech.
   - (D) R delivers the sixth speech.
   - (E) S delivers the fourth speech.

3. **If S delivers the third speech and T delivers the fourth speech, then which one of the following must be true?**
   - (A) H delivers the second speech.
   - (B) J delivers the fifth speech.
   - (C) K delivers the fifth speech.
   - (D) K delivers the first speech.
   - (E) R delivers the first speech.

4. **If K delivers the first speech and H delivers the fifth speech, which one of the following must be true?**
   - (A) R delivers the third speech.
   - (B) T delivers the fourth speech.
   - (C) J's speech is immediately before H's speech.
   - (D) K's speech is immediately before T's speech.
   - (E) R's speech is immediately before J's speech.

5. **If R's speech is immediately after S's speech and immediately before K's speech, then which one of the following could be true?**
   - (A) H's speech is immediately before S's speech.
   - (B) H's speech is immediately before T's speech.
   - (C) K's speech is immediately before J's speech.
   - (D) K's speech is immediately before T's speech.
   - (E) T's speech is immediately before S's speech.

6. **If K delivers the third speech, any of the following could be the student who makes the fourth speech EXCEPT**
   - (A) H
   - (B) J
   - (C) R
   - (D) S
   - (E) T

GO ON TO THE NEXT PAGE.

Questions 7–13

The country of Zendu contains exactly four areas for radar detection: R, S, T, and U. Each detection area is circular and falls completely within Zendu. Part of R intersects T; part of S also intersects T; R does not intersect S. Area U is completely within R and also completely within T. At noon exactly four planes—J, K, L, M—are over Zendu, in a manner consistent with the following statements:

Each plane is in at least one of the four areas.
J is in area S.
K is not in any detection area that J is in.
L is not in any detection area that M is in.
M is in exactly one of the areas.

7. Which one of the following could be a complete listing of the planes located in the four areas at noon, with each plane listed in every area in which it is located?

(A)	R: J, L;	S: J, M;	T: L;	U: L
(B)	R: J, L;	S: K;	T: M;	U: none
(C)	R: K;	S: J;	T: L;	U: M
(D)	R: K, M;	S: J, L;	T: J;	U: none
(E)	R: M;	S: J, K;	T: J, L;	U: none

8. If at noon K is within exactly two of the four areas, then which one of the following CANNOT be true at that time?

(A) J is within area T.
(B) K is within area R.
(C) K is within area T.
(D) L is within area R.
(E) L is within area T.

9. Which one of the following is a complete and accurate list of those planes any one of which could be within area T at noon?

(A) M
(B) J, L
(C) J, L, M
(D) K, L, M
(E) J, K, L, M

10. Which one of the following statements CANNOT be true at noon about the planes?

(A) K is within area T.
(B) K is within area U.
(C) L is within area R.
(D) M is within area R.
(E) M is within area U.

11. It CANNOT be true that at noon there is at least one plane that is within both area

(A) R and area T
(B) R and area U
(C) S and area T
(D) S and area U
(E) T and area U

12. If at noon M is within area T, then which one of the following statements CANNOT be true at that time?

(A) J is within area T.
(B) L is within area R.
(C) L is within area S.
(D) K is within exactly two areas.
(E) L is within exactly two areas.

13. If at noon plane L is within exactly three of the areas, which one of the following could be true at that time?

(A) J is within exactly two of the areas.
(B) J is within exactly three of the areas.
(C) K is within area S.
(D) M is within area R.
(E) M is within area T.

GO ON TO THE NEXT PAGE.

Questions 14–19

Four people—Fritz, Gina, Helen, and Jerry—have formed a car pool to commute to work together six days a week from Monday through Saturday. Each day exactly one of the people drives. The schedule of the car pool's drivers for any given week must meet the following conditions:

Each person drives on at least one day.
No person drives on two consecutive days.
Fritz does not drive on Monday.
Jerry drives on Wednesday or Saturday or both, and he may also drive on other days.
If Gina drives on Monday, then Jerry does not drive on Saturday.

14. Which one of the following could be the schedule of drivers for one week, for the days Monday through Saturday, respectively?

(A) Gina, Fritz, Jerry, Helen, Gina, Gina
(B) Gina, Fritz, Jerry, Helen, Fritz, Jerry
(C) Helen, Fritz, Gina, Jerry, Helen, Fritz
(D) Helen, Gina, Jerry, Fritz, Helen, Fritz
(E) Helen, Gina, Jerry, Helen, Jerry, Gina

15. Which one of the following could be true of one week's schedule of drivers?

(A) Fritz drives on both Wednesday and Saturday.
(B) Gina drives on both Monday and Wednesday.
(C) Jerry drives on both Tuesday and Friday.
(D) Gina drives on Monday and Jerry drives on Thursday.
(E) Jerry drives on Wednesday and Gina drives on Saturday.

16. If during one week Jerry drives on Wednesday and Saturday only, which one of the following must be true of that week?

(A) Fritz drives on Tuesday.
(B) Gina drives on Friday.
(C) Helen drives on Monday.
(D) Fritz drives on exactly two days.
(E) Helen drives on exactly two days.

17. If during one week Gina drives on Monday and Saturday only, which one of the following must be true of that week?

(A) One other person besides Gina drives on exactly two days.
(B) The person who drives on Wednesday does not drive on Friday.
(C) Helen drives on a day immediately before a day on which Fritz drives.
(D) Either Fritz or Helen drives on Friday.
(E) Either Helen or Jerry drives on Tuesday.

18. Which one of the following CANNOT be true of one week's schedule of drivers?

(A) Fritz drives on Tuesday and Gina drives on Friday.
(B) Gina drives on Monday and Jerry drives on Tuesday.
(C) Gina drives on Monday and Jerry drives on Friday.
(D) Helen drives on Monday and Jerry drives on Tuesday.
(E) Helen drives on Tuesday and Jerry drives on Friday.

19. If during one week Fritz drives exactly twice but he drives on neither Tuesday nor Wednesday, which one of the following could be true of that week?

(A) One person drives exactly three times during the week.
(B) Three people drive exactly one time each during the week.
(C) Jerry drives on no day that is immediately before a day on which Fritz drives.
(D) Gina drives on Wednesday.
(E) Jerry drives on Friday.

GO ON TO THE NEXT PAGE.

<u>Questions 20–24</u>

Five experienced plumbers—Frank, Gene, Jill, Kathy, and Mark—and four inexperienced plumbers—Roberta, Sally, Tim, and Vernon—must decide which of them will be assigned to four work teams of exactly two plumbers each. Assignments must meet the following restrictions:

Each plumber is assigned to at most one team.
At least one plumber on each team must be experienced.
Neither Mark nor Roberta nor Vernon can be assigned to a team with Frank.
If Tim is assigned to a team, either Gene or Kathy must be assigned to that team.
Jill cannot be assigned to a team with Roberta.

20. **Which one of the following is an inexperienced plumber who can be assigned to a team with Frank?**

(A) Kathy
(B) Roberta
(C) Sally
(D) Tim
(E) Vernon

21. **Which one of the following is a pair of plumbers who can be assigned together to a team?**

(A) Frank and Roberta
(B) Frank and Vernon
(C) Jill and Mark
(D) Roberta and Tim
(E) Sally and Vernon

22. **If Tim is assigned to a team, and if Sally is assigned to a team with a plumber who could have been assigned to a team with Tim, then the only plumber with whom Frank could be assigned to a team is**

(A) Gene
(B) Jill
(C) Mark
(D) Roberta
(E) Vernon

23. **If Gene is not assigned to a team, then Jill must be assigned to a team with**

(A) Vernon
(B) Tim
(C) Mark
(D) Kathy
(E) Frank

24. **If all of the inexperienced plumbers are assigned to teams, and neither Roberta nor Tim nor Vernon is assigned to a team with Gene, then Sally must be assigned to a team with either**

(A) Frank or else Gene
(B) Frank or else Mark
(C) Gene or else Mark
(D) Jill or else Kathy
(E) Jill or else Mark

S T O P

IF YOU FINISH BEFORE TIME IS CALLED, YOU MAY CHECK YOUR WORK ON THIS SECTION ONLY. DO NOT WORK ON ANY OTHER SECTION IN THE TEST.

SIGNATURE ______________________ __/__/__
DATE

LSAT WRITING SAMPLE TOPIC

Coach Mineko Sato is choosing members of her team to form a squad that will compete in this year's Big Basin International Games. Each squad member will compete in one event, and the overall prize goes to the squad whose members win the most events. With four of the five squad members chosen, Coach Sato is selecting a skier to compete in the 10K cross-country event. Write an argument supporting one of two candidates over the other based on the following criteria:

- To win the overall prize, Coach Sato needs a skier who is likely to win the 10K event.
- Coach Sato wants a skier who will provide leadership and inspire the squad to work well together.

One of cross-country skiing's all-time greats, Andrea Anderson has won the 10K event at the Big Basin games for four straight years, twice setting a new world record. Shortly after last year's games, Anderson suffered a serious knee injury that has hampered her performance for most of this season, although a team physician has predicted that her knee will be fully healed in time for the Big Basin games three months from now. Anderson is both outgoing and outspoken. Her vivid sense of humor and high energy have made her popular with teammates, yet several times in the last year she received bad press for publicly criticizing a teammate.

Undefeated so far this season, Bettina Schmidt is viewed by many as cross-country skiing's next great champion. Schmidt's recent achievements include her first-ever defeat of Anderson, a goal that had eluded her for several years. She performs best on hilly, winding courses like the one at Big Basin. She recently missed several team meetings, claiming that her time was better spent working out, and she rarely joins in the team's social activities. Her teammates, nonetheless, admire her skill and drive, and she is known for her encouragement during competition, especially when someone on the team suffers a difficulty or setback.

Computing Your Score

Directions:

1. Use the Answer Key on the next page to check your answers.
2. Use the Scoring Worksheet below to compute your raw score.
3. Use the Score Conversion Chart to convert your raw score into the 120-180 scale.

Scoring Worksheet

1. Enter the number of questions you answered correctly in each section.

	Number Correct
SECTION I	_____
SECTION II	_____
SECTION III	_____
SECTION IV	_____

2. Enter the sum here: _____
This is your Raw Score.

Conversion Chart

For Converting Raw Score to the 120-180 LSAT Scaled Score
LSAT Form 6LSS27

Reported Score	Raw Score Lowest	Raw Score Highest
180	100	101
179	99	99
178	–*	–*
177	98	98
176	97	97
175	–*	–*
174	96	96
173	95	95
172	94	94
171	93	93
170	92	92
169	91	91
168	89	90
167	88	88
166	87	87
165	85	86
164	84	84
163	82	83
162	80	81
161	78	79
160	77	77
159	75	76
158	73	74
157	71	72
156	69	70
155	67	68
154	65	66
153	63	64
152	61	62
151	59	60
150	57	58
149	55	56
148	54	54
147	52	53
146	50	51
145	48	49
144	46	47
143	44	45
142	43	43
141	41	42
140	39	40
139	38	38
138	36	37
137	35	35
136	33	34
135	32	32
134	30	31
133	29	29
132	28	28
131	26	27
130	25	25
129	24	24
128	23	23
127	22	22
126	21	21
125	20	20
124	19	19
123	–*	–*
122	18	18
121	17	17
120	0	16

*There is no raw score that will produce this scaled score for this form.

Answer Key

Section I

1. C
2. A
3. D
4. A
5. D
6. B
7. B
8. E
9. E
10. C
11. B
12. A
13. A
14. D
15. B
16. C
17. C
18. D
19. B
20. D
21. A
22. E
23. B
24. C
25. C
26. A
27. D

Section II

1. A
2. D
3. E
4. D
5. A
6. B
7. B
8. A
9. E
10. C
11. E
12. C
13. E
14. B
15. C
16. E
17. D
18. B
19. A
20. A
21. E
22. E
23. B
24. A

Section III

1. B
2. E
3. C
4. A
5. B
6. E
7. B
8. A
9. B
10. B
11. C
12. E
13. A
14. C
15. B
16. C
17. A
18. A
19. A
20. B
21. D
22. C
23. E
24. C
25. D
26. E

Section IV

1. D
2. B
3. C
4. A
5. D
6. A
7. D
8. A
9. E
10. E
11. D
12. E
13. A
14. D
15. E
16. C
17. A
18. B
19. E
20. C
21. C
22. B
23. A
24. A

Answers Explained

Section I

Passage 1

1. (C) It was the iridium found in clay deposits that, in part, led scientists during the 1980s to propose the meteorite-impact theory because the element was found in meteorites but rarely on the Earth's surface. Choices (A) and (D) are incorrect because earlier theories *did* propose a reason for the extinction of ocean species (the drop in sea level). The amount of carbon dioxide released (B) was not, according to the passage, in question. Choice (E) is incorrect because it was not the meteorite that released carbon dioxide, but rather volcanism.

2. (A) The passage specifically states, in the third paragraph, that "the lower regions of the Earth's mantle have roughly the same composition as meteorites."

3. (D) If iridium is "extremely rare in rocks on the Earth's surface," and if the diapirs emitted iridium hexafluoride, in large enough amounts to suddenly cause the extinction of the dinosaurs, there must have been more of it in the lava than on the surface.

4. (A) The author of the passage describes three theories concerning the extinction of the dinosaurs: a dramatic drop in sea level, meteorite impact, and volcanic eruption; each of these occurrences, it was said, could have resulted in the climatic changes that led to the dinosaurs' extinction. The author additionally explains why the latest of the three, the volcanic-eruption theory, appears to be the best theory, giving a number of reasons for that position.

5. (D) The theory described in the third paragraph is the volcanic-eruption theory. According to that theory, the iridium in question came from lava in the form of iridium hexafluoride, "a gas that would disperse more uniformly in the atmosphere than the iridium-containing matter thrown out from a meteorite impact." So the author implies that if the theory is true, then the iridium from lava would have been more uniformly dispersed. Choice (A) is incorrect because none of the theories mentions a "slow but steady increase" in iridium concentrations. There is no correlation suggested between iridium concentration and sea level (B), and the atmospheric iridium is not suggested as the cause of the extinction of ocean species (C), but rather a change in sea level caused by a distortion in the Earth's surface. Choice (E) is incorrect because volcanism *is* a normal geological process.

6. (B) The volcanic-eruption theory could explain why the sea level gradually fell prior to the extinction of the dinosaurs. The last paragraph states, "This change in sea level might well have been the result of a distortion in the Earth's surface that resulted from the movement of diapirs upward toward the Earth's crust." That *movement* could have preceded the eventual volcanic eruptions. None of the other choices is discussed concerning the volcanic-eruption theory.

7. (B) You are looking for the answer choice that would most call into doubt the volcanic-eruption theory (the theory described in the last paragraph). If other diapir eruptions are similar in size to the one that occurred in India before the extinction of the dinosaurs, and if *only* the India incident was followed by climatic change, then it is *unlikely* that volcanic eruption was the cause of the climatic change at the time of extinction. Therefore, the fact would call the theory into question. Choices (A) and (D) concern the meteorite-impact theory rather than the volcanic-eruption theory. The fact that marine species have perished at other times, (C) and (E), is irrelevant.

Passage 2

8. (E) The passage focuses on the recent changes in folklore studies, changes that (1) result in more attention being paid to women performers and (2) lead to a better understanding of

the context in which folklore in general is performed. Choices (A) and (B) are details of the passage rather than its main point. Choice (C) is untrue because it is the older studies rather than recent ones that focused primarily on repertoire analysis. Choice (D) is incorrect. The "life and cultural background" and the "role folklore plays in a culture" are basically the same thing, and so emphasis couldn't shift from one to the other.

9. **(E)** The *Dynamics of Folklore* is referred to as a recent text exemplifying the author's point that women are gaining increased critical attention in the folklore field. The author writes that "more telling is the focus" of this book because it "devotes many pages to women folk performers."

10. **(C)** The current interest of folklorists mentioned in the last paragraph is "viewing folklore in context and thus answering questions about what folklore means to the people who use it." The focus of the hypothetical book mentioned in (C) rephrases this point. The interest is not exclusively about women (A), on traditional versus nontraditional works (B), the changes in the folklore itself over time (D), or a comparison of folklore performers with writers (E).

11. **(B)** Prior to the 1970s, according to the passage, "folklorists concentrated on the folklore . . . and ignored the people who transmitted that lore as part of their oral culture." The change from that position is given in (B): "increased recognition of folk performers as creative individuals."

12. **(A)** If early folklorists tended to ignore the people who transmitted the folklore, it can be inferred that they found them in some way irrelevant to the content of the folklore, that is, that they did not play a creative role in its development. The general ignoring of the folk performers themselves would not support an inference that they were not conscious of their creative role (B) (they would be assumed to have none). And the concentration on the "lore" would not support the assumptions that it never changed (C), the role of women (D), or a variation in meaning given a male or a female performer (E).

13. **(A)** The folklore studies prior to the 1970s generally ignored the person (the performer) in favor of the product (the content of the folklore). Choice (A) is analogous to this situation—an anthropologist ignoring the person (the maker of implements) in favor of the product (the implement itself).

14. **(D)** The term *context* is used in this sentence: "These recent books reflect the current interest of folklorists in viewing folklore in context." The sentence begins a paragraph that follows a description of *these* books, a description that focuses on the books' attention to *details* of the performer's life and the *significance of traditional singing* in the performer's life. *Context,* then, refers to these details and this significance. Choice (D) restates this point: "the environment and circumstances in which a particular piece of folklore is used." All of the other choices reflect an interest in the piece of folklore itself, not in its cultural context.

15. **(B)** The author has this to say about Abraham's book: "Unfortunately . . . Abraham's study contains little repertoire analysis." This statement, specifically the word *unfortunately,* supports a description of the author's attitude as *qualified* admiration (B) rather than wholehearted approval (A). The more negative attitudes suggested by (C), (D), and (E) are not suggested by the passage.

Passage 3

16. **(C)** The passage has to do with the work of Pocock in suggesting that works of political thought should be analyzed by identifying the "language" or "vocabulary" of the writer. The author of the passage suggests that we should "applaud the historian [Pocock] who, though guilty of some exaggeration, has done the most to make us aware of their [vocabu-

laries'] importance." Choice (C) restates this main idea. The other choices are points made in the passage, but they reflect minor points, not the main idea.

17. **(C)** Pocock associates the use of a vocabulary of economic progress with the English Whigs, which is evident in the second paragraph. "On the other hand, Whig writers describe such virtue using a vocabulary of commerce and economic progress."

18. **(D)** The author of the passage refers to Pocock's ideas as *fertile* and suggests that Pocock should be *applauded*. The term *fruitful* refers to Pocock's work, but the term *cant* describes the view of other historians concerning eighteenth-century political language (A). The terms *sharp* and *elitist* (B) concern the contrast between historical assumptions and Jefferson's attitude, respectively, not the author's attitude toward Pocock. *Naively* is the author's term for the making of assumptions by earlier historians, although *controversial* does describe Pocock's ideas (C). The terms *simply* and *importance* do not refer to a person (E).

19. **(B)** The author states that in the 1950s it "was naively thought that the close reading of a text by an analytic philosopher was sufficient to establish its meaning, even if the philosopher had no knowledge of the period of the text's composition." Such analytic philosophers would think, then, that the meaning of the text could be definitively established without reference to the text's historical background (B). Literary historians (A) *did* attend to such background. These philosophers were reading in only one way, not several (C) and would have ignored the "linguistic preconceptions" and "historical context,"(D) and (E).

20. **(D)** While the author considers Pocock's work worthy of applause, the writer also qualifies admiration of Pocock's work by suggesting that it is more controversial when applied to Jefferson and comments that "it is not necessary to rate the relative importance of all the different vocabularies in which eighteenth-century political argument was conducted" but that it is enough to realize that "any interesting text is probably a mixture of several of these vocabularies." The author, then, would consider Pocock's point that Jefferson echoed the language of the Tories to be a weakness. That is, Pocock insisted on a single linguistic dichotomy for both English and U.S. political thought (before he changed his point of view somewhat).

21. **(A)** The passage presents Pocock's thesis concerning the understanding of political thought in light of linguistic constraints, goes on to consider the specific cases of the Whigs and Tories in England and Jefferson and the Federalists in the United States, and ends with an overall evaluation of the importance of Pocock's work.

Passage 4

22. **(E)** Title VII prohibited employers from making employment decisions on the basis of race. Executive Order 11,246 "prohibited discrimination by United States government contractors and emphasized direct monitoring of minority representation in contractors' work forces." Title VII, then, applied to hiring practices in a wider variety of workplaces, since it dealt with all employers, whereas the executive order applied only to United States government contractors.

23. **(B)** The passage states that "in the mid-1940s term length at black schools was approaching that in white schools." If the term length was *approaching* that in white schools, it can be assumed that the two were not yet equal. If the term length, then, in white schools was longer than that in black schools, teachers in white schools "had more time to cover material during a school year than did teachers in black schools." No *decreases* in school expenditures are mentioned or implied (A). Curriculum issues (C) are not dealt with, nor are any changes in white schools (D). We cannot assume any-

thing about relative salaries (E), only that salaries increased.

24. **(C)** The article specifically refutes the position of the proponents of the "continuous change" hypothesis, proceeding point by point to call their position into question, rather than simply saying it is *incomplete* (A). While the passage does touch on the impact of education (B) and black economic progress (D), these points are dealt with in the passage but are not its *primary purpose.* The passage also is not clarifying *the* current view (E) but rather refuting *a* current view.

25. **(C)** Proponents of the "continuous change" hypothesis concerning the relationship between law and racial discrimination can be summed up in choice (C). These theorists believe that legislation alone has had little effect on racially discriminatory behavior. In the words of the passage in the second paragraph, they "believe that United States federal law had a marginal impact on the economic progress made by black people in the United States." Whether individuals can be *forced* to behave in certain ways (A) is not mentioned. The theorists may well disagree with (B) and (D). The passage doesn't suggest, however, that these theorists would hold the view that legislation exacerbates discriminatory behavior (E).

26. **(A)** By conceding that there may be other reasons for black economic progress, the author anticipates a possible objection to the overall argument of the passage and deals with it directly. While the author does introduce another factor that may have influenced the progress (B), the introduction of the factor would not be a *primary reason* for admitting that the correlation in question could possibly be in error. The author is not conceding a point to the continuity theorists (C), who deal with long-term changes, not the specific attitude change introduced here, or in any way changing the argument to agree with the continuity theorists (D). The entire passage is a discussion of the impact of federal intervention, not just material introduced here (E).

27. **(D)** The "continuous change" hypothesis suggests that "slowly evolving historical forces, such as long-term trends in education" were responsible for black progress and that "federal law had a marginal impact." These theories would be compatible with the situation given in (D). The housing shortage in question is not remedied by laws mandating a change but rather by a change in the economy leading to private investment. Choices (A), (B), (C), and (E) all deal with *government* involvement, which the theorists would believe to be ineffective.

Section II

1. **(A)** The key words in this correct answer are *prohibited, legal,* and *unavoidably.* The point of the argument is that although cigarette smoking is *legal,* it should be *prohibited* on airplanes, because there the harmful exposure to others is *unavoidable* (they "cannot avoid" it). Choice (B) introduces the words *only, most situations,* and *inevitably,* all of which introduce points not made by the argument. There is no suggestion in the argument that the activity should be *modified* (C), that those who smoke elsewhere should be *excluded* from planes (D), or that because smoking is legal in some places it should be legal in all places (E).

2. **(D)** The chemist's response is a classic example of an *argument ad hominem,* that is, an argument against the person rather than appropriately against what the person has to say. The chemist does not restate a claim (A), confuse the meanings of the word *solve* (C), or employ a contradiction (E). Choice (B) is not relevant.

3. **(E)** The question asks for the answer choice that most supports the point that this bacterial strain likely induces ulcers. If a study finds that the study subjects who don't have the bacteria also don't have ulcers, that point strongly supports the argument for bacteria as the cause of ulcers. Kidney disease (A) has nothing to do with the argument, which

concerns ulcers, nor does the general health of the researcher (B). The fact that the researcher is an expert would have no impact on whether the researcher developed an ulcer or not (D). Choice (C) would weaken the argument rather than support it.

4. **(D)** The flaw in the argument is that it extrapolates results in a single instance to a wide, unsupported generalization. Just because an individual's blood pressure drops in an instance in which the person pets an animal does not mean that the same person would consistently experience such a drop simply because he or she owns a pet. And, indeed, the pressure drop could have been caused by something other than the petting to begin with. The flawed argument in (D) proceeds in exactly the same way. It suggests that an activity (riding in a boat) results in relaxation, so owning a boat would result in consistent relaxation. Here, too, there is no reason to assume necessarily that the boat ride was the cause of the initial relaxation. The reasoning of the other choices does not follow this pattern.

5. **(A)** The discrepancy here is that it would seem not to be possible that Mr. Young's "highest rate of unsuccessful collections" could be compatible with the fact that he is the best bill collector. However, the key here is the meaning of the word *best.* In this case, it can mean that Mr. Young can accomplish very difficult collections that others cannot, although because they are so difficult, more of them are not successfully resolved than in the easier situations handled by others. The other choices are all irrelevant to the seeming discrepancy—the opinion of the other collectors (B), the steadiness of Mr. Young's performance (C), Mr. Young's previous employment (D), and the length of service of the employees (E).

6. **(B)** In order to support the supposition that because these apes lived only in dense forests, this area in Namibia must at one time have been a dense forest, one would have to assume that the ape whose jawbone was found actually lived in this area of Namibia—that is, that the jawbone wasn't somehow moved to the area from some other locale. What modern apes do is not to the point (A), nor is the fact that there were no apes here prior to 15 million years ago (C) (the ape in question lived between 10 and 15 million years ago). And neither the diet (D) nor the number of apes (E) is central to the argument.

7. **(B)** Choice (B) most *weakens* the argument that because boredom was listed at the top of complaints, stress should not be considered the most serious problem for workers. If those who place boredom at the top of their list of problems (a majority of those surveyed) exhibit more stress-related symptoms than those who are not bored, then boredom and stress may well be correlated, thus weakening the argument. In (A), both boredom and stress are ruled out, making it irrelevant to the argument. And whether an experience is recent or in the past (C) or whether workers feel their jobs are secure (E) is not to the point either. Workers who are happy with their salaries (D) might not complain of boredom, but this fact doesn't affect the argument that boredom is most often complained about and that stress is therefore not a big problem.

8. **(A)** The main conclusion of this argument is that the government should continue trying to determine acceptable levels of toxic substances in foods. It makes the point that the only way this would not be true is if it were felt that such substances must be reduced to zero. Since it is not possible to determine whether such substances are reduced to zero, it follows that the government should not abandon its program. Choices (B), (C), and (D), then, are not main points but details of the argument. Choice (E) is not suggested in any way here.

9. **(E)** The point made here is that although workers' output per hour has increased, their leisure time has increased at only half the rate. This fact, if true, most supports the

Diagnostic Exam

statement made by (E). This is a straightforward question. The statements make exactly this point. If leisure time has increased at half the rate of hourly output, it follows that output must have increased also. The subjects of the other choices—money spent on leisure, the number of jobs, the number of those working, and the initial anticipation of hourly output—are not addressed by the original discussion.

10. (C) The question is why these people would not return to hunting and gathering if their agricultural pursuits left them with diet-related problems. Only (C) gives a plausible explanation for this phenomenon. If hunting and gathering could not supply enough food for the population but agriculture could, then this fact supplies a reason for the continuation of agricultural activities. Choices (A) and (B) both deal with experiences common to both types of communities. Whether similar shifts occurred elsewhere, (D) is irrelevant to the question. Choice (E) might explain the basis for the dietary problems inherent in the agricultural community but would not explain why these people didn't go back to hunting and gathering.

11. (E) The argument's conclusion is that using the phrase "in a surprise development" is not good journalistic practice. The argument gives three instances in which the phrase might be used in practice and, for each case, gives a reason that it should *not* be used in that instance, leaving no instances at all in which it should be used. All the other choices list times when it *would* be appropriate to use the phrase and consequently cannot be the correct answers here.

12. (C) Pyrrole-free zeolite is yellow, so, since the zeolite was yellow before it was submerged, polypyrroles could not already have formed on it (A). Lumps of polypyrrole could not have been responsible for the color change (B) because the statements tell us that there were not any on its outer surface (and interior pyrroles are not in the form of lumps). Since the zeolite turned from yellow to black, some pyrrole must have attached itself, so (D) and (E) cannot be true. But (C) must be true. Since it is clear the pyrrole was not on the surface of the zeolite, it must have been in its interior. If it is in the interior, it must be in the form of polypyrrole chains.

13. (E) The correct answer will be a principle that justifies the conclusion of the argument—that standards should be set for performance qualities as well as appearance qualities in dogs classified as working dogs. Choice (A) is incorrect because it suggests that standards for two types of characteristics, used at the same time, would be inappropriate, something not suggested by the argument. The argument has nothing to do with enforcement of standards now in effect, (B) and (C). Choice (D) is much too broad, having to do with *any* product or activity and suggesting that standards should reflect *only* use. Choice (E), however, would justify the argument because it states that the organization setting standards should be mindful of the purposes for which the products or activities were originally developed, in this case the working activities for which the dogs in question were originally bred.

14. (B) The phrase in question serves as a subsidiary conclusion to the main conclusion. The main conclusion is that standards should be set for the working qualities of these dogs. The phrase "certain traits like herding ability risk being lost among pedigreed dogs" is a secondary conclusion used as an example of an ability that is in risk of being lost if such standards are not set. The argument does not depend on this specific claim (A), raise any objection to the argument (C), summarize a position (D), or provide evidence for an earlier claim (E).

15. (C) The statements do not address the repair of damage to the joints (A) (only the avoidance of new pain and swelling), the balance of benefits and side effects (B), or adaptation of the medication to other disorders (D) and (E). But if the new medication contains a protein that inhibits pain and swelling, it

could well mean that a person who takes the medication could have an injury without being aware of it, since these injury indicators would be absent.

16. **(E)** If amaryllis plants in the wild go dormant in dry seasons, the argument states, they should sometimes be deprived of water in the home environment in order to thrive. For this supposition to be valid, it would have to be true that the dry period is of benefit to the plants, in addition to the benefit of keeping them alive in a drought period. If this is not true, then watering them consistently would not harm them and might be of benefit to them. The argument doesn't deal with other sorts of plants, the difficulty of keeping amaryllis plants, or the length of dormancy either in native habitats or in the house—(A), (B), and (D). Choice (C) looks more like a possibility here, but the time of year isn't specified in the argument, and it suggests only that houseplants should be deprived of water for "part of the year."

17. **(D)** The argument is most vulnerable to criticism because it assumes that what "most people believe" is true, without any real evidence to back up the assumption. Choice (D) reflects this criticism. The argument doesn't *restate* its conclusion (A); it states it only once. The reasons for yawning wouldn't be outside the expertise of historians of popular culture (B); it would be just the sort of thing they'd be likely to study. And the argument doesn't rely on a limited number of cases (C); it relies on no cases at all. While choice (E) may at first seem likely, the argument doesn't discount other possible causes for yawning; it says only that seeing others yawn is the *most irresistible cause.*

18. **(B)** The argument proceeds in this way: All A's (gourmet cooks) are B (those who enjoy a wide variety of foods and spices). No B is a C (one who prefers bland food to all other food). So those who are C's cannot be A's. The only answer choice in which the argument proceeds in exactly this way is choice (B). All A's (paintings in the Huang Collection) are B (abstract). No B (abstract painting) is a C (a painting included in next week's art auction). So those that are C's (paintings included in the auction) cannot be A's (paintings in the Huang Collection). The argument in no other answer choice proceeds in this way.

19. **(A)** The argument fails to consider that the information could have come from the leader of the opposition party or even from the finance minister himself. Choice (A) restates this failure. A conclusion is drawn from evidence that could support other conclusions. The other choices are all convoluted statements, but once they are deciphered, they are clearly incorrect. (B) and (E) suggest, in this case, that once the newspaper had the information, it necessarily had to result in the minister's political demise, which isn't the error committed by the argument. Choice (C) deals with separate occurrences, which is not the case in the argument. The evidence used in the argument isn't irrelevant (D). In this particular case, however, although usually it is best to read all the answer choices, it may be the best use of time to immediately recognize that (A) is correct and simply choose that option rather than reading through, and quite possibly being confused by, the remaining choices.

20. **(A)** Evans says that only true poets can judge poetic output. Evans then says that he or she has read the critics' works and judges them not to be poetic. The assumption here is that Evans is a true poet, one who is competent to judge the poetic creativity of the critics' works. Thus, Evans is presupposing what the argument sets out to prove, that Evans is a true poet. Evans's argument does not include any of the faults given by the other choices—suggesting that everyone falls into one category, dealing with judging a poet independent of the poet's work, saying that no critic can be a poet, or in any way implying that poets cannot improve their output.

21. **(E)** If the principle given is meant to *counter* the claim that Country X lowered tariff barriers to serve the interests of powerful foreign

companies, then the choice that could serve as a premise to this argument is (E). The application of the principle suggests that in order for the explanation to be valid, it must be shown how the foreign companies played a role in bringing about the lowering of tariffs. Choice (E) says that although the companies benefited, no evidence exists that they induced the change, an exact application of the principle. All of the other choices are irrelevant to both the claim and the principle—benefit to consumers (A), price competition (B), economic reforms (C), and competition among the foreign companies (D).

22. **(E)** If in the tropics food is more available in fresh water than in the ocean, that finding would square with the hypothesis that food availability is a determining factor in the migration of migratory fish. In both temperate and tropical zones, then, these fish would be spending their non-spawning time where most food is available. If this is not the case, then the hypothesis would be in question. The temperature of the water and the types of food eaten, (A) and (B), are not central to the scientist's hypothesis. The species of fish and their numbers are not important here, (C) and (D), only that the fish are migratory.

23. **(B)** The argument depends on the *assumption* that human minds, or at least one human mind, can solve a problem that is not solvable by applying mechanically applicable rules. No evidence for such an occurrence is given, making it an assumption. All of the other choices involve problems that are solvable by applying mechanically applicable rules, which computers *can* do. The point here is what computers *can't* do that humans *can* do.

24. **(A)** The argument takes a group of responses collected at one time in a survey ("responses collected at one time from many individuals of widely different ages") and then comments on responses an individual in the survey would have made at earlier times, responses that could not truly be known but only surmised. The argument, then, is "projecting . . . to hypothetical earlier responses." The argument does not reinterpret anyone's statement (B), uses no counterexamples (C), deals with no contradiction or pair of statements (D), and in no way suggests manipulation by survey questioners (E).

Section III

1. **(B)** The point of this argument is to discount the claim that appreciation for Shakespeare's plays has always, in England, extended beyond the educated elite. That is, the argument provides evidence to support those who are skeptical about the claim. Choice (B) exactly restates this point. The argument doesn't approach any method of distinguishing the uneducated from the educated (A) or what aspects of Shakespeare's work prompt appreciation at various times (C). The argument deals with a particular time in the past, the early eighteenth-century, so (D) is too broad, dealing with all of the time since Shakespeare lived. And (E) is incorrect because the argument doesn't suggest that it's the "elite" who are skeptical; it simply deals with "skepticism" from an unknown group.

2. **(E)** The argument is faulty because it bases the claim that appreciation for Shakespeare's work couldn't have extended to the relatively uneducated in the early eighteenth century simply because they couldn't have afforded to buy the beautifully bound books containing the works. It fails to consider that these people could have enjoyed the works by some other means, attending a play rather than reading it, for example. Popularity as a measure of quality (A) isn't addressed, nor is any aesthetic conclusion, (B) and (D). No twentieth-century standard is being used (C), but rather evidence from the eighteenth century.

3. **(C)** The president is assuming that because an item is made from recycled material that

same item can itself *be* recycled. Choice (C), then, is *one* assumption made here—that envelope windows made from recyclable materials are then recyclable themselves (the argument makes the same assumption about the other materials, but only the one concerning the windows is an option here). Since the argument deals with only this type of mailing and this particular type made by headquarters, (A) and (E) are incorrect. Whether all envelopes have windows is not to the point here (B). The president doesn't say the envelopes and stationary actually are *recycled* (D), only that they are *recyclable.*

4. **(A)** The point questioned by this argument is whether the expressed view that written constitutions are inherently more liberal than are unwritten ones is correct. The argument suggests that this is not the case. Choice (B) deals with self-contradiction, (D) with preservation, and (E) with evaluative criteria, none of which is mentioned in the argument. The argument does suggest that both types of constitution must be interpreted but doesn't suggest that one is less subject to misinterpretation (C).

5. **(B)** If it is true that a written constitution is a liberal constitution "only when it is interpreted and applied in a liberal way," it follows that by simply studying the words of that constitution one could not determine that it is a liberal constitution. The same statement in the argument makes (A) incorrect—one could not determine that a constitution is not a liberal one without also knowing how it is interpreted. The advantages of one type of constitution over the other are not discussed (C). The argument states that either written or unwritten constitutions may be equally liberal, so (D) is incorrect. And the argument further states that it is a liberal interpretation that makes a constitution liberal, *not* just the *possibility* of interpreting it in a liberal way (E).

6. **(E)** The argument suggests that efforts to establish the probability of extraterrestrial life should be based on the number of planets like Earth that exist, even though there could be non-carbon-based life forms on planets very unlike Earth. The only principle given in the answer choices that would support this claim is that in (E). This principle would support focusing efforts on identifying planets that would likely host carbon-based life forms such as we are familiar with on Earth—that is, estimates "closely tied to what is known." The argument doesn't suggest that life forms would resemble one another (A). The general principle in (B) would contradict the argument's assumption that the narrower path of focusing on carbon-based life is preferable. Any of the estimates in question will in part be based on unobservable phenomena (on planets we cannot observe), so the principle in (C) is not applicable. Whether principles used as the basis for scientific theories are few or many (D) doesn't have an impact on this particular argument.

7. **(B)** If the politician believes that inequities in the distribution of wealth will lead to violent attempts at social reform, and further that it is the nation's responsibility to avoid conditions that will lead to violent attempts at social reform, then the politician is committed to the conclusion that it is the "nation's responsibility to redistribute wealth." The argument doesn't comment on whether violence is ever justified (A) or on political expediency as distinguished from moral principles as a basis for action (C). And it is not suggested that simply because injustices don't lead to intolerable conditions they shouldn't be remedied (D)—the argument deals with those that lead to intolerable conditions but not with those that do not. The problem with (E) is the word *all,* which makes this choice too broad to be a correct answer.

8. **(A)** If these beetles are well camouflaged and difficult to see if they are stationary, then the researcher would logically see more of the beetles in a wet year when they are more active. This fact would support the conclusion that the difference in the number of beetles observed probably doesn't suggest a drop in their population. Choice (B), the habitat of

the beetles, is irrelevant, as is the reason for their movement in this case (C) and the fact that there is no predation on the beetles (E)—if there is *no* predation, there would be *no* effect on the beetle count in the two years. The argument deals with two specific years of counting the beetles, 1985 and 1989, so the fact that the second beetle wasn't seen until 1974 is not relevant to the conclusion.

9. (B) The argument makes the mistake of assuming that if characteristics are associated, one characteristic necessarily *causes* the other. In this case, the assumption is that low magnesium levels cause chronic fatigue syndrome when it is equally logical to assume that chronic fatigue syndrome causes low magnesium levels in the blood. The argument doesn't suggest that low magnesium levels are *always* caused by malabsorption (A). Fluctuation of magnesium levels is not the point in the argument (C), but rather levels that are too low. To be valid, the argument wouldn't necessarily have to state the exact concentration of magnesium needed to be considered normal (D). It would simply have to be correct in saying that the level in question is lower than normal. The method of raising the level is irrelevant to the argument (E).

10. (B) The argument is that explicit labels listing possible hazards would prevent injuries to children from these toys almost entirely. The present labels list appropriate age levels for the toys and are intended to suggest to parents that there are health hazards to children younger than the label indicates if they are allowed to play with these toys. But if parents believe that the labels are indicating appropriate cognitive age for toy use rather than appropriate age to avoid hazards, then changing the labels to specifically list the hazards instead might well result in substantially lowering the incidence of injury. The specific types of toys, the age at which most injuries occur, or the specific types of injuries—(A), (C), and (E)—are not central to the argument and would not strengthen it. Choice (D) would weaken the argument rather than strengthen it. If parents don't pay attention to the labels no matter what they say, there would be no point in changing the labels.

11. (C) The question asks for the *function* served by the statement that the law should require these labels. It is *not* a general principle supporting the conclusion (A) or evidence that must be refuted to support the conclusion (D); it *is* the conclusion. It is also *not* a compromise (B); it is the only proposal made. And it is *not* a particular instance of the position (E); it *is* the position (the conclusion). Here, the conclusion appears at the beginning of the argument rather than at the end as is often the case.

12. (E) If the argument is that because organic farming takes up more land to produce the same amount of food as that produced when using chemicals, there is less land available as animal habitat, it must be assumed that the land used by organic farming is *not* useable as habitat by wildlife. Choice (A) is incorrect both because it deals with both methods of farming and because the argument does not say that chemicals pose no threat to wildlife. Whether animals will or will not ingest food containing chemicals is not to the point either, (B)—the argument focuses only on the amount of land available to the animals in each case. Proponents of organic farming say that using chemicals and pesticides is harmful to wildlife, not the author of this argument, and neither side suggests that this is the *only* disadvantage (C). The types of crops grown (D) would have no bearing on the argument.

13. (A) The initial argument is actually missing one logical step. As it is, it proceeds in this way: A (reptiles) are B (air-breathing vertebrates with completely ossified skeletons). So C (alligators) are B. With the missing step included, the argument would go as follows: A (reptiles) are B (air-breathing vertebrates with completely ossified skeletons). C (alligators) are A (reptiles). So C are B. Choice (A) proceeds in exactly this way, leaving out the missing step. A (green plants) are B (those that take in carbon dioxide and release oxy-

gen back into the air). So C (grasses) are B. The missing step here would be C (grasses) are A (green plants). None of the other choices follows this pattern.

14. **(C)** The argument is dealing with the waste of taxpayer dollars, but its conclusion says that producing the weapons at a safer facility would cost the same as producing them in a nonsafe facility. So it is relying on evidence (the fact that the plant in question will violate 69 environmental, health, and safety laws) that doesn't directly address the issue of wasteful spending. The question of which facility is safer, then, (A) is not part of the argument. The argument is primarily about the cost of weapons production, not weapons research (B), and it does not approach in any way the necessity of either research or production (D)—only the cost of them. Since the argument is about waste of money only, the argument would not need to prove the two types of facilities similar (E).

15. **(B)** Dr. Godfrey contends that the long working hours are causative of lower academic performance. Dr. Nash contends that the work doesn't cause the lower academic performance but rather that the lower academic performance causes the longer hours of work. So Nash is offering another interpretation of the fact that those students who work longer hours show less interest in school and get lower grades. Neither speaker comments on the seriousness of the problem (A) or questions the accuracy of the evidence (C). And neither person discusses where the fault lies in the situation (D). Choice (E) is incorrect because both speakers suggest a relationship between academic problems and employment, but they have opposite interpretations of which is the cause and which the result.

16. **(C)** To determine whether Godfrey's conclusion could be defended against Nash's counterargument, one could determine whether the academic problems in question existed prior to the long work hours. If they did *not* exist prior to this time, Godfrey's point that the work causes the problems would be supported. Knowing what the future holds in store as far as the careers of these students, (A) and (E), wouldn't support either conclusion, nor would the time that students spend on other nonacademic activities (B). Work laws (D) are completely irrelevant to both conclusions, which both concern only time spent working.

17. **(A)** X's argument relies on the premise that there must be a "trade-off," that because research results in averting human suffering, the experiments on animals must be continued. But Y suggests that one can avert human suffering just as well without relying on animal experiments, and consequently the "trade-off" is not necessary at all. That is, Y is contradicting X's premise concerning the need for the "trade-off." Y doesn't disagree with the "weight" to be given to each type of suffering (B) but is instead saying that neither is necessary, and Y's argument doesn't follow from X's, (C) and (E), or strengthen it (D) but rather presents a different point of view that could serve to weaken X's argument.

18. **(A)** The conclusion of the argument is that *all* genetic mutation is random. The conclusion is based on an experiment that involved certain bacteria and certain nutrients and in which mutation was random. In order for this conclusion to be sound, we must be able to extend what happened in the experiment with particular bacteria to a universal statement about what will always happen with all genetic mutations. So, in this case, only if we accept the premise that genetic mutation *must* be *either* all random *or* never random, can we say on the basis of the experiment that all genetic mutation is random. Choices (B), (D), and (E) are irrelevant to the argument, which focuses on *all* genetic mutation, not just that of bacteria and not just in this particular experiment. Choice (C) is incorrect because it doesn't in any way rule out the possibility that in fact there could be both random and nonrandom mutations. It simply gives the possibility that *if all* genetic mutation in bacteria is random then all mutation in other life forms is random also, but here

there is nothing to say that all such mutations actually *are* random.

19. **(A)** What Thomas fails to recognize in his argument is that there may be other criteria used to determine voting eligibility in addition to the dues requirement. Choice (A) doesn't frame this lack in these words but approaches the problem from the same basis. Because Jeffrey has paid his dues, his voting is *not prohibited.* At the same time, his vote might not be *authorized* because he might not have met some other requirement. Althea recognizes this reasoning flaw when she compares another situation in which her two-year-old niece would not be *prohibited* from voting because of her citizenship but might not be *authorized* to vote for another reason, in this case her age. The other options here are all irrelevant to the issue raised in Thomas's argument. Choice (C) might at first look like a possibility here, but it only addresses the fact that Althea admitted to the regulation concerning dues, and it doesn't deal with the issue of other requirements.

20. **(B)** The discrepancy here is why some individuals who drink two or three alcoholic beverages and thereby *exceed* their calorie requirements do not gain weight when others who exceed their calorie requirements, we assume in different ways, do gain weight. If (B) is true, it could explain the discrepancy, suggesting that the calories consumed in this particular situation are dissipated and consequently would not actually add to the overall calorie count of the individual. Choice (A) is incorrect because it contradicts what is stated. The passage states that these drinks *do* cause the exceeding of caloric needs. Choices (C) and (E) don't affect the argument, simply stating that others don't gain weight either, for whatever reasons. Choice (D) simply expands on what is stated in the passage.

21. **(D)** Because of the word *therefore,* which starts the sentence in question, what is needed for the conclusion of the sentence is a statement that will qualify in some way the information concerning the *diagnosis of temporal lobe epilepsy* in this way. The only choice offered that would logically qualify this information is (D). We are told that the EEG *is a reasonably reliable indicator* that temporal lobe epilepsy is present. However, nothing in this information suggests that the test necessarily catches all instances of the disease, so (D) logically follows. Temporal lobe epilepsy may be present even if the test doesn't catch it. Positive readings are generally reliable, so (A) and (C) don't follow. (B) isn't the best answer because the disease in question is temporal lobe epilepsy, not other forms. It is not logical that a negative reading would be in any way a reliable indicator of a disease (E).

22. **(C)** The flaw in the reasoning given is that it doesn't follow that because most bicyclists over 18 have lights, more of them have lights than those under 18. There could be many fewer bicyclists who are over 18 than there are bicyclists under 18. So even if a lower percentage of those under 18 have lights, there could be numerically more of them. The most similar pattern of flawed reasoning is present in (C). Although most of those *who voted* were on the Conservative party's list, it doesn't follow that most of the people on the list *voted.* There could be many on the list who did not vote. The reasoning in (A) is not flawed. The flaw in (B) is one of ascribing a causal relationship without appropriate evidence. Choices (D) and (E) are flawed because they misread the evidence, but not in the same way as the original argument.

23. **(E)** The argument is that asbestos removal should not be mandated because it causes the asbestos to be disturbed, thus creating a health hazard. If the asbestos that is removed ends up in landfills where it may well be disturbed again, creating an additional health hazard, this fact would strengthen the argument that the asbestos is safer left in place. The fact is that asbestos is a danger, and its danger relative to other factors (A) is not to the point here and certainly wouldn't strengthen the argument. The fact that asbestos poses a health risk to those who remove it (B) might strengthen

the argument, but this is not the best answer because it goes on to say that it poses the risk only if proper equipment is not worn. The fact that there are occasions when asbestos in buildings is inevitably disturbed (D) would not strengthen the argument that it should not be required to be removed.

24. **(C)** The question focuses on one point—the argument that the Earth's magnetic field has *changed over time.* The evidence given for this fact is that solidified lava is magnetized in the direction in which the magnetic field points. Consequently, if the evidence is true, then the lava must *not* be unpredictable in its direction (it is *predicted* that it will point where the magnetic field points). In this case, the statement in choice (C) can be taken to mean either that the direction of some of the lava is predictable or that the direction of all of it is predictable. The negative framing of this choice is confusing, but none of the other choices would need to be assumed by this argument, and you could approach this question by eliminating all the obviously wrong answers, leaving only (C) as a possibility. The possibility of determining the magnetic field in other ways (A), the consistency of the lava (B), the number of eruptions (D), and the picking up of magnetized rocks (E) are all completely irrelevant to the argument.

25. **(D)** For this question, you are looking for the statement that *weakens* the conclusion that the change in the direction of the magnetic field happened *slowly.* If direction of magnification is different in two parts of a single lava flow, which had to have happened over a relatively short time, then the direction of the Earth's magnetic field must also have changed over a relatively short time. The reason for the change in direction (A), the fact that there has not been a recent change (B), the number of times of change (C), and the time taken for lava solidification (E) are not to the point here, only that there has been a change at some time in the past.

26. **(E)** You are looking here for the statement that *must* be true, not only for one that *may* be true. Choice (A) is incorrect because a company may have reasons other than lack of competition to raise its prices. Choices (B) and (D) are incorrect because there may be reasons other than competitors' quicker adoption of technology for these companies to have been squeezed out. Choice (C) is incorrect because the lowering of production costs may be made possible by something other than manufacturing techniques. Choice (E) is correct. The passage states "When the manufacturers in a given country are slower to adopt new technologies than their foreign competitors are, their production costs will fall more slowly than their foreign competitors' costs will . . . and they will be unable to lower their prices . . . ." In answering this question, you must accept this as a fact. So if the country in question is equal in the time needed to lower its prices, it must be at least as fast as the other countries in adopting the technology.

Section IV

Answers 1–6

The conditions have been numbered here to assist in locating the explanations.

(Initial set-up condition 1)
Six Speeches: H, J, K, R, S, T

(Condition 2)
H, J, K cannot be consecutive ~~H, J, K~~

(Condition 3)
R, S, T cannot be consecutive ~~R, S, T~~

(Condition 4)
H before S H ? S *or* H → S

(Condition 5)
J not 1st or 6th ~~J~~ ~~J~~
1 2 3 4 5 6

(Condition 6)
Not T J or J T ~~TJ~~

The organizer could look like this:

~~T~~ ~~J~~ | H ? S

~~HJK~~ ~~J~~ ~~J~~

~~RST~~ 1 2 3 4 5 6

1. (D) Which one COULD be true?

(A) HJRSTK	No: RST consecutive, condition 3
(B) HRTKSJ	No: J cannot be 6th, condition 5
(C) KJTHRS	No: J and T cannot be consecutive, condition 6
(D) RJKTHS	Yes: This could be the order
(E) TRJSKH	No: H must precede S, condition 4

2. (B) Which MUST be true?

1	2	3	4	5	6
		T		J	

J must be 5th. J cannot be 1st or 6th (condition 5) or immediately precede or follow T. Thus J must be 5th. Therefore, (B) must be true. If the order is as follows, we see that each of the other answer choices don't have to be true: KHTRJS

3. (C) Which MUST be true?

1	2	3	4	5	6
H	J	S	T	K	R

If S is 3rd and T is 4th, then J must be 2nd (J cannot be 1st or 6th, condition 5, or next to T), H must be 1st (H must precede S, condition 4), R must be 6th (R cannot be 5th which would result in STR consecutive, condition 3). Thus, K must be 5th. Therefore, (C) is correct. The other 4 answer choices are false.

4. (A) Which MUST be true?

1	2	3	4	5	6
K	J	R	T	H	S
	T		J		

Since H must precede S, S must be 6th (condition 4). Since J and T cannot be consecutive (condition 6), J and T must be 2nd and 4th or 4th and 2nd. Thus, R must be 3rd. Therefore, (A) is correct. The other answer choices COULD be true but don't have to be.

5. (D) Which COULD be true?

If SRK are consecutive and in that order, S cannot be 1st, since H must precede S. Therefore, there are three arrangements to consider:

1	2	3	4	5	6
H	S	R	K	J	T

This arrangement is NOT POSSIBLE, since J and T cannot be consecutive (condition 6).

1	2	3	4	5	6
H	J	S	R	K	T

Since J cannot be 1st or 6th (condition 5), J must be 2nd. Thus, H must be 1st (condition 4) and T is therefore 6th. This is a POSSIBLE order.

1	2	3	4	5	6
T	H	J	S	R	K

Since J and T cannot be consecutive (condition 6) and J cannot be 1st (condition 5), J must be 3rd, T must be 1st, and H must be 2nd. This is a POSSIBLE order.

Choice (D) COULD be true. The other answer choices are false.

6. **(A)** Who CANNOT be 4th?

1	2	3	4	5	6
		K	H		

If H were 4th, this would mean that J must be 2nd or 5th (J cannot be 1st or 6th from condition 5). In either case, this would result in HJK consecutively, which violates condition 2. Therefore, H CANNOT be 4th and (A) is thus correct.

The other four answer choices are possible, as follows:

1	2	3	4	5	6	
H	S	K	J	R	T	Choice (B)
H	T	K	R	J	S	Choice (C)
H	T	K	S	J	R	Choice (D)
R	J	K	T	H	S	Choice (E)

Answers 7–13

A Venn diagram is useful in organizing the information in this problem. The four regions, R, S, T, and U, can be drawn as follows to show the relationship among these four regions. Observe that regions R and S have no area in common. Also note that any plane in region U must also be in regions R and T.

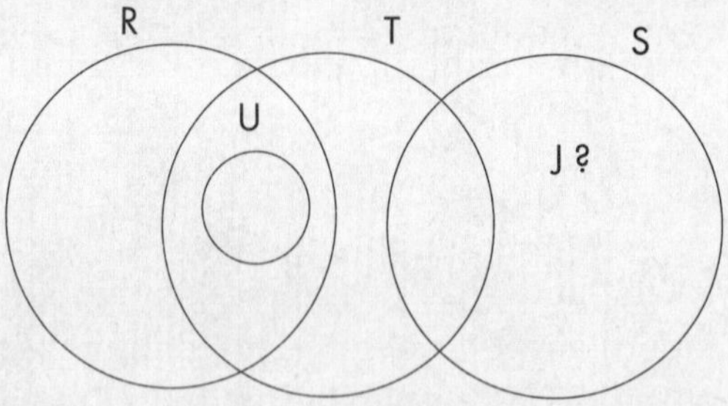

The conditions have been numbered here to assist in locating the explanations.

(Initial set-up)
(Condition 1)
Each plane (J, K, L, and M) in at least one region

(Condition 2)
J in S   J-S *or* J → S

(Condition 3)
K ≠ J (K and J are not in the same region) *or* ~~KJ~~

(Condition 4)
L ≠ M (L and M are not in the same region) *or* ~~LM~~

(Condition 5)
M in 1 (M is in exactly one of the regions)

7. **(D)** Eliminate those choices with conflicts.

(A) is incorrect, since J cannot be in both R and S (regions R and S do not intersect).
(B) is incorrect, since J must be in area S (condition 2).
(C) is incorrect, since M is in exactly one region, and any plane in region U must also be in regions R and S (condition 5).
(E) is incorrect, since J and K are in the same region (condition 3).
(D) is the correct listing.
The following diagram illustrates answer choice (D):

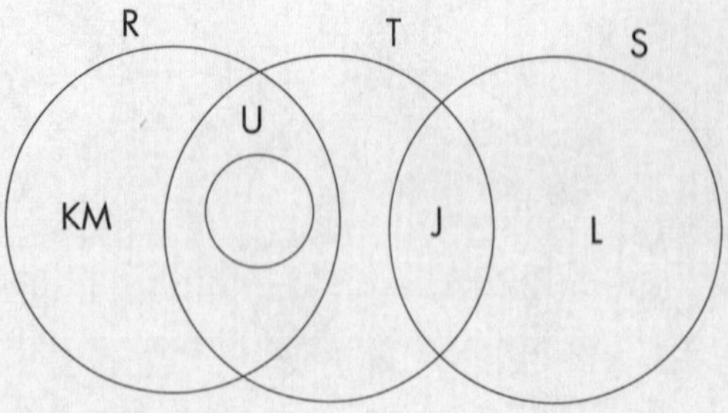

8. (A) Which CANNOT be true?

If K is in exactly two regions, then K must be in region T. Since J and K cannot be in the same region (condition 3), J cannot be in region T. Therefore, (A) is correct. The other answer choices are possible as illustrated below:

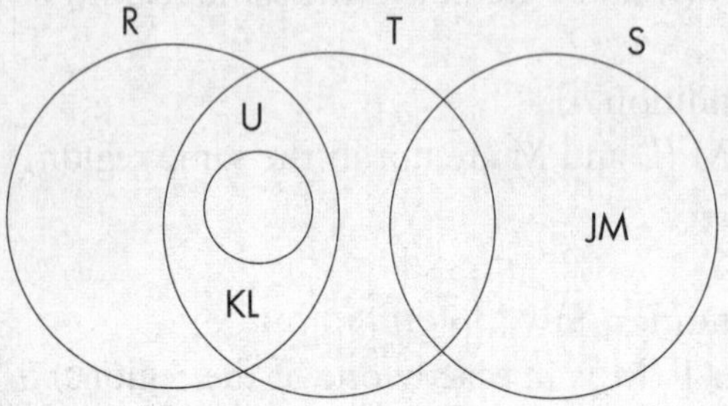

9. (E) Any of the four planes could be in region T as illustrated below:

Planes M or J in region T:

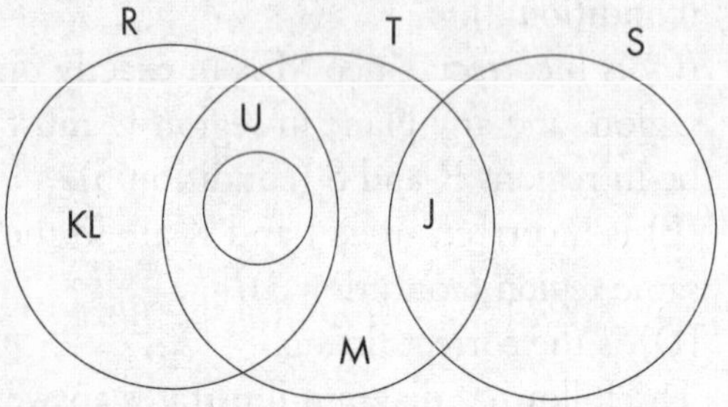

Planes K or L in region T:

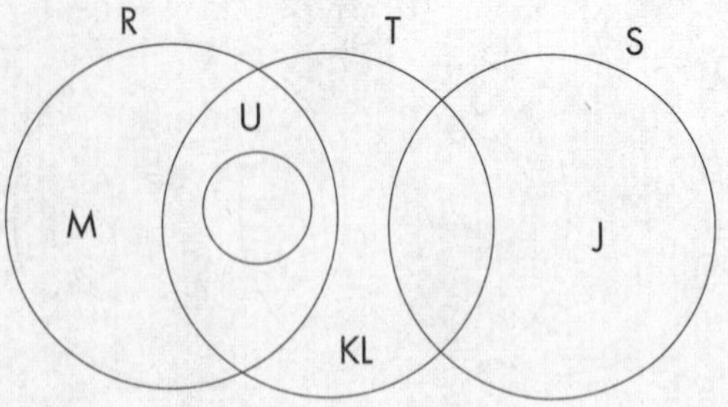

10. (E) Which CANNOT be true?

Plane M is in exactly one region. Since region U is a subset of both regions R and T, any plane in region U must also be in regions R and T. Thus, M cannot be in region U, since it would be in three regions. Therefore, (E) is correct. Each of the other answer choices COULD be true.

11. (D) Which CANNOT be true?

Region S does not intersect regions R or U. Therefore, it is not possible for a plane to be in both regions S and U at the same time. Thus, (D) is correct. Each of the other intersections exist, and could contain at least one plane.

12. (E) Which CANNOT be true?

If a plane is in exactly two regions, it must be in region T. If M is in region T, then L cannot be in region T (condition 4). Therefore, L CANNOT be in exactly two regions. Thus, (E) is correct. Each of the other answer choices is possible.

This diagram illustrates that (A) and (B) are possible:

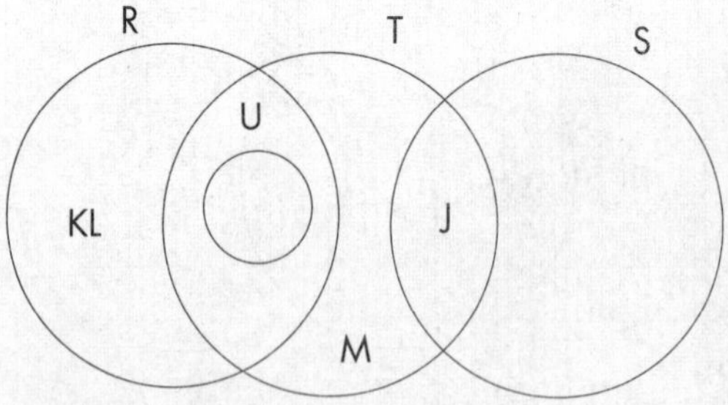

This diagram illustrates that (C) and (D) are possible:

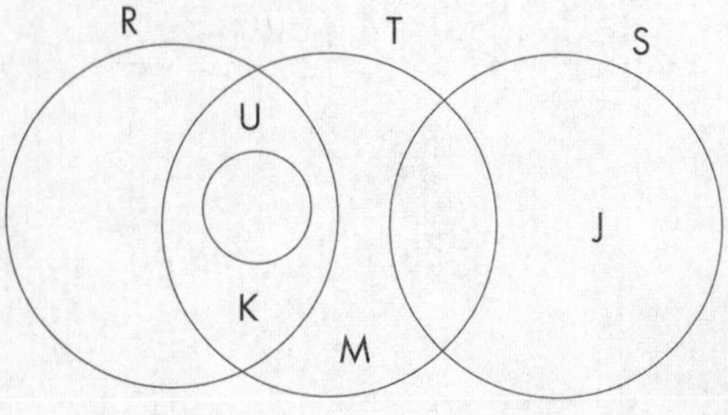

13. (A) Which COULD be true?

If L is within exactly three regions, it must be in region U as illustrated below:

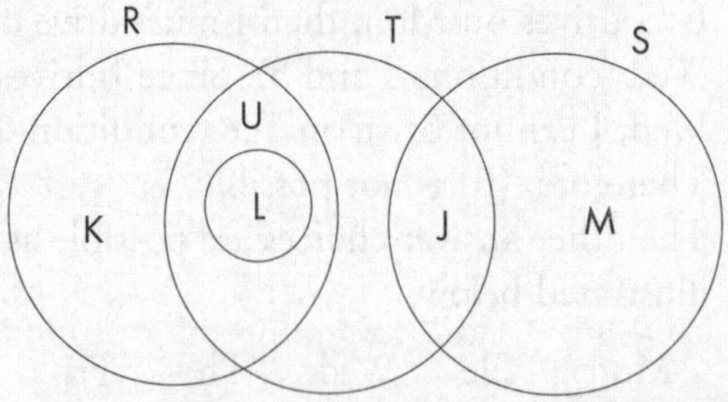

(A) is possible as illustrated above and is therefore the correct answer.
(B) is not possible, since if J is in exactly three regions, it must be in U. Regions U and S do not intersect, and since J must be in S (condition 2), this choice is not possible.
(C) is not possible, since J must be in S. If K were also in S, it would violate condition 3.
(D) is not possible, since L is in R. If M were also in R, it would violate condition 4.
(E) is not possible, since L is in T. If M were also in T, it would violate condition 4.

Answers 14–19

(Initial set-up information)

People: F, G, H, J
Days: Mon, Tue, Wed, Th, Fri, Sat

The conditions have been numbered here to assist in locating the explanations.

(Condition 1)
Each person drives on at least one day

(Condition 2)
Cannot drive on two consecutive days

(Condition 3)
F not on Mon

(Condition 4)
J on Wed or Sat or both or others ?

(Condition 5)
G on Mon implies J not on Sat

The organizer could look like this:

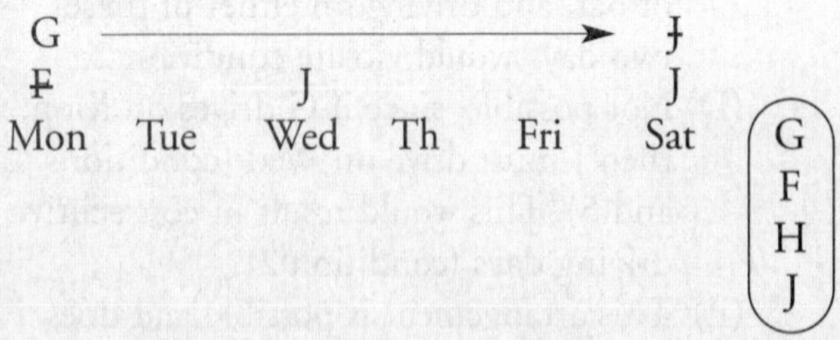

14. (D) Which COULD be the schedule?

	Mon	Tue	Wed	Th	Fri	Sat
(A)	G	F	J	H	G	G

Not possible, since G cannot drive on consecutive days (condition 2).

	Mon	Tue	Wed	Th	Fri	Sat
(B)	G	F	J	H	F	J

Not possible, since G is driving on Mon, and J is driving on Sat (condition 5).

	Mon	Tue	Wed	Th	Fri	Sat
(C)	H	F	G	J	H	F

Not possible, since J must drive on Wed or Sat (condition 4).

	Mon	Tue	Wed	Th	Fri	Sat
(D)	H	G	J	F	H	F

Possible. Does not violate any condition.

	Mon	Tue	Wed	Th	Fri	Sat
(E)	H	G	J	H	J	G

Not possible, since F does not drive (condition 1).

15. (E) Which COULD be true?

(A) Not possible, since J must drive on Wed or Sat (condition 4).
(B) Not possible, since if G drives on Mon, then J must drive on Wed, not G (conditions 4 and 5).
(C) Not possible, since J must drive on Wed or Sat, and driving on either of these two days would violate condition 2.
(D) Not possible, since if G drives on Mon, then J must drive on Wed (conditions 4 and 5). This would result in consecutive driving days (condition 2).
(E) This arrangement is possible and does not violate any conditions.

16. (C) Which MUST be true?

Mon	Tue	Wed	Th	Fri	Sat
H		J			J

Since J drives only on Wed and Sat, J cannot drive on Mon. Since J drives on Sat, G cannot drive on Mon (condition 5). F cannot drive on Mon (condition 3). This leaves H to drive on Mon. Thus, (C) MUST be true. The following schedule shows that the other answer choices do not have to be true:

Mon	Tue	Wed	Th	Fri	Sat
H	G	J	G	F	J

17. (A) Which MUST be true?

Mon	Tue	Wed	Th	Fri	Sat
G		J			G

Since G drives on Mon and Sat, J must drive on Wed (condition 4). Since three days remain to be assigned drivers, and only 2 drivers remain to be assigned, one must drive on 2 days. If J also drives on Fri, then J drives on two days. Thus, (A) must be true.
(B) is not correct, since J does not have to drive on Fri.
(C) is not correct, since H could drive on Fri and F could drive on Tue or Th.
(D) is not correct, since J could drive on Fri.
(E) is not correct, since F could drive on Tue.

18. (B) Which CANNOT be true?

Mon	Tue	Wed	Th	Fri	Sat
G		J			

If G drives on Mon, then J must drive on Wed (conditions 4 and 5). Since J drives on Wed, J cannot drive on Tue (condition 2). Therefore, (B) is not possible.
The other answer choices are possible as illustrated below:

	Mon	Tue	Wed	Th	Fri	Sat
(A)	H	F	J	H	G	J
(C)	G	F	J	F	J	H
(D)	H	J	G	F	G	J
(E)	G	H	J	F	J	F

19. (E) Which COULD be true?

Mon	Tue	Wed	Th	Fri	Sat
		J	F		F

F cannot drive on Mon (condition 3). If F does not drive on Tue or Wed, then only three days remain for F. If F drives exactly twice, it must be on Th and Sat and not Fri, since that would result in consecutive driving days (condition 2).
(A) is false, since none of the other three drivers besides F can drive on three days. This would result in one driver not driving (condition 1).
(B) is false, since if F drives exactly twice, this leave 4 days for the three remaining drivers.
(C) is false, since J must drive on Wed and F drives on Th.
(D) is false, since J must drive on Wed.
(E) is POSSIBLE, as illustrated below:

Mon	Tue	Wed	Th	Fri	Sat
H	G	J	F	J	F

Answers 20–24

(Initial set-up statement)

Experienced	Inexperienced
F	R
G	S
J	T
K	V
M	

The conditions have been numbered here to assist in locating the explanations.

(Condition 1)
Experienced ≥1 (At least one experienced)

(Condition 2)
4 teams, 2 each

(Condition 3)
M x F, R x F, V x F (F cannot be teams with M, R, or V)

(Condition 4)
T implies G or K (T on a team means that G or K must also be on that team)

(Condition 5)
J x R (J and R not on same team) ~~JR~~

The organizer could look like this:

Experienced	Inexperienced
F	R
G	S
J	T
K	V
M	

M x
R x → F
V x

T → G or K

J x R

20. (C) Choice (A) is not correct, since K is experienced.
(B) is not correct, since R cannot be assigned with F (condition 3).
(C) is correct. S can be assigned with F.
(D) is not correct, since T must be assigned to a team with either G or K, not F (condition 4).
(E) is not correct, since V cannot be assigned with F (condition 3).

21. (C) Choice (A) is not correct, since R cannot be assigned with F (condition 3).
(B) is not correct, since V cannot be assigned with F (condition 3).
(C) is POSSIBLE. One is experienced and one inexperienced, and no condition is violated.
(D) is not correct, since T must be assigned to either G or K (condition 4).
(E) is not correct, since they are both inexperienced (condition 1).

22. (B)

Experienced	Inexperienced
F	R (no)
G (no)	S (no)
J	T (no)
K (no)	V (no)
M (no)	

T must be assigned with either G or K (condition 4). Therefore, S is assigned to either K or G whichever one is not assigned to T. Since F cannot be assigned with M, R, or V (condition 3), F must be assigned with J. Thus, (B) is correct.

23. (A) If G is not assigned to a team, then each team must be made up of one experienced and one inexperienced plumber, and T must be assigned with K (condition 4). Since F cannot be assigned with either R or V (condition 3), F must be assigned with S. Since J cannot be assigned with R (condition 5), J must be assigned with V, and M must be assigned with R. Thus, (A) is correct.

Experienced		Inexperienced
F	-------	S
G		
J	-------	V
K	-------	T
M	-------	R

------- must be assigned together

24. (A) Since all inexperienced plumbers must be assigned, each team consists of one experienced and one inexperienced plumber. If T is not assigned to G, then T must be assigned to K (condition 4). Since R cannot be assigned with either F (condition 3) or J (condition 5) or G (stated condition in this problem), R must be assigned with M. Since V cannot be assigned with F (condition 3) or G (stated condition in this problem), V must be assigned with J. Therefore, S must be assigned with either F or G. Thus, (A) is correct.

Experienced		Inexperienced
F		S
G		
J	-------	V
K	-------	T
M	-------	R

------- must be assigned together

A Brief Reasoning Review (and Warm-Up)

CHAPTER 1

An Overview of the Key Strategies in the Chapter

Deductive and Inductive Reasoning
Some Types of Reasoning
- Reasoning from Signs or Symbols
- Cause–Effect Reasoning
- Reasoning by Analogy
- Reasoning from Statistics

Logical Fallacies
Conditional Statements (If–Then)

Before analyzing LSAT question types, let's review a few basics of logical and analytical reasoning. Keep in mind that formal logic is not necessary for this test. The LSAT won't ask whether you know the definition of a *universal syllogism,* for example.

These next few pages should get you to start thinking about some of the reasoning involved in LSAT Logical and Analytical Reasoning questions. The formal principles of logic (which are not required by the test) can be very complex and this short discussion is a simple illustration of a few of the basic concepts that should be helpful.

DEDUCTIVE AND INDUCTIVE REASONING

Although logical reasoning may take many forms, basically, it is either deductive or inductive.

Deductive reasoning goes from general to specific. A deduction, or deductive reasoning, can be demonstrated by a simple syllogism as follows:

Major Premise: A person cannot be a world traveler unless he or she has been out of the country.

Minor Premise: Bob has never been out of the country.

Conclusion: Bob is not a world traveler.

Notice that the major premise is followed by a particular instance, or minor premise, which is followed by a conclusion. The conclusion is only as valid as the major and minor premises. Therefore, a conclusion may be logical, but not necessarily true. Piano student A might reason, for example, that, if she spends four hours practicing the piano each week, while piano student B spends only one hour practicing the piano each week, then student A will be the better piano player. Student A is basing her conclusion on the hidden premise that the amount of practice is directly proportional to her improvement and becoming a better piano player. Although the conclusion is logically based, in actuality, she may find that student B is a better piano player because the major premise is incorrect; so the conclusion is invalid.

Inductive reasoning goes from specific to general. That is, inductive reasoning moves from a particular situation or fact to a generalization or conclusion. You might reason, for example, that because four hundred people are killed each year in boating accidents, boating is a dangerous activity. This conclusion is based on induction, moving from specific facts to a generalization. Notice that the larger the number of specific facts, the more valid the generalization or conclusion. If forty thousand people are killed each year in boating accidents, then the conclusion that boating is a dangerous activity becomes a more valid conclusion. An even more valid conclusion could be drawn as follows: If forty thousand people are killed worldwide each year in boating accidents, and twenty thousand of those occur in the small isolated Lake Tibar, then boating in Lake Tibar is probably very dangerous.

These simple examples of deductive and inductive reasoning are meant to give you some idea of how to examine the validity of generalizations or conclusions in Logical Reasoning questions. Is the conclusion warranted by the facts? Do the facts support the conclusion? Are the generalizations valid?

SOME TYPES OF REASONING

Four of the basic types of reasoning and inference include:

1. Reasoning from Signs or Symbols

You might reason that, because a woman wears expensive jewelry, she is wealthy. Your reasoning would be even stronger if she also drove an expensive car. Since these are signs of wealth, your reasoning might appear valid. But the jewelry and car may be borrowed, so your reasoning might not be valid. The more signs or symbols you have that are good indicators to support your inference or conclusion, the better your chance of a valid conclusion.

2. Cause–Effect Reasoning

You might reason that a healthy diet causes people to live longer. To reasonably make this assumption, you would need concrete evidence to support it. The reasoning that your essays were published by a major publisher because you started using a computer might be difficult to prove. Would this cause–effect reasoning be reasonable? Of course not.

3. Reasoning by Analogy

You might reason that, since your friend purchased a treadmill for exercising and lost ten pounds, you should also purchase one. To follow this line of reasoning, you must consider whether your needs are similar to your friend's needs. Do you want to lose weight? Do you have room for a treadmill? Establishing a solid basis for comparison with sufficient similarities is necessary to make reasoning by analogy valid.

4. Reasoning from Statistics

You might reason that, since nine out of the ten dentists surveyed recommended Popsodent toothpaste, it is the best toothpaste on the market. The strength of the reasoning will depend upon the validity of the facts and the authority behind them. Would the reasoning be more apt to be valid if 99 out of 100 dentists recommended Popsodent? Could you reason that, if nine out of the ten dentists surveyed recommended Popsodent toothpaste, most people buy Popsodent toothpaste? Since only ten dentists were surveyed, could you really make any strong conclusions? Probably not. From this survey of ten dentists, could you make a valid conclusion about *most* people? I don't think so. Since statistics are subject to interpretation, watch them carefully.

LOGICAL FALLACIES

Now let's take a quick look at some logical fallacies. These typical errors in logic come from problems in reasoning or connecting ideas. Some common errors include:

Argument Ad Hominem: This argument is based on name-calling or attacking a person either directly or indirectly. The attempt here is to avoid discussing the issue.

The candidate shouldn't be elected because his parents were convicted of tax evasion.

Sam would be a fine choice for principal if he didn't provide a bad example by sometimes eating fast food at lunch.

Bandwagon/Celebrity Appeal: This argument implies that the reader should agree with a premise because a celebrity or a majority agrees with it.

Our president said that it is the best plan.

Almost everyone agrees with the decision to change the speed limit.

Begging the Question: When a conclusion is presented as part of a premise, the writer is *begging the question.*

We must act immediately to stop violence on our campus.

The writer presumes that there is violence on the campus.

Circular Reasoning: The use of a statement to support itself is *circular reasoning.* The writer employs this type of reasoning by restating the original problem.

The witness's testimony was truthful because he said he was telling the truth.

Either/Or Reasoning or Oversimplification: This logical fallacy occurs when the writer assumes that there can be only one cause or one solution to a problem.

The only way to stop smokers is to outlaw cigarettes.

False Analogy: Comparing two objects or ideas that have too few similarities to establish a basis for a good comparison leads to a *false analogy.*

Ted will be an outstanding coach because he was a good player.

Non Sequitur: When the writer reaches a conclusion that does not follow or is not warranted by the evidence offered, he has committed a *non sequitur.*

Since crosswalks are designed for the safety of walkers, I don't need to watch for oncoming traffic before using the crosswalk.

In some ways, all logical fallacies are non sequiturs—they don't follow.

Post Hoc; Ergo Propter Hoc: The writer draws a conclusion based only on the assumption that the time sequence is sufficient proof for a particular deduction.

Janis drives the sporty, turbocharged Mach SKM and has a lot of dates. So, if you drive the Mach SKM, then you will be irresistible to the opposite sex.

Since President Reagan was in office during the hostage crisis, it must have been his fault.

The words "Post Hoc; Ergo Propter Hoc" mean "after this; therefore, because of it."

Slippery Slope/Unfounded Generalization: The writer assumes that because one minor fact is true, then, despite any further proof, a larger premise must also be true. When a conclusion is made on the basis of too little information, it is said to be *unfounded.*

School board member Heller voted for teacher pay raises at the last meeting; therefore, she will always vote for teacher pay raises.

Three math students were caught cheating on a test; therefore, all the math students cheated.

Don't worry about remembering the names of these logical fallacies, just understand *why* the reasoning is faulty.

CONDITIONAL STATEMENTS (IF–THEN)

Finally, let's take a quick look at conditional statements. *If–then statements* are called "conditional statements" or "conditionals." The part of the statement following *if* is called the hypothesis, and the part immediately following *then* is called the conclusion. For example:

If it is Saturday, then Andy plays tennis.

Hypothesis: *It is Saturday.*

Conclusion: *Andy plays tennis.*

If the hypothesis is true, then the conclusion must be true.

Some statements that are conditionals are not written in *if–then* form but could be easier to understand logically if they were. For example:

Cats have quick reflexes.

If–then form: *If it is a cat, then it has quick reflexes.*

Hypothesis: *It is a cat.*

Conclusion: *It has quick reflexes.*

When a statement is put into *if–then* form, it often becomes easier to reason from. So, in this case, use "If it is a cat, then it has quick reflexes" as the original conditional.

If you exchange the *if* (hypothesis) and the *then* (conclusion) in a conditional statement, you get the **converse** of the original conditional. For example:

Original conditional: *If it is a cat, then it has quick reflexes.*

Converse: *If it has quick reflexes, then it is a cat.*

The converse is not necessarily true because other animals have quick reflexes. So, the **converse of a true statement is not necessarily true.**

If you take the opposite (negative) of each of the parts of a conditional statement, then you get the **inverse** of the original conditional. For example:

Original conditional: *If it is a cat, then it has quick reflexes.*

Inverse: *If it is not a cat, then it does not have quick reflexes.*

The inverse is not necessarily true because other animals have quick reflexes. So, the **inverse of a true statement is not necessarily true.**

If you exchange and negate the parts of a conditional statement you get the **contrapositive** (that is, take both the converse and inverse of a conditional statement). For example:

Original conditional: *If it is a cat, then it has quick reflexes.*

Contrapositive: *If it does not have quick reflexes, then it is not a cat.*

The contrapositive of a true statement is always true. Keep this in mind as you work logical and analytical reasoning problems.

Let's take one more look using our first example:

Original conditional: *If it is Saturday, then Andy plays tennis.*
(This is a true statement.)

Converse: *If Andy plays tennis, then it is Saturday.*
(This is not necessarily true. Andy could also play tennis on other days.)

Inverse: *If it is not Saturday, then Andy does not play tennis.*
(This is not necessarily true. Andy could also play tennis on other days.)

Contrapositive: *If Andy does not play tennis, then it is not Saturday.*
(This must be true.)

Logical Reasoning

CHAPTER 2

An Overview of the Key Strategies in the Chapter

Introduction to Question Type

The LSAT will contain *two* Logical Reasoning sections that will count toward your score. The unscored experimental section could also be Logical Reasoning. Each Logical Reasoning section is 35 minutes in length and contains from 24 to 26 questions. *Since approximately half of your exam consists of Logical Reasoning questions, you should spend additional time reviewing, understanding, and practicing this question type.*

Logical Reasoning questions, which require you to apply your reading and reasoning skills, measure your aptitude for understanding, analyzing, utilizing, and criticizing various short passages and types of arguments. Your ability to reason logically and critically is tested by questions that require you to do the following:

- Recognize a point.
- Follow a chain of reasoning.
- Draw conclusions.
- Infer missing material.
- Apply principles from an argument.
- Identify methods.
- Evaluate arguments.
- Differentiate between fact and opinion.
- Analyze evidence.
- Assess claims critically.

Let's take a closer look:

First, let's check the approximate percentages of problem types.

Logical Reasoning Questions

Types	Approx. Frequency
Author's Main Point or Main Idea (Example of)	10–15%
Author Information or Author's Purpose	1–2%
Form of Argumentation (Vulnerable to criticism)	10–15%
Strengthening or Weakening Author's Statement or Conclusion (Undermines, supports)	20–25%
Author's Assumptions, Presuppositions, Underlying Principles (Justifies)	15–20%
Inferences and Implications	3–5%
Deductions	5–8%
Parallel Reasoning or Similarity of Logic	8–10%
Argument Exchange	5–8%
Syllogistic Reasoning	1–2%
Conclusions	5–10%
Logical Flaws	8–10%
Situation Analysis	*
Passage Completion	2–3%
Word Reference	**

*Appeared in recent bulletins
**Appeared infrequently in earlier exams

Now, let's preview the common question stems.

Sample Logical Reasoning Question Stems

- The statements above, if true, must support which one of the following?
- Each of the following, if true, strengthens the argument EXCEPT:
- Megan and Channen disagree over whether . . .
- Which one of the following, if true, most weakens the editorial's argument?
- The conclusion of the argument follows logically if which one of the following is assumed?
- The reasoning in the letter to the editor is vulnerable to criticism in that it
- Which one of the following, if true, would most seriously undermine the claim that the explanation given above is the only one available?

- Which one of the following, if true, most helps to resolve the apparent discrepancy described above?
- Which of the following is an assumption on which the author's argument relies?
- Which one of the following most accurately describes a flaw in the argument's reasoning?
- The pattern of reasoning in which one of the following arguments is most similar to the pattern of reasoning in the argument above?
- If the educator's statements are true, then which one of the following must be true?
- Which one of the following most accurately expresses the main conclusion of the editorialist's argument?

And finally, let's take a quick overview of the key strategies.

Overview of the Three (3) Key Strategies
Your Actions and . . . Reactions

Actions	Reactions
1. Read the question first	Mark the key word or words, circle or underline the reference points for the question (conclusion, first sentence) and tip word for the question (strengthens, weakens, assumes, flaw, main point)
2. Read the passage actively	Mark the main point and conclusion, focus on the logic of the argument or statement
3. Look for key words in choices	Spot and mark the essence of the choice, know what each choice means and how the choices differ

Logical reasoning questions may take many forms. In analyzing these forms, consider their basic component parts:

1. A *passage, argument,* or *discussion* followed by
2. A ***question*** **based upon the preceding text** followed by
3. The five *answer choices* (A, B, C, D, and E)

The following discussion offers some tips for each of these parts.

The Approach

THE BASIC COMPONENTS

1. The Passage, Argument, or Discussion

For the passage, read *actively;* that is, as you read, you should mark the important parts with circles, exclamation points, etc., directly on the page of your question booklet. Reading actively helps you stay involved in the passage, keeps you an active participant in the testing process, and helps you note and highlight the important points mentioned, should you need to refer to the passage.

As you read, you should also note the major issue being discussed, along with the few supporting points, if any.

2. The Question

For the question, it is often very helpful to *preread actively;* that is, to read the question first, *before* reading the passage. That way, you have an idea of what to look for as you read the passage. This is an effective technique only if the question is short. If the question is as long as (or longer than) the passage, this technique may not be helpful. Use your judgment.

As you read the question, note the key words and *circle* them, in the same manner as you mark the passage. Also note the *reference* of the question. Is it positive or negative? Is it asking what would strengthen the author's argument or what would weaken the author's argument? Is it asking what the author would agree or disagree with? Is it asking what the author believes, or what his critics would believe? Finally, be aware that questions often refer to *unstated* ideas: assumptions (a supposition or a truth taken for granted); implications/inferences (what would logically follow from a previous statement); and conclusions (the necessary consequence or result of the ideas in the passage). Assumptions and implications/inferences are usually not directly mentioned in the passage. Conclusions may or may not be mentioned. You must arrive at all three through logical thinking.

3. The Choices

For the choices, note that you must select the *best* of the five alternatives. Therefore, there might not be a perfect choice. There might also be two good choices. You are to pick the best of the five. Therefore, the elimination strategy (p. 11) is an effective way to approach the answer choices. Eliminate choices that are irrelevant (have nothing to do with the particular topic or issue), off-topic, or not addressed by the passage. Note that often a choice will be incorrect simply because one word in that choice is off-topic. Learn to look for and mark these off-topic key words.

Finally, be very careful as you read the passage, question, and choices, to watch for words that have very special meanings. The following words, for instance, are frequently used:

except some all none only one few no could must each

These types of words will often be the key to finding the best answer. Therefore, make sure to underline or circle them in your reading.

ANALYZING QUESTION CATEGORIES

The following sections give detailed examples of the most common types of Logical Reasoning questions, complete with important techniques and strategies. You should not try to memorize the different categories presented here, but rather use them as an aid in identifying strategies needed and in practicing techniques.

Author's Main Point or Main Idea

A very common Logical Reasoning question type will ask you to identify or understand the main point or main idea of the passage. This is also a common question type in the Reading Comprehension section.

As you read the short passage, focus on what the author is trying to say—the major issue. Each paragraph usually contains only one main idea, often stated in the first sentence.

Let's analyze the following passage:

EXAMPLE 1

Legal Analyst: **As the legal profession becomes more specialized and complex, clerical assistance must become more specialized as well. One legal secretary might be an expert in bankruptcy law, another an expert in criminal justice.**

Which one of the following is the main point of the passage?

(A) A legal secretary may understand subjects other than law.
(B) A legal secretary should have special training in a particular branch of law.
(C) A legal secretary must be an expert in several types of law.
(D) Attorneys will hire only secretaries without legal experience so they can be trained on the job.
(E) Attorneys will still need legal secretaries with a very general background.

STUDY TIP

About 10–15 percent of the questions have to do with the author's main point or main idea, or an example.

ANALYSIS

The first sentence of the passage, a general statement about increasing specialization in the legal profession, states the main idea. It is followed by a more specific statement, which gives you additional information.

To help you focus on the main point, you may wish to use the following technique when practicing this question type. As you finish reading each paragraph, try to mentally summarize the paragraph in a few words. For example, after reading

Example 1, you might summarize it by saying to yourself, "Legal secretaries should specialize in different types of law."

Next, note whether the paragraph states a particular attitude toward the subject. Typically the author will either approve or disapprove of the main point, or remain neutral. In the Example 1 passage, the author takes no position pro or con but delivers the additional information in a matter-of-fact way.

The correct answer is (B). In this case, the main point is that legal secretaries must become more specialized, and the correct answer emphasizes "special training." Notice also that the correct answer here refers as well to the second sentence, which contains additional information about particular branches of law.

(A) is irrelevant. Although particular types of law are mentioned, subjects other than law are not. Note that this statement may certainly be true for some legal secretaries, but it receives no support from the paragraph. (C) contradicts information in the passage; the passage discusses legal secretaries who specialize in one type of law, not several. (D) and (E) are not addressed in the passage. The passage does not discuss attorneys' hiring requirements or the need for legal secretaries with a very general background.

Remember, when asked for a main point, be sure to differentiate the main point from secondary or minor points.

EXAMPLE 2

The belief that positive thinking is the key to success can lead to laziness. It encourages some people to engage in slipshod work, in the hope that an optimistic mental attitude will take the place of hard, careful, dedicated work.

Which one of the following is the main idea of this passage?

(A) Laziness is always the result of positive thinking.
(B) Laziness is practiced by successful people.
(C) Laziness is only permissible after one has completed a hard day's work.
(D) Laziness may result from reliance on positive thinking.
(E) Laziness may result from an assortment of mental attitudes.

ANALYSIS

The correct answer is (D), which restates the opening statement that "positive thinking . . . can lead to laziness." However, the paragraph does not say that laziness is always the result; therefore (A) is incorrect. (B) is unreasonable and is contradicted by the paragraph. (C) is irrelevant; the paragraph does not discuss when laziness is permissible. (E) brings in an assortment of mental attitudes that are not addressed.

EXAMPLE 3

Few people understand poetry, and few prefer to read it. Although English professors speak in glowing terms about the greatness of Pope's *Rape of the Lock* and Tennyson's *Ulysses,* it seems that only other English professors share their enthusiasm. To appreciate the greatness of difficult poetry, readers must exercise great patience and concentration, and must tolerate the unusual, compressed language of rhythm and rhyme; with so many urgent issues demanding our attention almost every hour of the day, choosing to figure out a poem seems an unlikely possibility.

In the passage above, the writer makes which one of the following arguments?

(A) English professors pay lip service to great poetry but, in fact, rarely read it for pleasure.
(B) Even English professors might not really understand difficult poetry.
(C) Few laypeople will spend the time necessary to read difficult poetry.
(D) Simple poetry may continue to be popular, but only English professors now read difficult poetry.
(E) To read difficult poetry requires patience, concentration, and tolerance.

ANALYSIS

The correct answer is (C). The passage does not suggest that the English professors' enthusiasm is insincere (A) nor that they may fail to understand difficult poems (B). It argues that only English professors have the skills, time, and interest in poetry to deal with its difficulties and that laypeople are now unlikely to do so (C). The passage does not allude to simple poetry (D). (E) is tempting at first, but the argument of the passage is that understanding or appreciating poetry requires these skills, not simply reading it, so (C) is the best of the five choices.

Author Information or Author's Purpose

Another common Logical Reasoning question refers to a reading passage or paragraph and asks you to understand some things about the author. You may be asked to interpret what the author is trying to accomplish by this statement, or to predict the action and feeling of the author on similar or unrelated subject matter (i.e., to tell whether the author would agree or disagree with some idea).

To answer this type of question, first look for the values and attitudes of the author. (Ask yourself, "Where is the author coming from?") Second, watch for word connotation: The author's choice of words can be very important. Third, decide the author's purpose and point of view, but don't OVERREAD. Keep within the context of the passage. Sometimes it will be advantageous to skim some of the questions (not the answer choices) before reading the short passage so that you will know what to expect.

Remember while reading to mark the passage and look for *who, what, when, where, why,* and *how.* (See the section on "Active Reading" that begins on page 297.)

EXAMPLE 1

Recent studies show that the general public is unaware of most new legislation and doesn't understand 99% of the remaining legislation. This is mainly because of the public's inattention and lack of interest.

The author of this argument would most likely be

(A) in favor in new legislation
(B) against new legislation
(C) advocating public participation in legislation
(D) advocating the simplifying of the language of new legislation
(E) advocating more interesting legislation

ANALYSIS

The correct answer is (C). The statement does not imply that an increase or decrease in legislation would change the public awareness; therefore (A) and (B) are incorrect. (C) follows in the tenor of the argument because the author's purpose appears to be centered around involvement. He points out that the general public is unaware because of inattention and lack of interest. (D) would be possible, *but* the author is not focusing his criticism on the complex wording of legislation and does not mention it as a reason for unawareness. Remember (1) *whom* the author is talking about—the general public, (2) *what* he mentions—their unawareness of most new legislation, and (3) *why* they are unaware—because of inattention and lack of interest. The author is not advocating more interesting legislation (E).

EXAMPLE 2

***Writing Teacher:* There are advantages and disadvantages to clear, simple writing. Sentences that are easy to understand are processed more quickly and efficiently by readers; those who can express themselves in simple terms are rarely misunderstood. However, prose that is crystal clear often lacks both complexity and imagination. Whether one chooses a style that is simple and clear or complex and unusual often depends upon the tolerance of one's readers.**

The purpose of the writing teacher who makes this statement to a class is probably to

(A) encourage students to write more simply
(B) encourage students to imitate in their own pure style the points the teacher is making about pure style
(C) encourage students to be more imaginative in their writing
(D) remind students of the importance of the audience to a piece of writing
(E) urge students to combine simplicity and complexity, clarity and imagination in all their writing

ANALYSIS

The correct answer is (D). The passage points out the disadvantages and advantages of both simple and complex prose and concludes with the reminder that the readers will determine which is appropriate. The passage does not favor one style over another as in (A) and (C), nor does it say that all writing should be both simple and complex (E). It argues for a style suitable to the audience.

Form of Argumentation

In this type of question, you are asked to decide what type of argument, logic, or reasoning the author is using (e.g., example, exaggeration, deduction, or induction).

To answer this type of question, carefully follow the author's line of reasoning while focusing on his or her intent or purpose. Notice how the author starts and finishes the argument. Consider what the author has concluded or proved, or what point has been made or argued. Watch "if" and "how" specific points or examples are used in relation to more general statements.

STUDY TIP

About 10–15 percent of the questions have to do with the form of argumentation and the vulnerability to criticism.

EXAMPLE 1

Once again, refer to the argument used earlier concerning legislation.

Recent studies show that the general public is unaware of most new legislation and doesn't understand 99% of the remaining legislation. This is mainly because of the public's inattention and lack of interest.

To make the point, the author of this statement

(A) gives a general statement followed by supporting facts
(B) argues by pointing out the effects and then the cause
(C) uses specific examples to disprove an argument
(D) infers an outcome and then attempts to support that outcome
(E) assumes the conclusion is true and uses circular reasoning to state the premise

ANALYSIS

The correct answer is (B). The author starts by making specific points about the general public. It is "unaware of most new legislation and doesn't understand 99% of the remaining legislation." This is followed by a statement of the cause: "This is mainly because of the public's inattention and lack of interest."

EXAMPLE 2

***Editorial:* In the twelfth century, people used the abacus (a simple device made of beads strung on wire) to perform complex calculations. Today we use electronic calculators, and the abacus has become obsolete. In fifty or one hundred years, the calculator will be as quaint and outmoded as the abacus. Every invention of man, every breakthrough of science will, if we wait long enough, be out of date and used no longer.**

Which one of the following is a questionable technique used in the argument in this passage?

(A) It ignores the fact that the abacus is still in use in Asia.
(B) It generalizes from a single instance of obsolescence.
(C) It makes a prediction without specifying exactly when the prediction will come true.
(D) It mistakes a minor premise for a major premise and so deduces erroneously.
(E) It considers only scientific advances, but some inventions are not related to science.

ANALYSIS

The correct answer is (B). The question calls for a questionable technique. The error here is the hasty generalization, based on a single instance of obsolescence. (A), (C), and (E) may be true, but they do not point to a technique of argument. (D) is irrelevant and not true of this argument, which is not a syllogism.

Strengthening or Weakening the Author's Statement or Conclusion

STUDY TIP

Notice that about 20–25 percent of the questions have to do with strengthening, weakening, undermining, or supporting the author's statement or conclusion.

This question type is very common on the LSAT. Here you are given a short reading passage or paragraph followed by the question "Which of the following would strengthen the author's statement the most?" or "Which of the following would most weaken the author's statement?" (Both of these questions may be asked. There are many possible varieties of this question type: "least likely to weaken," "strongest criticism of," and so on).

You may find it helpful to preread, or to read the question before reading the short paragraph. Focus on the major point of the statement and "how" or "if" it is supported. Be aware of the strength of the statement or argument. Is it a harsh criticism of a certain system? Is it a mildly persuasive paragraph? What point is the author trying to make in supporting this cause?

Remember to always read actively, marking key words or phrases.

EXAMPLE 1

Psychiatrists and laypeople agree that the best sort of adjustment is founded upon an acceptance of reality, rather than an escape from it.

Which one of the following would probably most weaken the author's point?

(A) Psychiatrists and laypeople do not often agree.
(B) Reality is difficult to define.
(C) Escaping reality has worked for many.
(D) Accepting reality is often traumatic.
(E) Psychiatrists' definition of reality and laypeople's definition of reality are different.

ANALYSIS

The correct answer is (C). If escaping reality has worked for many, then it becomes more difficult to defend the acceptance of reality theory. (A) would probably strengthen the point being made. (B) could strengthen or weaken the point. (D) and (E) are irrelevant.

EXAMPLE 2

The likelihood of America exhausting her natural resources is growing less. All kinds of waste are being reworked, and new uses are constantly being found for almost everything. We are getting more use out of our goods and are making many new by-products out of what was formerly thrown away. It is, therefore, unnecessary to continue to ban logging in national parks, nature reserves, or areas inhabited by endangered species of animals.

Which one of the following most seriously undermines the conclusion of this argument?

(A) The increasing amount of recycled material made available each year is equal to one-tenth of the increasing amount of natural material consumed annually.
(B) Recent studies have shown that the number of endangered animals throughout the world fluctuates sharply and is chiefly determined by changes in weather conditions.
(C) The logging industry contributes huge sums of money to the political campaigns in states where it has a financial interest.
(D) The techniques that make recycling possible are constantly improved so that more is reclaimed for lower costs each year.
(E) Political contributions by the recycling industry are now greater than those of the logging or animal-protection interests.

ANALYSIS

The correct answer is (A). First, remember to circle the words "undermines" and "conclusion" to help you focus on what you're looking for. Now let's look at the choices. (D) would support, rather than undermine, the conclusion. (B), (C), and (E) neither support nor weaken the argument, though with more information (C) and (E) might be relevant. If the recycled materials are equal to only one-tenth of the natural materials lost each year, the argument is seriously injured.

EXAMPLE 3

Some scientists have proposed that, over two hundred million years ago, one giant land mass—rather than various continents and islands—covered one-third of the earth. Long before there was any human life, and over vast periods of time, islands and continents drifted apart. Australia was the first to separate, while South America and Africa were late in splitting apart. Some islands, of course, were formed by volcanoes and were never part of the great land mass.

All the following would support the author's claim EXCEPT:

(A) Many of the plants of the South American rain forests are markedly similar to those of the African rain forest.
(B) Australia has more animals that are not found on any other continent than have several of the much larger continents.
(C) Volcanic islands like Hawaii have ecosystems very different from those of continental lands with the same average temperature.
(D) The plants of similar conditions in South America have less in common with those of Australia than with those of Asia, Africa, or Europe.
(E) The primitive languages of Australia are unlike those of Africa, which resemble those of South America.

ANALYSIS

The correct answer is (E). If Australia was the first continent to separate, it would follow that its flora and fauna would develop in isolation over a longer period of time. Similarly, we may expect the plants and animals of South America and Africa that separated later to be more alike. (A), (B), and (D) support these ideas. That the separately developed islands are different is also in accord with the passage (C). However, the languages of all the continents would have developed in isolation, since man did not evolve until after the break-up of the land mass, and it is surprising that African and South American languages are similar. Human likeness or difference are irrelevant to the claims of the passage.

EXAMPLE 4

Columnist: **In America, a baseball game should be described as a series of solo performances: At any given moment, attention is focused on one player and one play. On the other hand, soccer involves all of the team most of the time: Each player interacts with others constantly so that no single individual seems responsible for success or failure. It is because spectators prefer concentrating on individual personalities that baseball remains a much more popular spectator sport than soccer.**

Which one of the following, if true, can best be used to undermine the conclusion of this argument?

(A) Soccer is more popular than baseball with spectators in France.
(B) Among the ten most televised sports in America, by far the most watched is football, and the least watched are tennis and bowling.
(C) Many people watch only the baseball teams of the city in which they live and for whom they root.
(D) Compared to football and basketball, baseball games are much cheaper to attend.
(E) In some sections of the United States, soccer leagues for children under fifteen are more popular than Little League baseball.

ANALYSIS

The correct answer is (B). The weakness of this argument is not its claim that baseball is more popular than soccer with spectators in America. This is true from the passage. The weakness is its claim that the reason for baseball's greater popularity is that it is an individual performance rather than a team sport. (B) cites a team sport that is more watched than baseball and two solo performance sports that are not very popular. (A) makes a good point, but the passage is concerned with spectators "in America." Even if (C) is true, it may be that these people watch the teams to see individual performances. (D) is true, but not as powerful a criticism as (B). (E) does not necessarily deal with spectators; popularity could refer to the number of participants.

Author Assumptions, Presuppositions, Underlying Principles

This is another very common question type in the Logical Reasoning section. Here you are again given a short reading passage or paragraph followed by questions asking about the author's possible assumptions, presuppositions, or underlying principles.

STUDY TIP

About 15–20 percent of the questions have to do with the author's assumptions, presuppositions, underlying principles, or justifications.

To answer this question type, you may wish to first read the question actively. Make a careful note of what part of the paragraph the question refers to. Is the question asking about the conclusion of the passage? (Which of the following assumptions must be made for the author to reasonably arrive at the stated conclusion?) Or about the opening statement? Or about the complete paragraph? (The complete paragraph may be only one or two sentences long.)

Keep in mind that assumptions and presuppositions are things taken for granted, or supposed as facts. In the same sense, an underlying principle is the basis for the original statement. It is necessary for the conclusion to be logical. There may be a number of assumptions possible, but in most cases you are looking for the major assumption, not a minor one. In some cases the major assumption will be evident; you will know what the author is assuming before you even get to the answer choices. In other cases, the assumptions are more subtle, and the answer choices will be helpful by stating them for you.

EXAMPLE 1

Use the statement in Example 1 on page 87:

Psychiatrists and laypeople agree that the best sort of adjustment is founded upon an acceptance of reality, rather than an escape from it.

The author of this statement assumes that

(A) there is only one sort of adjustment
(B) escaping reality is possible
(C) psychiatrists and laypeople disagree on most things
(D) psychiatrists never escape reality
(E) laypeople need many sorts of adjustments

ANALYSIS

The correct answer is (B). In stating "rather than an escape from it [reality]," the author is assuming that escaping reality is possible.

EXAMPLE 2

It has been said that a weed is a flower whose virtue has not yet been discovered. As if to prove this point, a homeowner who was tired of constantly maintaining a pretty lawn and shrubbery decided to let weeds run wild in his yard. The result, so far, has been an array of lively shapes and colors. If everyone in the neighborhood would follow this leader, we could save time, effort, money, and water, and soon have one of the most unusual neighborhoods in the city.

Which one of the following is a basic assumption on which this argument depends?

(A) The neighborhood values convenience more than maintaining an attractive environment.
(B) All the other yards will look like the first homeowner's if the weeds are allowed to run wild.
(C) Allowing the weeds to take over will save money spent on maintaining a lawn.
(D) Other neighborhoods in the city will not follow the example of this neighborhood.
(E) The loss of jobs or revenue to gardeners and garden supply businesses is not so important as the time and money that will be saved.

ANALYSIS

The correct answer is (A). Although all five of the propositions here may well be true, it is (A) that is the basic assumption of the argument. No one who highly values an attractive lawn and yard will want to let weeds take over, so for the argument to have any validity, its speaker must assume that an audience willing to allow the gain in convenience outweighs the loss in appearance of the neighborhood.

EXAMPLE 3

Political Analyst: **Four of the candidates for reelection in this state had been named among those who had more than 100 overdrafts on the House Bank. Of these four, two were Democrats, one was a Republican, and one an Independent. One other Republican incumbent candidate had bounced over 50 checks. All of the Democrats favored increased federal spending on education and increased government regulation of firearms, while the Republicans opposed these measures. Of the five incumbents, only the Independent candidate was reelected.**

Which one of the following is the most likely principle upon which the majority of voters cast their votes in the elections?

(A) The voters opposed any candidate who had more than 49 overdrafts on the House Bank.
(B) The voters opposed any candidates who favored increased federal spending.
(C) The voters opposed reelection of any members of the two major parties who bounced 50 or more checks.
(D) The voters opposed any candidate who favored increased firearms control.
(E) The voters opposed any candidate who opposed firearms legislation.

ANALYSIS

The correct answer is (C). Since the Independent also bounced more than 100 checks, that cannot be the reason for the defeat of the other four candidates. Since we do not know how the Independent candidate stands on spending for education or on firearms regulation, the only factor to explain his victory is his not belonging to one of the two major parties.

EXAMPLE 4

***Social Worker:* Time and again, studies have shown that 85 percent of the young adults sent to special juvenile prison farms lead productive lives after they are released. On the other hand, 85 percent of the young adults of the same age who are sent to prisons for adults later return to prisons. The bad influence of the older inmates is permanent. We must expand the number of special juvenile prison farms so that all young adults convicted of crimes can be sent to a penal institution that will not maim them for life.**

Which one of the following principles most helps to justify this argument?

(A) It is more expensive to house adult prisoners in prisons than to house young adults on prison farms.
(B) Young adults exposed to bad role models will imitate these models.
(C) Some young adults who are sent to prison farms later become criminals who are sent to prisons for adults.
(D) Some of the young adults who are sent to prisons for adults become productive members of society and never return to prison.
(E) Young adults who have been sent to prison farms on two occasions are more likely to return to prison than young adults who have been sent to prison farms only once.

ANALYSIS

The correct answer is (B). This principle is the basis of the argument to prevent young adults from being exposed to adult felons. If the hope of penologists is to reintegrate young adults into society, these young adults must be kept away from bad models they are likely to imitate. (C) and (D) may be true, but they do not justify the argument. (A) is a practical matter, not a principle to justify the case. (E) would not justify the argument, and might, in fact, be used against it.

EXAMPLE 5

Drunken drivers in our state kill or maim people every day. I understand that only one out of 500 drunken drivers on the highway is flagged down by the police. Also, 50 percent of these arrests are made on four holiday weekends when the policing of highways is greatly increased. With these odds, I can afford to drink heavily and drive, as long as I am careful not to do so on holiday weekends.

Which one of the following is a necessary premise for the speaker's conclusion in the paragraph above?

(A) The odds against being arrested from drunken driving are greater on weekends than on weekdays.
(B) Fear of arrest is a good reason not to drink and drive.
(C) All that drunken drivers need to fear is being arrested.
(D) The chances of being arrested for drunken driving are greatest on four holiday weekends.
(E) The penalties for drunken driving are often incommensurate with the dangers to the public.

ANALYSIS

The correct answer is (C). The speaker of this passage notes that drunk driving can kill and maim, but his concern is solely with the chances of his being arrested. His conclusion is based on the assumption that no other consequence of drunk driving need trouble him. (A), (B), (D), and (E) are not untrue, but they are not the underlying principle in the speaker's conclusion.

Inferences and Implications

In this very common question type, you are asked to "read between the lines." Inferences and implications are not expressed in words in the passage, but may be fairly understood from the passage. If you draw or infer something from a passage, it is called an *inference*. From the author's point of view, if he or she imparts or implies something, it is called an *implication*. For the purposes of your exam, you should not be concerned with the differences in the terms, but in understanding what unstated information is in the passage. As you read the passage, focus on the main idea, what the author is suggesting but not actually saying, and what information you can be drawing.

As you approach the choices in inference and implication questions, look for the most direct answer that is not explicitly stated. That is the one that most directly ties back into the passage. Remember that your inference is NOT directly stated in the passage but is implied by the passage.

EXAMPLE 1

Since 1890, the federal government and the individual states have passed a number of laws against corrupt political practices. But today, many feel that political corruption is a regular occurrence and deeply distrust their public leaders.

Each of the following can be reasonably inferred from the passage EXCEPT:

(A) Corrupt political practices have been going on for many years.
(B) The laws against corrupt political practices have not been effective.
(C) The federal government and the individual states are against corrupt political practices.
(D) Many public leaders may be distrusted even though they are not corrupt.
(E) Leaders in private industry are also involved in corrupt political practices.

ANALYSIS

The correct answer is (E). Since the passage does not address leaders in private industry, you could not reasonably make an inference regarding their practices. Though (A), (B), (C), and (D) are not stated, all of them are reasonable inferences from the passage.

EXAMPLE 2

Teacher: **The ability to recognize grammar and usage errors in the writing of others is not the same as the ability to see such errors in one's own writing.**

The author of this statement implies that

(A) a writer might not be aware of his own errors
(B) grammar and usage errors are difficult to correct
(C) grammar and usage errors are very common
(D) one often has many abilities
(E) recognizing grammar and usage errors and writing correctly use two different abilities

ANALYSIS

The correct answer is (A). The author's statement points out that recognizing errors in others' work involves a different ability from recognizing errors in one's own work. Since these abilities are different, writers might not possess both abilities and therefore might not be aware of their own errors. (B) is irrelevant because its focus is "difficulty to correct," which is not addressed. (C) and (D) are incorrect because they are too general, addressing items that are not specific to the statement. (E), which is a common mistake, simply restates information in the statement.

EXAMPLE 3

A poll of journalists who were involved in the Senate campaign revealed that 80 percent believed Senator Smith's campaign was damaged by press reports about his record during his last six years in office. His opponent, the recently narrowly elected Senator Jones, believes he was benefited by press coverage of his campaign. Journalists believe the election was covered without bias and that the Senator was defeated because of his record, not, as he insists, because of unfair press coverage. Ninety percent of the voters who supported Senator Smith believe that the press was unfair in this election, while 85 percent of the voters who supported Senator Jones thought the coverage was free of any bias.

Which one of the following can be inferred from this passage?

(A) The press coverage of the Senate election was free from bias.
(B) Senator Smith lost the election because the press reported his record accurately.
(C) The public's view of the objectivity of the press is likely to be influenced by the election results.
(D) The election was close because of different perceptions of the bias of the press.
(E) Journalists are probably the best judges of bias in political campaign reportage.

ANALYSIS

The correct answer is (C). We cannot be sure whether the reporting of the press was biased since the election was close and the pros and cons are nearly equal. The press cannot be counted on to be objective, so (A), (B), and (E) are not reasonable inferences. The large percentage of each candidate's supporters, whose views of the press coincide with the success or defeat of their candidates, strongly support the inference of (C). Whether (D) is true, we cannot tell.

Deductions

You may be asked to deduce information from a passage. Deductions are arrived at or attained from general premises—drawing information from a specific piece of information—from general laws to specific cases. In a deduction, if the general premises are true, then the deduction is necessarily true.

To answer this question type, you may wish to actively read the question first. Focus on the general premises to see where they lead. As you continue reading, try to follow the logic as it narrows the possibilities of what must be true.

EXAMPLE 1

Years ago, a nationwide poll concluded that there are more televisions than there are bathtubs in American homes. No doubt that fact remains today, especially in light of the growing popularity of home computers. Now, in addition to owning televisions for entertainment, more and more families are purchasing TV monitors for use with a personal computer. We can safely guess that there are still many more people staring at a picture tube than singing in the shower.

Which one of the following statements can be deduced from this passage?

(A) Personal computers probably cost less than installing a shower or a bathtub.
(B) People can wash themselves without a tub or shower, but they cannot watch television unless they own a television set.
(C) TV monitors will work with personal computers in place of regular computer monitors.
(D) As many computers are sold today as television sets a few years ago.
(E) More television monitors are now used with personal computers than are used to watch commercial television broadcasts.

ANALYSIS

The correct answer is (C). Though (A) and (B) may well be true, they are not deductions that we can make from the information in the passage. But (C) can be deduced since "more and more families are purchasing TV monitors for use with a personal computer." TV monitors must work with these computers. Otherwise, people would not buy them for that purpose. (D) and (E) may or may not be true, but they are not deductions from the passage, simply additional information.

EXAMPLE 2

Antifreeze lowers the melting point of any liquid to which it is added so that the liquid will not freeze in cold weather. It is commonly used to maintain the cooling system in automobile radiators. Of course, the weather may become so cold that even antifreeze is not effective, but such a severe climatic condition rarely occurs in well-traveled places.

Which one of the following can be deduced from the passage?

(A) Well-traveled places have means of transportation other than automobiles.
(B) Antifreeze does not lower the melting point of certain liquids in extreme conditions.
(C) Severe climatic conditions rarely occur.
(D) It is not often that many travelers who use antifreeze have their cooling systems freeze.
(E) Antifreeze raises the melting point of some liquids.

ANALYSIS

The correct answer is (D). Since severe climatic conditions rarely occur in well-traveled places, it is necessarily true that "It is not often that many travelers who use antifreeze have their cooling systems freeze." (A) mentions other means of transportation, which is not addressed in the passage. (B) refers to "certain" liquids, which again are not addressed. You cannot deduce that "severe climatic conditions rarely occur" (C), because the passage alludes to only well-traveled places. (E) discusses raising the melting point, which is irrelevant to the passage.

EXAMPLE 3

Sociologists have noted that children today are less "childish" than ever; when they are still very young, perhaps only six or seven years old, children are already mimicking adult fashions and leading relatively independent lives. Dressed in designer jeans, an elementary school child is likely to spend much of every day fending for herself, taking charge of her own life while waiting for her working parents to arrive home. Children become less dependent on adults for their day-to-day decisions.

From the passage above, since children are less dependent on adults for their day-to-day decisions, it must be true that

(A) children need more supervision
(B) children are growing up more quickly
(C) children should be completely independent
(D) parents should not leave children home alone
(E) parents need to spend more "quality time" with their children

ANALYSIS

The correct answer is (B). Since children today are "less childish than ever," and since they are "less dependent on adults for their day-to-day decisions," they must be "growing up" more quickly. Although (A), (D), and (E) are probably true, they are not necessarily true and therefore cannot be deduced from the passage.

Parallel Reasoning or Similarity of Logic

In this type, you will be given a statement or statements and asked to select the statements that most nearly parallel the originals or use similar logic. First, you should decide whether the original statement is valid. (But don't take too much time on this first step because some of the others may tip you off to the correct choice.) If the statement is valid, your choice must be a valid statement. If the statement is invalid, your choice must be an invalid one. Your choice must preserve the same relationship or comparison.

Second, the direction of connections is important—general to specific (deduction), specific to general (induction), quality to thing, thing to quality, and so on.

Third, the tone of the argument should be the same. If the original has a negative slant, has a positive slant, or changes from negative to positive, then so must your choice.

Fourth, the order of each element is important. Remember: Corresponding elements must be in the same order as the original.

It may be helpful to substitute letters for complex terms or phrases in order to simplify confusing situations and help you avoid getting lost in the wording. Direction and order are usually more easily followed by letter substitution.

Remember: Don't correct or alter the original; just reproduce the reasoning.

EXAMPLE 1

Alex said, "All lemons I have tasted are sour; therefore, all lemons are sour."

Which one of the following most closely parallels the logic of the above statement?

(A) I have eaten pickles four times and I have gotten sick each time; therefore, if I eat another pickle, I will get sick.
(B) My income has increased each year for the past four years; therefore, it will increase again next year.
(C) I sped to work every day last week and I did not get a ticket; therefore, they do not give tickets for speeding around here anymore.
(D) All flormids are green. This moncle is red; therefore, it is not a flormid.
(E) Every teacher I had in school was mean; therefore, all teachers are mean.

ANALYSIS

The correct answer is (E). First, the logic of the original is faulty; therefore, the correct choice must also be faulty, eliminating (D). Next, notice the direction of connections: generalization from a *few* experiences → generalization about *all* similar experiences. (A) and (B) each project the result of a few past experiences to only ONE similar experience. (C) starts from a few experiences, but finishes with a result that implies a change in a specific area. You could assume that "they" used to give tickets here.

EXAMPLE 2

Some serious novelists prefer scientific studies to literary studies. All science fiction writers are more interested in science than in literature. Therefore, some serious novelists are science fiction writers.

Which one of the following is most closely parallel to the flawed reasoning in the argument above?

(A) All trees have leaves. Some cactuses have leaves. Therefore, all trees are cactuses.
(B) All orchestras include violins, and all chamber groups include violins. Therefore, some chamber groups are orchestras.
(C) Some animals sleep through the winter and some animals sleep through the summer. Therefore, all animals sleep through either the summer or the winter.
(D) All hotels have restaurants. Some shopping malls have restaurants. Therefore, some shopping malls are hotels.
(E) Some sweaters in this store are made of cotton. All shirts in this store are made of cotton. Therefore, all the wearing apparel in this store is made of cotton.

ANALYSIS

The correct answer is (D). The stem asserts that all science fiction writers prefer science to literature and so do some serious novelists. It then concludes that some serious novelists must be science fiction writers. The "some serious novelists" who prefer science do not have to be science fiction writers, though they share a preference with them. The stem would have to say only science fiction writers prefer science to make this conclusion certain. The two terms used in the stem are "all" and "some," so we can exclude (B) and (C), which use "all" and "all" and "some" and "some." (E), though it gives the "some" term first and the "all" term second, is parallel to the passage.

EXAMPLE 3 (with a slight twist)

Why do you want to stop smoking?

Which one of the following most closely parallels the reasoning of this question?

(A) Why do you want to go to Italy?
(B) When will you decide on the offer?
(C) Will you ever play cards again?
(D) When do you want to learn to play tennis?
(E) Which desk do you like better?

ANALYSIS

The correct answer is (C). This response is the only one that implies that the *action has already taken place,* as in the original question. To stop smoking, one must have been smoking *before.* To stop playing cards, one must have been playing cards *before.* (A) appears to be the closest, but this is only true regarding sentence structure, not reasoning. (B) and (D) are asking about future plans without implying anything about past actions. (D) does imply past lack of action. (E) merely asks for a comparison.

Argument Exchange

In this question type, two or more speakers are exchanging arguments or merely discussing a situation. You will then be asked to choose the statement that most strengthens or weakens either argument. Or you may be asked to find the inconsistency or flaw in an argument, or to identify the form of argument. In some instances you will be asked to interpret what one speaker might have thought the other meant by his response.

To answer these questions, you should first evaluate the strength and completeness of the statements. Are they general or specific? Do they use absolutes? Are they consistent?

Second, evaluate the relationship between responses. What kind of response did the first statement elicit from the second speaker?

Third, evaluate the intentions of the author in making his remarks. What was his purpose?

EXAMPLE 1

Tom: **It is impossible to hit off the Yankee pitcher Turley.**
Jim: **You're just saying that because he struck you out three times yesterday.**

Which one of the following would strengthen Tom's argument most?

(A) Tom is a good hitter.
(B) Turley pitched a no-hitter yesterday.
(C) Tom has not struck out three times in a game all season.
(D) Tom has not struck out all season.
(E) Turley has not given up a hit to Jim or Tom all season.

ANALYSIS

The correct answer is (B). Tom's is a general statement about Turley's relationship to all hitters. All choices except (B) mention only Tom or Jim, not hitters in general.

EXAMPLE 2

Sid: **The recent popularity of hot-air ballooning and bungee-jumping are instances of the latest quest for new types of adventure in the modern world.**

Phil: **That's ridiculous! Certainly these brightly colored floating globes of air are not modern inventions; rather, they recall the spectacle of county fairs and carnivals from the turn of the century.**

Sid: **Well, bungee-jumping wasn't around at the turn of the century.**

Phil's best counter to Sid's last statement would be

(A) But bungee-jumping is used in fairs and carnivals.
(B) No, bungee-jumping is merely a newer version of a Polynesian ritual hundreds of years old.
(C) You do know that bungee-jumping is more dangerous than hot-air ballooning.
(D) Yes, but hot-air ballooning is more popular than bungee-jumping.
(E) No, but lots of other inventions are adventurous.

ANALYSIS

The correct answer is (B). Sid's point is that these modern adventures are had with modern inventions. His last statement is trying to say that bungee-jumping is modern. Phil's best counter would be to point out that bungee-jumping is not new.

EXAMPLE 3

Al: **To be a good parent, one must be patient.**

Bill: **That's not so. It takes much more than patience to be a good parent.**

Bill has understood Al's statement to mean that

(A) if a person is a good parent, he or she will be patient
(B) if a person is patient, he or she will make a good parent
(C) some patient people make good parents
(D) some good parents are patient
(E) a person cannot be a good parent unless he or she is patient

ANALYSIS

The correct answer is (B). This is a problem in grasping an understanding of necessary and sufficient conditions. Al states that if one is a good parent then one is patient. Patience is necessary to be a good parent. However, Bill's response shows that he (Bill) has inferred that Al considers patience to be sufficient to be a good parent, not just a necessary condition. (B) reflects Bill's mistaken inference. (A) is incorrect because it accurately describes Al's statement. (C) and (D) are incorrect because Al's statement concerns "any" or "all" persons and not "some." (E) is incorrect because it is equivalent to (A) and thus accurately describes Al's statement.

Syllogistic Reasoning

Syllogistic reasoning is a slightly more formal type of reasoning. It deals with an argument that has two premises and a conclusion. This type of question gives you short propositions (premises) and asks you to draw conclusions, valid or invalid. You may be expected to evaluate assumptions—information that is or is not assumed.

First, if possible, simplify the propositions to assist your understanding.
Second, draw diagrams (Venn diagrams; see p. 220 in Chapter 3), if possible.
Third, replace phrases or words with letters to help yourself follow the logic.

EXAMPLE 1

All couples who have children are happy.
All couples either have children or are happy.

Assuming the above to be true, which one of the following CANNOT be true?

(A) All couples are happy.
(B) Some couples who are happy have children.
(C) Some couples who have children are not happy.
(D) Some couples have happy children.
(E) Children of happy couples are happy.

ANALYSIS

The correct answer is (C). If all couples who have children are happy, and if all couples who don't have children are happy, then all couples are happy. Simplifying the two statements to "all couples are happy" makes this question much more direct and easier to handle. Thus, (C) is false, since it contradicts the first statement; we have no information about children.

EXAMPLE 2

All As are Bs.
Some Cs are As.

Which one of the following is warranted based upon the above?

(A) All Bs are As.
(B) Some Cs are Bs.
(C) All Bs are Cs
(D) No Bs are As.
(E) All Cs are Bs.

ANALYSIS

The correct choice is (B). Here is a diagram of the original information:

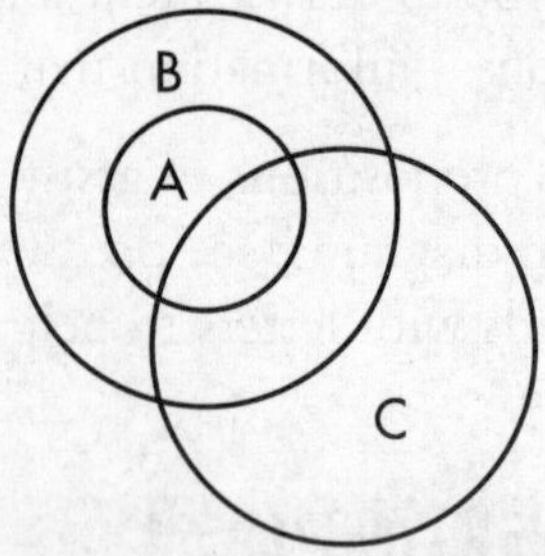

With this diagram, the following is evident:

(A) "All Bs are As" is false.
(B) "Some Cs are Bs" is true.
(C) "All Bs are Cs" is false.
(D) "No Bs are As" is false. If all As are Bs, then some Bs must be As.
(E) "All Cs are Bs" is false.

EXAMPLE 3

In this question, the second premise shows up in the actual question.

If the Dodgers do not finally win a championship for their fans this season, the team's manager will definitely not return to guide the club next year.

It follows logically from the statement above that, if the Dodgers win a championship this season, then next year the team's manager

(A) will definitely not return
(B) will probably not return
(C) will probably return
(D) will definitely return
(E) may or may not return

ANALYSIS

The correct answer is (E). The passage states that if the Dodgers do not win the championship [condition A], then the manager will not return [condition B]. Thus, we have "if A then B." The question then asks, "What follows if they *do* win the championship [a negation of condition A]?" If A implies B, the negation of A [if the Dodgers do win the championship] does *not* imply the negation of B [the manager will return]. Hence, condition A or not A (win or lose) may be the case; the manager may or may not return. (C) is possible, but he may also not return. All we know for sure is that if he loses, he positively won't return.

Conclusions

Here you will be given a list of conditionals, statements, or a short paragraph, and asked to follow the logic to reach a valid conclusion.

In this type, you will first want to underline key terms to eliminate looking at excess wording.

Second, mark the direction of each statement. Where does it start and end? What connection is it making?

Third, look for the "kicker" statement. That's the one that starts the chain reaction; it gives you the information to work with other statements.

If there is no "kicker" statement, carefully check how the information given in one statement is relative to the information given in the next statement. This relationship may be enough to help you understand the reasoning.

In checking the validity of a conclusion, you should be looking for a key statement that leads you as directly as possible to that conclusion. Sometimes, if the choices don't start with the word "therefore," you may wish to insert the word "therefore" before the answer choices to help you see which one follows logically.

EXAMPLE 1

Senator Jones will vote for the Pork bill if he is reelected. If the Pork bill passes, then Senator Jones will not have been reelected. Senator Jones was reelected.

Which one of the following can be concluded from these statements?

(A) Senator Jones assisted in the passage of the Pork bill.
(B) The passage of the Pork bill carried Senator Jones to victory.
(C) Senator Jones voted against the Pork bill, but it passed anyway.
(D) The Pork bill didn't pass, even though Senator Jones voted for it.
(E) The Pork bill was defeated by a large majority.

ANALYSIS

The correct answer is (D). Notice that the "kicker" statement that started the chain reaction is "Senator Jones was reelected." From this, we know that he voted for the Pork bill. But the Pork bill could not have passed; otherwise, he could not have been reelected.

EXAMPLE 2

Meteorology may qualify as a science, but there is a great deal of guesswork involved as well. Even with increased knowledge about wind currents and weather patterns, and the most sophisticated equipment, forecasters' predictions are often wrong. Even the movement of a phenomenon as prominent as a hurricane cannot be determined very far in advance.

Which one of the following is the best conclusion to the passage?

(A) Therefore, we should be especially skeptical of weather predictions for the distant future.
(B) Therefore, we cannot control the weather, but we can predict it.
(C) Therefore, even though we cannot accurately predict the weather now, it will be possible in the near future.
(D) Therefore, since we cannot predict the weather, our aim should be to control it.
(E) Therefore, meteorology is a worthless science.

ANALYSIS

The correct answer is (A). The passage points out that, although we can to some extent predict the weather, we are often wrong. This leads us to the conclusion that we cannot predict far in advance. (A) is the best answer. (B) and (D) do not follow since the passage does not mention controlling the weather. (C) does not follow since the passage does not address our gaining additional knowledge or more sophisticated equipment to help us in the future. The passage does not condemn meteorology, so (E) can be eliminated.

Logical Flaws

This common question type gives you a passage, statement, or argument and asks you to find, understand, analyze, or name the type of flaw in the reasoning.

As you watch for logical flaws, notice that some are very evident, especially if the passage or argument seems nonsensical. Others are very subtle and need a second look. If you don't spot the flaw immediately upon reading the passage, let the choices help. Remember, the choices are showing you some possibilities.

Reading the question first will stop you from trying to make complete sense of a nonsensical passage or from trying to follow the logic or reasoning when, by the design of the question, it does not follow. You see that the question itself warned you that there was a flaw in the reasoning.

EXAMPLE 1

The new American revolution is an electronic one. Advances in sophisticated circuitry have yielded more gadgets than anyone could have imagined only a few years ago: Calculators as small as a wristwatch and automobile dashboards full of digital readouts are two of the many products that have enhanced the quality of life. But we may become so dependent on solid-state circuits to do our thinking that we may forget how to do it ourselves. Certain birds living on islands where there were no predators have, in time, lost their ability to fly. We may just as easily lose the ability to perform even the simplest mathematical calculation without the aid of an electronic gadget.

Which one of the following best describes the flaw in the reasoning in this passage?

(A) It assumes that a temporal sequence implies a causal relation.
(B) It generalizes from one instance to every other instance of the same type.
(C) It draws an analogy between two very different situations.
(D) It wrongly assumes that no new and better electronic devices will be invented.
(E) It assumes that what happens in America also happens in the rest of the world.

ANALYSIS

The correct answer is (C). The flaw in the reasoning here is the comparison of two wholly unlike situations. The analogy compares men and birds and compares an event in the evolutionary history of certain birds that happened under unique circumstances over vast periods of time to what is supposed to be a similar situation in the modern world, but which has in fact no real similarity.

EXAMPLE 2

With the continued water shortage in our area, the Water Department has had to restrict the use of water during daylight hours and increase the cost of water to consumers. An average water bill has risen twenty-four dollars a year for three years in a row. Three years from now, our water costs will be astronomical.

A major flaw in the reasoning is that it

(A) relies upon figures that are imprecise to support a conclusion
(B) fails to indicate exactly how high expenses will be in three years
(C) assumes the conditions of the past three years will continue
(D) overlooks the possibility that conservation methods may improve in the next five years
(E) ignores the likelihood of the high cost driving down the water usage

ANALYSIS

The correct answer is (C). To follow the author's line of reasoning, the author must assume that "the conditions of the past three years will continue." This assumption is flawed since the conditions could change. The conclusion is, therefore, based on a faulty assumption.

EXAMPLE 3

***School Principal:* In 1992 and 1993, when the limit on class size in grades 7, 8, and 9 was 25, our junior-high-school students had an average reading score of 79 and an average math score of 75 on the state tests administered at the end of grade 9. But, in 1994 and 1995, when the limit on class size was raised to 28, our junior-high-school students had average scores of 75 on the state reading tests and 75 on the state math tests. The increase in class-size limitations has brought about the decline in state test scores.**

Which one of the following is a major flaw in the reasoning in this passage?

(A) The author believes that test scores are accurate.
(B) The author fails to realize that some students' math test scores have not declined, though the average has.
(C) The author regards scores in math tests as more important than scores in reading.
(D) The author assumes that class size has caused the variation in test scores.
(E) The author does not know whether class size actually increased.

ANALYSIS

The correct answer is (D). Since the class-size limitations were increased, and only the reading scores decreased, the author came to the conclusion that class-size limitations caused the decline. But the math scores did not decrease, which would lead one to believe that other factors are involved in the scores' decline. Also, the fact that there were different class-size limitations does not mean the sizes of the classes were different. The author's reasoning is flawed by his assumption that class size caused the variation. (E) is a fact, but is not the flaw in the author's reasoning.

Situation Analysis

This new question type requires you to select the situation, from the ones given, that most appropriately illustrates a principle expressed by the analysis of the situation in the passage.

To answer this question type, you should focus on the analysis and how it applies to the situation. After reading the situation, you may wish to read the analysis twice before proceeding to the question and the choices.

EXAMPLE 1

Situation: In order to discourage the use of tobacco products, the state imposes a 50-cent tax on each package of cigarettes. It employs the revenues generated by the cigarette tax to fund television advertisements whose purpose is to deter teenagers from smoking.
Analysis: The objective of both is to reduce smoking, and the success of the first may help to achieve the objective of the second.

The analysis provided for the situation above would be most appropriate in which one of the following situations?

(A) In order to reduce the number of cars on the five major highways into the city, the transportation board sets aside one lane in each direction for the exclusive use of cars carrying two or more passengers. To keep these lanes moving at higher speeds, taxis and buses are not allowed to use them.
(B) In order to stem the rising crime rate, the city council approves a budget that spends $600 million to increase the size of the police force. To avoid a tax increase, the money for the additional officers is provided by reducing the funding of gang-prevention and neighborhood-watch programs.
(C) In an effort to get rid of the rodents that have been feeding on the grain stored in his barn, Mr. McDonald buys five cats to live in the barn. To keep the cats warm and inside the barn, he carefully repairs all of the holes in the doors and walls where the wood has weathered.
(D) In order to reduce its liability insurance rates, the Ace Car Rental Agency no longer allows drivers under the age of twenty-one or over the age of seventy-five to drive its trucks and cars. To make up for the lost revenues, it offers lower rates on weekend rentals.
(E) To reduce the air pollution caused by automobile emissions, the city establishes bicycle lanes on many of the roads from the suburbs to the downtown working areas. To provide space for the bicycle lanes without the expense of widening the roads, the number of car lanes is reduced by one in all of the highways with multiple lanes.

ANALYSIS

The correct answer is (C). As the increased taxes and the television advertising both contribute to the reduction of smoking, so the use of cats to prey on the grain-eating rodents, and the repairs to the barn that will keep the cats in and keep rodents out will both contribute to the preservation of the grain.

In (A), the restriction may or may not reduce the number of cars on the highways. By denying buses and taxis the use of the faster lanes, the city may actually increase the number of cars on the highways. There is no certainty that either of the two steps will work, and the success of the one will not contribute to the success of the other.

In (B), the reduction of funds that support gang-prevention and neighborhood-watch programs will probably result in an increase in crime, rather than encourage its reduction.

Though it is possible that the reduction of weekend rental rates (D) may make up for lost revenues, the two objectives are not closely related, and success in the one will not contribute to success in the other.

In (E), if the automobiles must spend more time on the road because of increased congestion that results from the loss of a driving lane, air pollution will not be reduced.

EXAMPLE 2

Situation: In order to increase its advertising revenues, radio station WJBW changes its format from all news to the rap and salsa music that is popular with the younger listeners whom advertisers prefer. To accommodate the revised format, the station reduces the time for commercial messages from 16 to 12 minutes each hour.
Analysis: The success of the first objective is undermined by meeting the requirements of the second.

The analysis provided for the situation above would be most appropriate in which one of the following situations?

(A) In order to improve profitability, Fox Produce Company raises only a popular yellow tomato that sells at a higher price than the red. It uses the profits from sales to expand the greenhouses in which it develops seedlings of the yellow tomato.
(B) The aquarium raises its fees in order to finance the construction of a wing to exhibit tropical jellyfish. In order to educate the public, its new Web site is devoted to information about jellyfish of the world's oceans.
(C) In order to increase her disposable income, Mrs. Scudder gives used clothing, books, and furniture to the church thrift shop for which she receives both federal and state income tax deductions. She uses the money she saves on her taxes to buy tax-free-bond mutual funds.
(D) In order to increase its profits, a cable television company raises its fees to customers and adds an additional channel of nature programs. To make room for the new station, the company eliminates a popular classic movie channel, as well as a Spanish language station and a successful all-news channel.
(E) In order to increase the value of their stock holdings, members of the Key Investment Club contribute at least $500 dollars each month to buy additional shares in the stock portfolio of the club. In order to diversify its holdings, the club invests only in stocks that it does not already own.

ANALYSIS

The correct answer is (D). Though not an ideal answer, this is clearly the best of the five choices. In the original situation, the number of advertising minutes is reduced, and so the advertising revenues are likely to decline. In (D), though the station will increase revenues by raising its fees, the reduction in the number of channels and the elimination of two popular ones will probably lead to customer defections, and the plan to increase profits will be undermined.

In (A), the use of the profits to increase the availability of seedlings will contribute to, rather than undermine, the success of the first objective.

In (B), there is no reason to believe that information on the Internet will have an effect one way or the other on the aquarium's ability to finance new construction.

In (C), both the tax deductions and the mutual funds will contribute to the disposable income that is sought.

In (E), it is impossible to say how the choice of stocks that are not already in the portfolio will affect the value of the holdings. It is possible, but not certain, that previously owned stocks would be better investments, so we cannot be sure how the second factor will affect the first.

Passage Completion

This question type requires you to choose a phrase or sentence that best completes the passage.

It is initially important that you preserve the meaning of the passage, completing or maintaining the same thought. Unity (same subject) and coherence (order of thoughts) should be carefully noted. Second, it is important that the words you choose fit stylistically, use the same vocabulary, and are from the same context. Many times you will be able to eliminate some choices that "just don't sound good."

EXAMPLE 1

English, with its insatiable and omnivorous appetite for imported food, has eaten until it has become linguistically unbuttoned. And the glutton has cloaked his paunch with the pride of the gourmet. We would not imply that a large vocabulary is bad, but rather that it is self-destructive if uncontrolled by ______________________.

Which one of the following is the best completion according to the context of this passage?

(A) a smattering of slang
(B) a fine sense of distinction
(C) the removal of all but Anglo-Saxon derivatives
(D) a professor who knows the limits of good usage
(E) an unbuttoned tongue

ANALYSIS

The correct answer is (B). The passage describes the English language itself; therefore, references to individuals, (D) and (E), are inappropriate. They do not maintain the same general level of thought. Since the author does not condemn a large and distinguished vocabulary, (A) and (C), which do, are both poor choices. (B) preserves the meaning of the passage and fits stylistically.

EXAMPLE 2

In a reversal of past trends, last year more lawyers left courtroom practice to go into the teaching of law than vice versa. Since courtroom practice on average yields a much higher annual income, this shift discredits the theory that ______.

Which one of the following best completes the last sentence in the passage above?

(A) incomes in the teaching of law will at some future time match those of courtroom practice
(B) the change in profession by those lawyers who are likely to increase their incomes can be predicted in advance
(C) more lawyers have remained in the teaching of law in the past few years than previously was the case
(D) lawyers under 40 years of age are more likely to change professions for financial rather than other reasons
(E) lawyers are likely to move into those professions in which the income is highest

ANALYSIS

The correct answer is (E). The passage argues a connection among lawyers, profession changes, and income. Any answer choice that does not address those items cannot be a logical conclusion. (E) addresses the three key items and offers a conclusion that is logically consistent with the apparent change from higher to lower paying professions. (A) is irrelevant because the passage does not address the "future." (B) is irrelevant because the passage does not address "prediction." (C) is irrelevant because the passage does not address "remaining" in a profession, only changing. (D) is irrelevant because the passage does not address the "age" of lawyers.

Word Reference

Here a word, or a group of words, is taken out of context, and you are asked either what the word or words mean or what they refer to. In this type of question, first consider the passage as a whole, then carefully examine the key word or words surrounding the selected ones.

EXAMPLE

English, with its insatiable and omnivorous appetite for imported food, has eaten until it has become linguistically unbuttoned. And the glutton has cloaked his paunch with the pride of the gourmet. We would not imply that a large vocabulary is bad, but rather that it is self-destructive if uncontrolled by a fine sense of distinction.

As used here, the word "glutton" refers to

(A) an English language with a lack of Anglo-Saxon derivation
(B) one who never stops talking about foreign food
(C) an English language bursting with pride
(D) one who is bilingual
(E) an English language bursting with derivatives from foreign languages

ANALYSIS

The correct answer is (E). The passage, as a whole, is commenting on the English language, and (E) is the only choice that equates "glutton" with the subject of the passage.

IN CONCLUSION

As you have seen, Logical Reasoning includes a potpourri of problem types all requiring common sense and reasonableness in the answers. You should take care in underlining what is being asked so that you do not (for example) accidentally look for the valid conclusion when the invalid one is asked for. Because of the nature of the Logical Reasoning problems, it is very easy to get tangled in a problem and lose your original thought, spending too much time on the question. If you feel that you have become trapped or stuck, take a guess and come back later if you have time. Remember that you must work within the context of the question, so do not bring in outside experiences or otherwise complicate a problem. The Logical Reasoning question is looking not for training in formal logic, but just for common sense and reasonableness.

Remember: Logical Reasoning accounts for 50 percent of your LSAT score.

REVIEW OF SOME GENERAL STRATEGIES FOR LOGICAL REASONING

THE PASSAGE

Read *actively,* circling key words.

Note major issue and supporting points.

THE QUESTION

Preread (before reading the passage) *actively.*

Note its reference.

Watch out for *unstated* ideas:

assumptions, implications/inferences, and sometimes conclusions.

ANSWER CHOICES

Sometimes there will not be a *perfect* answer;

thus, choose the *best* of the five choices.

Use the elimination strategy.

Note that "wrong" words in a choice make that choice incorrect.

Watch for those off-topic key words.

Remove answer sheet by cutting on dotted line

Answer Sheet

EXTRA PRACTICE: LOGICAL REASONING

1 Ⓐ Ⓑ Ⓒ Ⓓ Ⓔ
2 Ⓐ Ⓑ Ⓒ Ⓓ Ⓔ
3 Ⓐ Ⓑ Ⓒ Ⓓ Ⓔ
4 Ⓐ Ⓑ Ⓒ Ⓓ Ⓔ
5 Ⓐ Ⓑ Ⓒ Ⓓ Ⓔ
6 Ⓐ Ⓑ Ⓒ Ⓓ Ⓔ
7 Ⓐ Ⓑ Ⓒ Ⓓ Ⓔ
8 Ⓐ Ⓑ Ⓒ Ⓓ Ⓔ
9 Ⓐ Ⓑ Ⓒ Ⓓ Ⓔ
10 Ⓐ Ⓑ Ⓒ Ⓓ Ⓔ
11 Ⓐ Ⓑ Ⓒ Ⓓ Ⓔ
12 Ⓐ Ⓑ Ⓒ Ⓓ Ⓔ
13 Ⓐ Ⓑ Ⓒ Ⓓ Ⓔ
14 Ⓐ Ⓑ Ⓒ Ⓓ Ⓔ
15 Ⓐ Ⓑ Ⓒ Ⓓ Ⓔ
16 Ⓐ Ⓑ Ⓒ Ⓓ Ⓔ
17 Ⓐ Ⓑ Ⓒ Ⓓ Ⓔ
18 Ⓐ Ⓑ Ⓒ Ⓓ Ⓔ
19 Ⓐ Ⓑ Ⓒ Ⓓ Ⓔ
20 Ⓐ Ⓑ Ⓒ Ⓓ Ⓔ
21 Ⓐ Ⓑ Ⓒ Ⓓ Ⓔ
22 Ⓐ Ⓑ Ⓒ Ⓓ Ⓔ
23 Ⓐ Ⓑ Ⓒ Ⓓ Ⓔ
24 Ⓐ Ⓑ Ⓒ Ⓓ Ⓔ
25 Ⓐ Ⓑ Ⓒ Ⓓ Ⓔ
26 Ⓐ Ⓑ Ⓒ Ⓓ Ⓔ
27 Ⓐ Ⓑ Ⓒ Ⓓ Ⓔ
28 Ⓐ Ⓑ Ⓒ Ⓓ Ⓔ
29 Ⓐ Ⓑ Ⓒ Ⓓ Ⓔ
30 Ⓐ Ⓑ Ⓒ Ⓓ Ⓔ
31 Ⓐ Ⓑ Ⓒ Ⓓ Ⓔ
32 Ⓐ Ⓑ Ⓒ Ⓓ Ⓔ
33 Ⓐ Ⓑ Ⓒ Ⓓ Ⓔ
34 Ⓐ Ⓑ Ⓒ Ⓓ Ⓔ
35 Ⓐ Ⓑ Ⓒ Ⓓ Ⓔ
36 Ⓐ Ⓑ Ⓒ Ⓓ Ⓔ
37 Ⓐ Ⓑ Ⓒ Ⓓ Ⓔ
38 Ⓐ Ⓑ Ⓒ Ⓓ Ⓔ
39 Ⓐ Ⓑ Ⓒ Ⓓ Ⓔ
40 Ⓐ Ⓑ Ⓒ Ⓓ Ⓔ
41 Ⓐ Ⓑ Ⓒ Ⓓ Ⓔ
42 Ⓐ Ⓑ Ⓒ Ⓓ Ⓔ
43 Ⓐ Ⓑ Ⓒ Ⓓ Ⓔ
44 Ⓐ Ⓑ Ⓒ Ⓓ Ⓔ
45 Ⓐ Ⓑ Ⓒ Ⓓ Ⓔ
46 Ⓐ Ⓑ Ⓒ Ⓓ Ⓔ
47 Ⓐ Ⓑ Ⓒ Ⓓ Ⓔ
48 Ⓐ Ⓑ Ⓒ Ⓓ Ⓔ
49 Ⓐ Ⓑ Ⓒ Ⓓ Ⓔ
50 Ⓐ Ⓑ Ⓒ Ⓓ Ⓔ
51 Ⓐ Ⓑ Ⓒ Ⓓ Ⓔ
52 Ⓐ Ⓑ Ⓒ Ⓓ Ⓔ
53 Ⓐ Ⓑ Ⓒ Ⓓ Ⓔ
54 Ⓐ Ⓑ Ⓒ Ⓓ Ⓔ
55 Ⓐ Ⓑ Ⓒ Ⓓ Ⓔ
56 Ⓐ Ⓑ Ⓒ Ⓓ Ⓔ
57 Ⓐ Ⓑ Ⓒ Ⓓ Ⓔ
58 Ⓐ Ⓑ Ⓒ Ⓓ Ⓔ
59 Ⓐ Ⓑ Ⓒ Ⓓ Ⓔ
60 Ⓐ Ⓑ Ⓒ Ⓓ Ⓔ
61 Ⓐ Ⓑ Ⓒ Ⓓ Ⓔ
62 Ⓐ Ⓑ Ⓒ Ⓓ Ⓔ
63 Ⓐ Ⓑ Ⓒ Ⓓ Ⓔ
64 Ⓐ Ⓑ Ⓒ Ⓓ Ⓔ
65 Ⓐ Ⓑ Ⓒ Ⓓ Ⓔ
66 Ⓐ Ⓑ Ⓒ Ⓓ Ⓔ
67 Ⓐ Ⓑ Ⓒ Ⓓ Ⓔ
68 Ⓐ Ⓑ Ⓒ Ⓓ Ⓔ
69 Ⓐ Ⓑ Ⓒ Ⓓ Ⓔ
70 Ⓐ Ⓑ Ⓒ Ⓓ Ⓔ
71 Ⓐ Ⓑ Ⓒ Ⓓ Ⓔ
72 Ⓐ Ⓑ Ⓒ Ⓓ Ⓔ
73 Ⓐ Ⓑ Ⓒ Ⓓ Ⓔ
74 Ⓐ Ⓑ Ⓒ Ⓓ Ⓔ
75 Ⓐ Ⓑ Ⓒ Ⓓ Ⓔ
76 Ⓐ Ⓑ Ⓒ Ⓓ Ⓔ
77 Ⓐ Ⓑ Ⓒ Ⓓ Ⓔ
78 Ⓐ Ⓑ Ⓒ Ⓓ Ⓔ
79 Ⓐ Ⓑ Ⓒ Ⓓ Ⓔ
80 Ⓐ Ⓑ Ⓒ Ⓓ Ⓔ
81 Ⓐ Ⓑ Ⓒ Ⓓ Ⓔ
82 Ⓐ Ⓑ Ⓒ Ⓓ Ⓔ
83 Ⓐ Ⓑ Ⓒ Ⓓ Ⓔ
84 Ⓐ Ⓑ Ⓒ Ⓓ Ⓔ
85 Ⓐ Ⓑ Ⓒ Ⓓ Ⓔ
86 Ⓐ Ⓑ Ⓒ Ⓓ Ⓔ
87 Ⓐ Ⓑ Ⓒ Ⓓ Ⓔ
88 Ⓐ Ⓑ Ⓒ Ⓓ Ⓔ
89 Ⓐ Ⓑ Ⓒ Ⓓ Ⓔ
90 Ⓐ Ⓑ Ⓒ Ⓓ Ⓔ

Extra Practice: Logical Reasoning

<u>Directions:</u> In this section you will be given brief statements or passages and will be required to evaluate the reasoning involved. In some instances, more than one choice will appear to be a possible answer. You are to choose the *best* answer. Use common sense and reasonableness in making your selection; then mark the correct answer.

<u>Questions 1–3</u>

Robots have the ability to exhibit programmed behavior. Their performance can range from the simplest activity to the most complex group of activities. They not only can build other robots but also can rebuild themselves. Physically they can resemble humans, yet mentally they cannot. Even the most highly advanced robot does not have the capacity to be creative, have emotions, or think independently.

1. From the passage above, which one of the following must be true?

   (A) Robots could eventually take over the world.
   (B) The most complex group of activities involves being creative.
   (C) A robot could last forever.
   (D) Emotions, creativity, and independent thought can be written as programs.
   (E) Building other robots involves independent thinking.

2. The author of this passage would agree that

   (A) robots would eventually be impossible to control
   (B) in the near future, robots will be able to think independently
   (C) robots have reached their peak of development
   (D) there are dangers in robots that think for themselves
   (E) there are some tasks that are better done by humans than by robots

3. The author's assertions would be weakened by pointing out that

   (A) humans exhibit programmed behavior for the first few years of life
   (B) robots' behavior is not always predictable
   (C) building other robots requires independent training
   (D) internal feeling is not always exhibited
   (E) the most complex group of activities necessitates independent thinking

4. The management of Trans-Caribbean Airways has announced that the airline's bonus-mileage program will be discontinued on July 1. A survey conducted on weekdays in February on the Miami to Port-of-Spain route asked passengers to rate, in order of importance: low fares, on-time performance, prompt baggage handling, quality in-flight refreshments, and bonus mileage. More than 95 percent of the respondents put low fares and on-time performance either first or second, whereas less than 1 percent placed the bonus-mileage program above fourth. Since bonus mileage is not important to Trans-Caribbean passengers, management has decided to eliminate it.

   The decision of the management is based on all the following assumptions EXCEPT:

   (A) that because the bonus-mileage program was not the passengers' first or second concern, it is not important to them
   (B) that the passengers on the Miami to Port-of-Spain route reflect the opinion of other passengers of Trans-Caribbean Airways
   (C) that the passengers flying in February are representative of the airline's passengers throughout the year
   (D) that other airlines will not attract Trans-Caribbean customers by offering attractive bonus-mileage plans
   (E) that the number of passengers who failed to complete the survey is statistically insignificant

5. *Botanist:* No plant in the botanical gardens blossoms twice in the same month. All of the plants in the botanical gardens that blossom in January are grown from either bulbs or tubers. None of the plants that blossom in January will flower again later in the year.

   If the statements above are true, which one of the following must also be true?

   (A) No plant in the botanical garden grown from a bulb will blossom in October.
   (B) No plants in the botanical garden blossom twice in the year if they blossom first in January.
   (C) None of the plants in the botanical gardens that blossom in June are grown from tubers.
   (D) All of the plants in the botanical gardens grown from bulbs or tubers that did not blossom in January will flower later in the year.
   (E) All plants in the botanical gardens grown from bulbs or tubers flower in January.

6. The simplest conceivable situation in which one human being may communicate with another is one in which structurally complementary communicants have been conditioned to associate the same words with the same things.

The sentence that would best complete this thought is:

(A) Therefore, dictionaries are of little value to foreigners.
(B) Therefore, man cannot communicate effectively with animals.
(C) Therefore, communication is a matter of relation.
(D) Therefore, communication is simplest following a common experience.
(E) Therefore, communication is dependent on complementary structures.

7. In a nationwide survey, four out of five dentists questioned recommended sugarless gum for their patients who chew gum.

Which one of the following would most weaken the above endorsement for sugarless gum?

(A) Only five dentists were questioned.
(B) The dentists were not paid for their endorsements.
(C) Only one of the dentists questioned chewed sugarless gum.
(D) Patients do not do what their dentists tell them to do.
(E) Sugarless gum costs much more than regular gum.

8. In Tom and Angie's class, everyone likes drawing or painting or both, but Angie does not like painting.

Which one of the following statements cannot be true?

(A) Angie likes drawing.
(B) Tom likes drawing and painting.
(C) Everyone in the class who does not like drawing likes painting.
(D) No one in the class likes painting.
(E) Tom dislikes drawing and painting.

9. *Mark:* The big test is tomorrow, and I didn't study. I suppose I'll just have to cheat. I know it is wrong, but I have to get a good grade on the test.
Amy: I don't think that's a good idea. Just go to the teacher, tell the truth, and maybe you can get a postponement.

Amy attacks Mark's argument by

(A) attacking his reasoning
(B) applying personal pressure
(C) implying that good triumphs over evil
(D) presenting another alternative
(E) suggesting a positive approach

Questions 10–11

The microwave oven has become a standard appliance in many kitchens, mainly because it offers a fast way of cooking food. Yet, some homeowners believe that the ovens are still not completely safe. Microwaves, therefore, should not be standard appliances until they are more carefully researched and tested.

10. Which one of the following, if true, would most weaken the conclusion of the passage above?

(A) Homeowners often purchase items despite knowing they may be unsafe.
(B) Those homeowners in doubt about microwave safety ought not to purchase microwaves.
(C) Research and testing of home appliances seldom reveal safety hazards.
(D) Microwaves are not as dangerous as steam irons, which are used in almost every home.
(E) Homeowners often purchase items that they do not need.

11. Which one of the following, if true, would most strengthen the conclusion of the passage above?

(A) Homeowners often doubt the advertised safety of all new appliances.
(B) Speed of food preparation is not the only concern of today's homeowner.
(C) Modern homeowners have more free time than ever before.
(D) Food preparation has become almost a science, with more complicated and involved recipes.
(E) Many microwave ovens have been found to leak radioactive elements.

12. Cats that eat Vitagatto Cat Food each day will have sleek coats and excellent night vision. Since Jane feeds her cats only white tuna or poached chicken breasts, they cannot have excellent night vision. Therefore they should be kept indoors at night to prevent injuries.

    Which one of the following contains a reasoning error most similar to that in the argument above?

    (A) Older houses in Canary Park sell for about $100,000, if the kitchen and bathrooms have been modernized. Arthur has put new fixtures in the bathrooms of his Canary Park house, but has not changed the kitchen. Therefore, the house will sell for less than $100,000 dollars.
    (B) Plants that have never been exposed to fungicides are especially susceptible to mildew. Since Jarmilla never uses any chemicals in her garden, her plants are susceptible to mildew in wet or cloudy weather.
    (C) Restaurants in Arlmont that buy their baked goods from Vonder's Bakery do brisk business at breakfast. Since Tamale Tom's restaurant does all its own baking, it will not have many breakfast customers and should not open until lunchtime.
    (D) Students who take the law exam preparation class offered by the English department receive scores above the national average. Sally has taken a more expensive and more time-consuming course from a private tutor. She will, therefore, receive a very high score and be accepted at Yale.
    (E) Police in Allentown solve most of the robberies that take place during daylight hours, but more than half of the robberies that take place after 6 P.M. go unsolved. Since the Borden Furniture Company was robbed at midnight, the thieves will probably not be caught.

13. According to a count of the men and women listed in the Glenarm Telephone Directory, there are 10,000 more men than women in this city of only 100,000. But according to the last census report, the population of Glenarm is 55 percent female. All of the following can be used to explain this discrepancy EXCEPT:

    (A) not all phone users list their names in the directory
    (B) married couples are more likely to use the husband's than the wife's name in the directory
    (C) the census report has been faulted for undercounting the minority population of large cities
    (D) the phone book count may be thrown off by initials or names that are not gender-specific
    (E) there are many more females under 14 than males

14. Given that this rock is white in color, it must be quartz.

    The foregoing conclusion can be properly drawn if it is true that

    (A) only quartz rocks are white in color
    (B) quartz rocks are generally white in color
    (C) other white rocks have proved to be quartz
    (D) few other types of rocks are white in color
    (E) all quartz rocks are white in color

<u>Questions 15–16</u>

"Even the smallest restaurant in Paris serves better breads than the best restaurants in New York," the visiting chef said. He was complaining about the quality of the bread available in America. "I was trained in France," he added, "so I understand bread-making. But in America, there are hardly any good bakers. You can tell just by looking at the roll baskets. In every restaurant I have visited in New York, the roll baskets are still full on every table at the end of the meal."

15. The chef's conclusions depend on all of the following assumptions EXCEPT

    (A) if the bread is good, at least some of it will be consumed
    (B) the quality of a restaurant can be determined by the quality of its breads
    (C) all good bakers work in restaurants
    (D) the standard for good bread-making is France
    (E) restaurants do not replenish roll baskets

16. All of the following are flaws in the reasoning of the speaker in the passage above EXCEPT:

    (A) the argument takes as fact what is unproven personal opinion
    (B) the argument assumes that New York restaurants represent American baking
    (C) the speaker claims complete knowledge of a large number of small restaurants in Paris
    (D) the speaker claims that he knows how to bake bread
    (E) the examples the speaker cites of good and bad bread makers are vague and unspecific

Questions 17–18

Some American auto factories are beginning to resemble their Japanese counterparts. In many Japanese factories, the workers enjoy the same status and privileges as their bosses. Everyone works in harmony, and there is much less of the tension and anger that results when one group dominates another.

17. With which one of the following would the author of the above passage most likely agree?

(A) American work environments ought to emulate Japanese auto factories.
(B) Japanese automobiles are better built than American automobiles.
(C) Tension in the workplace enhances worker productivity.
(D) Japanese culture differs so much from American culture that it precludes any overlap of styles.
(E) Striving for managerial status induces worker productivity.

18. The argument gives logically relevant support for which one of the following conclusions?

(A) Some American auto factories are experiencing changes in their work environments.
(B) American auto workers envy their Japanese counterparts.
(C) There is no tension or anger in Japanese factories.
(D) Decrease in tension leads to higher productivity.
(E) There is no tension or anger in American factories that follow Japanese models.

---

19. When we approach land, we usually sight birds. The lookout has just sighted birds.

Which one of the following represents the most logical conclusion based upon the foregoing statements?

(A) The conjecture that we are approaching land is strengthened.
(B) Land is closer than it was before the sighting of the birds.
(C) We are approaching land.
(D) We may or may not be approaching land.
(E) We may not be approaching land.

20. The presence of the gas Nexon is a necessary condition, but not a sufficient condition, for the existence of life on the planet Plex.

On the basis of the foregoing, which of the following would also be true?

(A) If life exists on Plex, then only the gas Nexon is present.
(B) If life exists on Plex, then the gas Nexon may or may not be present.
(C) If life exists on Plex, then the gas Nexon is present.
(D) If no life exists on Plex, Nexon cannot be present.
(E) If no life exists on Plex, Nexon is the only gas present.

21. The absence of the liquid Flennel is a sufficient condition for the cessation of life on the planet Fluke, but it is not a necessary condition.

On the basis of the foregoing, which of the following would also be true?

(A) If life on Fluke ceased to exist, there would have to have been an absence of the liquid Flennel.
(B) If all liquid Flennel were removed from Fluke, life there would surely perish.
(C) If all liquid Flennel were removed from Fluke, life there might or might not cease.
(D) If all liquid Flennel were removed from Fluke, the cessation of life would depend upon other conditions.
(E) Life on Fluke cannot cease so long as Flennel is present.

22. The gas rates in Edina are low only for the first 30 therms used each month; the next 30 cost twice as much, and all gas over 60 therms costs four times as much as the first 30. The city has very cold winters and warm summers. To heat an average-size two-bedroom home in the winter by gas is prohibitively expensive, but not as costly as electric heating. Consequently

All of the following are logical conclusions to this passage EXCEPT:

(A) most homeowners use oil heating
(B) many homes are kept at temperatures below 70 degrees in the winter
(C) the consumption of gas is lower in the winter than in the summer
(D) electric cooling is more common than electric heating
(E) many homes have wood-burning stoves and fireplaces

23. If the poodle was reared at Prince Charming Kennels, then it is a purebred.

The foregoing statement can be deduced logically from which one of the following statements?

(A) Every purebred poodle is reared at Prince Charming Kennels or at another AKC-approved kennel.
(B) The poodle in question was bred at either Prince Charming Kennels or at another AKC-approved kennel.
(C) The poodle in question either is a purebred or looks remarkably like a purebred.
(D) The majority of poodles reared at Prince Charming Kennels are purebred.
(E) There are no dogs reared at Prince Charming Kennels that are not purebred.

24. There is no reason to eliminate the possibility of an oil field existing beneath the Great Salt Lake. Therefore, we must undertake the exploration of the Great Salt Lake's bottom.

The foregoing argument assumes which one of the following?

(A) Exploration of the Great Salt Lake's bottom has not been previously proposed.
(B) An oil field located beneath the lake would be easy to identify.
(C) The Great Salt Lake is the only large, inland body of water beneath which an oil field may lie.
(D) The quest for oil is a sufficient motive to undertake exploration of the Great Salt Lake's bottom.
(E) An oil field exists beneath the Great Salt Lake.

Questions 25–26

My course of study had led me to believe that all mental and moral feelings and qualities, whether of a good or bad kind, were the results of association; that we love one thing and hate another, take pleasure in one sort of action or contemplation and pain in another sort, through the clinging of pleasurable or painful ideas to those things, from the effect of education or experience. As a corollary to this, I was convinced that the object of education should be to form the strongest possible associations of the salutary class; associations of pleasure with all things beneficial to the great whole. It now seemed to me, in retrospect, that my teachers had occupied themselves but superficially with the means of forming and keeping up these salutary associations. They seemed to have trusted altogether to the old, familiar instruments, praise and blame, reward and punishment. I did not doubt that by these means, begun early, and applied unremittingly, intense associations of pain and pleasure, especially of pain, might be created and might produce desires and aversions capable of lasting undiminished to the end of life. But there must always be something artificial and casual in associations thus produced.

25. By "salutary" the author means

(A) "the strongest possible associations"
(B) ideas that "salute" one's mind
(C) capable of giving pain
(D) promoting some good purpose
(E) those earning a middle-class income or better

26. All of the following questions are answered in the passage EXCEPT:

(A) Is there any sort of thinking that is not associational?
(B) Is schooling the only cause of our lifelong "desires and aversions"?
(C) What else besides education causes these associations?
(D) What do teachers praise, and what do they blame?
(E) How long would the desires and aversions last?

27. The San Diego Chargers practice expertly for long hours every day and keep a written log of their errors.

    The above statement is an example of which one of the following assumptions?

    (A) Practice makes perfect.
    (B) To err is human.
    (C) People make mistakes; that's why they put erasers on pencils.
    (D) Practice is what you know, and it will help to make clear what you do not know.
    (E) Writing is a mode of learning.

28. Pine trees may be taller than any other tree. Pines are never shorter than the shortest palms, and some palms may exceed the height of some pines. Pepper trees are always taller than palm trees. Peach trees are shorter than peppertrees but not shorter than all palms.

    Given the foregoing, which one of the following would be true?

    (A) Peach trees may be shorter than pine trees.
    (B) Pepper trees may be shorter than some peach trees.
    (C) Every pine is taller than every palm.
    (D) A particular palm could not be taller than a particular pine.
    (E) Now and then, a peach tree may be taller than a pepper tree.

29. Most popular paperback novels are of low intellectual quality; therefore, *Splendor Behind the Billboard,* an unpopular paperback novel, is probably of high intellectual quality.

    The foregoing argument is most like which one of the following?

    (A) Most locusts inhabit arid places; therefore, locusts are probably found in all deserts.
    (B) Most acts of criminal violence have declined in number during the past few years; therefore, law enforcement during this period has improved.
    (C) Most people who stop drinking gain weight; therefore, if Carl does not cease drinking, he will probably not gain weight.
    (D) Most nations run by autocratic governments do not permit a free press; therefore, the country of Endorff, which is run by an autocratic government, probably does not have a free press.
    (E) Most new motor homes are equipped with air conditioning; therefore, Jim's new motor home may not be equipped with air conditioning.

Questions 30–31

Jane states, "All mammals have hair. This creature possesses no hair. Therefore, it is not a mammal."

30. Which one of the following most closely parallels the logic of Jane's statement?

(A) All reptiles have scales. This creature possesses scales. Therefore, it is a reptile.
(B) All physics tests are difficult. This is not a physics test. Therefore, it is not difficult.
(C) All American cars are poorly constructed. Every car sold by Fred was poorly constructed. Therefore, Fred sells only American cars.
(D) All mammals do not have hair. This creature possesses hair. Therefore, it may be a mammal.
(E) All lubricants smell. This liquid does not have an odor. Therefore, it is not a lubricant.

31. Which one of the following, if true, would most weaken Jane's argument?

(A) Animals other than mammals have hair.
(B) Some mammals do not have hair.
(C) Mammals have more hair than nonmammals.
(D) One could remove the hair from a mammal.
(E) Reptiles may have hair.

Questions 32–33

A recent study of Hodgkin's disease in young adults has examined a large number of sets of twins, half of them identical and half nonidentical. Identical twins have the same genetic makeup, but like any other siblings nonidentical twins share only about 50 percent of their genetic material. In the study of twins with Hodgkin's disease, the researchers found that the chances of the second of a set of identical twins also developing the disease was 100 times higher than in the case of the sibling of a nonidentical twin, or of any other average individual. The number of cases where both identical twins were affected was, however, not a very large proportion of the identical twin pairs.

32. Based on the information in this passage, we can infer all of the following EXCEPT:

(A) Genetic inheritance is one factor in determining the susceptibility to Hodgkin's disease.
(B) If one twin of a set of nonidentical twins develops Hodgkin's disease, the chances of the second twin developing Hodgkin's disease are no greater than that of a person who is not a twin.

(C) Hodgkin's disease is more likely to appear first in a twin who is one of a pair of identical twins than one of a pair of nonidentical twins.
(D) Genetics alone is not sufficient to cause Hodgkin's disease.
(E) The chances of the second of a pair of identical twins whose twin has developed Hodgkin's disease also developing the disease are not very high.

33. For which one of the following reasons are studies of identical twins most likely to be valuable to medical research?

(A) Identical twins are usually raised in the same environments.
(B) Researchers using identical twins can discern differences more easily.
(C) Identical twins may differ psychologically, but not physically.
(D) Identical twins may reveal information related to genetics.
(E) It is easier to arrange medical examinations at the same hospital for identical twins than for unrelated persons.

---

34. The frog population in the lake each year is determined by the number of two avian predators: egrets and blue herons. The weather has little effect on the egret population, but the number of herons varies according to the rainfall in the area. Therefore, a greatly changing frog population in the lake three years in a row will probably occur when the annual rainfall fluctuates widely for three years.

Of the following arguments, which one most closely resembles this paragraph in the pattern of its reasoning?

(A) The annual profit or loss of Acme Desk Company depends chiefly on the number of new office buildings in the city and on the stability of the mortgage rates. In a year when mortgage rates fluctuate, the building rate is also likely to fluctuate.
(B) The parking lot at the university is filled to capacity on nights when the business school holds classes at the same hours as the extension college. If there are classes at the business school and no classes at the extension college, or classes at the extension college and no classes at the business school, the parking lots are three-quarters full.
(C) The restaurant can sell a beef-and-cheese pizza for a one-dollar profit if the price of cheese remains at less than two dollars per pound and the price of beef at less than one dollar per pound. For the last six months, cheese has sold at $1.95 per pound. Since the pizzas have failed to earn a profit of one dollar in this period, the price of beef must have risen above one dollar per pound.
(D) Farmers in the valley can legally purchase federal water at a reduced rate only if they raise cotton or if their farms are no larger than 960 acres. Several of the farmers who continue to purchase federal water at the reduced rate are raising only alfalfa. Therefore, their farms must be larger than 960 acres.
(E) A cake will not collapse in the oven if the eggs have been brought to room temperature before mixing or if the sugar syrup is at a temperature above 140 degrees. The cake must have collapsed because the eggs were too cold or the sugar was not hot enough.

35. *Editorial:* Scientific studies have shown that second-hand tobacco smoke in the workplace greatly increases the number of workers who take more than fifteen days of sick-leave and the number of workers who suffer serious respiratory ailments. It has also been shown that the number of workers who die of lung cancer is twice as high in workplaces that permit smoking than in workplaces that do not. Therefore, the state must pass laws that require all companies to forbid smoking in the workplace.

Which one of the following is the underlying principle in this argument?

(A) Every individual has a responsibility for the well-being of every other individual with whom he or she comes into daily contact.
(B) Employers who do not take care of the health of their workers risk increasing losses from absenteeism each year.
(C) States must be permitted to outlaw any dangerous substances or implements.
(D) States must be responsible for the safety of the workplace of all businesses in their jurisdiction.
(E) Workers must be permitted to make their own decisions about their workplace.

36. For the post-election festivities, no athlete was invited to the White House unless he or she was more than 35 years old. No one older than 35 was both an athlete and invited to the White House.

Which one of the following conclusions can be logically drawn from the statements above?

(A) No one but athletes were invited to the White House.
(B) No athlete was invited to the White House.
(C) Only persons older than 35 were invited to the White House.
(D) No one over 35 was invited to the White House.
(E) Some athletes over 35 were invited to the White House.

37. At the Brightman Diet Center, 20 men and women who wished to lose ten pounds undertook a program that included an hour of exercise and a limit of 200 calories for breakfast and lunch each day. A second group of 20 men and women, similar in age and weight to the first group, exercised for only half an hour and ate up to 500 calories for breakfast and lunch each day. Surprisingly, at the end of three weeks, all 20 who had exercised less and consumed more calories at breakfast and lunch had lost more weight than members of the other group.

Which one of the following best explains these unexpected results?

(A) Some of those who lost more weight exercised longer than the half hour.
(B) Forty people is too small a sample to produce any meaningful statistics.
(C) The exercise of some of the members of those who lost more weight was more vigorous than that of members of the other group.
(D) Those in the group that ate 500 calories for breakfast and lunch chose foods lower in fat and cholesterol than those in the other group.
(E) The group that had eaten more and exercised less during the day ate fewer calories at dinner than those in the other group.

38. Of the 8,000 American victims of isochemic optic neuropathy, most are over 60. The condition occurs suddenly, and normally in only one eye. Its cause is unknown, though doctors agree that an interruption of the blood flow to the optic nerve is a major factor. Untreated, most people recover full vision in six months. The most common treatment, an operation called "optic nerve decompression surgery," has proven to be less effective than no treatment at all. Fewer regain their sight after the operation, and those who do require nine months to do so.

    The conclusions of this paragraph would be most useful in support of an argument for

    (A) increasing federal supervision of surgical procedures
    (B) reducing the cost of surgical procedures
    (C) reducing the number of surgical procedures
    (D) expanding federal oversight of cosmetic surgery
    (E) funding a study of isochemic optic neuropathy in men and women under 40

39. No one who is a member of the tennis team will smoke cigarettes. No first-rate athlete smokes cigarettes. Therefore, only first-rate athletes will become members of the tennis team.

    The reasoning here is in error since the conclusion does not allow for the possibility of

    (A) a nonsmoker on the tennis team who is a second-rate athlete
    (B) a first-rate athlete who doesn't play tennis
    (C) an ex-smoker who is a first-rate athlete
    (D) a nonsmoker who is not a first-rate athlete
    (E) a smoker who is a first-rate tennis player

40. The sale of clothing featuring characters from children's television programs such as *Barney and Friends* or the *Power Rangers* has increased enormously in the last five years. The number of children who watch television must also have increased greatly in the same period.

    Which one of the following would fail to support this conclusion and at the same time explain the rise in clothing sales?

    (A) The relaxation of trade barriers has substantially reduced the cost of Asian-made clothes in the last five years.
    (B) Five years ago, the most popular children's television program, *Sesame Street*, was seen only on educational television stations.
    (C) In many areas, the three most popular children's television programs are carried on both cable and network television stations.
    (D) There are now several stations, such as the Disney Channel or Nickelodeon, that intend most or all of their programs for a young or very young audience.
    (E) Television programs directed at children, while growing more popular, have been increasingly attacked in the last five years for excessive violence.

41. Alfred Thomason, one of the ten brokers in the mortgage department of Kean and Landers, will certainly write more than $5 million in mortgages this year. Last year, the department's sales totaled more than $50 million, and this year's totals will be just as high.

    Which one of the following contains the same kind of reasoning error as this passage?

    (A) Jacobson expects the dahlias he exhibits in this year's flower show to win a prize. His dahlias failed to win in last year's exhibition, but he believes that the cause was a jealous judge who is not on this year's panel.
    (B) The debate squad is expected to win the state tournament in May. They have won all nine of their debates this year, including a large tournament in Memphis competing against most of the teams highly regarded in the state competition.
    (C) The Vasquez family plans to drive from Boston to Scottsdale in four days. Last winter, the drive took six days, but they were delayed by bad weather in New England, Pennsylvania, and New Mexico.
    (D) South Texas State's Edward Meany will represent his college in a two-day tournament for top golfers from 30 different colleges in the state. Since the team from South Texas State easily won the state intercollegiate golf championship, Meany should have no trouble winning this tournament.
    (E) Seeded first in the NCAA championships in Atlanta, Laura Lomax should breeze through the tournament. She already has won the two tournaments she has entered, and she has a 38-match winning streak.

42. Although it is subject to the variations of currencies and interest rates, the Asian influx is now a major factor in the Australian real estate market. Although many Australians are nervous about the waves of Asian immigration, their economy welcomes the purchase of Australian properties by investors from Asia who have no residential rights. Foreigners are permitted to purchase up to half of the units of a condominium, provided they do so before the condo is first occupied. They can also purchase real estate in areas designated as "integrated tourism resorts," though few exist at present. The average purchase price paid by foreign investors is 80 percent more than the average paid by Australian residents. The United States is still the largest foreign investor, and Singapore recently has replaced Britain in second place.

    From which one of the following can we infer that Australian regulations of foreign investments in real estate are not determined by a policy designed to exclude Asians?

    (A) Asians make purchases chiefly of the more expensive dwelling units.
    (B) Asians pay higher average purchase prices than Australians.
    (C) The largest foreign investor is the United States.
    (D) Traditional ties to Great Britain are no longer important to many Australians.
    (E) Asians can purchase property in "integrated tourism resorts."

43. Thirty-eight percent of people in America drink unfluoridated water and, as a result, have 25 percent more cavities. Early opponents of fluoridation, like the John Birch Society, claimed that it was a demonic, communist scheme to poison America. More recent opponents invoke the fear of cancer, though years of scientific studies have continued to declare fluoridation safe. Almost every dental and medical organization has endorsed the process, but cities as large as Los Angeles are still without it, though its yearly cost is about 50 cents per person.

The claim that fluoridation is a communist plot is cited here because

(A) it gives historic breadth to the argument
(B) it exemplifies the eccentricity of the opposition
(C) it is what the argument is attempting to refute
(D) it supports the assumption that fluoridation is dangerous
(E) it supports the conclusion of the argument

44. The sickle-cell trait is usually regarded as a characteristic of black Africans. As a single gene, it confers a resistance to malaria, but if the gene is inherited from two parents, it may lead to a dangerous form of anemia. That trait, however, is not a unique characteristic of black Africans but appears wherever malaria has been common. The gene occurs as often in areas of Greece and of southern Asia as it does in central Africa. A genetic grouping by how well they digest milk would separate Arabs and northern Europeans from southern Europeans, native Americans, and some Africans. Most Europeans, black Africans, and east Asians have a gene that determines how they inherit fingerprint patterns, but Mongolians and the Australian aborigines do not. We have the notion that race is important because the surface is what we see. We now have the means to look beneath the skin.

This paragraph is probably part of a longer article that seeks to show

(A) the importance of genetic inheritance in the incidence of disease
(B) the difficulty of finding a scientific definition of race
(C) the decline of parasitic diseases like malaria in the wake of the discovery of their causes
(D) that most of the genes in a member of one race are likely to be unique to that race
(E) the genetic determination of the higher incidence of certain diseases in different racial groups

Questions 45–46

Auto accident victims in this state can sue for both their medical costs and for "pain and suffering" awards. Because the "pain and suffering" awards can be very large, often when the medical expenses are high, victims have an incentive to inflate their medical needs and medical costs in order to receive a higher total payment. For the victims of automobile accidents of equivalent seriousness, medical costs in this state are 30 percent higher than in all four of the neighboring states that have no-fault insurance programs and do not make "pain and suffering" awards. Motorists in this state pay more than $300 more for the same insurance coverage of motorists in the four adjoining states. A no-fault insurance system eliminating the lawsuits for "pain and suffering" and fairly compensating victims for medical costs would save the insured drivers of the state medical costs of nearly $1 billion.

45. This argument depends on all of the following assumptions EXCEPT:

(A) Juries assume that a higher medical cost signifies greater pain and suffering.
(B) Accident victims may falsify the extent of their injuries.
(C) Doctors and lawyers have no incentives to keep costs low.
(D) Accident victims should not be rewarded for "pain and suffering."
(E) The medical costs of automobile accidents exceed their legal costs.

46. Which one of the following, if true, would weaken the persuasiveness of this argument?

(A) The per-vehicle accident rate in this state is 4 percent higher than in the four neighboring states.
(B) The average motorist in this state drives fewer miles than the average motorist in two of the four neighboring states.
(C) There are more state patrolmen per driver in this state than in any other in the region.
(D) Medical costs in the four neighboring states are 20 percent lower than in this state.
(E) Though the sales tax rate is lower, the income tax is higher in this state than in any other in the region.

47. In order for Agri-Cola Corporation to show a profit this year, it must again sell $10 million worth of soft drinks in the United States and an equal amount overseas. Though sales in this country will certainly be equal to last year's, market unrest in Asia and South America will limit this year's overseas sales to at least $2 million less than last year's. It is therefore impossible that the company can show a profit this year.

Which one of the following would support the conclusion?

(A) Last year's overseas sales were more than $10 million.
(B) This year's expenses on overseas sales can be reduced so that profits will increase.
(C) This year's sales of domestic soft drinks may surpass last year's.
(D) The margin of profit on this year's sales will not be higher than last year's.
(E) Both this year and last, sales in the overseas markets have been more profitable than sales in the domestic market.

Questions 48–49

Ecologist: It is true that the solution of the problem of global warming will require important changes in the way we use fossil fuels over the long term and that the free market must play an important role in making these changes possible. But these facts should not make us forget how crucial near-term limits on the emissions of "greenhouse gases" are to motivate these changes. When the issue was the limitation of ozone-reducing substances, it was short-term emissions limits that quickly brought the needed technologies to the marketplace. These technologies were not available until the international community had adopted specific limits on ozone-depleting substances.

48. By which one of the following means does the author of this passage make his case?

(A) making a careful distinction between two key terms
(B) questioning the accuracy of the evidence given to support the opposition's case
(C) using an appropriate analogy
(D) using the literal meaning of a word that could be construed as metaphoric
(E) using premises that are contradictory

49. The author's case would be weakened if it could be shown that

(A) the immediate economic consequences of reducing the emission of greenhouse gases will be catastrophic in both the industrialized world and developing countries
(B) there has been virtually no research to develop a technology to deal with global warming
(C) the long-term limits on greenhouse gas emissions may not be adopted for at least 25 years
(D) many multinational corporations are reluctant to abide by any international agreements to limit the use of oil and oil-based products
(E) many scientists are skeptical about the effect of fossil fuel use on global warming

---

50. *Robert:* Cattle are turning up dead all over the place with their eyes removed with surgical precision. Strange lights have been seen in the sky on the nights before the bodies were discovered, and no human culprits have ever been found. It must be extraterrestrial invaders.
June: Maybe it's some weird cult. Or a college student prank. I don't know all the facts of the story, and I have no certain explanation myself, but I am sure that it's not likely to be aliens who want to collect eyes from cattle.

June responds to Robert's explanation by

(A) demonstrating that his conclusion is inconsistent with the evidence that is advanced in its support
(B) questioning the accuracy of the evidence on which his argument depends
(C) providing evidence that contradicts his conclusion
(D) refusing to deal with the logic of his argument
(E) offering counter-explanations equally supported by the evidence

51. *Professor:* Did you study for this exam?
Student: Yes. And I spent at least two hours on the endocrine system alone.
Professor: And you reviewed the circulatory system?
Student: I read that chapter three times.
Professor: You aren't being honest here. If you'd studied, you wouldn't have confused such basic facts as the functions of the left and right ventricles.

The professor's reasoning is flawed for each of the following reasons EXCEPT:

(A) It does not consider the possibility that lack of concentration can cause poor retention.
(B) It assumes that the study regimen mentioned by the student would be effective.
(C) It assumes that basic facts are easy to remember.
(D) It connects repeated reading with retention.
(E) It ignores the possibility that the student may have been ill or tired during the exam, causing poor performance.

52. People who dream in color are creative. Conrad is a creative person. Therefore, Conrad must dream in color.

The pattern of reasoning in the argument above is flawed most similarly to which of the following arguments?

(A) Ants leave scent trails for other ants to follow to food. Food scent trails are common among social insects. Therefore, all social insects leave scent trails.
(B) Redwood is extremely weather-resistant. Cedar is less resistant but less expensive. Therefore, cedar is the choice of most builders.
(C) Plumbers and electricians often belong to unions. Sally wants to become an electrician. Therefore, Sally will probably join a union.
(D) Oak trees provide acorns as food for wildlife. Wildlife has many food sources. Therefore, oak trees are not necessary as a wildlife food source.
(E) Corn is not a good plant to grow in containers. Maize is not a good plant to grow in containers. Therefore, maize is corn.

Questions 53–54

Park visitor advisory: Chigger activity in the park is high. According to a popular misconception, chiggers burrow under one's skin, but they don't. They bite and hold on, exuding an enzyme that liquefies the skin so they can sip it up. The longer they stay attached and exude the enzyme, the more severe a person's reaction is likely to be. Chiggers, which are so small they can't be seen on the body without magnification, perch on the tops of weeds and other plants, particularly tall plants, and jump onto a person or animal coming close to them. They then often migrate to areas such as the ankles, waist, underarms, and groin because they are relatively weak and need something such as socks or a waistband to push against in order to bite into the skin. Preventive measures include spraying with an insect repellant and showering immediately upon returning from outside to dislodge the insects. If showering is not possible, a brisk rubdown with a rough towel is somewhat effective. Prophylactic measures after bites include application of an anti-itch medication and complete avoidance of scratching the bite, which causes more severe itching and may cause infection. The effects of chigger bites may last up to two weeks or more.

Parks and Recreation Supervisor

53. Which of the following assumptions is most likely being made by the Parks and Recreation Supervisor?

(A) Visitors to the park will invariably be bitten by chiggers but with varying levels of discomfort.
(B) Prophylactic measures are generally only marginally effective.
(C) Visitors to the park would like to avoid being bitten by chiggers.
(D) Showering will remove all chiggers from the body.
(E) Tight clothing will lessen the severity of chigger bites.

54. According to the information supplied by the supervisor, which one of the following descriptions would describe a person LEAST likely to be affected by chigger bites?

(A) Before going into the woods, Sheila sprays herself with insect repellant and then showers.
(B) Consuela picks blackberries in the woods and towels herself off when she reaches her cabin.
(C) George stays on the woodland paths, except for a strenuous climb up a rock face. He showers when he returns to his room.
(D) Dimitri makes sure to spray insect repellant on his waist, ankles, and wrists before taking his dirt bike up Thunder Mountain through the brush.
(E) During her walk through the forest, Connie briskly towels herself off and applies insect repellent.

---

55. There are now almost three million undocumented immigrants living in the United States. They are taking jobs that legal citizens should have and are using services that cost federal tax dollars to which they don't contribute. Consequently, these undocumented immigrants must be identified and deported immediately.

Which of the following, if true, would most call into question the speaker's conclusion?

(A) There are actually 3.2 million undocumented immigrants living in the United States.
(B) Undocumented immigrants do pay taxes in the form of local sales taxes on their purchases.
(C) Undocumented immigrants come primarily from Central and South America, important areas for the production of raw materials crucial to the United States.
(D) The jobs taken by undocumented immigrants are largely those low-paid positions that U.S. workers refuse to take.
(E) New laws would need to be passed in order to grant amnesty to undocumented immigrants.

56. The Woodward family, in reviewing their electricity cost for the month of August, discovered the following facts: The electric company's average charge per kilowatt hour throughout their area was the same as it was in July. The Woodwards' total kilowatt usage in August was higher than it was in July, but their total expenditure for August's electricity was less than their expenditure in July.

Of the following, which fact, if true, would most likely explain the difference between the July and August electricity charges?

(A) The Woodwards had to repair their air conditioner during July.
(B) The Woodwards' August electricity usage was more often at off-peak, lower-rate times than it was in July.
(C) The electric company began buying electricity from a different, lower-cost source in August.
(D) During August, the Woodwards lowered the temperature setting on their hot water heater and hung their clothes outside to dry rather than using the electric dryer.
(E) In July, the Woodwards were away on vacation for two weeks.

57. *Pete:* Although it's a mistake to equate the life of a spotted owl and the life of a human, I agree with the ecoterrorists' concerns for the planet. It's undeniable that burning down buildings can stop overbuilding in natural environments, and embedding spikes in trees to harm loggers and their equipment can slow down clear-cutting operations.
Anne: Then you think the ends can justify the means.

Anne's response indicates that she has most likely misunderstood Pete to believe which one of the following?

(A) Spotted owls are not as important as other endangered species.
(B) Spikes in trees unacceptably endanger human life, and arson unnecessarily endangers human possessions.
(C) Environmentalists share the concerns of ecoterrorists in that they realize that drastic measures must be taken to save the planet.
(D) Human life must take precedence over the lives of other animals.
(E) The need to stem the danger to the planet makes spiking trees acceptable.

58. In the United States, pharmaceutical plant research is hailed by most scientists as holding promise for important medical breakthroughs. Ninety percent of doctors actively promote the research. But the majority of people do not know enough about the process to make an informed decision on the necessity of protecting the rain forests in which most of the promising plants are discovered. Fewer than two out of a hundred can speak knowledgeably about the basics of the subject. Politicians in rain forest countries tend to denounce the research, stressing the economic needs of their citizens over the nebulous promise of new medicines.

    If the information given above is true, which one of the following must also be true?

    (A) No politician in a rain forest country is among those who can speak knowledgeably about pharmaceutical plant research.
    (B) Ten percent of doctors do not actively promote pharmaceutical plant research.
    (C) Ninety-eight percent of people oppose pharmaceutical plant research.
    (D) Most doctors are well informed about pharmaceutical plant research.
    (E) Some doctors oppose pharmaceutical plant research.

59. Although the regulation that airline pilots be provided nine hours of rest in a twenty-four-hour period seems reasonable and prudent, serious safety concerns remain due to pilot fatigue. The nine hours of rest may be on paper only because schedule delays often mean the pilot is in the airport hours before a flight, and the time traveling to, and checking into, a hotel is counted as part of the rest time.

    The argumentative technique used in the argument above is most accurately described by which of the following?

    (A) setting up a hypothesis and then giving examples to both support and refute it
    (B) citing specific information that calls a conclusion into question
    (C) contrasting the details of two opposing points of view
    (D) presenting an analogy between assumed and actual facts
    (E) comparing the general attitude of the public with the more informed attitude of a regulatory body

60. The penny coin ought to be discontinued. People no longer want pennies taking up space in pockets and purses, and the coins no longer serve any viable function in today's economy. There is no longer anything that can be purchased with a penny.

Of the following, which statement, if true, most strongly calls into question the above argument?

(A) The citizenry would not approve rounding up the sales tax to the nearest nickel, which would be necessary if the penny were eliminated.
(B) Pennies can be easily exchanged for other coins or bills.
(C) The elimination of the penny coin would immediately make coin collectors' penny mint sets more valuable.
(D) Penny candy has historically been widely available.
(E) Pennies cost the U.S. Mint more to make than they are worth.

61. *Janice:* Continued building on coastal shorelines is nothing but a recipe for disaster. The threat of hurricane destruction of homes and businesses is ever present, and erosion caused by construction activities is extremely destructive to the natural coastal environment. Both state and federal governments should take more decisive steps to stop U.S. coastal development.
Wayne: People have a right to their property, the use of it, and any benefit they may derive from its ownership. Such rights should never be abridged by government without a compelling reason.

Which one of the following best summarizes the point under discussion by Janice and Wayne?

(A) whether hurricane destruction and erosion constitute a compelling reason to ban coastal development
(B) the need for a ban on coastal development due to damage to property and the environment versus the property rights of individuals
(C) the possibility of a government buyout of existing private coastal property versus the grandfathering in of rights for existing property owners
(D) the need for a ban on coastal development based on the compelling reasons of loss of shore bird habitat and beach areas due to erosion
(E) whether the benefits derived from coastal property ownership offset the damage caused to the environment

62. State auto emission testing is less effective against air pollution than generally thought. Not all states require such testing before license renewal, and those that do may be more or less stringent in their checking procedures, allowing local garages, whose priorities may be earning the fee, not controlling emissions, to do the testing. It is clear that approximately 12 percent of vehicles, those that are older or malfunctioning, produce over 50 percent of emission pollution.

    Of the following, which one is most strongly supported by the information above?

    (A) Consistent auto emission checking by all states would result in less emission pollution.
    (B) Half of auto emission pollution is caused by 50 percent of older and malfunctioning vehicles.
    (C) The general thought concerning the effectiveness of emission testing is irrelevant to a constructive handling of the problem.
    (D) If checking stations themselves were regulated, making sure they efficiently enforced appropriate auto emission standards, the problem would be eliminated.
    (E) A stringent federal program to identify and repair or delicense vehicles with unacceptable emission levels would most likely lower emission pollution.

63. The venomous brown recluse spider, as its name indicates, is not regularly seen because of its reclusive habits. Outdoors, it may be discovered under stones and rocks, but it is more likely to inhabit indoor areas, particularly dark closet or drawer corners or any quiet and unused cranny. It is, however, also often seen in bathtubs.

    Which one of the following, if true, LEAST explains the fact that brown recluse spiders are found in bathtubs?

    (A) Although the brown recluse spider inhabits many indoor areas, it is most easily spotted in contrast to the often light-colored field of the bathroom fixtures.
    (B) The insects upon which the brown recluse spider preys are likely to inhabit the moist areas of a bathroom.
    (C) Since the brown recluse spider prefers to inhabit indoor areas, it can bite humans when they step into the tub, sometimes causing ulcerative sores that are slow to heal.
    (D) The brown recluse spider is unable to negotiate the slick surface of bathroom fixtures.
    (E) Since these spiders prefer to inhabit indoor areas, they are statistically likely to sometimes appear in bathtubs.

64. A research study on corporate behavior concludes that without the threat of government intervention, only a third as many recalls of dangerous products would occur as there are at present. Based on interoffice memos concerning products eventually recalled, the research finds that prior to recalling a product, company employees cite the possibility of government sanctions in two-thirds of the correspondence.

Based on the information above, the reasoning upon which the conclusion of the research study is based is likely to be flawed for all of the following reasons EXCEPT:

(A) The study makes the assumption that companies should recall dangerous products on their own, without the impetus of government intervention or sanctions.
(B) Interoffice memos may be sent and received by low-level employees who have little or no input into the decision-making process of a company.
(C) Of all the recalled products studied, those that are dangerous may constitute only a small percentage of the whole.
(D) Citing the possibility of government sanctions does not necessarily make such sanctions a consideration in making the decision whether to recall or not.
(E) The mention of the possibility of government sanctions in two-thirds of the correspondence does not necessarily equate to a reduction of two-thirds of recalled products.

65. *Political analyst:* Contributions to political campaigns carry with them not only the possibility but the near certainty of conflicts of interest for politicians elected to office. When a politician votes on issues that will have an impact on the business interests of wealthy, generous constituents, it is highly likely that the politician's vote will be influenced. But needed as it is, pending campaign-contribution-reform legislation is in for a rocky road because the very politicians who benefit from campaign donations would have to vote to discontinue them.

Upon which of the following assumptions does the political analyst's argument most depend?

(A) Public and private good are inevitably at odds with one another when conflicts of interest arise in the political arena.
(B) Campaign-contribution reform will be voted down by politicians in power because it is antithetical to their interests.
(C) Politicians, because they rely on contributions to their campaigns in order to be elected, would be ineffective champions for any sort of reform legislation while they are in office.
(D) Campaign contributors will make their points of view on legislation known to the politicians to whom they contributed.
(E) Those who receive campaign contributions are likely to adopt points of view reflecting those of the majority of their contributors.

66. Advertising and conducting closeout sales of summer merchandise should be banned until September. It's still hot in August, and people are still going on vacations, so they need the merchandise available to them.

Of the following principles, which one, if valid, most provides justification for the reasoning above.

(A) If closeout sales are advertised, they always take place.
(B) If closeout sales take place, they have not only been advertised, they are also successful.
(C) When one merchant has a closeout sale of summer merchandise, all other merchants have closeout sales of summer merchandise.
(D) After a closeout sale of summer merchandise, no summer merchandise remains for sale until the following year.
(E) Advertising of closeout sales is regulated by law, and merchants may not falsely depict what is for sale, its price, and how long the sale will continue.

67. Sales of SUVs (sport utility vehicles), which use twice the gas that compact cars do for the same mileage, have not decreased even in periods of high gas prices. Automobile manufacturers have continued to produce these vehicles at an escalating rate and without any new fuel-efficient features. So, the lowering of gas consumption is not a concern among purchasers and owners of these vehicles.

Which one of the following, if true, most weakens the argument above?

(A) In periods of high gas prices, owners of SUVs drive them twenty-five percent fewer miles than they do when gas prices fall.
(B) Fuel-efficient features were incorporated in the design of SUVs when they were first produced.
(C) SUV owners support the fact that manufacturers have designed many fuel-efficient features to use in these vehicles as soon as government regulations mandate them.
(D) The sales of SUVs in Europe have sharply declined compared to sales in the United States.
(E) SUV owners generally purchase the same lower-octane fuel as do drivers of compact cars.

68. The dry heat of the southwestern United States has long been touted as an excellent environment for alleviating respiratory problems such as asthma and emphysema. But with the growing air pollution problems in southwestern cities, retirees with such conditions should not plan for the Southwest as their retirement home.

Which one of the following is an assumption that the speaker above must make in order to appropriately draw his or her conclusion?

(A) Air pollution problems in the Southwest are as bad as or worse than those problems in other urban areas of the country.
(B) Retirees plan for housing and move to new areas when they stop working.
(C) The effect of air pollution on respiratory ailments offsets the benefit of dry heat for these ailments.
(D) Although respiratory problems have many causes, air pollution is certainly one of them.
(E) Air pollution problems in the Southwest reduce the dryness of the heat, causing it to be ineffective in alleviating respiratory problems.

69. Thirty minutes of exercise several times a week and, for those who are overweight, a reduction in weight of as little as 7 percent, can be effective in preventing or delaying the onset of adult type II diabetes. Therefore, if you are sedentary and obese, your chances of having this disease are higher than if you are thinner and active.

If the statements above are true, which one of the following must also be true?

(A) If you reduce your weight by 7 percent, your chances of remaining free of type II diabetes are enhanced.
(B) If you are not overweight, if you exercise, and if you don't have type II diabetes, your weight and exercise may be playing a role in your freedom from the disease.
(C) Thirty minutes of exercise several times a week and a reduction of weight by 7 percent will likely lengthen your life span.
(D) If you have type II diabetes, the addition of exercise and the careful attention to diet will make it more likely that your disease can be eliminated.
(E) If you do not have type II diabetes, you have controlled your weight and engaged in some exercise.

70. *Defense lawyer:* The releasing of computer viruses is a form of vandalism. That the vandalism is electronic does not change the fact that, like spray painting a wall or knocking down a mailbox, it is the destruction of property. So punishment for releasing computer viruses should be no harsher than for other types of vandalism.

Of the following, which most accurately describes the defense lawyer's argument?

(A) It draws a conclusion based on semantic differences in disparate points of view.
(B) It uses a metaphor to point out substantive variations in definition.
(C) It moves from a specific identification to general description.
(D) It proposes that seemingly unrelated events are members of the same larger category.
(E) It defines a principle and then posits an exception to that principle.

71. *Politician:* The Three Strikes Law is a failure! Imprisoning a person for life after he or she commits a third felony has filled our prisons with hundreds of people serving life sentences for trivial offenses and has strained state budgets, while the crime rate continues to rise.

Each of the following, if true, supports the politician's claim EXCEPT:

(A) Serious crimes, defined as those that have resulted in the perpetrator being sentenced to life in prison, have risen 13 percent in the last year.
(B) Prisoners are now being housed four to a cell, and the state is being sued by the federal government for violating prisoners' civil rights.
(C) More time in prison has increased educational opportunities, with many prisoners acquiring college degrees at taxpayers' expense.
(D) Violence in prisons is on the rise as more prisoners with three strikes are switched to maximum-security prisons with hardened criminals.
(E) Penalties for misdemeanors have also increased.

72. *Civil libertarian:* Many employers try to justify their prying into their employees' e-mails by pointing out that the equipment on which the e-mails are created, sent, and/or received is owned by the company. Additionally, the companies believe that monitoring employees' e-mails encourages employees to be more conscientious and hardworking and respectful of company property. All of these arguments are clearly false and are intended to obscure the fact that the companies in question are invading the privacy of their workers.

Which one of the following is a questionable technique used in the argument above?

(A) Making a generalization based on limited evidence.
(B) Questioning the employers' motives rather than examining their reasons for those arguments.
(C) Attempting to hold the companies in question to a much higher standard than is common to other businesses.
(D) Seeking to exculpate the workers by attacking the employers.
(E) Justifying the employees' actions on the basis that the actions are necessary for the continued health of these businesses.

73. If all well-executed architecture inspires lofty thoughts, and the Genesee Opera House is a well-executed example of architecture, then it follows that the Genesee Opera House inspires lofty thoughts. But the Genesee Opera House does not inspire lofty thoughts. So, either the Genesee Opera House is not an example of well-executed architecture or not all well-executed examples of architecture inspire lofty thoughts.

    Which one of the arguments below has the same pattern of reasoning as the reasoning illustrated above?

    (A) Poetry has the capacity to invoke emotions. "A Sunset Song" is a poem. Therefore, "A Sunset Song" invokes emotions.
    (B) If all penicillins have the capacity to destroy disease-causing bacteria, and Zencillin B is a penicillin, then Zencillin B has the capacity to destroy disease-causing bacteria. But Zencillin B does not destroy bacteria. So, either Zencillin B is not penicillin, or not all penicillins have the capacity to destroy bacteria.
    (C) If all trucks carrying propane have to use the overpass to cross the Little Eagle River, and the vehicle crossed the Little Eagle River by using the overpass, then the vehicle is a truck. But the vehicle is not a truck. So, either it did not cross the river or it was not carrying propane.
    (D) If all the butchers at the major supermarkets are union members, and John is a butcher, then it follows that John is a union member. But John is anti-union. So, John is either not a butcher at a major supermarket or he is lying about his hatred of the union.
    (E) If all Cub Scouts are obliged to take the Cub Scout Oath, and Kyle wishes to become a Cub Scout, Kyle will be obliged to take the Cub Scout Oath. But Kyle has yet to take the Cub Scout Oath. So, either Kyle is opposed to taking the Oath or he is opposed to becoming a Cub Scout.

74. The cliff dwellers of Arajaput live an average of 89 years, fifteen years longer than their low-land countrymen. This is due to the cleansing and life-enhancing effects of their yogurt, which is a staple of the Arajaput diet. Now that yogurt, created from the same cultures that have granted long life to generations of Arajaputians, is available here in the States.

    Which one of the following, if true, most seriously weakens the claim that their eating yogurt is responsible for the longer lives of Arajaputians as compared to their low-land countrymen?

    (A) Diseases have ravaged Arajaput in the last fifteen years, killing off people both in the mountains and the plains.
    (B) The largest cause of death in the cliff dwellers of Arajaput is cholera, a disease notably absent in many other parts of the country.
    (C) Due to the high altitude, few mountain-dwelling Arajaputians get malaria, the second-largest mortality factor elsewhere in the country.
    (D) The Arajaputians have not fought a war in this century.
    (E) Cuozo, a country remarkably like Arajaput, has a population with even longer life spans.

75. Illiteracy has long been acknowledged as one of the leading causes of crime. Scientists studying hundreds of career criminals at a series of prisons throughout the Southwest discovered that over half of those studied could neither read nor write. These findings form the basis for the governor's appeal to raise taxes to support primary education.

Which one of the following reasons, if true, most strengthens the governor's conclusion to appeal to the electorate to support primary education?

(A) The criminals studied committed more vicious crimes than any of their counterparts in prison.
(B) Particularly violent crimes are harder to obtain convictions for and thus cost the taxpayers more money to prosecute.
(C) Many criminals reported that negative experiences motivated early criminal acts.
(D) Prison classes are instrumental in preparing inmates for a successful return to society.
(E) Adult literacy is causally related to a strong elementary education.

76. Albert Goodman, a long-time student of the stock market, has recently published a study that claims to be able to predict when a rise in the market will occur. Goodman's study notes that substantial rises in the stock market for the last fifty years have occurred in years in which an American League team was victorious in the World Series. So, he argues, since an American League team won the Series this year, the prudent investor can count on substantial returns.

Which one of the following accurately describes the flaw in Goodman's reasoning?

(A) The argument fails to state just how much money the average investor made during these times of stock market increases.
(B) The argument's conclusion is simply a restatement of one of its premises.
(C) The argument implies that just because one event happened before another event, the first event caused the second.
(D) The argument goes on to say that depressions often occur when the National League wins.
(E) Baseball is no longer the most popular sport in America, which has greatly reduced the power of the World Series outcomes to predict trends in the stock market.

77. Throughout history, most generals in wartime have resisted transferring their military units to other generals who requested such transfers. These refusals have occurred even when the general who received the request for additional troops was in a relatively safe area and sometimes even when the requesting general's position was being attacked.

Each of the reasons below, if true, supports the decision of the general with the stronger force not to share his forces with the requesting generals EXCEPT:

(A) War is unpredictable, and situations can change in an instant.
(B) Generals with the largest armies are typically promoted faster than those commanding smaller armies.
(C) Moving troops from one place to another often unnecessarily exposes them to attack.
(D) Many of the greatest generals have waged successful campaigns with forces inferior to those of their adversaries.
(E) Transportation is always difficult in wartime because of destruction of roads and rail lines.

78. *Pundit:* The end of the recent recession has signaled the end of the truce between labor and management in many industries. Fearful of forcing already strapped businesses into insolvency, unions postponed wage demands and avoided strikes. With better times on the way, you can be sure that unions will be vigorous in demanding an increased share of corporate profits.

The action taken by the unions is most supported by which one of the following ideas?

(A) To combat recession, nothing is more important than teamwork.
(B) Unions never ask for something that a company doesn't have to give.
(C) In times of economic stress, unreasonable demands by unions could destroy the companies and thereby cost union members their jobs.
(D) Unions and management are, by their very natures, always at odds.
(E) To secure and retain their positions, union leaders must oppose management whenever they can.

79. Every angler in the Big Liar's Club exaggerates the size of every fish he or she catches. To hear a member talk, one would think that only large, record-sized fish are caught by club members. Yet some fish that are caught by club members are actually quite small, despite how they are described by the anglers who catch them.

For the statement that some fish caught by the members are small to be true, which one of the following has to be assumed?

(A) Every fish the angler catches is actually quite small.
(B) The only fish in the sample discussed are small fish.
(C) The anglers catch various sizes of fish.
(D) Exaggerating the size of the fish they catch is something that most anglers do.
(E) The size of the fish is unimportant given that all sizes are subject to the same degree of exaggeration.

80. Athletes are often encouraged to eat higher amounts of protein than would be indicated by their bodyweights in order to help build muscles broken down in strenuous workouts. But recent studies prove that any ingested protein that exceeds the body's maintenance needs is simply excreted. Therefore, athletes can safely ingest a normal amount of protein for their bodyweight without worrying about any extraordinary needs that their vigorous lifestyle may impose on them.

Which one of the following statements, if true, would most seriously weaken the argument that athletes need not ingest larger amounts of protein than normal for their bodyweights?

(A) Athletes are generally larger than non-athletic people, so they need more protein.
(B) A thick steak is extremely satisfying for many athletes.
(C) The dangers of excess protein intake are more substantial and longer-lasting than previously thought.
(D) These most recent studies were all funded by the beef industry.
(E) Vigorous lifestyles break down more muscle tissue than can be rebuilt by normal protein intake.

Questions 81–82

Juan said, "It takes a good swing to be a good golfer. It takes practice to develop a good swing. Thus, it takes practice to be a good golfer."

81. Which one of the following most closely parallels the logic of this statement?

(A) Betsy can bake a good cake if she wants to. Betsy baked a good cake. Thus, she must have wanted to bake a good cake.
(B) A vote for Senator Cobb is a vote for peace. I voted for Senator Cobb. Thus, I want peace.
(C) You must work to earn money. You need money to pay the rent. Thus, you must work to pay the rent.
(D) It costs $200 to buy the TV. It costs $50 to buy the radio. Thus, the TV costs more than the radio.
(E) It is important to be alert when you take an exam. If you take a cold shower, you will be alert. Thus, you should take a cold shower before you take your exam.

82. Which one of the following would weaken Juan's argument the most?

(A) It takes more than a good swing to be a good golfer.
(B) Some good golfers have average swings.
(C) Some people are born with a good golf swing.
(D) It takes strong forearms to have a good golf swing.
(E) Many good golfers lift weights.

83. The theory that the subconscious is simply the unsymbolized suggests the desirability of adequate verbalization at the earliest possible stage of emotional development. It is the nameless fears and frustrations that defy analysis.

The author of this passage would most likely agree that

(A) there is nothing to fear but fear itself
(B) emotional development starts at birth
(C) verbalization is the key to complete emotional development
(D) unsymbolized thoughts and emotions cannot be analyzed
(E) the subconscious initiates only nameless fears and frustrations

84. *Article:* Many studies have demonstrated that cardiovascular health is greatly improved by regular exercise. As little as a half-hour's walk three times a week is sufficient to strengthen the heart and to help control weight. Even men and women in their 50s and 60s who have not exercised regularly for many years show beneficial effects almost at once. But there may be a slight disadvantage.

Which one of the following most logically completes this paragraph?

(A) Their hearts will never be as strong as those of men and women who have exercised regularly throughout their lives.
(B) The half-hour's walk can be gradually extended to increase the cardiovascular benefit.
(C) Other exercises to increase lung and upper-body strength are also recommended.
(D) Weight control should combine moderate exercise with a carefully planned diet.
(E) Older people are likely to suffer from muscle aches, especially in the first few months of a new exercise program.

85. The most serious threat to modern man, it would seem, is not physical annihilation but the alleged meaninglessness of life. This latent vacuum becomes manifest in a state of boredom. Automation will lead to more and more free time, and many will not know how to use their leisure hours. This is evidenced today by what Dr. Frankl refers to as "Sunday Neurosis," the depression that afflicts people who become conscious of the lack of content in their lives when the rush of the busy week stops. Nothing in the world helps man to keep healthy so much as the knowledge of a life task. Nietzsche wisely said, "He who knows a Why of living surmounts every How."

Which one of the following is the best refutation of the above argument?

(A) The availability of free time does not afford people more opportunity to enjoy their blessings.
(B) Nuclear annihilation would vastly transcend the issue of personal meaningfulness.
(C) Automation may actually result in more people working in such fields as computer science and technology.
(D) The problem of personal meaning has existed since the beginning of modern times.
(E) Most people actually enjoy their weekends when their work week ends on Friday.

86. Reading is an activity involving the use of the visual apparatus by means of which printed words are recognized.

The above definition would be weakened most by pointing out that

(A) a "nonreader" can recognize words
(B) skimming is a form of reading
(C) some printed words can be difficult to interpret
(D) seeing is necessary for reading
(E) lengthy printed words are not easily recognized

87. Exercise is not positive for people because things that are positive never kill people, and many people have died because of exercise-induced trauma.

Which one of the following arguments demonstrates the same reasoning as that illustrated in the argument above?

(A) The animal in question is not a zebra because zebras do not climb trees, and we found this animal in the oak in John's front yard.
(B) The Surgeon General has determined that smoking is hazardous to your health. Therefore, you should stop smoking.
(C) Lifting weights is good for you. It creates stronger muscles, and a stronger body is deemed by many to be desirable.
(D) No one who saw the movie *The Pirate's Curse* asked for their money back. Therefore, *The Pirate's Curse* must be one of this year's best movies.
(E) This promotion is a scam. The prize is yours only when you send in three hundred box tops. But nobody can eat that much cereal.

88. *Jack:* Many discerning fans of our generation have an appreciation for the music of the Beatles, even though these fans were born long after the heyday of this great group.
Jill: It's immaterial when a person was born. Good music is good no matter when it was created or when its fans were born.

This conversation offers the most support for the claim that Jack and Jill agree on which one of the following statements?

(A) Appreciation of great music is possible for people of all ages.
(B) Great art transcends time.
(C) The Beatles' career, although great, was tragically short.
(D) Beatles' music is and was very good music.
(E) Nostalgia is an important part of a band's reputation.

Questions 89–90

A leading discount chain store recently held a large nationwide sale of reproductions of masterpieces of the past and present. In every city, by far the largest sales were of nineteenth-century realistic landscapes, while hardly any paintings by cubist and abstract artists of the twentieth century found buyers. Since all the paintings were inexpensive and of approximately the same size, it is clear that popular tastes have not caught up with the last hundred years in the development of painting. Attendance figures suggest that modern audiences are equally behind the times in their response to classical music and ballet.

89. If the statements above are true, which one of the following is also most likely to be true?

(A) At auctions, original paintings by leading artists of the twentieth century will sell for lower prices than nineteenth-century landscapes.
(B) Summer outdoor concerts of classical music attract larger crowds for programs of nineteenth-century music than for concerts of works by contemporary composers.
(C) The size of the audience for ballet and the number of professional ballet companies declined in the years between 1950 and 1990.
(D) Most interior decorators choose a painting for the suitability of its colors to the room in which it will be placed.
(E) There is rarely any clear relationship between the painting and the music of a particular era.

90. Upon which one of the following assumptions does this passage rely?

(A) A person who dislikes modern art will also dislike modern music.
(B) The rise in the cost of tickets does not explain the changing attendance patterns of ballet and opera.
(C) The decline in interest in serious art and music coincides with the rise in the popularity of television.
(D) The audience for art and music in the nineteenth century was more discriminating than the twentieth-century audience.
(E) Chain store sales are an adequate indicator of popular taste in art.

ANSWERS EXPLAINED

1. **(C)** The passage states that robots not only can build other robots but also can rebuild themselves; therefore, they could last forever. (B) is probably true, but (C) must be true. According to the passage, (A) and (E) are not implied, and (D) is probably not true.

2. (E) There are tasks that robots can do better than humans. But any task in which being able to think independently or creatively would have to be done by humans.

3. (E) The author states that the robot can do the most complex group of activities, but "does not have the capacity to . . . think independently." If the most complex group of activities necessitates independent thinking, then the author's assertions are in *direct* contradiction. (C) would be a good choice if it mentioned independent thinking, not training, as training is not mentioned in the passage.

4. **(D)** All of the four other answers are clearly assumptions that can be inferred from the details of the paragraph. Choice (D) may or may not be true, but unlike the other choices, there is nothing in the paragraph that supports it, since there is no reference to the policies of other airlines.

5. **(B)** Since none of the January blossoming plants will flower again later in the year, no plants that first blossom in January will flower twice in the year. (A), (C), and (E) may be untrue, because we are not told that all the bulbs and tubers in the garden blossom in January; we are told only that all the plants that blossom in January are from bulbs or tubers. (D) need not be true, since some bulbs may not flower every year.

6. **(D)** (A) and (B) are irrelevant, and (C) and (E) are not as effective as (D) because they are just restatements of the thought, rather than a clarification.

7. **(A)** The phrase "four out of five" implies 80% of a large sample (nationwide). If only five dentists were in the sample, the reliability would certainly be in question. (B) would strengthen the endorsement, while (D) and (E) are irrelevant. (C) could weaken it, but not nearly as much.

8. (E) (A) must be true by the first statement because everybody in the class likes drawing or painting or both, so if Angie does not like painting, she must like drawing. This same logic holds for (C). "Everyone in the class who does not like drawing" must like painting. As for (D), it is possible that no one in the class likes painting. But (E) cannot be true if everyone likes drawing or painting or both.

9. **(D)** (A) is incorrect, since there is no attack on Mark's reasoning. (B) is incorrect because personal pressure is not implied. (C) is incorrect since it is hearsay. (E) is incorrect because who is to say what a "positive" approach is? (E) could have been the correct choice if (D) were not a possibility.

10. (C) The conclusion of the passage is that, because of safety concerns, more research and testing ought to be done before microwaves become standard household appliances. If, however, research and testing are ineffective means of discerning safety problems, then research and testing would be irrelevant. This criticism seriously weakens the conclusion.

11. (E) If many microwave ovens have been found to leak radioactive elements, then the conclusion—that microwaves should not be standard appliances until they are more carefully researched and tested—is further strengthened because more safety concerns need to be addressed.

12. (C) The pattern of reasoning here is that since X follows from Y, if Y is absent, there will be no X. In choice (C), buying from the bakery (Y) results in good breakfast business (X). But the restaurant that does not buy from the bakery (Y is absent) will have poor breakfast business (X). In the original, the first step is an action (eating Vitagatto), whereas in choice (B) it is inaction that has a consequence.

13. (C) Choices (A), (B), (D), and (E) are all reasonable ways of explaining the discrepancies. If the census report did undercount, we would still need to know whether it undercounted one gender more than the other.

14. (A) The conclusion can be properly drawn only if the condition *"being white"* is sufficient to rule out all but quartz. (A) allows the conclusion, "*must* be quartz," to be reached.

15. (B) Though this chef probably believes that the restaurants of Paris are superior, the passage passes judgment only on the breads, not on the restaurants of New York. It does assume that good bread will be eaten, that, lacking French training, there are hardly any good bakers in America, and that if the bread is good, the roll basket will be empty. But it may have been refilled three times.

16. (D) The chef's claim to know how to bake bread is, no doubt, just, but the four other answers point to weaknesses to be seen in the passage. The speaker asserts American incompetence on the basis of flimsy evidence, and the assumption that American food can be judged on the basis of some New York restaurants generalizes about the small restaurants in Paris and is not specific about restaurants in New York or Paris.

17. (A) The tone of the passage is positive: Workers "enjoy" the same status; "harmony"; less "tension and anger." One can therefore conclude that the author approves of the work environment of the Japanese auto factory for the workers' well-being and that he believes that any resemblance of American factories to those of the Japanese ought to be encouraged. Note that there is no indication at all regarding the quality of the goods produced (B).

18. (A) Only (A) is logically supported by the passage. There is no direct support regarding worker envy for (B). There may be less tension and anger in Japanese auto factories; however, to conclude that there is no tension or anger is not logically sound. Nothing in the passage describes the relation of tension to productivity (D).

19. **(A)** The key word in the statements given is "usually." "Usually" suggests a frequent or regular phenomenon. It implies that an event may be normally expected and allows one to draw a conclusion *stronger than* those contained in (D) and (E). "Usually" does not mean "with certainty." Therefore, the categorical conclusions of (B) and (C) are not appropriate.

20. **(C)** (A) is not true, since Nexon is not a sufficient condition for life; that is, Nexon alone is not enough. (B) is not true because Nexon must be present if there is life (necessary condition). (C) is true; Nexon must be present (necessary condition). (C) does not suggest the absence of things other than Nexon and, therefore, does not contradict the original statement. (E) is untrue since Nexon alone is not a sufficient condition.

21. **(B)** (A) need not be true, because the absence of Flennel is not a necessary condition; that is, there can be other conditions that result in the end of life. (C) is not true, because the absence of Flennel is sufficient to end life (one cannot say that life may "not cease"). (B) is true, given that the absence of Flennel is sufficient to end life. Both (D) and (E) are untrue. The absence of Flennel is sufficient cause, (D) but there might be other causes as well (E).

22. **(C)** Choices (A), (B), (D), and (E) are all logical conclusions. Since electric heat is very expensive, and the winters are very cold but the summers are merely warm, choice (C) makes sense. But even with high costs, we expect gas consumption to be higher in the very cold winters.

23. **(E)** The statement presented can be logically made only if being reared at Prince Charming Kennels ensures that a poodle is purebred. (E) provides such assurance. (A) does not state that only purebreds are reared and, therefore, does not ensure that any given poodle from the kennels is purebred.

24. **(D)** (A) can be eliminated because the argument does not rule out a possible previous proposal. (B) may be eliminated as no suggestion of easy identification or the necessity of easy identification is presupposed. (C) can be eliminated because the argument is independent of any comparison between the Great Salt Lake and any other body of water. (E) can be eliminated because the argument presents the weaker claim of the *possibility* of oil. (D) allows, if true, the *possibility* of oil to be sufficient cause for exploration.

25. **(D)** The context suggests that salutary associations are positive ones, and the phrase *associations of pleasure* immediately following the first mention of *salutary* certifies (D) as the best choice.

26. **(D)** (A) is answered in the first sentence, as are (B) and (C). In the first sentence, we are told that all thinking is associational, and in the second, that both education and experience promote associations. Nowhere, however, does the author mention just what teachers blame and praise.

27. **(D)** Only this choice addresses both parts of the statement, which implies that expert practice helps to identify errors. (B) and (C) stress error only; (A) stresses practice only; and (E) stresses writing only.

28. **(A)** Refer to the following diagram:

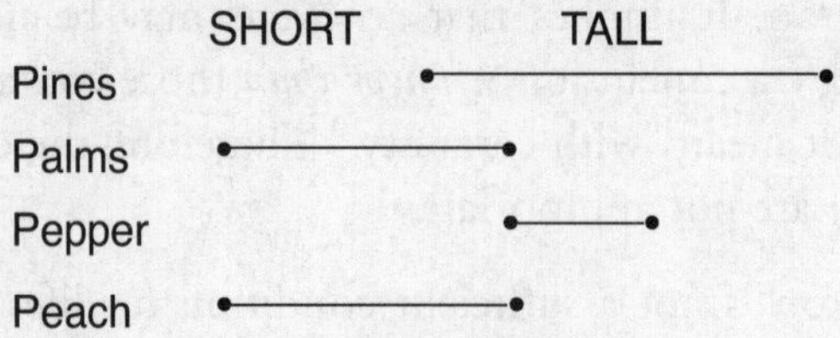

On the basis of the foregoing diagram, (B), (C), (D), and (E) are false.

29. **(C)** The structure of the given argument may be simplified:

    Most are popular and low.
    Splendor is not popular and high (not low).

    (C) parallels this structure:

    Most who stop do gain.
    Carl does not stop and will not gain.

30. **(E)** The statement given can be simplified:

    All have hair (mammal).
    This does not have hair.
    It is not (mammal).

    Only (E) can be reduced to this same form:

    All have smell (lubricants).
    This does not have smell.
    It is not (lubricant).

31. **(B)** (A) has no bearing because the argument is concerned only with mammals. (C) is not relevant; the argument does not address the amount of hair. (E) is likewise outside the argument's subject. (D) is a possible answer because the claim is that the absence of hair indicates a nonmammal. However, (B) is a better choice. (D) is a possibility—"One *could* remove." (B) points out that, without any other intervention, there *are* creatures with no hair that are also mammals.

32. **(C)** If the chances of a person with the same genetic makeup as someone who has developed the disease are 100 times higher than someone with different genes, genetic material must play some role. But if the proportion of people who do develop the disease is very small, genetics cannot be the only cause. The study supports (B) and (E) but gives no information on whether the disease is more likely to affect one identical twin than one nonidentical twin.

33. **(D)** Because they share the same genetic makeup, identical twins are especially useful in medical studies of the role of genes.

34. **(C)** The pattern of reasoning here is that X is caused by changes in either Y or Z. If Y is unchanged, and X happens, it must have been caused by Z. In (C), X is the rise in pizza costs, the steady Y is the cost of cheese, and the causative Z is the price of beef.

35. (D) Since the argument concerns state laws to be passed, the best choices must be those that refer to the responsibility of the state, (C) and (D). Of the two, (D) is clearly the more specific and directly relevant to the situation described in the paragraph.

36. (B) The first proposition states that if an athlete and invited, then over 35. The second proposition states that if over 35, then not both an athlete and invited. The propositions contradict each other. Therefore, no person can be both an athlete and invited.

37. (E) The most plausible answer here is that the group that lost more weight ate less at dinner. Presumably, members of the other group were much hungrier because they had exercised so much more and had less to eat at lunch, and so they ate more at dinner. (A) and (C) will not work if applied only to "some" of the group.

38. (C) If this surgical procedure does more harm than good, it would be wise not to perform it at all. This would reduce by one the number of needless surgical procedures.

39. (A) The passage insists that the tennis team will be composed only of first-rate athletes and nonsmokers. But there is no reason given to prevent a nonsmoker who is not a first-rate athlete from being on the team. Presumably he or she made up for lack of great natural ability with more practice.

40. (A) If the prices have gone down, the clothing sales might well increase, and television watching would be irrelevant. Options (B), (C), (D), and (E) have no information to explain the rise in sales apart from television.

41. (D) The error in the reasoning is the assumption that what was true of a group (the mortgage sales department) can predict something specific about a single member of that group (Thomason's presumed sales). The correct parallel is in (D), where the individual's performance (Meany's winning the golf championship) is based on the accomplishment of a group (the South Texas State golf team).

42. (C) If the largest foreign investor is the United States, and the third largest is Britain, it appears that the rules are not intended to exclude Asians, since the same rules apply even more extensively to Europeans and Americans.

43. (B) The author, whose position is clearly in favor of fluoridation, refers to the "demonic scheme" to suggest the irrationality of the opposition. Choice (C) is careless. The argument is not trying to refute the notion of a communist plot.

44. (B) Only the first example (sickle-cell) is related to disease. The second concerns the response to lactose, and the third to fingerprints. What all three have in common is that they cannot be predicted by race, and the passage is part of a consideration of the difficulty of providing a scientific definition of race.

45. (E) Options (A), (B), (C), and (D) assumptions are in the passage, but there is nothing here to support the idea that either medical or legal costs are greater.

46. (D) If all medical costs in the other states are much lower, the fact that the medical costs of automobile accident victims are also lower would be explained, and the argument that "pain and suffering" awards lead to higher medical costs would be weakened.

47. (D) Most of the paragraph is concerned with the sales figures. Only in the last sentence does the subject of profit arise, and we are never told exactly how sales relate to profit. To assume that there can be no profit with this decline in sales, we must also assume that the profit margin will not be higher.

48. (C) The author makes his point by using an analogy. That is, he argues that the passage of limits on ozone-depleting gases resulted in the rapid development of affordable technologies to deal with the problem and suggests that unless short-term limits on greenhouse gases are enacted, there will be no urgency to develop the necessary technologies.

49. (B) If there has been no research to develop a technology to deal with global warming, the enactment of short-term limits would not bring the needed technologies to the marketplace. Choice (A) deals with "immediate economic consequences," but the issue concerns short- and long-term limits, not immediate ones.

50. (E) The suggestions of a cult or college prank are alternate explanations that are supported by the evidence as well as the alien-invader notion. Though the evidence is questionable, the response here does not quarrel with its accuracy.

51. (C) The professor accuses the student of being less than honest about the study time mentioned and so is assuming that the two hours spent on the review of the endocrine system and the rereading of the chapter on the circulatory system three times would have been effective (A), which is not necessarily the case. Consequently, the professor is saying, the student must be less than honest about the study time. But the student's study time and methods might not have been effective through poor concentration (B), lack of attention perhaps during the rereading (D), or physical problems during the exam itself (E) and might not be dishonest at all. The passage assumes only that the "basic facts" could have been learned in the study time that the student had specified; there is no evidence to suggest, however, that the professor considers the learning of basic facts to be easy.

52. (E) The argument is in this form: A (people who dream in color) are B (creative). C (Conrad) is B (creative). Therefore, C (Conrad) is A (one who dreams in color). The final statement logically doesn't follow, because the first statement doesn't say *only* people who dream in color are creative. The only answer that follows this pattern is (E). A (corn) is B (not good in containers). C (maize) is B (not good in containers). Therefore, C (maize) is A (corn). This question is made more difficult by the fact that, in reality, maize actually is corn. But that doesn't change the flawed reasoning. Any other plant could have been substituted for maize in the pattern of this argument, producing a statement such as "tomatoes are corn." No other answer exhibits this flawed pattern of logic. Answer (C) is incorrect because Sally is not now an electrician, and there's nothing that suggests she will be, only that she wants to be.

53. (C) The only assumption made by the Parks and Recreation Supervisor is that visitors to the park would like to avoid being bitten. If the supervisor didn't make such an assumption, there would be no reason to write the advisory in the first place.

54. (C) Although George doesn't do all that he could to avoid bites, what he does is the most likely to be effective. By staying on the paths, he avoids the weeds and other plants that are likely to harbor chiggers. And climbing the rock face is unlikely to put him in harm's way from the insects because a rock face would not tend to have heavy plant growth. By showering when he returns, he's likely to dislodge any stray chiggers that might have gotten on his body. Sheila (A) showers after applying repellant, rendering it ineffective. Consuela (B), by venturing into a blackberry patch will probably have picked up chiggers, and toweling alone may not rid her of them. Dimitri (D) sprays only a few areas of his body and is going through heavy brush, where insects are likely to be. Connie (E) may be applying countermeasures too late into her walk.

55. (D) The fact that the immigrants are taking jobs that U.S. citizens won't take calls into question the speaker's statement that the immigrants are taking jobs away from legal citizens. It doesn't approach the speaker's contention that the immigrants use federal tax dollars for services, but it calls the conclusion into question more than does any other choice given. (B) is not correct because it mentions local taxes, not the federal taxes the speaker cites.

56. (B) Only this fact could explain the seeming inconsistency presented. The Woodwards used *more* kilowatt hours in August than in July, but they were charged *less* for those hours. The information given makes it clear that the electric company didn't lower their *average* rate. It remained the same as July's, so the company's buying cheaper electricity (C) isn't relevant. Neither is the fact that the Woodwards tried to conserve electricity in August. Since they used more hours in August than in July, they obviously weren't successful in that endeavor.

57. (E) Pete clearly says that he agrees with the *concerns* of the ecoterrorists. But he also suggests that the life of the spotted owl and the life of a human shouldn't be equated; in other words, methods used to save the planet should *not* endanger people (he doesn't comment on whether harming human possessions is unacceptable). The fact that Pete recognizes the effectiveness of the ecoterrorists' methods doesn't mean that he agrees with them. But Anne mistakenly believes that Pete agrees with the *methods* of the ecoterrorists, not only with their *concerns*.

58. (B) If ninety percent of doctors actively promote pharmaceutical plant research, then it can be assumed that ten percent do not. But it doesn't follow that those who don't actively promote the research are opposed to it (E). It also can't be known from the facts given that all politicians in rain forest countries are ignorant about the subject (A) or that ninety-eight percent of people oppose the research (C) (they simply aren't knowledgeable about it). And even though ninety percent of doctors actively promote the research, it doesn't necessarily follow that they are well informed about it (D).

59. (B) The argument uses specific information (schedule delays, travel and check-in time) to call into question the conclusion that the allowance of nine hours of rest in a twenty-four-hour period is reasonable and prudent. By this argumentative technique, the speaker suggests that pilots may not be getting the nine hours of rest they are thought to get. Although the argument does deal with a possible discrepancy between assumed and actual facts, it doesn't use an analogy (D).

60. (A) If the citizenry would not approve the rounding up of sales tax to the next nickel, then local government would have a real dilemma. They would lose money if the amount were rounded down, and they would be unable to collect their present sales tax if pennies were eliminated and consequently would lose needed revenue. Of the answers given, this problem would most strongly call the elimination of the penny coin into question. The other answer choices either support (mildly or strongly) the argument (choices (B) and (E)) or are irrelevant (choices (C) and (D)).

61. (B) Janice promotes a ban on coastal development. Wayne, however, raises the question of property rights of individuals in this matter. All the other choices go too far, given the discussion presented. The conversation might go on to discuss whether Janice's points constitute a compelling reason for the ban (A), but it doesn't do so as presented. A government buyout or grandfathering in of rights (C) might be options discussed as the conversation progresses, but they aren't here. The specific damage of lost shore bird habitat and beach areas isn't discussed (D), only erosion damage in general. And, although you might surmise that Wayne may contend that property rights offset the damage (E), he doesn't actually make that point.

62. (E) The passage states that not all states have emission testing. A first step in controlling the emission problem, then, would be to have testing on a national (federal) level. The fact that the testing program would be "stringent," that is, rigorous and exacting, indicates that it may be more effective than existing state programs. In addition, the choice suggests that these measures would "probably" be effective, not absolutely. Choice (A) isn't the best answer, because there is no indication of the level of effectiveness of the state programs. Checking can be consistently bad as well as good, in which case the problem would not be reduced. The general view of emission testing is not irrelevant (C), although it may be incorrect, as public opinion can be important in the passing of laws and the functioning of government. Choice (D) overstates the effect when it says the problem would definitely be "eliminated."

63. (C) For choice (C) to explain why the spiders are found in bathtubs, it would have to be assumed that they intentionally lie there awaiting a chance to bite humans, which is illogical considering that, first, the spiders prefer isolated, dark, unused areas and, second, that they would somehow consider humans prey, which is not likely, considering their size. All other choices give possible reasons for the phenomenon, although (E) does so fairly weakly. Choice (D) does explain the presence of the spiders, as they may fall into the tub and be unable to climb back out.

64. **(A)** According to the information, the study makes no ethical judgment on what the companies should or should not do; it simply reports, based on this research, on what is done. But given these facts, the other choices all indicate a likely flaw in the study's reasoning. The actual decision makers might not agree with the memo writers (B); the study seems to confuse dangerous recalled products with all recalled products (C); the awareness of possible sanctions doesn't automatically make them factors in the decision (D); and the assumption that mention of sanctions in two-thirds of the correspondence equates to a two-thirds reduction of dangerous products (or even of all recalled products) is illogical (E).
65. **(D)** If contributors don't somehow make their points of view known to the politicians, it would be difficult for those points of view to be influential at voting time. Although the discussion does seem to suggest that public and private good may sometimes be in conflict, it doesn't assume that it would be "inevitably" so (A). Nor does the analyst imply that campaign-contribution reform will necessarily be "voted down" (B), only that it will face challenges (a "rocky road"). Choice (C) mentions reform legislation in general, which isn't under discussion here. There is an assumption by the analyst that politicians may adopt the view of "wealthy, generous contributors," but choice (E) mentions the "majority" of contributors. The wealthy and generous donors might not be in the majority. Their number, as compared to, say, donors of small sums, isn't mentioned.
66. **(D)** Although there are several logical problems with the reasoning in the passage, and no choice fully justifies its reasoning, choice (D) at least in part justifies it. If people actually still need summer merchandise in August, and if no summer merchandise remains after a sale, then an argument might be made that no such closeout sales should be allowed until September. No other choice indicates that no summer merchandise remains for consumers to buy in August.
67. **(A)** Only this choice definitely suggests that the SUV owners are concerned about the lowering of gas consumption at least to some extent and at least during periods of high gas prices, and it weakens the argument that they are unconcerned. The fact that fuel-efficient features were originally incorporated in these vehicles (B) is irrelevant, as the SUVs are now high gas users. Choice (C) is also irrelevant; these owners may simply not want their vehicles banned and thus support features that will still allow them to drive them. Because the conclusion about SUV owners' lack of concern is not restricted to U.S. drivers, choice (D) may seem to be a good answer, because it indicates a drop in sales in Europe. But the choice doesn't say why the drop in sales has occurred. Perhaps it's just a cultural change in preference. The purchase of lower-octane fuel (E) doesn't necessarily have to do with the concern about the amount of gas consumption, only with the cost of that consumption, and nothing indicates that these vehicles would need higher-octane fuel in any case.
68. **(C)** If dry heat alleviates respiratory problems, and this speaker now recommends against the Southwest as a retirement destination for retirees with respiratory problems because of the air pollution, the speaker must make the assumption that the pollution substantially offsets the benefits of dry heat. Choice (D) is incorrect because air pollution is not listed as a *cause* of respira-

tory problems such as asthma or emphysema (although it could be), and such an assumption is not necessary to the argument, which addresses itself to those who already *have* respiratory difficulties. Choices (A), (B), and (E) are not assumptions that the speaker must make. Choice (A) deals with comparing pollution problems with those in other areas. Choice (B) deals with retirees' plans, and Choice (E) deals with the reduction of dryness of the heat.

69. **(B)** Choice (B) is the only choice that must be true if the statements are true. Note that the choice says that weight and exercise "may" be playing a role, which is true, given the fact that we know they are effective in preventing or delaying the onset of the disease. The choice would not necessarily be true if it said they "are" definitely playing a role, because other factors may be involved in the disease (say, genetic factors or simply your age). Choice (E) is incorrect for this same reason. Choice (A) is not necessarily true, because it discusses weight alone, and the original statements speak only of the combination of exercise and weight reduction. Choice (C) is incorrect because you may die from other causes, and life span would not be affected. Choice (D) introduces the elimination of the disease, which isn't discussed in the original statements, only the onset of the disease.

70. **(D)** The lawyer's argument proposes that seemingly unrelated events—the releasing of computer viruses, the spray painting of a wall, and the knocking over of a mailbox—are part of a larger category, vandalism. The argument doesn't deal with "disparate points of view" (A), a metaphor (B), a general description (C), or an exception to a principle (E). The argument goes on to draw a conclusion based on the fact that the events are part of one larger category, but even though choice (D) might not be a complete description of the lawyer's argument, it remains the best of the choices given.

71. **(E)** The argument says nothing about misdemeanors. (A) and (B) support the contention that prisons are more crowded now than ever and (A) also supports the idea that crime rates are rising. Prisoners whose sentences allow them to stay in prison long enough to earn college degrees (C) are an additional burden on state budgets, particularly because their severe sentences preclude them from returning as useful members of the society that educated them. (D) suggests that those who have been imprisoned for trivial offenses might become the victims of more ruthless criminals.

72. **(B)** The argument does make a generalization (A) but does not provide us with any information as to the breadth of the evidence on which it is based. There is nothing in the argument that would suggest either (C) or (D). (E) is false because the argument deals with the actions of the employers, not those of the employees.

73. **(B)** (A) lacks the form of the original. The argument says that "all well-executed architecture has the capacity to inspire lofty thoughts." None of the other choices has a similar clause.

74. **(C)** To weaken a claim, you are obliged to weaken the premises on which the claim is built. (C) offers an alternative reason that the mountain people do not die as early as their low-land countrymen. (A) does not specify the part of the

country in which the diseases raged and (B) does not mention which parts of the country did not experience cholera. (D) applies to the whole country, while (E) is totally irrelevant. We're talking about Arajaput—not another country.

75. (E) The governor proposes giving money to support primary education, which will, in turn, fight adult illiteracy, which is a major cause of crime. (A) is an irrelevant comparison. (B) is appealing because it shows how money can be saved, but the major issue is not saving money but rather combating crime by reducing illiteracy. (C) is too vague. The negative experiences could have happened anywhere and at any time, not just at school. Also, negative experiences are not directly related to illiteracy. The argument is about preventing crime, not rehabilitating criminals, thus ruling out (D).

76. (C) That which is correlative is not necessarily causative. (B) implies that the argument is a circular one, which it is not. (A), (D), and (E) are irrelevant.

77. (D) All of the others offer reasons for a general *not* to share his forces with other generals. (D) suggests that large forces are not an absolute necessity for a successful campaign and that a smaller force that emerges victorious over its larger foes may actually enhance a general's reputation.

78. (C) The unions acted in a way that is really out of character for unions and did so because of the threat that the recession posed to the welfare of their members. Although (D) is probably true, it doesn't explain why the union acted in the way it did. (B) does not seem supported by fact, and the word *never* makes it an absolute. (A) is unresponsive to the question, and (E) is unsupported by the pundit's statement.

79. (C) The statement says that some fish caught are actually quite small despite the descriptions given to them. For that to be true, there have to be small fish in the set of fish that are caught (along with fish of other sizes).

80. (E) The fact that athletes are larger than others (A) is immaterial; after all, the argument clearly states that protein intake should be relative to body size. (B) is also irrelevant. (C) is tempting but still leaves us the problem of what excess intake is. The fact that the beef industry underwrote these studies (D) would more likely strengthen, rather than weaken, the argument against excess protein intake, since the beef industry might have a vested interest in increasing the amount of beef (a rich source of protein) consumed. But (E) suggests that more protein than normal for a given bodyweight may be required by an athlete's lifestyle.

81. (C) Good swing implies good golfer, and practice implies good swing; therefore, practice implies good golfer. (*X* implies *Y*, and *Y* implies *Z;* therefore, *X* implies *Z*.) This is most closely paralleled by (C), even though the terms are in slightly different order, or not exactly parallel. (B) is wrong, since voting for peace and wanting peace are two different things. Betsy may have baked a good cake (A) even if she had not wanted to. (E), although in proper form, brings in excess subjectivity.

82. **(B)** This is the only answer that refutes the premise that you need a good swing. (A) talks about what else you need, and (C) says nothing about the need for a good swing.

83. **(D)** The passage states that nameless fears and frustrations defy analysis and implies that unsymbolized thoughts and emotions constitute nameless fears and frustrations. (C) and (E) are close, but note the absolute words "complete" and "only" in each.

84. **(E)** The final sentence is introduced by "But" and notice of a "slight disadvantage." The best example of a "slight disadvantage" in the five choices is the "muscle aches" of (E).

85. **(B)** The consequences of nuclear annihilation—namely the end of human life—would include the disappearance of all other human questions. Thus, the author's contention that the most serious threat to modern man may be the alleged meaninglessness of life is seriously challenged by the magnitude of nuclear annihilation.

86. **(A)** If a "nonreader" (one who cannot read) can recognize words, then reading cannot be defined as the act of recognizing words.

87. **(A)** The form of the argument is A is not B (exercise is not positive) because B doesn't C (positive things don't kill people), and lots of people have died while exercising. The animal is not a zebra (A is not B), because B doesn't C (zebras don't climb trees), yet this unidentified animal is in a tree.

88. **(D)** (A) and (B) are far too general to be the answer. Jack and Jill might very well agree on (C), but the argument specifically addresses the music and not the career of the band. The whole point of the argument is that the Beatles' music is great on its own, not because of its nostalgic value (E). Although Jack doesn't directly say that the music is good, the fact that he uses the word "discerning," which means showing outstanding judgment or understanding, indicates that he does believe the music of the Beatles to be good.

89. **(B)** The passage is dealing with the "popular tastes" in art and music, with the people who purchase paintings at discount stores rather than at auctions of original leading artists (A). The larger attendance figures for concerts of nineteenth-century music is a logical corollary. For (C) to be relevant, we would have to know which ballets were performed. (D) may be true, but it has no bearing on this passage. (E) contradicts the implications of this passage.

90. **(E)** The passage endorses the position of (A) but offers evidence to support the idea ("attendance figures") rather than assuming it to be true. (E) is an assumption of the writer, who concludes from the sales ("it is clear") that popular tastes have fallen behind. The other options may or may not be true; they are not assumptions underlying this paragraph.

Analytical Reasoning

CHAPTER 3

An Overview of the Key Strategies in the Chapter
Introduction to Question Type
The Approach
Analyzing Types of Displays
Key Symbols

Introduction to Question Type

The Analytical Reasoning section is designed to measure your ability to analyze, understand, and draw conclusions from a group of conditions and relationships. This section is 35 minutes long and contains from 22 to 24 questions (usually four sets of conditions, statements, or rules). Each set is followed by five to seven questions.

The Analytical Reasoning type of question first appeared officially on the LSAT in June 1982, but a similar form of Analytical Reasoning had been used on the Graduate Record Exam (GRE) since 1977. It was removed from the GRE in 2003.

Analytical Reasoning situations can take many forms, but you should be aware of some general things before reviewing the problem types.

Remember, even though Analytical Reasoning is the most difficult section for most students, it is also the most preparable.

Let's take a closer look:

First, let's check the approximate percentages of analytical reasoning displays.

Analytical Reasoning Displays

Types	Approx. Frequency
The Position Organizer (linear)	40–50%
The Position Organizer (Non-linear)	4–7%
The Position Organizer with Diagram Provided	*
The Group Organizer	20–25%
The Group Organizer (with several conditional statements)	20–25%
The Group Organizer (Venn diagrams/grouping arrows)	**
The Table Organizer (information table)	8–12%
The Table Organizer (elimination grid)	2–3%
The Spatial Organizer	4–5%
The General Organizer (simply pulling out information)	**
The General Organizer with Diagram Provided	**

*Appeared in recent bulletins
**Appeared infrequently in earlier tests

Now, let's preview the common question stems.

Sample Analytical Reasoning Question Stems

- Which one of the following is an acceptable order of students from first to last?
- Which one of the following is a complete and accurate list of athletes who could have been on the team?
- Which one of the following CANNOT be a complete and accurate list of the films shown?
- Which one of the following could be a complete and accurate matching of the clubs and their members?
- If two films in French are shown on the first day of the festival, which one of the following must be true?
- If the fall semester offers a history class, then which one of the following could be true?
- If Tim is faster than Sal, and Bill is not the third fastest, then which one of the following must be true?
- If J is taller than B, then the shortest member is …
- If Taylor is selected first, then any of the following could be selected sixth EXCEPT:

- Which one of the following must be false?
- Which one of the following must be true?
- Which one of the following could be true?
- Which one of the following CANNOT be true?
- Which one of the following bands marches earlier than ninth?
- Which one of the following pairs of jugglers CANNOT juggle together?

And finally, let's take a quick overview of the key strategies.

Overview of the Three (3) Key Strategies
Your Actions and . . . Reactions

Actions	Reactions
1. Start a Set Confidently	Read the conditions carefully Mark the conditions
2. Draw Your Organizer (Keep it simple)	Look for key items Draw and place information Reason from the conditions Look at some questions for help
3. Answer the Questions (Anticipate some of the question stems)	Read the questions carefully Work with the choices given Eliminate answer choices

WHEN YOU START A SET, FOCUS ON:

Reading the Conditions

1. Read each statement carefully and actively, marking important words.
2. As you read, learn to flow with the information given, looking for relationships between items.
3. Remember that making simple charts or diagrams, or simply displaying information, is essential on most sets, so read the conditions as though they are describing a display or diagram.
4. If you wish to read through all of the conditions of a set before starting a diagram, begin your diagram on the second reading.
5. If no diagram seems apparent or conducive to the information given, look at a few questions. Sometimes the questions can give you some good hints on how to display the information.

Marking the Conditions

1. Because you will probably be drawing some sort of diagram or display, place a check mark next to each statement or condition as you read it or use it in the diagram. This will help you avoid skipping a statement or condition as you work back and forth in setting up your diagram.
2. Put a star or an asterisk next to big, general, and important statements. Sometimes these statements will affect a group, category, or placement. (Examples include "No two people of the same sex are sitting in adjacent seats" and "All of the members of a department cannot take the same day off." Two other examples might include: "At least two graduate students must be on the team" and "People with pets with them must stay in hotel room 1 or 8.")
3. Put a star or an asterisk by statements that are difficult to understand. Try to rephrase these statements to yourself for better understanding.

WHEN YOU START DRAWING YOUR DISPLAY, FOCUS ON:

Finding Key Items

1. Look for a simple way to display the information. Don't complicate the issue.
2. Look for the setup, frame, or framework. Sometimes this is given in the first statement, but in other cases you may need to read a number of conditions before constructing the type of drawing that will be most effective.
3. If you discover the frame or framework, fill in as much of the diagram as possible, but do not spend a great deal of time trying to complete it. This may not be possible or necessary to answer the questions.
4. Be aware that you may have to redraw all or part of your diagram several times (typically, a few times for each set) as different conditional information is given for specific questions.
5. If a framework is not given, see whether the information can be grouped by similarities or differences.
6. As you read each statement, look for concrete information that you can enter into your chart or that you can simply display. (For example, "Tom sits in seat 4" or "Cheryl coaches swimming.")

Drawing and Placing Information

1. Locate off to the side any information that you cannot place directly into your chart. (Whatever you can't put in goes out; for example, "Jill will not sit next to Helen" or "A biology book must be next to a science book.")
2. Some very important statements might not fit into your chart. Remember to put a star or an asterisk by these big, general, and important statements.

3. If some statements are not immediately placeable in your chart (and if they are not the big, general statements), you may have to return to them for later placing, after you have placed other statements. Remember to mark such statements with an arrow or some other symbol so you don't forget to return to them.
4. As you place information, use question marks to mark information that is variable or that could be placed in a number of different places in the diagram.
5. Underline and abbreviate or write out column headings and labels. Don't use single letters as they may be confused with the actual items. (If you use "m" for males, it could be confused with an "m" for Manuel, one of the males.)
6. If, as is true in many cases, no standard type of chart will apply to the problem, be aware that you can merely pull out information in a simple display or through simple notes. Remember to flow with the information given, looking for relationships between items.

Reasoning from the Conditions

1. No formal logic is required.
2. Apply evidence in both directions. For instance, if a statement tells you that a condition must be true, consider whether this means that certain other conditions must not be true. (For example: "All blue cars are fast" tells you that a slow car is *not* blue.)
3. Notice what information is used and what is left to use. (For example, "Bob, Carl, Don, Ed, and Fred are riding the school bus home. Don, Ed, and Fred are sitting in seats one, two, and three, respectively." You should realize that Bob and Carl are left to be placed.)
4. Watch for actions and the subsequent reactions in initial conditions or from information given in the questions. (For example, "Dale, Ralph, and Art cannot be on the same team. Dale is on Team A." Your action is that Dale is on Team A; your immediate reaction is that Ralph and Art cannot be on Team A.)
5. Watch the number of items, places, and people (e.g., males to females, adults to children) you are working with. Sometimes these numbers are the basis for correct answers, and they can even tip you off as to how to construct a diagram.
6. If the diagram you construct shows positions or specific dates or other limits, watch for items that will force you off the end or out of the limits. (For example, "There are five houses in a row on the north side of the street numbered 1, 2, 3, 4, 5 consecutively. There is one yellow house that is between two blue houses." Therefore, the yellow house cannot be in place 1 or 5 because there would be no room for a blue house. It would be forced off the end or out of bounds.)

WHEN YOU START ANSWERING THE QUESTIONS, FOCUS ON:

Reading the Questions

1. Read the questions actively, marking the important words. You should first always circle what you are looking for (Which of the following must be true? All of the following are possible except . . .).
2. Notice and underline any *actions* given to you in a question. (If Bob is selected for the team, whom else must be selected?) Watch for any subsequent *reactions.* (If Bob is selected, Tom can't be selected.)
3. Keep in mind that any information given to you in a specific question (usually starting with the words "If . . . ," "Assume . . . ," "Suppose . . . ," "Given the fact that . . . ," and so on) can be used only for that question and not for any other questions.
4. Don't take any information from one question to another question. That is, if you get an answer on one question, don't use that information (answer) in any other questions.

Working with the Answer Choices

1. Using the elimination strategy mentioned in the introduction can be invaluable here. Watch for rule breakers, that is, statements that contradict initial conditions. If the conditions state, "X cannot sit next to Y," then any answer choice with X sitting next to Y can be eliminated (unless, of course, the initial condition was changed in the question for that particular question).
2. Watch for certain types of wrong answers known as *distracters.* Since *"could be"* and *"must be"* are often confused, a *"could be true"* answer choice is a great distracter (*attractive distracter*) for a question that asks what *"must be true."*

Understand the distinction between *must be* and *could be:*

Must Be	***Could Be***
No exceptions All the time Always	May be, but doesn't necessarily have to be

3. If a question looks like it's going to be difficult or time-consuming, you may wish to **scan the answer choices.** When you scan, **look for winners, losers, workers, and question marks:**

   Winners—right answers that jump out at you or are easy to spot (circle the answers in your question booklet, mark them on your answer sheet, and move on)

   Losers—answers that you can eliminate instantly or very easily (cross out these answer choices, and move on)

   Workers—answer choices that can be fairly easily worked out to determine whether they are right or wrong (go on and work these)

   Question Marks—answer choices that you either can't work or don't know what to do with (put a question mark, and move on)

AND A FINAL REMINDER: KEEP THE DRAWING SIMPLE; DON'T COMPLICATE YOUR THINKING.

The following sections provide some detailed examples of typical problem types and useful ways of organizing the information given. These examples are intended to give you insight into some efficient methods of organizing by presenting a variety of displays or organizers—e.g., charts, tables, grids, diagrams. Some of these terms may be used interchangeably, but don't get hung up on the names of the different types. You should practice enough to be comfortable with many different types of basic displays and variations and be able to adjust your display as needed. REMEMBER: Different students may prefer different types of displays or organizers. Use what is effective and efficient for you!

The Approach

ANALYZING TYPES OF DISPLAYS

Here are some key symbols you should use on the most common types of organizeres.

Key Symbols

Symbols	Meaning
In position organizers	
[AB]	A is to the left of and next to B.
A B (with arrows both ways)	A is next to B on either side.
~~AB~~	A is **not** next to B.
A → B	B is to the right of A.
A □ B (arrow from A to B)	A is to the left of B with one space in between.
A □ B (arrows both ways)	There is one space between A and B.
A ? B (arrow from A to B)	A is to the left of B, but there could be spaces between them.
B [C A] (arrow from A to B; C and A linked)	A is to the right of B and next to C.
□ 1	Space 1 is empty.
~~A~~ 2	A cannot be in space 2.
B 3	B is in space 3.
B above a line; below the line, C between arrows pointing up and down, A at the bottom	B is taller than A and C. C is shorter than B but could be taller, shorter, or the same height as A.
In group organizers	
x–y or [xy]	x is in the same group as y.
x ~~—~~ y or ~~xy~~	x is **not** in the same group as y.
x → y	If x is in the group, y must also be in the group.
~~y~~ → ~~x~~	Logically, if y is not in the group, then x cannot be either.
~~N~~ (under Reading)	N cannot be in the reading group.
<u>Reading</u> <u>Writing</u>	
O (under Writing)	O is in the writing group.
A → B and B → C , A → C	If A is in the group, then so is B, and if B is in the group, then so is C; therefore, if A is in the group, then so is C.

The Position Organizer (Linear)

This display is used for a problem set that can be organized in a straight line. This linear display is often the simplest to set up and tends to be very common on the LSAT. These problem sets can come in a variety of forms. In constructing this type of organizer, you should follow these steps:

1. Look for a frame or framework (often given in a statement preceding the conditions or in the first condition).
2. Look for key words to help you set up the frame, such as:
   - sequence
   - order
   - first
   - last
   - before
   - after
   - taller
   - shorter
   - in a row

   The words used in the problem set will often lead you toward setting up your organizer either horizontally or vertically.
3. Look for concrete information (that is, specific information to fill in the positions or information that shows restrictions or connections). Have techniques and symbols for showing restrictions (B cannot be next to A—BA) and connections (C is adjacent to D—CD) before you take the test.
4. List the items, people, or letters that will be used to fill in the positions, and mark the relationships and/or restrictions between them.
5. Watch for and mark large, general, important statements (statements that cover a group or category). Remember to place a small check mark next to each statement as you read it, and an asterisk next to general statements.
6. Fill in as many of the positions as possible, but don't be concerned if you can't fill in any immediately; the questions themselves may give you information to fill in the positions. (For example, if X sits in position 4, then which of the following sits in position 6?)
7. Watch for situations that push you out of bounds (for example, if Bill sits between Alice and Jan, then Bill cannot sit on either end—that would push Alice or Jan out of bounds).
8. Also watch for situations that lock you into certain positions. For example, consider this situation: There are seven seats in a row numbered 1 to 7 consecutively, and there are four boys and three girls to fill the seats. A statement like "No boys sit in adjacent seats" would lock you into certain positions because you would immediately know that the boys must be in positions 1, 3, 5, and 7.
9. If you can't fill in any positions from the initial conditions, read some of the questions to get a feel for how much you should know and should have filled in.

Keep in mind that whatever won't go in the chart immediately, goes out to the side for possible placement later. (Whatever won't go in, goes out.)

EXAMPLE

Seven poker players—Arlo, Biff, Chuckie, Dixie, Eunice, Fong, and Glenn—will play at the final table in a Texas Hold-'Em tournament. They will sit in a straight line next to each other on one side of the table, with seats numbered 1 through 7 from left to right. The following conditions apply:

> **Chuckie sits to the right of Biff and next to Glenn.**
> **Dixie sits to the left of Biff and next to Arlo.**
> **Eunice's seat has a lower number than both Fong's seat and Arlo's seat.**

ANALYSIS—THE SETUP

You should first number from 1 through 7.

1 2 3 4 5 6 7

Next, you should build a visual display that will show you the relationships.

"Chuckie sits to the right of Biff and next to Glenn." The display could start with:

B G C

STUDY TIP

Notice that about 40–50 percent of the displays are a form of Linear Position Organizer. Anticipate some Position Organizers.

Notice that G and C are next to each other and could swap places.

"Dixie sits to the left of Biff and next to Arlo." Adding this information gives:

A D B G C

Notice that D and A are next to each other and could swap places.

"Eunice's seat has a lower number than both Fong's seat and Arlo's seat." Adding this information gives:

E A D B G C
| – F →

1 2 3 4 5 6 7
E

Notice that E must sit in seat 1 and that spaces are left between some players because F still needs to be placed.

Question 1

If Arlo sits next to Biff, then each of the following could be true EXCEPT:

(A) Biff sits in seat 4.
(B) Chuckie sits in seat 6.
(C) Dixie sits in seat 4.
(D) Fong sits in seat 2.
(E) Glenn sits in seat 5.

ANALYSIS

The correct answer is (C). If Arlo sits next to Biff, then Dixie must sit in seat 2 or 3, depending on where Fong sits. The display would look like this:

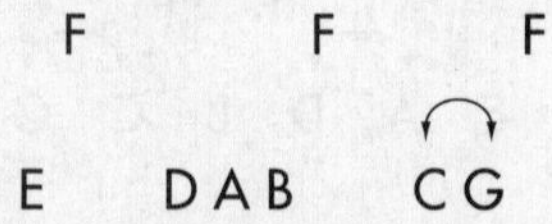

Notice that Fong could sit in seats 2, 5, or 7.

If you use an elimination approach, remember that you are looking for "could be true EXCEPT."

Choice (A), "Biff sits in seat 4," could be true: E, D, A, B, F, C, G. Eliminate (A).

Choice (B), "Chuckie sits in seat 6," could be true: E, D, A, B, G, C, F. Eliminate (B).

Choice (C), "Dixie sits in seat 4," can't be true; she must sit in seat 2 or 3. Stop here; you've found the EXCEPTION. Record your answer.

For your information:

Choice (D), "Fong sits in seat 2," could be true: E, F, D, A, B, C, G. Eliminate (D).

Choice (E), "Glenn sits in seat 5," could be true: E, D, A, B, G, C, F. Eliminate (E).

Note that once you have found the answer that could not be true, the EXCEPTION, you can stop, record your answer, and move on to the next question.

Question 2

If Fong sits next to Biff, then which one of the following seats could be occupied by Arlo?

(A) Seat 1
(B) Seat 2
(C) Seat 4
(D) Seat 5
(E) Seat 6

ANALYSIS

The correct answer is (B). If Fong sits next to Biff, you would have the following display:

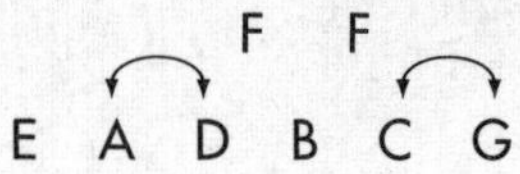

Notice that Arlo must sit in seat 2 or 3. Therefore, (B) is correct.

Question 3

Which one of the following players could sit in seat 3?

(A) Arlo
(B) Biff
(C) Chuckie
(D) Eunice
(E) Fong

ANALYSIS

The correct answer is (A). Using the original display, you can see that either Arlo or Dixie could sit in seat 3.

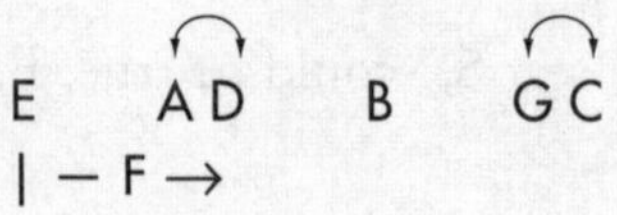

Notice that Biff, choice (B), could sit only in seat 4 or 5. Chuckie, choice (C), could sit only in seat 5, 6, or 7. Eunice, choice (D), must sit in seat 1. Fong, choice (E), could sit only in seat 2, 4, 5, or 7.

Question 4

Which one of the following could be a list of people sitting in seats 5, 6, and 7, respectively?

(A) Chuckie, Fong, Glenn
(B) Chuckie, Glenn, Fong
(C) Dixie, Biff, Chuckie
(D) Dixie, Biff, Glenn
(E) Glenn, Fong, Chuckie

ANALYSIS

The correct answer is (B). (A) and (E) are not correct, since Fong cannot sit in seat 6, between Chuckie and Glenn. (C) and (D) are not correct, since Dixie cannot sit in seat 5, only in seat 2, 3, or 4. And Biff cannot sit in seat 6 because there wouldn't be seats to the right of Biff for Chuckie and Glenn. (B) is possible.

Question 5

If Arlo sits in seat 4, then for exactly how many of the seven players are the seating positions determined?

(A) two
(B) three
(C) four
(D) five
(E) seven

ANALYSIS

The correct answer is (D). If Arlo sits in seat 4, then Biff must sit in seat 5, Dixie in seat 3, Fong in seat 2, and Eunice in seat 1. The only seat positions not determined are seats 6 and 7, which are occupied by Chuckie and Glenn (or Glenn and Chuckie).

The arrangement would look like this:

1	2	3	4	5	6	7
E	F	D	A	B	C ↔	G

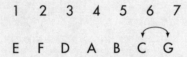

So, five positions are determined.

When a question gives you a placement, such as "Arlo sits in seat 4," immediately go to the display and make the placement.

Question 6

Which one of the following must be false?

(A) Arlo sits next to Biff.
(B) Biff sits next to Chuckie.
(C) Eunice sits next to Dixie.
(D) Fong sits next to Biff.
(E) Glenn sits next to Arlo.

ANALYSIS

The correct answer is (E). Note that you are looking for "must be false." Using the original display, you can determine that Biff sits between Arlo and Glenn; therefore, they cannot sit next to each other.

```
E   AD   B   GC
|  — F →
```

You could eliminate the other choices as follows:

Choice (A), "Arlo sits next to Biff," could be true, since Arlo and Dixie could swap places. Eliminate (A).

Choice (B), "Biff sits next to Chuckie," could be true, since Glenn and Chuckie could swap places. Eliminate (B).

Choice (C), "Eunice sits next to Dixie," could be true, since Arlo and Dixie could swap places. Eliminate (C).

Choice (D), "Fong sits next to Biff," could be true. A careful look at the display will make this evident. Eliminate (D).

Question 7

If there are exactly three seats between Arlo and Fong, then for exactly how many of the seven players are the seating positions determined?

(A) one
(B) three
(C) four
(D) five
(E) seven

ANALYSIS

The correct answer is (D.) If there are exactly three seats between Arlo and Fong, the display would look like this:

```
1 2 3 4 5 6 7
E D A B C G F
```

Notice that the only way there could be three seats between Arlo and Fong is if Arlo is in seat 3 and Fong is in seat 7. Only the positions of Chuckie and Glenn in seats 5 and 6 are not determined.

Question 8

Which one of the following players could sit in one of exactly two different seats?

(A) Arlo
(B) Biff
(C) Dixie
(D) Fong
(E) Glenn

ANALYSIS

The correct answer is (B). From the display, you can see that three or four players sit to the left of Biff and that two or three players sit to the right of Biff; so, Biff can sit in either seat 4 or 5.

```
E   AD   B   GC
|—F→
```

(A) is not correct, since Arlo can sit in seat 2, 3, or 4. (C) is not correct, since Dixie can sit in seat 2, 3, or 4. (D) is not correct, since Fong can sit in seat 2, 4, 5, or 7. (E) is not correct, since Glenn can sit in seat 5, 6, or 7.

EXAMPLE

In a parking lot, seven company automobiles are lined up in a row in seven adjacent parking spots.

> **There are two vans, which are both adjacent to the same sports car.**
> **There is one station wagon.**
> **There are two limousines, which are never parked adjacent to each other.**
> **One of the sports cars is always on one end.**

ANALYSIS—THE SETUP

From this information, you could have made the following display:

___	___	___	___	___	___	___
S			or			S

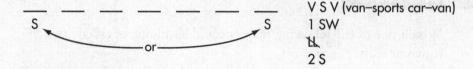

V S V (van–sports car–van)
1 SW
~~LL~~
2 S

Question 1

If the station wagon is on one end, then one of the sports cars must be in the

(A) 2nd spot
(B) 3rd spot
(C) 4th spot
(D) 5th spot
(E) 7th spot

ANALYSIS

The correct answer is (C). In this question, two charts are possible:

S						SW

and

SW						S

Now notice that for *both* of the vans to be adjacent to the same sports car, there must be another sports car, and they must always be in the order V S V. Thus, the only way to place V S V in either of the above diagrams so that two limousines are never adjacent is to place V, S, and V in spots 3, 4, and 5, as follows:

S		V	S	V		SW

or

SW		V	S	V		S

Thus, the limousines will not be adjacent if one of the sports cars is in the 4th spot.

Question 2

If one of the vans is on one end, then the station wagon must be

(A) only in the 4th spot
(B) either in the 2nd or the 6th spot
(C) only in the 3rd spot
(D) either in the 3rd or the 5th spot
(E) only in the 6th spot

ANALYSIS

The correct answer is (D). Again, there are two possible diagrams for this question:

V	S	V				S

and

S				V	S	V

Now notice that, in order for the limousines not to be adjacent, the station wagon must be in either the 5th spot or the 3rd spot.

Question 3

If a limousine is in the 7th spot, then the station wagon could be in

(A) the 2nd spot
(B) the 3rd spot
(C) the 6th spot
(D) either the 2nd or 6th spot
(E) either the 2nd, 3rd, or 6th spot

ANALYSIS

The correct answer is (E). If a limousine is in the 7th spot, then a sports car, to be on an end, must be in the 1st spot:

S						L

Notice that the station wagon could now be in the 6th spot:

		V	S	V	L	
S	L	V	S	V	SW	L

or else in either the 2nd or the 3rd spot:

	L	SW				
S	SW	L	V	S	V	L

So, the station wagon could be in either the 2nd, the 3rd, or the 6th spot.

Question 4

If one of the sports cars is in the 2nd spot, then the station wagon

(A) could be in the 5th spot
(B) could be in the 6th spot
(C) must be in the 5th spot
(D) must be in the 6th spot
(E) must be in the 3rd spot

ANALYSIS

The correct answer is (C). If one of the sports cars is in the 2nd spot, the other sports car must be in the 7th spot:

V	S	V				S

Thus, in order for the limousines not to be adjacent, the station wagon must be in the 5th spot.

Question 5

If both sports cars are adjacent to a van, the station wagon must be in

(A) the 2nd spot
(B) the 4th spot
(C) the 6th spot
(D) either the 2nd or 4th spot
(E) either the 2nd or 6th spot

ANALYSIS

The correct answer is (E). Two diagrams are necessary for this problem. If both sports cars are adjacent to a van, your diagrams will be:

S	V	S	V			

and

			V	S	V	S

Thus, in order for the limousines not to be adjacent, the station wagon must be in either the 2nd spot or the 6th spot.

Question 6

If an eighth car (a limousine) is added, and another parking spot is also added, then in order not to violate any of the original statements EXCEPT the number of limousines,

(A) a limousine must be parked in the 2nd spot
(B) the station wagon must be parked in the 2nd spot
(C) the station wagon must be parked in the 6th spot
(D) a limousine must be parked on one end
(E) a limousine cannot be parked on either end

ANALYSIS

The correct answer is D. If another limousine is added along with an eighth parking spot, all of the original statements can be obeyed ONLY if a limousine is parked on one end. For example:

S	L	V	S	V	L	SW	L

EXAMPLE

A graphic artist is designing a modern type style for the alphabet. This type style is based on artistic design and relative sizes of the letters. At this point, the relative sizes among the letters that the artist has designed are as follows:

A is taller than B but shorter than C.
B is shorter than D but taller than E.
F is shorter than A but taller than B.
G is taller than D but shorter than F.
H is shorter than B.

ANALYSIS—THE SETUP

From the information given, a simple display may be constructed using the following steps:

The first statement reads, "A is taller than B but shorter than C." Using a position chart where the top is the tallest and the bottom is the shortest, you have:

C

A

B

The first part of the second statement reads, "B is shorter than D. . . ." Notice that D can be *anywhere* taller than B, so a "range" for D has to be drawn:

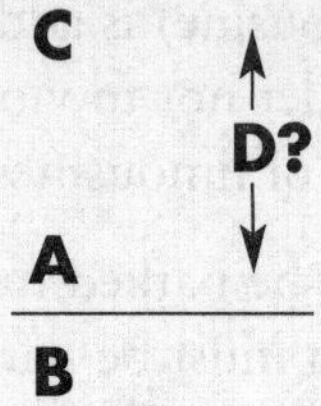

Adding the second part of the second statement gives "B is shorter than D but taller than E." Since B is taller than E, E will be placed under B:

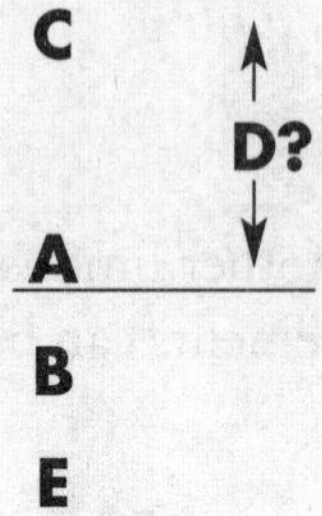

The third statement reads, "F is shorter than A but taller than B." Therefore, F must fit between A and B:

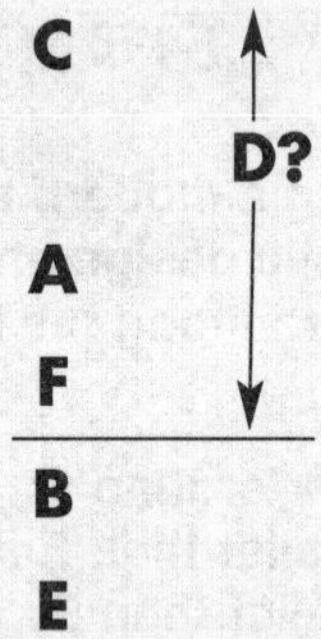

According to the fourth statement, "G is taller than D but shorter than F." Therefore, G is above D, but since it's below F, both G and D must fit between F and B:

The fifth statement reads, "H is shorter than B," so H must have a possible range anywhere under B:

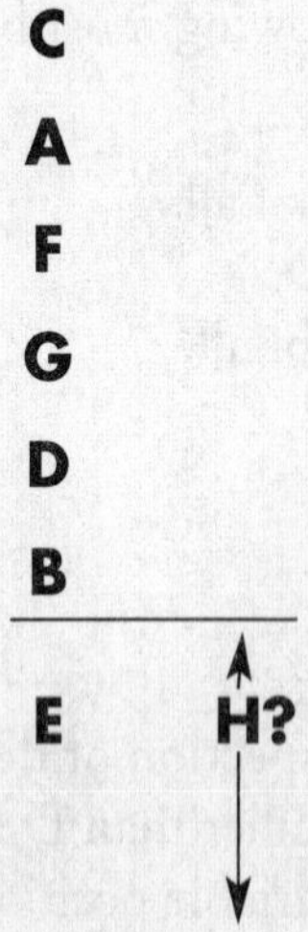

Note that H is in a variable position.

Question 1

Which one of the following could be false but is not necessarily false?

(A) E is shorter than D.
(B) C is taller than E.
(C) D is taller than F.
(D) H is taller than E.
(E) E is shorter than A.

ANALYSIS

The correct answer is (D). H may be taller than E, or it may be shorter than E. This is the only part of the chart that isn't definitely resolved.

Question 2

Which of the following could be true?

(A) D is taller than most of the others.
(B) A is the tallest.
(C) H is the shortest.
(D) D is not shorter than G.
(E) H is taller than F.

ANALYSIS

The correct answer is (C). H may be the shortest, because it could be shorter than E.

Question 3

Which one of the following must be true?

(A) F is taller than D.
(B) H is the shortest of all.
(C) H is taller than D.
(D) E is the shortest of all.
(E) E is taller than H.

ANALYSIS

The correct answer is (A). Inspection of the chart reveals that F is taller than D. It also reveals that H cannot be taller than D and that H or E *could* be the shortest of all, since H is in a relatively variable position.

Question 4

If Q is added to the group, and Q is taller than B but shorter than G, then Q must be

(A) taller than F
(B) shorter than D
(C) between D and F
(D) taller than only three of the others
(E) shorter than at least three of the others

ANALYSIS

The correct answer is (E). If Q is added to the group, it may be either taller or shorter than D. Therefore, only (E) is true.

Question 5

If Q and Z are both added to the group, and both are taller than H, then

(A) H is the shortest of all
(B) E is the shortest of all
(C) C is the tallest of all
(D) either Q or Z is the tallest of all
(E) either H or E is the shortest of all

ANALYSIS

The correct answer is (E). If Q and Z are added, and both are taller than H, we know little more except that H or E must still be the smallest. Q or Z could possibly be the tallest, but not necessarily so. Only (E) *must* be true.

EXAMPLE

The Rockford Tennis Club is composed of seven tournament players. Four of these players are women—Carol, Denise, Evelyn, and Gneisha. Three of these players are men—Abel, Ben, and Fritz. Each became a member of the club in a different year starting in 1990 and going through 1996. The following conditions apply:

Denise became a member before Evelyn.
Gneisha became a member after Fritz.
Abel and Ben became members before Carol.
Fritz and Gneisha became members after Evelyn.
None of the women became members in consecutive years.

ANALYSIS—THE SETUP

From the information given, you can set up the following list of years and relationships among the players:

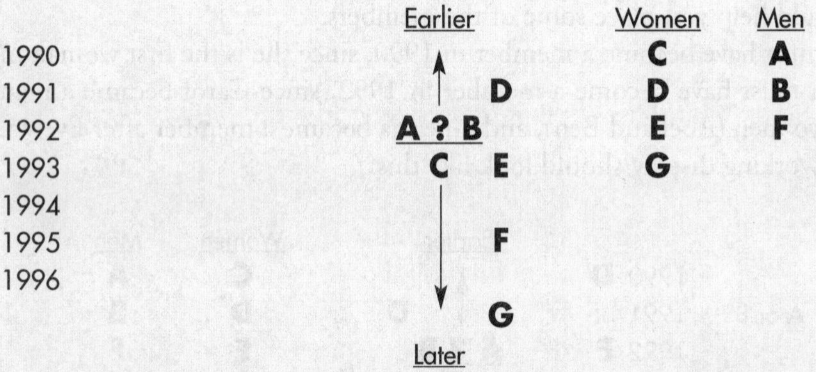

You may wish to scan the conditions before you begin. Let's build the setup from the start.

From the initial information, first list the years involved. Next, sort and list the men and women. Finally, apply the conditions.

"Denise became a member before Evelyn."

D

E

Notice the space between D and E because players could be in between.

"Gneisha became a member after Fritz."

D

E

F

G

Since a later condition states, "Fritz and Gneisha became members after Evelyn," scanning the conditions helped make the display above.

Finally, "Abel and Ben became members before Carol."

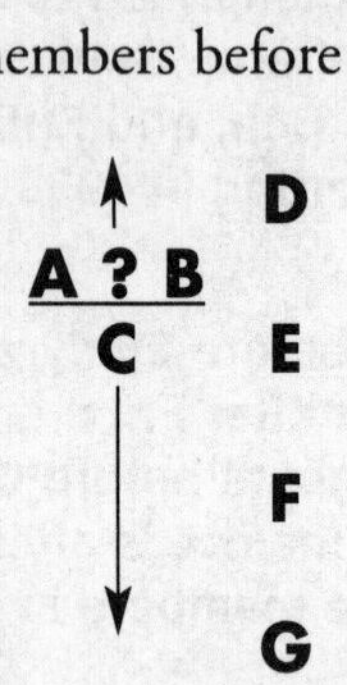

The final statement needs to be starred. It is an important statement. Since there are four women and seven years involved, and "None of the women became members in consecutive years," then the women must have joined the club in the even years—1990, 1992, 1994, and 1996. Mark this in the chart.

Now, taking a second look at the information as displayed and using some reasoning should help you place some of the members.

Denise must have become a member in 1990, since she is the first woman member. Evelyn must have become a member in 1992, since Carol became a member after the two men (Abel and Ben), and Gneisha became a member after Evelyn. So, your final working display should look like this:

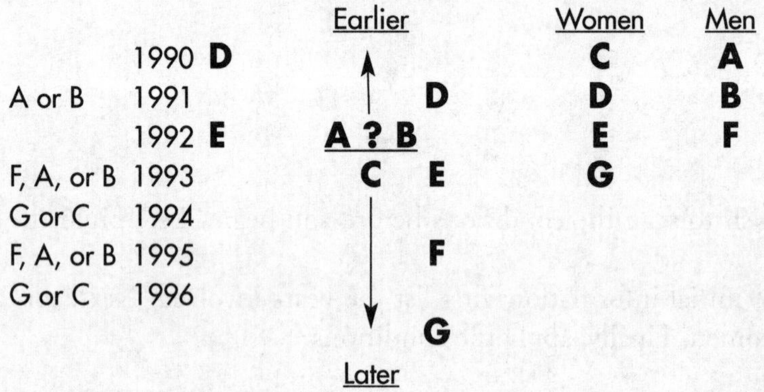

You could simplify the display with arrows, and you could circle the women in the middle display.

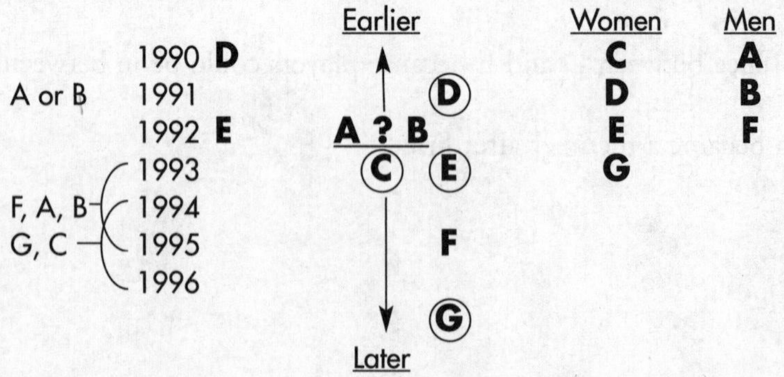

You may wish to list the years vertically at the bottom of the page of your test booklet in case you want to grid the scenerio for each question as follows:

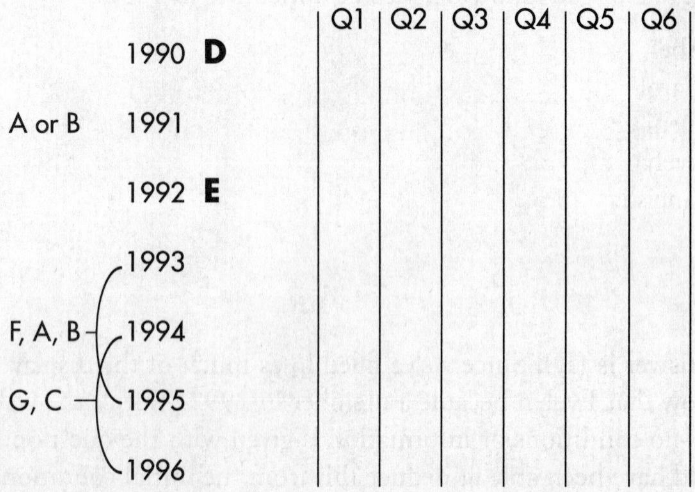

In this particular set, only two questions (questions 2 and 6) actually require that you identify a specific member in a specific year, so it's probably easier simply to list the years only next to each of those two problems.

Question 1

Which one of the following must be true?

(A) Carol became a member before Gneisha.
(B) Fritz became a member before Carol.
(C) Denise became a member before Carol.
(D) Gneisha became a member before Fritz.
(E) Ben became a member before Gneisha.

ANALYSIS

The correct answer is (C). Let's work through the choices and eliminate.

Choice (A), "Carol became a member before Gneisha," is possible, but we're looking for "must."

Choice (B), "Fritz became a member before Carol," is possible.

Choice (C), "Denise became a member before Carol," must be true, since Denise is in 1990. STOP! You have the right answer. No need to look at the rest.

For your information, here are the other two choices.

Choice (D), "Gneisha became a member before Fritz," is not possible.

Choice (E), "Ben became a member before Gneisha," is possible.

Question 2

Which one of the following became a member in 1992?

(A) Abel
(B) Carol
(C) Denise
(D) Evelyn
(E) Gneisha

ANALYSIS

The correct answer is (D). Since we've filled in as much of the display as possible, we already know that Evelyn became a member in 1992. Notice the way this question is asked—no conditions or information is given with the question. It tells you that you should have been able to deduce this from the initial conditions. It should have been in your original display. If you missed this information when setting up your display, this question alerts you to it.

Question 3

Suppose the original condition that Gneisha became a member after Fritz is replaced with "Gneisha became a member the year before or the year after Fritz." If all the other conditions remain in effect, and if Ben became a member in 1993, then which one of the following must be true?

(A) Abel became a member in 1991, and Carol became a member in 1994.
(B) Evelyn became a member in 1992, and Gneisha became a member in 1996.
(C) Abel became a member in 1991, and Fritz became a member in 1995.
(D) Fritz became a member in 1995, and Carol became a member in 1996.
(E) Denise became a member in 1992, and Gneisha became a member in 1994.

ANALYSIS

The correct answer is (C). For this question, you will need to go into the years chart:

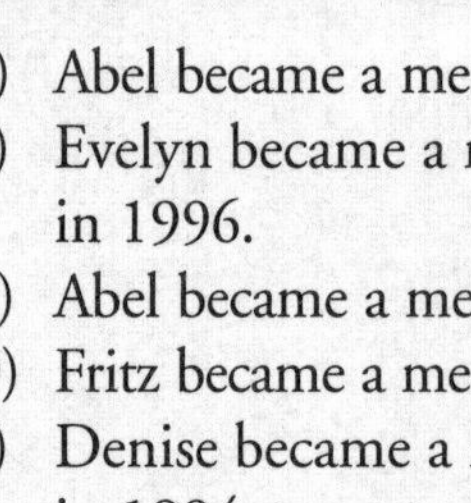

Since Ben is in 1993, Abel must be in 1991. Fritz must be in 1995, since that is the only remaining place for men.

(A), (B), and (D) could be true, while (E) is false. (C) *must* be true. A typical wrong answer to a "must be" question is a "could be" answer.

Notice that any change, replacement, or deletion of an original condition in a question applies only to that question.

Question 4

Which one of the following is a complete and accurate list of members who could have joined the club in 1994?

(A) Carol
(B) Denise, Evelyn
(C) Carol, Gneisha
(D) Carol, Denise, Gneisha
(E) Carol, Evelyn, Gneisha

ANALYSIS

The correct answer is (C). Since Denise and Evelyn are in 1990 and 1992, respectively, they could not join in 1994. Eliminate (B), (D), and (E). (A) is accurate, but not complete, since Gneisha could also have joined in 1994. On this type of question, be sure to look at all the choices. Remember, some answers might be accurate but not complete.

Question 5

Which one of the following is a possible order of players becoming members of the club from 1990 through 1996?

(A) Denise, Abel, Evelyn, Carol, Fritz, Gneisha, Ben
(B) Evelyn, Ben, Denise, Fritz, Carol, Abel, Gneisha
(C) Denise, Abel, Evelyn, Fritz, Carol, Ben, Gneisha
(D) Carol, Fritz, Ben, Evelyn, Gneisha, Abel, Denise
(E) Denise, Ben, Evelyn, Abel, Carol, Fritz, Gneisha

ANALYSIS

The correct answer is (E). Eliminate (B) and (D), since Denise must be first. Next, eliminate (A), since a man (Ben) cannot be in 1996. Finally, eliminate (C), because Ben became a member before Carol.

Question 6

If Fritz became a member in 1993, then which one of the following must be true?

(A) Gneisha became a member in 1994.
(B) Carol became a member in 1994.
(C) Ben became a member in 1995.
(D) Evelyn became a member in 1996.
(E) Abel became a member in 1995.

ANALYSIS

The correct answer is (A). For this question, you will need to go into the years chart as follows:

	1990	**D**
A or B	1991	
	1992	**E**
	1993	**F**
	1994	**G**
G, C	1995	**A** or **B**
	1996	**C**

Notice that if Fritz became a member in 1993, then either Abel or Ben became members in 1995. Carol became a member after Abel and Ben, so she must be in 1996. If Carol became a member in 1996, then Gneisha became a member in 1994.

EXAMPLE

Alice, Bobby, Carole, Dwight, and Elva were playing a game with marbles. When the game ended, Alice wrote down the following information:

Carole has more marbles than Alice and Bobby together.
Alice's total is the same as the total of Dwight and Elva together.
Alice has more marbles than Bobby.
Bobby has more marbles than Elva.
Everyone has at least one marble.

ANALYSIS—THE SETUP

From the information given, you can set up the following relationships:

C > A + B
A = D + E
A > B
B > E

Then you can construct the following diagram (Note: This chart is more easily realized by starting with the last condition and working up.):

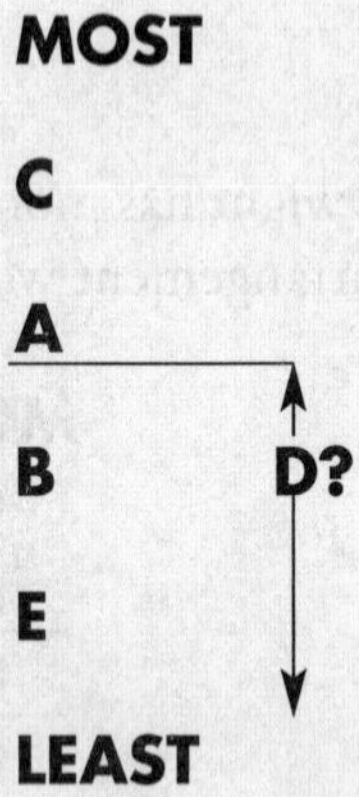

Question 1

Who ended the game with the most marbles?

(A) Alice
(B) Bobby
(C) Carole
(D) Dwight
(E) Elva

ANALYSIS

The correct answer is (C.) Using the relationships, you can see that Carole has more marbles than Alice and Bobby together. Because Alice has more marbles than Dwight, Elva, or Bobby each has alone, Carole must have the most of all.

Question 2

If Dwight has more marbles than Bobby, who ended the game with the fewest marbles?

(A) Alice
(B) Bobby
(C) Carole
(D) Dwight
(E) Elva

ANALYSIS

The correct answer is (E). If Dwight has more marbles than Bobby, then Elva must have the fewest marbles. The arrangement would be as follows:

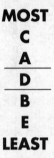

MOST
C
A
D
B
E
LEAST

Question 3

Which one of the following is a possible order of children going from most marbles to fewest?

(A) Alice, Bobby, Carole, Dwight, Elva
(B) Carole, Alice, Bobby, Elva, Dwight
(C) Carole, Bobby, Alice, Dwight, Elva
(D) Dwight, Carole, Alice, Bobby, Elva
(E) Carole, Alice, Elva, Bobby, Dwight

ANALYSIS

The correct answer is (B). From the original chart, we can see that Carole must have most of all, followed by Alice. Because Bobby has more marbles than Elva, only answer (B) can be a possible correct order.

Question 4

Which one of the following must be true?

(A) Elva has more marbles than Dwight.
(B) Dwight has fewer marbles than Bobby.
(C) Alice has more marbles than Elva.
(D) Dwight and Bobby have the same number of marbles.
(E) Elva and Dwight have the same number of marbles.

ANALYSIS

The correct answer is (C). Only (C) *must* be true. In (A) and (E), Elva *could* have more marbles than Dwight, but not necessarily. She could have fewer *or the same amount.* Notice the possible range of placement for Dwight on the original chart. Again, in (B) and (D), Dwight's placement is uncertain: Dwight could have fewer, *the same,* or more marbles than Bobby.

Question 5

If Elva has 3 marbles, and everyone has a different number of marbles, which one of the following could NOT be the number of marbles that Alice could have?

(A) 5
(B) 6
(C) 7
(D) 8
(E) 9

ANALYSIS

The correct answer is (B). Using the relationships, you can see that if Elva has 3 marbles, then Dwight can have any number *but* 3. Because Alice's total equals Dwight's and Elva's total together, Alice cannot have 3 + 3, or 6.

The Position Organizer (Non-linear)

EXAMPLE

John, Paul, George, and Herman sit around a square table with eight chairs, which are equally distributed.

Bob, Carol, Ted, and Alice join them at the table.
The two women (Carol and Alice) cannot sit next to each other.
John and Herman are seated on either side of George and are next to him.
Ted is seated next to Herman.
Carol is seated next to John but not directly across from George.
John is directly across from Alice.

ANALYSIS—THE SETUP

Note that the statement preceding the six conditions immediately suggests that you draw a square table with two spaces on each side. The first piece of concrete information is condition 3, which tells you to seat John, George, and Herman in that order. Next, seat Ted next to Herman (#4), seat Carol next to John (#5), and seat Alice across from John (#6). Note that Carol and Alice are not sitting next to each other (#2) and that Paul and Bob are in *variable* positions on either side of Alice. The resulting chart is as follows:

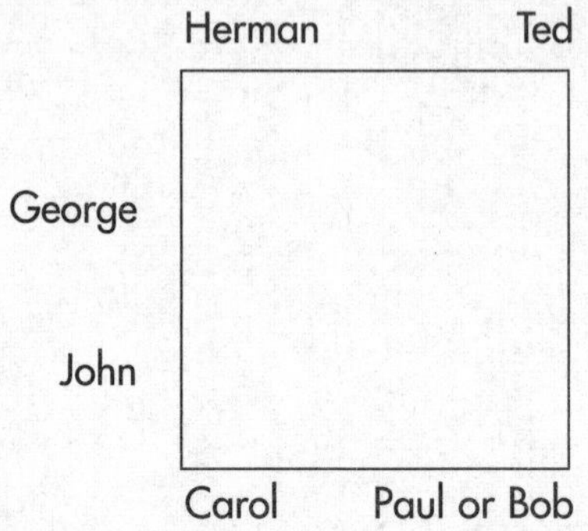

Question 1

Which men could switch positions without contradicting the seating arrangement?

(A) George and Herman
(B) John and George
(C) Paul and Ted
(D) Bob and Paul
(E) Bob and George

ANALYSIS

The correct answer is (D). As the chart points out, only Bob and Paul are in variable positions and, thus, interchangeable.

Question 2

Which of the following must be false?

(A) George is not next to Ted.
(B) Alice is not next to Carol.
(C) Herman is next to Carol.
(D) George is across from Paul.
(E) Bob is not next to Paul.

ANALYSIS

The correct answer is (C). Working from the answer choices and inspecting the chart, you see that (C) *must* be false in any case and that (D) *may* be false, depending upon where Paul is seated.

Question 3

Which of the following could be true?

(A) Herman sits next to Carol.
(B) Herman sits next to John.
(C) Ted sits next to Paul.
(D) John sits next to Paul.
(E) George sits next to Alice.

ANALYSIS

The correct answer is (C). From the diagram, you can see that Paul could be in the seat next to Ted. None of the other choices is possible.

Question 4

Which of the following must be true?

(A) Ted sits next to Paul.
(B) Alice sits next to Paul.
(C) George sits next to Carol.
(D) Ted sits next to Bob.
(E) Bob sits next to John.

ANALYSIS

The correct answer is (B). Since the two seats next to Alice are taken by Paul and Bob, then Alice must sit next to Paul.

Question 5

If Arnold were now to take Ted's seat, then Arnold

(A) must now be next to Bob
(B) must be next to Alice
(C) must be across from Bob
(D) is either next to or across from Paul
(E) is either next to or across from George

ANALYSIS

The correct answer is D. If Arnold takes Ted's seat, then either he is seated next to Paul or Paul is seated across from him.

The Position Organizer with the Diagram Provided

On occasion, the position chart or diagram will be provided. That is, instead of, or along with, a description of the setup, an actual diagram is given. Use the following steps if a chart or diagram is given:

1. Either redraw the chart or diagram, or mark the diagram dark enough so you can understand your notes but also so you can erase without losing information.
2. Follow the same procedures you would use in filling in or completing the position chart.

EXAMPLE

Nine guests—A, B, C, D, E, F, G, H, I—attend a formal dinner party. Ten chairs are arranged around the rectangular dining room table as follows:

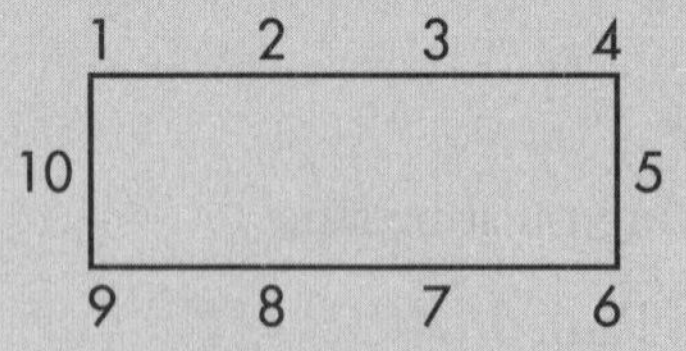

Seat 1 is directly across from seat 9.
Seat 2 is directly across from seat 8.
Seat 3 is directly across from seat 7.
Seat 4 is directly across from seat 6.
Seats 5 and 10 are at the ends of the table and are directly across from each other.

A, B, C, and D are females.
E, F, G, H, and I are males.
A and E are a married couple.
B and F are a married couple.
C and G are engaged to each other.
Each married couple always sits next to his or her spouse on one side of the table.
Members of the same sex never sit in adjacent seats.
Guests in end seats 5 and 10 are considered adjacent to seats on each side of them.
If G is in seat 10, then C is not in seat 5.
I is never in seat 6.
A is always in seat 1.

ANALYSIS—THE SETUP

From the initial conditions, the diagram and markings would look like this:

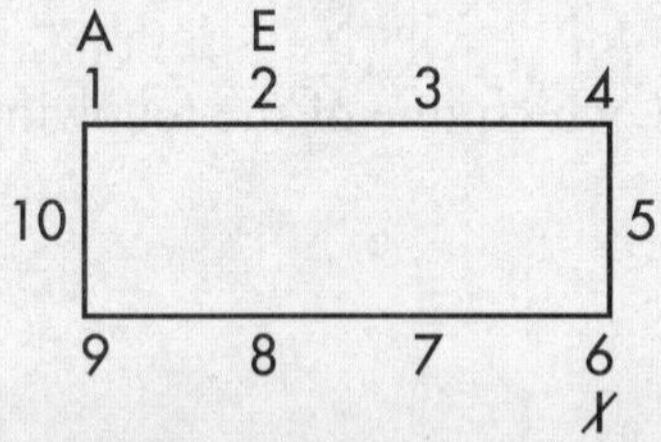

AE
BF
If G10, then C~~5~~

<u>Males</u>
F G H I

<u>Females</u>
A B C D

Question 1

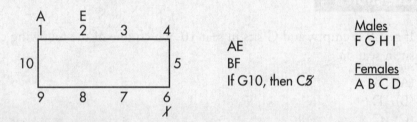

Which one of the following could sit in seat 10?

(A) A
(B) C
(C) D
(D) F
(E) H

ANALYSIS

The correct answer is (E). Since guest A sits in seat 1, a male must sit in seat 10 if it is not empty. This eliminates (A), (B), and (C) since guests A, C, and D are females. (A is in seat 1 anyway.) Since guests B and F are a married couple, they must sit next to each other on a side. This eliminates (D). Guest H is a male and could sit in seat 10.

Question 2

Which one of the following is a complete and accurate list of guests who could sit in seat 3?

(A) A, B, C, D, E, F, G
(B) B, C, D, E, F
(C) B, C, D, E
(D) B, C, D
(E) B, C

ANALYSIS

The correct answer is (D). Since guest E is in seat 2, only a female could sit in seat 3. Since guest A is in seat 1, the remaining females are guests B, C, and D.

Question 3

If seat 9 is empty, and G sits in seat 10, which one of the following could sit in seat 5?

(A) B
(B) D
(C) C
(D) H
(E) I

ANALYSIS

The correct answer is (B). From the information given in the question and the initial conditions, the diagram should look like this:

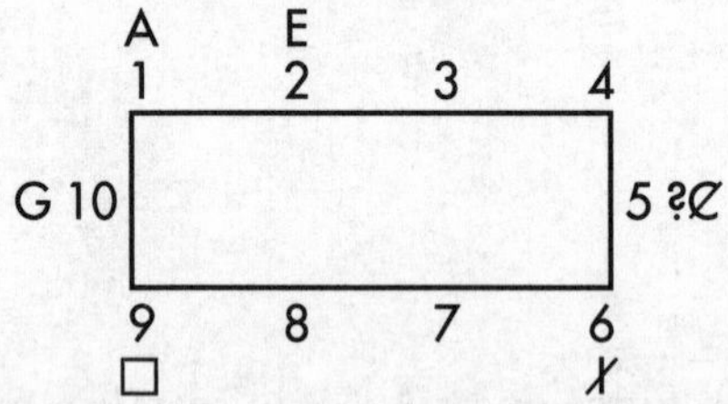

It can now be determined that seat 3 is a female, seat 4 is a male, and seat 5 is a female. You may have added to your diagram, so it would now look like this:

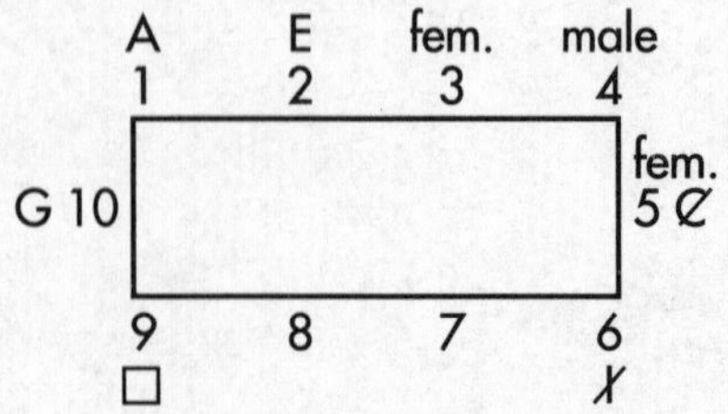

Seat 5 cannot be guest B, since guest B cannot be on the end. Guests H and I are males, so (D) and (E) are eliminated. Since guest G is in seat 10, then guest C cannot be in seat 5 (from initial conditions), so only guest D is left.

Question 4

If C sits in seat 5, and F sits in seat 4, which one of the following could be the arrangement of seats from 1 to 10, respectively?

	1,	2,	3,	4,	5,	6,	7,	8,	9,	10
(A)	A,	B,	E,	F,	C,	G,	__,	I,	D,	H
(B)	A,	E,	B,	G,	C,	F,	D,	H,	__,	I
(C)	A,	E,	B,	F,	C,	I,	D,	__,	G,	H
(D)	A,	E,	B,	F,	C,	H,	D,	I,	__,	G
(E)	A,	E,	B,	F,	C,	G,	D,	H,	__,	I

ANALYSIS

The correct answer is (E). From the information given, the diagram should look like this:

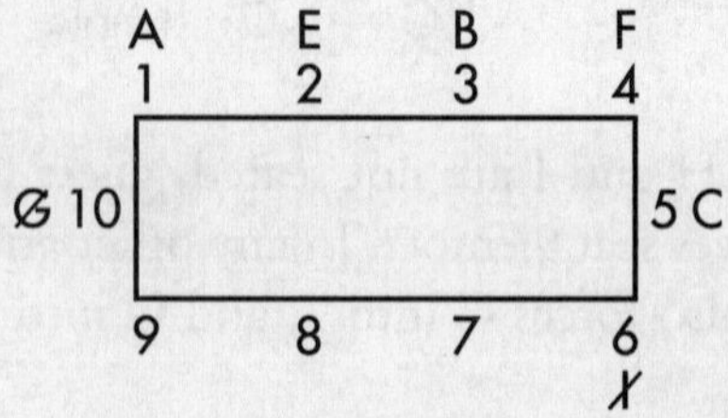

You could eliminate (A) because guest B cannot be in seat 2. Since guest F is in seat 4, guest B is in seat 3. This eliminates (B). (C) can be eliminated, since male guests G and H cannot be seated next to each other. Since guest C is in seat 5, guest G cannot be in seat 10, so (D) is eliminated. (E) is a possible arrangement.

Question 5

If D sits in seat 5, and the engaged couple sits together in seats 7 and 8, which one of the following seats must be empty?

(A) 3
(B) 4
(C) 6
(D) 9
(E) 10

ANALYSIS

The correct answer is (D). From the information given, your chart should now look like this:

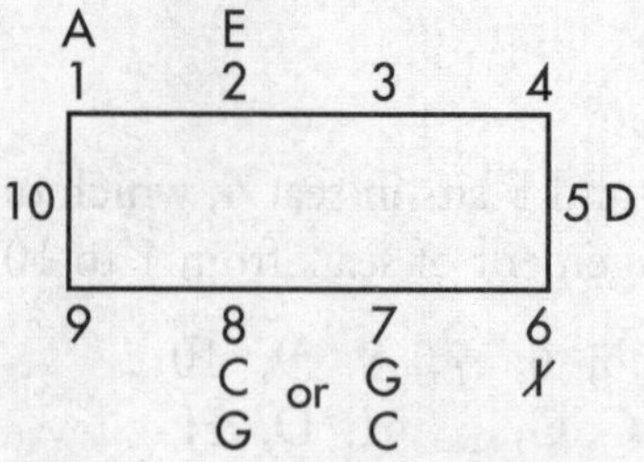

You should also be able to fill in seats 3 and 4 and determine that seats 6, and 10, if not empty, must be males. Your diagram should now have this information:

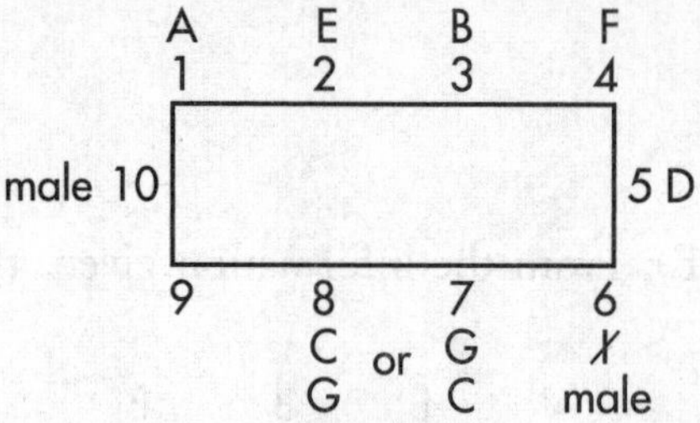

Since only male guests H and I are not seated, guest H must be in seat 6 and guest I in seat 10. This leaves seat 9 empty. In any other arrangement, two males are next to each other. (This also forces C into 7, and G into 8.)

Question 6

Which one of the following is a complete and accurate list of guests who could sit in seat 5?

(A) C
(B) D
(C) C, D
(D) B, C, D
(E) C, D, G

ANALYSIS

The correct answer is (C). First eliminate (D), since guest B must be on a side. If guest G is in seat 5, then the diagram would look like this:

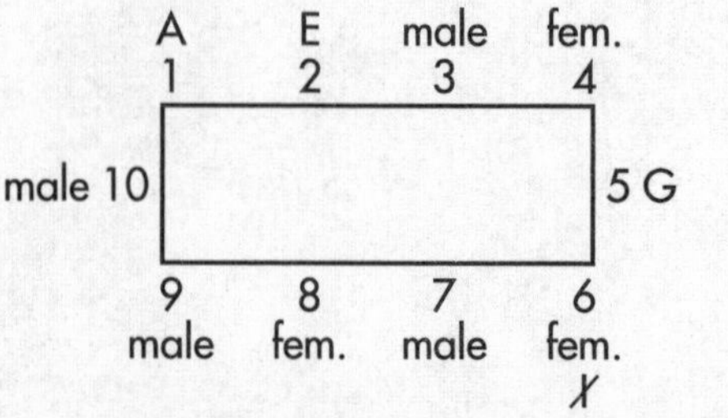

This requires two males to be next to each other, so seat 5 must be a female, either guest C or D.

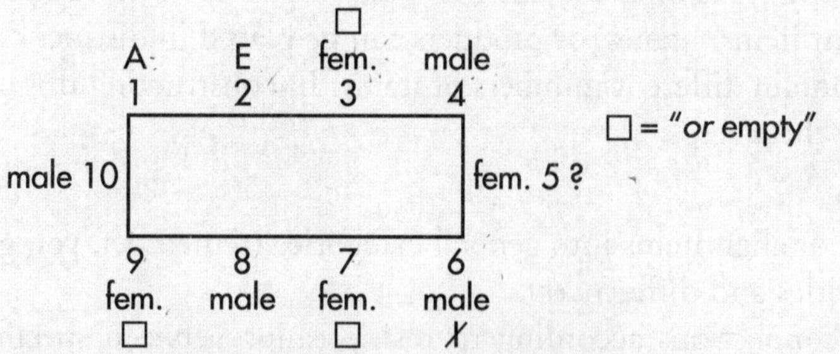

Question 7

If a female sits directly across from A, which one of the following must be true?

(A) Seat 3 is empty.
(B) Seat 4 is empty.
(C) Seat 6 is a female.
(D) Seat 7 is a female.
(E) Seat 8 is a male.

ANALYSIS

The correct answer is (E). If a female sits across from guest A, your diagram would now have the following information:

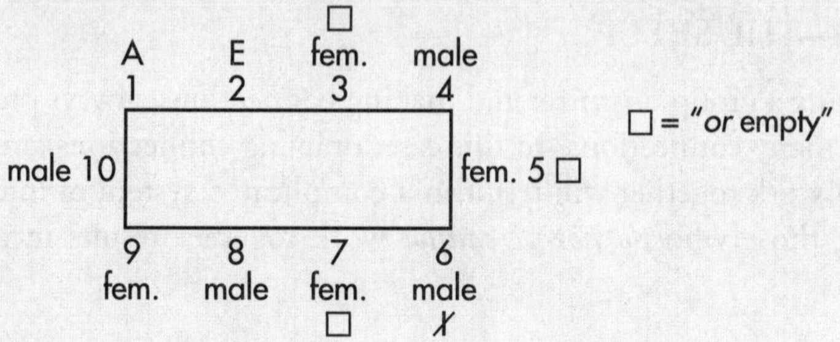

Since seat 3, 5, or 7 could be empty, only (E), a male is in seat 8, must be true.

The Group Organizer

One of the many types of displays is the group organizer. This is a problem set in which different items, names, or products can be placed in distinct categories, which may contain different numbers of items. In constructing this organizer, you should follow these steps:

1. Group or align items into general categories (remember, you group items by similarities and differences).
2. Draw connections according to relationships between specific items. Your markings should indicate whether items always go together (x—y), never go together (x-✕-y), are conditional (if x goes then y goes; x → y), and so on.

STUDY TIP

Notice that about 20–25 percent of the displays are a form of Group Organizer.

After you've drawn your chart, remember to take information forward and backward (what can and can't happen) and to watch for actions and subsequent reactions.

EXAMPLE

Sales manager Phil Forrester is trying to put together a sales team to cover the Los Angeles area. His team will consist of four members—two experienced and two new salesmen.

Sam, Fred, Harry, and Kim are the experienced salesmen.
John, Tim, and Dom are new.
Sam and Fred do not work together.
Tim and Sam refuse to work together.
Harry and Dom cannot work together.

ANALYSIS—THE SETUP

When drawing a group organizer and making connections, always prefer fewer connections to many connections. In this case, drawing connections among the workers who can work together will result in a complicated system of intersecting lines. Connecting those who *do not* or *cannot* work together results in a simple, clear chart:

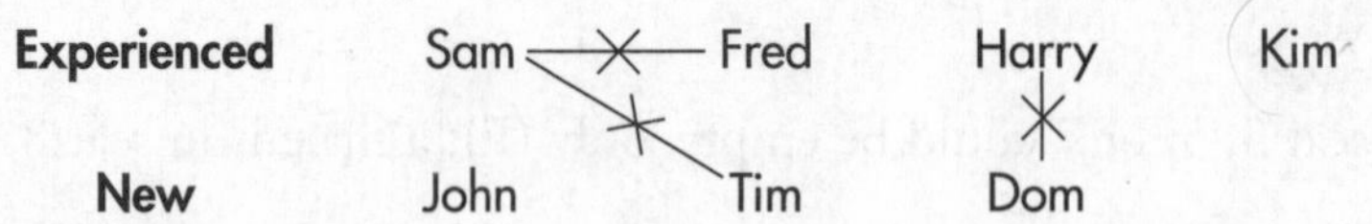

or

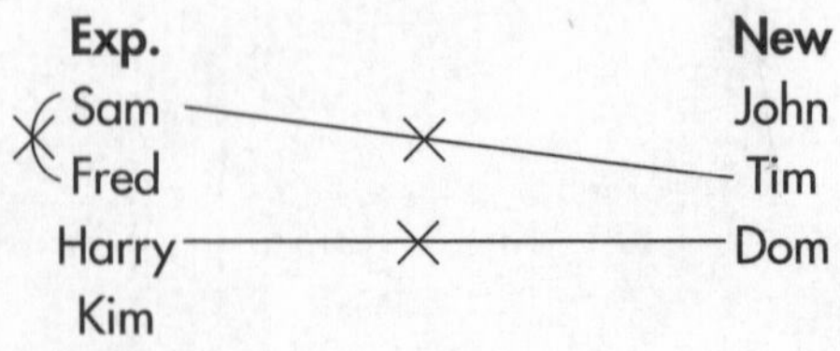

Each group organizer encourages you to use information in both directions, recognizing that, because connected workers *cannot* work together, unconnected workers *can* work together.

Notice that the conditions gave initial information about those who cannot work together, helping you to formulate the most efficient method of connecting the diagram. If the conditions had stated that some salesmen always work together and that some never work together, you would have used a different type of marking to denote each type of connection. Also notice that the labels or headings should be written out or abbreviated *and* underlined.

Question 1

If Sam is made part of the team, the following must be the other members:

(A) John, Tim, Dom
(B) John, Dom, Kim
(C) Tim, Harry, Kim
(D) Dom, John, Fred
(E) John, Dom, Harry

ANALYSIS

The correct answer is (B). The team must consist of two experienced and two new salesmen. Sam is experienced, so the rest of the team must include one experienced and two new salesmen. (C) should be eliminated both because it contains two experienced salesmen and because Sam does not work with Tim; also eliminate (A) because it includes Tim. Eliminate (D) because Sam does not work with Fred, and eliminate (E) because Dom does not work with Harry.

Question 2

If Sam is not chosen as part of the sales team and Tim is, then which one of the following must be true?

(A) Dom and Harry are on the team.
(B) Kim and John are on the team.
(C) Harry and Fred are on the team.
(D) John or Dom is not on the team.
(E) Fred or Kim is not on the team.

ANALYSIS

The correct answer is (D). With Tim on the team, there is room for one other new salesman. Therefore, *either* John *or* Dom is on the team, but not both.

Question 3

Which one of the following must be true?

(A) Fred and Sam always work together.
(B) Kim and Dom never work together.
(C) Kim and Fred always work together.
(D) If John works, then Kim doesn't work.
(E) If Sam works, then Dom works.

ANALYSIS

The correct answer is (E). The key word in this question is *must,* which excludes possible, but not necessary, combinations. (A) is false, as the chart reveals. (B) is false because they *could* work together if Harry does not work. (C) is false because Kim and Fred do not have to work together. You could have the team of Kim, Sam, John, and Dom. This also eliminates (D). (E) must be true since Sam and Tim never work together; Sam must always work with Dom and John.

Question 4

If Dom is chosen as part of the sales team but John is not, then the other three members must be

(A) Fred, Tim, and Harry
(B) Fred, Tim, and Kim
(C) Harry, John, and Tim
(D) Tim, Dom, and Kim
(E) Sam, Fred, and Harry

ANALYSIS

The correct answer is (B). If Dom is chosen as part of the team and John is not, then Tim must be the other inexperienced member. So, if Dom and Tim both are chosen, then Sam and Harry are not chosen. The team now consists of Dom, Tim, Fred, and Kim.

Question 5

Which one of the following must be true?

(A) If Harry works, then John works.
(B) If Kim works, then John works.
(C) If John works, then Dom works.
(D) If Dom works, then John works.
(E) If John works, then Kim works.

ANALYSIS

The correct answer is (A). Since Harry will not work with Dom, then John must be one of the other inexperienced members in the group when Harry works. The other combinations (Kim and John; John and Dom) do not always work together.

EXAMPLE

Seven students—John, Kim, Len, Molly, Neil, Owen, and Pam—will be assigned to three study stations—reading, writing, and math. Students are assigned to the stations under the following conditions:

Each student must be assigned to exactly one station.
Each station must have at least one student but cannot have more than three students.
Kim and Len are always assigned to the same station.
Len and Molly are never assigned to the same station.
Pam is assigned to the reading station.
If John is assigned to math, then Kim is assigned to reading.
Neil is never assigned to writing.
Owen is never assigned to math.

ANALYSIS—THE SETUP

Your first step should be to set up the placement categories—reading, writing, and math. Be sure to underline the categories.

Reading	**Writing**	**Math**

From the condition "Each station must have at least one student, but cannot have more than three students," you could add the following:

	Reading	**Writing**	**Math**
	____	____	____
?	____	____	____
?	____	____	____

Next, you could put information off to the side from the conditions "Kim and Len are always assigned to the same station" and "Len and Molly are never assigned to the same station."

	Reading	**Writing**	**Math**	
	____	____	____	
?	____	____	____	KL
?	____	____	____	~~LM~~

The statement "Pam is assigned to the reading station" gives you a quick placement as follows:

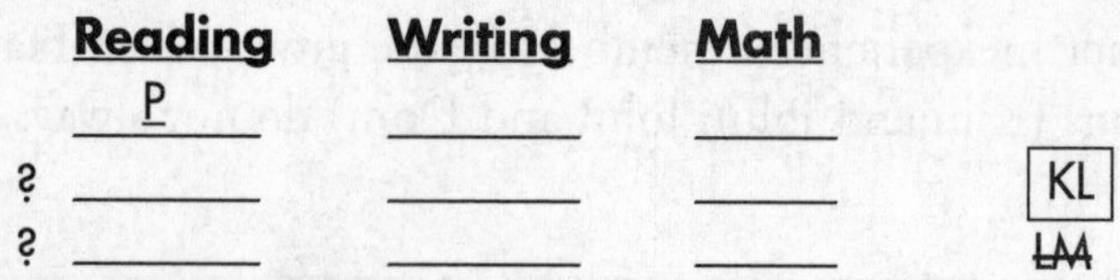

The conditional statement "If John is assigned to math, then Kim is assigned to reading" should be marked as follows:

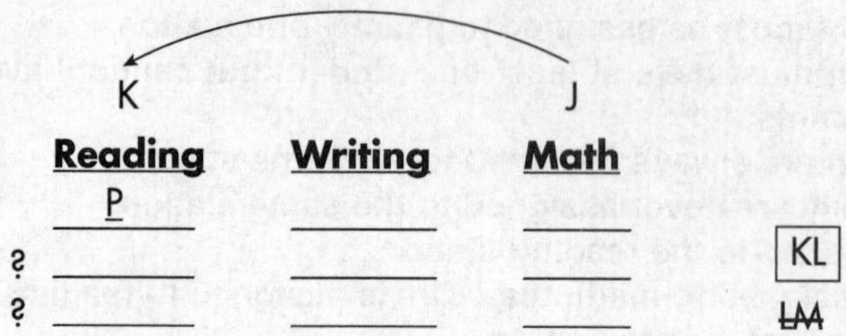

Notice that the arrow is pointing from J to K.

Finally, "Neil is never assigned to writing" and "Owen is never assigned to math" can be marked as follows:

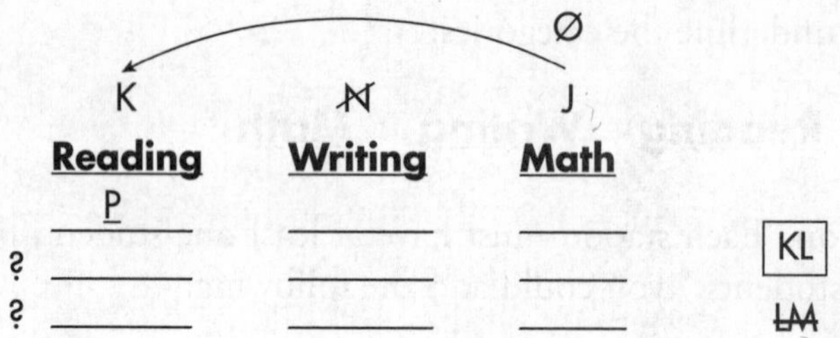

Question 1

Which one of the following is a complete and accurate list of the students who could be assigned to reading?

(A) JKL
(B) LMO
(C) KLMN
(D) JKLMOP
(E) JKLMNOP

ANALYSIS

The correct answer is (E). Since Pam is assigned to reading, you could eliminate any answer that does not include P. Choices (A), (B), and (C) should be eliminated. Now take a careful look at the difference between (D) and (E). The difference is that choice (E) contains N, and since there is no reason that N could not be assigned to reading, (E) is the correct answer.

Question 2

Which one of the following is an acceptable assignment of students to stations?

(A) Reading: PKLN; Writing: MO; Math: J
(B) Reading: KLN; Writing: PO; Math: JM
(C) Reading: PJN; Writing: MO; Math: KL
(D) Reading: PMO; Writing: JN; Math: KL
(E) Reading: PN; Writing: MO; Math: JKL

ANALYSIS

The correct answer is (C). Since the question asks you for "an acceptable assignment," you should look for unacceptable assignments (rule breakers) and eliminate them. (A) can be eliminated because there can't be four students in reading. (B) can be eliminated because P is in writing and must be in reading. (D) can be eliminated because N cannot be in writing. (E) can be eliminated since "If John is assigned to math, then Kim is assigned to reading," so J and K cannot both be in math.

Question 3

Which one of the following is a pair of students who could be assigned to math?

(A) OM
(B) JL
(C) JK
(D) JN
(E) LM

ANALYSIS

The correct answer is (D). Since the question asks, "who could be assigned to math?" you should again look for those who couldn't (rule breakers). (A) can be eliminated because O cannot be in math. (B) can be eliminated because if J is in math, K must be in reading, so L must then be in reading. And because if J is in math, K must be in reading, so (C) can be eliminated. (E) can be eliminated because L and M cannot be assigned to the same station.

Question 4

If John is assigned to math, then which one of the following must be true?

(A) Molly is assigned to reading.
(B) Neil is assigned to writing.
(C) Molly and Owen are assigned to writing.
(D) Neil is assigned to Math, and Owen is assigned to writing.
(E) Neil is assigned to Math, and Len is assigned to writing.

ANALYSIS

The correct answer is (D). Once John is assigned to math, Kim and Len are assigned to reading, and the display will look like this:

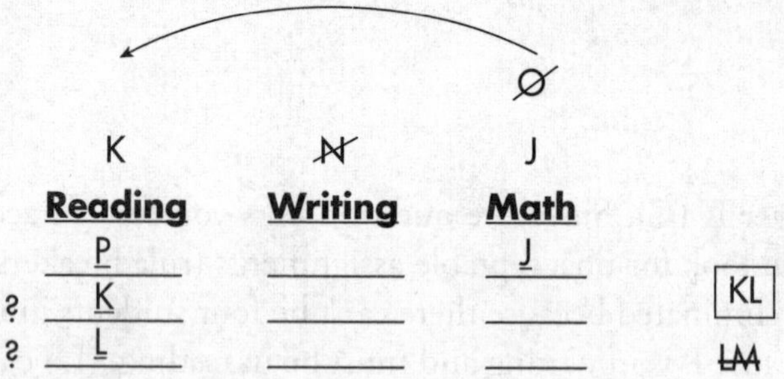

Therefore, Neil must be in math, and Owen must be in writing. Notice that (C) could be true but doesn't necessarily have to be true.

Question 5

If Neil is assigned to reading, then which one of the following could be true?

(A) John is assigned to math.
(B) Kim is assigned to reading.
(C) Molly is assigned to the same station as Kim.
(D) John is assigned to reading.
(E) Len is assigned to writing, and Molly is assigned to reading.

ANALYSIS

The correct answer is (D). Once again, you should probably be looking for what can't be true and eliminating. If you place Neil in reading, the display would look like this:

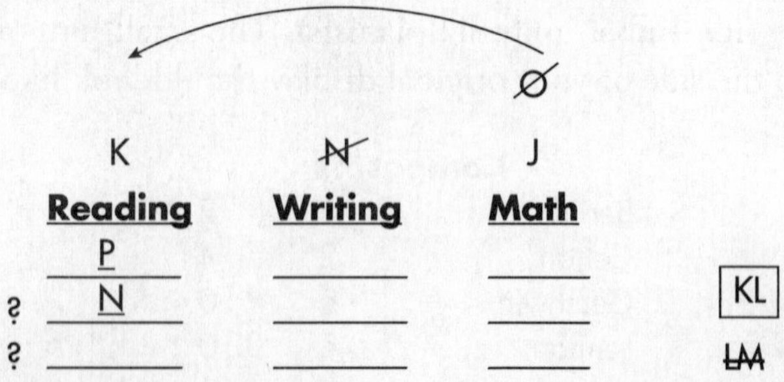

Now, since there are two students in reading, neither K nor L can be in reading, and therefore J can't be in math. You can eliminate (A) and (B). You can eliminate (C); because K and L must be together, and M cannot be with L, so M could never be with K. If L is assigned to writing, then K is assigned to writing. If M is assigned to reading, then O must be assigned to writing (O can't be in math, and reading already has three), and then J is assigned to math. But if J is assigned to math, K must be in reading; therefore, eliminate (E).

EXAMPLE

Six piano players—Moss, Nance, Odell, Parish, Quayle, Reed—are auditioning for a musical. Each pianist may choose to play one selection from one of four different composers—Berlin, Cohan, Gershwin, or Lennon. Exactly twice as many pianists choose a selection from Cohan as choose a selection from Berlin. The following conditions apply:

Moss and Nance choose selections from the same composer.
Odell chooses a selection from Berlin.
Parish and Quayle choose selections from different composers.
Quayle and Reed choose selections from different composers.

ANALYSIS—THE SETUP

From the information given, a simple display may be constructed. Since the first sentence mentions "six piano players," and the second sentence mentions one selection each, you might set up the following:

Next, pay special attention to the numerical relationship among the selections. "Exactly twice as many pianists choose a selection from Cohan as choose a selection from Berlin" is a key statement. Here's what it means: If exactly one pianist chooses a selection from Berlin, then exactly two choose a selection from Cohan. The remaining three would have to choose selections from Gershwin or Lennon. If exactly two pianists choose a selection from Berlin, then exactly four choose a selection from Cohan, and none chooses a selection from Gershwin or Lennon (remember, only six pianists). Three pianists could not choose a selection from Berlin because then six would have to choose a selection from Cohan, and that would be too many pianists (remember, only six pianists). The small, important chart that you should put to the side of your original display should look like this:

Composers

Berlin	1	2
Cohan	2	4
Gershwin	?	0
Lennon	?	0

These are the only two possible numbers of selections from Berlin and Cohan.

Now a closer look at the remaining conditions will help you mark the display as follows:

"Moss and Nance choose selections from the same composer."

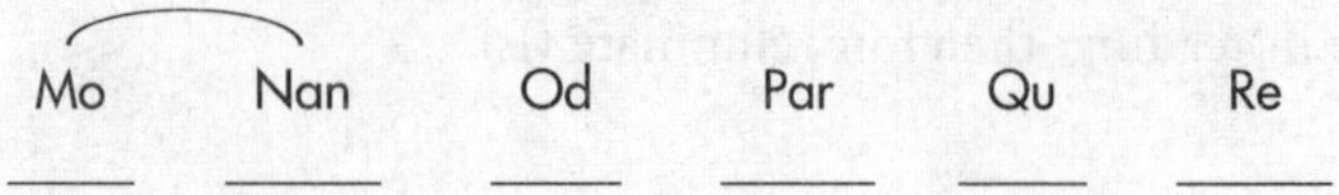

"Odell chooses a selection from Berlin."

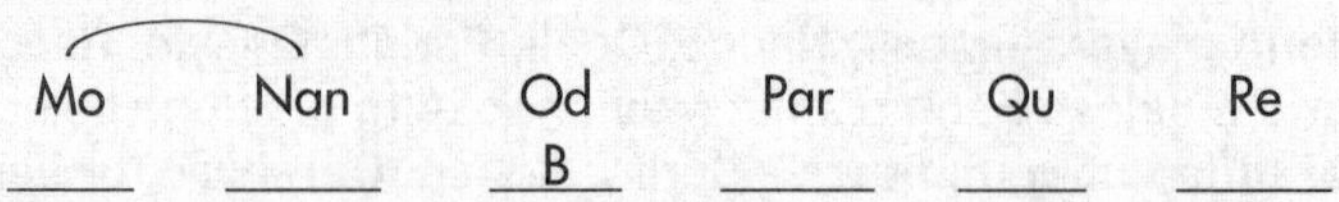

"Parish and Quayle choose selections from different composers."

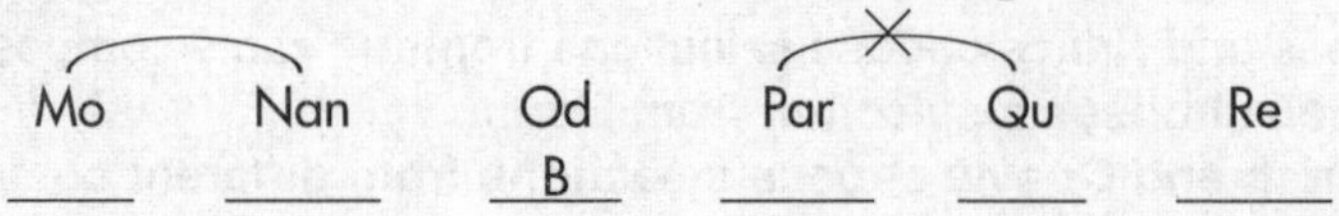

"Quayle and Reed choose selections from different composers."

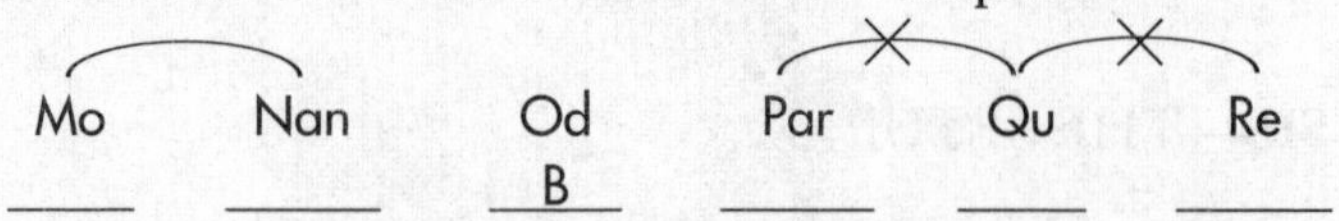

Simply from the initial conditions, the final display and chart would look like this:

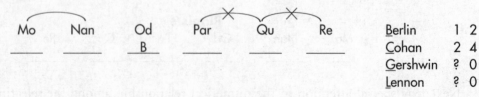

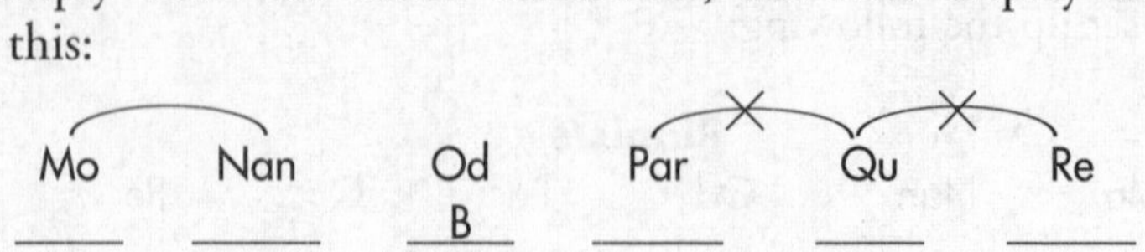

Berlin	1	2
Cohan	2	4
Gershwin	?	0
Lennon	?	0

Question 1

If Moss chooses a selection from Gershwin, then which one of the following must be true?

(A) Parish chooses a selection from Gershwin.
(B) Odell chooses a selection from Cohan.
(C) Quayle chooses a selection from Berlin
(D) Nance chooses a selection from Gershwin.
(E) Reed chooses a selection from Berlin.

ANALYSIS

The correct answer is (D). If Moss chooses a selection from Gershwin, then the first thing you should notice is that Nance must also choose a selection from Gershwin. At this point, scan your answers looking for Nance. Choice D is "Nance chooses a selection from Gershwin." Take it, and don't worry about the other choices, since this must be true. Go for the things you know.

Question 2

Which one of the following is a possible list of the pianist choices?

(A) Berlin: Moss, Nance, Odell
Cohan: Parish, Quayle
Gershwin: Reed
(B) Berlin: Odell
Cohan: Nance, Parish
Gershwin: Moss, Quayle
Lennon: Reed
(C) Berlin: Odell
Cohan: Parish, Quayle
Gershwin: Moss, Nance
Lennon: Reed
(D) Berlin: Parish, Reed
Cohan: Odell, Moss, Nance, Quayle
(E) Berlin: Odell
Cohan: Parish, Reed
Gershwin: Moss, Nance, Quayle

ANALYSIS

The correct answer is (E). Remember, the only two possible numbers of selections from Berlin and Cohan is 1 and 2, or 2 and 4. Now go through the choices using the elimination strategy.

(A) has too many Berlins, and Parish and Quayle can't choose from the same composer. Eliminate (A).
(B) has the right numbers, but Moss and Nance must choose the same composer. Eliminate (B).
(C) has the right numbers, but Parish and Quayle can't choose from the same composer. Eliminate (C).
(D) doesn't have Odell choosing a selection from Berlin. Eliminate (D).
(E) has the right numbers and doesn't break any of the conditions.

Question 3

If Nance chooses a selection from Cohan and no one chooses a selection from Lennon, then which one of the following CANNOT be true?

(A) Moss chooses a selection from Cohan.
(B) Parish chooses a selection from Cohan.
(C) Quayle chooses a selection from Berlin.
(D) Reed chooses a selection from Gershwin.
(E) Odell chooses a selection from Berlin.

ANALYSIS

The correct answer is (D). If Nance chooses a selection from Cohan, then with the help of a little reasoning the display should look like this:

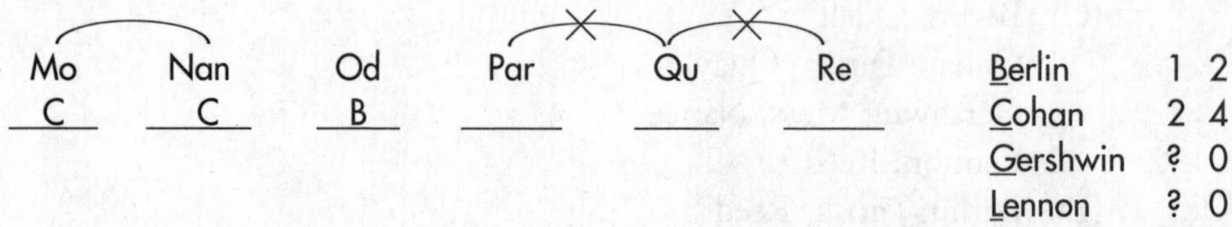

Now, since no pianist chooses Lennon, Gershwin must have either 3 spots or no spots, but the three spots cannot be Par, Qu, and/or Re because that would leave either Par and Qu or Qu and Re having a selection from the same composer, which would break a rule. At this point, you may have realized that, in this case, none of the pianists could choose Gershwin, so the answer is (D). For your information, the filled in display must be:

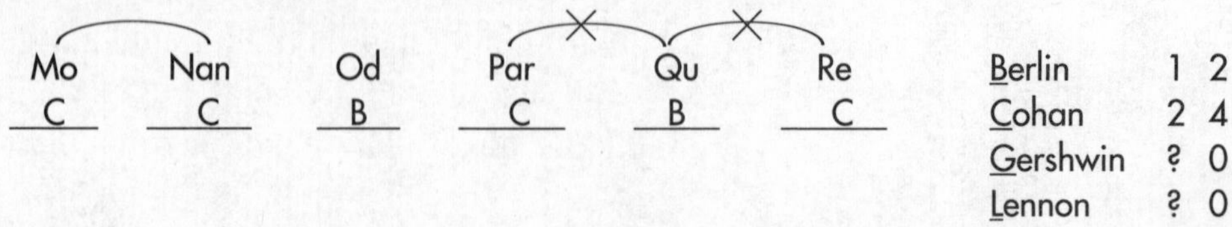

Remember, this question asks for what CANNOT be true.

Question 4

Which one of the following CANNOT be true?

(A) At least one selection is chosen from each composer.
(B) At least two selections are chosen from two composers.
(C) No selection is chosen from Gershwin.
(D) No selection is chosen from Cohan.
(E) Three selections can be chosen from one composer.

ANALYSIS

The correct answer is (D). This question is also asking for what CANNOT be true. Looking at the chart on the right, you know that either two or four selections are from Cohan. (D) cannot be true.

Question 5

Which one of the following could choose a selection from Berlin?

(A) Moss
(B) Nance
(C) Parish
(D) Quayle
(E) Reed

ANALYSIS

The correct answer is (D). If another pianist chooses Berlin, since Odell already chooses Berlin, there must be two selections from Berlin. Since you have two selections from Berlin, you must have four selections from Cohan, and the completed chart would have to be:

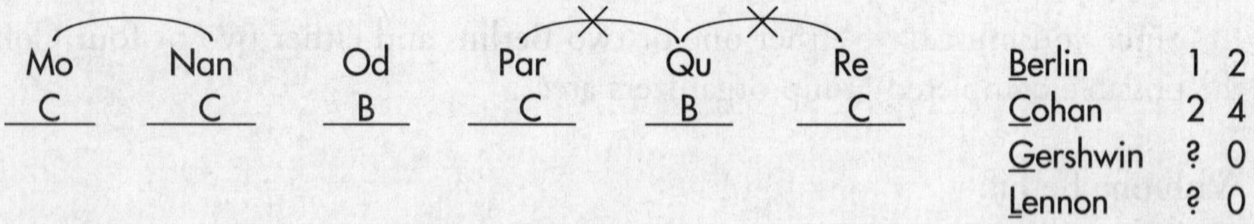

So, aside from Odell, Quayle is the only other pianist who can choose a selection from Berlin.

Question 6

Which one of the following pairs of pianists must choose a selection from the same composer?

(A) Odell and Reed
(B) Nance and Parish
(C) Parish and Reed
(D) Odell and Quayle
(E) Moss and Quayle

ANALYSIS

The correct answer is (C). You could work through the choices and eliminate as follows:

Choice (A): Odell and Reed cannot choose from the same composer because they would both have to choose from Berlin. If you have two from Berlin, you must have four from Cohan. But the four Cohans would have to include Parish and Quayle, who cannot choose from the same composer. Eliminate (A).

Choice (B): Nance and Parish could choose from the same composer, but they don't have to. Eliminate (B).

Choice (C): Parish and Reed have to choose from the same composer, which can be seen in the following charts.

Choice (D): Odell and Quayle could choose from the same composer (Berlin), but they don't have to. Eliminate (D).

Choice (E): Moss and Quayle could choose from the same composer, but they don't have to. Eliminate (E).

The choices can be more easily examined using the following information and charts.

Since you must have either one or two Berlins and either two or four Cohans, the possible completed group organizers are:

With one Berlin:

Mo	Nan	Od	Par	Qu	Re
G	G	B	C	G/L	C
L	L	B	C	L/G	C
C	C	B	L	G	L
C	C	B	G	L	G

Berlin	1	2
Cohan	2	4
Gershwin	?	0
Lennon	?	0

With two Berlins:

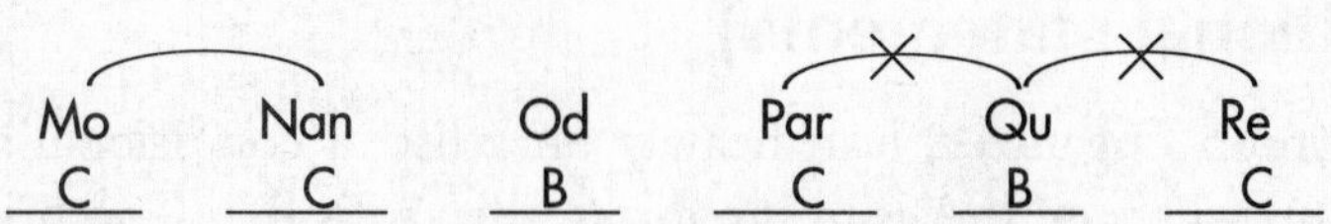

In each chart, Parish and Reed must choose a selection by the same composer.

Question 7

Which one of the following is a complete and accurate list of the pianists who could choose a selection from Cohan?

(A) Moss
(B) Moss, Nance
(C) Nance, Parish, Reed
(D) Moss, Nance, Parish, Quayle
(E) Moss, Nance, Parish, Reed

ANALYSIS

The correct answer is (E). If you realize that there must be four pianists who choose Cohan, you could immediately eliminate (A), (B), and (C). Then you could simply check (D) and (E). Otherwise, you could work through all the choices and eliminate as follows:

Choice (A): If Moss could choose Cohan, so could Nance. Also notice that there must be four possible pianists who choose Cohan. Eliminate (A).

Choice (B): Moss and Nance could both choose a selection from Cohan. This is accurate but not complete. Cohan must be chosen by two more pianists when two of the pianists choose Berlin. Eliminate (B).

Choice (C): If Nance could choose Cohan, so could Moss. Also notice that there must be four possible pianists who choose Cohan. Eliminate (C).

Choice (D): Quayle cannot choose a selection from Cohan. Since there are either two or four chosen from Cohan, the three possible arrangements for Cohan are:

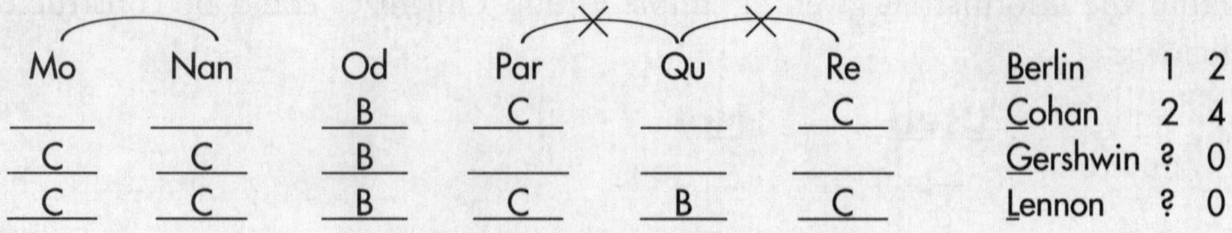

Eliminate (D).

Choice E: Moss, Nance, Parish, and Reed is a complete and accurate list of the pianists who could choose a selection from Cohan. This is evident from the group organizer above.

Remember, on a question that asks for a "complete and accurate" list, you must look at all the choices. An answer could be accurate but not complete.

The Group Organizer (with several conditional statements)

Some Group Organizers lean heavily on a list of conditional statements (if–then statements) such as "If A is in the forest, then so is B." (Conditional statements are reviewed in Chapter 2.) It can also be used with statements that show relationships between sets or groups of sets such as "All As are Bs." When putting together this type of Group Organizer, you should follow these steps:

1. When if–then statements are involved, mark them carefully, making sure that the arrow is going from the "if" to the "then" (if A then B should be noted as A → B).
2. Remember that whenever "If A then B" is true, then "If not B then not A" must also be true (this can be written $\not B \to \not A$). An example would be: If bluejays are in the forest, then so are sparrows. This statement also tells you that if sparrows are not in the forest, neither are bluejays. This second statement is called the *contrapositive* of the first statement. Make sure that you understand the original statement and the contrapositive. And remember, if the original statement is true, then the contrapositive must also be true.
3. Combine rules or make connections whenever possible. For example, A → B and B → C means that A → B → C.

STUDY TIP

Notice that about 20–25 percent of the displays are a form of Group Organizer with several conditional statements.

EXAMPLE

A landscape designer wishes to use roses of different colors in a large planter. Seven colors of roses are available for selection: lavender, orange, pink, red, tan, white, and yellow. Only certain color combinations will be used based on the following conditions:

If lavender is used, then so is tan.
If red is used, then yellow is not used.
If orange, tan, or both are used, then so is red.
If pink is not used, then neither is lavender.
If white is not used, then yellow is used.

ANALYSIS—THE SETUP

From the information given, a simple Group Organizer could be constructed as follows:

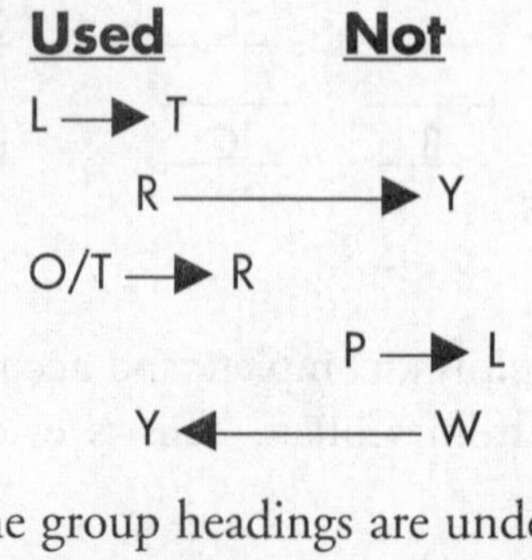

Notice that the group headings are underlined and that the arrows are pointing in one direction. "If–then" statements should be represented by arrows pointing from the "if" to the "then."

Now let's take a closer look at the following conditions and their contrapositives. Read each pair of statements carefully to make sure you understand the reasoning involved. Keep in mind that the contrapositive of an if–then statement is true.

"If lavender is used, then so is tan." Therefore, if tan is not used, then lavender is not used.

"If red is used, then yellow is not used." Therefore, if yellow is used, then red is not used.

"If orange, tan, or both are used, then so is red." Therefore, if red is not used, then neither orange nor tan is used.

"If pink is not used, then neither is lavender." Therefore, if lavender is used, then pink is used.

"If white is not used, then yellow is used." Therefore, if yellow is not used, then white is used.

Don't let additional information confuse you. A careful look at the reasoning involved should help you understand the following explanations. It should also give you some insight into this type of problem set.

Using this chart or display should make answering the questions much easier.

Question 1

If lavender is used, what is the least number of colors that can be used?

(A) 2
(B) 3
(C) 4
(D) 5
(E) 6

ANALYSIS

The correct answer is (D). If L is used, then so is T. If T is used, then so is R. If R is used, then Y is not. If Y is not used, then W is used. Since L is used, so must P be. Therefore, Y cannot be used, and O doesn't have to be used. Five is the correct answer. The following summarizes the results.

Used	**Not**
L	Y
T	O?
R	
W	
P	

Question 2

If tan is not used, which one of the following must be true?

(A) Pink is not used.
(B) Either lavender or red is used.
(C) Orange and red are the only two colors used.
(D) Either white or yellow or both are used.
(E) Both red and yellow are used.

ANALYSIS

The correct answer is (D). If T is not used, then neither is L. Since L is not used, P may or may not be used; therefore, answer (A) is incorrect. Since R may or may not be used, answer (B) is incorrect. Since R does not have to be used, answers (C) and (E) are incorrect. It is not possible for both W and Y not to be used; therefore, answer (D) is correct.

	Used		Not
			T
			L
		P?	
		R?	
Either	Y		W
or	W		Y
or	W, Y		

Question 3

Which one of the following sets of colors CANNOT be a complete set of colors used?

(A) orange, pink, red, and white
(B) yellow only
(C) lavender, red, tan, and white
(D) red and white
(E) pink, red, tan, and white

ANALYSIS

The correct answer is (C). Only answer choice (C) fails to meet the conditions. If P were not used, then L would not be used. Since L is used, so must P. All the other choices are possible.

Question 4

If exactly two colors are used, which of the following CANNOT be those two colors?

(A) red and white
(B) pink and white
(C) white and yellow
(D) orange and red
(E) pink and yellow

ANALYSIS

The correct answer is (D). If R is used, then Y is not used. If Y is not used, then W must be used. Therefore, if R is used, then so must W, and choice (D) is only O and R.

Question 5

If white is not used, then which one of the following must be true?

(A) Tan must be used.
(B) Pink must be used.
(C) Pink cannot be used.
(D) Yellow must be used.
(E) Yellow cannot be used.

ANALYSIS

The correct answer is (D). If W is not used, then Y must be used. T can't be used because then R would have to be used, and then Y couldn't be used (eliminate A). Eliminate choices (B) and (C) since either *could* be true. Choice (E) cannot be true since Y must be used.

The Group Organizer (Venn diagrams/grouping arrows)

Another type of less commonly used Group Organizer is Venn diagrams/grouping arrows (also mentioned in Chapter 2: Logical Reasoning). This type of diagram can be useful when information is given that shows relationships between sets or groups of sets. Keep in mind that:

1. Venn diagrams should be used only in *very simple situations* involving small numbers of items.
2. Grouping arrows seem to be *more effective and simpler* to work with, especially in complex situations.

Some very basic Venn diagrams and grouping arrows look like this:

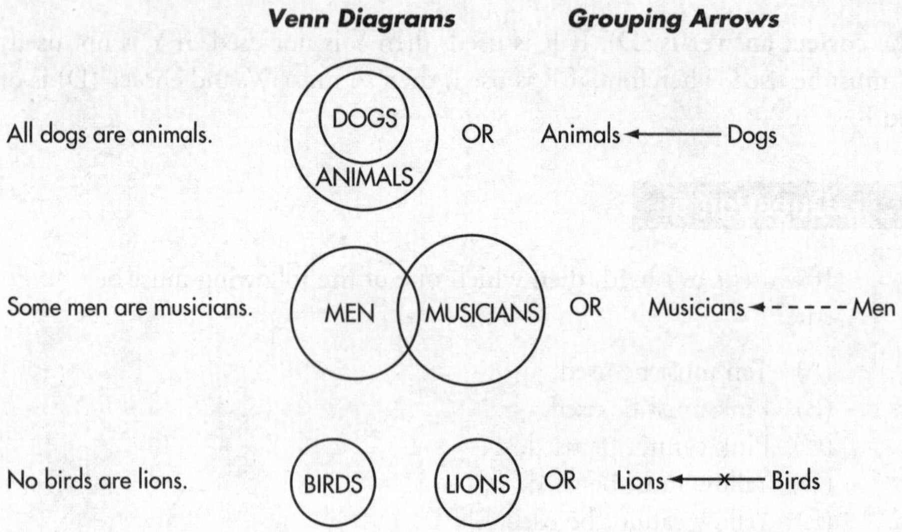

In diagramming more than two groups, you may find it helpful to draw the most general or largest category before drawing any of the others.

EXAMPLE

A pharmacist has labeled certain pills—A, B, C, D, and E—by the categories they fall into. Some of the categories overlap as follows:

(1) All As are Bs.
(2) All Bs are Cs.
(3) Some, but not all, Ds are As.
(4) All Ds are Bs.
(5) No Es are Cs.

ANALYSIS—THE SETUP

From statement 1, we may draw a Venn diagram or grouping arrows as follows:

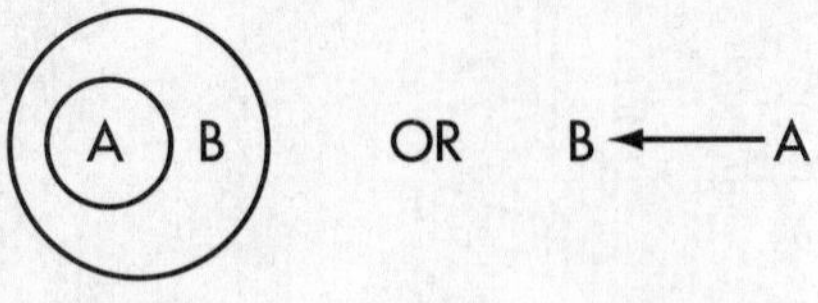

From statement 2, our diagrams or grouping arrows grow to look like this:

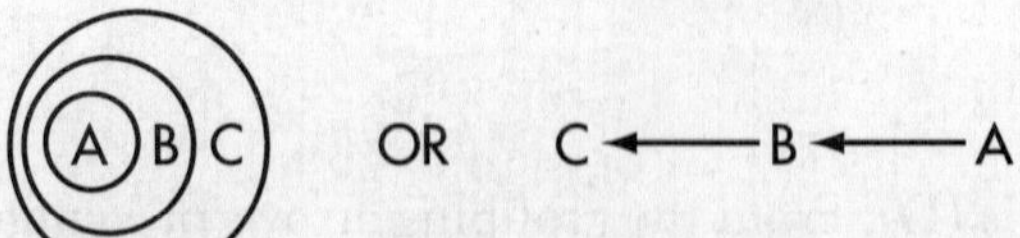

Now statements 3 and 4 add another circle in the Venn diagram (note that we need the fourth statement in order to "contain" the D circle within the B circle) or another element to the grouping arrows as follows:

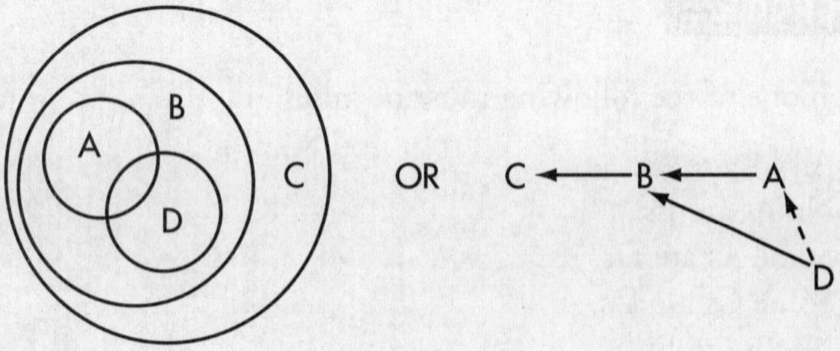

And, finally, from statement 5 we get:

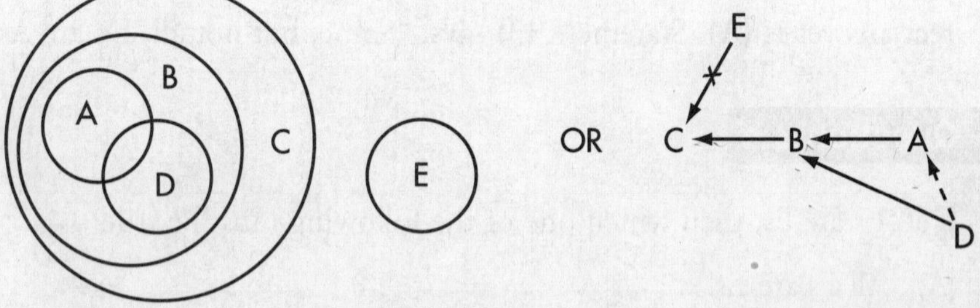

Now it will be relatively simple to answer the questions simply by referring to our final Venn ciagram or grouping arrows.

Remember that Venn diagrams can become unwieldy, while grouping arrows are usually much simpler to display and easier to use.

Question 1

Which one of the following must be true?

(A) All Cs are As.
(B) Some Es are Bs.
(C) All As are Ds.
(D) No Bs are Es.
(E) Some Es are As.

ANALYSIS

The correct answer is (D). From the grouping arrows or Venn diagram, you can see that Bs and Es do not connect, so "No Bs are Es" must be true. Notice that (A) is false, all As are Cs, but not all Cs are As. Choice (B) is false because the Es are separate from the Bs. Choice (C) could be true but doesn't have to be true. Choice (E) is false—since no Bs are Es, no Es are Bs.

Question 2

Which one of the following must be false?

(A) All Ds are As.
(B) No As are Es.
(C) Some As are Ds.
(D) Some Cs are Ds.
(E) No Bs are Es.

ANALYSIS

The correct answer is (A). Statement (3) says, "Some, but not all, Ds are As."

Question 3

If all Es are Fs, then which one of the following must be true?

(A) All Fs are Es.
(B) Some Fs are Es.
(C) All As are Fs.
(D) Some Bs are Fs.
(E) No Fs are Cs.

ANALYSIS

The correct answer is (B). Note that this problem requires us to add another circle to our Venn diagram as follows:

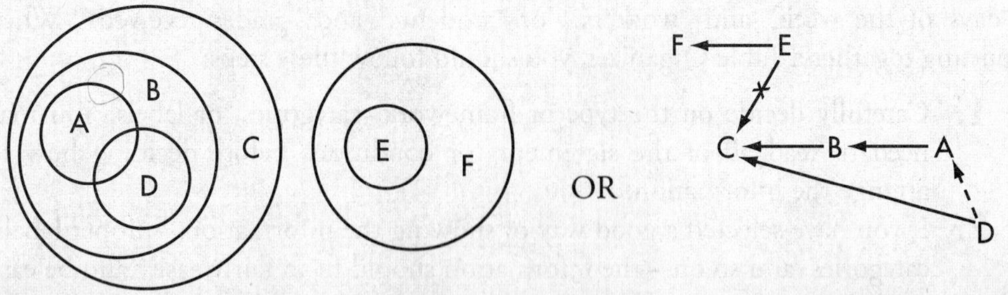

(Note that Fs must contain at least Es but could possibly also contain other circles.)

Question 4

If some Gs are As, then which one of the following must be true?

(A) Some Gs are Ds.
(B) All Ds are Gs.
(C) All Bs are Gs.
(D) Some Es are Gs.
(E) Some Gs are Cs.

ANALYSIS

The correct answer is (E). This problem, too, requires us to add to our original Venn diagram. If some Gs are As, our Venn diagram must *at least* contain some Gs in the A circle (x notes the location of some Gs):

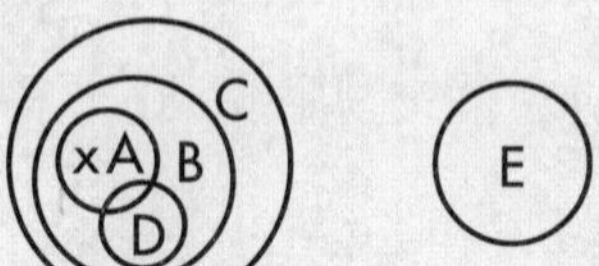

but it *could* also look like this:

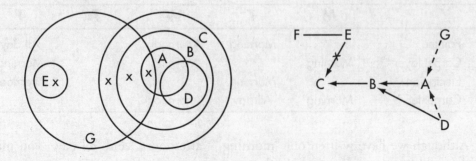

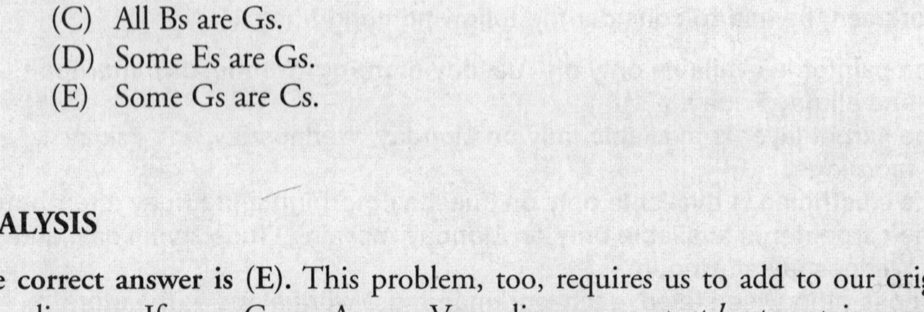

The Table Organizer (Information Table)

The Table Organizer is helpful for spotting information and making deductions quickly. This is a problem set that sets up in a row-and-column format. In this way, you can have categories in the rows and columns at the same time—for example, "days of the week" and "workers," or "students" and "grades received." When putting together a Table Organizer, you should follow these steps:

STUDY TIP

About 8–12 percent of the displays are a form of the Table Organizer (Information Table).

1. Carefully decide on the type of framework, categories, or labels. You may need to read all of the statements or conditions before deciding how to arrange the information.
2. If you have selected a good way of showing the information—proper labels, categories, and so on—the information should fit in fairly easily and be easy to understand and interpret.
3. Be sure to note variable positions or possibilities in your information chart (for example, Bob can work on Mondays or Tuesdays).

EXAMPLE

In order to open a new furniture store the following week, Mr. Worble hired a painter, a carpet layer, an electrician, and a carpenter. In scheduling the workmen, he had to consider the following conditions:

The painter is available only on Tuesday morning, Wednesday afternoon, and all day Friday.
The carpet layer is available only on Monday, Wednesday, and Friday mornings.
The electrician is available only on Tuesday morning and Friday afternoon.
The carpenter is available only on Monday morning, Tuesday all day, and Wednesday afternoon.
Unless otherwise stated, each workman must work alone in the store.
Unless otherwise stated, each workman is able to complete his own job in half a day.

ANALYSIS—THE SETUP

An information chart is suggested whenever you are trying to determine the points at which two sets of facts coincide. In this case, we chart the daily schedule of each worker, simply following the explicit information given.

	M	*T*	*W*	*T*	*F*
Painter		Morning	Afternoon		All day
Carpet layer	Morning		Morning		Morning
Electrician		Morning			Afternoon
Carpenter	Morning	All day	Afternoon		

Although we have written out "morning," "afternoon," and "all day," you may wish to abbreviate such terms. Another possible chart might look like this:

	Mon.	Tues.	Wed.	Thurs.	Fri.
A.M.	CL C	P E	CL		CL P
P.M.		C	P C		P C

Question 1

If the carpenter and the electrician must work on the same day to coordinate their efforts, but cannot work at the same time, who of the following will NOT be able to start work until Wednesday, at the earliest?

(A) painter
(B) carpet layer
(C) electrician
(D) carpenter
(E) carpet layer and electrician

ANALYSIS

The correct answer is (A). The carpet layer may work on Monday, and the carpenter and the electrician *must* work Tuesday (the only day they are available together). In this case, the painter (A) may not begin until Wednesday.

Question 2

If the painter needs the whole day on Friday to complete his job, the

(A) carpenter must work on Thursday
(B) electrician and carpet layer must work on the same day
(C) total job cannot be completed in one week
(D) electrician must work on Tuesday
(E) carpet layer and carpenter must work on the same day

ANALYSIS

The correct answer is (D). The electrician *must* work Tuesday, because his only other working day, Friday, interferes with the painter's work.

Question 3

Mr. Worble is expecting a supply of furniture on Thursday morning. Which one of the following must be true?

(A) The carpenter will be the only one finished before the merchandise arrives.
(B) Before the merchandise arrives, the painter will be finished, but the electrician will have to work Wednesday night.
(C) The carpet layer, the carpenter, and the electrician will be the only ones finished before the merchandise arrives.
(D) The carpet layer will have to work on the Tuesday before the merchandise arrives.
(E) All of the workers could have their jobs completed before the merchandise arrives.

ANALYSIS

The correct answer is (E). One possible plan is this: The carpet layer works Monday morning, the electrician works Tuesday morning, the carpenter works Tuesday afternoon, and the painter works Wednesday afternoon.

Question 4

If the store must be closed Monday and Tuesday and no worker may enter on those days, then, for all the work to be completed by the end of the week,

(A) the carpet layer must work Friday morning
(B) the painter must work Friday morning
(C) the painter must work Wednesday afternoon
(D) the painter must work Friday afternoon
(E) the carpet layer must work Friday afternoon

ANALYSIS

The correct answer is (B). If the store must be closed on Monday and Tuesday, then the carpenter must work Wednesday afternoon, and the electrician must work Friday afternoon, as these workers have no other available days to work. Since the painter cannot work Wednesday afternoon (the carpenter is already working then), he must work Friday morning. This leaves the carpet layer Wednesday morning to complete his work.

Question 5

If the store must be painted before any of the other work may begin, then, for all the work to be completed, all the following are true EXCEPT:

(A) the carpenter may work Tuesday or Wednesday afternoon
(B) the electrician must work Friday afternoon
(C) the carpet layer must work Wednesday or Friday morning
(D) the electrician and the carpet layer may work the same day
(E) the painter and the electrician may work the same day

ANALYSIS

The correct answer is (E). If the store must be painted first, then the painter could do his work Tuesday morning. All of the choices then are true, except (E). The painter and electrician may not work the same day, because if it's Tuesday, then they both would work in the morning, which is not allowed. The only other day they could both work is Friday, but that wouldn't allow all the work to be completed if the painter first works Friday morning.

The Table Organizer (Elimination Grid)

This type of chart will assist you in eliminating many possibilities, thus narrowing your answer choices and simplifying the reasoning process. To set up an elimination grid you should:

1. Decide on the column and row headings.
2. Mark X's in squares or situations that are not possible. You may use Y's and N's for yes and no.
3. Place check marks or fill in squares or situations that are possible.
4. Fill in any items that you can deduce or "eliminate" with the grid (for example, if Ann receives an A, she cannot receive a B, C, or D).

EXAMPLE

Two boys (Tom and Sal) and two girls (Lisa and Molly) each receive a different one of four passing grades (A,B,C,D) on an exam. The following information is known:

(1) Both boys receive lower grades than Lisa.
(2) Sal did not get a B.
(3) Tom got a B.
(4) Molly did not get an A.

ANALYSIS—THE SETUP

Although a chart is not necessary to answer question 1, you could have constructed the following using the information given in the statements:

First, since both boys received lower grades than Lisa, we know that Lisa could not have gotten the C or D, and that neither of the boys could have gotten the A. Thus, your chart will look like this:

	A	B	C	D
Tom	X			
Sal	X			
Lisa			X	X
Molly				

From statements 2 and 3, we can fill in that Tom received the B (and thus the others didn't):

	A	B	C	D
Tom	X	✓	X	X
Sal	X	X		
Lisa		X	X	X
Molly		X		

Statement 4 allows us to indicate on our chart that Molly didn't get an A. Thus, we can see from our chart that Lisa *must* have gotten the A:

	A	B	C	D
Tom	X	✓	X	X
Sal	X	X		
Lisa		X	X	X
Molly	X	X		

Notice that we could have deduced that even without statement 4, as there was no other grade Lisa could possibly have received.

Now we know that Lisa received the A and that Tom received the B. But we cannot deduce Sal's or Molly's grade. Be aware that, on many problems like this, you will have to proceed to the questions with an incomplete chart.

Question 1

Which statement(s) may be deduced from only one of the other statements?

(A) statement 1
(B) statement 2
(C) statement 3
(D) statement 4
(E) statements 1 and 3

ANALYSIS

The correct answer is (B). Statement 2 may be deduced from statement 3. If Tom got the B, it must be true that Sal did not get the B.

Question 2

If Molly received the lowest grade, then Sal must have received

(A) the A
(B) the B
(C) the C
(D) the D
(E) either the A or the B

ANALYSIS

The correct answer is (C). Using the chart, if Molly received the lowest grade (D), then Sal must have gotten the C. Note that by elimination on the grid, the only possibilities for Sal and Molly were Cs and Ds.

Question 3

Which one of the following is a complete and accurate list of the grades that Sal could have received?

(A) A
(B) A, C
(C) B, D
(D) C, D
(E) B, C, D

ANALYSIS

The correct answer is (D). From our chart we can easily see that Sal could have received either the C or the D.

Question 4

Which one of the following is a complete and accurate list of the grades that Molly could NOT have received?

(A) A
(B) B
(C) B, C
(D) C, D
(E) A, B

ANALYSIS

The correct answer is (E). From our chart we can easily see that Molly could not have received either the A or the B. We could also have determined this from statements 3 and 4.

Question 5

If Sal received the D, then Molly received

(A) the A
(B) the B
(C) the C
(D) the D
(E) either the A or the D

ANALYSIS

The correct answer is (C). From our chart we can easily see that, if Sal received the D, then Molly must have received the C.

Question 6

If the grades that Sal and Lisa received were reversed, then which one of the original statements would no longer be true?

(A) statement 1
(B) statement 2
(C) statement 3
(D) statement 4
(E) statements 2 and 3

ANALYSIS

The correct answer is (A). If Sal and Lisa reversed their grades, then

Sal would get the A.
Tom would get the B.
Lisa would receive either the C or the D.
Molly would receive either the C or the D.

Therefore, only statement 1 ("Both boys receive lower grades than Lisa") would no longer be true.

EXAMPLE

The Intermediate League board of directors is composed of exactly four members—Beals, Dunphy, Franks, and Mellon. Beals and Dunphy are the senior directors, whereas Franks and Mellon are the new directors. At the off-season meeting, the directors must consider three proposed changes to the league rules. The changes to be voted on are these: fee increases, fewer players on a team, and a longer season. The following conditions apply:

Each proposed change must have three votes to pass.
None of the changes has a unanimous vote, either for or against.
Exactly three directors vote for the fee increases.
Both of the senior directors vote against fewer players on a team.
Both new directors vote against a longer season.
Beals and Mellon vote for fee increases.

ANALYSIS—THE SETUP

In setting up this chart, you should list the directors across the top and the proposed changes along the side (or vice versa). Mark the senior directors and the new directors.

	Senior		New	
	B	D	F	M
Fees				
Players				
Season				

Next, quickly fill in as much information as possible. Use Y for "for" and N for "against."

	Senior		New	
	B	D	F	M
3 for Fees	Y			Y
Players	N	N		
Season			N	N

Since "None of the changes has a unanimous vote," you can add the following notations to the chart:

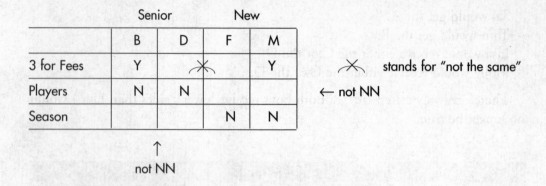

	Senior		New	
	B	D	F	M
3 for Fees	Y	✕ (D, F)		Y
Players	N	N		
Season			N	N

✕ stands for "not the same"

← not NN (Players)

↑ not NN (D)

Question 1

Which one of the following statements could be true?

(A) One director votes for all the changes.
(B) One director votes against all the changes.
(C) Two directors vote for all the changes.
(D) Two directors vote against all the changes.
(E) Three directors vote against all the changes.

ANALYSIS

The correct answer is (B). Notice that you are looking for what "could be true." Using the chart, you can quickly eliminate (A) and (C), since each director votes against at least one change. (D) and (E) can be eliminated, since there are three votes for the fee increase. Either Franks or Dunphy could vote against all the changes, but not both. So only one director could vote against all the changes.

Question 2

Which one of the following statements must be true?

(A) The fee increase change does not pass.
(B) The fewer-players change passes.
(C) The longer-season change and the fewer-players change pass.
(D) The fee-increase change and the longer-season change pass.
(E) The fee-increase change passes.

ANALYSIS

The correct answer is (E). Using the chart, since the fewer-players change and the longer-season change each have at least two against votes, then neither of them could pass. The only change that passes is the fee-increases change, since one of the conditions stipulates that there are exactly three votes for that change.

Question 3

If Dunphy votes for the fee increase and against the longer season, then which one of the following must be true?

(A) Beals votes for the longer season.
(B) Franks votes for the fee increase.
(C) Mellon votes for fewer players.
(D) Franks votes against all the changes.
(E) Mellon votes for all the changes.

ANALYSIS

The correct answer is (A). Filling in the Dunphy votes and using some reasoning gives the following chart:

	Senior		New		
	B	D	F	M	
3 for Fees	Y	Y	N	Y	
Players	N	N			← not NN
Season	Y	N	N	N	

Since Dunphy votes for fee increases, Franks must vote against fee increases. Since Dunphy votes against a longer season, Beals must vote for a longer season.

Question 4

If the new directors vote the same on only one change, and the senior directors vote the same on only two changes, then which one of the following must vote for a longer season?

(A) Beals
(B) Dunphy
(C) Franks
(D) Mellon
(E) Beals or Dunphy

ANALYSIS

The correct answer is (E). If the new directors vote the same on only one change, it must be the longer season, so they must vote differently on fewer players and fee increases. Since Mellon votes for fee increases, Franks must vote against fee increases. Since three directors must vote for fee increases, Dunphy must vote for them. Since the senior directors vote the same on only two changes, they must vote differently on the longer season. So either Beals or Dunphy must vote for a longer season. The following shows how the chart is completed:

	Senior		New	
	B	D	F	M
3 for Fees	Y	Y	N	Y
Players	N	N		
Season			N	N

← YN or NY (Players row)

↑ YN or NY (Senior columns)

Question 5

Which one of the following is a complete and accurate list of directors who could possibly vote for a longer season?

(A) Beals
(B) Dunphy
(C) Beals, Dunphy
(D) Beals, Franks
(E) Beals, Dunphy, Mellon

ANALYSIS

The correct answer is (C). Using the chart, you can see that only Beals or Dunphy could possibly vote for a longer season. Choices A and B are accurate but not complete.

	Senior		New	
	B	D	F	M
3 for Fees	Y			Y
Players	N	N		
Season			N	N

← not NN (Players row)

↑ not NN (Senior columns)

Question 6

Which one of the following is a possible vote outcome on the fee increase?

(A)	Beals: for	Dunphy: for	Franks: for	Mellon: for
(B)	Beals: for	Dunphy: for	Franks: for	Mellon: against
(C)	Beals: for	Dunphy: against	Franks: against	Mellon: for
(D)	Beals: for	Dunphy: for	Franks: against	Mellon: for
(E)	Beals: against	Dunphy: for	Franks: for	Mellon: for

ANALYSIS

The correct answer is (D). Using the chart, you can easily eliminate choices (A), can't pass unanimously; (B), Mellon is against; (C), need three votes for; and (E), Beals is for.

The Spatial Organizer

The spatial organizer is used when a problem set describes the relative positions of different items to each other. These items with relative positions may simply have connections between them or overlapping areas. When putting together a spatial organizer, you should follow these steps:

1. Look for key words to tip off the type of "simple map" you should be drawing.
2. As you place the objects, islands, cities, and so on, watch for relative positions.
3. Placements of items will sometimes be relative to a central location or other placements.
4. In some instances, you may be placing houses, cities, objects, or people in general areas, limited areas, or zones—north, south, east, west, northeast, southwest, and so on.
5. Sometimes the items will be placed directly north (due north), directly southeast, and so on.
6. Watch for limited areas or zones rather than exact locations. This takes careful reading, reasoning, and placement.
7. Place question marks next to items that are movable (that is, not stuck in one spot).
8. If appropriate, mark connections from one item to the next.
9. If appropriate, mark overlapping areas.
10. Watch for items, areas, or connections that have special restrictions—e.g., a connecting bridge that only goes in one direction, an island that can only be visited once, or a route that only goes to certain places.

EXAMPLE

LSAT Airlines flies to and from exactly eight cities—A, B, C, D, E, F, G, and H—using exactly five flight paths—1, 2, 3, 4, and 5. The flight paths are described as follows:

Flight Path 1: Connects Cities A and C with its only stop in City G
Flight Path 2: Connects Cities A and H with its only stop in City F
Flight Path 3: Connects Cities D and H with its only stop in City B
Flight Path 4: Connects Cities A and E with its only stop in City D
Flight Path 5: Connects Cities D and G with its only stop in City F

A direct connection is a flight between two cities that does not require a stop. An indirect connection is a flight between two cities that requires at least one stop.

ANALYSIS—THE SETUP

From the flight path descriptions, the following diagrams can be drawn:

Flight Path 1:	A – G – C
Flight Path 2:	A – F – H
Flight Path 3:	D – B – H
Flight Path 4:	A – D – E
Flight Path 5:	G – F – D

Combining these diagrams gives the following complete map:

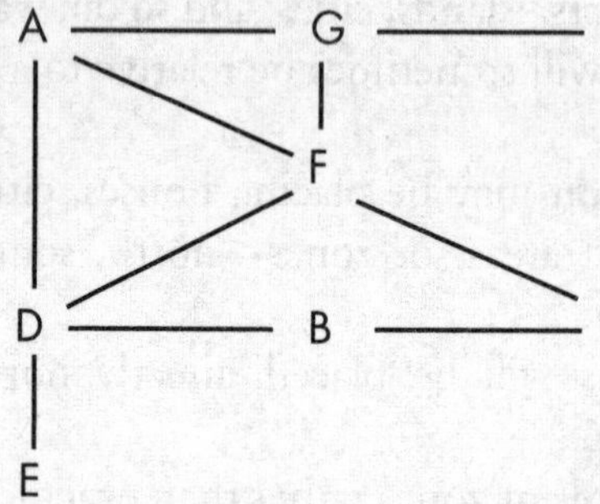

Combine diagrams whenever possible to get a complete picture of what you have to work with and the relative positions of each item.

Question 1

Without stopping in City A, what is the fewest number of stops necessary to travel between Cities C and E?

(A) 1
(B) 2
(C) 3
(D) 4
(E) 5

ANALYSIS

The correct answer is (C). Notice that you are looking for the fewest number of stops necessary, *without stopping at City A.* By carefully following the map, you can see that to get from City C to City E requires at least three stops—Cities G, F, and D.

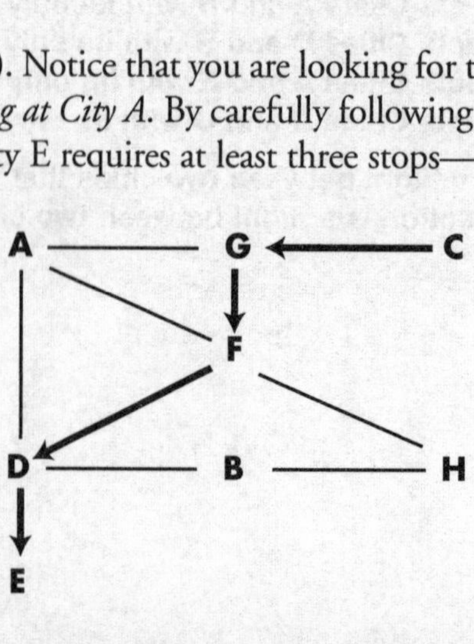

Question 2

Which one of the following cities is directly connected to the most number of cities?

(A) City A
(B) City B
(C) City C
(D) City D
(E) City E

ANALYSIS

The correct answer is (D). Make sure that you underline "directly connected to the most." From the original completed map, you can see that City D is directly connected to four other cities. City A is directly connected to three other cities. City B is directly connected to two other cities. Cities C and E are directly connected to only one other city.

Question 3

Using only Flight Paths 2, 4, and 5, which of the following is a complete and accurate list of the other cities that can be reached from City A by taking an indirect connection and making exactly one stop?

(A) D, F
(B) E, G, H
(C) C, D, F, H
(D) B, C, E, G, H
(E) D, E, F, G, H

ANALYSIS

The correct answer is (E). Using only Flight Paths 2, 4, and 5 gives the following map:

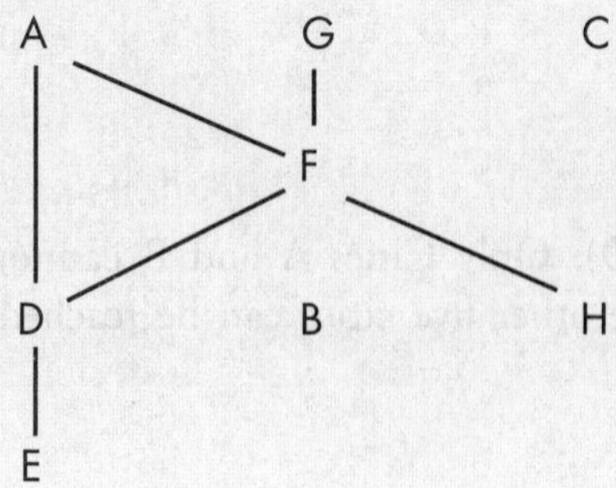

Starting from City A:

City D can be reached by making one stop at City F.
City E can be reached by making one stop at City D.
City F can be reached by making one stop at City D.
City G can be reached by making one stop at City F.
City H can be reached by making one stop at City F.

Question 4

Which one of the following is a complete and accurate list of the flight paths that must be used to travel from City C to City H?

(A) 1
(B) 1, 2
(C) 1, 2, 3, 4
(D) 1, 3, 4
(E) 2, 3

ANALYSIS

The correct answer is (A). From the original completed map, you can see that only Flight Path 1 must be used. Flight Paths 2, 3, and 4 could be used, but they do not have to be used. Flight Path 1 must be used, since it is the only flight path that flies to City C.

Question 5

How many other cities can be reached from City F after using an indirect connection and making exactly two stops?

(A) 2
(B) 3
(C) 4
(D) 5
(E) 6

ANALYSIS

The correct answer is (D). Only Cities A and B **cannot** be reached by making exactly two stops. So, the other five cities can be reached by making exactly two stops.

Question 6

If no city is stopped at more than once, then which one of the following is a possible order of cities stopped at when traveling from City G to City E?

(A) H, F, A, D, B
(B) F, C, H, B, D
(C) A, F, D, A, D
(D) A, F, H, B, D
(E) F, A, H, B, D

ANALYSIS

The correct answer is (D). Since the question is asking for a "possible" order, using the original map you could eliminate choices that are **not** possible as follows:

Eliminate (A) because Cities G and H do not connect directly.
Eliminate (B) because Cities F and C do not connect directly.
Eliminate (C) because Cities A and D are stopped at more than once.
Eliminate (E) because Cities A and H do not connect directly.

Question 7

If the airline adds a new flight path, Flight Path 6, connecting Cities C and E and stops only at City H, then which one of the following must be true?

(A) City H can only be reached by exactly two direct connections.
(B) City E can only be reached by exactly two direct connections.
(C) City H cannot be reached by an indirect connection.
(D) City G cannot be reached by an indirect connection.
(E) City C can only be reached by exactly one direct connection.

ANALYSIS

The correct answer is (B). First, add the new information and redraw the map as follows:

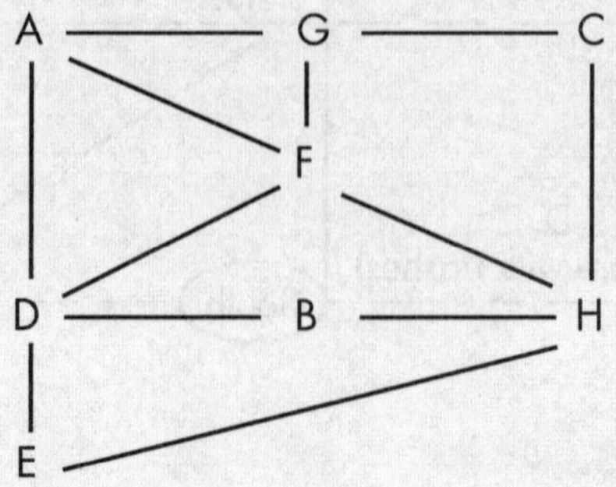

Now using this new map, review each of the choices.

Eliminate (A) because City H can be reached by three direct connections.

(B) is correct because City E is directly connected to Cities D and H.

You could stop here and mark your answer.

(C) could be eliminated because City H can be reached by many indirect connections (for example, A to F to H, or D to B to H).

(D) could be eliminated because City G can be reached by many indirect connections (for example, A to F to G, or D to F to G).

(E) could be eliminated because City C can be reached by two direct connections, one from City H, and one from City G.

EXAMPLE

Six cabins—A, B, C, D, E, and F—were constructed on a small flat area in the mountains. The focal point of the area was a statue that was constructed years before the cabins were constructed. The cabins are positioned as follows:

Cabin A is directly north of the statue.
Cabin C is directly west of the statue.
Cabin D is south of Cabin C.
Cabin E is west of Cabin A.
The statue is directly southeast of Cabin B and directly northwest of Cabin F.

ANALYSIS—THE SETUP

From the information given, a simple display may be constructed as follows (possible ranges are denoted with arrows):

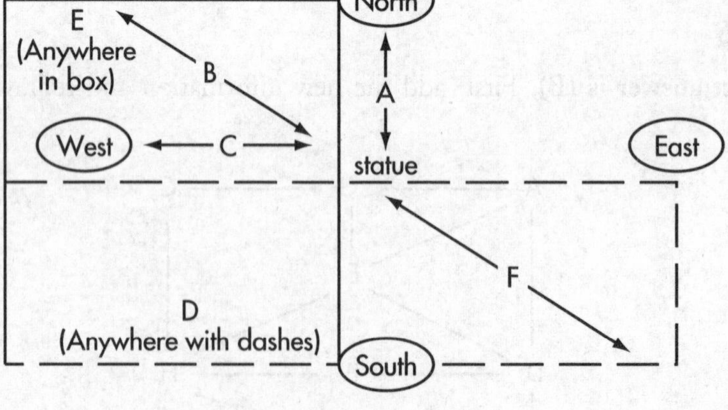

Or an even simpler map (if you can remember the zones) is possible:

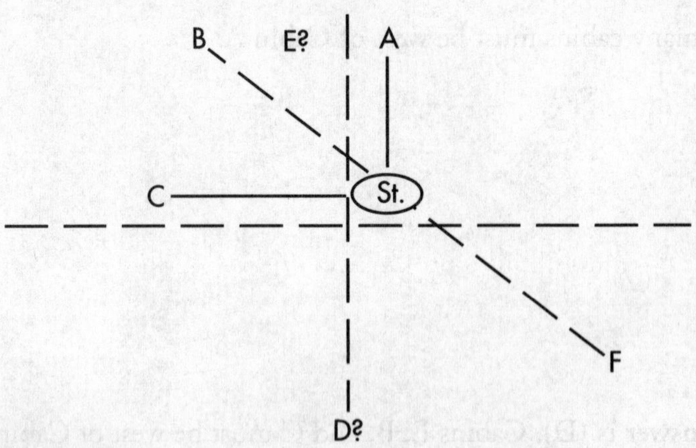

Question 1

Which one of the following must be true?

(A) Cabin B is east of Cabin C.
(B) Cabin B is west of Cabin C.
(C) Cabin F is west of Cabin E.
(D) Cabin D is south of Cabin B.
(E) Cabin D is east of Cabin A.

ANALYSIS

The correct answer is (D). Statements (A), (B), and (E) *could* be true but do not necessarily have to be true. (C) is false. Only (D) must be true.

Question 2

Which one of the following must be false?

(A) Cabin A is north of Cabin E.
(B) Cabin C is east of Cabin E.
(C) Cabin B is south of Cabin F.
(D) Cabin D is north of Cabin F.
(E) Cabin D is east of Cabin E.

ANALYSIS

The correct answer is (C). Choices (A), (B), (D), and (E) *could* be true, but (C) *must* be false.

Question 3

How many cabins must be west of Cabin A?

(A) 0
(B) 1
(C) 2
(D) 3
(E) 4

ANALYSIS

The correct answer is (D). Cabins E, B, and C must be west of Cabin A. Cabin D does not have to be west of Cabin A.

Question 4

What is the maximum number of cabins you could encounter traveling directly east from Cabin C?

(A) 0
(B) 1
(C) 2
(D) 3
(E) 4

ANALYSIS

The correct answer is (B). Traveling directly east from Cabin C, you could encounter Cabin E.

Question 5

If another cabin, Cabin G, is constructed directly north of Cabin F, then all of the following must be true EXCEPT:

(A) Cabin A is west of Cabin G
(B) Cabin G is east of Cabin C
(C) Cabin D is south of Cabin G
(D) Cabin G is east of Cabin A
(E) Cabin B is west of Cabin G

ANALYSIS

The correct answer is (C). Adding Cabin G to the display results in:

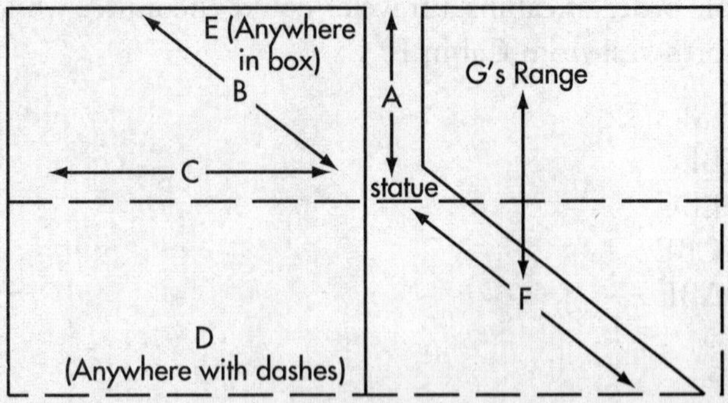

Statements (A), (B), (D), and (E) must be true. Statement (C) could be true but does not necessarily have to be true.

Question 6

If Cabins H and J are constructed so that Cabin H is directly east of Cabin J, and Cabin H is directly north of Cabin A, then which one of the following must be true?

(A) Cabin H is north of Cabin B.
(B) Cabin C is west of Cabin J.
(C) Cabin H is south of Cabin D.
(D) Cabin E is south of Cabin H.
(E) Cabin F is east of Cabin J.

ANALYSIS

The correct answer is (E). Adding Cabins H and J to the chart results in:

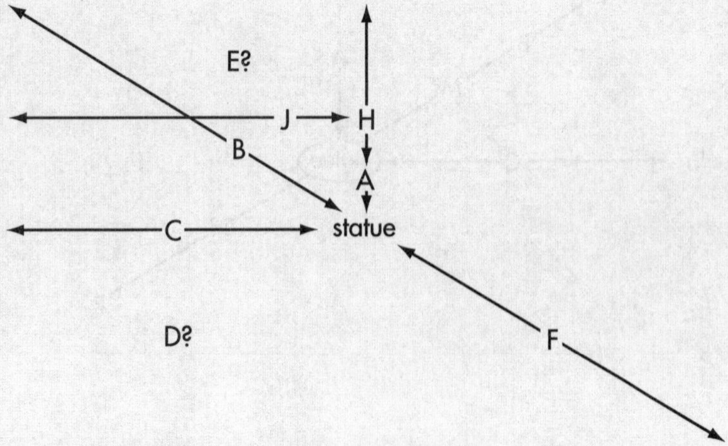

From the display, Cabin F must be east of Cabin J. Choices (A), (B), and (D) could be true but do not necessarily have to be true. Choice (C) must be false.

Question 7

If Cabin M is constructed west of Cabin A, which one of the following is a possible order of cabins a traveler could encounter while traveling directly northwest from Cabin F?

(A) BEDM
(B) DMBE
(C) MDEBC
(D) DMCBE
(E) MDABE

ANALYSIS

The correct answer is (B). Adding Cabin M to the display results in:

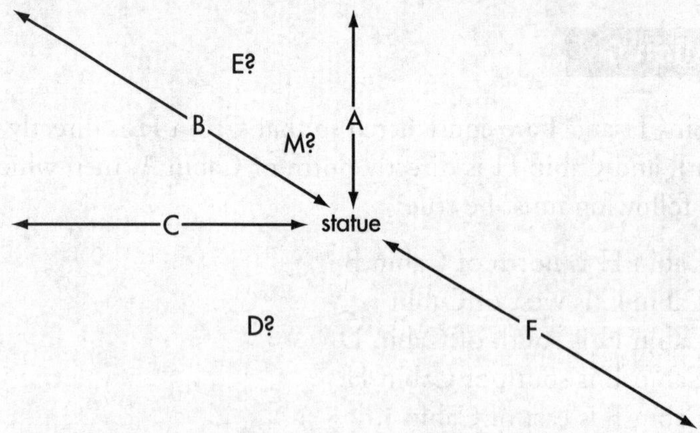

From the display, you could possibly encounter DMBE while traveling northwest from F.

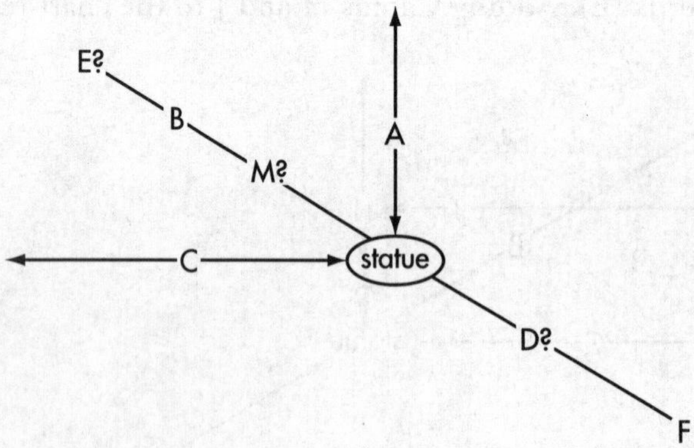

EXAMPLE

Five school playground aides—Alice, Bert, Carrie, Diego, and Emma—are each given one circular area to supervise. Because some of the areas are used more often than others, they overlap as follows:

Alice's area overlaps part of Bert's area.
Bert's area overlaps part of Emma's area.
Emma's area overlaps part of Alice's area.
Part of Alice's and Bert's overlapping area is also overlapped by part of Emma's area.
Carrie's area overlaps part of Bert's area but no one else's area.
Diego's area overlaps part of Emma's area but no one else's area.

The playground aides must follow these rules:

An aide may only treat a student who is injured in that aide's area.
No more than two aides may ever treat an injured student.
An injured student may not be taken out of the aide's area.

ANALYSIS—THE SETUP

From the information given, you should have made a display similar to this:

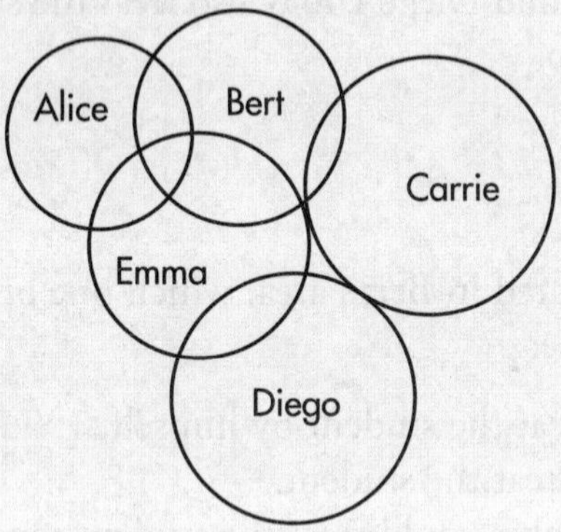

Check the overlaps carefully.

Question 1

Which one of the following must be true?

(A) Alice and Carrie could treat an injured student together.
(B) Bert and Diego could treat an injured student together.
(C) Emma could treat an injured student with Carrie.
(D) Alice and Bert could treat an injured student together.
(E) Diego and Alice could treat an injured student together.

ANALYSIS

The correct answer is (D). Since Alice and Bert's areas overlap, Alice and Bert could treat an injured student together. You could have eliminated each of the other choices because they don't overlap.

Question 2

If a student is injured in Emma's area, which one of the following is a complete and accurate list of the aids who could possibly treat the student?

(A) Emma
(B) Alice, Bert
(C) Alice, Bert, Emma
(D) Bert, Diego, Emma
(E) Alice, Bert, Diego, Emma

ANALYSIS

The correct answer is (E). Since Emma's area is overlapped by Alice, Bert, and Diego's areas, Alice, Bert, and Diego could also treat the student if the student happened to be in the overlap.

Question 3

If a student is injured in Bert's area, which one of the following CANNOT be true?

(A) Bert must treat the student by himself.
(B) Alice could treat the student.
(C) Alice and Emma could treat the student together.
(D) Diego may not treat the student.
(E) Carrie could treat the student.

ANALYSIS

The correct answer is (A). Since Bert's area is overlapped by other areas, Bert wouldn't have to treat the student by himself.

Question 4

If a student is injured in Bert's area, how many different possible combinations of one or two aides could treat the student?

(A) 3
(B) 4
(C) 5
(D) 7
(E) 8

ANALYSIS

The correct answer is (E). The possibilities are: (1) Bert; (2) Alice; (3) Emma; (4) Carrie; (5) Bert and Alice; (6) Bert and Emma; (7) Bert and Carrie; and (8) Alice and Emma.

Question 5

If another school playground aide, Frank, is hired and assigned to supervise part of the areas supervised by Bert, Carrie, Diego, and Emma, then which one of the following must be true?

(A) Frank supervises all of Diego's area.
(B) Most of Emma's area is supervised by Frank.
(C) Part of Alice's area could be supervised by Frank.
(D) None of Alice's area is supervised by Frank.
(E) More of Bert's area is supervised by Frank than any other aide's area.

ANALYSIS

The correct answer is (C). Part of Alice's area could be supervised by Frank because the display could look like this:

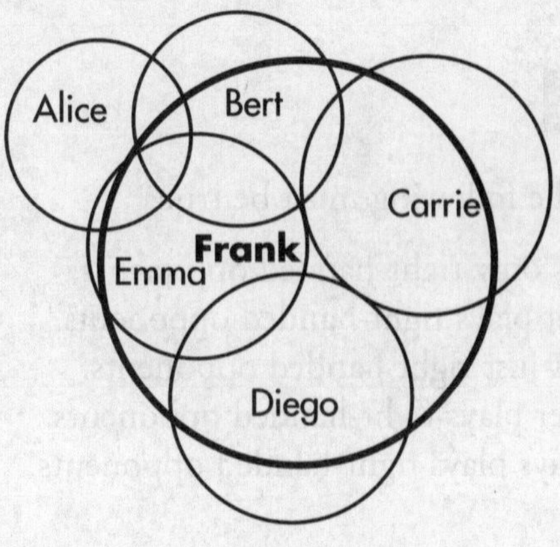

The General Organizer (Simply pulling out information)

In most cases, you will be able to construct some sort of organized display, but on a rare occasion no chart or diagram will appear to fit the situation. If this is the case, then:

1. Simply pull out or note whatever information seems important to you.
2. Mark any relationships between the items you have pulled out.
3. Go on to the questions.

EXAMPLE

Tongo is a sport similar to racquetball, except in each game three players oppose each other. Sandy, Arnie, and Betsy are the only entrants in a tongo tournament. Sandy is a left-handed tongo player, while Arnie and Betsy are right-handed tongo players. The players must compete in the tournament according to the following rules:

The winner of each game receives 5 points; the second-place finisher gets 3 points; and the third-place finisher gets 1 point.
There are no tie games.
The one player with the most game points at the end of the tournament is the grand winner.
If, at the end of the tournament, two or more players have the same total number of points, there will be a playoff.

ANALYSIS—THE SETUP

You probably found that this set of conditions was not conducive to constructing any standard chart. As soon as this was evident, you should have simply pulled out information as follows:

L—Sandy	**1st—5 pts.**
R—Arnie	**2nd—3 pts.**
R—Betsy	**3rd—1 pt.**

Question 1

Which one of the following must be true?

(A) Betsy plays only right-handed opponents.
(B) Arnie never plays right-handed opponents.
(C) Arnie plays just right-handed opponents.
(D) Sandy never plays right-handed opponents.
(E) Sandy always plays right-handed opponents.

ANALYSIS

The correct answer is (E). Since Sandy is the only left-handed player, then she must play only right-handed opponents.

Question 2

If, after three games, both right-handed players have each scored 9 points, which one of the following could be true?

(A) One of the right-handed players finished first twice.
(B) At least one of the right-handed players finished second three times.
(C) Both right-handed players each finished first, second, and third.
(D) The left-handed player finished first twice.
(E) The left-handed player was ahead after three games.

ANALYSIS

The correct answer is (C). Only (C) may be true. (A) is blatantly false, since two first-place wins would result in 10 points. (B) is incorrect because, if one player finished second in all three games, then there is no way a second player could score exactly 9 points in three games. (D) and (E) are incorrect since there must be 27 points scored during the three games with each player scoring 9 points.

Question 3

Which one of the following must be true?

(A) A player with no first-place game points cannot win the tournament.
(B) A player with only second-place game points can win the tournament.
(C) A player with no first-place game points can win the tournament.
(D) A player with no third-place game points must win the tournament.
(E) A player with no second-place game points cannot come in second.

ANALYSIS

The correct answer is (A). Only (A) is true. With no first-place game points, the most a player could score per game is 3 points. The best that that player could hope for would be that the other two players would split first place and third place on all the games. But even then, the other two players would average 3 points per game. At best, a playoff would be necessary, and the player without a first-place finish would thus lose the tournament. (D) and (E) are false by example.

Question 4

If, after three games, Arnie has 11 points, Betsy has 9 points, and Sandy has 7 points, which one of the following must be false?

(A) After four games, there is a three-way tie.
(B) After four games, Betsy is alone in first place.
(C) After four games, Betsy is alone in third place.
(D) After four games, Sandy is alone in first place.
(E) After four games, Sandy is alone in third place.

ANALYSIS

The correct answer is (D). The only statement that could not be true is (D). Since the most Sandy could score after four games would be 12 points, Betsy and/or Arnie will at least tie her for first place.

Question 5

If, just before the last game, it is discovered that the left-handed player has finished first in every even-numbered game, then

(A) Sandy must win the tournament
(B) Sandy cannot win the tournament
(C) Arnie may win the tournament
(D) Betsy can't win the tournament
(E) Betsy must win the tournament

ANALYSIS

The correct answer is (C). Even though Sandy may have scored 5 points in every even-numbered game, she will not necessarily win the tournament. For instance, if Arnie scores 5 points in every odd-numbered game, and if the tournament consists of an odd number of games, then Arnie will win the tournament. Sandy *can* win the tournament, but not necessarily *must* win the tournament. Betsy, also, could win the tournament if she scores first-place wins in every odd-numbered game.

The General Organizer with Diagram Provided

EXAMPLE

A puzzle in a local newspaper gave a series of numerals in the following four four-letter sequences:

A B C D
D E H G
F B A K
H C F J

The rules for answering questions about the puzzle are as follows:

Each row represents a sequence, and some sequences could be the same.
Any letter that occurs in more than one sequence represents the same numeral in each of those sequences.
The numerals 6, 7, 8, and 9 are each represented once in each of the four sequences—no other numerals are represented.
The first letter of any sequence can represent only 6 or 7.
The last letter of any sequence cannot be 6.

ANALYSIS—THE SETUP

Since the display is already given, you should simply pull out information from the conditions and mark in or make notes as follows:

```
6/7    6̸
 A B C D     6, 7, 8, 9
 D E H G
 F B A K
 H C F J
```

You may have deduced some additional information from the conditions given. If you haven't, read a few questions to get a sense of what you need to know.

Question 1

What numeral is represented by A?

(A) 6
(B) 7
(C) 8
(D) 9
(E) 6 or 7

ANALYSIS

The correct answer is (A). This particular question is asking you something that you should have been able to deduce from the initial conditions. So, in this case, you can actually put your answer into the display. Otherwise, you cannot take information from one question and use it in another question.

Since A is in column 1, it must represent 6 or 7. Since D is in column 1, it must represent 6 or 7, but because D is in column 4, it cannot be 6. So, D is 7. Since A and D are in row 1, and D is 7, A must represent 6.

Your display should now look like this:

6/7			$\not{6}$	
A^6	B	C	D^7	6, 7, 8, 9
D^7	E	H	G	
F	B	A^6	K	
H	C	F	J	

Notice that if A is 6 in row 1, then it is also 6 in row 3. Since D is 7 in row 1, it is 7 in row 2. Notice that you could have also figured out the value for F at this point.

Question 2

What numeral is represented by D?

(A) 6
(B) 7
(C) 8
(D) 9
(E) 6 or 7

ANALYSIS

The correct answer is (B). Since D is in column 1, it must represent 6 or 7, but because D is in column 4, it cannot be 6. So, D must represent 7. You already knew this from finding A in the previous problem.

Question 3

Which one of the following is a possible order of the numerals for the last sequence?

(A) 6, 7, 8, 9
(B) 8, 6, 7, 9
(C) 7, 9, 6, 8
(D) 7, 8, 6, 9
(E) 6, 8, 7, 9

ANALYSIS

The correct answer is (E). From the display, since A is 6 (in row 3), F must represent 7. In the last row, if F is 7, H must be 6. The only sequences possible for HCFJ are 6, 8, 7, 9 or 6, 9, 7, 8.

Question 4

Which one of the following CANNOT be true?

(A) H represents 6.
(B) F represents 7.
(C) C represents 8.
(D) B represents 7.
(E) G represents 9.

ANALYSIS

The correct answer is (D). In row 1, since A is 6 and D is 7, B cannot be 7.

Question 5

If the additional rule is given that K represents 9, which one of the following must be true?

(A) G represents 8.
(B) E represents 8.
(C) B represents 8.
(D) J represents 9.
(E) F represents 9.

ANALYSIS

The correct answer is (C). Notice that in row 3, if K represents 9, A must be 6, and F must be 7. Then B represents 8.

IN CONCLUSION

You have just worked through some of the basic types of displays that you may encounter on the LSAT. Be aware that there are *many other possible displays and modifications of the displays presented.* In the following practice tests, as you work through some of the other possible displays, carefully review the explanations of each to assist you in understanding these other types.

Remember that the exact type of display you make is not of critical importance. What is important is that you can get the necessary information from your display, and that it is simple to understand. Do not spend a great deal of time trying to make an elaborate display; a simple one will usually serve the purpose.

An Alternative General Approach

Some students, regardless of how much they review, analyze, and practice, cannot seem to finish the Analytical Reasoning section. They simply cannot work fast enough or make displays or rough diagrams quickly enough to see relationships and maintain a high level of correct answers. If you find that you consistently have a problem getting to or into the fourth set, you may wish to try this alternative approach: Focus your time on only three of the four sets. That is, try to set up and do well on the three sets and the questions that follow, and simply guess at the questions to the remaining set. You can skip one of the four sets and still receive a good score. The idea is to significantly raise your percentage of correct answers on the questions you *are* attempting. Remember, this is an alternative approach that you may wish to try if you are having a real problem getting to all four sets and maintaining a good level of correct answers. In using this method, you may wish to decide which set of questions you are going to skip after you have read the conditions and realize that the set is going to be problematic and difficult to complete.

Answer Sheet

EXTRA PRACTICE: ANALYTICAL REASONING

1 Ⓐ Ⓑ Ⓒ Ⓓ Ⓔ	22 Ⓐ Ⓑ Ⓒ Ⓓ Ⓔ	43 Ⓐ Ⓑ Ⓒ Ⓓ Ⓔ	64 Ⓐ Ⓑ Ⓒ Ⓓ Ⓔ
2 Ⓐ Ⓑ Ⓒ Ⓓ Ⓔ	23 Ⓐ Ⓑ Ⓒ Ⓓ Ⓔ	44 Ⓐ Ⓑ Ⓒ Ⓓ Ⓔ	65 Ⓐ Ⓑ Ⓒ Ⓓ Ⓔ
3 Ⓐ Ⓑ Ⓒ Ⓓ Ⓔ	24 Ⓐ Ⓑ Ⓒ Ⓓ Ⓔ	45 Ⓐ Ⓑ Ⓒ Ⓓ Ⓔ	66 Ⓐ Ⓑ Ⓒ Ⓓ Ⓔ
4 Ⓐ Ⓑ Ⓒ Ⓓ Ⓔ	25 Ⓐ Ⓑ Ⓒ Ⓓ Ⓔ	46 Ⓐ Ⓑ Ⓒ Ⓓ Ⓔ	67 Ⓐ Ⓑ Ⓒ Ⓓ Ⓔ
5 Ⓐ Ⓑ Ⓒ Ⓓ Ⓔ	26 Ⓐ Ⓑ Ⓒ Ⓓ Ⓔ	47 Ⓐ Ⓑ Ⓒ Ⓓ Ⓔ	68 Ⓐ Ⓑ Ⓒ Ⓓ Ⓔ
6 Ⓐ Ⓑ Ⓒ Ⓓ Ⓔ	27 Ⓐ Ⓑ Ⓒ Ⓓ Ⓔ	48 Ⓐ Ⓑ Ⓒ Ⓓ Ⓔ	69 Ⓐ Ⓑ Ⓒ Ⓓ Ⓔ
7 Ⓐ Ⓑ Ⓒ Ⓓ Ⓔ	28 Ⓐ Ⓑ Ⓒ Ⓓ Ⓔ	49 Ⓐ Ⓑ Ⓒ Ⓓ Ⓔ	70 Ⓐ Ⓑ Ⓒ Ⓓ Ⓔ
8 Ⓐ Ⓑ Ⓒ Ⓓ Ⓔ	29 Ⓐ Ⓑ Ⓒ Ⓓ Ⓔ	50 Ⓐ Ⓑ Ⓒ Ⓓ Ⓔ	71 Ⓐ Ⓑ Ⓒ Ⓓ Ⓔ
9 Ⓐ Ⓑ Ⓒ Ⓓ Ⓔ	30 Ⓐ Ⓑ Ⓒ Ⓓ Ⓔ	51 Ⓐ Ⓑ Ⓒ Ⓓ Ⓔ	72 Ⓐ Ⓑ Ⓒ Ⓓ Ⓔ
10 Ⓐ Ⓑ Ⓒ Ⓓ Ⓔ	31 Ⓐ Ⓑ Ⓒ Ⓓ Ⓔ	52 Ⓐ Ⓑ Ⓒ Ⓓ Ⓔ	73 Ⓐ Ⓑ Ⓒ Ⓓ Ⓔ
11 Ⓐ Ⓑ Ⓒ Ⓓ Ⓔ	32 Ⓐ Ⓑ Ⓒ Ⓓ Ⓔ	53 Ⓐ Ⓑ Ⓒ Ⓓ Ⓔ	74 Ⓐ Ⓑ Ⓒ Ⓓ Ⓔ
12 Ⓐ Ⓑ Ⓒ Ⓓ Ⓔ	33 Ⓐ Ⓑ Ⓒ Ⓓ Ⓔ	54 Ⓐ Ⓑ Ⓒ Ⓓ Ⓔ	75 Ⓐ Ⓑ Ⓒ Ⓓ Ⓔ
13 Ⓐ Ⓑ Ⓒ Ⓓ Ⓔ	34 Ⓐ Ⓑ Ⓒ Ⓓ Ⓔ	65 Ⓐ Ⓑ Ⓒ Ⓓ Ⓔ	76 Ⓐ Ⓑ Ⓒ Ⓓ Ⓔ
14 Ⓐ Ⓑ Ⓒ Ⓓ Ⓔ	35 Ⓐ Ⓑ Ⓒ Ⓓ Ⓔ	56 Ⓐ Ⓑ Ⓒ Ⓓ Ⓔ	77 Ⓐ Ⓑ Ⓒ Ⓓ Ⓔ
15 Ⓐ Ⓑ Ⓒ Ⓓ Ⓔ	36 Ⓐ Ⓑ Ⓒ Ⓓ Ⓔ	57 Ⓐ Ⓑ Ⓒ Ⓓ Ⓔ	78 Ⓐ Ⓑ Ⓒ Ⓓ Ⓔ
16 Ⓐ Ⓑ Ⓒ Ⓓ Ⓔ	37 Ⓐ Ⓑ Ⓒ Ⓓ Ⓔ	58 Ⓐ Ⓑ Ⓒ Ⓓ Ⓔ	79 Ⓐ Ⓑ Ⓒ Ⓓ Ⓔ
17 Ⓐ Ⓑ Ⓒ Ⓓ Ⓔ	38 Ⓐ Ⓑ Ⓒ Ⓓ Ⓔ	59 Ⓐ Ⓑ Ⓒ Ⓓ Ⓔ	80 Ⓐ Ⓑ Ⓒ Ⓓ Ⓔ
18 Ⓐ Ⓑ Ⓒ Ⓓ Ⓔ	39 Ⓐ Ⓑ Ⓒ Ⓓ Ⓔ	60 Ⓐ Ⓑ Ⓒ Ⓓ Ⓔ	81 Ⓐ Ⓑ Ⓒ Ⓓ Ⓔ
19 Ⓐ Ⓑ Ⓒ Ⓓ Ⓔ	40 Ⓐ Ⓑ Ⓒ Ⓓ Ⓔ	61 Ⓐ Ⓑ Ⓒ Ⓓ Ⓔ	82 Ⓐ Ⓑ Ⓒ Ⓓ Ⓔ
20 Ⓐ Ⓑ Ⓒ Ⓓ Ⓔ	41 Ⓐ Ⓑ Ⓒ Ⓓ Ⓔ	62 Ⓐ Ⓑ Ⓒ Ⓓ Ⓔ	83 Ⓐ Ⓑ Ⓒ Ⓓ Ⓔ
21 Ⓐ Ⓑ Ⓒ Ⓓ Ⓔ	42 Ⓐ Ⓑ Ⓒ Ⓓ Ⓔ	63 Ⓐ Ⓑ Ⓒ Ⓓ Ⓔ	84 Ⓐ Ⓑ Ⓒ Ⓓ Ⓔ

Remove answer sheet by cutting on dotted line

Extra Practice: Analytical Reasoning

<u>Directions:</u> In this section you will be given a group of questions based on a specific set of conditions. Drawing a simple diagram may be helpful in answering some of the questions. You are to choose the best answer and mark the corresponding space on your answer sheet.

<u>Questions 1–4</u>

There are four books standing next to each other on a shelf. The books are in order from left to right. The colors of the books are red, yellow, blue, and orange, but the placement of these books has not been determined. The following is known about the placement of the books:

The red book is between the yellow and blue books.
The blue book is between the orange and red books.
The orange book is not fourth.

1. If the orange book could be fourth, then which one of the following can be deduced?

   (A) The red book is fourth.
   (B) The blue book is not third.
   (C) The red book is next to the orange book.
   (D) The blue book is next to the yellow book.
   (E) The yellow book is not second.

2. If a white book is added to the shelf, and the fourth book is not necessarily an orange book, then which one of the following is a possible order of the books?

   (A) yellow, red, orange, blue, white
   (B) white, yellow, blue, red, orange
   (C) yellow, red, blue, white, orange
   (D) orange, blue, red, yellow, white
   (E) blue, red, yellow, orange, white

3. Which one of the following pairs are next to each other on the shelf?

   (A) yellow and blue
   (B) blue and orange
   (C) yellow and orange
   (D) red and orange
   (E) No books are next to each other on the shelf.

4. If a green book were placed just to the left of the blue book, what position would it be in (counting from the left)?

 (A) first
 (B) second
 (C) third
 (D) fourth
 (E) fifth

Questions 5–13

A head counselor is choosing people to go on a hiking trip. The head counselor must choose from among 3 adult counselors (A, B, C) and 9 campers (boys D, E, F, G, H, and girls J, K, L, M).

At least two adult counselors must go on the hike.
Camper D will not go without friends E and F.
Campers J and L will not hike together.
Camper M will not hike with counselor C.
There can never be more boy campers than girl campers.

5. If camper D is chosen for the hike

 (A) camper L must be chosen
 (B) camper J cannot be chosen
 (C) camper L cannot be chosen
 (D) camper G cannot be chosen
 (E) camper H must be chosen

6. If camper K is NOT chosen for the hike

 (A) camper G cannot be chosen
 (B) camper H cannot be chosen
 (C) camper E cannot be chosen
 (D) camper D cannot be chosen
 (E) camper L cannot be chosen

7. If camper D is chosen for the hike, which one of the following CANNOT be true?

 (A) Camper H goes on the hike.
 (B) Camper K goes on the hike.
 (C) Counselor A goes on the hike.
 (D) Counselor B goes on the hike.
 (E) Camper M goes on the hike.

8. An acceptable combination of campers and counselors is

(A) A B C D E F J K M
(B) A B D E F J L M
(C) A B G H J K M
(D) A C D E F J K
(E) A C E F G K L M

9. If counselor A is NOT chosen for the hike, then

(A) camper D must be chosen
(B) camper D cannot be chosen
(C) camper J must be chosen
(D) camper L cannot be chosen
(E) camper F cannot be chosen

10. If counselor A is NOT chosen for the hike, then which one of the following must be true?

(A) If camper E is chosen, camper K must be chosen.
(B) If camper F is chosen, camper K must be chosen.
(C) Camper J cannot be chosen.
(D) Camper D cannot be chosen.
(E) If camper L is chosen, camper F must be chosen.

11. If camper D is chosen for the hike, which one of the following could represent the other hikers?

(A) A C E F J K M
(B) A B G H K M L
(C) A B E F J K M
(D) A B F G J K L
(E) A C E F G K L M

12. What is the largest number of hikers who can go on the hike?

(A) 5
(B) 6
(C) 7
(D) 8
(E) 9

13. Which one of the following must be true?

(A) Campers K and M never hike together.
(B) Campers E and G never hike together.
(C) Campers D and G never hike together.
(D) Campers J and M never hike together.
(E) Campers D and M never hike together.

Questions 14–19

There are exactly six people waiting in line to buy tickets for a play. The names of the six people are Alexis, Brady, Hal, Len, Phyllis, and Sandy, not necessarily in that order. Their placement in line is governed by the following set of conditions:

One person stands in each place in line, no people are side by side.
Alexis is in front of Brady with more than one person separating them.
Sandy is either the second, fourth, or sixth person in line.
Phyllis is in front of Hal with exactly one person separating them.

14. If Brady is the next person in line behind Phyllis, then who could be the fifth person in line?

(A) Alexis
(B) Hal
(C) Len
(D) Phyllis
(E) Sandy

15. If Len is the second person in line, then which one of the following must be true?

(A) Alexis is the first person in line.
(B) Brady is the sixth person in line.
(C) Hal is the sixth person in line.
(D) Phyllis is the fifth person in line.
(E) Sandy is the fourth person in line.

16. Which person CANNOT be the person immediately in front of Sandy?

(A) Alexis
(B) Brady
(C) Hal
(D) Len
(E) Phyllis

17. Which one of the following could be a list of the names of the people ordered from first in line to last in line?

(A) Len, Sandy, Alexis, Phyllis, Brady, Hal
(B) Phyllis, Alexis, Hal, Sandy, Brady, Len
(C) Alexis, Len, Sandy, Hal, Brady, Phyllis
(D) Phyllis, Hal, Alexis, Len, Brady, Sandy
(E) Brady, Sandy, Hal, Len, Phyllis, Alexis

18. If Sandy is the next person in line behind Phyllis, then who must be the third person in line?
    (A) Alexis
    (B) Brady
    (C) Len
    (D) Phyllis
    (E) Sandy

19. Which one of the following is NOT a true statement?
    (A) Alexis cannot be the third person in line.
    (B) If Phyllis is the second person in line, then there is only one possible order of the six people in line.
    (C) If Hal is the sixth person in line, then there is only one possible order of the six people in line.
    (D) If Phyllis is the first person in line, then Len may be either the fourth, fifth, or sixth person in line.
    (E) If Sandy is the sixth person in line, then Len must be either the second or fourth person in line.

<u>Questions 20–26</u>

The last names of six card players are: Axelrod, Benton, Carlton, Dexter, Elliott, and Fellows. Three of the card players are male, and three are female. The six card players have formed three teams of two players each, comprising one female and one male. In an upcoming tournament, each team will play in one of exactly three rounds; first (earliest), second, and third (latest). The following conditions will apply for team composition and round of play:

Elliott will not play in the first or third rounds.
Dexter will not play in a later round than Axelrod.
Fellows, who is female, will play in a later round than Carlton, who is male.

20. If Elliott is female, and Axelrod plays in an earlier round than Carlton, then which one of the following must be true?
    (A) Axelrod is male.
    (B) Benton is male.
    (C) Carlton plays in the third round.
    (D) Dexter is female.
    (E) Fellows plays in the second round.

21. If Fellows plays in round 2, then which one of the following players could play in the round immediately following Dexter's round and be the same gender as Dexter?

(A) Axelrod
(B) Benton
(C) Carlton
(D) Elliott
(E) Fellows

22. Which one of the following is a complete and accurate list of the players, any one of whom could be female and playing in round 3?

(A) Axelrod, Benton, Carlton, and Fellows
(B) Alexrod, Benton, Dexter, and Fellows
(C) Axelrod, Dexter, and Fellows
(D) Benton and Dexter
(E) Elliott and Fellows

23. If Fellows plays in round 2, then which of the following could be two of the three female players?

(A) Axelrod and Benton
(B) Axelrod and Carlton
(C) Benton and Carlton
(D) Benton and Elliott
(E) Carlton and Dexter

24. If Carlton is the same gender as Axelrod and plays in the round immediately following Axelrod's round, then which one of the following must be true?

(A) Benton plays in the first round.
(B) Benton is the same gender as Elliott.
(C) Benton is female.
(D) Dexter plays in the first round.
(E) Dexter is male.

25. Which one of the following could be an accurate list of the male and female players listed in the round in which they will play?

		Round 1	Round 2	Round 3
(A)	Male:	Benton	Axelrod	Carlton
	Female:	Dexter	Elliott	Fellows
(B)	Male:	Carlton	Dexter	Axelrod
	Female:	Elliott	Benton	Fellows
(C)	Male:	Carlton	Elliott	Dexter
	Female:	Axelrod	Fellows	Benton
(D)	Male:	Dexter	Carlton	Benton
	Female:	Axelrod	Elliott	Fellows
(E)	Male:	Dexter	Carlton	Fellows
	Female:	Benton	Elliott	Axelrod

26. If Benton and Dexter are on the same team, then which one of the following statements must be true?

(A) Axelrod and Carlton are on the same team.
(B) Axelrod and Fellows are on the same team.
(C) Carlton and Fellows are on the same team.
(D) Elliott is male.
(E) Fellows plays in a later round than Axelrod.

Questions 27–34

Four men, A, B, C, and D, and three women, E, F, and G, are auditioning for a new TV pilot. The director is deciding the order in which they should audition. Since many of the actors have other auditions to attend at different locations, the director must observe the following restrictions:

A must audition first or last.
D and E must audition consecutively, but not necessarily in that order.
Neither F nor G can audition last.
E cannot audition until B has auditioned.

27. Which one of the following must be true?

(A) F cannot audition first.
(B) D cannot audition first.
(C) B cannot audition first or second.
(D) A must audition before D auditions.
(E) G must audition second.

28. If A auditions first, which one of the following CANNOT be true?

(A) G auditions second.
(B) F auditions before B auditions.
(C) D auditions second.
(D) B auditions fifth.
(E) G auditions before B auditions.

29. If F and G audition first and second, respectively, then which one of the following must be false?

(A) C auditions fourth.
(B) B auditions fourth.
(C) E auditions sixth.
(D) D auditions fifth.
(E) B auditions fifth.

30. Assume that B auditions first and that F and G audition second and third, respectively. Which one of the following must be false?

(A) E auditions sixth.
(B) C auditions fifth.
(C) D auditions fourth.
(D) C auditions sixth.
(E) E auditions fifth.

31. Suppose that D auditions ahead of E. If A auditions first, and B auditions fifth, who must audition sixth?

(A) D
(B) E
(C) F
(D) G
(E) C

32. Which one of the following is a possible order of auditions?

(A) A, E, B, D, F, G, C
(B) A, B, D, E, C, F, G
(C) C, B, G, F, E, A, D
(D) B, F, G, D, E, C, A
(E) F, B, E, G, D, A, C

33. If the director decides NOT to audition two men consecutively, and if C auditions first, which one of the following must be true?

(A) F auditions second.
(B) G auditions second.
(C) E auditions fifth.
(D) D auditions fourth.
(E) B auditions third.

34. Assume that all the women must audition consecutively. If F auditions third, and G does NOT audition second, then which one of the following must be true?

(A) A auditions first.
(B) B auditions second.
(C) C auditions seventh.
(D) G auditions fifth.
(E) D auditions sixth.

Questions 35–40

Eight weight lifters, Aaron, Bryan, Clifford, David, Ellen, Jason, Logan, and Prescott, have joined a local gym. No two of these lifters lift the same weight. The following statements describe the relative strength of the lifters:

Ellen lifts more than Aaron.
Bryan lifts less than Logan but more than Prescott.
David lifts more than Logan.
Jason lifts less than Aaron but more than Clifford.
Logan lifts more than Jason.

35. Which one of the following statements must be true?

(A) David lifts more than Jason.
(B) Jason lifts more than Prescott.
(C) Ellen lifts more than Bryan.
(D) Clifford lifts more than Ellen.
(E) Bryan lifts more than David.

36. If Prescott lifts more than Aaron, then which one of the following must be true?

(A) Logan lifts more than Aaron.
(B) Aaron lifts more than Bryan.
(C) Ellen lifts more than Bryan.
(D) David lifts more than Ellen.
(E) Clifford lifts more than Logan.

37. If Aaron lifts more than David, what is the maximum number who can lift more than Logan?

(A) 0
(B) 1
(C) 2
(D) 3
(E) 4

38. If 5 people lift less than Logan, then which one of the following must be true?

(A) Bryan lifts more than Aaron.
(B) Prescott lifts more than Aaron.
(C) Clifford lifts more than Prescott.
(D) Jason lifts more than David.
(E) David lifts more than Aaron.

39. If Bryan lifts more than Aaron and Jason lifts more than Prescott, then who can lift more than Ellen?

(A) Prescott, Bryan, and Logan.
(B) David, Prescott, and Clifford.
(C) Logan, Bryan, and Prescott.
(D) David, Logan, and Jason.
(E) Logan, David, and Bryan.

40. If Prescott lifts more than Jason, then which one of the following must be false?

(A) Bryan lifts more than Aaron.
(B) Prescott lifts more than Ellen.
(C) Ellen lifts more than David.
(D) Aaron lifts more than Logan.
(E) Bryan lifts more than David.

Questions 41–46

There are nine cans of soft drinks lined up on a shelf. The cans are numbered from 1 to 9, from left to right.

The first and fourth are different brands of cola.
The sixth and eighth are different brands of root beer.
The second, fifth, sixth, seventh, and ninth are the only caffeine-free soft drinks.
The second, third, fifth, seventh, and ninth cans contain unflavored beverages.

41. How many of the cans contain unflavored beverages that contain caffeine?

(A) 0
(B) 1
(C) 2
(D) 3
(E) 4

42. In which one of the following places is a beverage that contains caffeine?

(A) second
(B) fourth
(C) fifth
(D) sixth
(E) ninth

43. Which place contains a caffeine-free beverage that is not unflavored?

(A) first
(B) third
(C) fourth
(D) sixth
(E) seventh

44. If the two root beers were replaced with two cans of orange flavored beverage containing caffeine, how many cans would contain either cola or caffeine but not both?

(A) 0
(B) 1
(C) 2
(D) 3
(E) 4

45. If someone randomly chose two cans of caffeine-free beverage, which places could they be?

(A) second and third
(B) fourth and fifth
(C) third and seventh
(D) sixth and ninth
(E) eighth and ninth

46. How many cans of flavored beverage are next to at least one can of caffeine-free beverage?

(A) 0
(B) 1
(C) 2
(D) 3
(E) 4

<u>Questions 47–50</u>

Eight people—A, B, C, D, E, F, G, and H—are to be seated at a square table, two people on each side.

B must sit directly across from H.
A must sit between and next to F and G.
C cannot sit next to F.

47. Which one of the following must be true?

(A) C sits next to either B or H.
(B) H must sit next to G.
(C) F sits next to D or E.
(D) A sits directly across from B.
(E) F sits directly across from C or D.

48. If B does not sit next to G, then which one of the following is NOT possible?

(A) If C sits next to B, then D could sit directly across from F.
(B) If C sits next to D, then E could sit directly across from G.
(C) C could sit next to G.
(D) If C sits next to H, then B could sit between D and E.
(E) If C sits next to B, then A could sit next to H.

49. If C sits directly across from F, who could NOT sit next to H?

(A) C
(B) D
(C) E
(D) G
(E) A

50. How many different people could be seated directly across from A?

(A) 1
(B) 2
(C) 3
(D) 4
(E) 5

Questions 51–57

Three division office managers, Fred, Al, and Cynthia, draw office assistants each day from the clerical and typing pools available to them. The clerical pool consists of Lyndia, Jim, Dennis, and Sylvia. The typing pool consists of Edra, Gene, and Helen. The office assistants are selected according to the following conditions:

Fred always needs at least one typist but never more than two assistants.
Al always needs at least two assistants but never more than three.
Sylvia or Gene and one other assistant always work for Cynthia.
Gene and Lyndia always work together.
Dennis and Edra will not work together.
No more than two typists work for the same manager, but all three typists must work each day.

51. If Gene works for Fred, and all of the assistants work, then which one of the following must be false?

(A) Jim works for Cynthia.
(B) Sylvia works for Cynthia.
(C) Lyndia works for Fred.
(D) Dennis works for Al.
(E) Edra works for Al.

52. If Sylvia doesn't work for Cynthia, then which one of the following must be true?

(A) Edra works for Fred.
(B) Gene works for Al.
(C) Lyndia works for Cynthia.
(D) Dennis works for Al.
(E) Helen works for Cynthia.

53. Assume that Lyndia and Jim work for Al. Which one of the following must be true?

(A) Gene works for Al.
(B) Edra works for Cynthia.
(C) Helen works for Fred.
(D) Edra works for Fred.
(E) Helen works for Cynthia.

54. Assume that Sylvia and Jim work for Al. If all of the assistants work, then which one of the following must be true?

(A) Edra works for Al.
(B) Gene works for Fred.
(C) Lyndia works for Al.
(D) Helen works for Fred.
(E) Dennis works for Fred.

55. Which one of the following must be false?

(A) Helen and Edra never work for Cynthia on the same day.
(B) Edra can work for Cynthia.
(C) Dennis and Gene never work for Fred on the same day.
(D) Jim and Sylvia never work for Fred on the same day.
(E) Lyndia and Sylvia can work for Al on the same day.

56. If Jim works for Cynthia, and all of the assistants work, then

(A) Dennis works for Al.
(B) Edra works for Al.
(C) Helen works for Al.
(D) Lyndia works for Al.
(E) Sylvia works for Fred.

57. Assume that Al needs only two assistants, and Fred needs only one assistant. If Helen works for Fred, then which one of the following must be true?

(A) Jim works for Al.
(B) Sylvia doesn't work.
(C) Dennis doesn't work.
(D) Edra works for Al.
(E) Edra works for Cynthia.

Questions 58–64

During a trip to a museum, Jilian and Mark each attend three historical lectures (D, E, and F) and three scientific lectures (R, S, and T). They do not attend the same lecture at the same time, although they both attend all six one-hour lectures. The lecture schedule must conform to the following conditions:

Mark must attend each scientific lecture prior to Jilian attending that same lecture.
Jilian must attend each historical lecture prior to Mark attending that same lecture.
Mark cannot attend two historical lectures consecutively.
Jilian must attend lecture T third.

58. Which one of the following could be true?

(A) Mark attends lecture R fourth.
(B) Mark attends lecture D fifth.
(C) Mark attends lecture E first.
(D) Jilian attends lecture T fifth.
(E) Jilian attends lecture F fourth.

59. If Jilian attends lecture E second, and Mark attends lecture D second, which one of the following must be true?

(A) Mark attends lecture E fourth.
(B) Jilian attends lecture F fourth.
(C) Mark attends lecture S fifth.
(D) Mark attends lecture F fourth.
(E) Jilian attends lecture R sixth.

60. Which one of the following is an acceptable lecture schedule ordered from 1st to 6th?

(A) Jilian: D, E, T, R, S, F
Mark: T, D, R, E, F, S
(B) Jilian: D, E, T, F, R, S
Mark: R, T, E, S, D, F
(C) Jilian: E, S, D, T, F, R
Mark: S, E, T, D, R, F
(D) Jilian: D, E, T, R, F, S
Mark: T, D, R, F, S, E
(E) Jilian: D, E, T, F, R, S
Mark: T, D, R, E, S, F

61. Which one of the following is a complete and accurate list of when Jilian must attend a historical lecture?

(A) first, second
(B) second, third
(C) first, second, fifth
(D) first, third, fourth
(E) first, fourth, fifth

62. If Mark attends lecture F fourth, and Jilian attends lecture D first, which one of the following CANNOT be true?

(A) Mark attends lecture R before lecture F.
(B) Jilian attends lecture E after lecture R.
(C) Lecture R is the fifth lecture attended by Jilian.
(D) Lecture E is the second lecture attended by Mark.
(E) Lecture D is the second lecture attended by Mark.

63. Which one of the following must be true?

(A) Mark must attend lecture S fifth.
(B) Jilian cannot attend lectures D and E consecutively.
(C) Mark must attend lecture T first.
(D) Jilian must attend lecture R before Mark attends lecture F.
(E) Mark attends lecture S sixth.

64. If Mark attends lecture R third, then Jilian must attend which lecture sixth?

(A) D
(B) E
(C) F
(D) R
(E) S

Questions 65–70

Kevin Kissalot, famous hairdresser to the stars, has scheduled eight one-hour appointments, one for each of his best customers: Arnie, Betah, Coco, Dodi, Elvis, Fetina, Greg, and Hector. Scheduling of appointments must conform to the following conditions:

Elvis is scheduled immediately before Dodi.
Fetina's appointment must be scheduled before Arnie's but after Greg's.
Fetina's appointment must be scheduled either 3rd or 7th.
Betah is scheduled 2nd only if Coco is scheduled 3rd or Arnie is scheduled 8th.

65. Which one of the following is an acceptable appointment schedule?

(A) B C G F E D A H
(B) E D B G C H F A
(C) H B C G E A F D
(D) H B F C G E D A
(E) G B F C E D A H

66. It would NOT be possible for Arnie to be scheduled

(A) 3rd
(B) 4th
(C) 5th
(D) 6th
(E) 7th

67. If Arnie is scheduled 6th, and Hector is scheduled after Dodi, which one of the following could be true?

(A) Greg is scheduled 5th.
(B) Hector is scheduled 2nd.
(C) Betah is scheduled 7th.
(D) Dodi is scheduled 2nd.
(E) Coco is scheduled 4th.

68. If Hector is scheduled 8th and Coco is scheduled 7th, which one of the following must be true?

(A) Betah is scheduled 1st.
(B) Dodi is scheduled 5th.
(C) Greg is scheduled 1st.
(D) Elvis is scheduled 6th.
(E) Arnie is scheduled 6th.

69. If Betah is scheduled 2nd, and Arnie is scheduled immediately after Coco, Hector could be scheduled

(A) 1st
(B) 3rd
(C) 4th
(D) 5th
(E) 7th

70. Which one of the following is NOT an acceptable schedule of appointments from 1st to 8th?

(A) G C F E D A B H
(B) H G F A B C E D
(C) B H C G E D F A
(D) G B F H A E D C
(E) H B C E D G F A

Questions 71–77

Teams A and B play a series of 9 games. To win the series, a team must win the most games but must also win a minimum of 3 games.

There are no ties in the first 3 games.
Team A wins more of the last 3 games than team B.
Team B wins more of the last 5 games than team A.
The last game is a tie.
Games 1 and 3 are won by the same team.

71. Which one of the following must be true?

(A) One team must win 5 games to win the series.
(B) There are no ties.
(C) One team wins at least 2 of the first 3 games.
(D) The same team wins the last 5 games.
(E) The last three games are won by one team.

72. Considering all of the conditions mentioned above, game 6

(A) could be won by team A
(B) could be won by team B
(C) could be a tie
(D) must be won by team A
(E) must be won by team B

73. If game 7 is won by team A, then

(A) game 8 is a tie
(B) game 2 is a tie
(C) game 4 is won by team A
(D) game 5 is a tie
(E) game 6 is won by team A

74. Which one of the following must be true?

(A) There is only 1 tie in the last 5 games.
(B) Team A wins 2 of the first 3 games.
(C) Team B can win 3 of the last 5 games.
(D) Game 4 is a tie.
(E) Team A can win only 1 of the last 5 games.

75. If team A wins game 1 and game 4, then which one of the following must be false?

(A) Team A wins game 3.
(B) Team A wins game 2.
(C) Team B wins game 2.
(D) Team A wins the series.
(E) Team B wins the series.

76. Assume that game 4 is won by the winner of game 5. If game 2 is not won by the winner of game 3, then which one of the following must be true?
    - (A) Team A wins game 7.
    - (B) Team B is the winner of the series.
    - (C) Team A wins game 2.
    - (D) Team B wins game 1.
    - (E) Team A wins game 3.

77. Which one of the following must be true?
    - (A) For team A to win the series, it must win exactly two of the first four games.
    - (B) For team B to win the series, it must win exactly one of the first four games.
    - (C) For team A to win the series, it must win only three of the first seven games.
    - (D) For team B to win the series, it must win at least three of the first four games.
    - (E) For team A to win the series, it must win two consecutive games.

<u>Questions 78–84</u>

The Raxmeyers have seven daughters, each born two years apart. Their ages are 7, 9, 11, 13, 15, 17, and 19. Their names are Hilda, Ida, Joy, Kim, Loren, Marsha, and Nicole. The following conditions must be met:

Joy is older than Marsha.
Hilda is older than Loren but younger than Ida.
Either Ida or Loren is 13 years old.
Nicole is younger than Joy.
The difference in ages between Marsha and Nicole is at least three years.

78. Which one of the following must be true?
    - (A) Hilda is the oldest.
    - (B) Kim is older than Joy.
    - (C) Hilda is younger than Joy.
    - (D) Ida is older than Loren.
    - (E) Marsha is older than Loren.

79. If Loren is 4 years younger than Ida, then which one of the following could be true?
    - (A) Marsha is 9 years old.
    - (B) Hilda is 17 years old.
    - (C) Joy is 15 years old.
    - (D) Hilda is 9 years old.
    - (E) Joy is 19 years old.

80. Which one of the following could be the order of the ages of the seven daughters from youngest to oldest?

(A) L, H, K, I, M, N, J
(B) M, H, N, L, J, I, K
(C) N, K, M, L, H, I, J
(D) M, L, N, H, I, J, K
(E) L, M, H, I, J, N, K

81. If Ida is older than Joy, then how many different possible orders are there for the ages of the seven daughters?

(A) three
(B) four
(C) five
(D) six
(E) seven

82. Which one of the following could be true?

(A) Kim is two years older than Hilda.
(B) Joy is two years younger than Marsha.
(C) Loren is two years younger than Kim.
(D) Joy is two years older than Hilda.
(E) Hilda is two years older than Kim.

83. All of the following could be true EXCEPT:

(A) If Loren is 13 years old, then Marsha is 7 years old.
(B) If Hilda is 15 years old, then Nicole is 7 years old.
(C) If Ida is 13 years old, then Kim is 7 years old.
(D) If Ida is 17 years old, then Kim is 9 years old.
(E) If Hilda is 11 years old, then Marsha is 7 years old.

84. If Kim is older than Joy, then Ida must be

(A) 9 years old
(B) 11 years old
(C) 13 years old
(D) 15 years old
(E) 17 years old

ANSWERS EXPLAINED

Answers 1–4

By following statements 1–3, you could have made these two possible orders:

Y R B O or O B R Y

but statement 4 eliminates the first order, Y R B O.

1. **(E)** From statements 2 and 3, the red and blue books are between other books; thus, they cannot be first or fourth and are second and third. This leaves the first and fourth positions for the orange and yellow books.

2. **(D)** Orange, blue, red, yellow, white is a possible order. Notice that each of the other orders could have been eliminated because each broke an initial statement:

   (A) Orange and blue are switched.
   (B) Blue and red are switched.
   (C) White must be on an end since the other four must be next to each other.
   (E) Blue cannot be on an end.

3. **(B)** This follows the order discovered from the initial conditions, YRBO.

4. **(B)** Because the blue book was in the second position, it will move to the third position, and the green book will take the second.

Answers 5–13

Drawing the simple diagram, below, will help answer the questions.

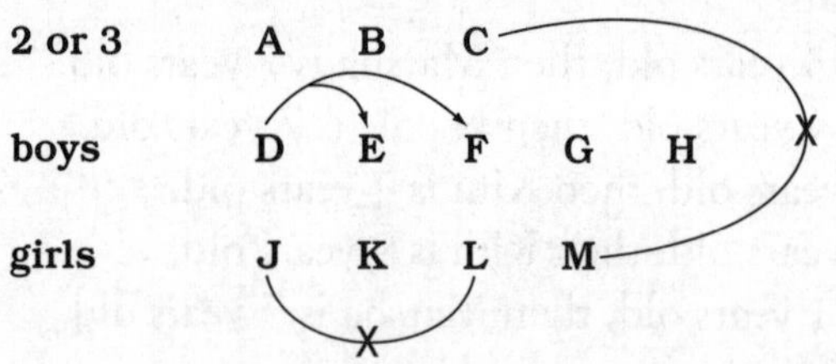

5. **(D)** If camper D is chosen, then campers E and F are also chosen. Thus, three boys have been picked to go on the hike. Note that three girls, at most, can go on the hike. Since boys cannot outnumber girls, no other boys can be chosen.

6. **(D)** If camper K is not chosen, the maximum number of girls chosen can be two. Therefore, since boys cannot outnumber girls, D cannot be chosen, since selecting D means also selecting two more boys, E and F.

7. **(A)** If camper D is chosen, then boys E and F are also chosen. Since the maximum number of girls chosen can be three, no other boys may be chosen, since boys may not outnumber girls.

8. **(C)** Choices (A) and (E) include both C and M, which is not permitted. Choice (B) includes J and L, who will not hike together. In choice (D), boys outnumber girls, which is not permitted. Only choice (C) is an acceptable combination of campers and counselors.

9. **(B)** If counselor A is not chosen for the hike, then counselors B and C are chosen, as there must be at least two counselors on the hike. Since counselor C is chosen, camper M (a girl) cannot be chosen. Therefore, the maximum number of girls on the hike can be two. Since boys cannot outnumber girls, D cannot be chosen, since selecting D would mean also selecting E and F, a total of three boys.

10. **(D)** If counselor A is not chosen, then counselors B and C will be chosen, as there must be at least two counselors on the hike. If counselor C is chosen, camper M cannot be chosen, leaving the maximum number of girls possible on the hike at two. Therefore, since boys may not outnumber girls, D cannot be chosen, as choosing D would mean also selecting E and F, thus outnumbering the girls.

11. **(C)** Choices (A) and (E) included both C and M, which is not permitted. Choices (B) and (D) do not include camper E, who must accompany camper D. Only choice (C) includes acceptable companions for a hike with camper D.

12. **(D)** The largest number of hikers who can go on the hike is eight, as follows: three boys, three girls, and counselors A and B. (Example: A, B, D, E, F, J, K, and M)

13. **(C)** The maximum number of girls possible for the hike is three. Therefore, since choosing camper D means also choosing campers E and F, no other boys (for instance, G) can be chosen, as boys would then outnumber girls.

Answers 14–19

The conditions are summarized as follows:

	1	A	P
S?	2	*	*
	3	* (2 or more)	H
S?	4	B	
	5		
S?	6		

14. **(B)** If Brady is behind Phyllis, then there are only two possible arrangements for Phyllis, Brady, and Hal.

1	Alexis	Alexis
2	Sandy	Sandy or Len
3	Len	Phyllis
4	Phyllis	Brady
5	Brady	Hal
6	Hal	Len or Sandy

The possible candidates for the fifth person in line are Brady and Hal. Since Brady is not one of the choices, it must be Hal.

15. **(A)** If Len is second, Alexis must be first. If Alexis were third, then Brady would be sixth, Phyllis and Hal would be second and fourth, and there would be no place for Sandy. Hal cannot be sixth because Phyllis would then be fourth, and there would be no place for Sandy. Phyllis cannot be fifth because there would be no place for Hal. The other choices MAY be true, but they do not have to be, as shown in the following arrangement.

1	Alexis
2	Len
3	Phyllis
4	Brady/Sandy
5	Hal
6	Sandy/Brady

16. **(D)** Sandy must be either second, fourth, or sixth. If Len were immediately in front of Sandy, there would not be enough spaces left to accommodate the other people properly as shown:

1	Len	*	Alexis
2	Sandy	*	*
3	Alexis	Len	*
4	*	Sandy	Brady
5	*	*	Len
6	Brady	*	Sandy

17. **(B)** (A) is not correct, since there must be at least two people between Alexis and Brady. (C) is not correct, since Phyllis must be in front of Hal, and Sandy cannot be third. (D) is not correct, since there must be one person between Phyllis and Hal. (E) is not correct, since Phyllis must be in front of Hal, and Alexis must be in front of Brady. (B) is a possible ordering of the people.

18. **(D)** If Sandy is the next person in line behind Phyllis, then Sandy is between Phyllis and Hal. This means Sandy cannot be sixth. Remember, Sandy must be second, fourth, or sixth. If Sandy were second, then Phyllis would be first and Hal would be third. This would result in only one person between Alexis and Brady. Therefore, Sandy must be fourth. This implies that Phyllis is the third person in line.

1	Alexis or Len
2	Len or Alexis
3	Phyllis
4	Sandy
5	Hal
6	Brady

19. (E) (A) is a true statement. If Alexis were third, then Brady would have to be sixth. Since Sandy must then be second or fourth, this leaves no room for Phyllis and Hal. (B) is a true statement. If Phyllis were second, Hal would be fourth, and Sandy would be sixth. Also, Alexis would have to be first, and Brady would have to be fifth. This implies that Len must be third. (C) is a true statement. If Hal were sixth, then Phyllis must be fourth. This implies that Sandy must be second. Then Alexis must be first and Brady fifth. This leaves Len third. (D) is a true statement. If Phyllis were first, then Hal would be third, and Alexis second. Len can be either fourth, fifth, or sixth. (E) is NOT a true statement. If Sandy were sixth, Len MAY be second or fourth, but Len COULD be third.

1	Alexis	Alexis	Phyllis	Alexis
2	Phyllis	Sandy	Alexis	Phyllis
3	Len	Len	Hal	Len
4	Hal	Phyllis	Len or Sandy or Sandy	Hal
5	Brady	Brady	Brady or Brady or Len	Brady
6	Sandy	Hal	Sandy or Len or Brady	Sandy

Answers 20–26

The conditions lead to the following:

"Fellows, who is female, will play in a later round than Carlton, who is male" can be illustrated as:

Male—C C ← F
Female—F

So, C can play in rounds 1 or 2, and F can play in rounds 2 or 3. But if C plays in 2, then F plays in 3.

"Dexter will not play in a later round than Axelrod" can be illustrated as:

← D
A

"Elliott will not play in the first or third rounds," so Elliott plays in round 2 and can be illustrated in the complete display as follows:

	~~F~~		~~C~~
	~~E~~	E	~~E~~
	1	2	3
Male	__	__	__
Female	__	__	__

Male—C C ← F
Female—F
← D
A

Notice that since Fellows plays in a later round than Carlton, Fellows cannot play in round 1, and Carlton cannot play in round 3.

20. **(B)** If Elliott is female and plays in the second round, then Fellows, who is female and plays in the second or third round, must play in the third round. If Fellows plays in the third round, then Carlton must play in the second round. If Axelrod plays in an earlier round than Carlton, then Axelrod and Dexter must play in the first round. Thus, Benton must be male and plays in the third round. Axelrod could be male, and Dexter could be female, or vice versa.

	1	2	3
Male:	A/D	C	B
Female:	D/A	E	F

21. **(E)** If Fellows, who is female, plays in the second round, then Elliott, who also plays in the second round, must be male. If Fellows plays in the second round, then Carlton, who plays in an earlier round than Fellows, must play in the first round. If someone follows Dexter, then Dexter cannot play in the third round. Therefore, Dexter must be female and play in the first round. Thus, Fellows is the same gender as Dexter and plays in the round immediately following Dexter.

	1	2	3
Male:	C	E	A/B
Female:	D	F	B/A

22. **(B)** The right answer cannot include Elliott, since Elliott plays in round 2. Eliminate (E). The right answer cannot include Carlton, because he is a male and cannot play in the third round. Eliminate (A). Each of the other players (Axelrod, Benton, Dexter, and Fellows) could be female and play in the third round as illustrated in the following four possible diagrams:

	1	2	3
Male:	C	E	B
Female:	D	F	**A**

	1	2	3
Male:	C	E	A
Female:	D	F	**B**

	1	2	3
Male:	C	E	A
Female:	B	F	**D**

	1	2	3
Male:	A	C	B
Female:	D	E	**F**

23. **(A)** The answer cannot be (B), (C), or (E), since Carlton is male. If Fellows, who is female, plays in round 2, then Elliott, who also plays in round 2, must be male. Therefore, (D) cannot be correct. Both Axelrod and Benton could be female.

24. **(D)** Carlton, who is male, can only play in rounds 1 or 2. If Axelrod is the same gender as Carlton and plays in a round preceding Carlton, then Axelrod is male and plays in round 1, with Carlton playing in round 2. Since Elliott plays in round 2, Elliott must be female. If Carlton is playing in round 2, then Fellows, who follows Carlton, is female and plays in round 3. If Axelrod plays in round 1, so must Dexter. Benton must then be male and playing in round three. (D) is the only accurate choice.

	1	2	3
Male:	A	C	B
Female:	D	E	F

25. **(D)** (A) is not correct, since Carlton must play in an earlier round than Fellows. (B) is not correct since Elliott plays in round 2. (C) is not correct, since Axelrod, playing in round 1, would imply that Dexter plays in round 1 also. (E) is not correct, since Fellows is female.

26. **(B)** If Benton and Dexter play on the same team, then they cannot play in the second round, since Elliott is playing in the second round. Benton and Dexter cannot play in the third round, since that would imply that Fellows must play in round 2, forcing Axelrod into round 1. If Axelrod plays in round 1, then so must Dexter. Therefore, Benton and Dexter must play in round 1. Carlton, who cannot play in round 3, must play in round 2. Thus, Elliott is female. Since Fellows must play in round 2 or 3, Fellows must play in round 3. Therefore Axelrod is male and plays in round 3. Thus, (B) is correct.

	1	2	3
Male:	B/D	C	A
Female:	D/B	E	F

Answers 27–34

From the information given, you could have constructed a diagram similar to this:

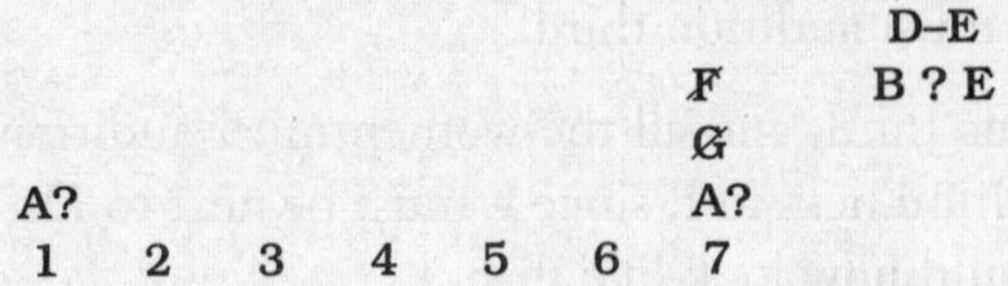

Notice the information listed off to the side of the diagram.

27. **(B)** D cannot audition first, since D and E have to audition consecutively, and B must audition before E.

28. **(C)** If A auditions first, then D cannot audition second because B must audition before E, and therefore also before D.

29. **(E)** If F and G audition first and second respectively, then A must audition last, and the diagram for this question would look like this:

F	G					A
1	2	3	4	5	6	7

Therefore, A must audition last, and B cannot audition fifth (no room for D and E to follow B). C could possibly audition fourth.

30. **(B)** If B auditions first, and F and G audition second and third, respectively, then A must audition last, and the diagram for this question would look like this:

B	F	G				A
1	2	3	4	5	6	7

Therefore, "E auditions sixth" could be true. "C auditions fifth" must be false because D and E must be next to each other. If C were fifth, he would split D and E. "D auditions fourth" could be true.

31. **(A)** If D auditions ahead of E, and if A auditions first and B fifth, then the diagram for this question would look like this:

A				B	D	E
1	2	3	4	5	6	7

Since B auditions fifth, then D must be sixth and E seventh.

32. **(D)** This question is most easily answered by eliminating the orders that are not possible. Choice (A) can be eliminated because E is ahead of B and not next to D. Choice (B) can be eliminated because G cannot audition last. Choices (C) and (A) can be eliminated because A is not first or last.

33. **(E)** From the new information given, men cannot audition consecutively; the diagram for this question would now look like this:

C		B		D		A
1	2	3	4	5	6	7

Therefore, B must audition third.

34. **(E)** If F auditions third, and all the women must audition consecutively, then G must audition next to F, since E must be next to D. The diagram for this question would now look like this:

		F	G	E	D	
1	2	3	4	5	6	7
	~~D~~					
	~~E~~					

Therefore, D must audition sixth.

Answers 35–40

The following diagram may prove helpful:

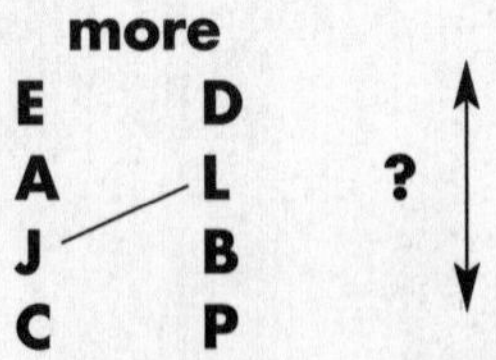

35. (A) Because David lifts more than Logan, and Logan lifts more than Jason, David lifts more than Jason. Prescott and Bryan lift less than Logan, but we cannot say anything about their relationship to Jason. It is possible for Prescott to lift more than Ellen.

36. (A) Logan lifts more than Prescott. If Prescott lifts more than Aaron, so must Logan.

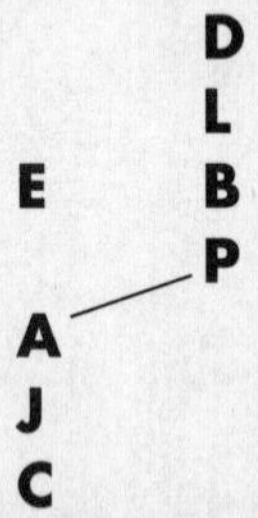

37. (D) If Aaron lifts more than David, then Aaron, Ellen, and David each lift more than Logan.

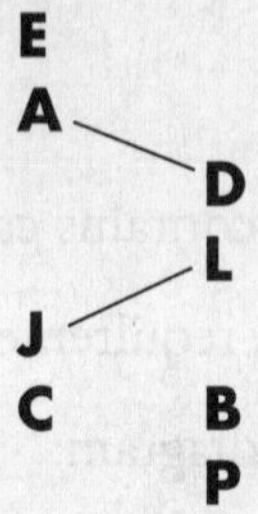

38. (E) If 5 people lift less than Logan, they must be Bryan, Prescott, Clifford, Jason, and Aaron. Thus, David and Ellen lift more than Logan, and David lifts more than Aaron. Answer (C) may be true but doesn't have to be.

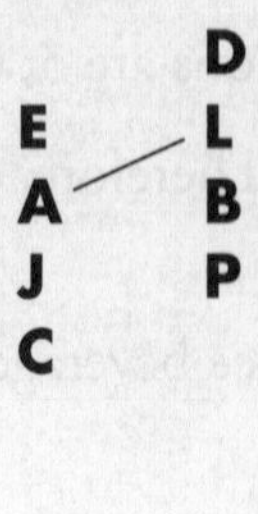

39. (E) Given these additional facts, we can redraw the diagram as follows:

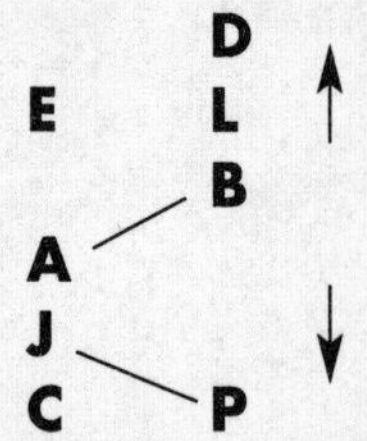

Thus, Logan, David, and Bryan can each lift more than Ellen.

40. (E) From the diagram, all of the following could be true:

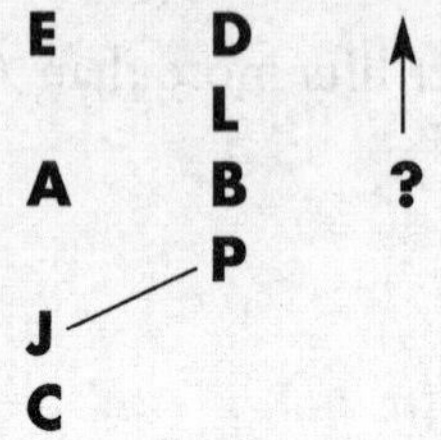

Answers 41–46

This diagram shows these relationships:

	CF			CF	CF	CF		CF
1	2	3	4	5	6	7	8	9
Cola			Cola		RB		RB	

41. (B) Can 3 is the only one.

42. (B) Of the cans listed, only the fourth place (can 4) contains caffeine.

43. (D) The sixth place (can 6) is the can that meets the requirements.

44. (D) For this question, you should use the following diagram:

	CF			CF		CF		CF
1	2	3	4	5	6	7	8	9
Cola			Cola		O		O	

After the replacement, the cans that meet the conditions are 3, 6, and 8.

45. (D) The five caffeine-free cans are 2, 5, 6, 7, and 9. Therefore, choice (D), the sixth and ninth places, is the only valid one.

46. (E) All four flavored beverages are next to caffeine-free beverages.

Answers 47–50

From the information given, it would be helpful to construct a diagram to answer the questions.

NOTE: When more than one letter appears at a seat, those letters represent all the possible occupants of that seat.

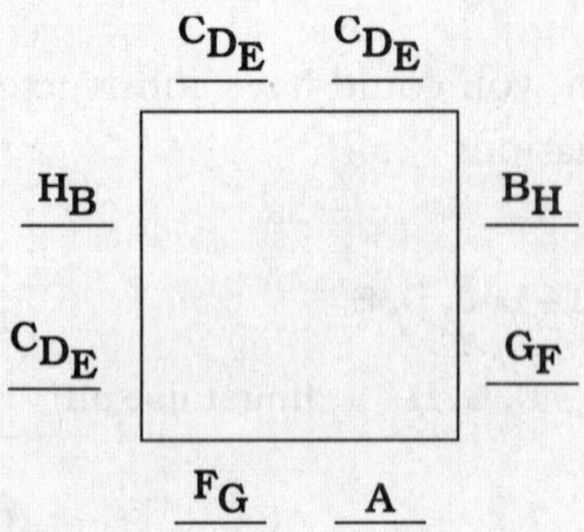

47. (A) From the diagram, C must sit next to B or H; therefore, (A) is true. Taking a second look at the diagram, we can see that H doesn't have to sit next to G, and F doesn't have to sit next to D or E. Therefore, (B) and (C) are not necessarily true. Also, (D) is false, since H sits directly across from B. Statement (E) is false, since F could sit across from E.
48. (E) If B does not sit next to G, then we should adjust the diagram as follows:

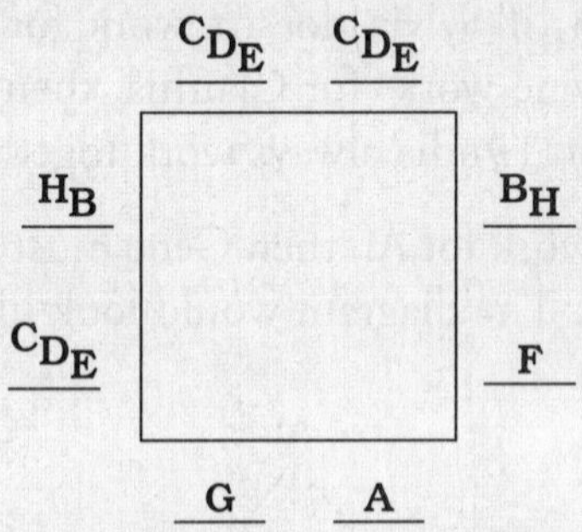

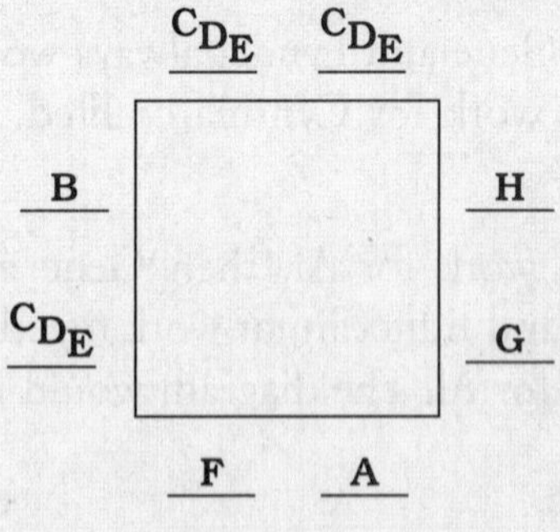

From these diagrams, we see that all statements are possible except (E). Since A sits between G and F, A cannot sit next to H under any circumstances.

49. (E) If C sits across from F, then H could sit next to any of these four (C, D, E, and G) depending on the positions of B and H. A cannot sit next to H, since A sits between G and F.

50. (C) B and H can't, since they must sit opposite each other. F and G can't, since they must sit next to A. That leaves only C, D, and E.

Answers 51–57

From the information given, you could have constructed the following simple diagram and display of information:

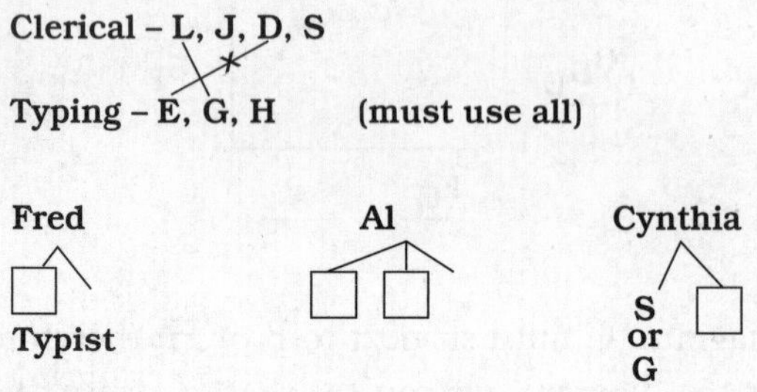

51. (A) From the diagram and information above, if Gene works for Fred, then Lyndia also works for Fred, and Sylvia must work for Cynthia. Since Dennis and Edra will not work together, one of them must work for Cynthia; therefore, choice (A) must be false. Jim cannot work for Cynthia.

52. (C) Using the diagram, if Sylvia doesn't work for Cynthia, then Gene must work for Cynthia. If Gene works for Cynthia, then Lyndia must also work for Cynthia, since Gene and Lyndia always work together.

53. (A) If Lyndia and Jim work for Al, then Gene must also work for Al, and Sylvia must work for Cynthia. The diagram would look like this:

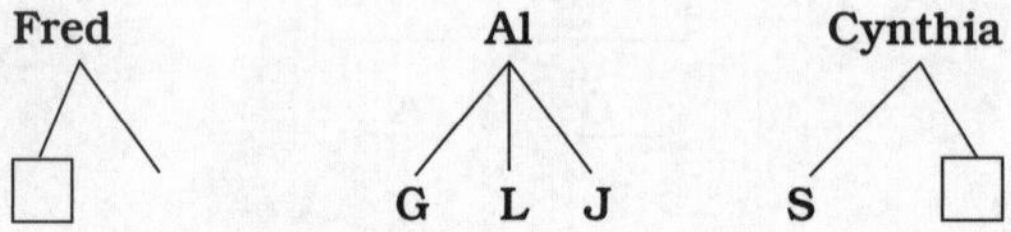

First, (A) is true, since Gene and Lyndia always work together. Stop there. Go no further. Edra could work for Cynthia or Fred, and Helen could work for Cynthia or Fred.

54. (D) If Sylvia and Jim work for Al, then Gene and Lyndia must work for Cynthia. Since Dennis and Edra cannot work together, one of them must work for Fred, and the other for Al. The diagram would now look like this:

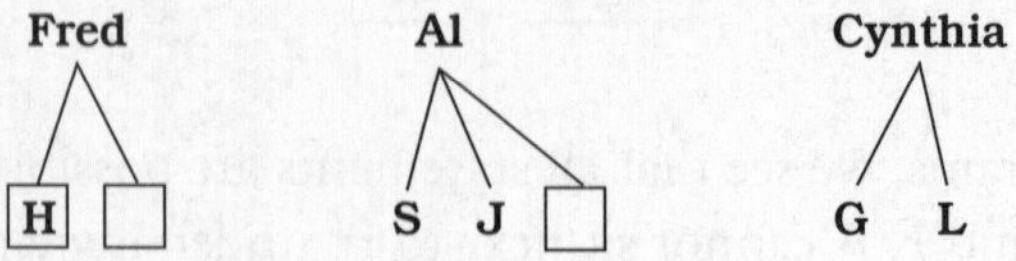

Therefore, only (D) is true.

55. (E) From the diagram, if Lyndia and Sylvia work for Al, then Gene also must work for Al. But either Sylvia or Gene must work for Cynthia. Therefore, (E) must be false.

56. (D) From the diagram, if Jim works for Cynthia, then Sylvia must also work for Cynthia, since Gene and Lyndia must work together. Gene and Lyndia cannot work for Fred, because then Dennis and Edra (who cannot work together) would work for Al. Therefore, Lyndia must work for Al. The diagram would look like this:

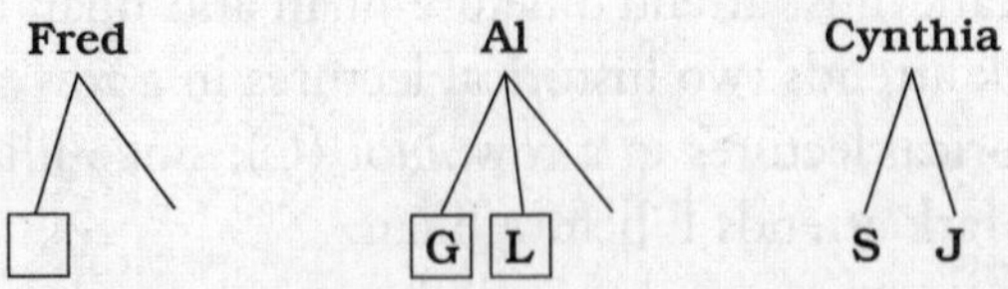

57. (C) If Al needs only two assistants, and Fred needs only one, and if Helen works for Fred, then the diagram would look like this:

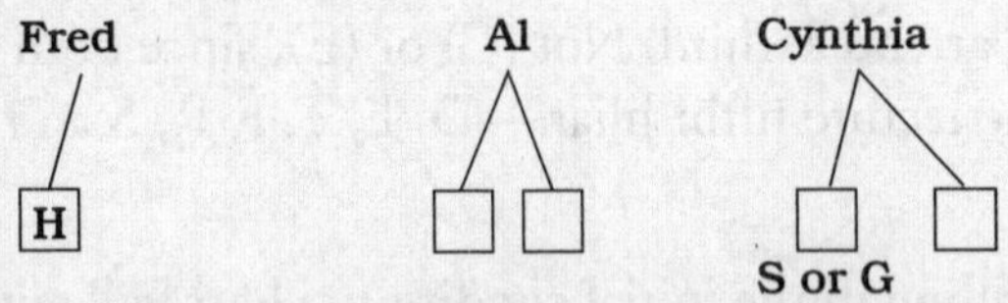

Since Gene and Lyndia must work together, they can work for either Al or Cynthia. Since Edra (typist) must work, and Dennis and Edra cannot work together, then Dennis doesn't work. Otherwise, Dennis and Edra would work together. Statements A, B, D, and E *could* be true.

Answers 58–64

58. (E) From the initial conditions, the following chart can be drawn:

	1	2	3	4	5	6
Jilian	D,E,F		T			R,S
Mark		D,E,F		D,E,F		D,E,F

Not (D), since Jilian attends T third. Not (A), (B), or (C), since Mark must attend historical lectures second, fourth, and sixth so that no two historical lectures are attended consecutively.

59. (A) Filling in Mark's possible schedule gives:

	1	2	3	4	5	6
Jilian	D,E,F		T			R,S
Mark	T	D,E,F	R,S	D,E,F	R,S	D,E,F

If Jilian attends E second, and Mark attends D second, we get:

	1	2	3	4	5	6
Jilian	D	E	T	F,R,S	F,R,S	R,S
Mark	T	D	R,S	E	R,S	F

Notice that Mark must attend F sixth, after it is attended by Jilian.

E must therefore be attended fourth by Mark. Now choices can be eliminated. Not (B), since Jilian could attend F fourth or fifth. Not (C), since Mark could attend S third or fifth. Not (D), since Mark attends F sixth. Not (E), since Jilian could attend R fourth, fifth, or sixth.

60. **(E)** Referring to the initial chart and conditions, the unacceptable choices can be eliminated.

Not (A), since Mark must attend S before Jilian and Jilian must attend F before Mark. Also, Mark attends two historical lectures in a row. Not (B), since Mark attends two historical lectures in a row. Not (C), since Jilian attends T fourth. Not (D), since Mark attends F before Jilian.

61. **(A)** Using the initial chart and the conditions will give the following:

Jilian cannot attend a scientific lecture first, since Mark must attend all scientific lectures first. Thus, Jilian must attend an historical lecture first. Not (D) since Jilian must attend T third. Not (C) or (E), since both Jilian and Mark can attend a scientific lecture fifth: Jilian—D, E, T, F, R, S and Mark—T, D, R, E, S, F.

62. **(D)** Using and filling in the initial conditions chart will give the insight needed for this question.

	1	2	3	4	5	6
Jilian	D,E,F		T			R,S
Mark		D,E,F		D,E,F		D,E,F

If Mark attends lecture F fourth, and Jilian attends lecture D first:

	1	2	3	4	5	6
Jilian	D	F	T	E,R,S	E,R,S	R,S
Mark	T	D	R,S	F	R,S	E

Lecture E is the sixth lecture attended by Mark; therefore, choice (D) is false. Each of the other four choices is possible.

63. **(C)** Not (A), (B), or (D) as the following counterexample illustrates:

Jilian: D, E, T, S, F, R and
Mark: T, D, S, E, R, F.

Not (E), since Mark must attend an historical lecture sixth. The answer must be (C), since Mark must attend scientific lectures first, third, and fifth and must attend T before Jilian. Thus, first is the only possibility for T.

64. (E) Using the initial conditions chart, the following information can be included:

	1	2	3	4	5	6
Jilian	D,E,F		T			R,S
Mark	T	D,E,F	R	D,E,F	S	D,E,F

Mark attends lecture T first since he must attend it before Jilian. If he attends lecture R third, he must attend lecture S fifth. Since he must attend S before Jilian, Jilian must attend S sixth.

From the initial conditions, a simple display could have been drawn.

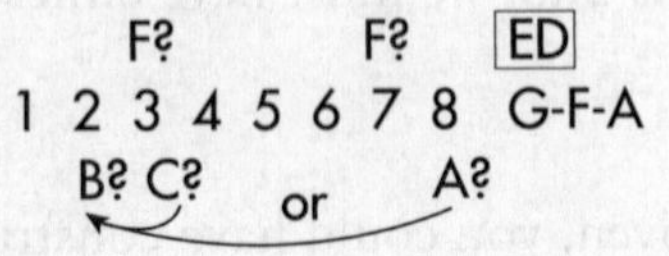

Answers 65–70

65. (B) Using the simple display and the initial conditions makes eliminating the wrong answers much easier to do.

Not (A), since F is 4th and must be either 3rd or 7th. Not (C), since D does not immediately follow E. Also GFA is not in the correct order. Not (D), since GFA not in the correct order. Not (E), since C is not 3rd, and A is not 8th, but B is 2nd.

66. (A) Using the initial conditions: Since Fetina's appointment must be before Arnie's, and Fetina must be either 3rd or 7th, it is not possible for Arnie to be scheduled 3rd.

67. (C) Using the simple display and the initial conditions: Since Arnie is 6th, Fetina must be 3rd. Since Greg's appointment is before Fetina's, it must be either 1st or 2nd. Since Hector's appointment is after Dodi's, it must be either 7th or 8th. Therefore, the answer is not (A), since Greg must be 1st or 2nd. Not (B), since Hector is either 7th or 8th. Not (D), since Dodi is 5th. Not (E), since Coco must be either 7th or 8th.

1	2	3	4	5	6	7	8
B,C,G	B,C,G	F	E	D	A	B,C,H	B,C,H

68. (A) Using the simple display and the initial conditions: If Coco is 7th, then Fetina must be 3rd. Since Greg must be scheduled before Fetina, the only appointments open for Elvis and Dodi are 4th, 5th, and 6th, with Arnie taking the remaining slot. This leaves 1st and 2nd available for Betah. Betah cannot be 2nd, since Coco is not 3rd, and Arnie is not 8th. Thus, Betah must be 1st. The display would look like this:

1	2	3	4	5	6	7	8
B	G	F	A,E	D,E	A,D	C	H

69. (C) Using the simple display and the initial conditions: Since Arnie is scheduled after Coco, Arnie must be 8th, and Coco must be 7th and Fetina 3rd. Since Betah is 2nd, Greg must be 1st. Since Dodi must immediately follow Elvis, Elvis is 4th, and Dodi is 5th, or Elvis is 5th, and Dodi is 6th. Therefore, Hector must be either 4th or 6th. The display would look like this:

1	2	3	4	5	6	7	8
G	B	F	E,H	E,D	D,H	C	A

70. (D) Using the initial conditions and simple display: Answer choice (D) is not valid, since if Betah is 2nd, we must have either Coco 3rd or Arnie 8th.

Answers 71–77

From the information given, you could have constructed the following diagram:

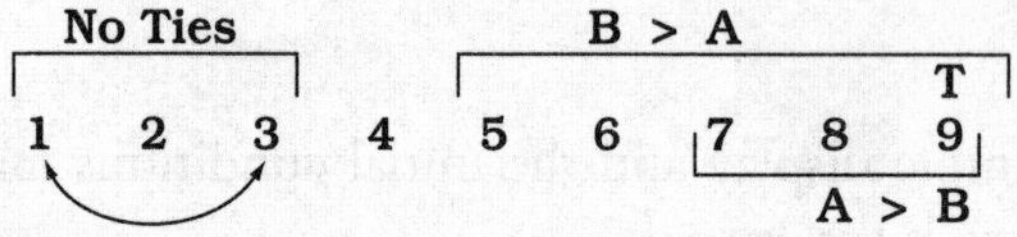

Notice the simple markings to show:

There are no ties in the first 3 games.
Team A wins more of the last 3 games than team B.
Team B wins more of the last 5 games than team A.
The last game is a tie.
Games 1 and 3 are won by the same team.

From this information you could deduce that team A wins either game 7 or 8, but not both, and team B cannot win any of the last 3 games. (If team A wins both, team B could not win more of the last 5 games.) If team A wins game 7, then 8 is a tie, and if team A wins game 8, then 7 is a tie.

You could also deduce that team B must win games 5 and 6. Your diagram now looks like this:

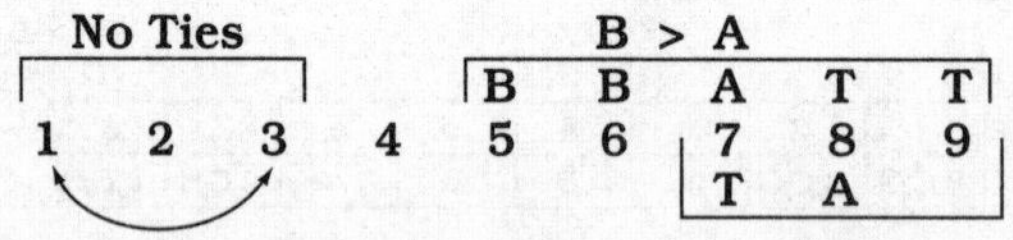

71. (C) From the information given, since games 1 and 3 are won by the same team, then one team wins at least 2 of the first 3 games.

72. (E) From the diagram, game 6 must be won by team B.

73. (A) From the diagram, if game 7 is won by team A, then game 8 must be a tie.

74. (E) From the diagram, you can see that (E) must be true.

75. **(E)** If team A wins games 1 and 4, then it must also win game 3. This would give team A four wins total, and team B could only win three, therefore team B could not win the series. For this question, the diagram would now look like this:

A		A	A	B	B	A ⌒		T
1	2	3	4	5	6	7	8	9

76. **(B)** If game 4 is won by the winner of game 5, then team B wins game 4. If game 2 is not won by the winner of game 3, then team B wins either game 2 or 3. This gives team B at least four wins and team A only a possible three wins. Therefore, B is the winner of the series.

77. **(E)** From the original diagram, team A must win either games 1, 2, and 3, or games 1, 3, and 4 to win the series. [This also eliminates choice (A).] If team B wins exactly one of the first four games [choice (B)], then team B cannot win the series, as team A will win at least three games. If team A wins only three of the first seven games [choice (C)], then team A could still lose the series, as team B could win games 2, 4, 5, and 6, with team A winning only games 1, 3, and 7. Team B could win the series by winning two of the first four games, eliminating choice (D).

Answers 78–84

The six conditions could give the following display:

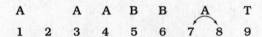

7	9	11	13	15	17	19
			L/I			

~~MN~~ or ~~NM~~
N–J
M–J
L–H–I

You may have been able to deduce additional information.

78. **(D)** Choice (A) is incorrect, since H is between L and I. Choice (B) is incorrect, since Kim could be younger than Joy, as follows:

7	9	11	13	15	17	19
N	K	M	L	H	J	I

Choice (C) is incorrect, since Hilda could be older than Joy, as follows:

7	9	11	13	15	17	19
N	K	M	L	J	H	I

Choice (E) is incorrect, because Marsha could be younger than Loren, as illustrated above. Choice (D) is correct, since Hilda is older than Loren but younger than Ida.

79. (E) The correct answer is (E). Because there are only two possible basic setups, this could be true as follows:

7	9	11	13	15	17	19
M?	K	N?	L	H	I	J
M?	L	H	I	N?	K	J

Choice (A) is incorrect, since if M were 9, it would be consecutive with N. Choice (B) is incorrect, since if H were 17, L would be 15, which would violate a condition. Choice (C) is incorrect, since if J were 15, there would not be enough slots to the left of J for five daughters. Choice (D) is incorrect since if H were 9, I would be 11, which would violate a condition.

80. (C) Choice (A) is incorrect, since M and N are consecutive. Choice (B) is incorrect, since H is not between L and I. Choice (D) is incorrect, since I or L must be 13. Choice (E) is incorrect, since N is older than J. Only choice (C) meets all the conditions.

81. (B) The correct choice is four. These four possibilities are shown below. If I is 19, L is 13, so H must be 15 or 17. Remember, M and N can't be next to each other.

7	9	11	13	15	17	19
N	K	M	L	H	J	I
M	K	N	L	H	J	I
N	K	M	L	J	H	I
M	K	N	L	J	H	I

82. (D) Choices (A) and (E) are incorrect. If Kim were two years older than Hilda, or if Hilda were two years older than Kim, the following arrangements would result. In either case, M and N would be consecutive.

7	9	11	13	15	17	19
M	N	J	L	H?	K?	I
L	H?	K?	I	M	N	J

Choice (B) is incorrect, since Joy is older than Marsha. Choice (C) is incorrect, since M and N would be consecutive as follows:

7	9	11	13	15	17	19
M	N	J	L	K	H	I
L	K	H	I	M	N	J

Choice (D) is the correct choice as follows:

7	9	11	13	15	17	19
M	K	N	L	H	J	I

83. (C) Choice (C) is correct, since if I is 13 and K is 7, you end up with M and N consecutive, as follows:

7	9	11	13	15	17	19
K	L	H	I	M	N	J

The other four choices are all possible, as follows:

	7	9	11	13	15	17	19
(A) & (D)	M	K	N	L	H	I	J
(B)	N	K	M	L	H	I	J
(E)	M	L	H	I	N	K	J

84. (C) Choice (C) is correct because, from the conditions, I must always be either 13, 17, or 19. If I were 17 or 19, M and N would be 7 and 9 and therefore consecutive. Thus, I must be 13. If I is 13, we could get the following:

7	9	11	13	15	17	19
M	L	H	I	N	J	K

Reading Comprehension

CHAPTER **4**

An Overview of the Key Strategies in the Chapter
Introduction to Question Type
Four-Step Approach
- Skim the Questions
- Skim the Passage
- Read and Mark the Passage
- Answer the Questions

Comparative Reading

Introduction to Question Type

The entire LSAT is, generally speaking, a test of reading and reasoning skills. However, the Reading Comprehension section itself is a test of general reading skills rather than the more particular analytical skills stressed in the Analytical Reasoning Section.

Each Reading Comprehension section consists of four (and in one case five) passages that range in length from 400 to 600 words. In past years there have been four passages, but this year the LSAT has added a "Comparative Reading," where one of the four sets will have two shorter passages (Passage A and B). Each passage or "comparative reading" will be followed by five to eight questions relating to the passage or passages. These 26–28 questions are to be answered in 35 minutes.

The new "comparative reading" will be similar to the traditional reading; however, the questions will be based on the two shorter passages and will contain questions comparing the passages and items in the passages. Most questions should be about both passages and how they compare to each other.

The passages are drawn from the humanities, the natural sciences, the social sciences, and law. No specialized knowledge is necessary to answer any of the questions. All questions can be answered by referring to the passage or passages.

Reading Comprehension Questions

Types	Approx. Frequency
Main Point or Primary Purpose	27–28%
Meaning of Words or Phrases in Context	6–8%
Explicitly Stated	10–15%
Inferences or Implications	20–25%
Agree or DIsagree (Support, Weaken)	20–25%
Author's Tone or Attitude	3–6%
Function of Part of the Passage	4–7%
Organization of Passage	3–6%

Common Reading Comprehension Question Stems

- Which one of the following most accurately states the main point of the passage?
- The author states which one of the following about . . . ?
- Which one of the following most accurately describes the organization of the passage?
- Based on the passage, with which one of the following statement would the author be most likely to agree?
- Which one of the following titles most completely and accurately describes the contents of the passage?
- The author's primary purpose in the passage is to . . .
- The passage provides the most support for which one of the following inferences?
- Which one of the following most accurately expresses what the author means by ". . ." (line 20)?
- Which one of the following most accurately describes the author's attitude toward . . . ?
- Which one the following could most logically be appended to the end of the final paragraph?
- The passage most strongly supports which one of the following inferences about . . . ?
- The passage provides the most support for which one of the following statements?
- The passage contains information sufficient to justify inferring which one of the following?

Overview of the Four (4) Key Strategies Your Actions and . . . Reactions

Actions	Reactions
1. Skim the questions	Mark the key word or words (main point, purpose, strengthens, weakens, assumes)
2. Skim the passage (optional)	Some students like to skim the passage quickly, reading the first sentence in each paragraph to see the structure of the passage as a whole
3. Read the passage actively	Mark the main point, important points and support, and note the structure, tone, and purpose of the passage
4. Look for key words in choices	Spot and mark the essence of the choice, know what each choice means and how the choices differ

Active Reading

The Reading Comprehension section presents long passages demanding your steady concentration. Because such passages are complex, you must approach them actively, focusing on a specific plan of attack.

Suppose that midway through the first paragraph of a passage you encounter a sentence like this:

Ordinarily, of course, we are invited only to criticize the current neglect of government programs; politicians cling to their own fringe benefits while the strife in our inner cities is only nominally contained with a plethora of half-baked local projects whose actual effect is the gradual erosion of trust in the beneficence of the republic.

Different students may respond in different ways:

"What? Let me read that again" (and again and again).
"I used to know what *beneficence* meant; uh . . . ."
"Boy, am I tired."
"I should have eaten a better breakfast; my head aches."
"I wonder what I'll do tonight. . . ."
"This writer is screwy; I was a senator's aide, and I know he's wrong."
"How can I read this!? It's written so poorly; that word *plethora* is a terrible choice."

These typical responses—getting stuck, getting distracted, getting angry—all work against your purpose: understanding the information given in the passage to answer the questions that follow. The techniques described below should help you avoid some common reading-test pitfalls.

Essentially, active reading consists of marking as you read. But the marking you do must be strategic and efficient. To present some effective active reading techniques, we will consider seven typical LSAT questions and a sample reading passage that is shorter and less complex than those in the exam.

EXAMPLE

With the possible exception of equal rights, perhaps the most controversial issue across the United States today is the death penalty. Many argue that it is an effective deterrent to murder, while others maintain there is no conclusive evidence that the death penalty reduces the number of murders, and go on to contend that it is cruel and inhuman punishment, that it is the mark of a brutal society, and finally, that it is of questionable effectiveness as a deterrent to crime anyway.

But, the death penalty is a necessary evil. Throughout recorded history there have always been those extreme individuals who were capable of terribly violent crimes such as murder. But some are more extreme, more diabolical than others. It is one thing to take the life of another in a momentary fit of blind rage, but quite another to coldly plot and carry out the murder of one or more people in the style of an executioner. Thus, murder, like all other crimes, is a matter of relative degree. While it could be argued with some conviction that the criminal in the first instance should be merely isolated from society, such should not be the fate of the latter type of murderer. To quote Moshe Dayan, "Unfortunately, we must kill them." The value of the death penalty as a deterrent to crime may be open to debate, but there remains one irrefutable fact: Gary Gilmore will never commit another murder. Charles Manson and his followers, were they to escape, or—God forbid—be paroled, very well might.

The overwhelming majority of citizens believe that the death penalty protects them. Their belief is reinforced by evidence that shows that the death penalty deters murder. For example, the Attorney General points out that from 1954 to 1963, when the death penalty was consistently imposed in California, the murder rate remained between three and four murders for each 100,000 population. Since 1964 the death penalty has been imposed only once (in 1967), and the murder rate has skyrocketed to 10.4 murders for each 100,000 population. The sharp climb in the state's murder rate, which commenced when executions stopped, is no coincidence. It is convincing evidence that the death penalty does deter many murderers. If the governor were to veto a bill reestablishing the death penalty, an initiative would surely follow. However, an initiative cannot restore the death penalty for six months. In the interim, innocent people will be murdered—some whose lives may have been saved if the death penalty were in effect.

1. The primary purpose of the passage is to

(A) criticize the governor
(B) argue for the value of the death penalty
(C) initiate a veto
(D) speak for the majority
(E) impose a six-month moratorium on the death penalty

2. The passage attempts to establish a relationship between

(A) Gary Gilmore and Charles Manson
(B) the importance of both equal rights and the death penalty
(C) the murder rate and the imposition of the death penalty
(D) executions and murders
(E) the effects of parole and the effects of isolation

3. It can be inferred that the author assumes which one of the following about a governor's veto of the death penalty legislation?

(A) It might be upheld.
(B) It will certainly be overridden.
(C) It represents consultation with a majority of citizens.
(D) The veto is important, but not crucial.
(E) It is based on the principle of equal protection for accused murderers.

4. The author's response to those who urge the death penalty for all degrees of murder would most likely be

(A) strongly supportive
(B) noncommittal
(C) negative
(D) supportive
(E) uncomprehending

5. In the passage the author is primarily concerned with

(A) supporting a position
(B) describing an occurrence
(C) citing authorities
(D) analyzing a problem objectively
(E) settling a dispute

6. In line 36 "initiative" refers to

(A) a demonstration against the governor's action
(B) a rise in the murder rate
(C) a more vocal response by the majority of citizens
(D) the introduction of legislation to reinstate the death penalty
(E) overriding the governor's veto

7. The passage provides answers to all of the following questions EXCEPT:

(A) Are all murders equally diabolical?
(B) Does the public believe the death penalty deters murder?
(C) What happened to Gary Gilmore?
(D) Will Charles Manson be paroled?
(E) Should the governor support the death penalty?

Four-Step Approach

STEP ONE: SKIM THE QUESTIONS

Before reading the passage, spend a short time familiarizing yourself with the questions. You should preread or "skim" the questions for two reasons: (1) to learn what *types* of questions are being asked; and (2) to learn what specific *information* to look for when you do read the passage. In order to skim efficiently and effectively, you should read over only the portion of each question that *precedes* the multiple choices, and you should mark *key words* as you do so.

A *key word* or phrase is any segment that suggests what you should look for when you read the passage. Marking these key words will help you remember them as you read (luckily, the questions will be printed directly below and alongside the passage, so that as you read the passage you will be able to glance at the questions and remind yourself about what you've marked). In order to further explain and clarify these tips on skimming, let's examine the questions that follow the preceding passage.

The key words for each of them are circled.

1. The primary purpose of the passage is to . . . .

This is a "main idea" or "primary purpose" question; most LSAT reading passages are followed by at least one of these. You are asked what the passage is trying to *do* or *express,* as a whole. Here is a list of possible purposes that may be embodied in a reading passage:

to inform	to criticize	to show
to persuade	to argue for or against	to question
to analyze	to illustrate	to explain
to change	to represent	to prove
to restore	to parody	to describe

This list is by no means exhaustive; the possible purposes are almost endless, and you might try thinking of some yourself.

The main idea or primary purpose of a passage is usually stated or implied in the *thesis sentence* of one or more of the paragraphs. A thesis sentence tells what the paragraph as a whole is about; it states a main idea or primary purpose. For example, the second sentence of paragraph 3 in the passage is the thesis sentence; it sums up the evidence of that paragraph into a single statement.

A primary purpose or main idea question should direct your attention to the thesis sentences in the passage, that is, the *general statements* that sum up the specific details.

2. The passage attempts to establish a relationship between . . . .

This question requires that you locate *explicit* (established) *information* in the passage, information that defines a relationship. The question allows you to anticipate the mention of at least one relationship in the passage and warns you through its wording that the relationship is not "hidden" but that it is instead one that the author deliberately attempts to establish.

3. It can be inferred that the author assumes which one of the following about the veto of a governor's death penalty legislation?

This question requires that you locate *implicit,* rather than *explicit*, information; you are asked to draw an *inference* (a conclusion based on reasoning), not just to locate obvious material. It is more difficult than question 2. When you read about the governor's veto in the passage, you should take mental note of any unstated assumptions that seem to lie behind the author's commentary.

4. The author's response to those who urge the death penalty for all degrees of murder would most likely be . . . .

This question type, usually more difficult than the types previously discussed, requires you to *apply* the information in the passage itself. As you read the passage, you should pay special attention to the author's attitude toward types, or degrees, of murder; applying this attitude to the situation described in the question should lead to the answer.

5. In the passage the author is primarily concerned with. . . .

This is another variety of the "primary purpose" or "main idea" question.

6. In line 36, "initiative" refers to . . . .

The question requires you to focus on specific language in the passage and define it in context. Such a question is relatively easy insofar as it specifies just where to look for an answer; its difficulty varies according to the difficulty of the word or phrase you are asked to consider.

7. The passage provides answers to all of the following questions EXCEPT: . . . .

Although many questions that you skim will lead you to useful information in the passage, some, like this one, do not. It is still important, however, to circle key words in the question to avoid the *misread.*

In general, spend only a few seconds skimming the questions. Read each question, mark key words, and move on.

DO NOT:

- dwell on a question and analyze it extensively.
- be concerned with whether you are marking the "right" words (trust your intuition).
- read the multiple choices (this wastes time).

STEP TWO (OPTIONAL): SKIM THE PASSAGE

Some students find skimming the passage helpful. Skimming the passage consists of quickly reading the first sentence of each paragraph and marking key words and phrases. This will give you an idea of what the paragraph as a whole is about. The first sentence is often a general statement or thesis sentence that gives the gist of the paragraph.

Consider the passage given above. Reading the first sentence of each paragraph, we mark the key words and phrases and may draw the following conclusions:

Paragraph 1: "With the possible exception of equal rights, perhaps the most controversial issue across the United States today is the death penalty." This sentence suggests that the passage will be about the death penalty, and the word "controversial" suggests that the author is about to take a stand on the controversy.

". . . that it is cruel and inhuman punishment, that it is the mark of a brutal society, and finally that it is of questionable effectiveness as a deterrent to crime anyway." This sentence presents opposition arguments, and because those arguments are presented as the views of others, not the views of the author, we begin to suspect that he does not align himself with the opposition.

Paragraph 2: "But, the death penalty is a necessary evil." This confirms our suspicion; the author is beginning an argument *in favor of* the death penalty.

"For example, it is one thing to take the life of another in a momentary fit of blind rage but quite another to coldly plot and carry out the murder of one or more people in the style of an executioner." Here the author is distinguishing between *degrees* of murder, and you may at this point recall question 4; this information seems relevant to that question.

"The value of the death penalty as a deterrent to crime may be open to debate, but there remains one irrefutable fact: Gary Gilmore will never commit another murder." The most significant feature of this sentence is that the author's tone is so absolute, indicating his strong belief in his own position.

Paragraph 3: "The overwhelming majority of citizens believe that the death penalty protects them." This sentence points toward statistical evidence in favor of the author's view.

"If the governor were to veto a bill reestablishing the death penalty, an initiative will surely follow." Coincidentally with the author's faith in the will of the majority, here he suggests that the death penalty will be upheld one way or another, by overriding a veto or through initiative.

Do not expect your own skimming of the passage to necessarily yield a series of conclusions such as those expressed above. Most of the knowledge you gather as you skim will "happen" without a deliberate effort on your part to translate your intuitions into sentences. Just read and mark the sentences, without slowing yourself down by analyzing each sentence. The preceding analysis suggests some possible conclusions that may occur to a reader, but drawing such full conclusions from sentence clues will take both practice and a relaxed attitude; don't push yourself to make sense out of everything and don't reread sentences (skimming the passage should take only a few seconds). Some sentences you read may be too difficult to make sense of immediately; just leave these alone and move along. Remember that getting stuck wastes time and raises anxiety.

STEP THREE: READ AND MARK THE PASSAGE

Now you are ready to read the entire passage. To read quickly, carefully, and efficiently, you must be *marking* important words and phrases while you read. At least such marking will keep you alert and focused. At most it will locate the answers to many questions.

Skimming the questions will have helped you decide what to mark. If a question refers to a specific line, sentence, or quotation from the passage, you will want to mark this reference and pay special attention to it. Whenever a key word from a question corresponds with a spot in the passage, mark the spot. In the scheme for marking a passage, these spots are called, simply, ANSWER SPOTS. There are two other kinds of "spots" that you should mark as you read: REPEAT SPOTS and INTUITION SPOTS. Repeat spots are sections of the passage in which the same type of information is repeated.

As you read and mark the passage, you may also wish to paraphrase the main idea of each paragraph. This enables some students to better comprehend the organization and main idea of the passage.

Consider the following excerpt from a passage:

Proposed cutbacks in the Human Resources Agency are scheduled for hearing 9 A.M. on the 17th. Included in possible program reductions are cutbacks in the veterans' affairs program, including closure of the local office; in potential support for the county's Commission on the Status of Women; and in payments provided by the county for foster home care, which are not being adjusted for cost-of-living increases this year.

Programs in the Environmental Improvement Agency will be examined by the board beginning 9 a.m. Friday, August 18. The milk and dairy inspection program has been recommended by County Administrative Officer Fred Higgins for transfer to state administration. In addition, budget recommendations do not include funds for numerous community general plans which have been discussed previously by the board of supervisors. Such areas as Joshua Tree, Crestline, Lytle Creek, and Yucaipa are not included in the Planning Department's program for the upcoming year.

A special session to discuss proposed budget cuts in the county's General Services Agency will be conducted at 9 a.m. Saturday, August 19. A number of county branch libraries have been proposed for closure next year, including the Adelanto, Bloomington, Crestline, Joshua Tree, Mentone, Morongo, Muscoy, and Running Springs locations. A rollback in hours of operation will also be considered. Branches now open 60 hours a week will be cut to 52 hours. Other 50-hour-a-week branches will be reduced to 32 hours a week. Testimony will be heard on cutbacks in various agricultural service programs, including the county trapper program in the Yucaipa region and support for 4-H activities.

Generally, this excerpt stresses information about times, dates, and locations; we are conscious of repeated numbers and repeated place names. Marking the spots in which such information is found will help you to sort out the information, and also to answer more efficiently a question that addresses such information, a question such as "Which of the following cities are (is) *not* included in the Planning Department's program and *are* (is) liable to lose a branch library?" Having marked the REPEAT SPOTS that contain location names, you may be better able to focus on the appropriate information quickly.

INTUITION SPOTS are any spots that strike you as significant, for whatever reason. As we read, we tend to pay special attention to certain information; marking those spots that your intuition perceives as important will help increase your comprehension and will therefore contribute to correct answers.

You may notice that ANSWER SPOTS, REPEAT SPOTS, and INTUITION SPOTS are not necessarily different spots. An answer spot may also be a spot that contains repeat information AND appeals to your intuition.

Don't overmark. Some students, fearing that they will miss an important point, underline everything. Such misplaced thoroughness makes it impossible to find any specific word or phrase. Just mark the main idea of each paragraph and several important words or phrases. And vary your marks. You may want to underline main ideas, use circles or brackets or stars to indicate other important spots, and jot some notes to yourself in the margin. Here is how you might mark the death penalty passage:

With the possible exception of equal rights, perhaps the most controversial issue across the United States today is the death penalty. Many argue that it is an effective deterrent to murder, while others maintain there is no conclusive evidence that the death penalty reduces the number of murders, and go on to contend that it is cruel and inhuman punishment, that it is the mark of a brutal society, and finally that it is of questionable effectiveness as a deterrent to crime anyway.

* **But, the death penalty is a necessary evil. Throughout recorded history there have always been those extreme individuals who were capable of terribly violent crimes such as murder. But some are more extreme, more diabolical than others. It is one thing to take the life of another in a momentary fit of blind rage, but quite another to coldly plot and carry out the murder of one or more people in the style of an executioner. Thus, murder, like all other crimes, is a matter of relative degree. While it could be argued with some conviction that the criminal in the first instance should be merely isolated from society, such should not be the fate of the latter type of murderer. To quote Moshe Dayan, "Unfortunately, we must kill them." The value of the death penalty as a deterrent to crime may be open to debate, but**

contrast

opposition points

degrees of murder

penalty

there remains one irrefutable fact: Gary Gilmore will never commit another murder. Charles Manson and his followers, were they to escape, or—God forbid—be paroled, very well might.

The overwhelming majority of citizens believe that the death penalty protects them. Their belief is reinforced by evidence that shows that the death penalty deters murder. For example, the Attorney General points out that from 1954 to 1963, when the death penalty was consistently imposed in California, the murder rate remained between three and four murders for each 100,000 population. Since 1964 the death penalty has been imposed only once (in 1967), and the murder rate has skyrocketed to 10.4 murders for each 100,000 population. The sharp climb in the state's murder rate, which commenced when executions stopped, is no coincidence. It is convincing evidence that the death penalty does deter many murderers. If the governor were to veto a bill reestablishing the death penalty, an initiative would surely follow. However, an initiative cannot restore the death penalty for six months. In the interim, innocent people will be murdered—some whose lives may have been saved if the death penalty were in effect.

STATS

veto effects

Your marking method should be active, playful, and personal. While you are marking, don't worry about whether you are doing it correctly. You may notice that, in the discussion of skimming the passage, some sentences are marked differently from the way they are here, in order to stress that there is no single, "correct" method.

Remember not to react subjectively to the passage, or add to it. Your own background may have you disagreeing with the passage, or you may be tempted to supply information from your own experience in order to answer a question. You must use only the information you are given, and you must accept it as true.

Avoid wasting time with very difficult or technical sentences. Concentrating on the sentences and ideas you do understand will often supply you with enough material to answer the questions. Rereading difficult sentences takes time and usually does not bring greater clarity.

STEP FOUR: ANSWER THE QUESTIONS

As you attempt to answer each question, follow these steps:

1. Focus on the key words.
2. Eliminate unreasonable and incorrect answer choices.
3. Make certain that information in the passage supports your answer.
4. Don't get stuck; assess the level of difficulty, and skip the question if necessary.

We will follow this procedure, using the questions on the "death penalty" passage as examples.

Question 1

The primary purpose of the passage is to

(A) criticize the governor
(B) argue for the value of the death penalty
(C) initiate a veto
(D) speak for the majority
(E) impose a six-month moratorium on the death penalty

ANALYSIS

The correct answer is B. Remember that this sort of question asks for the *primary* purpose, not a subsidiary purpose. Often the incorrect answer choices will express minor or subsidiary purposes; this is true of (A) and (D). Another type of incorrect answer choice *contradicts* the information in the passage. So it is with (C) and (E). Both contradict the author's expressed support of the death penalty. Having marked thesis sentences in the passage, you should be aware of the author's repeated arguments for the value of the death penalty, and choose (B).

Question 2

The passage attempts to establish a relationship between

(A) Gary Gilmore and Charles Manson
(B) the importance of both equal rights and the death penalty
(C) the murder rate and the imposition of the death penalty
(D) executions and murders
(E) the effects of parole and the effects of isolation

ANALYSIS

The correct answer is C. "Equal rights" is mentioned only in passing, and a relationship between parole and isolation is scarcely even implied; therefore (B) and (E) should be eliminated. (A) is not a good answer because, strictly speaking, Gary Gilmore and Charles Manson are not compared; their *sentences* are. (D) is a true answer, but not the best one because it is more vague and general than the best choice, (C); paragraph 3 makes this specific comparison.

Question 3

It can be inferred that the author assumes which of the following about a governor's veto of the death penalty legislation?

(A) It might be upheld.
(B) It will certainly be overridden.
(C) It represents consultation with a majority of citizens.
(D) The veto is important, but not crucial.
(E) It is based on the principle of equal protection for accused murderers.

ANALYSIS

The correct answer is A. We are looking for information that is (1) assumed but not explicit, and (2) relevant to the governor's veto. Having marked the appropriate section of the passage, you are able to return immediately to the final two paragraphs, which discuss the veto. (B), (C), and (D) contradict passage information. (C) contradicts the author's earlier explanations that most citizens approve of the death penalty, and (D) contradicts the author's final statement. (B) contradicts the author's assumption that the veto might be upheld. (E) is irrelevant to the veto issue. (A) is correct because the assumption that the veto might be upheld would certainly underlie an argument against it.

Question 4

The author's response to those who urge the death penalty for all degrees of murder would most likely be

(A) strongly supportive
(B) noncommittal
(C) negative
(D) supportive
(E) uncomprehending

ANALYSIS

The correct answer is C. Having marked the section that refers to different degrees of murder, you are once again able to focus on the appropriate section. In paragraph 2 the author argues that unpremeditated murder might not warrant the death penalty. This argument suggests his negative attitude toward someone who urges the death penalty for all murderers.

Question 5

In the passage the author is primarily concerned with

(A) supporting a position
(B) describing an occurrence
(C) citing authorities
(D) analyzing a problem objectively
(E) settling a dispute

ANALYSIS

The correct answer is A. With your general knowledge of the passage, you should immediately eliminate (B) and (D), because the author is *argumentative* throughout, never merely descriptive or objective. Citing authorities (C) is a *subsidiary* rather than a *primary* concern; the author does so in paragraph 3. (E) is incorrect because it is the author himself who is *creating* a dispute over the death penalty. A review of the thesis sentences alone shows that the author is consistently supporting a position; (A) is certainly the best answer.

Question 6

In line 36 "initiative" refers to

(A) a demonstration against the governor's action
(B) a rise in the murder rate
(C) a more vocal response by the majority of citizens
(D) the introduction of legislation to reinstate the death penalty
(E) overriding the governor's veto

ANALYSIS

The correct answer is D. Skimming this question has allowed you to pay special attention to "initiative" as you read the passage. The sentence suggests that the initiative is a response to a governor's veto of the death penalty; and it is a *certain* response, as indicated by "surely." It is also an action that can eventually restore the death penalty; this fact especially signals (D) as the answer. (B) states information mentioned apart from the initiative; the murder rate will rise "in the interim." Demonstrations (A) or vocal responses (C) are not suggested as possibilities anywhere. (E) is eliminated because the last sentence of the passage urges an override, thus distinguishing this action from an initiative.

Question 7

The passage provides answers to all of the following questions EXCEPT:

(A) Are all murders equally diabolical?
(B) Does the public believe the death penalty deters murder?
(C) What happened to Gary Gilmore?
(D) Will Charles Manson be paroled?
(E) Should the governor support the death penalty?

ANALYSIS

The correct answer is D. The passage answers all of these questions except the question of Manson's parole, which remains a possibility.

COMPARATIVE READING

As mentioned earlier, the new "comparative reading" will be similar to the traditional reading; however, the questions will be based on the two shorter passages and will contain questions comparing the passages and items in the passages. Most questions should be about both passages and how they compare to each other.

The passages will be labeled "Passage A" and "Passage B" and will be numbered continuously. The passages will be on the same topic and will have a case in common or have some sort of commonality. There may be a short introduction to the passages. The following is a sample of a "comparative reading" set.

Tuna Fishing

These passages cover events before an international agreement to limit dolphin mortality during tuna fishing was reached. By 1994, only dolphin-safe tuna could be sold in the United States.

Passage A

Just as the members of the Inter-American Tropical Tuna Commission have subscribed to annual quotas on the tuna harvest, they are agreed that cooperation is essential in limiting the dolphin kill. The common interest is preservation of the tuna industry, and since modern fishing methods exploit the cozy relationship between the yellowfin tuna and the dolphin, tuna fishing would become less profitable if the number of dolphins decreased. Tuna and dolphin are often found together at sea, and the fishermen have learned to cast their nets where they see the dolphin, using them to locate the tuna. The problem is that many dolphins die in the nets.

The commission deliberations acknowledged the environmental pressures that have led to strict regulation of U.S. tuna crews under federal law. Delegates also recognized that dolphin protection goals are relatively meaningless unless conservation procedures are adopted and followed on an international basis. Commission supervision of survey, observer, and research programs won general agreement at the eight-nation conference. The method and timetable for implementing the program, however, remain uncertain.

Thus the federal regulation that leaves U.S. crews at a disadvantage in the tuna-harvest competition remains a threat to the survival of the tuna fleet. Still, the commission meetings have focused on the workable solution. All vessels should be equipped with the best dolphin-saving gear devised; crews should be trained and motivated to save the dolphin; a system must be instituted to assure that rules are enforced. Above all, the response must be international. Dolphin conservation could well be another element in an envisioned treaty that remains unhappily elusive at the continuing Law-of-the-Sea Conference.

The tuna industry's interest in saving dolphins is bothersome to many who also want to save the dolphin but object to the industry's motivation for doing so. For fishermen, saving the dolphin is valuable only because the dolphins lead them to tuna. For more compassionate souls, however, the dolphin is not just a tuna finder but, more important, the sea creature that seems most human.

Passage B

At one time, tropical tuna were caught with poles and fishing lines. Then, in the 1950s, a synthetic netting was developed that wouldn't rot in tropical waters. A hydraulically driven power block could haul the large synthetic nets and deploy them around entire schools of tuna, which resulted in being able to catch many tons of fish at one time. This method of tuna fishing is called "purse seining," and the ships that are equipped to do it are "purse seiners."

During "porpoise fishing" (the fishermen's term for purse seining), schools of tuna are located by spotting dolphins or seabird flocks, often by a helicopter that takes off from the purse seiner's upper deck. Tuna and the dolphin travel together—usually accompanied by sea birds—for reasons that are not completely understood but that are probably associated with areas of food supply. Once the dolphin are spotted, speedboats are used by the fishermen to chase them down, herd them into a group, and set the net around them. The chase takes place over many miles of ocean and can take as long as several hours. Once the dolphins have been herded, cables draw the net taut at the bottom, like drawstrings on a purse. The purse seiner's powerful hydraulic system then pulls the net upward. Once the net is hauled back on board, the captain puts the seiner into reverse, which is called the "backdown" procedure. As the slack of the net eases, a panel of webbing designed to not snag the dolphins drops them back into the ocean. Back on deck the tuna are scooped out of the net and put into storage wells on a lower deck.

The backdown procedure to release the dolphins doesn't always go smoothly, sometimes because of human error and sometimes because of strong rip tides and currents. The dolphins, caught in a canopy of netting, can suffocate. Because of their struggle in the net, they can be badly injured and will die later. It is estimated that since the introduction of the purse-seining method of catching tuna, over six million dolphins have been killed. This is by far the largest documented cetacean kill in the world. In comparison, the total number of whales of all species killed during commercial whaling in the twentieth century is about two million.

Efforts first in the United States and then internationally have reduced the dolphin kill substantially in the last thirty years. Since 1993, reported dolphin mortality has been a small fraction of the population size, so that recovery of the dolphin population has been expected. But by 2002, this hadn't occurred. There are several hypotheses, among which are the negative effects of repeated chases on dolphin survival or reproduction, the separation of suckling calves from their mothers during the fishing process, environmental changes, and unobserved or unreported mortality.

Question 1

Which of the following best contrasts the main ideas of Passage A and Passage B?

(A) Passage A presents the reasons an international agreement to protect dolphins is needed while Passage B details the fishing methods that endanger dolphins.
(B) While Passage A focuses on the effects of U.S. dolphin legislation on the tuna fishing industry, Passage B focuses on the reasons dolphins are valuable.
(C) Passage A presents two sides of the dolphin legislation controversy, while Passage B presents only one side.
(D) Passage A explains the international program for protecting dolphins, while Passage B explains the program's failure.
(E) While Passage A criticizes the U.S. dolphin protection legislation because it negatively affects the tuna fishing industry, Passage B criticizes it for failing to protect dolphins.

ANALYSIS

The correct answer is (A). Passage A is concerned primarily with the importance of an international agreement about dolphin protection, and the main subject in Passage B is the method of tuna fishing that endangers dolphins. Choice (D) may seem like a good answer because Passage A does outline ideas for an international program and Passage B indicates that the dolphin population has not recovered in spite of a reduction in dolphin mortality. But this answer is not as good as (A) because it covers only parts of each passage.

Question 2

The author of Passage A, unlike the author of Passage B,

(A) believes that international laws will help reduce dolphin mortality
(B) states that U.S. laws covering dolphin protection have been unsuccessful
(C) mentions a noncommercial motivation for protecting dolphins
(D) criticizes the Inter-American Tropical Tuna Commission
(E) insists on a timetable for international supervision of the tuna industry

ANALYSIS

The correct answer is (C). In the last paragraph of Passage A, the author mentions that some "compassionate souls" are interested in saving the dolphin for reasons having nothing to do with commerce, making (C) the best answer, since Passage B doesn't consider motivations for saving dolphins. Neither passage claims that U.S. laws have been unsuccessful (B), and Passage A doesn't criticize the Inter-

American Tropical Tuna Commission or "insist" on a timetable (D and E). Both passages see international laws as beneficial.

Question 3

The author presents the information in Passage A

(A) angrily
(B) cynically
(C) ironically
(D) indifferently
(E) objectively

ANALYSIS

The correct answer is (E). The information is presented objectively, even though the author in the last paragraph suggests that some people are bothered by the tuna industry's commercial motivations. This fact is presented in a straightforward, not emotional, manner.

Question 4

The author of Passage A implies that the government and industry representatives concerned with dolphin conservation may lack which one of the following?

(A) knowledge
(B) altruism
(C) influence
(D) compassion
(E) efficiency

ANALYSIS

The correct answer is D. The author uses this word in line 29, and implies that although some people's interest in saving dolphins is based on an appreciation for the animals, the tuna industry's motivations have nothing to do with compassion.

Question 5

Which one of the following in NOT described in Passage A?

(A) the relationship between dolphins and tuna
(B) the requirements that must be met for tuna to be labeled dolphin-safe
(C) why dolphin protection is of international concern
(D) elements of a solution to the dolphin conservation problem
(E) the items that won general agreement at the Law-of-the-Sea conference

ANALYSIS

The correct answer is (B). All of the statements are items considered in Passage A except for (B), making this the correct answer. The relationship between dolphins and tuna is mentioned in line 5, the importance of an international agreement is stated in lines 12–14, elements of a solution are touched on in lines 19–22, and the items that won general agreement are mentioned in lines 14–15.

Question 6

In Passage B, the "backdown" procedure is described as a way to

(A) protect dolphins from injury
(B) separate dolphin calves from their mothers
(C) return dolphins to the ocean
(D) ensure the safety of the tuna catch
(E) meet requirements of U.S. legislation

ANALYSIS

The correct answer is (C). The backdown procedure is explained in lines 49–54, and its purpose is clearly to return the dolphins to the sea, making (C) the best answer. The procedure doesn't protect the dolphins from injury (A), as is made clear in the third paragraph. Nothing in the passage suggests either (D) or (E).

Question 7

According to Passage B, dolphin mortality became a major problem after

(A) tuna fishermen recognized that tuna and dolphin swam together
(B) the purse-seining method of tuna fishing was introduced
(C) tuna fishing became an international industry
(D) poor netting was used to catch tuna
(E) it became more economical to destroy dolphins rather than to save them

ANALYSIS

The correct answer is (B). The passage shows that it was the introduction of purse seining, not tuna fishing itself, that presented a problem because it involved actually trapping the dolphins in netting, not merely using them as a means to spot tuna (A). Synthetic netting, not poor netting (D), allowed purse seining and, therefore, led to increases in dolphin mortality.

Question 8

Which of the following can be inferred from the last paragraph of Passage B?

(A) Improved fishing methods to reduce dolphin kill haven't succeeded.
(B) International agreements have not been effective in protecting dolphins.
(C) The fact that the dolphin population hasn't recovered needs further study.
(D) A large percentage of the dolphin population has been destroyed.
(E) Observers on purse seiners are often bribed to under-report the number of dead dolphins.

ANALYSIS

The correct answer is (C). Lines 68–71 suggest several hypotheses that might explain why the dolphin population hasn't recovered even though dolphin mortality figures have been significantly reduced. The inference can be made from these hypotheses that further study is required, making (C) the best answer. (A), (B), and (D) are contradicted in the passage, and bribery (E), while possibly true, is not implied.

ACTIVE READING—A SUMMARY CHART

SKIM THE QUESTIONS
(Mark the key words and phrases.)

↓

SKIM THE PASSAGE
—OPTIONAL—
(Quickly read and mark the first sentence of each paragraph.)

↓

READ AND MARK THE PASSAGE
- Answer Spots
- Repeat Spots
- Intuition Spots
- Paraphrase

↓

ANSWER THE QUESTIONS
- Focus on key words.
- Eliminate weak choices.
- Don't "read into" the passage.
- Don't get stuck.
- Skip if necessary.

An Alternative General Approach

Some students, regardless of how much they review, analyze, and practice, cannot seem to finish the Reading Comprehension section. They simply cannot work fast enough and continue to maintain a high level of comprehension. If you find that you consistently have a problem getting to or into the fourth passage, you may wish to try this alternative approach: Focus your time on three of the four passages. That is, try to do well on the three passages and the questions that follow, and simply guess at the questions for the remaining passage. You can skip a passage and still receive a good score. The idea is to significantly raise your percentage of correct answers on the passages and questions you *are* completing. Remember, this is an alternative approach that you may wish to try if you are having a real problem getting to all four passages and maintaining a good level of comprehension.

Basic Training: Extra, Effective Practice

The following procedure, *practiced daily,* should strengthen precisely the kinds of skills that you will need for the Reading Comprehension section of the LSAT:

1. Locate the editorial page in your daily newspaper. There you will probably find three or four editorials on different subjects.
2. Read several editorials at your normal reading speed, marking them if possible.
3. Set the editorials aside, and try to write a summary sentence describing each editorial. Make your summary as precise as possible. Do not write, "This editorial was about the economy." Instead, try to write something like this: "This editorial argued against the value of supply-side economics by referring to rising unemployment and interest rates."

   You may not be able to write so precise a summary right away, but after a few days of practicing this technique, you will find yourself better able to spot and remember main ideas and specific details, and to anticipate and understand the author's point of view.

   It is most important that you *write down* your summary statements. This takes more time and effort than silently "telling" yourself what the editorial means, but the time and effort will pay off.
4. Every few days, create some of your own multiple-choice questions about an editorial. What would you ask if you were a test maker? Putting yourself in the test maker's shoes can be very instructive. You will realize, for instance, how weak or incorrect answer choices are constructed, and that realization will help you to eliminate such choices when you take the LSAT.

Answer Sheet

EXTRA PRACTICE: READING COMPREHENSION

1	(A) (B) (C) (D) (E)	23	(A) (B) (C) (D) (E)	45	(A) (B) (C) (D) (E)	67	(A) (B) (C) (D) (E)
2	(A) (B) (C) (D) (E)	24	(A) (B) (C) (D) (E)	46	(A) (B) (C) (D) (E)	68	(A) (B) (C) (D) (E)
3	(A) (B) (C) (D) (E)	25	(A) (B) (C) (D) (E)	47	(A) (B) (C) (D) (E)	69	(A) (B) (C) (D) (E)
4	(A) (B) (C) (D) (E)	26	(A) (B) (C) (D) (E)	48	(A) (B) (C) (D) (E)	70	(A) (B) (C) (D) (E)
5	(A) (B) (C) (D) (E)	27	(A) (B) (C) (D) (E)	49	(A) (B) (C) (D) (E)	71	(A) (B) (C) (D) (E)
6	(A) (B) (C) (D) (E)	28	(A) (B) (C) (D) (E)	50	(A) (B) (C) (D) (E)	72	(A) (B) (C) (D) (E)
7	(A) (B) (C) (D) (E)	29	(A) (B) (C) (D) (E)	51	(A) (B) (C) (D) (E)	73	(A) (B) (C) (D) (E)
8	(A) (B) (C) (D) (E)	30	(A) (B) (C) (D) (E)	52	(A) (B) (C) (D) (E)	74	(A) (B) (C) (D) (E)
9	(A) (B) (C) (D) (E)	31	(A) (B) (C) (D) (E)	53	(A) (B) (C) (D) (E)	75	(A) (B) (C) (D) (E)
10	(A) (B) (C) (D) (E)	32	(A) (B) (C) (D) (E)	54	(A) (B) (C) (D) (E)	76	(A) (B) (C) (D) (E)
11	(A) (B) (C) (D) (E)	33	(A) (B) (C) (D) (E)	55	(A) (B) (C) (D) (E)	77	(A) (B) (C) (D) (E)
12	(A) (B) (C) (D) (E)	34	(A) (B) (C) (D) (E)	56	(A) (B) (C) (D) (E)	78	(A) (B) (C) (D) (E)
13	(A) (B) (C) (D) (E)	35	(A) (B) (C) (D) (E)	57	(A) (B) (C) (D) (E)	79	(A) (B) (C) (D) (E)
14	(A) (B) (C) (D) (E)	36	(A) (B) (C) (D) (E)	58	(A) (B) (C) (D) (E)	80	(A) (B) (C) (D) (E)
15	(A) (B) (C) (D) (E)	37	(A) (B) (C) (D) (E)	59	(A) (B) (C) (D) (E)	81	(A) (B) (C) (D) (E)
16	(A) (B) (C) (D) (E)	38	(A) (B) (C) (D) (E)	60	(A) (B) (C) (D) (E)	82	(A) (B) (C) (D) (E)
17	(A) (B) (C) (D) (E)	39	(A) (B) (C) (D) (E)	61	(A) (B) (C) (D) (E)	83	(A) (B) (C) (D) (E)
18	(A) (B) (C) (D) (E)	40	(A) (B) (C) (D) (E)	62	(A) (B) (C) (D) (E)	84	(A) (B) (C) (D) (E)
19	(A) (B) (C) (D) (E)	41	(A) (B) (C) (D) (E)	63	(A) (B) (C) (D) (E)	85	(A) (B) (C) (D) (E)
20	(A) (B) (C) (D) (E)	42	(A) (B) (C) (D) (E)	64	(A) (B) (C) (D) (E)	86	(A) (B) (C) (D) (E)
21	(A) (B) (C) (D) (E)	43	(A) (B) (C) (D) (E)	65	(A) (B) (C) (D) (E)	87	(A) (B) (C) (D) (E)
22	(A) (B) (C) (D) (E)	44	(A) (B) (C) (D) (E)	66	(A) (B) (C) (D) (E)	88	(A) (B) (C) (D) (E)

Remove answer sheet by cutting on dotted line

Extra Practice: Reading Comprehension

Directions: Read the passages and answer the questions following each passage by blackening the appropriate space on the answer sheet. You may refer back to the passages when answering the questions. Answer all questions on the basis of what is stated or implied.

Passage 1 (Written in 1982)

A recent Harris Survey revealed that a majority of Americans say the price of gasoline would have to go to $1.50 a gallon before they would cut back on the use of their automobiles for pleasure driving. The survey, conducted among 1,517 adults nationwide, also found that gasoline prices would have to go to $1.85 per gallon before adults would cease to use their own cars to go to work and would turn to public transportation and car pooling.

In fact, the price of gasoline is presently going *down* rather than up. Major oil companies have announced plans to reduce wholesale prices by as much as eight cents a gallon. As a result, those drivers who insisted that only rising gasoline costs would cut their consumption will now probably begin to drive more rather than less. Already, according to the Highway Patrol, highways are becoming more crowded with cars carrying only one passenger, and with gas-guzzling recreational vehicles.

These results are interesting when one considers that we are presently at the height of the smog season. As most of us know by now, the majority of our smog problem is caused by exhaust emissions from cars. Yet how many of us have actually made an effort to drive less? In fact, how many of us have even made an effort to drive more slowly to help conserve gasoline? Unfortunately, the answer to both questions is: not very many. Even though we all are aware—or certainly should be by now—that there is a desperate need both to conserve fuel and to clean up our air, far too few of us are willing to make even a small sacrifice to help.

Recently, we read that a small group of botanists is busily attempting to develop a strain of pine tree that can resist the smog. It seems that as the smog has gotten worse each year it has taken an increasingly greater toll on the pines in mountain areas. Now the situation is becoming critical, either we develop a hardier tree or they will all die. It's sad to think that in a country which professes so much love for nature, and where so much natural beauty abounds, we have to develop a breed of "supertrees" which can cope with the polluted air we create.

The solution to our smog problem lies not in eliminating the steel industry's coke oven emissions, or any other industrial emissions, but in convincing the millions of people who traverse our freeways daily to try at least to drive less. Obviously, it's necessary to drive in order to get to and from work, but if each of us could at least reduce the pleasure driving a little, drive the speed limit, and have our automobile engines tuned regularly, the improvement would be immediately noticeable. If we make these small sacrifices we won't have to worry about eventually paying $1.85 per gallon for gasoline. The reduced consumption will keep prices low because there will be enough for everyone without having to increase prices to "force" us to use less.

1. The primary purpose of this passage is to
   (A) convince smog producers to reduce emissions
   (B) convince drivers to reduce smog
   (C) convince drivers to drive less
   (D) describe an instance of the supply/demand phenomenon
   (E) argue against higher gasoline prices

2. The author puts the blame for air pollution on
   (A) individuals
   (B) institutions
   (C) corporations
   (D) botanists
   (E) pollsters

3. With which one of the following statements about the effects of smog would the author be most likely to agree?
   (A) A greater number of vans and campers at our national parks threatens the parks' beauty.
   (B) Smog encourages the survival of hardy vegetation.
   (C) The price of gasoline may rise in the future.
   (D) People who drive alone have no respect for nature.
   (E) Smog will gradually become something we can live with.

4. Who of the following would be most likely to object to the author's argument?
   (A) an industrialist
   (B) an auto mechanic
   (C) a botanist
   (D) a Highway Patrol officer
   (E) a manufacturer of recreational vehicles

5. The author implies which one of the following in his argument?
   (A) Industrial emissions are uncontrollable.
   (B) Reduced driving will occur even if drivers do not follow his advice.
   (C) Reduced driving will not inconvenience drivers.
   (D) The diminishing supply of fuel is not a problem.
   (E) Gasoline prices should not go down.

6. The author's tone in this passage is

   (A) cynical
   (B) analytical
   (C) satirical
   (D) urgent
   (E) objective

7. To accept the author's argument, we must assume which one of the following about the Harris Survey?

   (A) The people conducting the survey were opposed to pleasure driving.
   (B) The people conducting the survey were not drivers.
   (C) The survey was conducted recently.
   (D) The 1,517 adults actually represent a majority of Americans.
   (E) The people conducting the survey were not employed by the steel industry.

Passage 2

A recent study surveyed 3,576 trials in two reporting samples. Over 500 judges cooperated in the study. The survey was conducted using judges as reporters for jury trials. Two major questions were explored in the survey, "First, what is the magnitude and direction of the disagreement between judge and jury? And, second, what are the sources and explanations of such disagreement?"

The study found that judges and juries agree (would decide the same case the same way) in 75.4 percent of the cases. If cases in which the jury hung are eliminated, the overall agreement rate rises to 78 percent. Thus at the outset, whatever the defects of the jury system, it can be seen that the jury at least arrives at the same result as the judge in over three-fourths of the cases.

The direction of disagreement is clearly toward a more lenient jury than judge. The trend was not isolated to any particular type of offense but was spread throughout crime categories. Additionally, the pattern found was that in convictions, juries tended to be more lenient as far as counts, degrees, and sentencing.

For civil cases the percentage of agreement and disagreement was about the same except that there did not appear to be any strong sentiment in favor of plaintiff over defendant (or vice versa) by the jury.

In cases decided differently because the judge had facts the jury did not, generally, these facts related to suppressed evidence, personal knowledge of the defendant's prior record, etc. The factors that made the difference between judge and jury in these cases, then, were all facts that we as a society purposefully keep from juries because the information is irrelevant or because it is highly prejudicial. From the study it can be assumed that the judge, hearing the information, did not disregard it but, quite the contrary, used it in reaching his (harsher) judgment.

The overwhelming number of cases in which judge and jury agree argue for the jury's understanding of the evidence because it is not to be expected that a jury deciding cases it does not understand and a judge deciding cases he does understand (we presume) would not agree in their results so often. Also, judges themselves generally did not identify "jury misunderstood the facts" as the reason for disagreement.

The level of sympathy that the jury had with the defendant did make some difference. Although generally the jury was neutral, in about 36 percent of the cases the jury had some reaction (positive or negative) because of the personal characteristics, occupation, family, or court appearance. These factors affected juries differently depending on the age, race, or sex of the defendant. Through various statistical evaluations the study is able to state that "the sympathetic defendant causes disagreement in . . . 4 percent of all cases." Similar figures apply for the unsympathetic defendant.

8. This passage was probably written in response to an argument for

(A) the appointment rather than the election of judges
(B) the election rather than the appointment of judges
(C) the wider use of the trial by jury
(D) the reduced use of the trial by jury
(E) the increased use of statistics in the courts

9. According to the passage, judge and jury are likely to reach the same verdict in

(A) criminal cases rather than in civil cases
(B) civil cases rather than in criminal cases
(C) cases where the judge has facts denied to the jury
(D) cases in which the jury hung
(E) roughly three-quarters of the cases

10. The results of this study suggest that, when there is disagreement between a judge and a jury, the judgments of the judge are

(A) harsher than those of juries
(B) less harsh than those of juries
(C) very nearly the same as those of juries
(D) less likely to be influenced by irrelevant or prejudicial information
(E) less harsh than those of juries in criminal cases only

11. From the results of the study we can infer that withholding from a jury information that is irrelevant or prejudicial to a defendant

(A) has no significant effect on the results of a trial
(B) works to the disadvantage of most defendants
(C) works to the advantage of most defendants
(D) works to increase the objectivity of the judge
(E) works to decrease the objectivity of the jury

12. The author's argument for the jury's understanding of the evidence presented in trial is based upon
    (A) his assumption that the judge understands the evidence
    (B) his assumption that evidence too complex for the jury to understand would not be admitted
    (C) the fact that evidence is rarely complex
    (D) the fact that juries are able to reach verdicts
    (E) the fact that no judges have accused juries of misunderstanding

13. With which one of the following statements would the author be most likely to disagree?
    (A) Juries are likely to be influenced by the personal characteristics, occupation, family, or court appearance of defendants.
    (B) Juries are influenced by the age, race, or sex of the defendant.
    (C) The judge's misunderstanding the evidence is not a likely cause of judge-jury disagreements.
    (D) The jury's misunderstanding the evidence is not a likely cause of judge-jury disagreements.
    (E) The jury's sympathy with a defendant is a major cause of judge-jury disagreements.

14. By including the information in the final paragraph about the effect of sympathy with the defendant upon the jury, the author of the passage
    (A) unfairly denigrates the opposing argument
    (B) undermines the case he has presented
    (C) suggests that his arguments are objective
    (D) conceals a weakness in his case
    (E) underscores the lack of objectivity in judges

15. The author includes statistical information in the passage chiefly in order to
    (A) demonstrate his familiarity with social science research methods
    (B) support his case for the use of juries
    (C) make what is really a hypothesis appear to be factual
    (D) give an appearance of objectivity to a subjective view
    (E) support a case against the use of juries

Passage 3

The last twenty years of the 19th century were to become the pinnacle of success for big business. The legal climate was most conducive to enterprise. The courts of that time interpreted the 14th Amendment demand for "due process of law" in state action to include corporations as "citizens" and hence made them virtually immune to state regulation. Cases involving business occupied the Supreme Court continuously. The states had never had the power to regulate interstate railroads, although they frequently tried to do so, and the Interstate Commerce Act of 1887 attempted to do so. The income tax law of 1894 and the Sherman Antitrust Act of 1890 were Congressional attempts to moderate the abuses of the new industrial giants, but the Court continued to favor business interest and eviscerated all of the acts.

The 1872 *Slaughterhouse* case was the first blow to federal regulation of business. The Louisiana legislature had given a monopoly on slaughtering animals in New Orleans to one company and hundreds of butchers found themselves without facilities. They asked the federal courts to interpret the "privileges and immunities" clause of the 14th Amendment to incorporate a new federally protected right to make a living, which in turn would declare the monopoly unconstitutional. However, the Supreme Court held that the clause did not add any rights, it merely protected pre-existing federal ones, such as the right of interstate travel; therefore the monopoly was a valid use of state power.

In 1876 in *Munn v. Illinois*, the Supreme Court upheld a state's right of regulation. Chicago was the hub of the grain storage industry, since grain was stored there upon receipt from the Midwest's farmers until it could be distributed through the East. Munn and other warehousemen made agreements with railroads to get a monopoly on each line's incoming shipments and then fixed prices. This was most damaging to the grain merchants, who pressured the Illinois legislature into legislating against these practices in 1871. Warehouse owners claimed that these regulations deprived them of their property rights without due process of law. The Supreme Court decision was rendered by Chief Justice Morrison Waite, who had been appointed by President Grant. He announced that although railroads were interstate commerce, grain storage was not and therefore the state regulations were valid. This was the last case in which the Supreme Court upheld any state regulation of business until 1937.

In addition to business cases, there were other problems as well. After Reconstruction officials left the South, the states began passing laws directed at the removal of the political rights the blacks had gained. For the first decade after the war, there were few "Jim Crow" laws requiring segregation, and integration was at least tolerated. However, persistent denials of the right to vote alarmed Congress and in 1875 the Civil Rights Act was enacted, which protected the franchise and prohibited segregation in places of public accommodation. Several cases involving blacks who had been denied access to theaters and restaurants in New York City and other areas were decided by the Supreme Court in the *Civil Rights* cases of 1883. The Court (delaying as long as possible) did not hear a case of this type during the 1870s. The Court held that the 14th Amendment, providing that "no state shall deny to any citizen the equal protection of the laws" applied only to state action and therefore, although official discrimination was prohibited, attempts to regulate private discrimination, as in restaurants, were unconstitutional. The results of this decision were the immediate segregation laws passed by every Southern state. Since political parties were not state organizations, the "white primary," in which the political party became a private club, was invented.

16. Based on the passage, which one of the following is an accurate statement about the Interstate Commerce Act of 1887?

(A) The act was not supported by a majority in Congress.
(B) The act was intended to increase the states' regulatory powers.
(C) The act was intended to support the growth of interstate railroads.
(D) The act favored federal regulation over state regulation.
(E) The act was ruled unconstitutional.

17. In the 1872 *Slaughterhouse* case, the Supreme Court's decision achieved all of the following EXCEPT:

(A) helping big business
(B) allowing a monopoly
(C) upholding states' rights
(D) narrowly interpreting a clause of the 14th Amendment
(E) protecting Congress's right to regulate industry

18. According to the passage, the Supreme Court's decision in *Munn v. Illinois* was based on

(A) a state's right to regulate business.
(B) a person's federally protected right to make a living.
(C) a company's right to fix prices.
(D) the federal government's right to regulate interstate commerce.
(E) the negative effect of regulation on grain merchants.

19. Which one of the following interpretations can we infer was most important in the Supreme Court's pro-business decisions?

(A) Corporations were to be viewed as "citizens" and given the same rights and privileges.
(B) "Due process" was to be applied only to state actions.
(C) All rights not specified in the Constitution were reserved for the individual states.
(D) "Privileges and immunities" were to include the right to make a living.
(E) Regulation was to be limited to interstate commerce.

20. The Supreme Court's ruling in the *Civil Rights* cases of 1883 can best be characterized as

    (A) the result of intimidation by the South.
    (B) progressive for its time.
    (C) the result of compromise.
    (D) the inevitable result of an all-white Court.
    (E) a victory for segregationists.

21. According to the passage, the "white primary" was introduced in the South to

    (A) defy the Supreme Court's authority.
    (B) prevent the election of African-Americans to state offices.
    (C) provide a way around the prohibition of official discrimination.
    (D) return authority for election procedures to individual states.
    (E) redefine the 14th Amendment to exclude certain rights.

22. The main purpose of the first three paragraphs of the passage is to

    (A) show that corruption of the Supreme Court in the late 19th century had far-reaching effects.
    (B) illustrate how Supreme Court decisions generally favored big business in the late 19th century.
    (C) analyze the pros and cons of two important Supreme Court decisions relating to big business.
    (D) explain why no regulatory legislation was passed during the late 19th century.
    (E) argue against the Supreme Court's decisions in the late 19th century.

23. The author's attitude expressed in this passage can best be described as

    (A) bitterly cynical.
    (B) thoughtfully positive.
    (C) mildly judgmental.
    (D) strictly objective.
    (E) harshly negative.

Passage 4

No sooner had the British forces in June 1944 carried out their part in the Allied invasion of Germany than they were faced with the fact that among the prisoners of war captured there were Russians in German uniforms. By the time the war in Europe ended, between two and three million Soviet citizens had passed through Allied hands. This extraordinary situation, certainly never before known in the history of war, was the consequence of the policy of both the Soviet and the German regimes. On the Soviet side, the very existence of prisoners of war was not recognized: the Soviet government refused to adhere to the Geneva Convention, and washed its hands of the millions who fell into German power.

The Germans, in turn, treated their Soviet prisoners with such callous brutality that only a relatively small number of them survived. For a Soviet prisoner in German hands to enlist in the German armed forces was about the only way open to him of saving his life. There were also Soviet citizens whose hatred of the Communist regime was so strong that they were prepared to fight alongside the Germans in order to overthrow Stalin: nominally headed by General Andrey Vlasov, they saw little combat until the end of the war, largely because of Hitler's suspicion of Vlasov's claims to maintain his political independence of the National Socialist regime even as a prisoner of war. There were also some other combat units composed of Russians, some of them noted for their savagery. Then there were hordes of civilians in German hands—some compulsorily swept into the German labor mobilization drive, many more borne along the wave of the German retreat from Russia and thereafter drafted for labor duties. These civilians included many women and children.

The problem facing the British government from the outset was what policy to adopt toward this mass of humanity that did not fall into any of the accepted categories thrown up by war. Quite apart from the logistic problems, there existed a well-established tradition in Britain which refused to repatriate against their will people who found themselves in British hands and the nature of whose reception by their own government was, to say the least, dubious. The first inclination of the Cabinet—to send all captured Russians back to the Soviet Union—was challenged by the minister of economic warfare, Lord Selborne, who was moved by the fact that the Russians in British hands had only volunteered to serve in German uniforms as an alternative to certain death; and that it would therefore be inhuman to send them back to be shot or to suffer long periods of forced labor. Winston Churchill was also swayed by this argument.

24. The primary purpose of this passage is to
    (A) explain one of the problems facing British forces near the end of World War II
    (B) reveal the savagery of both the German and the Russian forces
    (C) stress America's noninvolvement
    (D) detail a "war within a war"
    (E) give evidence for Churchill's position

25. "Repatriate" in paragraph 3 means to
    (A) send back to the country of birth
    (B) send back to the country of allegiance
    (C) send back to the victorious country
    (D) reinstill patriotism
    (E) reinstill British patriotism

26. The author's position is
    (A) pro-Russian
    (B) anti-Russian
    (C) anti-British
    (D) pro-German
    (E) neutral

27. The problem in World War II concerning the disposition of Soviet prisoners of war was very similar to
    (A) the plight of Armenian refugees
    (B) Hitler's own loss of identity after 1944
    (C) the plight of British prisoners of war
    (D) no previous situation
    (E) several instances in the history of war

28. Lord Selborne's opinion disregards which one of the following facts?
    (A) The Soviet Union posed a nuclear threat to the United States.
    (B) Traditionally, repatriation was not imposed by Great Britain.
    (C) Certain Soviet citizens wanted to overthrow Stalin.
    (D) General Andrey Vlasov was politically independent.
    (E) Soviet prisoners were treated brutally.

29. The German labor mobilization drive consisted partly of
    (A) women and children
    (B) retreating German soldiers
    (C) followers of General Andrey Vlasov
    (D) savage combat units
    (E) those born during the retreat

30. The Soviet policy toward their prisoners of war was one of

(A) nonrecognition
(B) nonaggression
(C) nonproliferation
(D) noncontempt
(E) nonadherence

Passage 5

The right to an unbiased jury is an inseparable part of the right to trial by jury as guaranteed by the Seventh Amendment of the United States Constitution. This right guarantees that twelve impartial jurors will hear and "truly try" the cause before them.

In September 1982, the California Supreme Court upheld a lower court's $9.2 million verdict against Ford Motor Company despite the fact that three jurors had been working crossword puzzles and one juror had been reading a novel during the presentation of testimony. Four of the twelve jurors hearing the case were admittedly participating in the activities charged and were clearly guilty of misconduct, yet the California Supreme Court found no resultant prejudice against Ford's position.

In the United States, citizens are called upon by the government to serve as jurors. Only under extraordinary circumstances may a citizen be excused from such service. Juries are therefore not necessarily composed of willing volunteers, but instead, are sometimes made up of individuals who are serving against their will, and justice is adversely affected when citizens are "forced" to serve on juries. In "Reflections of a Juror," the author, who served as a juror himself, recognized two distinct perspectives shared among jurors. Some jurors have a very positive attitude about their being asked to serve on a jury. Their perspective is that of rendering a public service by fulfilling their jury duties. On the other hand, some jurors view their obligation as just that, a burdensome obligation, and nothing more. Their attitude is one of getting through with the ordeal as soon as possible, a let's-get-out-of-here-by-this-afternoon approach.

A study conducted with mock juries, concerned specifically with the issue of juror prejudgment, revealed that 25 percent of the jurors polled reached their decision early in the trial. The jurors in the study who admitted to having made up their minds before having heard all the evidence also stated that they generally held to their first-impression assessments. By prejudging the outcome of the case the jurors had, in effect, breached their sworn duty.

From a reading of the California Supreme Court's opinion, it appears that the Court itself has committed the one form of conduct universally prohibited, that of prejudgment. Ford's battle was lost before it had even begun to present its case. In the first place, Ford is a multibillion-dollar international corporation with "pockets" deeper than most. Secondly, Ford had experienced a great deal of negative publicity resulting from recent jury verdicts awarding large sums of money to victims of Pinto automobile accidents wherein it was determined that Ford had defectively designed the Pinto's gasoline tank so that it was prone to explode upon rear-end impacts. Finally, the plaintiff was a nineteen-year-old college freshman whose pursuit of a medical career was abruptly ended when he suffered extensive brain damage after the brakes on his 1966 Lincoln failed, causing him to crash into a fountain after careening down a steeply curving hillside street. Ford presented a considerable amount of evidence in an attempt to prove that the cause of the accident was driver error and faulty maintenance and not defective design. The Supreme Court responded to Ford's arguments by stating that the jury was responsible for judging the credibility of witnesses and it would be wholly improper for the Court to usurp that function by reweighing the evidence. How ironic that the Court should so gallantly refuse to upset the decision of the jury, a jury wherein four members admittedly were engaging in extraneous activities when they were supposed to be "judging the credibility of witnesses." It would appear from the misconduct of the jury and the conclusionary statements of the California Supreme Court that Ford's liability was indeed a predetermined, prejudged fact.

If the decision has any impact upon our present system of justice, it will regretfully be a negative one. The California Supreme Court has, in effect, approved a standard of jury conduct so unconscionable as to, in the words of dissenting Justice Richardson, "countenance such a complete erosion of a constitutional command," namely, the right to a fair and impartial jury trial.

31. Which one of the following best states the central idea of the passage?

(A) By not questioning the decision in the Ford case, the California Supreme Court, like the jury, was guilty of prejudgment.
(B) There are serious defects in the system of trial by jury.
(C) The jury in the Ford case was guilty of prejudging the case.
(D) The Supreme Court's handling of the Ford case may lead to an erosion of the constitutional right to a fair and impartial jury trial.
(E) Studies suggest that a large number of the men and women serving on juries fail to "truly try" the cases they hear.

32. All of the following data from the passage could be used to argue against the jury system EXCEPT:

(A) in the Ford case, three jurors were working crossword puzzles and one was reading a novel during the presentation of testimony
(B) juries are likely to include individuals who are serving against their will
(C) in a study of mock jurors, 25 percent reached a decision early in the trial
(D) pretrial publicity about Ford Pintos resulting in large jury verdicts to victims influenced the Supreme Court's decision
(E) some jurors view their service as an ordeal to be ended as quickly as possible

33. The author's belief that Ford was denied a fair trial in the lower court is best supported by the fact that

(A) the jury was unduly sympathetic to the nineteen-year-old accident victim who suffered extensive brain damage
(B) the jury was influenced by unfavorable publicity about the defective gas tanks on the Ford Pinto
(C) three of the jurors were admittedly working crossword puzzles during the testimony
(D) the California Supreme Court refused to reverse the decision of the jury
(E) the California Supreme Court refused to judge the credibility of the witnesses

34. An argument in favor of the Supreme Court decision in the Ford case might include all of the following EXCEPT:

(A) if the case were retried, the jury would probably include jurors who were serving against their will
(B) it is probable that the jurors working puzzles and reading were also paying attention to the testimony
(C) if the case were retried, some members of the jury are likely to come to a decision early in the trial
(D) if the case were retried, those jurors who made up their minds early would be unlikely to alter their verdicts later in the trial
(E) the jury at the original trial is in a better position to judge the credibility of the witnesses than the Supreme Court

35. The author suggests that the California Supreme Court reached its decision in the Ford case for all of the following reasons EXCEPT:

(A) a prejudice against Ford because of its wealth
(B) a prejudice against Ford because of recent negative publicity
(C) an agreement with the lower court's evaluation of the credibility of the witnesses
(D) a bias in favor of the young accident victim
(E) a refusal to find fault with deplorable jury conduct

36. In the next to last paragraph of the passage, the author uses irony when he writes

(A) "Ford's battle was lost before it had even begun to present its case."
(B) "Ford is a multibillion-dollar international corporation with 'pockets' deeper than most."
(C) The plaintiff's "pursuit of a medical career was abruptly ended when he suffered extensive brain damage . . ."
(D) ". . . the Court should so gallantly refuse to upset the decision of the jury. . . ."
(E) ". . . Ford's liability was indeed a predetermined, prejudged fact."

37. From information given in lines 58–62, it is clear that the Supreme Court decision

(A) was unanimous
(B) was not unanimous
(C) will have a significant impact on the justice system
(D) reverses that of the lower court
(E) will be appealed

Passage 6

In 1957, Congress passed the Price-Anderson Act, which provides a current limitation of $665 million on the liability of nuclear power companies in the event of a "nuclear incident." The dual purpose of the Act is to "protect the public and encourage the development of the atomic energy industry." While the objective of encouraging the development of atomic energy has been achieved, it is not yet known if Price-Anderson would fully compensate the public in the event of a serious nuclear accident.

In the event that a major accident does occur in this country, would the victims be adequately compensated for their injuries? The nuclear industry is promoted under Price-Anderson by having a limit on potential liability even if the accident was the result of gross negligence or willful misconduct. Victims are protected by having an asset pool of at least $665 million in which to recover for damages. This amount will undoubtedly be raised when Price-Anderson is renewed. Victims are also protected if an accident is deemed to be an "extraordinary nuclear occurrence" by the requirement that certain defenses be waived by the utility company. However, the victims would still substantially bear the risk because of the uncertainty of recovery for radiation injuries. This is contrary to the tort (wrongful act) concept that "he who breaks must pay."

The Price-Anderson Act does not disturb the common law rule of causation. A person injured in a nuclear incident has the burden of proving a causal relationship between the incident and his alleged injury. While the plaintiff does not have to show that the conduct of the defendant was the sole cause of the injury, the plaintiff must prove that it is more likely than not that the conduct of the defendant was a substantial factor in bringing about the injury. The plaintiff has the burden of showing that there is a high probability (i.e., 51 percent or more) that the defendant's conduct caused his alleged injury. A mere possibility of such causation is not enough; and when the matter remains one of pure speculation or conjecture, or the probabilities are at least evenly balanced, it becomes the duty of the court to direct a verdict for the defendant. In the event of a nuclear incident involving a large release of radioactive material, such as Chernobyl, it would probably not be difficult for immediate victims to demonstrate a causal link between the accident and their injuries. Scientists are able to detect approximately how much radiation was released into the atmosphere, and how surrounding areas are affected by it.

An argument in favor of Price-Anderson is that it ensures that claimants have an asset pool of at least $665 million in which to recover for damages. Without Price-Anderson, the possibility is very real that the utility company would be unable to pay claims arising out of a major accident. If the claims were sufficiently large or numerous, a private company could well choose bankruptcy over paying the claims. For example, the Planex Corporation, a defendant in thousands of asbestos cases, filed for reorganization under Chapter 11 of the Bankruptcy Code in 1982.

38. The primary purpose of the passage is to

(A) describe the Price-Anderson Act
(B) criticize the Price-Anderson Act
(C) support the Price-Anderson Act
(D) analyze and then condemn the Price-Anderson Act
(E) present the advantages and disadvantages of the Price-Anderson Act

39. The advantages to the nuclear industry in the United States of the Price-Anderson Act include all of the following EXCEPT:

(A) the limitation of the liability to $665 million
(B) some injuries may not be apparent until after the statute of limitations has expired
(C) the potential liability far exceeds the limit fixed
(D) the plaintiff must show the high probability that the defendant's conduct caused the injury
(E) the ceiling on liability will probably be raised when Price-Anderson is renewed

40. If there were a major nuclear accident in the United States equal in size to the Chernobyl incident, we can infer that under the rules of the Price-Anderson Act

(A) there would be difficulty in proving causation
(B) the asset pool would be exhausted
(C) victims with latent injuries would be able to collect damages
(D) the liability would not apply if the accident was caused by provable negligence
(E) the concept of "he who breaks must pay" would be applied

41. Which one of the following is an advantage of the Price-Anderson Act to the general public?

(A) The liability pool of $665 million would pay many victims of a nuclear accident.
(B) A utility company responsible for a nuclear accident would not need to file for bankruptcy if the claim exceeded the $665 million in the asset pool.
(C) A claim against a company responsible for a nuclear accident could be filed under relaxed common law rules of causation.
(D) Injuries caused by nuclear exposure might not be apparent for many years.
(E) Victims of an accident could collect punitive damages if an accident is caused by industry negligence.

42. Under the terms of the Price-Anderson Act, in the case of a minor nuclear accident a successful plaintiff would have to show that the defendant's conduct was the

(A) sole cause of his injury
(B) probable cause of his injury
(C) possible cause of his injury
(D) contributing cause of his injury
(E) cause of his injury through negligence

43. According to the passage, the Planex Corporation (line 44) filed for bankruptcy

(A) after paying damages in a nuclear accident case
(B) after paying damages in a toxic waste case
(C) after paying damages in an asbestos case
(D) to avoid paying damages in a toxic waste case
(E) to avoid paying damages in an asbestos case

44. With which one of the following statements would the author of the passage be most likely to disagree?

(A) Attitudes toward nuclear energy have changed dramatically since the incidents at Three Mile Island and Chernobyl.
(B) The radioactive contamination from Chernobyl may result in thousands of cancer deaths in the next 50 years.
(C) Congress should disallow any expansion of the nuclear power industry.
(D) The size of the asset pool under Price-Anderson should be increased.
(E) The 20-year statute of limitations under the Price-Anderson Act is too short.

Passage 7

In order to appreciate the reasons for the Electoral College, it is essential to understand its historical context and the problem that the Founding Fathers were trying to solve. They faced the difficult question of how to elect a president in a nation that was composed of thirteen large and small states jealous of their own rights and powers and suspicious of any central national government, and one that contained only 4,000,000 people spread up and down a thousand miles of Atlantic seaboard barely connected by transportation or communication (so that national campaigns were impractical even if they had been thought desirable). In addition, under the influence of such British political thinkers as Henry St. John Bolingbroke, the Founding Fathers believed that political parties were mischievous if not downright evil, and that gentlemen should not campaign for public office. (The saying was "The office should seek the man, the man should not seek the office.") How, then, to choose a president without political parties, without national campaigns, and without upsetting the carefully designed balance between the presidency and the Congress on one hand and between the states and the federal government on the other?

The Constitutional Convention considered several possible methods of selecting a president. One idea was to have the Congress choose the president. This idea was rejected, however, because some felt that making such a choice would be too divisive an issue and leave too many hard feelings in the Congress. Others felt that such a procedure would invite unseemly political bargaining, corruption, and perhaps even interference from foreign powers. Still others felt that such an arrangement would upset the balance of power between the legislative and executive branches of the federal government.

A second idea was to have the state legislatures select the president. This idea, too, was rejected out of fears that a president so beholden to the state legislatures might permit them to erode federal authority and thus undermine the whole idea of a federation.

A third idea was to have the president elected by a direct popular vote. Direct election was rejected not because the framers of the Constitution doubted public intelligence but rather because they feared that without sufficient information about candidates from outside their state, people would naturally vote for a "favorite son" from their own state or region. At worst, no president would emerge with a popular majority sufficient to govern the whole country. At best, the choice of president would always be decided by the largest, most populous states, with little regard for the smaller ones.

Finally, a so-called "Committee of Eleven" in the Constitutional Convention proposed an indirect election of the president through a college of electors. The function of the college of electors in choosing the president can be likened to that in the Roman Catholic Church of the College of Cardinals selecting the Pope. The original idea was for the most knowledgeable and informed individuals from each state to select the president based solely on merit and without regard to state of origin or political party.

The structure of the electoral college can be traced to the centurial assembly system of the Roman Republic. Under that system, the adult male citizens of Rome were divided, according to their wealth, into groups of 100 (called "centuries"). Each group of 100 was entitled to cast only one vote either in favor or against proposals submitted to them by the Roman senate. In the Electoral College system, the states serve as the centurial groups (though they are not, of course, based on wealth), and the number of votes per state is determined by the size of each state's Congressional delegation. Still, the two systems are similar in design and share many of the same advantages and disadvantages.

45. The primary purpose of the passage is to

(A) examine the history of the Electoral College in the United States.
(B) describe the issues faced by the Constitutional Convention in deciding how to elect a president.
(C) explain why the idea of a direct popular vote for the presidency was rejected by the Constitutional Convention.
(D) illustrate the conflict between the states and the federal government on the issue of electing a president.
(E) explain the structure of the Electoral College and how delegates are chosen.

46. The passage provides information that answers which one of the following questions?

(A) Which plan for selecting the president was supported by the public?
(B) Which plan for selecting the president created the most conflict between delegates?
(C) Why was the idea of having state legislatures choose the president rejected?
(D) Who opposed the decision to create a college of electors?
(E) How did presidential candidates campaign in the thirteen states?

47. It can be inferred from the passage that the author

(A) admires the Founding Fathers for their approach to choosing a president.
(B) believes the creation of political parties adversely affected the election process.
(C) sees some disadvantages with the college of electors system.
(D) feels that maintaining the balance of power between the legislative and executive branches of the government is essential.
(E) believes that Congress choosing the president would lead to corruption and possible influence by foreign powers.

48. According to the passage, which one of the following was an influence on the Founding Fathers' decision to create a college of electors?
    (A) the structure of the College of Cardinals in the Catholic Church
    (B) a desire to give power to state legislatures
    (C) the model of the Roman Republic's centurial assembly system
    (D) a desire to create a system not dependent on political parties or national campaigns
    (E) the belief that the public's intelligence was inadequate for a direct method of election

49. The passage provides most support for which one of the following inferences?
    (A) To be fair, direct election of the president would first require good methods of communication among the thirteen states.
    (B) Election of a state's "favorite son" to the presidency would ensure corruption.
    (C) The largest states would favor the system of a college of electors.
    (D) Anyone who would actively seek the presidency of the federation would be considered evil.
    (E) The first college of electors consisted of the most knowledgeable individuals in each state legislature.

50. According to the passage, the college of electors created by the Constitutional Convention and the centurial assembly system created by the Roman Republic are similar because
    (A) both are based on the intelligence of groups of electors.
    (B) neither embodies the idea of "one man, one vote."
    (C) the number of votes is dependent on the size of each group.
    (D) each favors a balance of power between a central government and individual groups.
    (E) neither is based on wealth.

Passage 8

The role that the Wall Street stock market crash of 1929 played in causing the Great Depression has been exaggerated in the popular mind. But that the Great Crash has become a symbol for the Depression, the event that one associates with the onset of bad times, is beyond argument. Why this should be is not hard to understand. Black Tuesday, October 29, was, in John Kenneth Galbraith's words, "the most devastating day in the history of the New York stock market"; the securities making up *The New York Times* industrial averages lost all they had gained in a whole year of boom. The market rebounded the next day, but the respite was temporary. By mid-November, stock prices were nearly 40 percent lower than they had been in September.

The financial losses that this swift decline reflected and the panic and despair it generated among investors account for the association that people made between the Great Crash and the long depression of the 1930s. As a matter of fact, the American economy had begun to decline during the early summer, well before the crash.

Furthermore, stock prices rebounded between late November and the following April. By the end of 1929, the October collapse no longer seemed particularly significant (except to those who had lost their shirts). In November 1929 the left-leaning commentator Stuart Chase expressed the opinion that "we probably have three more years of prosperity ahead of us" before the next cyclical downturn. A month later, the editor-in-chief of the conservative French newspaper *Le Temps* predicted that "the turmoil that has just shaken New York would probably not have deep or lasting repercussions."

The general opinion of supposedly informed people early in l930 was that the United States had experienced no more than a minor recession, a typical stock market "panic." In June a delegation of American clergymen obtained an interview with President Hoover in order to urge him to undertake an expanded public works program. "You have come sixty days too late," he told them. "The Depression is over."

Of course these words were scarcely out of the president's mouth when the bottom fell out of the American economy, along with the economies of most other nations. By the end of 1930, no one doubted any longer that a worldwide depression was in progress. Looking back from that vantage point, the Wall Street crash seemed the place where it had all begun.

Now, these many years later, this no longer seems correct. Scholars generally agree that American stock prices were not unreasonably high in 1929 and that the October collapse had little or no effect on the level of industrial activity in the United States or anywhere else. No effect, that is, except psychological; it is possible, though impossible to demonstrate convincingly, that the shock of the October crash so discouraged investors and consumers that a recession was turned into an economic collapse.

While all the nations experienced the same kinds of economic problems during the Depression (e.g., industrial stagnation, soaring unemployment, shrinking agricultural prices, and financial collapse), these problems manifested themselves in different ways in different places. What attracted the deepest concern at any given time and place appeared less pressing at others.

51. Which one of the following most accurately states the main point of the passage?

(A) The stock market crash in 1929 was the indirect cause of the Great Depression because people lost faith in the economy.
(B) Although the crash of the stock market has become a symbol of the Great Depression, it was not the cause.
(C) Overpriced stocks led to the events of Black Tuesday, 1929, and the ensuing panic that turned a recession into the Great Depression.
(D) Most well-informed people believed at the time of the Great Depression that the downturn of the economy was temporary.
(E) At the end of 1929, people realized that the economy was in the throes of an economic depression.

52. The passage provides the most support for which one of the following inferences?

(A) Even before the stock market crash, economic experts predicted a recession.
(B) Industrial stagnation immediately followed the stock market crash.
(C) Although most experts saw the stock market crash as a minor recession, the average citizen suffered extreme losses.
(D) When stock prices rebounded in late November of 1929, it appeared that the crash was not catastrophic but a short-lived downturn.
(E) When stock prices are seriously inflated, economic depression is inevitable.

53. The quotations from Stuart Chase (lines 21–22) and the editor-in-chief of *Le Temps* (lines 23–25) are offered as evidence that

(A) commentators across the political spectrum didn't at first realize the seriousness of the economic situation in 1929.
(B) the stock market crash triggered both a national and an international panic.
(C) economic downturns were cyclical events that occurred relatively frequently in the United States.
(D) news organizations could not be counted on to tell the public the truth about the economic situation.
(E) commentators initially disagreed about what the stock market crash meant in America and abroad.

54. According to the passage, President Hoover's attitude toward the economic situation in mid-1930

(A) reflected the optimistic attitudes of commentators and scholars
(B) was characterized by a "wait-and-see" view of events
(C) demonstrated an unwillingness to admit that there had been a depression
(D) showed a callous disregard for the plight of the unemployed
(E) was that the economy would heal itself and didn't require governmental intercession

55. The author of the passage would be most likely to agree with all of the following statements EXCEPT:

(A) Signs of an economic slow-down began months before the stock market crash.
(B) The nations of the world were affected by the Great Depression, though not necessarily in the same way or to the same degree as the United States.
(C) Industrial stagnation was one of the first results of the stock market crash.
(D) The psychological effect of the October 29 stock market crash may have been greater than the immediate financial loss.
(E) Immediately following the crash, stock prices temporarily rebounded.

56. According to the passage, people have probably mistakenly identified "Black Tuesday's" stock market crash as the cause of the Great Depression because it

(A) marked, in hindsight, the beginning of the devastating events that followed.
(B) immediately triggered a rapid decline in industrial activity and a decline in agricultural prices.
(C) was the first sign of an economic decline in U.S. history.
(D) was the worst day in the history of the New York stock market.
(E) caused nations around the world to question the stability of the U.S. economy.

Passage 9

Punitive satire is distinguished from the comic by the presence of both the historically authentic and the historically particular; in the absence of either, the satiric quality disappears. In other words, the satiric is lost when the object of attack is entirely imaginary (or "false" with respect to historical reality) or when, as a phenomenon so persistently recurrent and widespread as to be regarded as "universal," it cannot, without further qualification, be assigned specific historical identity. The first condition is easy enough to understand. Falstaff, Tony Lumpkin, and Donald Duck are, for all their appealing "humanity," manifest fabrications, composites of qualities which, though each may be very familiar to us, are here joined in synthetic combination. It is sometimes said that each of these figures inhabits his own "world" of fantasy; if true, this suggests how very far from satiric is the appeal which they have for us. If, in their presence, our world and our preoccupations tend to slip away from us for the time, then, in a frame of mind which is almost the antithesis of that invited by satire, we rejoice in our escape from the issues and problems and "significance" of ordinary existence.

But aside from these rare, and, in a sense, "unlikely" creations, most comic characters may be said to have a crucial correspondence with reality and to derive verisimilitude from our worldly familiarity with the most important qualities they display. The moralistic critic of comedy, moreover, often insists that it is precisely because basic human weaknesses and the dilemmas to which they lead are represented by the comic artist that his work deserves our serious attention. If, therefore, the great majority of comedies can be said to expose very real and familiar human frailties, why are they not, for this reason, satiric? And if this is true, is there not, at the least, a satiric element in most of the literature which moves us to laughter?

To these questions, the answer appears to be that between sheer comedy and those satires which produce laughter by the employment of comic formulas the difference is one of particularity in the object of attack. It is true that the most common sort of comic dupe is the character who, we suggest as we look around at our neighbors, might well have been Smith or Jones or Robinson. This is, indeed, an appropriate reaction, for the credibility and interest of such figures depend heavily upon their conforming to our own knowledge of human nature. But in such states, the "might have been" is of central importance. In satire, the victim is Smith, Jones, or Robinson or, if not, belongs to a particular group or embraces a particular view which can be isolated, for the purpose of receiving our unflattering attention, from the rest of the world about us.

Of the several assertions which are here made about satire, it is likely that this insistence upon the particularity of the satiric object will prove most controversial. Traditionally, satire has more often than not been discussed as though its principal function were to oppose vice and folly, if not in the abstract, then at least in terms sufficiently general to admit wide and profitable application to common human problems.

Satirists themselves (Swift among them, at times) have tended to insist that their assaults are prompted not by limited and specific aversions but by a hatred of evil, however and in whomever manifested. This is a position with which it is easy to sympathize; a serious writer cannot be expected to relish the role of a mere controversialist. It is similarly understandable that audiences conspire in this lofty view of the satiric mission, since most of us find gratification in the belief that our entertainment can provide us with "insights" into profound questions of human conduct.

57. Which one of the following most accurately states the author's main argument in the passage?

(A) Comedy is a less effective tool than satire for encouraging social reform.
(B) Satire is directed toward a particular object of attack that exists or existed in the real world.
(C) Comedy's central purpose is to offer an escape from the world's problems rather than to encourage reform.
(D) Satire relies more on wit for its effects, whereas comedy is broader and more universal.
(E) Comedy addresses universal human traits rather than particular ones.

58. According to the author, Donald Duck isn't a satirical object because he

(A) appears in animated form
(B) is an animal who is given human traits
(C) is more of a lovable than a foolish character
(D) doesn't represent a real historical character
(E) doesn't serve as a comment on society

59. The main function of the second paragraph of the passage is to

(A) present possible objections to the author's thesis
(B) define comedy in greater detail
(C) explain the most significant differences between satire and comedy
(D) describe what is meant by "synthetic combination" in paragraph one
(E) support the author's central argument

60. The passage most strongly supports which one of the following inferences?

(A) Satire is a more significant literary form than comedy.
(B) Many critics and satirists wouldn't agree with the author's view of satire.
(C) The distinction between comedy and satire is arbitrary.
(D) Comedy does not have serious intentions.
(E) Audiences enjoy the rewards of comedy more than the rewards of satire.

61. In line 50, the author uses the term "mere controversialist" to

(A) demean the status of authors who write comedy rather than satire
(B) underline the role of satiric writers
(C) emphasize the fact that satirists disagree among themselves
(D) designate a view of satire that serious writers might not like
(E) describe the way most audiences view satirists

62. According to the passage, which one of the following does the author attribute to satire's audience?

(A) a belief that satire can lead to important social reform
(B) an appreciation of satire's comic possibilities
(C) a belief that satire is a more intellectual form than comedy
(D) a conviction that satire represents a biased view of mankind
(E) a belief that satire can provide profound insights into behavior

63. Based on the author's argument in the passage, which one of the following would be most likely to be a satire?

(A) a skit in which the Republican and Democratic candidates for president are represented as squabbling children
(B) a comic novel poking fun at people's search for eternal youth at a luxurious health spa
(C) a television series about a confidence man in a small town who is mistaken for a priest
(D) a parody of "The Three Little Pigs" in which the wolf is the hero and the pigs are the villains
(E) a comedy in which the greedy children of an old man scheme to take his fortune

Passage 10

Art, since its very beginning in prehistoric caves, has been what our modern political parlance would define as "conservative." It has served to preserve the status quo. It has been a signal to future generations. It attempts to prolong the present to the detriment of the future. In ancient Egypt it served to banish death and the passage of time at the same time that it extolled the dynasty. In Greece it raised monuments that made visible lasting ideas and glorified victories and gods. In Rome it first turned ancestors into gods and then, during the Empire, gave lasting expression to a dominant political principle of Roman authority. This system was gradually transferred to Christianity and again served God, who in turn lent power to the emperor and his enterprises. The relationship between religion, dynasty, and art changes constantly in its proportionate emphasis according to the political moment. Sometimes it is religion that dominates, sometimes it is the dynasty. But always, art is called upon to memorialize, to eternalize certain principles, certain personalities, and certain events that are deemed to be of lasting importance and that tend to stand in the way of further developments. If we call Giotto or Titian revolutionary, we use the word only in the esthetic, not in its political or spiritual, meaning. Giotto and Titian and other artists who introduce new notions into art do so in the name of those forces that, ever since the beginning of Western civilization, have supported and needed art.

In exchange, the belief in higher powers gave art a grandeur and a secure significance that it could not have attained in any other way. Since art was the interpreter of communal religious ideals, it could count on speaking clearly to all reaches of society, and it could also count on going beyond the material essence, and thus it distinguished itself from the limited world of artifacts. For the image, whether it was of stone, of metal, or painted on terra cotta tablets, automatically became a symbol of an ordered universe in which the power of divinity was manifest at all times. Art, in short, showed mankind that life was a meaningful, divinely ordained gift which was part of a vast scheme of things that could be understood and, within limits, controlled by faith and by ritual.

From the time of the unification of Upper and Lower Egypt (about 3000 B.C.), which also marks the beginning of a truly Western point of view in art though dynasties and religious ideals kept changing, the major premise of each succeeding culture remained the same. There were, of course, certain moments in this immense stretch of time that did not conform to this pattern. Of these, the closest to us in time and best known by us today is the short period that saw the flowering of Dutch art in the 17th century. But even here, where secular rather than dynastic or religious ideals were predominant, there still remained an abstract, otherworldly, and universal principle on which art fed: patriotism and love of those homely Protestant virtues on which the unity of the community was based. Pride in the land, devotion to the domestic scene, an emphasis on virtue that was universally believed in even though it promised no concrete rewards in the hereafter were the keynote. But in any case, such short periods are freaks of art history and not the rule. Religion and dynasty were the dominant forces that gave art substance over the centuries.

This state of political and cultural balance broke down toward the end of the 18th century. Questioned by the major figures of the Enlightenment, the system was destroyed by the French, American, and industrial revolutions. Art, an activity that had always been reactionary, was suddenly immersed in a revolutionary epoch. The Church and the dynasty, which needed the artist as much as the artist needed them, were no longer there to sponsor art, and the artist was cut off from financial support and from spiritual response. Up to this time all important works of art had been produced on request; in other words, the artist knew before he set hand to his work that there was a real need for what he was about to produce. Now, with the coming of revolution, the artist produced his work in the void and hoped that his painting or sculpture (now reduced to the level of merchandise) would find an appreciative or at least a generous buyer.

64. Which of the following most accurately states the main idea of the passage?

(A) Throughout history, art has glorified heroic deeds and religious belief but ignored the plight of the common man.
(B) While artists traditionally served the forces in power, revolutions late in the eighteenth century changed the role of art.
(C) Art's role has always been to show mankind that there is order in the universe and that life has a divinely ordained purpose.
(D) Titian and Giotto are among the few artists who have rebelled against the conservative nature of art.
(E) The emphasis on religion and dynasty in art changed dramatically and permanently with the flowering of Dutch art in the seventeenth century.

65. According to the author, artists benefited most from the "conservative" nature of art because of which of the following?

(A) Art and artists were considered to be of great significance.
(B) Artists could confidently rely on accepted techniques.
(C) An artist could become wealthy and famous.
(D) Artists wouldn't be censored or persecuted for their ideas.
(E) Art's audience included all levels of the society.

66. The passage most strongly supports which of the following inferences about Dutch art of the seventeenth century?

(A) Although technically proficient, Dutch artists lacked a belief in religious ideals.
(B) Artists often painted simple domestic scenes.
(C) Dutch art is of minor interest in terms of its subject matter.
(D) Dutch artists were not popular with the ruling class.
(E) Dutch artists scorned visions of heaven and an afterlife.

67. In context, the author's use of the phrase "reduced to the level of merchandise" (line 62) emphasizes which of the following points?

(A) Artists were no longer respected members of the society.
(B) Religious art was unpopular after the eighteenth century.
(C) When art was not motivated by religion, its quality deteriorated.
(D) Technique became more important than subject matter in a work of art.
(E) To make a living, artists had to seek their own buyers.

68. The author of the passage would be most likely to agree with which of the following statements?

(A) The advent of Christianity changed the nature of art.
(B) Religion has been more important in the history of art than politics.
(C) Early artists supported the existing power structure out of fear and intimidation.
(D) Most artists after the eighteenth century were considered radical and dangerous.
(E) Art in ancient Egypt, Greece, and Rome protected the ruling powers.

69. Which of the following most accurately describes the organization of the passage?

(A) The first three paragraphs present first a generalization about the nature of art and then supporting evidence; the fourth paragraph introduces a change.
(B) The first two paragraphs support a generalization about art history, and the last two paragraphs present exceptions.
(C) The first three paragraphs present general statements about the nature of art, and the fourth paragraph draws a conclusion.
(D) The first paragraph presents the author's point of view about the history of art; the following three paragraphs present arguments against that point of view.
(E) After an introductory paragraph, three paragraphs present examples that support the central thesis.

Passage 11

Every animal is familiar with those variables in the environment that register through its senses, but what is a stimulus to one animal may not be a stimulus to another. Man perceives external senses of sight, sound, touch, pain, pressure, odors, and temperature, as well as internal senses of balance, hunger, thirst, kinesthesia, nausea, sex, suffocation, pain, and fullness of bladder and stomach. Sensations are not always interpreted correctly by the brain. Sometimes hot may feel like cold or cold like hot.

In initiations people have been blindfolded and given the suggestion that they were going to be branded. Then when an ice cube was put to the skin it felt hot rather than cold. Sometimes food is thought to have a taste when the sensation is really smell. Pain may be felt in a part of the body remote from where it actually occurs. Such pain is well known to doctors and is termed referred pain. In these cases, the misinterpretation results from conditions arising during embryological development. Usually the pained area is innervated by the same nerve that supplies the organ causing the trouble. For example, a pain in the heart may be felt on the median surface of the left arm, or a pain in the liver may be felt above the right shoulder blade. That there are variations in sensitivity of stimulus reception among humans is well known. To some people PTC (phenylthio-carbamide) is tasteless; to others it is bitter, salty, sour, or sweet. Some people see several colors; others are colorblind. Some hear a wide range of sound vibrations; others are tone deaf.

Thus if variations occur in humans, there may be even greater variations between humans and some other species of animal. The dog hears sounds of a frequency too high for human beings to hear, and its sense of smell is keen enough to track animals. Bees detect members of their own colony with their acute sense of smell, and female moths attract males at distances of three miles. The fact that responses of many animals are different from those of man leads many to attribute to animals a "sixth" sense. No one knows how many unknown variables are in our environment because we have no sense organs to receive them. Many animals have a time sense. Fiddler crabs become more active when the tide is out. Strangely, they also become more active during the same period of time in laboratories away from the ocean. When the sun rises, they somehow darken their skin whether they are on the beaches or enclosed in an unlighted laboratory. Bats dart through totally dark caves without striking anything. They avoid objects by listening to echoes of their shrieks. Because the frequency of their voices is fifty thousand cycles per second, which is above man's range of audible sensitivity, man does not hear the sound. Salmon depend on their olfactory sense to guide them to a spawning site. Tagged salmon generally return to the same stream where they were spawned or to a similar stream a short distance away. Much is still unknown about bird migrations. Length of day, food supply, and temperature are known to be influential. But homing pigeons can and do fly over country totally new to them.

Because of man's intelligence, he can reach beyond his natural senses. He does it by constructing sensitive apparatuses that convert imperceptible environmental variations into forms that he can receive. An example of how man makes such changes from one form to another is the transmission and reception of pictures by television. Visible images are changed to invisible electrical impulses, then converted again to visible images.

70. Which one of the following most accurately states the main point of paragraph one?

(A) Not all animals respond to the same stimuli.
(B) Factors in the immediate environment may affect the interpretation of stimuli.
(C) People can misinterpret stimuli or interpret them in different ways.
(D) Failure to correctly interpret sensory stimuli results from conditions during development of the embryo.
(E) What is a stimulus to one animal might not be a stimulus to another.

71. The author uses the example of PTC in lines 19–21 to

(A) show that humans may experience the same sensory stimulus differently
(B) indicate that different species react to the same stimulus in different ways
(C) emphasize humans' inability to accurately describe their reactions to a stimulus
(D) explain how phenomena such as referred pain can occur
(E) illustrate how senses such as taste can be affected by an individual's unique experience

72. The passage most strongly supports which one of the following inferences?

(A) Intelligence makes responses to sensory stimuli less important.
(B) Even though animals possess a "sixth sense," they often misinterpret sensory stimuli.
(C) People should never trust their responses to sensory stimuli.
(D) Damage to one of the senses is often compensated for by development of another.
(E) The environment may offer sensory stimuli to which humans can't respond.

73. The author covers all of the following in the passage EXCEPT:

(A) how salmon locate particular streams
(B) why individual humans respond to PTC differently
(C) how bees detect members of their colonies
(D) how bats are able to navigate in dark caves
(E) why a pain in the liver may be felt above the right shoulder blade

74. Which one of the following most accurately describes the organization of the passage?

(A) Paragraph one deals with human senses. Paragraph two deals with the senses of other animals. Paragraph three introduces the role of human intelligence.
(B) Paragraph one covers variations in human sensitivity to sensory stimuli. Paragraphs two and three compare humans' senses to those of other animals.
(C) Paragraphs one and two present examples of variations of sensitivity to particular sensory stimuli. Paragraph three draws generalizations from the examples presented.
(D) The first two paragraphs focus on the variety and superiority of animals' senses. The third paragraph focuses on man's intelligence.
(E) Paragraph one presents a thesis about responses to sensory stimuli. Paragraph two provides arguments to support the thesis. Paragraph three draws a conclusion.

75. Information in the passage most strongly supports which one of the following statements?

(A) Color blindness is most likely a genetic trait.
(B) Animals have several more sense organs than people.
(C) A person who has lost a leg might still experience pain from the area.
(D) Bats hear sound frequencies higher than any other animal.
(E) The phenomenon of referred pain is most likely psychosomatic.

76. The author's purpose in the passage can best be described as

(A) supporting a theory
(B) presenting a new perspective
(C) answering an unstated question
(D) disputing a widely accepted theory
(E) presenting a broad overview

Passage 12

In the early part of the thirteenth century, the Mongolian tribes in Central Asia were united under the leadership of Genghis Khan, and within a few years the Mongols conquered all their neighbors, including Russia. Because there were no barriers in the steppe to bar their way, they were able to march right in. Many historians claim that this invasion retarded Russia's development by two hundred years.

Among the results of the Mongol invasion were the deaths of thousands of Russians and the enslavement of ten percent of the population. Russia's most important cities were burned to the ground. A Catholic missionary traveling through the country in 1246 found countless bones and skulls lying by the wayside, while Kiev, once a city with a large population, contained only two hundred houses.

The effects on Russian politics and culture were equally devastating. The Mongols permitted no democracy in Russia, and the assembly, where formerly Russians were able to vote on their laws, was no longer allowed to meet. Russian communication with the outside world, which had already been limited by unfriendly Germans, Poles, and Swedes, was further discouraged by the Mongols. As a result, the European Renaissance (1300–1600 A.D.), with its great progress in science, mathematics, and art, didn't reach Russia.

As is frequently the case, in time the conqueror and the conquered influenced each other. The Mongols gave up their nomadic ways, settled down among the Russians, and even intermarried with them. Soon, many Mongol words became part of the Russian language. However, the Mongols weren't really interested in ruling Russia and didn't set up a real government there. Their primary interest was to get rich. How? By collecting taxes from the Russians. At first they collected the taxes themselves, but later they allowed the Russian princes, who still existed, to become the tax collectors. These princes were even allowed to rule their small regions, although the Mongols remained the real masters.

At the beginning of the fourteenth century, the Prince of Moscow received the title of Grand Prince from the Mongols and was given the right to collect taxes all over Russia. The princes of Moscow usually kept part of the money for themselves and as a result became the strongest princes in the country. Finally, in 1380, the current Prince of Moscow refused to turn over any of the tax money to the Mongols. In the battle that followed, the Mongols were defeated, and the people of Russia began to look at the princes of Moscow as the leaders of all Russia. It took, however, another one hundred years for the Russians to finally free themselves from the Mongols. By the middle of the sixteenth century, the Moscow princes had succeeded in uniting all the Russian lands under their rule and making Moscow their capital, with the Prince of Moscow becoming the tsar, or king, of Russia. The Mongol invasion, however, had cost the country two hundred years of development.

The new Russian state, with Moscow as its capital, was very different from the Kievan Russia before the Mongols. In the Russia with Kiev as its center, there had been some democracy, people were in some ways free to do as they pleased, and the power of the ruler was limited. In the new Russia, the people were considered servants of the state and the power of the tsar was unlimited and absolute.

77. Which of the following most accurately states the main point of the passage?

(A) The Mongols were not interested in providing a government for Russia but hoped to enrich themselves by taxing the people.
(B) The Mongol invasion of Russia resulted not only in physical destruction but also in political and cultural stagnation.
(C) The tsar system in Russia was established after the Moscow princes defeated the Mongols.
(D) To some extent, the Mongols in Russia were directly responsible for their own defeat because of their greed.
(E) Russia was unable to repel the Mongols both because of the country's physical location and its lack of a central government.

78. The passage provides the most support for which one of the following inferences?

(A) The Mongol invasion of Russia was made possible by the lack of a Russian military.
(B) Before the Mongol invasion, Russia had a democratically elected government and an assembly that met regularly.
(C) The nomadic ways of the Mongols hindered their ability to become part of Russian society.
(D) Moscow, rather than Kiev, became the central city in Russia after the Mongols were defeated.
(E) The Moscow princes were more successful as tax collectors than the Mongols had been.

79. The author attributes all of the following to the Mongols in Russia EXCEPT

(A) the enslavement of many Russians
(B) the contribution of Mongol words to the Russian language
(C) the destruction of Russian cities
(D) discouraging Russian contact with western Europe
(E) a powerful central government

80. Which of the following could most likely be added to the passage as the first sentence of paragraph 5?

(A) Giving the Moscow princes the power to collect taxes proved to be a mistake for the Mongols.
(B) Russian influence on the Mongols after the invasion was slight but not insignificant.
(C) What the Mongols wanted most from Russia was money and land.
(D) The isolation of Russia from the outside world had begun before the Mongols' invasion but became more severe under their rule.
(E) In spite of the fact that Russian princes were allowed to exist under the Mongols, they had almost no power.

81. According to the passage, which of the following most accurately describes the Russian political scene after the Mongols were defeated?

(A) Regional princes vied for authority, resulting in local skirmishes and more hardships for the peasantry.
(B) Absolute power was centralized in the person of the tsar.
(C) Limited democracy returned, but the Russian assembly was not reconvened.
(D) For many years anarchy reigned in most of the Russian provinces.
(E) The countries in Western Europe became models for Russian government.

82. According to the passage, which of the following was the most serious result of the Mongols' invasion in the thirteenth century?

(A) a 200-year hiatus in Russia's development
(B) an influx of Mongol values and practices
(C) the loss of major cities such as Kiev
(D) the loss of the Russian assembly
(E) a significant increase in poverty and serfdom

Passage 13

Following the early recognition that organisms were composed of cells, scientists turned their attention to these units as holding the answer to the meaning of life. From the time that Robert Hook first saw the cell wall in 1665 to the present time, the trend has been for scientists to focus their interests on smaller and smaller physiological and structural units within cells. It soon became evident that the cellular organization of organisms was essentially universal and that the living part of the cell was its contents (protoplasm) rather than its wall. In 1839 the name *protoplasm* was given to the living substance by Purkinje, a Bohemian. This period was also approximately the same time of Schleiden's and Schwann's publications, which more or less clinched the acceptance of the cell theory. Of course, inevitably protoplasm itself would come under the scrutiny of investigators. Indeed, in 1831—even before the coining of the word *protoplasm* by Purkinje—Robert Brown had discovered the specialized central part of protoplasm that is now called the nucleus.

For a period of time, interest was focused on the larger elements of the cell, like the nucleus and other parts visible under the microscope. But scientists then began to turn to other aspects, for example, the cell's physiology, method of division, origin, and its submicroscopic structure. About the middle of the nineteenth century, Virchow, a German physician, concluded that all cells came from pre-existing cells. By 1888 the process of cell division had been worked out in fair detail. Of course, interpretations have undergone refinements since that time.

The discovery of the electron microscope and the phase microscope was a boon to the study of cells. The electron microscope brought into view very small structures that the light microscope could not resolve. Whereas under average conditions the ordinary light microscope can magnify about one thousand times, the electron microscope in conjunction with photographic enlargement can magnify more than five hundred thousand times or, in linkage with a television system, up to two million times. Such magnification reveals the inner structure of chloroplasts, mitochondria, and the like, which previously, with the light microscope, had appeared to be without structure. The phase microscope of more recent development improves further the visibility of living cells. It makes use of an oblique source of light to clearly delimit transparent structures in the cell. With the transmitted light of the light microscope, many living structures are invisible. To make them visible, it has been the custom to kill, preserve, and color them with dyes. Certain of the parts have affinities for specific dyes. While processing cells in this manner has been useful to research, the cells themselves are altered and are no longer exactly like the living ones.

The knowledge of structure is not complete without relating it to the chemical matters of function. Therefore the level of exploration is shifting more to the invisible molecular level. The functions of all visible structures are not yet known, and even for those that are known the details of complex processes are often obscure at best.

83. Which one of the following most accurately expresses the main point of the passage?

(A) The recognition of the cell's importance in human physiology has been the most important step in the history of biology.
(B) The development of the electron microscope was the most important advance in helping us understand the cell.
(C) Since the identification of the cell as the basic unit of organisms, scientists have focused their attention on smaller units within cells and on function.
(D) Cell division, first recognized in the middle of the nineteenth century, explains how cells are produced.
(E) Studying the chemical matters of function is more important than simply having knowledge of a cell's structure.

84. Based on information in the passage, why was the development of the phase microscope significant to the study of cells?

(A) It led to the discovery of chloroplasts, mitochondria, and other parts of the cell's nucleus.
(B) In linkage with a television system, it could magnify a cell up to two million times.
(C) It provided visibility of cells colored with dye.
(D) Using the phase microscope, transparent structures could be viewed in living cells.
(E) It allowed the discovery of cell division as well as other cell functions.

85. The passage suggests that the author would be most likely to agree with which of the following statements?

(A) Nineteenth-century scientists provided the basic knowledge of the cell's structure.
(B) Robert Hook was the first to recognize the significance of the cell's nucleus.
(C) The functions of the cell's visible structures are well known, but the functions at the invisible molecular level remain to be discovered.
(D) Mitochondria would not have been identified had it not been for the development of the phase microscope.
(E) Protoplasm has come to mean the cell's entirety, not just its wall.

86. According to the passage, cells processed by preserving and coloring them

(A) do not duplicate exactly living cells
(B) are of little help in studying the submicroscopic structures
(C) have provided most of our knowledge of protoplasm
(D) can be easily viewed by any microscope
(E) are too distorted to be used in research

87. By "an oblique source of light" (lines 34–35), the author means a source of light that is

(A) perpendicular
(B) distant
(C) indirect
(D) parallel
(E) filtered

88. Which of the following best describes the type of organization the author uses in the passage?

(A) Generalizations about cells are followed by specific examples of researchers' findings.
(B) The history of cell research is presented chronologically.
(C) Questions are posed about the cell in the first half of the passage, and the answers provided in the second half.
(D) The first part of the passage deals with facts, and the second with theories.
(E) Cell structure is analyzed point by point, and a conclusion is presented in the final paragraph.

ANSWERS EXPLAINED

Passage 1

1. (C) This purpose is stated most explicitly in paragraph 5, although there are several other points in the passage where the author urges drivers to drive less. (A) is weak because it is too general and inclusive; (B) is vague about the means of reducing smog; (D) and (E) are very minor points.

2. (A) This is stated explicitly in paragraph 5, where the author blames individual drivers rather than industry.

3. (A) The second paragraph implies that recreational vehicles create more smog, and the fourth paragraph describes smog's effects on nature; therefore, we may conclude that gas-guzzling vacation vehicles help to damage the natural beauty of vacation spots. The author *might* also agree with (D), but the evidence in the passage itself points more substantially to (A).

4. (E) The author criticizes the increased use of recreational vehicles (see explanation for question 3).

5. (B) The final sentence in the passage implies that we will be "forced" to conserve if we do not do so voluntarily. (A) is neither stated nor implied; the author does imply that industrial emissions *should not be controlled,* but this is not the same as suggesting that they are *uncontrollable.*

6. (D) The author is almost pleading that drivers make immediate changes in their habits; the urgency of his purpose coincides with the urgency of his tone.

7. (D) The author begins the passage by claiming that the Harris Survey represents a "majority of Americans"; we must share that assumption in order to accept the importance of his argument. All other choices are irrelevant.

Passage 2

8. (D) The passage is part of a longer essay written to refute the arguments of Judge Jerome Frank, who holds that a judge alone is likely to be more reliable than a jury.

9. (E) The second paragraph says that judges and juries agree in 75.4 percent of the cases, according to the study.

10. (A) The third paragraph discusses the greater harshness of judges in all categories of crime—in counts, degrees, and sentencing.

11. (C) Because the effect of this information upon judges is to make their judgments harsher, we can infer it would have the same effect on juries and the withholding of this information is, predictably, to the defendant's advantage.

12. (A) The author assumes the judge understands the evidence, and because the juries agree with the judge so often, he argues the juries must also have understood the evidence to come to the same conclusion as the judge.

13. (E) The passage supports each of the first four statements, but the jury's sympathy with a defendant according to the last paragraph leads to judge-jury differences in only 4 percent of all the cases studied and so could not be called a "major" cause of disagreement.

14. (C) By admitting frankly that juries are not always fully objective, the author demonstrates a willingness to discuss facts that might not advance his case. All of the four other options are false.

15. (B) The statistics are used to support the author's case for the use of juries. Because the statistics are the result of other writers' research and are based upon a large sample, they give more than an "appearance" of objectivity.

Passage 3

16. (B) According to Paragraph 1, the states had never had the power to regulate interstate railroads, and the Interstate Commerce Act was an attempt to change this situation. (A) is an inference not supported by the passage, and although the passage says the Court "eviscerated" regulatory acts, it does not state or imply that this act was ruled unconstitutional (E). Both (D) and (C) are factually incorrect; the act was designed to provide state (not federal) regulation, and its purpose was to regulate railroads, not support their growth.

17. (E) The decision did not protect Congress's right to regulate industry. All of the other answers are true; the *Slaughterhouse* decision gave the state power (C) to give a monopoly to one company, (A, B). By refusing to extend the "privileges and immunities" clause of the 14th amendment to add the right to make a living, the Court was narrowly interpreting the clause (D).

18. **(A)** The Court found for Illinois, thereby confirming a state's right to regulate business. (B) was not considered in this decision. (D) is incorrect because the Court ruled that grain storage was not interstate commerce and therefore not under federal jurisdiction. Whereas grain merchants would be helped by Illinois regulating warehousemen, this fact did not serve as the basis for the Court's decision (E). Because the Court ruled for the state, (C) is simply incorrect.

19. **(A)** This is the best answer. By giving corporations the same rights and privileges as citizens, the Court made it almost impossible for states to regulate them. (B) was an important interpretation for cases involving private discrimination but not for cases involving regulation of business. (D) is incorrect; the Court ruled that the "privileges and immunities" clause did not include the right to make a living. (C) would not support business (and is not addressed in the passage), and the Court did not issue the ruling stated in (E).

20. **(E)** The ruling in the *Civil Rights* cases aided segregationists by limiting the 14th Amendment's application to state actions, thereby allowing private discrimination. There is no evidence that the ruling was the result of compromise (C), although it may have been, and it was definitely not a progressive decision, since official discrimination was already forbidden by the 14th Amendment (B). No evidence supports (A), and although the Justices were all white, that fact does not make the ruling "inevitable" (D).

21. **(C)** By making political parties private clubs, Southerners were able to circumvent the prohibition of official discrimination. Rather than defying the Court (A), they took advantage of its ruling on private discrimination. Although the "white primary" would prevent the election of African-Americans, that was not the reason it was created (B). (D) is irrelevant; the authority for election procedures was not in question. (E) is both vague and incorrect.

22. **(B)** The first three paragraphs illustrate by citing examples that the Court's decisions generally favored big business. The pros and cons of the decisions are neither addressed nor analyzed (C). The author does not suggest corruption in the Court nor does he describe "far-reaching effects" of any of the decisions (A). (D) is inaccurate; some regulatory legislation was passed during this period. (Beware of words like "no," "none," and "never.") The passage does not argue a point of view (E).

23. **(C)** Certain phrases indicate that the author is mildly judgmental; see lines 5, 10, 29, 37, and 47. (D) is a possible answer except for the use of the word "strictly." Connotations of words chosen by the author indicate some degree of judgment. Both (A) and (E) overstate the author's slightly judgmental attitude; he is neither cynical nor "harshly" negative. Nothing in the passage suggests (B).

Passage 4

24. **(A)** The passage discusses the past and present facts contributing to the British problem with captured Russians.

25. **(A)** The final paragraph discusses at length the question of whether to send Russians back to Russia despite their lack of allegiance to Russia. This is the repatriation question and is consistent with the dictionary definition of *repatriate*—to send back to the country of birth.

26. **(E)** The author does not himself argue for or against a particular position or nationality. He simply presents facts and the arguments of others. His comments in paragraph 2 might be called anti-German, but this attitude is not one of the choices.

27. **(D)** Paragraph 1 states, "This extraordinary situation [was] . . . never before known in the history of war."

28. **(C)** Selborne argued that Russians served the Germans only "as an alternative to certain death" (paragraph 3). But paragraph 2 states that some Russians fought with the Germans "in order to overthrow Stalin."

29. **(A)** Paragraph 2 says that "the German labor mobilization drive . . . included many women and children."

30. **(A)** Paragraph 1 states, "On the Soviet side, the very existence of prisoners of war was not recognized."

Passage 5

31. **(A)** The author wishes to criticize both the jury, which was inattentive, and the Supreme Court, which allowed the jury's decision to stand. Some of the other options are stated or implied ideas of the passage but not its central idea.

32. **(D)** (D) is relevant to the Supreme Court decision but not to the jury system. (A), (B), (C), and (E) all expose deficiencies in the jury system.

33. **(C)** The inattentiveness of four jurors is explicit support for a charge that Ford's case was not fairly heard. We don't know for certain whether (A) or (B) is true. (D) and (E) are true but do not support the author's belief in the unfairness of the trial.

34. **(B)** The limitations of all juries discussed in the passage would apply as well to the jury retrying the case as to the jury who reached a decision already. The Supreme Court's argument that the original jury was in a better position to judge the credibility of the witnesses is surely correct; the Supreme Court did not see the witnesses who testified. Though (B) is remotely possible, it is not a point one would wish to use in support of the Supreme Court decision.

35. **(C)** Though the Supreme Court agreed with the lower court jury, it specifically asserted the impropriety of its attempting to reweigh the evidence and the credibility of the witnesses.

36. **(D)** A case could be made that (B), an understatement, is ironic, but a clearer instance is the sarcasm of "gallantly"; the author does not believe the Supreme Court acted gallantly.

37. **(B)** Because Justice Richardson dissented, the decision cannot have been unanimous.

Passage 6

38. (E) Though the author has reservations about the Price-Anderson Act, the passage presents both the advantages and suggestions to rectify what the author sees as disadvantages.

39. (E) All of the first four items are advantageous financially to the industry. The rise in the ceiling on liability will raise the potential costs to the industry in the event of an "incident."

40. (B) The number of deaths, injuries, and damages caused by the accident at Chernobyl would surely cost more than $665 million in the asset pool. The other four answers are false.

41. (A) Only (A) is true and an advantage to the public. (B) is an advantage to the company, not to the public. (C) and (E) are untrue. (D) is true, but because the injuries might be slow to be recognized, the victim might not be able to qualify for reparations before the statute of limitations expired.

42. (B) The plaintiff under common law rules of causation would have to show a probability of 51 percent or more.

43. (E) The passage asserts that Planex declared bankruptcy to avoid the damages in a large number of suits involving asbestos.

44. (C) Though the author points to faults in Price-Anderson, he never suggests that the nuclear power industry's growth should be restricted. All of the other statements are either factual or opinions specifically supported in the passage.

Passage 7

45. (B) In the first paragraph the author states the issues faced by the delegates in deciding how to select a president, and the passage as a whole presents the various methods that were considered. (A) is too extensive; the passage doesn't examine the entire history of the Electoral College, only the initial decision by the Convention. (C) is a secondary point in the passage, as is choice (D). (E) is inaccurate; the author doesn't explain the structure of the Electoral College.

46. (C) See lines 20–26. The author doesn't discuss conflicts between delegates (B) or address public reaction to any of the plans (A). No opposition to the college of electors is mentioned (D). Also, according to the passage, national campaigning was considered undesirable and was also impractical; (E) is therefore not addressed.

47. (C) Although the author doesn't specify any disadvantages, in the last sentence of the passage he/she notes that the centurial system and the college of electors system share "many of the same advantages and disadvantages." (A) may be a true statement, but the author's opinion of the Founding Fathers is not implied in the passage. (B) is also inaccurate; the author states the Founding Fathers frowned on political parties but does not indicate his/her own opinion. Similarly, whereas the author indicates that the Founding Fathers agreed with the statements in (D) or (E), his/her own attitude cannot be inferred. Always focus on what the author implies rather than on what may or may not be a true statement.

48. (D) See lines 12–15. Both (A) and (C) may seem to have influenced the Founding Fathers, but it is the author of the passage not the Founding Fathers who draws comparisons between the College of Cardinals, the centurial system, and the college of electors. Nothing indicates that the Founding Fathers used these models. (B) is contradicted in lines 27–30, and (E) in lines 32–39.

49. (A) According to lines 33–35, the delegates to the Convention feared that because of a lack of communication among the thirteen states, people would vote for candidates from their own states ("favorite sons") merely because they had insufficient information about the other candidates. The inference in (B) is not warranted; the use of the word *ensure* is too strong. (C) is inaccurate; the college of electors envisioned by the Founding Fathers did not favor the larger states. (D) is also inaccurate; the Founding Fathers disapproved of anyone actively seeking public office, but, according to lines 11–12, it was political parties they saw as "mischievous if not downright evil." The original idea of the Convention was that the "most knowledgeable and informed individuals" from each state would make up the college of electors; nothing implies that this is what actually happened. Also, nothing implies that the electors came from the state legislatures (E).

50. (B) Direct election is based on "one man, one vote." But the college of electors uses indirect election; each state has a certain number of votes, depending on the size of its Congressional delegation. (C) is inaccurate; the centurial system was made up of groups of 100, whereas the size of the electoral groups depended on the size of a state's delegation (lines 55–56). (D) is irrelevant to the comparison, and (E) is inaccurate; the centurial system was based on wealth. (A) is also inaccurate; neither group is based on intelligence.

Passage 8

51. (B) Because of its dramatic nature, people came to view the stock market crash as the beginning of the Great Depression, but the sixth paragraph makes it clear that scholars today do not agree. It is a symbol rather than a cause. (A) is not the main point; the sixth paragraph suggests that the psychological effects of the crash might have contributed to a recession becoming a depression (lines 41–43), but this is a secondary point. (C) is not accurate (line 38). (D) is the second best answer; it is not the main point, however. (E) is inaccurate; according to the passage, it wasn't until the latter half of 1930 that people recognized the extent of the economic depression.

52. (D) From the evidence in lines 17–25, it is clear that the fear created by the October crash receded when stock prices rebounded. Nowhere in the passage is there the suggestion that experts predicted a recession before the crash (A), and in line 39 the author states that the crash had "little or no effect" on industry (B). (C) might possibly be true, but nothing in the passage itself indicates that "the average citizen" suffered extreme losses. (E) is far too broad. (When answering questions about inferences, beware of words such as "inevitable," "always," and "never.")

53. (A) The key words are "left-wing" to describe Chase and "conservative" to describe *Le Temps*. The author chooses these words to emphasize that the early reaction to the crash was the same across the political spectrum. (B) and (E) are inaccurate; neither quotation reflects a panic, and the two sources agree about the economic outlook. (C), while an accurate description of the quotations, does not explain why the author chooses a "left wing" and a "conservative" source. There is no evidence for (D).

54. (A) Hoover's belief that the economic depression had been short-lived agreed with the beliefs of most well-informed people, as evidenced by his response to the clergymen who urged him to expand a public works program. None of the other choices is accurate. While (D) might seem a possible answer, Hoover's statement that "The depression is over" was based on information he had at the time, not on callousness.

55. (C) See lines 37–40. (A) is supported in lines 15–16, (B) in the last paragraph, (D) in lines 39–43, and (E) in line 9. Notice the word "EXCEPT" in the question. It is important to understand exactly what the question is asking.

56. (A) See lines 35–36. The crash did not, according to the passage, immediately trigger industrial decline (lines 39–40) (B). The author doesn't state or imply that the crash was the first sign of economic decline in U.S. history (C), though, according to John Kenneth Galbraith, it was the worst day in history for the New York stock market (D). Therefore, (D) might seem like the best answer, but it was only in hindsight that the crash was viewed as the cause of the Great Depression. (E) is inaccurate; the quotation from a French newspaper in lines 23–25 indicates that the international view saw the crash as a temporary decline.

Passage 9

57. (B) (E), according to the passage, may be accurate, but it is not the best statement of the author's position. The author is most concerned with satire and with differentiating it from comedy. The first sentence of the passage states that satiric quality depends on both historical authenticity (the "real world") and historical particularity. Nowhere in the passage does the author deal directly with the relative effectiveness of comedy and satire, although there is a suggestion in lines 13–17 that (A) may be true. (C) may also be an accurate statement, but the author's main argument deals with satire, not comedy. (D) is not addressed in the passage.

58. (D) Donald Duck, along with Falstaff and Tony Lumpkin, is cited as an imaginary or fantasy character; historical reality is, according to the author, the first requirement of satire. A satirical character *could* be either (A) or (B), as satirical characters have been—but only if the character who is represented is an actual historical figure. Fantasy characters can serve to comment on society, but that does not, according to the author, make them satirical (E). (C) is irrelevant.

59. (A) After the author states in the first paragraph his/her definition of true satire, the second paragraph introduces what may be the objections to this position. The two questions at the end of the paragraph make it clear that the author is preparing to cover these objections. Comedy is further defined in this

paragraph (B), but that isn't the paragraph's main function. The difference between the two genres (C) is not addressed here, and both (D) and (E) are simply incorrect.

60. **(B)** In the last paragraph, the author states that the position presented in this passage is not the traditional view of satire, and that even the satirist Jonathan Swift would probably disagree with it. The author does not believe that the distinction between comedy and satire is arbitrary (C) but presents an argument that satire can be distinguished by the particularity and historical reality of its object of attack. Also, the author doesn't suggest that all comedy lacks serious intention (D); see the second paragraph. Nor does he/she judge the relative significance of either form. Nothing in the passage suggests (E).

61. **(D)** The author states that a satirist would rather not be seen as motivated by "limited and specific aversions" but instead by "a hatred of evil." "Mere controversialist" is a reference to the former. The term has nothing to do with authors of comedy (A), and it is not "underlining" the satirist's role (B); the use of the word *mere* rules this out. (E) is inaccurate; the author suggests in lines 51–53 the opposite view. (C) is irrelevant in the passage.

62. **(E)** See lines 51–53. (A), (B), (C), and (D) may be true statements about audiences' beliefs, but the author cites only one: that audiences "conspire in" a "lofty view" that satire can provide profound insights. In choosing an answer, focus on what is stated or implied in the passage, not on what may or may not be accurate in its own right.

63. **(A)** Choice (A) is based on the author's central point. The Republican and Democratic candidates are particular historical figures. (B) may be comedy with strongly satirical elements, but according to the author, the object of a satire should be particular and actual rather than representing general human foibles. (C) and (E) may also point up human foibles, but again there is no particular satirical object. (D) is about fantasy characters like Donald Duck, not real ones. Unless the pigs and the wolf are clearly based on actual, particular people, (D) would be a comedy, not a satire, according to the author's position.

Passage 10

64. **(B)** Most of the passage deals with art's support of the status quo, until the last paragraph, where the author indicates a breakdown in the status quo and a change in the role of the artist. The plight of the common man (A) is not alluded to in the passage. (C) is only partially correct, since the passage also deals with the change in art's purpose. (D) is inaccurate because the author specifically mentions Titian and Giotto as revolutionary only in the aesthetic sense. (E) is also inaccurate; Dutch art, according to the author, is a "freak of art history," not the rule.

65. **(A)** See lines 22–23. (E) is the second best answer, but it is not as encompassing as (A). (B) and (D) are not implied in the passage, nor does the passage state that artists became wealthy because of the importance of their work.

66. (B) The inference is supported by the reference to the secular nature of Dutch painting and to the statement that the art showed "devotion to the domestic scene." Although the passage does indicate that the Dutch artists did not deal with "rewards in the hereafter," it doesn't imply scorn (E), and "homely Protestant virtues" were a keynote of the artists' work, making (A) inaccurate. No judgment is implied (C), and there is no evidence to support (D).

67. (E) The Church and the dynasty in power had once commissioned art, so the artists knew what to produce and were guaranteed a living. But once the status quo had been destroyed by the Enlightenment and revolutions, artists had to produce their work "in the void" and then find buyers. There is no implication that the quality of the art deteriorated (C), nor does the passage suggest that religious art became unpopular (B). (D) is also not stated or implied. (A) might seem a plausible answer, but although artists might no longer be considered interpreters of "communal religious ideals," nothing suggests that they were no longer respected.

68. (E) The description of Egyptian, Greek, and Roman art in the first paragraph makes it clear that the art "extolled the dynasty," "glorified victories," and "gave lasting expression" to dominant political principles. According to the author, the conservative nature of art was "transferred" to Christianity, not changed by it (A). (B) is contradicted in lines 11–13. There is no evidence in the passage for the statements in (C) and (D).

69. (A) Although (B) may seem a good answer because the third paragraph does present an exception (Dutch art), the last paragraph presents not just an exception but rather an actual change in the nature of art because of a breakdown in "the political and cultural balance." (C) is not accurate because the last paragraph doesn't draw a conclusion. The structures suggested in (D) and (E) are wrong; arguments against the author's point of view are not included in the passage, and the final paragraph is not an example of the generalization made in the first paragraph.

Passage 11

70. (C) Although the first sentence of the paragraph may indicate that (A) or (E) is the answer, the rest of the sentences concern how sensory stimuli are interpreted differently—or misinterpreted—by the brain. (B) is a detail of the main point, and (D) isn't accurate in all cases.

71. (A) The author states that some people find PTC without taste, whereas to others it seems bitter, salty, sour, or sweet. Different species (B) are not involved, and referred pain (D) is a different issue. Both (C) and (E), while perhaps true, are not mentioned by the author in the example of PTC. When choosing an answer, rule out choices that, while they may be accurate, are not part of the passage.

72. (E) This point is implied in lines 30–31. Neither (A) nor (B) is directly stated or implied, and (D), while it may be accurate, cannot be inferred from information in the passage. (C) is too extreme; the passage gives examples of how sensory stimuli can be misinterpreted but does not support the broad inference that people should never trust their responses.

73. **(B)** The passage states that people experience PTC differently, but it does not suggest or provide a reason for this. (A) is explained in lines 40–43, (C) in lines 26–27, (D) in lines 36–37, and (E) in lines 15–18.

74. **(A)** All information in the first paragraph relates to human response to sensory stimuli; information in the second paragraph covers animal responses. The third paragraph deals with human intelligence and its ability to go beyond the senses. (E) is inaccurate; no thesis and no conclusion are presented in the passage, nor are generalizations drawn from the examples (C). Paragraph one covers human sensory response, not animal response (D), and paragraph two, while mentioning man's smaller range of audible sensitivity in lines 39–40, does not compare animal and human responses (B).

75. **(C)** While this specific phenomenon is not covered in the passage, paragraph one deals with misinterpretation of pain by the human brain. None of the other statements is supported in the passage. Genetics (A) are not mentioned, and there is no evidence that (B) is true. That bats hear high-frequency sounds is covered, but nothing suggests they hear frequencies higher than all other animals (D). Referred pain is explained as a physiological phenomenon, not as a psychosomatic condition (E).

76. **(E)** The passage is simply a broad overview of human and animal responses to sensory stimuli. It doesn't support or dispute any theory (A, D). The information in the passage is basic; it does not provide a new perspective (B), nor is there an unstated question that it answers (C).

Passage 12

77. **(B)** (C) may seem a tempting choice because it represents a major result of the ultimate defeat of the Mongols, but most of the passage focuses on the negative effects of the invasion itself, both the physical destruction (lines 7–12) and the political and cultural stagnation (lines 4–6, 13–18, 38–40). (A), (C), and (D), while accurate, are secondary points. (E) is not a main point, and the fact that Russia lacked a central government before the invasion is not mentioned.

78. **(D)** (lines 40–42). (E) might be accurate, but the passage provides no basis for this inference. The existence of a Russian military is never mentioned (A), and (C) is contradicted in lines 22–24. (B) might seem a plausible choice, but although "some democracy" and an assembly existed in Russian before the invasion, there is no indication that the country had "a democratically elected government" or indeed any elections at all.

79. **(E)** The passage states that the Mongols weren't interested in governing Russia and that they set up no real government (lines 25–26). They did, however, enslave ten percent of the population (line 8), contribute words to the language (lines 23–24), destroy cities (lines 8–9), and discourage contact with the outside world (lines 16–18). Remember to watch for words like "EXCEPT" in questions.

80. (A) The rest of the paragraph develops the point that giving the Russian princes the power to collect taxes ultimately led to the defeat of the Mongols. (B) and (D) are irrelevant to this paragraph, and (E) is contradicted in the paragraph by the description of how the Moscow princes were able to gain power by collecting taxes.

81. (B) See the last two lines of the passage. (A) isn't accurate, although it might seem like a plausible state of affairs after the defeat of the Mongols at the hands of the Moscow princes. But note lines 35–36. (C) and (D) are specifically contradicted, and there is no evidence for (E).

82. (A) Answer (A) is mentioned in lines 5–6 and restated in lines 43–44. (B) is not supported anywhere in the passage. Both (C) and (D) are accurate statements, but the author of the passage emphasizes the retardation of Russian development as the invasion's most serious effect. (E) is also possibly an accurate statement, but again, according to the passage, not the most significant result from a historical perspective.

Passage 13

83. (C) The passage deals with the progress of cell research, with an emphasis on studying smaller structural units and function. The development of microscopes (B) is an important secondary point, but not the main point. (D) and (E) are also secondary points. (A) is not a point that is developed in this passage.

84. (D) The chief asset of the phase microscope is described in lines 33–35. The electron microscope, not the phase microscope, allowed viewing of small structures (A and B). (C) is inaccurate; the phase microscope allowed for the viewing of cell parts without coloring them. (E) is not accurate; cell division was recognized in 1888, before the development of the phase microscope.

85. (A) (paragraphs 1 and 2). "Basic" is the key word in this answer. (B) and (C) are contradicted in the passage (lines 3 and 43–45). (E) is also contradicted; *protoplasm* is defined as the living part of the cell. There is no indication in the passage that (D) is an accurate statement. Credit for viewing of mitochondria is given to the magnification of the electron microscope.

86. (A) The passage states that processing cells in this way makes them "no longer exactly like the living ones." (B) is contradicted in line 39, (C) and (D) are not supported by the passage, and (E) overstates the effects of cell processing.

87. (C) *Oblique* means indirect or inclined. It is a contrast to both (A) and (D). In context, the point is made that indirect lighting makes the transparent structures visible. The direct "transmitted" light of the light microscope renders transparent structures of living cells invisible. (B) and (E) are not definitions of oblique, nor are these meanings suggested in the passage.

88. (B) Of the choices, it most accurately describes the movement of the passage, from the first viewing of the cell wall to the current study of cell function. The third paragraph dealing with microscopes is part of the chronological organization. Generalizations or questions are not presented (A and C). The passage is factual; it does not deal with theories (D).

CHAPTER 5

Writing Sample

Analyzing the Writing Sample Topic
The Decision Prompt
An Overview of the Three Key Strategies
The Phases of Writing
- Phase 1–Prewriting
- Phase 2–Writing
- Phase 3–Proofreading

Two Completed Writing Samples with Outlines

Introduction

The LSAT will include a 35-minute writing sample. You will be asked to respond to a decision prompt.

The decision prompt requires that you write an argument for selecting between two people, positions, items, or courses of action based on the given criteria. No specialized knowledge is required for the writing prompt, but you should express yourself clearly and effectively.

You will write the essay on the lined area on the front and back of the separate writing sample response sheet. Anything you write outside the restricted space will not be reproduced. Space will be provided below the general directions and topic for scratch work, such as organizing and/or outlining your ideas. For practice purposes, restrict yourself to about two lined pages so that you will be more comfortable writing under the exam conditions.

Following are general directions for the writing sample, a careful analysis of the writing prompt, and a short review of the writing process. Next, you will examine completed essays and then be given topics for writing your own essays.

General Directions

You have 35 minutes to plan and write an essay on the topic given. Take a few minutes to consider the topic and organize your thoughts before you begin to write your essay. As you write your essay, be sure to develop your ideas fully. Try to leave time to review your essay. DO NOT WRITE ON A TOPIC OF YOUR OWN CHOICE. ESSAYS THAT DO NOT ADDRESS THE GIVEN TOPIC ARE UNACCEPTABLE.

You will not be expected to display any specialized knowledge in your essay. Law schools are interested in the reasoning, clarity, organization, language use, and writing mechanics that you display. The quality of your writing is more important than the length of your response.

Only the lined area on your response sheets will be reproduced for the law schools, so do not write outside this space. Make sure that your handwriting is legible.

The Approach

ANALYZING THE WRITING SAMPLE TOPIC

The Decision Prompt

You will be asked to write an argument for hiring, promoting, or selecting one of two candidates or items based on two criteria and two descriptions of the choices or courses of action.

Either one of the two choices can be supported based on the information given. You should consider both choices and argue *for* one and *against* the other, based on the two specific criteria and the facts provided. There is no "right" or "wrong" selection.

Some recent topics have included writing arguments in support of:

- Purchasing one of two films for a public television station
- Selecting one of two designs submitted for a commemorative sculpture
- Selecting one of two retirement communities for a retiree
- Selecting one of two ways of investing money inherited from an uncle
- Deciding which one of two schools to enter for an undergraduate business degree
- Selecting one of two proposals for an introductory course in computer training
- Selecting one of two athletes for a team

In each case, the initial introductory statement or statements were followed by two criteria, and then the background of each candidate, or a description of each film, or a description of each school, or a description of each option.

Let's take a closer look. A recent topic gave us its two criteria for hiring a mathematics teacher: (1) the high school's increased concern with computers, and (2) its wish to develop the mathematics program at the school to incorporate work-study projects in the business community. The first candidate had a solid educational background, high-school teaching and minor administrative experience, good references, and recent training in computers. The second candidate had a slightly different, but equally good educational background and no high-school teaching experience but had worked as a teaching assistant in college and a tutor in community programs, as well as having solid credentials in computers and experience as an employee in financial work for a retail store and a bank.

What should be apparent is that it DOES *NOT* matter which candidate you choose. The principles and qualifications will be written in such a way that you can write in favor of *EITHER* candidate. Make your choice, and stick to it. You should mention the other candidate to show either some of his or her weaknesses or how the candidate you selected is more qualified. What your readers will be looking for are clarity, consistency, relevance, and correctness of grammar and usage. Since you have only one-half hour to read the topic and to plan and write your essay, you will not be expected to produce a long or a subtle essay. You must write on the topic clearly and correctly.

The questions will make clear the sort of audience you are writing for, and you can be sure that this audience is literate and informed about the issues in your paper. In the math teacher topic, for example, the assumed audience is whoever is to hire the math teacher. You do not need to tell this audience what they already know, but you do want to make them focus upon the issues that support your case. Let us assume you are making the case for the experienced teacher with some computer training. Your essay should stress the obvious qualifications—his teaching experience and computer training. Where you have no direct evidence of expertise, you can invent, so long as you do so plausibly and work from details that are given in the question. You could, for example, argue that, although there are two criteria, the computer issue is really the more important, since the students will not be able to find good work-study projects in the community until they have a greater knowledge of computers.

STUDY TIP

Write an argument for hiring, promoting, or selecting one of two candidates or items.

Assume you have chosen the second candidate. Your essay should focus upon her strengths (for example, her experience in business will help her in setting up a business-related program for the students). Where her qualifications are weaker (for example, her lack of high-school teaching experience), your essay can emphasize the other kind of teaching experience she has had. Do not be afraid to introduce details to support your argument that are your own ideas. Just be sure that, when you do present additional information, it is consistent with, and arises plausibly from, the information on the test.

So far, the writing topics have used two slightly different forms. The first (the math teachers) used two sentences, one for each of two equally weighted criteria, and then described the two equally qualified candidates. Another sample topic type also uses two sentences to describe the principles, but the first contains the two criteria, and the second sentence elaborates on one of them. For example, the two principles might be (1) lifeguards are promoted on the basis of years of service and community activities; and (2) community activities include lifesaving clinics, talks to school children, waterfront safety seminars, and high-school swim-team coaching. The biographies would then describe two candidates whose years of service differ slightly, and each of whom has some strength in the areas listed under (2). Since you are not told which of the two criteria is the more important, or which of the various sorts of community service is most important, you can decide for yourself how to weigh these factors, as long as you do so plausibly. You cannot contradict the question—for example, by saying that length of service is not important—but you can argue that, although your candidate's length of service is slightly less than that of her competition, her overwhelming superiority in community service is more important.

Here is a suggested plan for approaching any writing sample of this sort.

Overview of the Three (3) Key Strategies
Your Actions and . . . Reactions

Actions	Reactions
1. Prewrite (organize your thoughts)	Read the criteria and biographies at least twice, and mark the key word or words. Select your candidate or item, and list the strengths and weaknesses of each.
2. Write (with a purpose).	Write the opening paragraph with direction and purpose; support with specific examples; conclude or review your elements.
3. Proofread.	Edit, making changes and corrections. Make sure you leave time to read your work.

Now take one more careful look at the writing process.

THE PHASES OF WRITING

Phase 1—Prewriting

1. Read the introductory statements carefully as they lay out the argument that follows. Circle or underline key words.
2. Read the two statements of policy or criteria at least twice, *actively.* (Circle or mark the essential points of the topic.) Are they equally weighted? If not, clarify the difference.
3. Read the biographies or descriptions at least twice, *actively.* Test them carefully against the policy or criteria statements.
4. Choose your candidate or item. Again set the qualifications or qualities beside those of the statements. Decide exactly what your choice's greatest strengths are. What are the limitations? Think about how these limitations can be invalidated or turned into strengths. You may want to list some of the weaknesses of the other candidate. Which of these do you want to mention to strengthen your position?
5. Outline your essay. Your essay should be four or five paragraphs long. Paragraph 1 should be a short introductory paragraph that lays out the argument that follows. If you are selecting a candidate, paragraph 2 might focus on his or her obvious strengths that meet the given criteria. Paragraph 3 might deal with how the candidate also shows promise of fulfilling the other requirements. Paragraph 4 might discuss some of the weaknesses of the other candidate or might com-

pare the two candidates. Paragraph 5 might pull together and amplify the reasons for your selection.

Phase 2—Writing

1. Do *not* waste time with a fancy opening paragraph on an irrelevant topic like the importance of math teachers or lifeguards in this complex, modern world.
2. Start with a direction. Your first sentence should serve a purpose.
3. Support your argument with examples or other specifics.
4. Do *not* write a closing paragraph that simply repeats what you have already said.
5. Write legibly. Write clearly. Write naturally. Do *not* use big words for their own sake. Do not try to be cute or ironic or funny.
6. Remember that the assumed purpose of this paper is to convince a reader to prefer one candidate or item to another. Your real purpose, of course, is to show a law school that you can follow instructions and write an essay that is well organized, adheres to the point, and is grammatically correct.

Phase 3—Proofreading

1. Allow sufficient time to proofread your essay. At this point, add any information that is vital, and delete any information that seems confusing or out of place.
2. Don't make extensive changes that will make your writing less readable.
3. Check each sentence for mechanical errors (spelling, punctuation, grammar). Some common types of errors are these:
   - using pronouns with no clear antecedents;
   - lack of agreement between subject and verb;
   - using the wrong verb tense;
   - faulty parallelism in a series of items;
   - misplaced or dangling modifiers;
   - adjective-adverb confusion;
   - misuse of comparative terms or comparisons.

These elements should always be kept in mind as you write your essay.

The Elements of an Outstanding Essay

- On topic
- Well organized
- Well developed with examples
- Logically sound
- Grammatically sound with few errors
- Interesting to read, with a variety of sentence types
- Clear, neat, and easy to read

TWO COMPLETED DECISION WRITING SAMPLES

Following are two handwritten "model" essays, written on LSAT Writing Sample booklet-type pages. Notice that each of the two sample essays is written from a different perspective.

Sample Topic

Read the following descriptions of Bergquist and Kretchmer, applicants for the job of Assistant Director on a major motion picture. *Then, in the space provided, write an argument for hiring one over the other.* The following criteria are relevant to your decision:

- In addition to working closely with and advising the Director on creative decisions, the Assistant Director must work with all types of individuals—from stars to Teamster truck drivers—and elicit the best from every cast and crew member for the good of the motion picture.
- The Assistant Director is responsible for all the planning and organization—including paperwork, travel itinerary and meals—of the entire film project. He/she lays the groundwork for a successful "shoot."

BERGQUIST began her career in film as an Administrative Assistant to the president of a major film studio. As such, she often accompanied her employer in his wining and dining of stars, or to the set when problems arose. She double-checked contracts, shooting schedules, and cast and crew checks and kept a close eye on the budget of several multimillion-dollar films. When her boss was subsequently fired due to a poor season of films, Bergquist was able to secure a position as Assistant Editor at the studio, helping several highly respected film editors "cut" feature films. It was there that she learned about the creative end of the business, and soon after became the chief editor of an hour-long studio documentary, which won several awards. After two years, Bergquist was accepted into the Assistant Directors Training Program, and she is presently a candidate for Assistant Director of this new $15,000,000 motion picture.

KRETCHMER was a principal/teacher for 12 years before embarking on a film career. She taught math at the New York School for the Creative Arts and also worked with parents in the community, the board of education, and local government representatives in securing financing for the $20,000,000 school building. As Chairperson of the New Building Committee, she worked closely with architects, townspeople, contractors, and even children to understand their needs for the building. Today the building stands as a model for such schools everywhere. Eight years ago Kretchmer came to Hollywood and, through persistence and charm, secured a studio position and worked her way up to Chief Auditor, where she oversaw budgets on several multimillion-dollar films. She enrolled in the Assistant Directors Training Program, which she recently completed, and is now a candidate for the position of Assistant Director of this new film.

Scratch Paper

Do not write your essay in this space

Sample Topic

Read the following descriptions of Bergquist and Kretchmer, applicants for the job of Assistant Director on a major motion picture. *Then, in the space provided, write an argument for hiring one over the other.* The following criteria are relevant to your decision:

- In addition to working closely with and advising the Director on creative decisions, the Assistant Director must work with all types of individuals—from stars to Teamster truck drivers—and elicit the best from every cast and crew member for the good of the motion picture.
- The Assistant Director is responsible for all the planning and organization—including paperwork, travel itinerary and meals—of the entire film project. He/she lays the groundwork for a successful "shoot."

BERGQUIST began her career in film as an Administrative Assistant to the president of a major film studio. As such, she often accompanied her employer in his wining and dining of stars, or to the set when problems arose. She double-checked contracts, shooting schedules, cast and crew checks and kept a close eye on the budget of several multimillion-dollar films. When her boss was subsequently fired due to a poor season of films, Bergquist was able to secure a position as Assistant Editor at the studio, helping several highly respected film editors "cut" feature films. It was there that she learned about the creative end of the business, and soon after became the chief editor of an hour-long studio documentary, which won several awards. After two years, Bergquist was accepted into the Assistant Directors Training Program, and is presently a candidate for Assistant Director of this new $15,000,000 motion picture.

KRETCHMER was a principal/teacher for 12 years before embarking on a film career. She taught math at the New York School for the Creative Arts and also worked with parents in the community, the board of education, and local government representatives in securing financing for the $20,000,000 school building. As Chairperson of the New Building Committee, she worked closely with architects, townspeople, contractors, and even children to understand their needs for the building. Today the building stands as a model for such schools everywhere. Eight years ago Kretchmer came to Hollywood and, through persistence and charm, secured a studio position and worked her way up to Chief Auditor, where she oversaw budgets on several multimillion-dollar films. She enrolled in the Assistant Directors Training Program, which she recently completed, and is now a candidate for the position of Assistant Director of this new film.

Scratch Paper

Do not write your essay in this space

job requires
1) creative input on film
2) work w. variety of people
3) plan/organize paperwork, travel, etc. for whole project

For Berg
1) creative input most important
Berg knows creative side
Film editor—knows shots, moods, sequences
2) organization important
Kretch has org. background (but areas not connected w. film—educational, financial
Berg has org. background directly connected to job

Writing Sample 1

What sets Bergquist apart from Kretchmer is her understanding of, and experience in, the creative elements of filmmaking.

An Assistant Director (AD) advises the Director in key creative decisions: how to best structure and order the shooting schedule, how to begin and end scenes, and how best to shoot a scene or sequence. While the ultimate decision rests with the Director, the AD's input is vital. Like a caddy advising a golfer of the distance and terrain of the course, the AD's knowledge of the creative elements of filmmaking enhances her abilities in these tasks. Since a film's success often hinges on these creative decisions, the AD's contributions can be critical.

As an editor, Bergquist learned how a film is cut together and how the pieces must fit coherently. She cut her own films and won numerous awards, thus reflecting her understanding of good creative choices. This special knowledge of film (which Kretchmer lacks)—how shots must match, how moods and sequences build upon each other—is essential to the

Writing Sample 1 (continued)

final success of any film.

This is not to say that Kretchmer has no special talents to bring to this job. She does, in fact, have considerable organizational experience, an important area of expertise for an AD in that the AD must consistently deal effectively with complex schedules and budget concerns. And without that organizational ability, schedules and shoots can end in chaos, no matter how creatively planned. But the fact remains that Kretchmer's experience is primarily in areas far removed from the world of filmmaking—education and financing. Even in her Hollywood career, her responsibilities have centered on financial rather than creative matters.

Bergquist, however, while having excellent creative experience in her editing work, does not lack organizational expertise. In fact, her organizational experience is more likely to mesh with the requirements of the Assistant Director's job than Kretchmer's because that experience has been within the filmmaking community rather than in an area far removed from these concerns.

Sample Topic

Read the following descriptions of Bergquist and Kretchmer, applicants for the job of Assistant Director on a major motion picture. *Then, in the space provided, write an argument for hiring one over the other.* The following criteria are relevant to your decision:

- In addition to working closely with and advising the Director on creative decisions, the Assistant Director must work with all types of individuals—from stars to Teamster truck drivers—and elicit the best from every cast and crew member for the good of the motion picture.
- The Assistant Director is responsible for all the planning and organization—including paperwork, travel itinerary, and meals—of the entire film project. He/she lays the groundwork for a successful "shoot."

BERGQUIST began her career in film as an Administrative Assistant to the president of a major film studio. As such, she often accompanied her employer in his wining and dining of stars, or to the set when problems arose. She double-checked contracts, shooting schedules, and cast and crew checks and kept a close eye on the budget of several multimillion-dollar films. When her boss was subsequently fired due to a poor season of films, Bergquist was able to secure a position as Assistant Editor at the studio, helping several highly respected film editors "cut" feature films. It was there that she learned about the creative end of the business, and soon after became the chief editor of an hour-long studio documentary, which won several awards. After two years, Bergquist was accepted into the Assistant Directors Training Program, andshe is presently a candidate for Assistant Director of this new $15,000,000 motion picture.

KRETCHMER was a principal/teacher for 12 years before embarking on a film career. She taught math at the New York School for the Creative Arts and also worked with parents in the community, the board of education, and local government representatives in securing financing for the $20,000,000 school building. As Chairperson of the New Building Committee, she worked closely with architects, townspeople, contractors, and even children to understand their needs for the building. Today the building stands as a model for such schools everywhere. Eight years ago Kretchmer came to Hollywood and, through persistence and charm, secured a studio position and worked her way up to Chief Auditor, where she oversaw budgets on several multimillion-dollar films. She enrolled in the Assistant Directors Training Program, which she recently completed, and is now a candidate for the position of Assistant Director of this new film.

Scratch Paper

Do not write your essay in this space

Job requires:
1) creative input
2) work w. variety of people
3) plan/org. paperwork, travel, etc.

For Kretchmer
1) work w. variety of people
Films are collab.
Kretch has best collab. background—
chair of bldg. comm., work w. parents, etc.
understands indiv. strengths, goals, talents
2) Berg in film, but work w. pres. ≠ work w. director
overseeing, not direct involvement
Film editors isolated, not w. people on set
3) Kretch — bus. sense + ability to work w. diff. goals, personalities

Writing Sample 2

Kretchmer has what Bergquist seriously lacks: the experience and ability to work well with all kinds of people—a crucial skill in the collaborative art/business of filmmaking.

Any film's lengthy end-credits attest to the huge number of people contributing talent—technicians, laborers, performing artists, and others. As the Director's right-hand person, the Assistant Director (AD) must help orchestrate that effort. She must "read" the personalities of different individuals and know how to appeal to each ego ~~and~~ to garner the best from each.

As chairperson of a building committee, Kretchmer worked successfully with dozens of different personalities in pursuit of a common goal, not unlike a film project. In working with diverse personalities (parents, administrators, children, teachers, architects, and builders, each with different goals), Kretchmer had to have a keen understanding of people and be able to know their strengths and limitations. This is precisely her most important task as a

Writing Sample 2 (continued)

motion picture AD.

On first glance, it might seem that Bergquist's background is overall more suited to the job of AD. She has, in fact, been involved in aspects of filmmaking for much of her career. A closer look, however, would suggest that the specific responsibilities of her previous positions do not translate well to the requirements of the AD's work. Her resume emphasizes her work as Administrative Assistant to a film studio president. But a studio president's work is quite unlike that of a Director. It is an overseeing position rather than one that requires active and knowledgeable decisions before the fact. Similarly, film-editing experience, while it helps in understanding the elements of filmmaking, is generally accomplished in relative isolation and has little to do with the ability to work effectively in the diverse and chaotic world of a film set.

Kretchmer's background indicates not only the hard-headed business sense to effectively plan and organize a film project but also the essential ability to do so in the midst of the various and competing goals and beliefs of people involved in the film project.

REVIEW OF GENERAL TIPS

1. Read the topic question at least twice, *actively:* Circle or mark the essential points of the question. Note the main question or parts to be discussed, the audience you are addressing, and the persona or position from which you are writing.
2. Remember to *prewrite,* or plan before you write. Spend at least five minutes organizing your thoughts by jotting notes, outlining, brainstorming, and clustering.
3. As you write, keep the flow of your writing going. Don't stop your train of thought to worry about the spelling of a word. You can fix little things later.
4. Leave a few minutes to reread and edit your paper after you finish writing. A careful rereading will often catch careless mistakes and errors in punctuation and spelling that you didn't have time to worry about as you wrote.
5. Remember that a good essay will be

   - on topic,
   - well organized,
   - well developed with examples,
   - grammatically sound with few errors,
   - interesting to read, with a variety of sentence types,
   - clear, neat, and easy to read.

A SUMMARY OF THE PROCESS

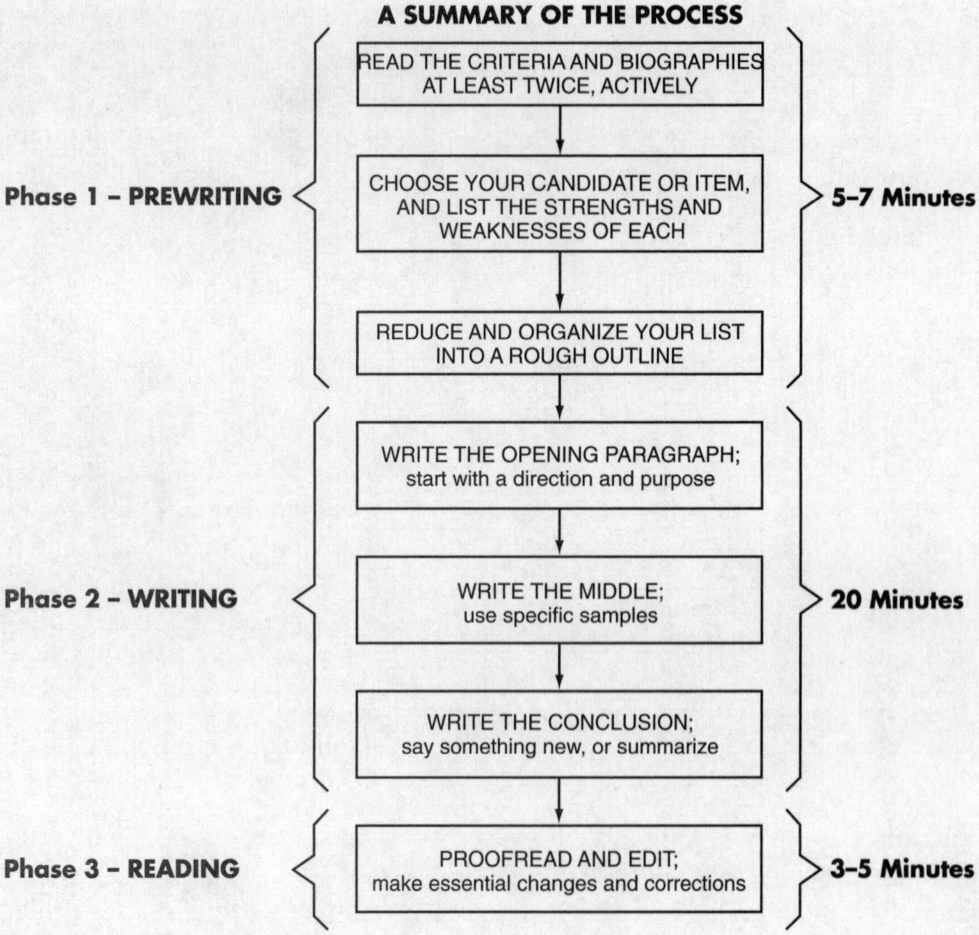
READ THE CRITERIA AND BIOGRAPHIES AT LEAST TWICE, ACTIVELY
CHOOSE YOUR CANDIDATE OR ITEM, AND LIST THE STRENGTHS AND WEAKNESSES OF EACH
REDUCE AND ORGANIZE YOUR LIST INTO A ROUGH OUTLINE
Phase 1 – PREWRITING
5–7 Minutes
WRITE THE OPENING PARAGRAPH; start with a direction and purpose
WRITE THE MIDDLE; use specific samples
WRITE THE CONCLUSION; say something new, or summarize
Phase 2 – WRITING
20 Minutes
PROOFREAD AND EDIT; make essential changes and corrections
Phase 3 – READING
3–5 Minutes

Practice: Writing Sample

After reviewing the completed essays, try some practice on your own. We have provided sample topics. Use two sides of an 8½ × 11 lined sheet of paper to write your essay.

Try following the steps we have suggested, varying them slightly, if necessary, to suit your personal style. Have an honest critic read and respond to each practice essay you complete.

Writing Sample Topic 1

Read the following description of Arbit and Blatas, candidates for your party's nomination to the city council. *Then, in the space provided, write an argument for nominating one candidate over the other.* Use the information in this description, and assume that two general policies guide your party's decision on nomination:

- Nominations are based upon a combination of the probable success in the election and party service.
- Party service includes seniority, committee work, and fund raising.

Arbit, a Romanian-American, has lived in the district and worked for the party for fifteen years. He is chairman of two key party committees and a member of two others. His fund raising picnic, begun ten years ago, now raises at least $10,000 every year. Arbit is 47, a trial lawyer, and has no prior experience in elective office. Twenty percent of the district is Romanian-American, almost all of whom support the party in every election.

Blatas, of Hungarian background, moved to the district seven years ago. She has worked for the party for seven years as a member of several party committees and as Arbit's assistant in arranging the fund-raising picnic. A graduate of law school, she is 35 and was recently promoted to director of the city's real estate research office. She narrowly lost an election for city assessor two years ago. Thirty-five percent of the voters in the district are Hungarian-American.

Scratch Paper

Do not write your essay in this space

Writing Sample Topic 2

The *Times-Herald,* a large metropolitan newspaper, is about to add a new strip to its comic page. The editorial board must decide between two features that do not now appear in any of the city's other newspapers. *In the space provided, write an argument to be presented to the editorial board in support of one comic strip over the other.* Two considerations should guide your decision:

- The newspaper wishes to improve its reputation for serious journalism.
- The newspaper wishes to increase its circulation.

Described by *Time* magazine as "America's most beloved comic strip," *Tom Jordan, M.D.* is a serial that depicts the life of a handsome, young doctor at a large New York hospital. It appears in more newspapers in the United States than any other comic. Its stories combine medical information, romance, and moral uplift. Each story takes thirty-two weeks to complete. An especially popular recent episode dealt with Tom Jordan saving the life of an orphaned leukemia victim; others in the recent past have dealt with drug addiction among the very rich, kidney transplants, and anorexia. *Tom Jordan, M.D.* is the work of a group of four cartoonists.

Bart Pollard's comic, *D.C.,* was the first strip cartoon to win a Pulitzer Prize. Its satiric treatment of Democrats and Republicans, of clergymen, doctors, lawyers, and athletes, has at one time or another given such offense that a number of newspapers that had contracted to run the feature have refused to print it. In Washington, Pollard's *D.C.* is called the "comic strip that everyone hates, but everyone reads." A cabinet officer who closely resembled a character pilloried in the comic has recently filed a libel suit against Pollard. Readership of the strip is especially high on college campuses.

Scratch Paper

Do not write your essay in this space

Writing Sample Topic 3

The Animal Protection Society must decide on a speaker to address its annual fund-raising dinner. *In the space provided, write an argument in support of one of the two following choices over the other.* Two considerations guide your decision:

- The society must immediately raise as much money as possible to support an emergency airlift to save an endangered species of crane.
- The society wishes to increase the number of life members, subscribers who can be counted on to give money every year.

Jan Gilbert is a comedienne and the star of a popular television talk show. On her program, she frequently invites keepers from the San Diego Zoo, who bring with them lion cubs, talking mynah birds, lemurs, and other small animals that appeal to large audiences. A dog lover, she often appears in public and on television with her miniature poodle, who travels with her wherever she goes. She is an active fund raiser for conservative political causes. Because of her love of animals, she has agreed to waive half of her usual personal appearance fee of $12,000.

Katrina Nelson is a distinguished zoologist. She is an adjunct research professor at Cambridge University and has spent fourteen years in Africa observing the behavior of packs of Cape hunting dogs, jackals, and hyenas. A film she made on the scavengers and predators of Africa has been shown on educational television stations. She is the author of five books, including one on the animals of Africa that have become extinct in this century. She is an experienced and skillful public speaker. Her lecture fee is $500.

Scratch Paper

Do not write your essay in this space

Writing Sample Topic 4

The Sundown Realty Company has purchased a large parcel of land for development in Date City. The company must decide between two building plans. *In the space provided, write an argument in support of one of the plans over the other.* Base your decision on the following considerations:

- The design of the development must be approved by an environmental commission that is likely to be unsympathetic to radical changes in the landscape.
- The construction must be completed, and at least half of the units sold, within eighteen months. All of the units must be sold within two years.

Plan One calls for the building of fifty free-standing one-story units distributed along the fairways of a newly constructed nine-hole golf course. Three of the nine holes will have small water hazards. Buyer studies of the area have shown clearly that the highest demand for new homes is for those on golf courses. The fifty houses will be well within the density limit set by the environmental committee, and none of the houses would be visible from outside the development. The units will be built of local wood and stone. Each will cost $200,000.

Plan Two calls for five multi-storied buildings, each containing twenty units built around an activities building, tennis courts, and a pool. The five buildings will be placed far apart in natural wooded areas on the property. Only the top stories will be visible above the trees, and only a few trees on the property will have to be removed for the construction. The units will sell for $100,000 or $150,000 each and will be constructed from aged brick.

Scratch Paper

Do not write your essay in this space

Writing Sample Topic 5

Southwest Pacific University is facing a severe budget crisis and must make up for a shortfall of $1,000,000 in the next fiscal year. *In the space provided, write an argument for Plan A or Plan B.* Keep in mind that the Board of Trustees has determined that the savings must be made under the following conditions:

- Direct and indirect costs to the students should be avoided as much as possible.
- The quality of academic instruction at the school must in no way be compromised.

Plan A would discontinue several campus services that are now running at a loss, including all the food services on campus that are now subsidized by the university. Any student activities such as band, debate, drama, and men's and women's athletics, which are now financially dependent on the university, must become self-supporting, and student admission fees will be charged for all activities that are not operating at a profit. A fund-raising drive among parents and alumni is the first priority of the administration.

Plan B would freeze all faculty and staff salaries and cancel all paid sabbatical leaves for two years. Throughout the university, a 10% reduction in non-academic staff will take place at once. Tuition fees will remain unchanged, but student users' fees will be assessed for laboratory equipment, printing costs, and computer time. Obtaining state and federal grants is the first priority of the administration.

Scratch Paper

Do not write your essay in this space

Writing Sample Topic 6

The Black Hills County Art Museum, a small, well-run institution, must decide how to spend a large state grant. The money was given with the understanding that the museum would accomplish two objectives. *In the space provided, write an argument in favor of Plan A or Plan B.* Keep these objectives in mind:

- The museum will open an area for the display of Native American artifacts.
- The museum will substantially increase its revenues from memberships, contributions, and sales.

Plan A: The museum will use all of the money to construct a display space large and secure enough to attract several of the major popular traveling art exhibits each year. At present, the display space at the museum is too small to be used to present the art exhibits that attract attention in the national media. With the large university population in the area, there is a local audience for such shows, and with the new galleries, the museum could become the most important exhibition space in a six-state area. A leading modern architect has expressed interest in designing the new gallery at a greatly reduced fee. By selling some of the museum's permanent collection, space could be made available for Native American art exhibits.

Plan B: The museum will use the money to construct a new, small gallery for the display of Native American art, and to construct classrooms, a sculpture garden, a museum shop, and a restaurant. The museum has never sponsored a program of art education for either its adult supporters or local schoolchildren, but the many college teachers, along with the museum staff, would provide a fine core of instructors. The museum has never had a shop or a restaurant, though many of its wealthiest supporters have encouraged these additions. The sculpture garden would also serve as an ideal place to display the large Native American carvings that are too tall to be shown inside the buildings.

Scratch Paper

Do not write your essay in this space

CHAPTER 6

A Summary of Strategies

Directions and Strategies

GENERAL TIPS

- Use the "one-check, two-check" system, doing the easier questions first, and saving the time-consuming and difficult questions for later.
- Don't leave any blank answer spaces. At least guess on your unanswered questions.
- Eliminate unreasonable or irrelevant answers immediately, crossing them out on your question booklet.
- Highlight key words and phrases by marking right in your question booklet. Use the margins to draw diagrams, set up charts, and so on.
- Mark "T" and "F" (for "True" and "False") alongside the Roman numeral statements in "multiple-multiple-choice" questions. Often these will allow you to immediately eliminate incorrect answer choices. This type of question has not appeared recently.
- Watch out for the common mistake—the MISREAD.
- Spend some extra time reviewing Logical Reasoning problems. Remember, Logical Reasoning will comprise two of the four scored sections of your exam.

REVIEW OF LSAT AREAS

Logical Reasoning

Directions: In this section you will be given brief statements or passages and will be required to evaluate the reasoning involved. In some instances more than one choice will appear to be a possible answer. You are to choose the *best* answer. Use common sense and reasonableness in making your selection; then mark the proper space on the answer sheet.

Strategies:

- Read the question first; then go back and read the argument or statement. This will give insight into what is going to be asked.
- Watch for items in the answer choices that are irrelevant or not addressed in the given information. Eliminate these immediately.
- Notice the overall tone of the question: Positive or negative? Agreeing with and strengthening the author's argument or criticizing and weakening the statement?
- Watch for important words: *some, all, none, only, one, few, no, could, must, each, except.*

Analytical Reasoning

Directions: In this section you will be given groups of questions based on different sets of conditions. Drawing a simple diagram may be helpful in answering some of the questions. You are to choose the *best* answer and mark the corresponding space on your answer sheet.

Strategies:

- No formal logic is required.
- Make simple charts or diagrams.
- Fill in as much of the diagram as possible, but don't worry if you cannot complete it.
- Look for the framework of the diagram that would be most effective.
- Apply evidence in both directions, that is, also use what you know is *not* true.
- Use question marks for information that is variable.
- Sometimes looking at the questions can tip off the framework of the diagram that would be most helpful.
- Sometimes no standard chart will apply. Then simply pull out information or use simple notes.

Reading Comprehension

Directions: Read the passages and answer the questions following each passage by blackening the appropriate space on the answer sheet. You may refer to the passages when answering the questions.

Strategies:

- Skim the questions first, marking key words and phrases. (Don't read the answer choices.)
- Skim the passage (optional). Read and mark the first sentence of each paragraph.
- Read actively, marking the passage. In particular, look for answer spots, repeat spots, and intuition spots.
- Answer the questions. Skip if necessary. Eliminate weak choices. Don't "read into" the passage.

Writing Sample

Directions: You have 35 minutes to write an essay in response to a given topic. Take a few minutes to plan your work before you begin writing. DO NOT WRITE ON A TOPIC OF YOUR OWN CHOICE. ESSAYS THAT DO NOT ADDRESS THE GIVEN TOPIC ARE UNACCEPTABLE.

The quality of your writing is more important than the length of your response or the content. Pay attention to organization, appropriate diction, and correct usage. You will not be expected to display any specialized knowledge in your response, nor will you be expected to write a "perfect" essay; law schools understand that you are writing under a time constraint, and will allow for the minor lapses in writing ability that might occur under this circumstance.

Only the lined area on your response sheets will be reproduced for the law schools, so do not write outside this space. Make sure your handwriting is legible.

Strategies:

- Read statements and biographies, descriptions, or arguments at least twice, actively.
- Choose your candidate or item, or list the argument's weaknesses.
- Outline your essay.
- Start with a direction. Your first sentence should serve a purpose.
- Support your argument or critique with examples or other specifics.
- You should mention the other candidate to show either some of his or her weaknesses or how the candidate you selected is more qualified.
- Do *not* write a closing paragraph that simply repeats what you have already said.
- Write legibly. Write clearly. Write naturally.
- Proofread and edit your essay.

A FINAL CHECKLIST

A Few Days before the Test

- Review the test directions and strategies for each area.
- Become familiar with the test site; visit it if necessary.
- Follow your normal daily routine; don't make drastic changes.

The Night before the Test

- Review briefly, but don't cram.
- Get a normal night's sleep; don't go to bed too early or too late.

On the Day of the Test

- Eat a high-protein breakfast, unless you never eat breakfast.
- Arrive on time, equipped with three or four sharpened No. 2 pencils, a good eraser, proper identification, your admission ticket, and a watch.
- Dress comfortably. (You may wish to dress in "layers" so that you can add or remove a sweater or jacket if the room temperature changes.)
- Read the test directions carefully.
- Use the "one-check, two-check" system.
- Read *actively.*
- In Reading Comprehension and Logical Reasoning, remember to look at all choices before marking your answer.
- In Analytical Reasoning, be aware that you may not always need to review all of the choices before marking your answer.
- Before you leave a problem, be sure to take a guess. Try to make it an educated guess by eliminating some choices.
- If there are only a few minutes left for a section, fill in the remaining problems with guesses before time is called.
- Remember: Look for problems that you CAN DO and SHOULD GET RIGHT, and DON'T GET STUCK on any one problem.

Model Test One

This chapter contains an actual LSAT, minus the experimental section It is geared to the format of the LSAT. It is complete with answers and explanations.

Model Test One should be taken under strict test conditions. Use the charts provided at the end of the test to score yourself. The test ends with a 35-minute Writing Sample, which is not scored.

Model Test One

Section	Description	Number of Questions	Time Allowed
I.	Analytical Reasoning	24	35 minutes
II.	Logical Reasoning	24	35 minutes
III.	Logical Reasoning	26	35 minutes
IV.	Reading Comprehension	27	35 minutes
	Writing Sample		35 minutes
TOTALS:		101	175 minutes

Now please turn to the next page, remove your answer sheet, and begin Model Test One.

Answer Sheet

MODEL TEST ONE

Section I Reading Comprehension	Section II Logical Reasoning	Section III Logical Reasoning	Section IV Analytical Reasoning
1 Ⓐ Ⓑ Ⓒ Ⓓ Ⓔ	1 Ⓐ Ⓑ Ⓒ Ⓓ Ⓔ	1 Ⓐ Ⓑ Ⓒ Ⓓ Ⓔ	1 Ⓐ Ⓑ Ⓒ Ⓓ Ⓔ
2 Ⓐ Ⓑ Ⓒ Ⓓ Ⓔ	2 Ⓐ Ⓑ Ⓒ Ⓓ Ⓔ	2 Ⓐ Ⓑ Ⓒ Ⓓ Ⓔ	2 Ⓐ Ⓑ Ⓒ Ⓓ Ⓔ
3 Ⓐ Ⓑ Ⓒ Ⓓ Ⓔ	3 Ⓐ Ⓑ Ⓒ Ⓓ Ⓔ	3 Ⓐ Ⓑ Ⓒ Ⓓ Ⓔ	3 Ⓐ Ⓑ Ⓒ Ⓓ Ⓔ
4 Ⓐ Ⓑ Ⓒ Ⓓ Ⓔ	4 Ⓐ Ⓑ Ⓒ Ⓓ Ⓔ	4 Ⓐ Ⓑ Ⓒ Ⓓ Ⓔ	4 Ⓐ Ⓑ Ⓒ Ⓓ Ⓔ
5 Ⓐ Ⓑ Ⓒ Ⓓ Ⓔ	5 Ⓐ Ⓑ Ⓒ Ⓓ Ⓔ	5 Ⓐ Ⓑ Ⓒ Ⓓ Ⓔ	5 Ⓐ Ⓑ Ⓒ Ⓓ Ⓔ
6 Ⓐ Ⓑ Ⓒ Ⓓ Ⓔ	6 Ⓐ Ⓑ Ⓒ Ⓓ Ⓔ	6 Ⓐ Ⓑ Ⓒ Ⓓ Ⓔ	6 Ⓐ Ⓑ Ⓒ Ⓓ Ⓔ
7 Ⓐ Ⓑ Ⓒ Ⓓ Ⓔ	7 Ⓐ Ⓑ Ⓒ Ⓓ Ⓔ	7 Ⓐ Ⓑ Ⓒ Ⓓ Ⓔ	7 Ⓐ Ⓑ Ⓒ Ⓓ Ⓔ
8 Ⓐ Ⓑ Ⓒ Ⓓ Ⓔ	8 Ⓐ Ⓑ Ⓒ Ⓓ Ⓔ	8 Ⓐ Ⓑ Ⓒ Ⓓ Ⓔ	8 Ⓐ Ⓑ Ⓒ Ⓓ Ⓔ
9 Ⓐ Ⓑ Ⓒ Ⓓ Ⓔ	9 Ⓐ Ⓑ Ⓒ Ⓓ Ⓔ	9 Ⓐ Ⓑ Ⓒ Ⓓ Ⓔ	9 Ⓐ Ⓑ Ⓒ Ⓓ Ⓔ
10 Ⓐ Ⓑ Ⓒ Ⓓ Ⓔ	10 Ⓐ Ⓑ Ⓒ Ⓓ Ⓔ	10 Ⓐ Ⓑ Ⓒ Ⓓ Ⓔ	10 Ⓐ Ⓑ Ⓒ Ⓓ Ⓔ
11 Ⓐ Ⓑ Ⓒ Ⓓ Ⓔ	11 Ⓐ Ⓑ Ⓒ Ⓓ Ⓔ	11 Ⓐ Ⓑ Ⓒ Ⓓ Ⓔ	11 Ⓐ Ⓑ Ⓒ Ⓓ Ⓔ
12 Ⓐ Ⓑ Ⓒ Ⓓ Ⓔ	12 Ⓐ Ⓑ Ⓒ Ⓓ Ⓔ	12 Ⓐ Ⓑ Ⓒ Ⓓ Ⓔ	12 Ⓐ Ⓑ Ⓒ Ⓓ Ⓔ
13 Ⓐ Ⓑ Ⓒ Ⓓ Ⓔ	13 Ⓐ Ⓑ Ⓒ Ⓓ Ⓔ	13 Ⓐ Ⓑ Ⓒ Ⓓ Ⓔ	13 Ⓐ Ⓑ Ⓒ Ⓓ Ⓔ
14 Ⓐ Ⓑ Ⓒ Ⓓ Ⓔ	14 Ⓐ Ⓑ Ⓒ Ⓓ Ⓔ	14 Ⓐ Ⓑ Ⓒ Ⓓ Ⓔ	14 Ⓐ Ⓑ Ⓒ Ⓓ Ⓔ
15 Ⓐ Ⓑ Ⓒ Ⓓ Ⓔ	15 Ⓐ Ⓑ Ⓒ Ⓓ Ⓔ	15 Ⓐ Ⓑ Ⓒ Ⓓ Ⓔ	15 Ⓐ Ⓑ Ⓒ Ⓓ Ⓔ
16 Ⓐ Ⓑ Ⓒ Ⓓ Ⓔ	16 Ⓐ Ⓑ Ⓒ Ⓓ Ⓔ	16 Ⓐ Ⓑ Ⓒ Ⓓ Ⓔ	16 Ⓐ Ⓑ Ⓒ Ⓓ Ⓔ
17 Ⓐ Ⓑ Ⓒ Ⓓ Ⓔ	17 Ⓐ Ⓑ Ⓒ Ⓓ Ⓔ	17 Ⓐ Ⓑ Ⓒ Ⓓ Ⓔ	17 Ⓐ Ⓑ Ⓒ Ⓓ Ⓔ
18 Ⓐ Ⓑ Ⓒ Ⓓ Ⓔ	18 Ⓐ Ⓑ Ⓒ Ⓓ Ⓔ	18 Ⓐ Ⓑ Ⓒ Ⓓ Ⓔ	18 Ⓐ Ⓑ Ⓒ Ⓓ Ⓔ
19 Ⓐ Ⓑ Ⓒ Ⓓ Ⓔ	19 Ⓐ Ⓑ Ⓒ Ⓓ Ⓔ	19 Ⓐ Ⓑ Ⓒ Ⓓ Ⓔ	19 Ⓐ Ⓑ Ⓒ Ⓓ Ⓔ
20 Ⓐ Ⓑ Ⓒ Ⓓ Ⓔ	20 Ⓐ Ⓑ Ⓒ Ⓓ Ⓔ	20 Ⓐ Ⓑ Ⓒ Ⓓ Ⓔ	20 Ⓐ Ⓑ Ⓒ Ⓓ Ⓔ
21 Ⓐ Ⓑ Ⓒ Ⓓ Ⓔ	21 Ⓐ Ⓑ Ⓒ Ⓓ Ⓔ	21 Ⓐ Ⓑ Ⓒ Ⓓ Ⓔ	21 Ⓐ Ⓑ Ⓒ Ⓓ Ⓔ
22 Ⓐ Ⓑ Ⓒ Ⓓ Ⓔ	22 Ⓐ Ⓑ Ⓒ Ⓓ Ⓔ	22 Ⓐ Ⓑ Ⓒ Ⓓ Ⓔ	22 Ⓐ Ⓑ Ⓒ Ⓓ Ⓔ
23 Ⓐ Ⓑ Ⓒ Ⓓ Ⓔ	23 Ⓐ Ⓑ Ⓒ Ⓓ Ⓔ	23 Ⓐ Ⓑ Ⓒ Ⓓ Ⓔ	23 Ⓐ Ⓑ Ⓒ Ⓓ Ⓔ
24 Ⓐ Ⓑ Ⓒ Ⓓ Ⓔ	24 Ⓐ Ⓑ Ⓒ Ⓓ Ⓔ	24 Ⓐ Ⓑ Ⓒ Ⓓ Ⓔ	24 Ⓐ Ⓑ Ⓒ Ⓓ Ⓔ
25 Ⓐ Ⓑ Ⓒ Ⓓ Ⓔ	25 Ⓐ Ⓑ Ⓒ Ⓓ Ⓔ	25 Ⓐ Ⓑ Ⓒ Ⓓ Ⓔ	25 Ⓐ Ⓑ Ⓒ Ⓓ Ⓔ
26 Ⓐ Ⓑ Ⓒ Ⓓ Ⓔ	26 Ⓐ Ⓑ Ⓒ Ⓓ Ⓔ	26 Ⓐ Ⓑ Ⓒ Ⓓ Ⓔ	26 Ⓐ Ⓑ Ⓒ Ⓓ Ⓔ
27 Ⓐ Ⓑ Ⓒ Ⓓ Ⓔ	27 Ⓐ Ⓑ Ⓒ Ⓓ Ⓔ	27 Ⓐ Ⓑ Ⓒ Ⓓ Ⓔ	27 Ⓐ Ⓑ Ⓒ Ⓓ Ⓔ
28 Ⓐ Ⓑ Ⓒ Ⓓ Ⓔ	28 Ⓐ Ⓑ Ⓒ Ⓓ Ⓔ	28 Ⓐ Ⓑ Ⓒ Ⓓ Ⓔ	28 Ⓐ Ⓑ Ⓒ Ⓓ Ⓔ
29 Ⓐ Ⓑ Ⓒ Ⓓ Ⓔ	29 Ⓐ Ⓑ Ⓒ Ⓓ Ⓔ	29 Ⓐ Ⓑ Ⓒ Ⓓ Ⓔ	29 Ⓐ Ⓑ Ⓒ Ⓓ Ⓔ
30 Ⓐ Ⓑ Ⓒ Ⓓ Ⓔ	30 Ⓐ Ⓑ Ⓒ Ⓓ Ⓔ	30 Ⓐ Ⓑ Ⓒ Ⓓ Ⓔ	30 Ⓐ Ⓑ Ⓒ Ⓓ Ⓔ

Remove answer sheet by cutting on dotted line

SECTION I
Time—35 minutes
24 Questions

Directions: Each group of questions in this section is based on a set of conditions. In answering some of the questions, it may be useful to draw a rough diagram. Choose the response that most accurately and completely answers each question and blacken the corresponding space on your answer sheet.

Questions 1–6

Eight new students—R, S, T, V, W, X, Y, Z—are being divided among exactly three classes—class 1, class 2, and class 3. Classes 1 and 2 will gain three new students each; class 3 will gain two new students. The following restrictions apply:

R must be added to class 1.
S must be added to class 3.
Neither S nor W can be added to the same class as Y.
V cannot be added to the same class as Z.
If T is added to class 1, Z must also be added to class 1.

1. Which one of the following is an acceptable assignment of students to the three classes?

	1	2	3
(A)	R, T, Y	V, W, X	S, Z
(B)	R, T, Z	S, V, Y	W, X
(C)	R, W, X	V, Y, Z	S, T
(D)	R, X, Z	T, V, Y	S, W
(E)	R, X, Z	V, W, Y	S, T

2. Which one of the following is a complete and accurate list of classes any one of which could be the class to which V is added?

(A) class 1
(B) class 3
(C) class 1, class 3
(D) class 2, class 3
(E) class 1, class 2, class 3

3. If X is added to class 1, which one of the following is a student who must be added to class 2 ?

(A) T
(B) V
(C) W
(D) Y
(E) Z

4. If X is added to class 3, each of the following is a pair of students who can be added to class 1 EXCEPT

(A) Y and Z
(B) W and Z
(C) V and Y
(D) V and W
(E) T and Z

5. If T is added to class 3, which one of the following is a student who must be added to class 2 ?

(A) V
(B) W
(C) X
(D) Y
(E) Z

6. Which one of the following must be true?

(A) If T and X are added to class 2, V is added to class 3.
(B) If V and W are added to class 1, T is added to class 3.
(C) If V and W are added to class 1, Z is added to class 3.
(D) If V and X are added to class 1, W is added to class 3.
(E) If Y and Z are added to class 2, X is added to class 2.

GO ON TO THE NEXT PAGE.

Questions 7–12

Four lions—F, G, H, J—and two tigers—K and M—will be assigned to exactly six stalls, one animal per stall. The stalls are arranged as follows:

First Row: 1 2 3

Second Row: 4 5 6

The only stalls that face each other are stalls 1 and 4, stalls 2 and 5, and stalls 3 and 6. The following conditions apply:

The tigers' stalls cannot face each other.
A lion must be assigned to stall 1.
H must be assigned to stall 6.
J must be assigned to a stall numbered one higher than K's stall.
K cannot be assigned to the stall that faces H's stall.

7. Which one of the following must be true?
   (A) F is assigned to an even-numbered stall.
   (B) F is assigned to stall 1.
   (C) J is assigned to stall 2 or else stall 3.
   (D) J is assigned to stall 3 or else stall 4.
   (E) K is assigned to stall 2 or else stall 4.

8. Which one of the following could be true?
   (A) F's stall is numbered one higher than J's stall.
   (B) H's stall faces M's stall.
   (C) J is assigned to stall 4.
   (D) K's stall faces J's stall.
   (E) K's stall is in a different row than J's stall.

9. Which one of the following must be true?
   (A) A tiger is assigned to stall 2.
   (B) A tiger is assigned to stall 5.
   (C) K's stall is in a different row from M's stall.
   (D) Each tiger is assigned to an even-numbered stall.
   (E) Each lion is assigned to a stall that faces a tiger's stall.

10. If K's stall is in the same row as H's stall, which one of the following must be true?
   (A) F's stall is in the same row as J's stall.
   (B) F is assigned to a lower-numbered stall than G.
   (C) G is assigned to a lower-numbered stall than M.
   (D) G's stall faces H's stall.
   (E) M's stall is in the same row as G's stall.

11. If J is assigned to stall 3, which one of the following could be true?
   (A) F is assigned to stall 2.
   (B) F is assigned to stall 4.
   (C) G is assigned to stall 1.
   (D) G is assigned to stall 4.
   (E) M is assigned to stall 5.

12. Which one of the following must be true?
   (A) A tiger is assigned to stall 2.
   (B) A tiger is assigned to stall 4.
   (C) A tiger is assigned to stall 5.
   (D) A lion is assigned to stall 3.
   (E) A lion is assigned to stall 4.

GO ON TO THE NEXT PAGE.

Questions 13–18

On an undeveloped street, a developer will simultaneously build four houses on one side, numbered consecutively 1, 3, 5, and 7, and four houses on the opposite side, numbered consecutively 2, 4, 6, and 8. Houses 2, 4, 6, and 8 will face houses 1, 3, 5, and 7, respectively. Each house will be exactly one of three styles—ranch, split-level, or Tudor—according to the following conditions:

Adjacent houses are of different styles.
No split-level house faces another split-level house.
Every ranch house has at least one Tudor house adjacent to it.
House 3 is a ranch house.
House 6 is a split-level house.

13. Any of the following could be a Tudor house EXCEPT house

(A) 1
(B) 2
(C) 4
(D) 7
(E) 8

14. If there is one ranch house directly opposite another ranch house, which one of the following could be true?

(A) House 8 is a ranch house.
(B) House 7 is a split-level house.
(C) House 4 is a Tudor house.
(D) House 2 is a split-level house.
(E) House 1 is a ranch house.

15. If house 4 is a Tudor house, then it could be true that house

(A) 1 is a Tudor house
(B) 2 is a Tudor house
(C) 5 is a ranch house
(D) 7 is a Tudor house
(E) 8 is a ranch house

16. On the street, there could be exactly

(A) one ranch house
(B) one Tudor house
(C) two Tudor houses
(D) four ranch houses
(E) five ranch houses

17. If no house faces a house of the same style, then it must be true that house

(A) 1 is a split-level house
(B) 1 is a Tudor house
(C) 2 is a ranch house
(D) 2 is a split-level house
(E) 4 is a Tudor house

18. If the condition requiring house 6 to be a split-level house is suspended but all other original conditions remain the same, then any of the following could be an accurate list of the styles of houses 2, 4, 6, and 8, respectively, EXCEPT:

(A) ranch, split-level, ranch, Tudor
(B) split-level, ranch, Tudor, split-level
(C) split-level, Tudor, ranch, split-level
(D) Tudor, ranch, Tudor, split-level
(E) Tudor, split-level, ranch, Tudor

GO ON TO THE NEXT PAGE.

Questions 19–24

Within a tennis league each of five teams occupies one of five positions, numbered 1 through 5 in order of rank, with number 1 as the highest position. The teams are initially in the order R, J, S, M, L, with R in position 1. Teams change positions only when a lower-positioned team defeats a higher-positioned team. The rules are as follows:

Matches are played alternately in odd-position rounds and in even-position rounds.

In an odd-position round, teams in positions 3 and 5 play against teams positioned immediately above them.

In an even-position round, teams in positions 2 and 4 play against teams positioned immediately above them.

When a lower-positioned team defeats a higher-positioned team, the two teams switch positions after the round is completed.

19. Which one of the following could be the order of teams, from position 1 through position 5 respectively, after exactly one round of even-position matches if no odd-position round has yet been played?

(A) J, R, M, L, S
(B) J, R, S, L, M
(C) R, J, M, L, S
(D) R, J, M, S, L
(E) R, S, J, L, M

20. If exactly two rounds of matches have been played, beginning with an odd-position round, and if the lower-positioned teams have won every match in those two rounds, then each of the following must be true EXCEPT:

(A) L is one position higher than J.
(B) R is one position higher than L.
(C) S is one position higher than R.
(D) J is in position 4.
(E) M is in position 3.

21. Which one of the following could be true after exactly two rounds of matches have been played?

(A) J has won two matches.
(B) L has lost two matches.
(C) R has won two matches.
(D) L's only match was played against J.
(E) M played against S in two matches.

22. If after exactly three rounds of matches M is in position 4, and J and L have won all of their matches, then which one of the following can be true?

(A) J is in position 2.
(B) J is in position 3.
(C) L is in position 2.
(D) R is in position 1.
(E) S is in position 3.

23. If after exactly three rounds M has won three matches and the rankings of the other four teams relative to each other remain the same, then which one of the following must be in position 3 ?

(A) J
(B) L
(C) M
(D) R
(E) S

24. If after exactly three rounds the teams, in order from first to fifth position, are R, J, L, S, and M, then which one of the following could be the order, from first to fifth position, of the teams after the second round?

(A) J, R, M, S, L
(B) J, L, S, M, R
(C) R, J, S, L, M
(D) R, L, M, S, J
(E) R, M, L, S, J

S T O P

IF YOU FINISH BEFORE TIME IS CALLED, YOU MAY CHECK YOUR WORK ON THIS SECTION ONLY. DO NOT WORK ON ANY OTHER SECTION IN THE TEST.

SECTION II

Time—35 minutes

24 Questions

Directions: The questions in this section are based on the reasoning contained in brief statements or passages. For some questions, more than one of the choices could conceivably answer the question. However, you are to choose the best answer; that is, the response that most accurately and completely answers the question. You should not make assumptions that are by commonsense standards implausible, superfluous, or incompatible with the passage. After you have chosen the best answer, blacken the corresponding space on your answer sheet.

1. The city's center for disease control reports that the rabies epidemic is more serious now than it was two years ago: two years ago less than 25 percent of the local raccoon population was infected, whereas today the infection has spread to more than 50 percent of the raccoon population. However, the newspaper reports that whereas two years ago 32 cases of rabid raccoons were confirmed during a 12-month period, in the past 12 months only 18 cases of rabid raccoons were confirmed.

   Which one of the following, if true, most helps to resolve the apparent discrepancy between the two reports?

   (A) The number of cases of rabies in wild animals other than raccoons has increased in the past 12 months.
   (B) A significant proportion of the raccoon population succumbed to rabies in the year before last.
   (C) The symptoms of distemper, another disease to which raccoons are susceptible, are virtually identical to those of rabies.
   (D) Since the outbreak of the epidemic, raccoons, which are normally nocturnal, have increasingly been seen during daylight hours.
   (E) The number of confirmed cases of rabid raccoons in neighboring cities has also decreased over the past year.

2. Recently, reviewers of patent applications decided against granting a patent to a university for a genetically engineered mouse developed for laboratory use in studying cancer. The reviewers argued that the mouse was a new variety of animal and that rules governing the granting of patents specifically disallow patents for new animal varieties.

   Which one of the following, if true, most weakens the patent reviewers' argument?

   (A) The restrictions the patent reviewers cited pertain only to domesticated farm animals.
   (B) The university's application for a patent for the genetically engineered mouse was the first such patent application made by the university.
   (C) The patent reviewers had reached the same decision on all previous patent requests for new animal varieties.
   (D) The patent reviewers had in the past approved patents for genetically engineered plant varieties.
   (E) The patent reviewers had previously decided against granting patents for new animal varieties that were developed through conventional breeding programs rather than through genetic engineering.

GO ON TO THE NEXT PAGE.

Questions 3–4

Although water in deep aquifers does not contain disease-causing bacteria, when public water supplies are drawn from deep aquifers, chlorine is often added to the water as a disinfectant because contamination can occur as a result of flaws in pipes or storage tanks. Of 50 municipalities that all pumped water from the same deep aquifer, 30 chlorinated their water and 20 did not. The water in all of the municipalities met the regional government's standards for cleanliness, yet the water supplied by the 20 municipalities that did not chlorinate had less bacterial contamination than the water supplied by the municipalities that added chlorine.

3. Which one of the following can properly be concluded from the information given above?
   (A) A municipality's initial decision whether or not to use chlorine is based on the amount of bacterial contamination in the water source.
   (B) Water in deep aquifers does not contain any bacteria of any kind.
   (C) Where accessible, deep aquifers are the best choice as a source for a municipal water supply.
   (D) The regional government's standards allow some bacteria in municipal water supplies.
   (E) Chlorine is the least effective disinfecting agent.

4. Which one of the following, if true, most helps explain the difference in bacterial contamination in the two groups of municipalities?
   (A) Chlorine is considered by some experts to be dangerous to human health, even in the small concentrations used in municipal water supplies.
   (B) When municipalities decide not to chlorinate their water supplies, it is usually because their citizens have voiced objections to the taste and smell of chlorine.
   (C) The municipalities that did not add chlorine to their water supplies also did not add any of the other available water disinfectants, which are more expensive than chlorine.
   (D) Other agents commonly added to public water supplies, such as fluoride and sodium hydroxide, were not used by any of the 50 municipalities.
   (E) Municipalities that do not chlorinate their water supplies are subject to stricter regulation by the regional government in regard to pipes and water tanks than are municipalities that use chlorine.

5. The population of songbirds throughout England has decreased in recent years. Many people explain this decrease as the result of an increase during the same period in the population of magpies, which eat the eggs and chicks of songbirds.

   Which one of the following, if true, argues most strongly against the explanation reported in the passage?
   (A) Official records of the population of birds in England have been kept for only the past 30 years.
   (B) The number of eggs laid yearly by a female songbird varies widely according to the songbird's species.
   (C) Although the overall population of magpies has increased, in most areas of England in which the songbird population has decreased, the number of magpies has remained stable.
   (D) The population of magpies has increased because farmers no longer shoot or trap magpies to any great extent, though farmers still consider magpies to be pests.
   (E) Although magpies eat the eggs and chicks of songbirds, magpies' diets consist of a wide variety of other foods as well.

6. The introduction of symbols for numbers is an event lost in prehistory, but the earliest known number symbols, in the form of simple grooves and scratches on bones and stones, date back 20,000 years or more. Nevertheless, since it was not until 5,500 years ago that systematic methods for writing numerals were invented, it was only then that any sort of computation became possible.

   Which one of the following is an assumption on which the argument relies?
   (A) Grooves and scratches found on bones and stones were all made by people, and none resulted from natural processes.
   (B) Some kinds of surfaces upon which numeric symbols could have been made in the period before 5,500 years ago were not used for that purpose.
   (C) Grooves and scratches inscribed on bones and stones do not date back to the time of the earliest people.
   (D) Computation of any sort required a systematic method for writing numerals.
   (E) Systematic methods for writing numerals were invented only because the need for computation arose.

GO ON TO THE NEXT PAGE.

7. Politician: Now that we are finally cleaning up the industrial pollution in the bay, we must start making the bay more accessible to the public for recreational purposes.

   Reporter: But if we increase public access to the bay, it will soon become polluted again.

   Politician: Not true. The public did not have access to the bay, and it got polluted. Therefore, if and when the public is given access to the bay, it will not get polluted.

   Which one of the following most closely parallels the flawed pattern of reasoning in the politician's reply to the reporter?

   (A) If there had been a full moon last night, the tide would be higher than usual today. Since the tide is no higher than usual, there must not have been a full moon last night.
   (B) The detective said that whoever stole the money would be spending it conspicuously by now. Jones is spending money conspicuously, so he must be the thief.
   (C) When prisoners convicted of especially violent crimes were kept in solitary confinement, violence in the prisons increased. Therefore, violence in the prisons will not increase if such prisoners are allowed to mix with fellow prisoners.
   (D) To get a driver's license, one must pass a written test. Smith passed the written test, so she must have gotten a driver's license.
   (E) In order to like abstract art, you have to understand it. Therefore, in order to understand abstract art, you have to like it.

8. Because learned patterns of behavior, such as the association of a green light with "go" or the expectation that switches will flip up for "on," become deeply ingrained, designers should make allowances for that fact, in order not to produce machines that are inefficient or dangerous.

   In which one of the following situations is the principle expressed most clearly violated?

   (A) Manufacturers have refused to change the standard order of letters on the typewriter keyboard even though some people who have never learned to type find this arrangement of letters bewildering.
   (B) Government regulations require that crucial instruments in airplane cockpits be placed in exactly the same array in all commercial aircraft.
   (C) Automobile manufacturers generally design for all of their automobiles a square or oblong ignition key and a round or oval luggage compartment key.
   (D) The only traffic signs that are triangular in shape are "yield" signs.
   (E) On some tape recorders the "start" button is red and the "stop" button is yellow.

9. From 1973 to 1989 total energy use in this country increased less than 10 percent. However, the use of electrical energy in this country during this same period grew by more than 50 percent, as did the gross national product—the total value of all goods and services produced in the nation.

   If the statements above are true, then which one of the following must also be true?

   (A) Most of the energy used in this country in 1989 was electrical energy.
   (B) From 1973 to 1989 there was a decline in the use of energy other than electrical energy in this country.
   (C) From 1973 to 1989 there was an increase in the proportion of energy use in this country that consisted of electrical energy use.
   (D) In 1989 electrical energy constituted a larger proportion of the energy used to produce the gross national product than did any other form of energy.
   (E) In 1973 the electrical energy that was produced constituted a smaller proportion of the gross national product than did all other forms of energy combined.

10. A fundamental illusion in robotics is the belief that improvements in robots will liberate humanity from "hazardous and demeaning work." Engineers are designing only those types of robots that can be properly maintained with the least expensive, least skilled human labor possible. Therefore, robots will not eliminate demeaning work—only substitute one type of demeaning work for another.

   The reasoning in the argument is most vulnerable to the criticism that it

   (A) ignores the consideration that in a competitive business environment some jobs might be eliminated if robots are not used in the manufacturing process
   (B) assumes what it sets out to prove, that robots create demeaning work
   (C) does not specify whether or not the engineers who design robots consider their work demeaning
   (D) attempts to support its conclusion by an appeal to the emotion of fear, which is often experienced by people faced with the prospect of losing their jobs to robots
   (E) fails to address the possibility that the amount of demeaning work eliminated by robots might be significantly greater than the amount they create

GO ON TO THE NEXT PAGE.

11. If the needle on an industrial sewing machine becomes badly worn, the article being sewn can be ruined. In traditional apparel factories, the people who operate the sewing machines monitor the needles and replace those that begin to wear out. Industrial sewing operations are becoming increasingly automated, however, and it would be inefficient for a factory to hire people for the sole purpose of monitoring needles. Therefore a sophisticated new acoustic device that detects wear in sewing machine needles is expected to become standard equipment in the automated apparel factories of the future.

Which one of the following is most strongly supported by the information above?

(A) In automated apparel factories, items will be ruined by faulty needles less frequently than happens in traditional apparel factories.
(B) In the automated apparel factories of the future, each employee will perform only one type of task.
(C) Traditional apparel factories do not use any automated equipment.
(D) The needles of industrial sewing machines wear out at unpredictable rates.
(E) As sewing machine needles become worn, the noise they make becomes increasingly loud.

Questions 12–13

Alexander: The chemical waste dump outside our town should be cleaned up immediately. Admittedly, it will be very costly to convert that site into woodland, but we have a pressing obligation to redress the harm we have done to local forests and wildlife.

Teresa: But our town's first priority is the health of its people. So even if putting the dump there was environmentally disastrous, we should not spend our resources on correcting it unless it presents a significant health hazard to people. If it does, then we only need to remove that hazard.

12. Teresa's statement most closely conforms to which one of the following principles?

(A) Environmental destruction should be redressed only if it is in the economic interest of the community to do so.
(B) Resources should be allocated only to satisfy goals that have the highest priority.
(C) No expense should be spared in protecting the community's health.
(D) Environmental hazards that pose slight health risks to people should be rectified if the technology is available to do so.
(E) It is the community as a whole that should evaluate the importance of eliminating various perceived threats to public health.

13. Which one of the following is the point at issue between Alexander and Teresa?

(A) whether the maintenance of a chemical waste dump inflicts significant damage on forests and wildlife
(B) whether it is extremely costly to clean up a chemical waste dump in order to replace it by a woodland
(C) whether the public should be consulted in determining the public health risk posed by a chemical waste dump
(D) whether the town has an obligation to redress damage to local forests and wildlife if that damage poses no significant health hazard to people
(E) whether destroying forests and wildlife in order to establish a chemical waste dump amounts to an environmental disaster

GO ON TO THE NEXT PAGE.

14. In 1980, Country A had a per capita gross domestic product (GDP) that was $5,000 higher than that of the European Economic Community. By 1990, the difference, when adjusted for inflation, had increased to $6,000. Since a rising per capita GDP indicates a rising average standard of living, the average standard of living in Country A must have risen between 1980 and 1990.

Which one of the following is an assumption on which the argument depends?

(A) Between 1980 and 1990, Country A and the European Economic Community experienced the same percentage increase in population.
(B) Between 1980 and 1990, the average standard of living in the European Economic Community fell.
(C) Some member countries of the European Economic Community had, during the 1980s, a higher average standard of living than Country A.
(D) The per capita GDP of the European Economic Community was not lower by more than $1,000 in 1990 than it had been in 1980.
(E) In 1990, no member country of the European Economic Community had a per capita GDP higher than that of Country A.

15. Municipal officials originally estimated that it would be six months before municipal road crews could complete repaving a stretch of road. The officials presumed that private contractors could not finish any sooner. However, when the job was assigned to a private contractor, it was completed in just 28 days.

Which one of the following, if true, does most to resolve the discrepancy between the time estimated for completion of the repaving job, and the actual time taken by the private contractor?

(A) Road repaving work can only be done in the summer months of June, July, and August.
(B) The labor union contract for road crews employed by both municipal agencies and private contractors stipulates that employees can work only eight hours a day, five days a week, before being paid overtime.
(C) Many road-crew workers for private contractors have previously worked for municipal road crews, and vice versa.
(D) Private contractors typically assign 25 workers to each road-repaving job site, whereas the number assigned to municipal road crews is usually 30.
(E) Municipal agencies must conduct a lengthy bidding process to procure supplies after repaving work is ordered and before they can actually start work, whereas private contractors can obtain supplies readily as needed.

16. Researchers in South Australia estimate changes in shark populations inhabiting local waters by monitoring what is termed the "catch per unit effort" (CPUE). The CPUE for any species of shark is the number of those sharks that commercial shark-fishing boats catch per hour for each kilometer of gill net set out in the water. Since 1973 the CPUE for a particular species of shark has remained fairly constant. Therefore, the population of that species in the waters around South Australia must be at approximately its 1973 level.

Which one of the following, if true, most seriously weakens the argument?

(A) The waters around South Australia are the only area in the world where that particular species of shark is found.
(B) The sharks that are the most profitable to catch are those that tend to remain in the same area of ocean year after year and not migrate far from where they were born.
(C) A significant threat to shark populations, in addition to commercial shark fishing, is "incidental mortality" that results from catching sharks in nets intended for other fish.
(D) Most of the quotas designed to protect shark populations limit the tonnage of sharks that can be taken and not the number of individual sharks.
(E) Since 1980 commercial shark-fishing boats have used sophisticated electronic equipment that enables them to locate sharks with greater accuracy.

GO ON TO THE NEXT PAGE.

Questions 17–18

Winston: The Public Transportation Authority (PTA) cannot fulfill its mandate to operate without a budget deficit unless it eliminates service during late-night periods of low ridership. Since the fares collected during these periods are less than the cost of providing the service, these cuts would reduce the deficit and should be made. Transit law prohibits unauthorized fare increases, and fare-increase authorization would take two years.

Ping: Such service cuts might cost the PTA more in lost fares than they would save in costs, for the PTA would lose those riders who leave home during the day but must return late at night. Thus the PTA would lose two fares, while realizing cost savings for only one leg of such trips.

17. The relationship of Ping's response to Winston's argument is that Ping's response

(A) carefully redefines a term used in Winston's argument
(B) questions Winston's proposal by raising considerations not addressed by Winston
(C) supplies a premise that could have been used as part of the support for Winston's argument
(D) introduces detailed statistical evidence that is more persuasive than that offered by Winston
(E) proposes a solution to the PTA's dilemma by contradicting Winston's conclusion

18. Which one of the following, if true, most strongly supports Ping's conclusion?

(A) Over 23 percent of the round trips made by PTA riders are either initiated or else completed during late-night periods.
(B) Reliable survey results show that over 43 percent of the PTA's riders oppose any cut in PTA services.
(C) The last time the PTA petitioned for a 15 percent fare increase, the petition was denied.
(D) The PTA's budget deficit is 40 percent larger this year than it was last year.
(E) The PTA's bus drivers recently won a new contract that guarantees them a significant cash bonus each time they work the late-night shifts.

19. The Volunteers for Literacy Program would benefit if Dolores takes Victor's place as director, since Dolores is far more skillful than Victor is at securing the kind of financial support the program needs and Dolores does not have Victor's propensity for alienating the program's most dedicated volunteers.

The pattern of reasoning in the argument above is most closely paralleled in which one of the following?

(A) It would be more convenient for Dominique to take a bus to school than to take the subway, since the bus stops closer to her house than does the subway and, unlike the subway, the bus goes directly to the school.
(B) Joshua's interest would be better served by taking the bus to get to his parent's house rather than by taking an airplane, since his primary concern is to travel as cheaply as possible and taking the bus is less expensive than going by airplane.
(C) Belinda will get to the concert more quickly by subway than by taxi, since the concert takes place on a Friday evening and on Friday evenings traffic near the concert hall is exceptionally heavy.
(D) Anita would benefit financially by taking the train to work rather than driving her car, since when she drives she has to pay parking fees and the daily fee for parking a car is higher than a round-trip train ticket.
(E) It would be to Fred's advantage to exchange his bus tickets for train tickets, since he needs to arrive at his meeting before any of the other participants and if he goes by bus at least one of the other participants will arrive first.

GO ON TO THE NEXT PAGE.

20. Students from outside the province of Markland, who in any given academic year pay twice as much tuition each as do students from Markland, had traditionally accounted for at least two-thirds of the enrollment at Central Markland College. Over the past 10 years academic standards at the college have risen, and the proportion of students who are not Marklanders has dropped to around 40 percent.

Which one of the following can be properly inferred from the statements above?

(A) If it had not been for the high tuition paid by students from outside Markland, the college could not have improved its academic standards over the past 10 years.
(B) If academic standards had not risen over the past 10 years, students who are not Marklanders would still account for at least two-thirds of the college's enrollment.
(C) Over the past 10 years, the number of students from Markland increased and the number of students from outside Markland decreased.
(D) Over the past 10 years, academic standards at Central Markland College have risen by more than academic standards at any other college in Markland.
(E) If the college's per capita revenue from tuition has remained the same, tuition fees have increased over the past 10 years.

21. Several years ago, as a measure to reduce the population of gypsy moths, which depend on oak leaves for food, entomologists introduced into many oak forests a species of fungus that is poisonous to gypsy moth caterpillars. Since then, the population of both caterpillars and adult moths has significantly declined in those areas. Entomologists have concluded that the decline is attributable to the presence of the poisonous fungus.

Which one of the following, if true, most strongly supports the conclusion drawn by the entomologists?

(A) A strain of gypsy moth whose caterpillars are unaffected by the fungus has increased its share of the total gypsy moth population.
(B) The fungus that was introduced to control the gypsy moth population is poisonous to few insect species other than the gypsy moth.
(C) An increase in numbers of both gypsy moth caterpillars and gypsy moth adults followed a drop in the number of some of the species that prey on the moths.
(D) In the past several years, air pollution and acid rain have been responsible for a substantial decline in oak tree populations.
(E) The current decline in the gypsy moth population in forests where the fungus was introduced is no greater than a decline that occurred concurrently in other forests.

22. Director of personnel: Ms. Tours has formally requested a salary adjustment on the grounds that she was denied merit raises to which she was entitled. Since such grounds provide a possible basis for adjustments, an official response is required. Ms. Tours presents compelling evidence that her job performance has been both excellent in itself and markedly superior to that of others in her department who were awarded merit raises. Her complaint that she was treated unfairly thus appears justified. Nevertheless, her request should be denied. To raise Ms. Tours's salary because of her complaint would jeopardize the integrity of the firm's merit-based reward system by sending the message that employees can get their salaries raised if they just complain enough.

The personnel director's reasoning is most vulnerable to criticism on the grounds that it

(A) fails to consider the possibility that Ms. Tours's complaint could be handled on an unofficial basis
(B) attempts to undermine the persuasiveness of Ms. Tours's evidence by characterizing it as "mere complaining"
(C) sidesteps the issue of whether superior job performance is a suitable basis for awarding salary increases
(D) ignores the possibility that some of the people who did receive merit increases were not entitled to them
(E) overlooks the implications for the integrity of the firm's merit-based reward system of denying Ms. Tours's request

GO ON TO THE NEXT PAGE.

23. S: People who are old enough to fight for their country are old enough to vote for the people who make decisions about war and peace. This government clearly regards 17 year olds as old enough to fight, so it should acknowledge their right to vote.

T: Your argument is a good one only to the extent that fighting and voting are the same kind of activity. Fighting well requires strength, muscular coordination, and in a modern army, instant and automatic response to orders. Performed responsibly, voting, unlike fighting, is essentially a deliberative activity requiring reasoning power and knowledge of both history and human nature.

T responds to S's argument by

(A) citing evidence overlooked by S that would have supported S's conclusion
(B) calling into question S's understanding of the concept of rights
(C) showing that S has ignored the distinction between having a right to do something and having an obligation to do that thing
(D) challenging the truth of a claim on which S's conclusion is based
(E) arguing for a conclusion opposite to the one drawn by S

24. The role of the Uplandian supreme court is to protect all human rights against abuses of government power. Since the constitution of Uplandia is not explicit about all human rights, the supreme court must sometimes resort to principles outside the explicit provisions of the constitution in justifying its decisions. However, human rights will be subject to the whim of whoever holds judicial power unless the supreme court is bound to adhere to a single objective standard, namely, the constitution. Therefore, nothing but the explicit provisions of the constitution can be used to justify the court's decisions. Since these conclusions are inconsistent with each other, it cannot be true that the role of the Uplandian supreme court is to protect all human rights against abuses of government power.

The reasoning that leads to the conclusion that the first sentence in the passage is false is flawed because the argument

(A) ignores data that offer reasonable support for a general claim and focuses on a single example that argues against that claim
(B) seeks to defend a view on the grounds that the view is widely held and that decisions based on that view are often accepted as correct
(C) rejects a claim as false on the grounds that those who make that claim could profit if that claim is accepted by others
(D) makes an unwarranted assumption that what is true of each member of a group taken separately is also true of the group as a whole
(E) concludes that a particular premise is false when it is equally possible for that premise to be true and some other premise false

S T O P

IF YOU FINISH BEFORE TIME IS CALLED, YOU MAY CHECK YOUR WORK ON THIS SECTION ONLY. DO NOT WORK ON ANY OTHER SECTION IN THE TEST.

SECTION III

Time—35 minutes

26 Questions

Directions: The questions in this section are based on the reasoning contained in brief statements or passages. For some questions, more than one of the choices could conceivably answer the question. However, you are to choose the best answer; that is, the response that most accurately and completely answers the question. You should not make assumptions that are by commonsense standards implausible, superfluous, or incompatible with the passage. After you have chosen the best answer, blacken the corresponding space on your answer sheet.

1. The painted spider spins webs that are much stickier than the webs spun by the other species of spiders that share the same habitat. Stickier webs are more efficient at trapping insects that fly into them. Spiders prey on insects by trapping them in their webs; therefore, it can be concluded that the painted spider is a more successful predator than its competitors.

   Which one of the following, if true, most seriously weakens the argument?

   (A) Not all of the species of insects living in the painted spider's habitat are flying insects.
   (B) Butterflies and moths, which can shed scales, are especially unlikely to be trapped by spider webs that are not very sticky.
   (C) Although the painted spider's venom does not kill insects quickly, it paralyzes them almost instantaneously.
   (D) Stickier webs reflect more light, and so are more visible to insects, than are less-sticky webs.
   (E) The webs spun by the painted spider are no larger than the webs spun by the other species of spiders in the same habitat.

2. Despite the best efforts of astronomers, no one has yet succeeded in exchanging messages with intelligent life on other planets or in other solar systems. In fact, no one has even managed to prove that any kind of extraterrestrial life exists. Thus, there is clearly no intelligent life anywhere but on Earth.

   The argument's reasoning is flawed because the argument

   (A) fails to consider that there might be extraterrestrial forms of intelligence that are not living beings
   (B) confuses an absence of evidence for a hypothesis with the existence of evidence against the hypothesis
   (C) interprets a disagreement over a scientific theory as a disproof of that theory
   (D) makes an inference that relies on the vagueness of the term "life"
   (E) relies on a weak analogy rather than on evidence to draw a conclusion

GO ON TO THE NEXT PAGE.

Questions 3–4

Bart: A mathematical problem that defied solution for hundreds of years has finally yielded to a supercomputer. The process by which the supercomputer derived the result is so complex, however, that no one can fully comprehend it. Consequently, the result is unacceptable.

Anne: In scientific research, if the results of a test can be replicated in other tests, the results are acceptable even though the way they were derived might not be fully understood. Therefore, if a mathematical result derived by a supercomputer can be reproduced by other supercomputers following the same procedure, it is acceptable.

3. Bart's argument requires which one of the following assumptions?

(A) The mathematical result in question is unacceptable because it was derived with the use of a supercomputer.
(B) For the mathematical result in question to be acceptable, there must be someone who can fully comprehend the process by which it was derived.
(C) To be acceptable, the mathematical result in question must be reproduced on another supercomputer.
(D) Making the mathematical result in question less complex would guarantee its acceptability.
(E) The supercomputer cannot derive an acceptable solution to the mathematical problem in question.

4. The exchange between Bart and Anne most strongly supports the view that they disagree as to

(A) whether a scientific result that has not been replicated can properly be accepted
(B) whether the result that a supercomputer derives for a mathematical problem must be replicated on another supercomputer before it can be accepted
(C) the criterion to be used for accepting a mathematical result derived by a supercomputer
(D) the level of complexity of the process to which Bart refers in his statements
(E) the relative complexity of mathematical problems as compared to scientific problems

5. It is commonly held among marketing experts that in a nonexpanding market a company's best strategy is to go after a bigger share of the market and that the best way to do this is to run comparative advertisements that emphasize weaknesses in the products of rivals. In the stagnant market for food oil, soybean-oil and palm-oil producers did wage a two-year battle with comparative advertisements about the deleterious effect on health of each other's products. These campaigns, however, had little effect on respective market shares; rather, they stopped many people from buying any edible oils at all.

The statements above most strongly support the conclusion that comparative advertisements

(A) increase a company's market share in all cases in which that company's products are clearly superior to the products of rivals
(B) should not be used in a market that is expanding or likely to expand
(C) should under no circumstances be used as a retaliatory measure
(D) carry the risk of causing a contraction of the market at which they are aimed
(E) yield no long-term gains unless consumers can easily verify the claims made

6. Recent unexpectedly heavy rainfalls in the metropolitan area have filled the reservoirs and streams; water rationing, therefore, will not be necessary this summer.

Which one of the following, if true, most undermines the author's prediction?

(A) Water rationing was imposed in the city in three of the last five years.
(B) A small part of the city's water supply is obtained from deep underground water systems that are not reached by rainwater.
(C) The water company's capacity to pump water to customers has not kept up with the increased demand created by population growth in the metropolitan area.
(D) The long-range weather forecast predicts lower-than-average temperatures for this summer.
(E) In most years the city receives less total precipitation in the summer than it receives in any other season.

GO ON TO THE NEXT PAGE.

7. John: In 80 percent of car accidents, the driver at fault was within five miles of home, so people evidently drive less safely near home than they do on long trips.

Judy: But people do 80 percent of their driving within five miles of home.

How is Judy's response related to John's argument?

(A) It shows that the evidence that John presents, by itself, is not enough to prove his claim.
(B) It restates the evidence that John presents in different terms.
(C) It gives additional evidence that is needed by John to support his conclusion.
(D) It calls into question John's assumption that whenever people drive more than five miles from home they are going on a long trip.
(E) It suggests that John's conclusion is merely a restatement of his argument's premise.

8. Reasonable people adapt themselves to the world; unreasonable people persist in trying to adapt the world to themselves. Therefore, all progress depends on unreasonable people.

If all of the statements in the passage above are true, which one of the following statements must also be true?

(A) Reasonable people and unreasonable people are incompatible.
(B) If there are only reasonable people, there cannot be progress.
(C) If there are unreasonable people, there will be progress.
(D) Some unreasonable people are unable to bring about progress.
(E) Unreasonable people are more persistent than reasonable people.

9. Theater critic: The theater is in a dismal state. Audiences are sparse and revenue is down. Without the audience and the revenue, the talented and creative people who are the lifeblood of the theater are abandoning it. No wonder standards are deteriorating.

Producer: It's not true that the theater is in decline. Don't you realize that your comments constitute a self-fulfilling prophecy? By publishing these opinions, you yourself are discouraging new audiences from emerging and new talent from joining the theater.

Which one of the following is a questionable technique employed by the producer in responding to the critic?

(A) focusing on the effects of the critic's evaluation rather than on its content
(B) accusing the critic of relying solely on opinion unsupported by factual evidence
(C) challenging the motives behind the critic's remarks rather than the remarks themselves
(D) relying on emphasis rather than on argument
(E) invoking authority in order to intimidate the critic

10. Michelangelo's sixteenth-century Sistine Chapel paintings are currently being restored. A goal of the restorers is to uncover Michelangelo's original work, and so additions made to Michelangelo's paintings by later artists are being removed. However, the restorers have decided to make one exception: to leave intact additions that were painted by da Volterra.

Which one of the following, if true, most helps to reconcile the restorers' decision with the goal stated in the passage?

(A) The restorers believe that da Volterra stripped away all previous layers of paint before he painted his own additions to the Sistine Chapel.
(B) Because da Volterra used a type of pigment that is especially sensitive to light, the additions to the Sistine Chapel that da Volterra painted have relatively muted colors.
(C) Da Volterra's additions were painted in a style that was similar to the style used by Michelangelo.
(D) Michelangelo is famous primarily for his sculptures and only secondarily for his paintings, whereas da Volterra is known exclusively for his paintings.
(E) Da Volterra's work is considered by certain art historians to be just as valuable as the work of some of the other artists who painted additions to Michelangelo's work.

11. A controversial program rewards prison inmates who behave particularly well in prison by giving them the chance to receive free cosmetic plastic surgery performed by medical students. The program is obviously morally questionable, both in its assumptions about what inmates might want and in its use of the prison population to train future surgeons. Putting these moral issues aside, however, the surgery clearly has a powerful rehabilitative effect, as is shown by the fact that, among recipients of the surgery, the proportion who are convicted of new crimes committed after release is only half that for the prison population as a whole.

A flaw in the reasoning of the passage is that it

(A) allows moral issues to be a consideration in presenting evidence about matters of fact
(B) dismisses moral considerations on the grounds that only matters of fact are relevant
(C) labels the program as "controversial" instead of discussing the issues that give rise to controversy
(D) asserts that the rehabilitation of criminals is not a moral issue
(E) relies on evidence drawn from a sample that there is reason to believe is unrepresentative

GO ON TO THE NEXT PAGE.

12. The retina scanner, a machine that scans the web of tiny blood vessels in the retina, stores information about the pattern formed by the blood vessels. This information allows it to recognize any pattern it has previously scanned. No two eyes have identical patterns of blood vessels in the retina. A retina scanner can therefore be used successfully to determine for any person whether it has ever scanned a retina of that person before.

The reasoning in the argument depends upon assuming that

(A) diseases of the human eye do not alter the pattern of blood vessels in the retina in ways that would make the pattern unrecognizable to the retina scanner
(B) no person has a different pattern of blood vessels in the retina of the left eye than in the retina of the right eye
(C) there are enough retina scanners to store information about every person's retinas
(D) the number of blood vessels in the human retina is invariant, although the patterns they form differ from person to person
(E) there is no person whose retinas have been scanned by two or more different retina scanners

13. There are just two ways a moon could have been formed from the planet around which it travels: either part of the planet's outer shell spun off into orbit around the planet or else a large object, such as a comet or meteoroid, struck the planet so violently that it dislodged a mass of material from inside the planet. Earth's moon consists primarily of materials different from those of the Earth's outer shell.

If the statements above are true, which one of the following, if also true, would most help to justify drawing the conclusion that Earth's moon was not formed from a piece of the Earth?

(A) The moons of some planets in Earth's solar system were not formed primarily from the planets' outer shells.
(B) Earth's moon consists primarily of elements that differ from those inside the Earth.
(C) Earth's gravity cannot have trapped a meteoroid and pulled it into its orbit as the Moon.
(D) The craters on the surface of Earth's moon show that it has been struck by many thousands of large meteoroids.
(E) Comets and large meteoroids normally move at very high speeds.

14. Caffeine can kill or inhibit the growth of the larvae of several species of insects. One recent experiment showed that tobacco hornworm larvae die when they ingest a preparation that consists, in part, of finely powdered tea leaves, which contain caffeine. This result is evidence for the hypothesis that the presence of non-negligible quantities of caffeine in various parts of many diverse species of plants is not accidental but evolved as a defense for those plants.

The argument assumes that

(A) caffeine-producing plants are an important raw material in the manufacture of commercial insecticides
(B) caffeine is stored in leaves and other parts of caffeine-producing plants in concentrations roughly equal to the caffeine concentration of the preparation fed to the tobacco hornworm larvae
(C) caffeine-producing plants grow wherever insect larvae pose a major threat to indigenous plants or once posed a major threat to the ancestors of those plants
(D) the tobacco plant is among the plant species that produce caffeine for their own defense
(E) caffeine-producing plants or their ancestors have at some time been subject to being fed upon by creatures sensitive to caffeine

15. The only plants in the garden were tulips, but they were tall tulips. So the only plants in the garden were tall plants.

Which one of the following exhibits faulty reasoning most similar to the faulty reasoning in the argument above?

(A) The only dogs in the show were poodles, and they were all black poodles. So all the dogs in the show were black.
(B) All the buildings on the block were tall. The only buildings on the block were office buildings and residential towers. So all the office buildings on the block were tall buildings.
(C) All the primates in the zoo were gorillas. The only gorillas in the zoo were small gorillas. Thus the only primates in the zoo were small primates.
(D) The only fruit in the kitchen was pears, but the pears were not ripe. Thus none of the fruit in the kitchen was ripe.
(E) All the grand pianos here are large. All the grand pianos here are heavy. Thus everything large is heavy.

GO ON TO THE NEXT PAGE.

16. Scientific research will be properly channeled whenever those who decide which research to fund give due weight to the scientific merits of all proposed research. But when government agencies control these funding decisions, political considerations play a major role in determining which research will be funded, and whenever political considerations play such a role, the inevitable result is that scientific research is not properly channeled.

Which one of the following can be properly inferred from the statements above?

(A) There is no proper role for political considerations to play in determining who will decide which scientific research to fund.
(B) It is inevitable that considerations of scientific merit will be neglected in decisions regarding the funding of scientific research.
(C) Giving political considerations a major role in determining which scientific research to fund is incompatible with giving proper weight to the scientific merits of proposed research.
(D) When scientific research is not properly channeled, governments tend to step in and take control of the process of choosing which research to fund.
(E) If a government does not control investment in basic scientific research, political consideration will inevitably be neglected in deciding which research to fund.

17. A new silencing device for domestic appliances operates by producing sound waves that cancel out the sound waves produced by the appliance. The device, unlike conventional silencers, actively eliminates the noise the appliance makes, and for that reason vacuum cleaners designed to incorporate the new device will operate with much lower electricity consumption than conventional vacuum cleaners.

Which one of the following, if true, most helps to explain why the new silencing device will make lower electricity consumption possible?

(A) Designers of vacuum cleaner motors typically have to compromise the motors' efficiency in order to reduce noise production.
(B) The device runs on electricity drawn from the appliance's main power supply.
(C) Conventional vacuum cleaners often use spinning brushes to loosen dirt in addition to using suction to remove dirt.
(D) Governmental standards for such domestic appliances as vacuum cleaners allow higher electricity consumption when vacuum cleaners are quieter.
(E) The need to incorporate silencers in conventional vacuum cleaners makes them heavier and less mobile than they might otherwise be.

18. Because dinosaurs were reptiles, scientists once assumed that, like all reptiles alive today, dinosaurs were cold-blooded. The recent discovery of dinosaur fossils in the northern arctic, however, has led a number of researchers to conclude that at least some dinosaurs might have been warm-blooded. These researchers point out that only warm-blooded animals could have withstood the frigid temperatures that are characteristic of arctic winters, whereas cold-blooded animals would have frozen to death in the extreme cold.

Which one of the following, if true, weakens the researchers' argument?

(A) Today's reptiles are generally confined to regions of temperate or even tropical climates.
(B) The fossils show the arctic dinosaurs to have been substantially smaller than other known species of dinosaurs.
(C) The arctic dinosaur fossils were found alongside fossils of plants known for their ability to withstand extremely cold temperatures.
(D) The number of fossils found together indicates herds of dinosaurs so large that they would need to migrate to find a continual food supply.
(E) Experts on prehistoric climatic conditions believe that winter temperatures in the prehistoric northern arctic were not significantly different from what they are today.

GO ON TO THE NEXT PAGE.

Questions 19–20

Maria: Calling any state totalitarian is misleading: it implies total state control of all aspects of life. The real world contains no political entity exercising literally total control over even one such aspect. This is because any system of control is inefficient, and, therefore, its degree of control is partial.

James: A one-party state that has tried to exercise control over most aspects of a society and that has, broadly speaking, managed to do so is totalitarian. Such a system's practical inefficiencies do not limit the aptness of the term, which does not describe a state's actual degree of control as much as it describes the nature of a state's ambitions.

19. Which one of the following most accurately expresses Maria's main conclusion?

(A) No state can be called totalitarian without inviting a mistaken belief.
(B) To be totalitarian, a state must totally control society.
(C) The degree of control exercised by a state is necessarily partial.
(D) No existing state currently has even one aspect of society under total control.
(E) Systems of control are inevitably inefficient.

20. James responds to Maria's argument by

(A) pointing out a logical inconsistency between two statements she makes in support of her argument
(B) offering an alternative explanation for political conditions she mentions
(C) rejecting some of the evidence she presents without challenging what she infers from it
(D) disputing the conditions under which a key term of her argument can be appropriately applied
(E) demonstrating that her own premises lead to a conclusion different from hers

21. The similarity between ichthyosaurs and fish is an example of convergence, a process by which different classes of organisms adapt to the same environment by independently developing one or more similar external body features. Ichthyosaurs were marine reptiles and thus do not belong to the same class of organisms as fish. However, ichthyosaurs adapted to their marine environment by converging on external body features similar to those of fish. Most strikingly, ichthyosaurs, like fish, had fins.

If the statements above are true, which one of the following is an inference that can be properly drawn on the basis of them?

(A) The members of a single class of organisms that inhabit the same environment must be identical in all their external body features.
(B) The members of a single class of organisms must exhibit one or more similar external body features that differentiate that class from all other classes of organisms.
(C) It is only as a result of adaptation to similar environments that one class of organisms develops external body features similar to those of another class of organisms.
(D) An organism does not necessarily belong to a class simply because the organism has one or more external body features similar to those of members of that class.
(E) Whenever two classes of organisms share the same environment, members of one class will differ from members of the other class in several external body features.

GO ON TO THE NEXT PAGE.

22. Further evidence bearing on Jamison's activities must have come to light. On the basis of previously available evidence alone, it would have been impossible to prove that Jamison was a party to the fraud, and Jamison's active involvement in the fraud has now been definitively established.

The pattern of reasoning exhibited in the argument above most closely parallels that exhibited in which one of the following?

(A) Smith must not have purchased his house within the last year. He is listed as the owner of that house on the old list of property owners, and anyone on the old list could not have purchased his or her property within the last year.
(B) Turner must not have taken her usual train to Nantes today. Had she done so, she could not have been in Nantes until this afternoon, but she was seen having coffee in Nantes at 11 o'clock this morning.
(C) Norris must have lied when she said that she had not authorized the investigation. There is no doubt that she did authorize it, and authorizing an investigation is not something anyone is likely to have forgotten.
(D) Waugh must have known that last night's class was canceled. Waugh was in the library yesterday, and it would have been impossible for anyone in the library not to have seen the cancellation notices.
(E) LaForte must have deeply resented being passed over for promotion. He maintains otherwise, but only someone who felt badly treated would have made the kind of remark LaForte made at yesterday's meeting.

23. Reporting on a civil war, a journalist encountered evidence that refugees were starving because the government would not permit food shipments to a rebel-held area. Government censors deleted all mention of the government's role in the starvation from the journalist's report, which had not implicated either nature or the rebels in the starvation. The journalist concluded that it was ethically permissible to file the censored report, because the journalist's news agency would precede it with the notice "Cleared by government censors."

Which one of the following ethical criteria, if valid, would serve to support the journalist's conclusion while placing the least constraint on the flow of reported information?

(A) It is ethical in general to report known facts but unethical to do so while omitting other known facts if the omitted facts would substantially alter an impression of a person or institution that would be congruent with the reported facts.
(B) In a situation of conflict, it is ethical to report known facts and unethical to fail to report known facts that would tend to exonerate one party to the conflict.
(C) In a situation of censorship, it is unethical to make any report if the government represented by the censor deletes from the report material unfavorable to that government.
(D) It is ethical in general to report known facts but unethical to make a report in a situation of censorship if relevant facts have been deleted by the censor, unless the recipient of the report is warned that censorship existed.
(E) Although it is ethical in general to report known facts, it is unethical to make a report from which a censor has deleted relevant facts, unless the recipient of the report is warned that there was censorship and the reported facts do not by themselves give a misleading impression.

GO ON TO THE NEXT PAGE.

24. A birth is more likely to be difficult when the mother is over the age of 40 than when she is younger. Regardless of the mother's age, a person whose birth was difficult is more likely to be ambidextrous than is a person whose birth was not difficult. Since other causes of ambidexterity are not related to the mother's age, there must be more ambidextrous people who were born to women over 40 than there are ambidextrous people who were born to younger women.

The argument is most vulnerable to which one of the following criticisms?

(A) It assumes what it sets out to establish.
(B) It overlooks the possibility that fewer children are born to women over 40 than to women under 40.
(C) It fails to specify what percentage of people in the population as a whole are ambidextrous.
(D) It does not state how old a child must be before its handedness can be determined.
(E) It neglects to explain how difficulties during birth can result in a child's ambidexterity.

Questions 25–26

The government has no right to tax earnings from labor. Taxation of this kind requires the laborer to devote a certain percentage of hours worked to earning money for the government. Thus, such taxation forces the laborer to work, in part, for another's purpose. Since involuntary servitude can be defined as forced work for another's purpose, just as involuntary servitude is pernicious, so is taxing earnings from labor.

25. The argument uses which one of the following argumentative techniques?

(A) deriving a general principle about the rights of individuals from a judgment concerning the obligations of governments
(B) inferring what will be the case merely from a description of what once was the case
(C) inferring that since two institutions are similar in one respect, they are similar in another respect
(D) citing the authority of an economic theory in order to justify a moral principle
(E) presupposing the inevitability of a hierarchical class system in order to oppose a given economic practice

26. Which one of the following is an error of reasoning committed by the argument?

(A) It ignores a difference in how the idea of forced work for another's purpose applies to the two cases.
(B) It does not take into account the fact that labor is taxed at different rates depending on income.
(C) It mistakenly assumes that all work is taxed.
(D) It ignores the fact that the government also taxes income from investment.
(E) It treats definitions as if they were matters of subjective opinion rather than objective facts about language.

S T O P

IF YOU FINISH BEFORE TIME IS CALLED, YOU MAY CHECK YOUR WORK ON THIS SECTION ONLY. DO NOT WORK ON ANY OTHER SECTION IN THE TEST.

SECTION IV

Time—35 minutes

27 Questions

Directions: Each passage in this section is followed by a group of questions to be answered on the basis of what is stated or implied in the passage. For some of the questions, more than one of the choices could conceivably answer the question. However, you are to choose the best answer; that is, the response that most accurately and completely answers the question, and blacken the corresponding space on your answer sheet.

Three kinds of study have been performed on Byron. There is the biographical study—the very valuable examination of Byron's psychology and the events in his life; Escarpit's 1958 work is an example of this kind of study, and biographers to this day continue to speculate about Byron's life. Equally valuable is the study of Byron as a figure important in the history of ideas; Russell and Praz have written studies of this kind. Finally, there are studies that primarily consider Byron's poetry. Such literary studies are valuable, however, only when they avoid concentrating solely on analyzing the verbal shadings of Byron's poetry to the exclusion of any discussion of biographical considerations. A study with such a concentration would be of questionable value because Byron's poetry, for the most part, is simply not a poetry of subtle verbal meanings. Rather, on the whole, Byron's poems record the emotional pressure of certain moments in his life. I believe we cannot often read a poem of Byron's, as we often can one of Shakespeare's, without wondering what events or circumstances in his life prompted him to write it.

No doubt the fact that most of Byron's poems cannot be convincingly read as subtle verbal creations indicates that Byron is not a "great" poet. It must be admitted too that Byron's literary craftsmanship is irregular and often his temperament disrupts even his lax literary method (although the result, an absence of method, has a significant purpose: it functions as a rebuke to a cosmos that Byron feels he cannot understand). If Byron is not a "great" poet, his poetry is nonetheless of extraordinary interest to us because of the pleasure it gives us. Our main pleasure in reading Byron's poetry is the contact with a singular personality. Reading his work gives us illumination—self-understanding—after we have seen our weaknesses and aspirations mirrored in the personality we usually find in the poems. Anyone who thinks that this kind of illumination is not a genuine reason for reading a poet should think carefully about why we read Donne's sonnets.

It is Byron and Byron's idea of himself that hold his work together (and that enthralled early-nineteenth-century Europe). Different characters speak in his poems, but finally it is usually he himself who is speaking: a far cry from the impersonal poet Keats. Byron's poetry alludes to Greek and Roman myth in the context of contemporary affairs, but his work remains generally of a piece because of his close presence in the poetry. In sum, the poetry is a shrewd personal performance, and to shut out Byron the man is to fabricate a work of pseudocriticism.

1. Which one of the following titles best expresses the main idea of the passage?
   - (A) An Absence of Method: Why Byron Is Not a "Great" Poet
   - (B) Byron: The Recurring Presence in Byron's Poetry
   - (C) Personality and Poetry: The Biographical Dimension of Nineteenth-Century Poetry
   - (D) Byron's Poetry: Its Influence on the Imagination of Early-Nineteenth-Century Europe
   - (E) Verbal Shadings: The Fatal Flaw of Twentieth-Century Literary Criticism

2. The author's mention of Russell and Praz serves primarily to
   - (A) differentiate them from one another
   - (B) contrast their conclusions about Byron with those of Escarpit
   - (C) point out the writers whose studies suggest a new direction for Byron scholarship
   - (D) provide examples of writers who have written one kind of study of Byron
   - (E) give credit to the writers who have composed the best studies of Byron

GO ON TO THE NEXT PAGE.

3. Which one of the following would the author most likely consider to be a valuable study of Byron?
   (A) a study that compared Byron's poetic style with Keats' poetic style
   (B) a study that argued that Byron's thought ought not to be analyzed in terms of its importance in the history of ideas
   (C) a study that sought to identify the emotions felt by Byron at a particular time in his life
   (D) a study in which a literary critic argues that the language of Byron's poetry was more subtle than that of Keats' poetry
   (E) a study in which a literary critic drew on experiences from his or her own life

4. Which one of the following statements best describes the organization of the first paragraph of the passage?
   (A) A generalization is made and then gradually refuted.
   (B) A number of theories are discussed and then the author chooses the most convincing one.
   (C) Several categories are mentioned and then one category is discussed in some detail.
   (D) A historical trend is delineated and then a prediction about the future of the trend is offered.
   (E) A classification is made and then a rival classification is substituted in its place.

5. The author mentions that "Byron's literary craftsmanship is irregular" (lines 27–28) most probably in order to
   (A) contrast Byron's poetic skill with that of Shakespeare
   (B) dismiss craftsmanship as a standard by which to judge poets
   (C) offer another reason why Byron is not a "great" poet
   (D) point out a negative consequence of Byron's belief that the cosmos is incomprehensible
   (E) indicate the most-often-cited explanation of why Byron's poetry lacks subtle verbal nuances

6. According to the author, Shakespeare's poems differ from Byron's in that Shakespeare's poems
   (A) have elicited a wider variety of responses from both literary critics and biographers
   (B) are on the whole less susceptible to being read as subtle verbal creations
   (C) do not grow out of, or are not motivated by, actual events or circumstances in the poet's life
   (D) provide the attentive reader with a greater degree of illumination concerning his or her own weaknesses and aspirations
   (E) can often be read without the reader's being curious about what biographical factors motivated the poet to write them

7. The author indicates which one of the following about biographers' speculation concerning Byron's life?
   (A) Such speculation began in earnest with Escarpit's study.
   (B) Such speculation continues today.
   (C) Such speculation is less important than consideration of Byron's poetry.
   (D) Such speculation has not given us a satisfactory sense of Byron's life.
   (E) Such speculation has been carried out despite the objections of literary critics.

8. The passage supplies specific information that provides a definitive answer to which one of the following questions?
   (A) What does the author consider to be the primary enjoyment derived from reading Byron?
   (B) Who among literary critics has primarily studied Byron's poems?
   (C) Which moments in Byron's life exerted the greatest pressure on his poetry?
   (D) Has Byron ever been considered to be a "great" poet?
   (E) Did Byron exert an influence on Europeans in the latter part of the nineteenth century?

GO ON TO THE NEXT PAGE.

The United States Supreme Court has not always resolved legal issues of concern to Native Americans in a manner that has pleased the Indian nations. Many of the Court's decisions have been products of political compromise that looked more to the temper of the times than to enduring principles of law. But accommodation is part of the judicial system in the United States, and judicial decisions must be assessed with this fact in mind.

Despite the "accommodating" nature of the judicial system, it is worth noting that the power of the Supreme Court has been exercised in a manner that has usually been beneficial to Native Americans, at least on minor issues, and has not been wholly detrimental on the larger, more important issues. Certainly there have been decisions that cast doubt on the validity of this assertion. Some critics point to the patronizing tone of many Court opinions and the apparent rejection of Native American values as important points to consider when reviewing a case. However, the validity of the assertion can be illustrated by reference to two important contributions that have resulted from the exercise of judicial power.

First, the Court has created rules of judicial construction that, in general, favor the rights of Native American litigants. The Court's attitude has been conditioned by recognition of the distinct disadvantages Native Americans faced when dealing with settlers in the past. Treaties were inevitably written in English for the benefit of their authors, whereas tribal leaders were accustomed to making treaties without any written account, on the strength of mutual promises sealed by religious commitment and individual integrity. The written treaties were often broken, and Native Americans were confronted with fraud and political and military aggression. The Court recognizes that past unfairness to Native Americans cannot be sanctioned by the force of law. Therefore, ambiguities in treaties are to be interpreted in favor of the Native American claimants, treaties are to be interpreted as the Native Americans would have understood them, and, under the reserved rights doctrine, treaties reserve to Native Americans all rights that have not been specifically granted away in other treaties.

A second achievement of the judicial system is the protection that has been provided against encroachment by the states into tribal affairs. Federal judges are not inclined to view favorably efforts to extend states' powers and jurisdictions because of the direct threat that such expansion poses to the exercise of federal powers. In the absence of a federal statute directly and clearly allocating a function to the states, federal judges are inclined to reserve for the federal government—and the tribal governments under its charge—all those powers and rights they can be said to have possessed historically.

9. According to the passage, one reason why the United States Supreme Court "has not always resolved legal issues of concern to Native Americans in a manner that has pleased the Indian nations" (lines 1–4) is that

(A) Native Americans have been prevented from presenting their concerns persuasively
(B) the Court has failed to recognize that the Indian nations' concerns are different from those of other groups or from those of the federal government
(C) the Court has been reluctant to curtail the powers of the federal government
(D) Native Americans faced distinct disadvantages in dealing with settlers in the past
(E) the Court has made political compromises in deciding some cases

10. It can be inferred that the objections raised by the critics mentioned in line 18 would be most clearly answered by a United States Supreme Court decision that

(A) demonstrated respect for Native Americans and the principles and qualities they consider important
(B) protected the rights of the states in conflicts with the federal government
(C) demonstrated recognition of the unfair treatment Native Americans received in the past
(D) reflected consideration of the hardships suffered by Native Americans because of unfair treaties
(E) prevented repetition of inequities experienced by Native Americans in the past

GO ON TO THE NEXT PAGE.

11. It can be inferred that the author calls the judicial system of the United States "accommodating" (line 10) primarily in order to
    (A) suggest that the decisions of the United States Supreme Court have been less favorable to Native Americans than most people believe
    (B) suggest that the United States Supreme Court should be more supportive of the goals of Native Americans
    (C) suggest a reason why the decisions of the United States Supreme Court have not always favored Native Americans
    (D) indicate that the United States Supreme Court has made creditable efforts to recognize the values of Native Americans
    (E) indicate that the United States Supreme Court attempts to be fair to all parties to a case

12. The author's attitude toward the United States Supreme Court's resolution of legal issues of concern to Native Americans can best be described as one of
    (A) wholehearted endorsement
    (B) restrained appreciation
    (C) detached objectivity
    (D) cautious opposition
    (E) suppressed exasperation

13. It can be inferred that the author believes that the extension of the states' powers and jurisdictions with respect to Native American affairs would be
    (A) possible only with the consent of the Indian nations
    (B) favorably viewed by the United States Supreme Court
    (C) in the best interests of both state and federal governments
    (D) detrimental to the interests of Native Americans
    (E) discouraged by most federal judges in spite of legal precedents supporting the extension

14. The author's primary purpose is to
    (A) contrast opposing views
    (B) reevaluate traditional beliefs
    (C) reconcile divergent opinions
    (D) assess the claims made by disputants
    (E) provide evidence to support a contention

15. It can be inferred that the author believes the United States Supreme Court's treatment of Native Americans to have been
    (A) irreproachable on legal grounds
    (B) reasonably supportive in most situations
    (C) guided by enduring principles of law
    (D) misguided but generally harmless
    (E) harmful only in a few minor cases

GO ON TO THE NEXT PAGE.

When catastrophe strikes, analysts typically blame some combination of powerful mechanisms. An earthquake is traced to an immense instability along a fault line; a stock market crash is blamed on the destabilizing effect of computer trading. These explanations may well be correct. But systems as large and complicated as the Earth's crust or the stock market can break down not only under the force of a mighty blow but also at the drop of a pin. In a large interactive system, a minor event can start a chain reaction that leads to a catastrophe.

Traditionally, investigators have analyzed large interactive systems in the same way they analyze small orderly systems, mainly because the methods developed for small systems have proved so successful. They believed they could predict the behavior of a large interactive system by studying its elements separately and by analyzing its component mechanisms individually. For lack of a better theory, they assumed that in large interactive systems the response to a disturbance is proportional to that disturbance.

During the past few decades, however, it has become increasingly apparent that many large complicated systems do not yield to traditional analysis. Consequently, theorists have proposed a "theory of self-organized criticality": many large interactive systems evolve naturally to a critical state in which a minor event starts a chain reaction that can affect any number of elements in the system. Although such systems produce more minor events than catastrophes, the mechanism that leads to minor events is the same one that leads to major events.

A deceptively simple system serves as a paradigm for self-organized criticality: a pile of sand. As sand is poured one grain at a time onto a flat disk, the grains at first stay close to the position where they land. Soon they rest on top of one another, creating a pile that has a gentle slope. Now and then, when the slope becomes too steep, the grains slide down, causing a small avalanche. The system reaches its critical state when the amount of sand added is balanced, on average, by the amount falling off the edge of the disk.

Now when a grain of sand is added, it can start an avalanche of any size, including a "catastrophic" event. Most of the time the grain will fall so that no avalanche occurs. By studying a specific area of the pile, one can even predict whether avalanches will occur there in the near future. To such a local observer, however, large avalanches would remain unpredictable because they are a consequence of the total history of the entire pile. No matter what the local dynamics are, catastrophic avalanches would persist at a relative frequency that cannot be altered. Criticality is a global property of the sandpile.

16. The passage provides support for all of the following generalizations about large interactive systems EXCEPT:

(A) They can evolve to a critical state.
(B) They do not always yield to traditional analysis.
(C) They make it impossible for observers to make any predictions about them.
(D) They are subject to the effects of chain reactions.
(E) They are subject to more minor events than major events.

17. According to the passage, the criticality of a sandpile is determined by the

(A) size of the grains of sand added to the sandpile
(B) number of grains of sand the sandpile contains
(C) rate at which sand is added to the sandpile
(D) shape of the surface on which the sandpile rests
(E) balance between the amount of sand added to and the amount lost from the sandpile

GO ON TO THE NEXT PAGE.

18. It can be inferred from the passage that the theory employed by the investigators mentioned in the second paragraph would lead one to predict that which one of the following would result from the addition of a grain of sand to a sandpile?
    (A) The grain of sand would never cause anything more than a minor disturbance.
    (B) The grain of sand would usually cause a minor disturbance, but would occasionally cause a small avalanche.
    (C) The grain of sand would usually cause either a minor disturbance or a small avalanche, but would occasionally cause a catastrophic event.
    (D) The grain of sand would usually cause a catastrophic event, but would occasionally cause only a small avalanche or an even more minor disturbance.
    (E) The grain of sand would invariably cause a catastrophic event.

19. Which one of the following best describes the organization of the passage?
    (A) A traditional procedure is described and its application to common situations is endorsed; its shortcomings in certain rare but critical circumstances are then revealed.
    (B) A common misconception is elaborated and its consequences are described; a detailed example of one of these consequences is then given.
    (C) A general principle is stated and supported by several examples; an exception to the rule is then considered and its importance evaluated.
    (D) A number of seemingly unrelated events are categorized; the underlying processes that connect them are then detailed.
    (E) A traditional method of analysis is discussed and the reasons for its adoption are explained; an alternative is then described and clarified by means of an example.

20. Which one of the following is most analogous to the method of analysis employed by the investigators mentioned in the second paragraph?
    (A) A pollster gathers a sample of voter preferences and on the basis of this information makes a prediction about the outcome of an election.
    (B) A historian examines the surviving documents detailing the history of a movement and from these documents reconstructs a chronology of the events that initiated the movement.
    (C) A meteorologist measures the rainfall over a certain period of the year and from this data calculates the total annual rainfall for the region.
    (D) A biologist observes the behavior of one species of insect and from these observations generalizes about the behavior of insects as a class.
    (E) An engineer analyzes the stability of each structural element of a bridge and from these analyses draws a conclusion about the structural soundness of the bridge.

21. In the passage, the author is primarily concerned with
    (A) arguing against the abandonment of a traditional approach
    (B) describing the evolution of a radical theory
    (C) reconciling conflicting points of view
    (D) illustrating the superiority of a new theoretical approach
    (E) advocating the reconsideration of an unfashionable explanation

GO ON TO THE NEXT PAGE.

Historians have long accepted the notion that women of English descent who lived in the English colonies of North America during the seventeenth and eighteenth centuries were better off than either the contemporary women in England or the colonists' own nineteenth-century daughters and granddaughters. The "golden age" theory originated in the 1920s with the work of Elizabeth Dexter, who argued that there were relatively few women among the colonists, and that all hands—male and female—were needed to sustain the growing settlements. Rigid sex-role distinctions could not exist under such circumstances; female colonists could accordingly engage in whatever occupations they wished, encountering few legal or social constraints if they sought employment outside the home. The surplus of male colonists also gave women crucial bargaining power in the marriage market, since women's contributions were vital to the survival of colonial households.

Dexter's portrait of female colonists living under conditions of rough equality with their male counterparts was eventually incorporated into studies of nineteenth-century middle-class women. The contrast between the self-sufficient colonial woman and the oppressed nineteenth-century woman, confined to her home by stultifying ideologies of domesticity and by the fact that industrialization eliminated employment opportunities for middle-class women, gained an extraordinarily tenacious hold on historians. Even scholars who have questioned the "golden age" view of colonial women's status have continued to accept the paradigm of a nineteenth-century decline from a more desirable past. For example, Joan Hoff-Wilson asserted that there was no "golden age" and yet emphasized that the nineteenth century brought "increased loss of function and authentic status for" middle-class women.

Recent publications about colonial women have exposed the concept of a decline in status as simplistic and unsophisticated, a theory that based its assessment of colonial women's status solely on one factor (their economic function in society) and assumed all too readily that a relatively simple social system automatically brought higher standing to colonial women. The new scholarship presents a far more complicated picture, one in which definitions of gender roles, the colonial economy, demographic patterns, religion, the law, and household organization all contributed to defining the circumstances of colonial women's lives. Indeed, the primary concern of modern scholarship is not to generalize about women's status but to identify the specific changes and continuities in women's lives during the colonial period. For example, whereas earlier historians suggested that there was little change for colonial women before 1800, the new scholarship suggests that a three-part chronological division more accurately reflects colonial women's experiences. First was the initial period of English colonization (from the 1620s to about 1660); then a period during which patterns of family and community were challenged and reshaped (roughly from 1660 to 1750); and finally the era of revolution (approximately 1750 to 1815), which brought other changes to women's lives.

22. Which one of the following best expresses the main idea of the passage?
    (A) An earlier theory about the status of middle-class women in the nineteenth century has been supported by recent scholarship.
    (B) Recent studies of middle-class nineteenth-century women have altered an earlier theory about the status of colonial women.
    (C) Recent scholarship has exposed an earlier theory about the status of colonial women as too narrowly based and oversimplified.
    (D) An earlier theory about colonial women has greatly influenced recent studies on middle-class women in the nineteenth century.
    (E) An earlier study of middle-class women was based on insufficient research on the status of women in the nineteenth century.

23. The author discusses Hoff-Wilson primarily in order to
    (A) describe how Dexter's theory was refuted by historians of nineteenth-century North America
    (B) describe how the theory of middle-class women's nineteenth-century decline in status was developed
    (C) describe an important influence on recent scholarship about the colonial period
    (D) demonstrate the persistent influence of the "golden age" theory
    (E) provide an example of current research on the colonial period

24. It can be inferred from the passage that the author would be most likely to describe the views of the scholars mentioned in line 32 as
    (A) unassailable
    (B) innovative
    (C) paradoxical
    (D) overly sophisticated
    (E) without merit

GO ON TO THE NEXT PAGE.

25. It can be inferred from the passage that, in proposing the "three-part chronological division" (lines 60–61), scholars recognized which one of the following?
    - (A) The circumstances of colonial women's lives were defined by a broad variety of social and economic factors.
    - (B) Women's lives in the English colonies of North America were similar to women's lives in seventeenth- and eighteenth-century England.
    - (C) Colonial women's status was adversely affected when patterns of family and community were established in the late seventeenth century.
    - (D) Colonial women's status should be assessed primarily on the basis of their economic function in society.
    - (E) Colonial women's status was low when the colonies were settled but changed significantly during the era of revolution.

26. According to the author, the publications about colonial women mentioned in the third paragraph had which one of the following effects?
    - (A) They undermined Dexter's argument on the status of women colonists during the colonial period.
    - (B) They revealed the tenacity of the "golden age" theory in American history.
    - (C) They provided support for historians, such as Hoff-Wilson, who study the nineteenth century.
    - (D) They established that women's status did not change significantly from the colonial period to the nineteenth century.
    - (E) They provided support for earlier theories about women colonists in the English colonies of North America.

27. Practitioners of the new scholarship discussed in the last paragraph would be most likely to agree with which one of the following statements about Dexter's argument?
    - (A) It makes the assumption that women's status is determined primarily by their political power in society.
    - (B) It makes the assumption that a less complex social system necessarily confers higher status on women.
    - (C) It is based on inadequate research on women's economic role in the colonies.
    - (D) It places too much emphasis on the way definitions of gender roles affected women colonists in the colonial period.
    - (E) It accurately describes the way women's status declined in the nineteenth century.

S T O P

IF YOU FINISH BEFORE TIME IS CALLED, YOU MAY CHECK YOUR WORK ON THIS SECTION ONLY. DO NOT WORK ON ANY OTHER SECTION IN THE TEST.

SIGNATURE ______________________ / / DATE

LSAT WRITING SAMPLE TOPIC

Zelmar Corporation, an advertising company, must move its offices from their current downtown location. The company is considering an alternate building downtown and a suburban location. Write an argument favoring one of these choices over the other based on the following considerations:

- Zelmar wants as many employees as possible to remain with the company.
- Due to recent financial setbacks, Zelmar wants to make the coming year as profitable as possible.

The downtown location is in a somewhat smaller building a few blocks away from Zelmar's current offices and within the general area where a large proportion of the company's clients have offices. Rental costs would be slightly lower than those of its current location. Near a subway stop and close to numerous shops and restaurants, the building is located one block from a day care center that promises discounts to Zelmar employees, many of whom have preschool children. Because of space restrictions, about half of Zelmar's employees would have to give up their offices and work in a large open area subdivided by portable walls.

The suburban location is twenty miles from downtown, and the commute for many employees would at least double. While there is ample free parking, the subway line does not extend to this location; there is a bus stop directly outside the building. Zelmar would pay far less in rent than it currently does, and most employees could have their own offices. Located in an office park complex, this building has excellent facilities for large meetings and ample space for Zelmar to expand its business. A large cafeteria in the building offers food from 7 A.M. until 6 P.M. at a cost considerably below that of commercial restaurants. Employees from other offices have proposed a day care center to serve the entire complex.

Computing Your Score

Directions:

1. Use the Answer Key on the next page to check your answers.
2. Use the Scoring Worksheet below to compute your raw score.
3. Use the Score Conversion Chart to convert your raw score into the 120-180 scale.

Scoring Worksheet

1. Enter the number of questions you answered correctly in each section.

	Number Correct
SECTION I	_____
SECTION II	_____
SECTION III	_____
SECTION IV	_____

2. Enter the sum here: _____
   This is your Raw Score.

Conversion Chart

For Converting Raw Score to the 120-180 LSAT Scaled Score
LSAT Form 4LSS25

Reported Score	Raw Score Lowest	Raw Score Highest
180	98	101
179	97	97
178	96	96
177	95	95
176	94	94
175	93	93
174	92	92
173	90	91
172	89	89
171	88	88
170	87	87
169	86	86
168	84	85
167	83	83
166	82	82
165	80	81
164	79	79
163	77	78
162	76	76
161	74	75
160	73	73
159	71	72
158	69	70
157	68	68
156	66	67
155	65	65
154	63	64
153	61	62
152	60	60
151	58	59
150	56	57
149	55	55
148	53	54
147	51	52
146	50	50
145	48	49
144	46	47
143	45	45
142	43	44
141	42	42
140	40	41
139	39	39
138	37	38
137	36	36
136	34	35
135	33	33
134	31	32
133	30	30
132	29	29
131	27	28
130	26	26
129	25	25
128	24	24
127	23	23
126	22	22
125	21	21
124	20	20
123	18	19
122	17	17
121	—*	—*
120	0	16

*There is no raw score that will produce this scaled score for this form.

Answer Key

Section I

1. D	5. C	9. C	13. D	17. E	21. A
2. E	6. D	10. E	14. B	18. A	22. C
3. A	7. E	11. C	15. A	19. D	23. A
4. E	8. B	12. B	16. A	20. E	24. C

Section II

1. B	5. C	9. C	13. D	17. B	21. A
2. A	6. D	10. E	14. D	18. A	22. E
3. D	7. C	11. D	15. E	19. A	23. D
4. E	8. E	12. B	16. E	20. E	24. E

Section III

1. D	6. C	11. E	16. C	21. D	26. A
2. B	7. A	12. A	17. A	22. B	
3. B	8. B	13. B	18. D	23. D	
4. C	9. A	14. E	19. A	24. B	
5. D	10. A	15. C	20. D	25. C	

Section IV

1. B	6. E	11. C	16. C	21. D	26. A
2. D	7. B	12. B	17. E	22. C	27. B
3. C	8. A	13. D	18. A	23. D	
4. C	9. E	14. E	19. E	24. C	
5. C	10. A	15. B	20. E	25. A	

Answers Explained

Section I

Answers 1–6

The conditions have been numbered here to assist in locating the explanations.

(Initial set-up statement)

Eight students (R, S, T, V, W, X, Y, and Z) divided into three classes (1, 2, and 3).

(Condition 1)
Classes 1 and 2 gain 3 students

(Condition 2)
Class 3 gains 2 students

(Condition 3)
R into 1 $R \rightarrow 1$

(Condition 4)
S into 3 $S \rightarrow 3$

(Condition 5)
S ≠ Y (S and Y in different classes) ~~SY~~

(Condition 6)
W ≠ Y (W and Y in different classes) ~~WY~~

(Condition 7)
V ≠ Z (V and Z in different classes) ~~VZ~~

(Condition 8)
T into 1 implies Z into 1 If $T \rightarrow Z$

The organizer could look like this:

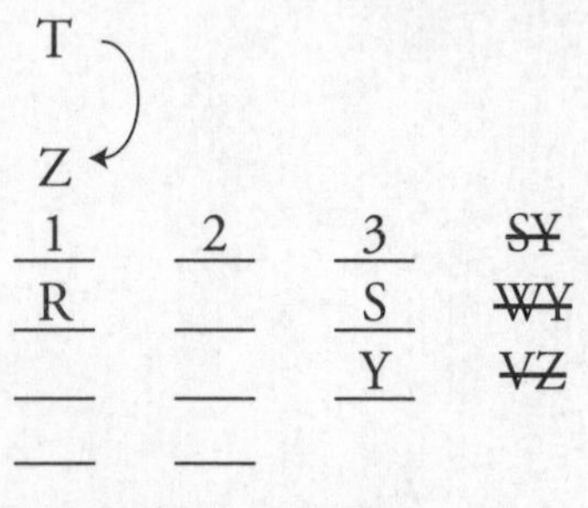

1. **(D)** Which is acceptable?
(A) is not correct, since if T is in class 1, then Z must also be in class 1 (condition 8).
(B) is not correct, since S must be in class 3 (condition 4).
(C) is not correct, since V and Z cannot both be in the same class (condition 7).
(D) is acceptable. It does not violate any of the conditions.
(E) is not correct, since W and Y cannot both be in the same class (condition 6).

2. **(E)** Student V could be added to any of the three classes. Therefore, (E) is correct.
The main issue is that V cannot be in the same class as Z. The following examples illustrate arrangements where V is in class 1, 2, and 3. Make sure that the conditions are not violated.

1	2	3	
RVW	XYZ	ST	V in class 1
RTZ	VXY	SW	V in class 2
RYZ	TWX	SV	V in class 3

3. **(A)** If X is added to class 1, then this is the resulting arrangement:

1	2	3
RX		S

Student T cannot be added to class 1, since there would be no room for Z (condition 8). Student T cannot be added to class 3 either. If T were placed in class 3, then there would be one available space in class 1 and three available spaces in class 2. Since the remaining students (V, W, Y, and Z) must be split in two groups of 2 (conditions 6 and 7), they will not fit in the available spaces. Therefore, T MUST be placed in class 2. Thus, (A) is correct.
For each of the other four answer choices, an arrangement is possible as follows:

1	2	3	
RVX	TYZ	SW	V, W not in class 2
RXY	TVW	SZ	Y, Z not in class 2

4. (E) Which pair CANNOT be added to class 3?

	1	2	3	
(A)	RYZ	TVW	SX	OK
(B)	RWZ	TVY	SX	OK
(C)	RVY	TWZ	SX	OK
(D)	RVW	TYZ	SX	OK
(E)	RTZ	VWY	SX	No

None of the conditions are violated for each of the first four choices. For (E), putting T and Z in class 1 forces W and Y into class 2. This violates condition 6. Therefore, (E) is the correct answer.

5. (C) Who MUST be added to class 2?
If student T is added to class 3, the following arrangement results:

1	2	3
R		ST

Students V and Z must be in different classes (condition 7). Students Y and W must be in different classes (condition 6). Therefore, the two empty spaces in class 1 must be for one student from each of these two groups. The last student (X) must be placed in the 3rd space in class 2. Thus, (C) is the correct answer.

6. (D) Which MUST be true?

	1	2	3	
(A)	RVW	TXY	SZ	V not in 3
(B)	RVW	TXY	SZ	T not in 3
(C)	RVW	TYZ	SX	Z not in 3
(D)	RVX	TYZ	SW	W MUST be in 3
(E)	RVX	TYZ	SW	X not in 2

(D) is the correct answer. Student Y cannot be in class 3 (condition 5). Student Y must therefore be in class 2. If Y is in class 2, then W cannot be in class 2 (condition 6). Therefore, W must be in class 3. For each of the other answer choices, an arrangement (illustrated above) can be found to negate the claim.

Answers 7–12

(Initial set-up statement)

Lions:	F, G, H, J
Tigers:	K, M

Row 1:	1	2	3
Row 2:	4	5	6

The conditions have been numbered here to assist in locating the explanations.

(Condition 1) Tigers (K and M) cannot face each other

(Condition 2) Lion in 1

(Condition 3) H in 6

(Condition 4) KJ consecutive in this order

(Condition 5) K not in 3

Since K is a tiger, K cannot be in stalls 1 (condition 2), 3 (condition 5), 5 (condition 4), or 6 (condition 3). Two basic arrangements are possible, K in 2 or K in 4:

1 (L)	2	3
F G	K	J
M	G F	H
4	5	6 (L)

or

1 (L)	2	3
G F	M G F	M G F
K	J	H
4	5	6 (L)

The organizer could have looked like this:

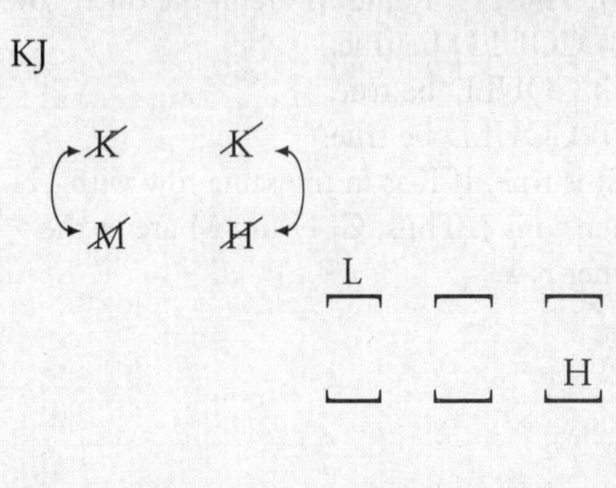

7. (E) Which MUST be true?

Given the two arrangements above, K must be in stall 2 or 4.
(A) is false, since F can be in stalls 1, 2, 3, or 5.
(B) COULD be true, but not necessarily.
(C) is false, since J must be assigned to stall 3 or 5.
(D) is false, since J must be assigned to stall 3 or 5.
(E) MUST be true, since K must be in stall 2 or 4.

8. (B) Which COULD be true?

(A) is false. If J is in 3, then M is in 4. If J is in 5, H is in 6. Therefore, F cannot be numbered one higher than J.
(B) is possible. Choice (B) is the correct answer.
(C) is false. J must be assigned to either stall 3 or 5.
(D) is false. The stalls for J and K are consecutive, not across.
(E) is false. If K is in 2, then J is in 3. If K is in 4, then J is in 5. They are in the same row.

9. (C) Which MUST be true?

(A) COULD be true.
(B) is false. A lion (F, G, or J) is in stall 5.
(C) MUST be true. This is the correct answer.
(D) COULD be true. If K is in 4 then M could be in 2 or 3.
(E) is false. There are 4 lions and only 2 tigers.

10. (E) Which MUST be true?

(A) is false. If K is in the row with H, then so is J. Thus, G, F, and M are in the other row.
(B) COULD be true.
(C) COULD be true.
(D) COULD be true.
(E) is true. If K is in the same row with H, then so is J. Thus, G, F, and M are in the other row.

11. (C) Which COULD be true?

(A) is false. If J is assigned to 3, then K is in 2.
(B) is false. If J is assigned to 3, then M is in 4.
(C) COULD be true. If J is assigned to 3, then F and G are assigned to stalls 1 and 5, in either order. Thus, G could be assigned to stall 1, and F assigned to stall 5. Therefore, (C) is the correct answer choice.
(D) is false. G is assigned to either stall 1 or 5.
(E) is false. If J is assigned to 3, M (Tiger) is assigned to 4.

12. (B) Which MUST be true?

(A) COULD be true, but not necessarily. F or G (Lions) or K or M (Tigers) could be in 2.
(B) must be true. Choice (B) is the correct answer choice.
(C) is false. Only Lions can be in 5.
(D) COULD be true, but not necessarily. M (Tiger) could be in 3.
(E) is false. A tiger is in stall 4.

Answers 13–18

(Initial set-up statement)

Three styles (R, S, T)
Eight houses (1 through 8)

The conditions have been numbered here to assist in locating the explanations.

(Condition 1) Adjacent not the same style
(Condition 2) S's don't face each other
(Condition 3) R has at least one T adjacent
(Condition 4) 3 is R
(Condition 5) 6 is S

The initial conditions could produce the following diagram:

1	3	5	7
	R		
2	4	6	8
		S	

House 5 cannot be R (condition 1) or S (condition 2). Therefore, 5 must be T. House 8 cannot be S (condition 1) or R (condition 3). Therefore, 8 must be T.

We now produce an updated diagram:

1	3	5	7
	R	T	
2	4	6	8
		S	T

13. **(D)** House 7 cannot be T, since it would violate condition 1. Choice (D) is the correct choice. Houses 1, 2, and 4 COULD be T. House 8 must be T.

14. **(B)** Which COULD be true?

Since houses 1 and 2 cannot both be R (condition 1), house 4 is R. It follows that house 2 is T (condition 3). This yields the following diagram:

1	3	5	7
	R	T	
2	4	6	8
T	R	S	T

(A) is not correct, since 8 is T.
(B) COULD be true. House 7 could be S. Choice (B) is correct.
(C) is not correct, since 4 is R.
(D) is not correct, since 2 is T.
(E) is not correct, since 1 cannot be R (condition 1).

15. **(A)** Which COULD be true?

If 4 is T, then we have the following diagram:

1	3	5	7
S, T	R	T	S, R
2	4	6	8
R, S	T	S	T

(A) COULD be true. House 1 could be S or T. Choice (A) is the correct answer.
(B) is not correct, since 2 cannot be T (condition 1).
(C) is not correct, since 5 is T.
(D) is not correct, since 7 cannot be T (condition 1).
(E) is not correct, since 8 is T.

16. **(A)** Which COULD be true?

Choice (A) COULD be true, as follows:

1	3	5	7
T	R	T	S
2	4	6	8
S	T	S	T

(B) is not possible, since houses 5 and 8 must be T.
(C) is not possible. Two houses, 5 and 8, must be T. In order for there to be exactly two T, each of the remaining houses cannot be T. This would mean that house 1 would have to be S. (Cannot be R from condition 1.) If house 1 is S, then house 2 would have to be R. (Cannot be S from condition 2.) This would mean that house 4 must be T (condition 3). This would result in more than two T.
(D) is not possible. House 1 cannot be R, and houses 2 and 4 cannot both be R (condition 1).
(E) is not possible. House 1 cannot be R, and houses 2 and 4 cannot both be R (condition 1). The maximum number of R is 3.

17. (E) Which MUST be true?

If no house faces a house of the same style, then house 4 must be T.

1	3	5	7
S, T	R	T	R, S
2	4	6	8
R, S	T	S	T

(A) COULD be true. House 1 could be T.
(B) COULD be true. House 1 could be S.
(C) COULD be true. House 2 could be S.
(D) COULD be true. House 2 could be R.
(E) must be true. Choice (E) is the correct answer.
Note: Choice (E) follows directly from the initial conditions on the problem. Check for restatements of given conditions.

18. (A) Which CANNOT be true?

Choice (A) is the correct answer. Condition 3 states that each R must have at least one T next to it. Choice (A) violates this condition. The other choices do not violate any of the given conditions.

Answers 19–24

(Initial set-up statement)

Five teams (R, J, S, M, and L)

Initial order:

1	R
2	J
3	S
4	M
5	L

(Conditions given)

Odd Position Round

3 – 2
5 – 4

Even Position Round

2 – 1
4 – 3

Matches alternate odd, even, in either order
Teams switch if lower wins

19. (D) After one even-position round, teams 1 and 2 could switch position, and teams 3 and 4 could switch position. Team 5 does not play and therefore would remain in position 5. The only answer choice where L remains in position 5 is choice (D). Therefore, (D) is the answer.

20. (E) After one odd-position round and then one even-position round with all lower-position teams winning, positions would change as follows:

	Init.	Odd	Even
1	R	R	S
2	J	S	R
3	S	J	L
4	M	L	J
5	L	M	M

(A) is true.
(B) is true.
(C) is true.
(D) is true.
(E) is false. Team M is in position 5.

21. (A) Which COULD be true?

In order for a team to win twice in two rounds, they must play both rounds. Choice (A) (J wins twice) COULD be true. It is possible for J to win two matches.

	Init.	Odd	Even
1	R	R	J
2	J	J	R
3	S	S	S
4	M	M	M
5	L	L	L

(B) (L lost both rounds) is not possible. If L loses the first (odd) round, L won't play in the second round. If the first round is even, L won't play the first round.
(C) (R wins both rounds) is not possible. If R wins the first (even) round, R won't play in the second round. If the first round is odd, R won't play the first round.
(D) is not possible. L is in position 5, and J is in position 2. They cannot play each other during the first 2 rounds.

(E) is not possible. If M plays S in the first (even) round and loses, M will play L in the second round. If M plays S in the first (even) round and wins, then M will play team 2, not M.

22. (C) Which can be true?

If J wins all matches, then J will end up in position 1. Therefore, choices (A), (B), and (D) are all false.
(C) is possible. Choice (C) is the correct answer.

	Init.	Odd	Even	Odd
1	R	R	J	J
2	J	J	R	L
3	S	S	L	R
4	M	L	S	M
5	L	M	M	S

(E) is not correct. If the rounds are odd, even, odd, as shown above, then S must finish in position 5, and M in position 4.

	Init.	Even	Odd	Even
1	R	J	J	J
2	J	R	R	R
3	S	M	M	L
4	M	S	L	M
5	L	L	S	S

If the rounds are even, odd, even, as shown above, then S will finish in position 5.

23. (A) After three rounds, M will end up in position 1 or 2, depending on the order of the odd and even rounds. In either case, J will move down to position 3. Therefore, the correct answer is (A).

24. (C) Each team can change, at most, one position per round. Since R and J end up in positions 1 and 2, they cannot be in position 5 after the previous round. Therefore, (B), (D), and (E) cannot be correct. Since L ends up in position 3 after three rounds, L cannot be in position 5 in the previous round. Therefore, (A) cannot be correct. Thus, the correct answer is (C). This arrangement is possible, since only two adjacent teams switch positions.

Section II

1. (B) If the rabies epidemic is more serious now than it was two years ago, and if more than 50 percent of the raccoon population is now infected, it would seem to be a discrepancy that only 18 cases were confirmed during the past 12 months as compared to 32 cases confirmed two years ago. However, if many more cases were identified during the year prior to the last 12 months, this fact would account for the seeming discrepancy. The number of other types of animals with rabies (A) is not relevant to this discussion, which focuses on raccoons. And (C) and (D) have nothing to do with the *number* of infected raccoons. (E) does have to do with number, but it involves other cities, not the one in question in the passage.

2. (A) The patent reviewers' argument is based on their determination that the mouse in question is a new type of animal. But if their regulations pertain only to domesticated farm animals, then the mouse would not come under this classification and thus would not, based on this regulation, be denied the patent. The fact that the patent application is unique (B) would have no bearing on the granting of the patent. While (C) or (E) might at first seem like possibilities, the reviewers could have been mistaken in the past in exactly the same ways. (D) is incorrect because the facts in question have to do with animals, not plants.

3. (D) Of the choices given, one could conclude only that some level of bacteria is allowed in the water supplies in question. If all the municipalities met the standards, and 20 had less bacterial contamination than the others, at the very least it would have to be assumed that the others had *some* contamination and still met standards. The statements

in the other choices could not be concluded from the information given.

4. (E) The question here is why the unchlorinated water might have less bacterial contamination that the chlorinated water, even though it is drawn from the same aquifer. Choice (E) supplies a logical reason for this occurrence. If those municipalities that do not use chlorine are subject to stronger regulations concerning pipes and water tanks, then they might have a lower bacteria level than others who do use chlorine but may have tanks and pipes that are in need of repair and are open to bacterial contamination. The dangers of chlorine to humans (A), the reason for not chlorinating (B), and the *lack* of use of other agents by all municipalities, (C) and (D), would have no bearing on the *difference* of bacteria levels in question.

5. (C) The argument is that the growth of the magpie population is responsible for the decline in the songbird population. This argument would be undercut, however, if it is shown that in the areas in which the songbirds live, the magpie population has not increased. The argument deals only with recent years, so the fact that population records have been kept for only 30 years (A) is not germane. The argument deals with songbirds as a group, so the variation in egg laying among songbird varieties (B) has no bearing on the argument. The argument deals only with the fact of magpie population increase, not the reasons for it (D). And the fact that magpies also eat things other than eggs and chicks (E) would not mean that they couldn't still have been responsible for the decline in songbirds.

6. (D) The argument suggests that only with systematic methods for writing numerals can computation take place. Conversely, it suggests that the symbols used earlier could not have been used for computation. The reason for all grooves and scratches on items is not discussed or assumed here, nor are various surfaces that symbols could have been written on, (A) and (B). The argument does state that the grooves and scratches date back 20,000 years, but no mention is made that this was the time of the earliest people (C). While the argument is made that computation is not possible without systematic methods for writing numerals, it does not stipulate or assume anything about the *only reason* for the invention of these methods (E).

7. (C) The politician's reply to the reporter is flawed because he or she doesn't seem to realize that just because the bay was polluted by industry (and wasn't at the time polluted by the public), it couldn't now be polluted by recreational use by the public. The one fact doesn't rule out the possibility of the other. The argument in (C) follows the same pattern. Fact 1: Violence in prison increased when prisoners convicted of violent crimes were kept in solitary. Possible fact 2: When these violent prisoners are not in solitary, violence may go up even more. The speaker here, as in the passage, does not see that the one fact doesn't rule out the possibility of the other. None of the other choices follows this pattern. (B) might seem at first like a good answer. But its pattern is not quite right. Politician's flawed pattern in the original: This is true, so this *won't* be true. The flawed pattern in choice (B): This is true, so this *will* be true.

8. (E) The principle states that designers should take ingrained habits into account so as to avoid inefficiency and danger. The situation that most clearly violates this principle is (E). While the LSAT does not ask for outside knowledge in order to answer questions, it does require you to use very broad, general knowledge such as the fact that "red" usually means "stop." And here, even if you didn't know this, you have a clue to that fact in the passage, which specifically states that "green" means "go." So, if the tape recorder has a "go" button that is red, the situation clearly violates the principle. Choices (A), (B), (C), and (D) are all incorrect because they are in accord with the principle rather than in violation of it.

9. **(C)** Choices (A), (D), and (E) are incorrect because there is no way to tell from the passage what most of the energy used in 1989 or 1973 was. We know only that during this period the use of electric energy grew by more than 50 percent. For all we know from the information given, the use of electric energy might have started at a very low level, and, consequently, a 50 percent rise would not amount to a great proportion of total energy use. (B) is incorrect because a decline in the use of any type of energy is not mentioned. (C) is correct. Electrical energy use did grow by 50 percent during this period, while the use of other energy grew by less than 10 percent, so use of electrical energy would constitute a larger proportion of total energy use.

10. **(E)** The argument fails to realize that robots may eliminate demeaning work other than that needed for their maintenance, which may be considerably greater than the amount done for their maintenance. The argument doesn't deal with job loss, (A) and (D), only types of work. It doesn't set out to prove that robots create demeaning work (B) (it simply states it) but rather to prove that they won't eliminate demeaning work. (C) is irrelevant to the argument.

11. **(D)** The information doesn't support choice (A) because it gives no indication of *how often* items have been, or will be, ruined by faulty needles. The type of task that eventually will be performed by workers in automated factories (B) or noise made by needles that are wearing out (E) are not mentioned or implied in any way by the information. While in traditional factories the new acoustic device is not used, that fact does not lead to the assumption that such factories use *no* automated equipment (C). But the information does support the assumption that the sewing machine needles wear out at an unpredictable rate. If they didn't, then neither the workers in the traditional factories nor the new acoustic device would be needed to detect wear. That is, if the needles wear out at a predictable rate, they could simply be replaced at a predictable rate.

12. **(B)** Teresa contends that the dump should be cleaned up *only* if it poses a health threat to people. A principle upon which she could be basing this contention is found in choice (B). Teresa says that the *first priority* is people's health, and the principle states that funds should be used *only* for the highest priority goals. Choices (A) and (C) deal with economic interest, (D) with level of health hazard, and (E) with who should make decisions, none of which Teresa addresses.

13. **(D)** There are two points of view in the dialogue: Alexander's point is that the dump should be cleaned up for ecological reasons. Teresa's point is that it should be cleaned up only if it poses a health risk. Those differing points of view are given only in choice (D).

14. **(D)** If the difference between the GDP of Country A and the European Economic Community was $5,000 in 1980 and $6,000 in 1990, it follows that the GDP of the European Economic Community could not have dropped more than the difference of $1,000 over this period. (A) is incorrect because we cannot know from the information what the population increase might have been in either case. (B) could not be assumed from the information. We cannot know from the information that the GDP of the European Economic Community dropped at all, and consequently, that the standard of living dropped at all. We know only what the *difference* between the two is—that is, from the information given, both may have risen, with one simply rising farther than the other, accounting for the greater gap between them. The standard of living in other member countries and their per capita GDP, (C) and (E), are not relevant to a comparison of Country A and the European Economic Community as a whole.

15. (E) The question asks for a possible resolution of the discrepancy between an estimate of six months for municipal crews and a reality of 28 days for a private contractor to complete this job. The difference could be accounted for if the municipality had to spend a great deal of time on bidding and supply procurement but the private contractor didn't. The months in which work could be done (A), the labor union contract (B), and the shift in workers from one entity to another (C) would apply to both the city and the contractor, so they aren't relevant to the difference in work time issue. (D) not only wouldn't resolve the discrepancy, it would make it more glaring. One would think that if the municipality had more workers it would be faster, not slower, in completing the work.

16. (E) The species population is being estimated from a particular catch rate by shark-fishing boats, and the argument suggests that since the catch rate has been fairly constant since 1973, so must the population be fairly constant for this species. (E) most weakens this argument because if the boats can more efficiently locate sharks, then they logically can catch more of whatever sharks exist. That is, there may well be fewer sharks, but these boats are now better at catching them, so the catch rate could remain the same. It doesn't matter that this is the only place these sharks are found (A) because the argument is *about* this place. Since the argument concerns *only* the numbers in the shark population, information concerning profitability (B), other reasons for shark mortality (C), or the tonnage of fish taken (D) are irrelevant to the argument and consequently could not weaken it.

17. (B) Ping introduces another way of looking at the question of whether there would be cost savings by cutting the services in question, suggesting that there would not be because fares would be lost—fares that Winston didn't consider. That is, Ping is questioning Winston's proposal by raising considerations that Winston did not address. Neither speaker defines a term (A) or uses statistics (D). Nothing Ping says supports Winston's argument (C), but Ping doesn't offer an alternative solution either (E).

18. (A) Ping bases the counterargument on the supposition that ridership could be lost if riders are completing only half of their travels during the late-night periods in question and would then perhaps find other transportation for the other half of their travels. (A) best supports this contention, providing the statistic that over 23 percent of round trips would fit in this category. The statistic could mean that the PTA would lose the fares of these people during the times that service would still be provided. Whether riders would oppose any cut in services (B) or the fact that PTA was turned down for a rate increase (C) wouldn't affect Ping's argument. (D) is counter to the information given, which states that the PTA is not allowed to operate at a deficit. (E) might support Winston's argument, providing another instance of cost saving by cutting service, but it wouldn't support Ping's.

19. (A) The pattern of reasoning is the statement of a point of view followed by the presentation of two reasons for that point of view. In the original argument, the point of view is that Dolores should replace Victor. The two reasons are (1) that Dolores is better at securing financing and (2) that Dolores doesn't alienate volunteers. The pattern in (A) is most closely parallel to this pattern. The point of view is that it would be more convenient for Dominique to take the bus. The two reasons given are (1) the bus stops closer to her house and (2) the bus goes directly to school. No other argument follows this point-of-view/reason/reason pattern. For this type of question it may be most efficient and less confusing to jot very quick notes to yourself outlining the pattern in the original before you consider the answer choices.

20. (E) From the original discussion we know these facts: (1) Outside students pay twice as much as Markland students. (2) Outside stu-

dents used to account for two-thirds of the enrollment or more. (3) Academic standards have risen at Markland. (4) Outside students now account for 40 percent of enrollment. Only these facts can figure into a correct inference. (A) is incorrect. We know only fact (3) concerning standards, which does not support any inference concerning reasons for the rise. (B) is incorrect because facts (2), (3), and (4) are not necessarily related. (C) is incorrect because the facts deal only with percentages of each type of student and not with the total number of students enrolled. (D) is incorrect because the facts deal only with Markland College, not with other colleges. (E) can be inferred from the facts. If the average revenue from students has not changed, and there are now more students who pay a lower fee (a higher percentage of students from Markland now), then for that average to remain the same, the fees must have increased.

21. (A) Since the entomologists conclude that the fungus is responsible for the decline in the population of caterpillars and adults, a supporting fact would somehow help to rule out other causes of the decline. Only (A) provides such a fact: If another strain of moth known to be unaffected by the fungus continues to thrive, then it is more likely that the fungus has been the cause of this strain's decline. That is, if other factors caused the decline of the strain in question, one might logically conclude that those other factors might well cause the decline of the second strain also. Other questions would have to be answered as well, but of the choices given, only this one strongly supports the conclusion. Because the argument concerns only these moths, not other insects or other moth species, (B) and (C) are incorrect. (D) would support a drop in both strains of moth, not one. (E) would weaken the argument, not support it.

22. (E) The director fails to consider that the denial of a justified claim could undermine the integrity of the company's merit-raise system—possibly much more than granting the *appropriate* raises. Whether the complaint is handled officially or unofficially (A) and the performance of other employees receiving raises (D) are not relevant to the director's argument. The director doesn't dismiss Ms. Tours's evidence (B) but rather admits it as true, and doesn't sidestep the argument concerning superior job performance (C) but rather agrees with it.

23. (D) T's response to S challenges the truth of S's claim that because a person is old enough to fight that person should be allowed to vote. T's evidence would not support S's argument, so (A) is incorrect. T doesn't call into question S's understanding of the concept of *rights* (B) or the distinction between rights and responsibilities (C), but rather S's understanding of necessary *qualifications* for both types of activity. (E) is a more difficult choice to eliminate here than the others. T suggests that S's *argument* is possibly incorrect. But suggesting that the argument is incorrect does not *necessarily* suggest that T *supports* the *opposite* view. T may, for example, simply be logically pointing out the problems with this *particular* argument for allowing 17-year-olds to vote and could, for all we know, actually support the position that they should vote.

24. (E) The argument concludes that a premise is false (the premise that the role of the supreme court is to protect all human rights). But it is equally possible for that premise to be true and another premise (for example, here, that it is not their role) false. What is important to realize here is that the argument isn't about how well the court functions in that role, but whether it is their role at all. The argument doesn't employ any examples (A), comment on a widely held view (B), deal in any way with profit (C), or have to do with individuals versus the group (D).

Section III

1. (D) The argument is that the painted spiders are more successful predators than their competitors because their stickier webs are more efficient at trapping their insect food than are the webs of other spiders in this habitat. The statement that most *weakens* this argument is found in choice (D). If the light-reflecting webs of these spiders are more easily seen by insects than are other webs, then that fact could offset the advantage gained by the stickiness of the webs because more insects could then avoid the webs and the entrapment. Whether *all* insects are flying insects (A) is irrelevant, as is the *time* of death *after* insects are trapped (C). Choice (B) would support the argument rather than weaken it. (C) would have an equal effect on painted spiders and on their competitors if the webs are the same size, and might strengthen the argument if the painted spiders' webs are smaller.

2. (B) The reasoning is flawed because it bases its conclusion that there *is no* intelligent life anywhere but on Earth on the fact that it hasn't yet been *proved* that there *is*. That is, it confuses the *absence* of evidence with *negative* evidence. The argument doesn't speculate on the possibility of intelligence in nonliving beings (A), include a disagreement over a theory (C), concern itself with the meaning of "life" (D), or use an analogy (E).

3. (B) This question focuses on Bart's argument *only*. He argues that because the process is so complex that it can't be comprehended, the result is not acceptable. Bart wouldn't have to assume that the unacceptability is because a supercomputer was used (A). The argument deals with complexity, no matter its cause. (C) is Anne's point, not Bart's. Bart would not assume that lessening the complexity would necessarily result in acceptance (D). The results still might not be able to be comprehended. (E) is tempting, since Bart is saying that the computer's work is too complex to be understood, so we might think that it would follow that the computer can't derive an acceptable solution. But there is nothing in the argument that would preclude the possibility that the computer might be able to arrive at a solution in a different, much less complex, way that could be comprehended. Bart does, however, assume that in order for the result to be acceptable it must be able to be comprehended by someone.

4. (C) Bart and Anne disagree on what constitutes an acceptable result, in this case, one arrived at by a supercomputer—that is, they disagree on what criterion should be employed to determine acceptability. Replication of the result, (A) and (B), the level of complexity (D), or mathematical, as distinguished from scientific, problems (E) aren't points of disagreement; the point is whether human comprehension of the process is a requirement for accepting the result.

5. (D) From the information given, one can determine, concerning comparative advertisements, only something based on these particular advertisements of particular products. The correct conclusion concerning comparative advertisements must then be derived from just these elements. The only choice that can be concluded from the experience of these two companies is (D). The companies were after a larger market share by using comparative advertisements, but instead their market shares shrank. So, it can be concluded that *sometimes* these techniques do not work as expected. The incorrect choices all have to do with conclusions that are extraneous to the information in the statements—conclusions concerning the superiority of a product (A), an expanding, versus stagnant, market (B), retaliation (C), and customer verification of claims (E).

6. (C) The author predicts that water rationing will not be necessary this summer, based on the recent filling of the reservoirs and streams. You are looking for the answer that will most *undermine* (that is, *weaken*) this prediction. What happened over the last five years (A) has no identifiable bearing on what

will happen this year. Since only a *small* part of the city's water comes from the underground systems (B), that fact would tend to strengthen the prediction rather than weaken it. Choice (D) might also strengthen the prediction because if the temperatures are lower, less water might evaporate and also less water might be required by the customers. (E) would have no effect on the prediction; it simply states what happens generally in the summer. But (C) would weaken the prediction. If the water company can't get the water to the customers, then even if there is an abundance of water, the company might have to ration it because of its inability to deliver.

7. **(A)** Judy is criticizing John's conclusion by suggesting that there is a reason other than the one he proposes for the greater number of accidents near the drivers' homes. So, she is suggesting that John's evidence is not sufficient to prove his claim that people drive less safely near home. Judy doesn't restate John's evidence (B), but rather gives her own point of view, and her evidence wouldn't support John's claim (C), but rather contradicts it. Judy doesn't deal with what is and what isn't a long trip (D) or claim that John restates anything (E).

8. **(B)** If the statement that all progress must depend on unreasonable people is true, then it must be concluded from the argument that progress occurs only when people try to adapt the world to themselves, which only unreasonable people do. From this fact follows the conclusion that if only reasonable people exist, there can be no progress. We don't know how these people get along with one another (A). Nor do we know whether unreasonable people always create progress, (C) and (D), only that unreasonable people never do. From the statements, we also know nothing about the persistence of unreasonable people (E).

9. **(A)** The producer is suggesting that by simply stating the facts as the critic feels they exist, the critic is making these outcomes true. By doing so, the producer attacks the effects of the critic's evaluation rather than the truth of it—that is, its content. And because the producer is not attending to the argument itself, he or she couldn't be accusing the critic of relying on opinion, emphasis, or authority, (B), (D), or (E). The producer doesn't suggest the critic's reasons (motives) for making the evaluation (C), only the effect of it.

10. **(A)** The question is why the restorers would leave intact only one artist's additions to the paintings while removing all others. The correct choice will give a reasonable explanation for this seemingly unusual behavior, given their stated goal of uncovering Michelangelo's original work. But if da Volterra stripped away all previous layers of paint before proceeding, the removing of his work would simply leave a blank surface, which wouldn't meet their goal of uncovering Michelangelo's work. That is, there would be no point to removing it. None of the other choices have anything to do with the *stated goal* of the restorers.

11. **(E)** If the argument stated that the plastic surgery was given to *any* inmate who wanted it, then the sample in question (those who had received plastic surgery) might be a much better representative of the general prison population than is the actual case here. The problem with the sample actually used is that the surgery was offered only to inmates who *behave particularly well.* Inmates who behave particularly well in prison might be expected to behave particularly well on the outside, so there is reason to believe that the group is not a representative one. Choices (A) and (B) cannot be right because the argument is *putting these moral issues aside.* The argument *does* deal with the issues of the controversy (C) and doesn't suggest that rehabilitation might not also be a moral issue (D); it only puts the moral issues discussed previously aside.

12. **(A)** If the machine can identify previously scanned individuals, it would have to be assumed that the blood vessel pattern of the retinas of the individuals does not change over time. The only choice that deals with the

matter of *change* in the pattern of an individual's retina is (A). Choice (B) deals with differences *between* eyes. The number of scanners (C) and the use of different scanners on a single individual (E) are irrelevant to the question of identification. The argument is about identifiable patterns, not the number of vessels (D).

13. (B) There are only two ways a moon can be formed from its planet. (1) Part of the outer shell spins off. But this cannot be the case here if the Earth's moon consists of elements primarily different from those in the Earth's outer shell. (This fact is given in the statements.) So, we are left with only one possibility if the moon is derived from the Earth: (2) that a large object dislodged a mass of material from inside the planet. Choice (B) adds the information that the moon consists primarily of elements that differ from those *inside* Earth as well. Adding this information would most justify the conclusion that the moon was not formed from a piece of Earth. Choices (A), (D), and (E) don't add information relevant to the forming of Earth's moon. (C) simply deals with *one* alternative way the moon could have been formed and thus also is irrelevant.

14. (E) The argument is made that caffeine in many species of plants *evolved* as a defense for those plants. If it *evolved,* then it at one time was not present, and some event began the evolution. If the plants developed a defense, then there was something that needed to be defended against. In this case, the argument assumes that the event was the feeding upon the plants by insects sensitive to caffeine. If the insects were *not* those sensitive to caffeine, then the development by the plants would *not* have been a defense against them. Choices (A), (B), and (C) do not deal with the evolution of this defense mechanism. (D) deals with defense, not the self-defense of the caffeine-containing plants but of indigenous plants in general.

15. (C) This is a difficult question because the flaw in the reasoning has to do with confusing something that may be true with something that has been proved through a valid pattern of reasoning. While it may be true that all the plants in the garden are tall plants, the argument does not appropriately prove this fact; it is not a valid syllogism. The argument could be simplified in this way: "All plants in the garden are tall tulips. So, all plants in the garden are tall plants." There is no middle term to unite "tall tulips" with "tall plants." It is easier to see the flaw in the argument if you look at another argument in this form: "All plants in the garden are perfect pictures. So, all plants in the garden are perfect plants." In this changed form, it is more apparent that there is a logical problem. The word *perfect* has different meanings in each case. Choice (C) follows exactly this flawed pattern. It is a good idea to review syllogistic form before taking the LSAT.

16. (C) The argument says that when political considerations play a role, scientific research is not properly channeled—that is, due weight is not given to the scientific merits of such research before funding it. So, it can be inferred that political considerations are incompatible with giving proper weight to the research. The argument doesn't go so far as to say there is *no* proper role for political considerations in determining who will decide (A), only that those with political considerations shouldn't do it. (B) leaves out any mention of *political* considerations, which are at the heart of the argument. (D) implies a chronological order of decision making not implied by the argument. (E) makes a point opposite to that of the argument.

17. (A) You are looking for the answer that will explain the lower electricity consumption in vacuum cleaners using the silencing device. (A) provides such an explanation by saying that typically, that is, without the new device, makers of these vacuums have less efficient motors because of noise-reduction techniques. If they don't have to use those old

techniques, then the motors will be more efficient and will use less power. Choices (B), (D), and (E) could suggest higher electricity usage, not lower. (C) is irrelevant because both the old and the new vacuum cleaners could operate in this way.

18. **(D)** The correct choice must *weaken* the argument that some dinosaurs might have been warm-blooded because their fossils were found in the arctic, where cold-blooded animals could not survive. Choices (A) and (E) could strengthen the argument. The size of the dinosaurs (B) would not affect whether they would freeze to death in arctic weather. Plant fossils found in the same frigid areas would be expected to be from cold-resistant plants (C), but that would have no bearing on the argument concerning dinosaurs. If, however, the dinosaurs were migrating animals, they could have been cold-blooded and could have followed the warmer temperatures—going to the colder regions when the low temperatures abated and to warmer regions when it was very cold.

19. **(A)** Maria concludes that no state can be called totalitarian because the term means exercising total control and no state is truly able to do that. So, she is saying that calling a state totalitarian invites the mistaken belief that the state does, in fact, exercise that control. All of the other choices are points Maria makes, but they are not the *main conclusion* of her argument.

20. **(D)** James argues that states can appropriately be called *totalitarian* because he differs from Maria in his definition of the term, saying that it can be applied in instances other than that given by Maria. James does not deal with inconsistencies of Maria's argument (A), offer alternative explanations for conditions she mentions (B), or point out a conflict between her premises (E). James *does* challenge Maria's inference (C).

21. **(D)** If the argument is that ichthyosaurs and fish are members of different classes but still developed similar external body features, it can be inferred that membership in a class does not necessarily rely on the presence of such similar features. Nothing in the discussion implies that members of a class must be *identical* in body features (A) or that one class's body features must differentiate it from all other classes (B). The problem with (C) is the word *only*. The discussion suggests that adaptation to environment *can* result in similar body features, but it does *not* go so far as to say that only adaptation will have that result. The argument deals only with development of similarities, not with differences (E), and nothing about such differences can be inferred from the information given.

22. **(B)** The argument proceeds by beginning with the conclusion (that further evidence must have come out on Jamison's activities), then suggesting that a particular fact could *not* have been established otherwise (that he was a party to the fraud), and finally stating that this particular fact *has* been established. Choice (B) also proceeds in this way. It begins with the conclusion (Turner must not have taken her usual train), follows that with a particular fact that could not have been true otherwise (she could not have been in Nance till this afternoon), and concludes with the statement that this fact has been established (she was there at 11:00 A.M.). All the other choices similarly begin with a conclusion but thereafter do not follow this pattern. The second part of the original pattern suggests that a fact could not have been established if the conclusion is not true, and none of the other answer choices makes this assertion.

23. **(D)** There are two criteria that must be used here to determine the correct answer: (1) It must *support* the journalist's conclusion that it was ethical to file the *censored* report because the news agency would precede it with the notice "Cleared by government censors," *and* (2) it must place the *least* constraint on the

flow of reported information. You need to determine only that it doesn't meet one of these to eliminate the answer. Choices (A), (B), and (C) don't meet the first requirement because this report fails to include known facts, which makes it unethical according to these criteria. (E) could be correct if it did not include the stipulation that "the reported facts do not by themselves give a misleading impression." All of these choices interfere with the flow of information also because they would not allow the report to be published. (D) is true because it includes an exception to its rule that it is unethical to make the report in a situation of censorship by adding "unless the recipient of the report is warned that censorship existed." In this case, that warning is given by the fact of the notice "Cleared by government censors." This choice also meets the second requirement of the least interference with the flow of information because it allows the report to be published.

24. **(B)** The conclusion is that more ambidextrous people are born to women over 40 because women over 40 are more likely to have difficult births. If there are more children born to women under 40, however, it could be that the total number of difficult births is higher among women under 40. The argument doesn't assume its conclusion (A); it provides evidence for it, although not all the evidence needed. The argument wouldn't have to mention the total number of ambidextrous people in the population (C) because it proposes only that more are born to women over 40. Both the time at which handedness is determined (D) and reasons why difficult births result in ambidexterity (E) are irrelevant to the argument.

25. **(C)** The argument doesn't address the obligations of government (A), the past versus the present (B), economic theory (D), or class systems (E). It does argue, though, that because part of a worker's salary goes to the government for taxes, and an entity employing involuntary servitude forces work for its own purpose, the two institutions both create pernicious situations of forced servitude. The argument assumes, then, that because each entity benefits from the work, they equally are instrumental in creating forced servitude.

26. **(A)** The argument tries to parallel the taxing of earnings by the government with the forcing of labor in involuntary servitude. It ignores, however, how the idea of forced work applies in each case. In the case of taxes, for example, it ignores the fact that the worker has a choice about working or not. And many other differences between the two situations might be pointed out. The argument concerns *any* taxing of earnings from labor, so the rates of tax (B), the fact that not all is taxed (C), and other types of taxes (D) are not relevant. There is no indication in the argument that the definition of *involuntary servitude* (the only definition given) is subjective (E).

Section IV

Passage 1

1. **(B)** The entire thrust of the passage is to present Byron as a poet whose "close presence" is always in the poems. So (B) is the best title given. The passage mentions both the absence of method and the fact that Byron is perhaps not a "great" poet (A), but these are minor points and don't reflect the passage as a whole. The passage deals specifically with Byron, not the larger issues of nineteenth-century poetry (C), early nineteenth-century Europe (D), or twentieth-century literary criticism (E).

2. **(D)** Russell and Praz are mentioned as authors of studies that treat "Byron as a figure important in the history of ideas." Such a study is one of three types mentioned in the first paragraph (D). They aren't, then, contrasted with one another (A), but rather are linked. Their conclusions are not presented at

all, much less contrasted with those of Escarpit (B), and their types of studies are not mentioned as taking a "new direction" (C) or being the "best" (E).

3. (C) The author makes the point that a study of Byron that focuses only on analyzing his "verbal shadings" is *not* valuable and thus would not consider either (A) or (D) to be of value. The author does suggest that analyzing Byron's thought relative to the history of ideas *is* valuable, so (B) is incorrect. Because it is the fact that the persona of Byron is present in the poems that is important, studying Byron by drawing on one's own life would not be appropriate (E), but identifying Byron's emotions at a particular time in his life (C) would be.

4. (C) The first paragraph names, and briefly defines, three types of studies of Byron, qualifies the value of the third type presented, and gives evidence on which this qualification is based. Choice (C) most closely reflects this progression.

5. (C) The author makes the point that because "Byron's poems cannot be convincingly read as subtle verbal creations," this indicates that he is not a "great" poet. The author then goes on to add other reasons why Byron would not be considered great, among them the fact that his "literary craftsmanship is irregular." Byron is contrasted with Shakespeare (A), not because his poetry is "irregular," but because Shakespeare can be read without our wondering what in his life prompted him to write a particular piece. Nothing says that poets shouldn't be judged by their craftsmanship (B), only that judging Byron like that isn't valuable. (D) would have nothing to do with irregular craftsmanship, and *why* the poetry lacks nuances is not discussed (E).

6. (E) Shakespeare's poems, according to the passage, can be read without our wondering what in his life prompted him to write them (end of the first paragraph), while the study of Byron's poems should always include "biographical considerations."

7. (B) The first paragraph specifically states that "biographers to this day continue to speculate about Byron's life." We do not know from information in the passage when speculation began in earnest about Byron's life (A), how satisfactory the speculation is, (D), or whether literary critics object to it (E). The author of the passage would disagree with (C), believing just the opposite.

8. (A) The author states, "Our main pleasure in reading Byron's poetry is the contact with a singular personality" and goes on to illustrate this point in detail. The passage mentions some literary critics who have focused on Byron but doesn't mention who might have focused *primarily* on with Byron (B). Also, the fact that Byron's life experiences have a great impact on his poetry is made clear, but precisely which moments are not investigated (C). Both whether anyone has considered Byron a "great" poet (D) or what his influence may or may not have been on Europeans in the latter part of the nineteenth century (E) are both irrelevant to the discussion and are not mentioned.

Passage 2

9. (E) The passage states that the Court may not have pleased Native Americans because of the necessity for political compromise and the temper of the times. It further suggests that "accommodation is part of the judicial system." Only (E) mentions one of these issues.

10. (A) The critics mentioned disagree with the assertion that Court decisions have usually been beneficial to Native Americans, at least in more minor issues, and not wholly detrimental on larger issues. Such critics point out the "patronizing tone" of opinions and the "apparent rejection of Native American values." If, however, a Court decision demonstrated respect and considered "principles and qualities" that Native Americans consider important, that would most clearly, among the choices given, answer the critics' objections. Protecting the rights of states (B)

would not answer these specific objections. The Court has recognized previous unfair treatment of Native Americans (C), (D), and (E), so a new case based on this recognition would not answer the critics either, and in any case, that recognition doesn't directly concern a patronizing tone or Native American values.

11. (C) The term *accommodating* is used in the context of explaining why the Court has sometimes engaged in "political compromise," thus suggesting a reason that decisions of the Court have not always favored Native Americans. The Court is "accommodating" the wishes of a number of varying groups at varying times. In context, the word doesn't refer only to Native Americans (A), (B), or (D). Choice (E) is a harder option to eliminate, but the general meaning of the word *accommodating* has to do with giving in, or giving preference, to a particular point of view. If one point of view is favored, then fairness to all may not be possible.

12. (B) The author, overall, suggests that the Supreme Court has made some good and helpful decisions regarding Native American rights. So *restrained appreciation* is an apt term for the author's attitude. The attitude is not one of wholehearted endorsement (A), since the author realizes that political compromise has been necessary. And because the author clearly favors a position opposite that of the critics in question, the attitude can't be described as *detached* or *cautious*, (C) or (D). *Suppressed exasperation* (E) is much too strong a term here.

13. (D) The discussion has to do with the Court's avoidance of the *encroachment* of states' rights and occurs as part of the author's evidence that the Court has, overall, done reasonably well for Native Americans. It is presented as an "achievement of the judicial system" in protecting Native American rights. So, it follows that the author would consider an extension of state power to be detrimental to the interests of Native Americans.

14. (E) The author clearly favors a particular view, a contention, making choice (E) the only reasonable answer. While critics' views are mentioned, the *purpose* of the passage is not to contrast the author's point of view with theirs (A), to reconcile them (C), or assess their claims (D), but to promote the author's point of view. No mention is made of traditional beliefs (B).

15. (B) The author believes that the Court decisions have, overall, been reasonably supportive (B), although clearly not "irreproachable" (A). The Court is described as "accommodating," not necessarily always "guided by enduring principles of law" (C). The phrase "misguided but generally harmless" (D) is entirely inappropriate in this case, and no decision is mentioned as actually causing harm (E) although some may not have been entirely supportive of Native American interests.

Passage 3

16. (C) In the words of the passage, "By studying a specific area of the pile, one can even predict whether avalanches will occur there." Consequently, observers *can* make *some* predictions, even though the large, catastrophic occurrences would remain unpredictable. All of the other choices *are* supported by the passage concerning large interactive systems. They can, and do, evolve to a critical state (as in the sand example) (A); they sometimes do not yield to traditional analysis (as in the avalanche example) (B); they are subject to chain reactions (as in the sand example) (D); and they are subject to more minor events than major ones (E)—"Although such systems produce more minor events than catastrophes . . . ."

17. (E) The criticality of the sandpile is determined by the balance between the amount of sand added and the amount lost. "The system reaches its critical state when the amount of sand added is balanced, on average, by the amount falling off the edge of the disk." The size of the grains (A), number of them (B),

rate of addition (C), and shape of the grains (D) do not contribute to criticality.

18. (A) The investigators mentioned in the second paragraph are the traditional analysts who predict the behavior of a large interactive system by studying its elements separately. They "assumed that in large interactive systems the response to a disturbance is proportional to that disturbance." Consequently, these analysts would believe that the addition of a single grain of sand (a small disturbance) would cause a proportional (small) disturbance. They would not believe that it would ever cause a catastrophic disturbance, choices (B), (C), (D), and (E).

19. (E) The passage begins by discussing traditional analysis of systems and the reasons why such analysis has been used. The passage then goes on to describe an alternative systems analysis theory called the "theory of self-organized criticality" and then provides examples of how this type of analysis works. This progression is outlined in (E).

20. (E) Again, the analysts mentioned in the second paragraph are the traditional analysts. The best analogous situation given in the answer choices is that in (E). The engineer in this answer choice is focusing on the elements of the bridge independent of one another, which is exactly what the traditional systems analysts do. The pollster, the historian, the meteorologist, and the biologist in the other examples are not dealing with interactive systems analysis but are simply noting specific occurrences.

21. (D) This author is showing why the newer "theory of self-organized criticality" is superior to the previous traditional approach. The author would probably argue for, rather than against, the abandonment of the traditional theory, (A) and (E), and would not call either theory "radical" (B). The point here is proposing the superiority of one theory, not reconciling the two (C).

Passage 4

22. (C) The newer theory concerning colonial women's lives presents a more complicated picture than the older "golden age" theory did. Thus, it suggested that the older theory was "too narrowly based and oversimplified." The theories in question are discussed primarily concerning their views of the seventeenth and eighteenth centuries, but choices (A), (B), (D), and (E) also concern the nineteenth century. Although the nineteenth century is mentioned, it isn't the focus of the discussion. And all of these choices have other problems as well, making each of them inappropriate as the main idea.

23. (D) Joan Hoff-Wilson is discussed as a historian who, while questioning the "golden age," still felt that women lost ground in the nineteenth century when compared to women in colonial times. The author thus illustrates the "tenacious hold," the "persistent influence," of the earlier theory. Because Hoff-Wilson still subscribed to at least part of the earlier theory, she didn't "refute" it (A), nor was she instrumental in developing that theory (B). She also is not among the recent writers who are questioning the early theory (C). The current researchers are those discussed in the last paragraph, not Hoff-Wilson (E).

24. (C) The scholars mentioned are those who, although they have questioned the "golden age," still "have continued to accept the paradigm of a nineteenth-century decline from a more desirable past." We can infer from the passage that the author would describe the views of these scholars as paradoxical, that is, as self-contradictory, holding two opposing views at the same time.

25. (A) The newer scholars proposed a three-part chronological division, which "more accurately reflects colonial women's experiences." Their focus is on change over these periods, first in early colonial times, then a time in which "patterns of family and community were challenged and reshaped," and the revolutionary

times, "which brought other changes to women's lives." The emphasis is on "change" and what that change meant in women's lives. It can be inferred that those changes occurred in "a broad variety of social and economic factors." There is no reason to assume that these newer scholars would feel that women's lives in England and in the colonies were similar (B). And we don't know precisely what the new scholarship has identified in women's lives, (C) and (E), only the method of study. It was the older type of scholarship that focused on economic issues (D).

26. **(A)** The publications mentioned in the third paragraph reflect the new scholarship. Since that scholarship called into question earlier types of scholarship, it would necessarily undermine that of Dexter, who was one of the traditional scholars who argued that "women of English descent who lived in the English colonies of North America during the seventeenth and eighteenth centuries were better off" than were women living later. The new scholarship didn't hold to earlier theories, so (B), (C), and (E) are incorrect. The scholarship also suggested that there were significant changes, so (D) is incorrect.

27. **(B)** The new scholarship signaled a change from traditional views. So, these scholars would most likely agree with the statement found in choice (B) concerning Dexter's argument. Dexter's argument hinges on the fact that the less complex society of colonial times resulted in higher status for women. But the new scholarship suggests a "far more complicated picture, one in which definitions of gender roles, the colonial economy, demographic patterns, religion, the law, and household organization all contributed" to the realities of women's lives.

Model Test Two

This chapter contains full-length Model Test Two. It is geared to the format of the LSAT, and it is complete with answers and explanations. It is equivalent to the LSAT in question structure, number of questions, level of difficulty, and time allotments. (The questions used are not taken directly from the LSAT, as those questions are copyrighted and may not be reproduced.)

Model Test Two should be taken under strict test conditions. The test ends with a 35-minute Writing Sample, which is not scored.

Model Test Two

Section	Description	Number of Questions	Time Allowed
I.	Reading Comprehension	28	35 minutes
II.	Analytical Reasoning	24	35 minutes
III.	Logical Reasoning	26	35 minutes
IV.	Analytical Reasoning	24	35 minutes
V.	Logical Reasoning	25	35 minutes
	Writing Sample		35 minutes
TOTALS:		127	3 hours 30 minutes

Now please turn to the next page, remove your answer sheet, and begin Model Test Two.

Remove answer sheet by cutting on dotted line

Answer Sheet

MODEL TEST TWO

Section I	Section II	Section III	Section IV	Section V
1 Ⓐ Ⓑ Ⓒ Ⓓ Ⓔ	1 Ⓐ Ⓑ Ⓒ Ⓓ Ⓔ	1 Ⓐ Ⓑ Ⓒ Ⓓ Ⓔ	1 Ⓐ Ⓑ Ⓒ Ⓓ Ⓔ	1 Ⓐ Ⓑ Ⓒ Ⓓ Ⓔ
2 Ⓐ Ⓑ Ⓒ Ⓓ Ⓔ	2 Ⓐ Ⓑ Ⓒ Ⓓ Ⓔ	2 Ⓐ Ⓑ Ⓒ Ⓓ Ⓔ	2 Ⓐ Ⓑ Ⓒ Ⓓ Ⓔ	2 Ⓐ Ⓑ Ⓒ Ⓓ Ⓔ
3 Ⓐ Ⓑ Ⓒ Ⓓ Ⓔ	3 Ⓐ Ⓑ Ⓒ Ⓓ Ⓔ	3 Ⓐ Ⓑ Ⓒ Ⓓ Ⓔ	3 Ⓐ Ⓑ Ⓒ Ⓓ Ⓔ	3 Ⓐ Ⓑ Ⓒ Ⓓ Ⓔ
4 Ⓐ Ⓑ Ⓒ Ⓓ Ⓔ	4 Ⓐ Ⓑ Ⓒ Ⓓ Ⓔ	4 Ⓐ Ⓑ Ⓒ Ⓓ Ⓔ	4 Ⓐ Ⓑ Ⓒ Ⓓ Ⓔ	4 Ⓐ Ⓑ Ⓒ Ⓓ Ⓔ
5 Ⓐ Ⓑ Ⓒ Ⓓ Ⓔ	5 Ⓐ Ⓑ Ⓒ Ⓓ Ⓔ	5 Ⓐ Ⓑ Ⓒ Ⓓ Ⓔ	5 Ⓐ Ⓑ Ⓒ Ⓓ Ⓔ	5 Ⓐ Ⓑ Ⓒ Ⓓ Ⓔ
6 Ⓐ Ⓑ Ⓒ Ⓓ Ⓔ	6 Ⓐ Ⓑ Ⓒ Ⓓ Ⓔ	6 Ⓐ Ⓑ Ⓒ Ⓓ Ⓔ	6 Ⓐ Ⓑ Ⓒ Ⓓ Ⓔ	6 Ⓐ Ⓑ Ⓒ Ⓓ Ⓔ
7 Ⓐ Ⓑ Ⓒ Ⓓ Ⓔ	7 Ⓐ Ⓑ Ⓒ Ⓓ Ⓔ	7 Ⓐ Ⓑ Ⓒ Ⓓ Ⓔ	7 Ⓐ Ⓑ Ⓒ Ⓓ Ⓔ	7 Ⓐ Ⓑ Ⓒ Ⓓ Ⓔ
8 Ⓐ Ⓑ Ⓒ Ⓓ Ⓔ	8 Ⓐ Ⓑ Ⓒ Ⓓ Ⓔ	8 Ⓐ Ⓑ Ⓒ Ⓓ Ⓔ	8 Ⓐ Ⓑ Ⓒ Ⓓ Ⓔ	8 Ⓐ Ⓑ Ⓒ Ⓓ Ⓔ
9 Ⓐ Ⓑ Ⓒ Ⓓ Ⓔ	9 Ⓐ Ⓑ Ⓒ Ⓓ Ⓔ	9 Ⓐ Ⓑ Ⓒ Ⓓ Ⓔ	9 Ⓐ Ⓑ Ⓒ Ⓓ Ⓔ	9 Ⓐ Ⓑ Ⓒ Ⓓ Ⓔ
10 Ⓐ Ⓑ Ⓒ Ⓓ Ⓔ	10 Ⓐ Ⓑ Ⓒ Ⓓ Ⓔ	10 Ⓐ Ⓑ Ⓒ Ⓓ Ⓔ	10 Ⓐ Ⓑ Ⓒ Ⓓ Ⓔ	10 Ⓐ Ⓑ Ⓒ Ⓓ Ⓔ
11 Ⓐ Ⓑ Ⓒ Ⓓ Ⓔ	11 Ⓐ Ⓑ Ⓒ Ⓓ Ⓔ	11 Ⓐ Ⓑ Ⓒ Ⓓ Ⓔ	11 Ⓐ Ⓑ Ⓒ Ⓓ Ⓔ	11 Ⓐ Ⓑ Ⓒ Ⓓ Ⓔ
12 Ⓐ Ⓑ Ⓒ Ⓓ Ⓔ	12 Ⓐ Ⓑ Ⓒ Ⓓ Ⓔ	12 Ⓐ Ⓑ Ⓒ Ⓓ Ⓔ	12 Ⓐ Ⓑ Ⓒ Ⓓ Ⓔ	12 Ⓐ Ⓑ Ⓒ Ⓓ Ⓔ
13 Ⓐ Ⓑ Ⓒ Ⓓ Ⓔ	13 Ⓐ Ⓑ Ⓒ Ⓓ Ⓔ	13 Ⓐ Ⓑ Ⓒ Ⓓ Ⓔ	13 Ⓐ Ⓑ Ⓒ Ⓓ Ⓔ	13 Ⓐ Ⓑ Ⓒ Ⓓ Ⓔ
14 Ⓐ Ⓑ Ⓒ Ⓓ Ⓔ	14 Ⓐ Ⓑ Ⓒ Ⓓ Ⓔ	14 Ⓐ Ⓑ Ⓒ Ⓓ Ⓔ	14 Ⓐ Ⓑ Ⓒ Ⓓ Ⓔ	14 Ⓐ Ⓑ Ⓒ Ⓓ Ⓔ
15 Ⓐ Ⓑ Ⓒ Ⓓ Ⓔ	15 Ⓐ Ⓑ Ⓒ Ⓓ Ⓔ	15 Ⓐ Ⓑ Ⓒ Ⓓ Ⓔ	15 Ⓐ Ⓑ Ⓒ Ⓓ Ⓔ	15 Ⓐ Ⓑ Ⓒ Ⓓ Ⓔ
16 Ⓐ Ⓑ Ⓒ Ⓓ Ⓔ	16 Ⓐ Ⓑ Ⓒ Ⓓ Ⓔ	16 Ⓐ Ⓑ Ⓒ Ⓓ Ⓔ	16 Ⓐ Ⓑ Ⓒ Ⓓ Ⓔ	16 Ⓐ Ⓑ Ⓒ Ⓓ Ⓔ
17 Ⓐ Ⓑ Ⓒ Ⓓ Ⓔ	17 Ⓐ Ⓑ Ⓒ Ⓓ Ⓔ	17 Ⓐ Ⓑ Ⓒ Ⓓ Ⓔ	17 Ⓐ Ⓑ Ⓒ Ⓓ Ⓔ	17 Ⓐ Ⓑ Ⓒ Ⓓ Ⓔ
18 Ⓐ Ⓑ Ⓒ Ⓓ Ⓔ	18 Ⓐ Ⓑ Ⓒ Ⓓ Ⓔ	18 Ⓐ Ⓑ Ⓒ Ⓓ Ⓔ	18 Ⓐ Ⓑ Ⓒ Ⓓ Ⓔ	18 Ⓐ Ⓑ Ⓒ Ⓓ Ⓔ
19 Ⓐ Ⓑ Ⓒ Ⓓ Ⓔ	19 Ⓐ Ⓑ Ⓒ Ⓓ Ⓔ	19 Ⓐ Ⓑ Ⓒ Ⓓ Ⓔ	19 Ⓐ Ⓑ Ⓒ Ⓓ Ⓔ	19 Ⓐ Ⓑ Ⓒ Ⓓ Ⓔ
20 Ⓐ Ⓑ Ⓒ Ⓓ Ⓔ	20 Ⓐ Ⓑ Ⓒ Ⓓ Ⓔ	20 Ⓐ Ⓑ Ⓒ Ⓓ Ⓔ	20 Ⓐ Ⓑ Ⓒ Ⓓ Ⓔ	20 Ⓐ Ⓑ Ⓒ Ⓓ Ⓔ
21 Ⓐ Ⓑ Ⓒ Ⓓ Ⓔ	21 Ⓐ Ⓑ Ⓒ Ⓓ Ⓔ	21 Ⓐ Ⓑ Ⓒ Ⓓ Ⓔ	21 Ⓐ Ⓑ Ⓒ Ⓓ Ⓔ	21 Ⓐ Ⓑ Ⓒ Ⓓ Ⓔ
22 Ⓐ Ⓑ Ⓒ Ⓓ Ⓔ	22 Ⓐ Ⓑ Ⓒ Ⓓ Ⓔ	22 Ⓐ Ⓑ Ⓒ Ⓓ Ⓔ	22 Ⓐ Ⓑ Ⓒ Ⓓ Ⓔ	22 Ⓐ Ⓑ Ⓒ Ⓓ Ⓔ
23 Ⓐ Ⓑ Ⓒ Ⓓ Ⓔ	23 Ⓐ Ⓑ Ⓒ Ⓓ Ⓔ	23 Ⓐ Ⓑ Ⓒ Ⓓ Ⓔ	23 Ⓐ Ⓑ Ⓒ Ⓓ Ⓔ	23 Ⓐ Ⓑ Ⓒ Ⓓ Ⓔ
24 Ⓐ Ⓑ Ⓒ Ⓓ Ⓔ	24 Ⓐ Ⓑ Ⓒ Ⓓ Ⓔ	24 Ⓐ Ⓑ Ⓒ Ⓓ Ⓔ	24 Ⓐ Ⓑ Ⓒ Ⓓ Ⓔ	24 Ⓐ Ⓑ Ⓒ Ⓓ Ⓔ
25 Ⓐ Ⓑ Ⓒ Ⓓ Ⓔ	25 Ⓐ Ⓑ Ⓒ Ⓓ Ⓔ	25 Ⓐ Ⓑ Ⓒ Ⓓ Ⓔ	25 Ⓐ Ⓑ Ⓒ Ⓓ Ⓔ	25 Ⓐ Ⓑ Ⓒ Ⓓ Ⓔ
26 Ⓐ Ⓑ Ⓒ Ⓓ Ⓔ	26 Ⓐ Ⓑ Ⓒ Ⓓ Ⓔ	26 Ⓐ Ⓑ Ⓒ Ⓓ Ⓔ	26 Ⓐ Ⓑ Ⓒ Ⓓ Ⓔ	26 Ⓐ Ⓑ Ⓒ Ⓓ Ⓔ
27 Ⓐ Ⓑ Ⓒ Ⓓ Ⓔ	27 Ⓐ Ⓑ Ⓒ Ⓓ Ⓔ	27 Ⓐ Ⓑ Ⓒ Ⓓ Ⓔ	27 Ⓐ Ⓑ Ⓒ Ⓓ Ⓔ	27 Ⓐ Ⓑ Ⓒ Ⓓ Ⓔ
28 Ⓐ Ⓑ Ⓒ Ⓓ Ⓔ	28 Ⓐ Ⓑ Ⓒ Ⓓ Ⓔ	28 Ⓐ Ⓑ Ⓒ Ⓓ Ⓔ	28 Ⓐ Ⓑ Ⓒ Ⓓ Ⓔ	28 Ⓐ Ⓑ Ⓒ Ⓓ Ⓔ
29 Ⓐ Ⓑ Ⓒ Ⓓ Ⓔ	29 Ⓐ Ⓑ Ⓒ Ⓓ Ⓔ	29 Ⓐ Ⓑ Ⓒ Ⓓ Ⓔ	29 Ⓐ Ⓑ Ⓒ Ⓓ Ⓔ	29 Ⓐ Ⓑ Ⓒ Ⓓ Ⓔ
30 Ⓐ Ⓑ Ⓒ Ⓓ Ⓔ	30 Ⓐ Ⓑ Ⓒ Ⓓ Ⓔ	30 Ⓐ Ⓑ Ⓒ Ⓓ Ⓔ	30 Ⓐ Ⓑ Ⓒ Ⓓ Ⓔ	30 Ⓐ Ⓑ Ⓒ Ⓓ Ⓔ

1 1 1 1 1

SECTION I

Time—35 minutes
28 Questions

Directions: Read the passages and answer the questions following each passage by blackening the appropriate space on the answer sheet. You may refer back to the passages when answering the questions. Answer all questions on the basis of what is stated or implied.

The Constitution of the United States protects both property rights and freedom of speech. At times these rights conflict. Resolution then requires a determination as to the type of property involved. If the property is private and not open to the general public, the owner may absolutely deny the exercise of the right of free speech thereon. On the other hand, if public land is at issue, the First Amendment protections of expression are applicable. However, the exercise of free speech thereon is not absolute. Rather it is necessary to determine the appropriateness of the forum. This requires that consideration be given to a number of factors including: character and normal use of the property, the extent to which it is open to the public, and the number and types of persons who frequent it. If the forum is clearly public or clearly private, the resolution of the greater of rights is relatively straightforward.

In the area of quasi-public property, balancing these rights has produced a dilemma. This is the situation when a private owner permits the general public to use his property. When persons seek to use the land for passing out handbills or picketing, how is a conflict between property rights and freedom of expression resolved?

The precept that a private property owner surrenders his rights in proportion to the extent to which he opens up his property to the public is not new. In 1675, Lord Chief Justice Hale wrote that when private property is "affected with a public interest, it ceases to be private." Throughout the development of Anglo-American law, the individual has never possessed absolute dominion over property. Land becomes clothed with a public interest when the owner devotes his property to a use in which the public has an interest. In support of this position the chairman of the board of the Wilde Lake Shopping Center in Columbia, Maryland said:

> The only real purpose and justification of any of these centers is to serve the people in the area—not the merchants, not the architects, not the developers. The success or failure of a regional shopping center will be measured by what it does for the people it seeks to serve.

These doctrines should be applied when accommodation must be made between a shopping center owner's private property rights and the public's right to free expression. It is hoped that when the Court is asked to balance these conflicting rights it will keep in mind what Justice Black said in 1945: "When we balance the Constitutional rights of owners of property against those of the people to enjoy (First Amendment) freedom(s) . . . we remain mindful of the fact that the latter occupy a preferred position."

GO ON TO THE NEXT PAGE.

Model Test 2

1 1 1 1 1

1. In which one of the following cases would the owner of the property probably be most free to restrict the freedom of speech?
(A) an amusement park attended by five million people each year owned by a multinational company
(B) a small grocery store owned by a husband and wife
(C) an enclosed shopping mall owned by a single woman
(D) a fenced public garden and park owned by a small town
(E) an eight-unit residential apartment building owned by a large real estate company

2. A conflict between property rights and freedom of speech might arise in all of the following situations, EXCEPT:
(A) protesters carrying signs outside a cinema in an enclosed shopping mall
(B) a disgruntled employee passing out leaflets in front of a hairdresser's salon
(C) a religious order soliciting funds and converts in the swimming pool area of a condominium
(D) a candidate for mayor handing out flyers in front of his opponent's headquarters
(E) environmentalists carrying signs at the entrance to an oil refinery

3. According to the passage, an owner's freedom to deny freedom of speech on his property is determined by all of the following EXCEPT:
(A) whether or not the land is open to the public
(B) the nature of and the usual use of the property
(C) the type of person who frequents the land
(D) the nature of character of the owner
(E) how many people use the property

4. We can infer from the passage that the author believes that shopping malls in America
(A) should be in the service of the people who frequent them
(B) have a right to prohibit distribution of advertising handbills
(C) have a right to prohibit the distribution of religious printed matter
(D) have a right to control any distributed materials
(E) should permit any charitable solicitations

5. According to the passage, the idea that a property owner's rights decline as the property is more used by the general public
(A) is peculiar to recent Supreme Court decisions
(B) is attested to by a three-hundred-year-old opinion
(C) conflicts with the idea that property affected with a public interest ceases to be private
(D) is in accord with the idea that ownership confers absolute dominion
(E) is now universally accepted in Great Britain and in Canada

6. All other things being equal, the courts must favor
(A) First Amendment rights over property rights
(B) Fourth Amendment rights over property rights
(C) property rights over First Amendment rights
(D) property rights and First Amendment rights equally
(E) property rights and Fourth Amendment rights equally

GO ON TO THE NEXT PAGE.

1 1 1 1 1

Passage A

Understanding copyright law is a little like wandering in a maze and hoping that you find the right outlet. As of 1976, the basic copyright law (and there are many qualifications and exceptions) is that an original work is the property of the author from the time of its creation to 70 years after the author's death, at which time it becomes part of the public domain and may be used by others. For over two hundred years, copyright has protected intellectual property from unauthorized use. This encourages creators because it ensures that they control the use of their works and the profits that may accrue from those works.

Then came the Internet. Is it a whole new ball game? Some people believe that anything on the Internet is in the public domain. Not true. Congress passed the Digital Millennium Copyright Act (DMCA) in 1998, and this act set standards for protecting software, written works, and music on the Internet. It also made illegal any technology used to break copyright-protection devices. (One provision of the act, however, exempts Internet service providers—America Online and Earthlink are just two examples—from lawsuits based on copyright violations that occur on their networks.)

Copyright protection of material on the Internet hasn't been completely successful. For example, book publishers complained that professors cost their industry at least $20 million a year by posting long excerpts of texts on the Internet, making material free to students rather than having them buy textbooks. Cornell University was the first school to respond to textbook publishers by agreeing that legal guidelines for copyright should apply to Web use. But faculty members from some schools complain that this restricts the free flow of ideas. Publishers, on the other hand, say that they must protect $3.35 billion in college textbook sales.

Copyright protection on the Internet is justified. The Internet is an impressive tool for distributing ideas, publications, music, art, and so on. But should it allow stealing? Instead, copyright laws should protect intellectual property wherever it is published and distributed. These laws encourage creative thinkers, and creative thinkers help drive the United States economy. If intellectual property is protected, the Internet's commercial possibilities will be fully realized.

Passage B

The idea that the Internet should be subject to increasingly rigid copyright laws is a bad one. It's true that not having copyright apply to the Internet means less profit for some including entities such as the motion picture and recording industries, who lobbied furiously for new copyright legislation in 1998. But the profit motive shouldn't be the sole consideration.

The world is a different place in the twenty-first century. Accessibility and instant communication are the attributes that make the Internet such a powerful new force, and we shouldn't interfere with this means of passing information, ideas, movies, art, and music from person to person around the world. Traditional barriers such as copyright laws don't belong. If copyright laws are strictly enforced on the Internet—and it is doubtful whether they even can be—we could end up being unable to send a copy of our favorite poem or short story to a friend without risking a lawsuit.

What about the concept of "fair use," which is part of the existing copyright laws? "Fair use" is meant to protect the financial stake of creators and publishers while allowing a limited use of material for primarily educational or artistic purposes, as for example, when reviewers quote passages from works they review. Unfortunately, according to Kenneth D. Crews, a law professor at

GO ON TO THE NEXT PAGE.

1 1 1 1 1

Indiana University and director of its Copyright Management Center, fair use is an "inherently flexible doctrine. It can be interpreted differently by different courts under the same circumstances." Copyright law doesn't state where fair use ends and where copyright infringement begins. It isn't hard to imagine an endless stream of lawsuits.

Recently the Australian government announced that it was planning to update their copyright law to keep up with the changing digital landscape. The head of public policy at Google, the giant Internet search engine, took issue with the proposed changes. If proposed new Australian copyright laws were to be adopted, Google warned, copyright owners could take action against search engines for caching and archiving material. This would "condemn the Australian public to the pre-Internet era." "Given the vast size of the Internet it is impossible for a search engine to contact personally each owner of a web page to determine whether the owner desires its web page to be searched, indexed or cached," Google wrote in its submission to the Senate Legal and Constitutional Affairs Committee.

Google's point about the proposed Australian update illustrates only one of many problems with stricter copyright laws on the Internet. Exclusive ownership of intellectual property is inimical to the Internet.

7. The authors of Passage A and Passage B would most likely agree with which of the following statements?

(A) Without copyright protection, creators of material on the Internet will be unable to fully profit from their creations.
(B) Copyrights are cumbersome tools for protecting intellectual property.
(C) Traditional copyright laws are too rigid.
(D) Strict copyright laws will negatively affect the commercial possibilities of the Internet.
(E) The use of "stealing" as a term for unauthorized use of materials on the Internet is misleading.

8. Which of the following statements best characterizes the main difference between the arguments in Passage A and B?

(A) Passage A argues that copyright protection on the Internet is a necessary evil, while Passage B argues that the copyright laws need to be changed.
(B) The author of Passage A believes copyright laws are outdated, while the author of Passage B believes they are adequate.
(C) The author of Passage A believes copyright laws encourage creators of original material, while the author of Passage B believes they limit the free flow of ideas.
(D) The author of Passage A believes that current enforcement of copyright laws on the Internet is successful, while the author of passage B believes that enforcement has been impossible.
(E) Passage A supports copyright laws because they favor business, while Passage B argues against them for the same reason.

1 1 1 1 1

9. The author of Passage B would be most likely to identify which of the following as the basis for the argument set forth in Passage A?

(A) tradition
(B) rejection of "fair use"
(C) regulation of the Internet
(D) the profit motive
(E) practicality

10. According to Passage A, the Digital Millennium Copyright Act

(A) protects material on the Internet for an indefinite period of time.
(B) solves the copyright issue for all materials on the Internet.
(C) has proved to be ineffective for Internet services such as AOL and Earthlink.
(D) is considerably more limiting than the copyright law of 1976.
(E) forbids breaking copyright-protection devices.

11. In line 59, which is the best meaning for the word *cached*?

(A) placed in a hidden file
(B) accessed by password only
(C) stored in memory
(D) deleted from memory
(E) integrated into existing files

12. In line 63, the word "inimical" probably means

(A) illegal
(B) unfriendly
(C) opposite
(D) synonymous
(E) related

13. According to Passage B, Google's negative response to the Australian government's proposed changes to Internet copyright laws was in part based on the

(A) fear of censorship
(B) objections from other governments
(C) impossibility of compliance
(D) danger of misinterpretation
(E) belief in voluntary adherence to guidelines

Much as they may deplore the fact, historians have no monopoly on the past and no franchise as its privileged interpreters to the public. It may have been different once, but there can no longer be any doubt about the relegation of the historian to a back seat. Far surpassing works of history, as measured by the size of their public and the influence they exert, are the novel, works for the stage, the screen, and television. It is mainly from these sources that millions who never open a history book derive such conceptions, interpretations, convictions, or fantasies as they have about the past. Whatever gives shape to popular conceptions of the past is of concern to historians, and this surely includes fiction.

Broadly speaking, two types of fiction deal with the past—historical fiction and fictional history. The more common of the two is historical fiction, which places fictional characters and events in a more or less authentic historical background. Examples range from War and Peace to Gone With the Wind. Since all but a few novelists must place their fictional characters in some period, nearly all fiction can be thought of as in some degree historical. But the term is applied as a rule only to novels in which historical events figure prominently. Fictional history, on the other hand, portrays and focuses attention upon real historical figures and events, but with the license of the

GO ON TO THE NEXT PAGE.

novelist to imagine and invent. It has yet to produce anything approaching Tolstoy's masterpiece. Some fictional history makes use of invented characters and events, and historical fiction at times mixes up fictional and nonfictional characters. As a result the two genres overlap sometimes, but not often enough to make the distinction unimportant.

Of the two, it is fictional history that is the greater source of mischief, for it is here that fabrication and fact, fiction and nonfiction, are most likely to be mixed and confused. Of course, historians themselves sometimes mix fact with fancy, but it is a rare one who does it consciously or deliberately, and he knows very well that if discovered he stands convicted of betraying his calling. The writer of fictional history, on the other hand, does this as a matter of course and with no compunction whatever. The production and consumption of fictional history appear to be growing of late. Part of the explanation of this is probably the fragmentation of history by professionals, their retreat into specializations, their abandonment of the narrative style, and with it the traditional patronage of lay readers. Fictional history has expanded to fill the gap thus created but has at the same time gone further to create a much larger readership than history books ever had.

14. We can infer from the passage that the author is probably
    (A) a historian
    (B) a historical novelist
    (C) a literary critic
    (D) a social commentator
    (E) a literary historian

15. According to the passage, which one of the following is likely to have contributed to the increasing popularity of fictional history?
    (A) a change in the demographics of lay readers of history
    (B) an increase in the audience for movies and television
    (C) a decline in historians' use of a storytelling style
    (D) an increase in historians' mixing fact and fancy
    (E) a decline in the writing ability of professional historians

16. The author's attitude toward fictional history can best be summarized in which one of the following statements?
    (A) Masterpieces such as War and Peace and Gone With the Wind could not be created in the fictional history genre.
    (B) Fictional history is responsible for leading the reading public away from traditional historical works.
    (C) Fictional history provides a useful service by filling the gap for readers not interested in traditional history.
    (D) Writers of fictional history should not mix historical figures with fictional characters.
    (E) Fictional history can mislead readers about actual historical events.

Model Test 2

GO ON TO THE NEXT PAGE.

1 1 1 1 1

17. Of the following, which one would the author consider most likely to cause a reader to confuse fact and fiction?
(A) a book about the Watergate scandal with fictionalized dialogue between President Nixon and his attorney general, John Mitchell
(B) a book about a fictional platoon in Vietnam during the last days of the war
(C) a fictional account of the adventures of a group of servants in the White House under Eisenhower, Kennedy, Johnson, and Nixon
(D) an account of the assassination of President Kennedy as viewed by a Texas adolescent on the parade route
(E) a book based on newspaper accounts about the reaction to the Cuban missile crisis in the United States, the U.S.S.R., and Western Europe

18. The function of the second paragraph of the passage is to
(A) reinforce the argument about fictionalized history presented in the first paragraph
(B) define and contrast fictional history and historical fiction
(C) emphasize the superiority of historical fiction to fictional history
(D) provide context for the analysis in the third paragraph
(E) clarify the difference between history and fiction

19. According to the passage, the author would agree with all of the following statements EXCEPT:
(A) historical fiction and fictional history are of concern to the professional historian
(B) the works of today's professional historians tend to be more specialized than historical works of the past
(C) professional historians understand that they should not mix fact and fiction in their works
(D) a historical event presented as a TV miniseries is likely to be accepted as true by many people
(E) fictional history has succeeded because of a failure of the academic history curriculum

20. The author's attitude about the issue of fiction and history is presented most clearly in
(A) paragraph 1, lines 1–7
(B) paragraph 1, lines 17–20
(C) paragraph 2, lines 35–41
(D) paragraph 3, lines 49–53
(E) paragraph 3, lines 62–64

21. The tone of this passage could best be described as
(A) hostile and didactic
(B) moderate and concerned
(C) pedantic and detached
(D) ironic and condescending
(E) philosophical and enlightened

GO ON TO THE NEXT PAGE.

Faith healing, or spirit healing, by definition, is the physical healing of the body of an individual by means of that individual's religious faith and the consequent intervention by deities in the healing process, spiritual intervention of other sorts in the course of a disease, or the efficacious effect on the physical body by force of will, either the will of the affected person or that of another person who has such power or who can channel such power from elsewhere. While looked upon by "hard" science as worthy of no attention other than the heaping upon it of denigration and a dismissive shake of the head, faith healing has enjoyed a long and continuous history of practice and acceptance among the peoples of the world. And debunking and calumny notwithstanding, it remains in many people a deep-seated belief in modern society, and elements of the practice find their way even into "standard" medical therapies.

Faith healing advocates point to historical practices, reputed to have been successful in treating a myriad of illnesses, to bolster their cases. Native American "medicine," for example, in which the medicine man, or shaman, functioned as a combination of priest, physician, and magician, relied, at least in part, on the shaman's ability to create belief by the sick individual in either cure or curse, and is said to have been highly effective in producing either recovery or descent into greater illness and death, whichever was desired by the shaman. While certain herbs or other substances as well as such devices as drums, rattles, and totems were used in treatment, it was the shaman's force of will and its effect on the strength of the belief system of the treated person that was paramount. Voodoo practices share some of the points of view found in ancient Native American healing, using dolls, fetishes, charms, and cabalistic totems in causing belief in the sufferer, as do the practices of certain fundamentalist religions—for example, in the ritual of the "laying on of hands," in which a deity's intervention is channeled through a minister and in which a sufferer believes himself or herself to be cured and so apparently is cured.

Modern proponents of forms of faith healing most often now promote a combination of spirituality, which does not necessarily involve religion, and science as the most effective team in the process of combating disease. One point of view suggests that modern society has lost its connection with its community and its strong belief in the religion and tradition of that community. Because of that weakened belief system, the real-world therapeutic effects of healing rituals have been lost, and only the strengthening of belief will reclaim the beneficial results produced historically by faith healing, whether that belief is in the force of an individual's own will or in outside healing forces. Holistic medicine, in which the emphasis is on treating the "whole" individual, not only the person's disease, shares at least in part some of these modern faith healers' points of view in that it does not discount the importance of the mindset of the ill person, nor does it discount the truism of "healthy mind, healthy body" or the effect on the physical body of the will to live. And while faith healing undoubtedly is often practiced by those most of society is convinced are charlatans, self-promoting and self-defined psychics, and those motivated simply by greed, some of its tenets are finding their way into the mainstream of medical practice, just as certain medicinal herbs used by ancient healers, "medicines" once ridiculed, have now been found to have curative powers previously unknown and unappreciated.

GO ON TO THE NEXT PAGE.

1 1 1 1 1

22. The main point of the passage is most accurately expressed by which one of the following?
    (A) If modern society has lost its faith in the force of will to heal disease, then it can reclaim that faith by studying the effects faith healers have had throughout history and in various cultures.
    (B) Holistic medicine has its roots in the practices of shamans, voodoo priests, and other religious figures and not in the practices of psychics and other charlatans.
    (C) Practices of using totems, herbs, charms, and other devices are central to the effect faith healing has on the ill person and are effective even in modern medical practices when the desired result is to strengthen the individual's belief system.
    (D) Faith healing is a long-accepted ritual that some have thought to be beneficial in combating disease, and although it may or may not have been effective, some of the beliefs of faith healing advocates have been incorporated into modern medical practice.
    (E) Modern medical practitioners have been remiss in dismissing the claims of faith healing because scientists have been surprised by the effectiveness of some of the ancient medicines used by healers.

23. Each of the following is indicated by the passage EXCEPT:
    (A) some faith healing is practiced by charlatans
    (B) the rituals of voodoo practitioners share some elements of Native American medicine
    (C) the term "holistic" is a modern term
    (D) faith healing can be based strictly on religious belief
    (E) faith healing may have been historically paired with drug treatment

24. The primary purpose of the concluding paragraph is to
    (A) combine historical and modern perspectives on the effectiveness of faith healing
    (B) discuss spirituality and faith as a basis for the efficacy of faith healing
    (C) differentiate historical attitudes of faith healers from the attitudes of modern medical practitioners
    (D) provide a synthesis of scientific objections to spirit healing
    (E) discuss elements of faith healing in modern medicine and suggest some reasons for the inclusion of those elements

25. The author would be most likely to agree with which one of the following?
    (A) There is no proof that faith healing has ever been effective; consequently, the inclusion of elements of faith healing in modern medicine is without rational foundation.
    (B) Open-minded behavior on the part of scientists may lead to some important discoveries in medicine; simply because something has not been rigorously tested may not mean it isn't effective.
    (C) The "laying on of hands" is a delusion in the ill person produced by the force of the minister's will.
    (D) "Healthy mind, healthy body" is a truism believed by ancient practitioners of faith healing as well as modern ones.
    (E) The belief in a deity's intervention in the healing process is as much an indication of rational thought processes as is the belief in "healthy mind, healthy body."

Model Test 2

GO ON TO THE NEXT PAGE.

1 1 1 1 1

26. The passage suggests that which one of the following is true about practitioners of holistic medicine?

(A) Practitioners of holistic medicine are well aware of the lost opportunities in treatment because effective, natural medicines have gone unrecognized.
(B) Because holistic medicine involves treating the whole person rather than simply the person's disease, it necessarily involves trained psychological intervention in the healing processes.
(C) Practitioners of holistic medicine are likely to refer some cases to faith healers when hard science fails to effect a cure.
(D) Practitioners of holistic medicine, in treating the whole person rather than simply the person's disease, are likely to investigate the mindset of the individual in the context of that mindset's effect on the course of a disease, even though the individual in question may disagree with the connection between the will to live and the outcome of treatment.
(E) Holistic medicine and the practices of ancient faith healers have little in common because the point of modern medical science, of whatever kind, is to use all available methods to competently treat patients.

27. According to the passage, modern practitioners of faith healing would be likely to engage in all of the following activities EXCEPT:

(A) relying on surgery and radiation alone to cure an individual of cancer
(B) the laying on of hands in order to effect an immediate and startling cure without recourse to more traditional medical treatment
(C) creating an atmosphere in which a patient feels free to discuss an illness at length, even to the point of admitting despair and suicidal thoughts
(D) calling upon deities to intervene in the healing process and channeling the power of the deities to effect healing
(E) referring patients to licensed medical doctors for long-term care

28. The author's primary purpose in the passage is to

(A) compare and contrast the methods of faith healers in the past and the methods of faith healers today
(B) explain some of the practices of faith healers both now and in the past and suggest the part of faith healers in modern medicine
(C) promote the acceptance of faith healers as viable alternatives to "standard" medical therapies
(D) identify those practices of faith healers that are unacceptable in modern society and those that are slowly gaining acceptance, even among promoters of "hard" science
(E) present medical alternatives for the reader who is searching for methods of treating his or her illness or that of another

STOP

IF YOU FINISH BEFORE TIME IS CALLED,
YOU MAY CHECK YOUR WORK ON THIS SECTION ONLY.
DO NOT WORK ON ANY OTHER SECTION IN THE TEST.

2 2 2 2 2

SECTION II

Time—35 minutes
24 Questions

Directions: In this section you will be given groups of questions based on different sets of conditions. Drawing a simple diagram may be helpful in answering some of the questions. You are to choose the best answer and mark the corresponding space on your answer sheet.

Questions 1–6

The Bell Canyon Condominium is a four-story building with a single penthouse apartment on the fourth floor. There are two apartments on each of the three other floors. The apartments are owned by A, B, C, D, E, F, and G.

A's apartment is on one of the floors higher than B's.

C's apartment is on one of the floors lower than D's.

C's apartment is on one of the floors lower than E's.

F and G's apartments are on the same floor.

1. Which one of the following could be the owner of the penthouse?
   (A) B
   (B) C
   (C) E
   (D) F
   (E) G

2. If F's apartment is on the second floor, which one of the following must be true?
   (A) C's apartment is on the first floor.
   (B) D's apartment is on the third floor.
   (C) A's apartment is on the fourth floor.
   (D) G's apartment is on the first floor.
   (E) B's apartment is on the third floor.

3. If D owns the penthouse apartment, on which floor or floors could G's apartment be located?
   (A) the first floor only
   (B) the second floor only
   (C) the third floor only
   (D) the second or the third floor
   (E) the first, second, or third floor

4. If D's and E's apartments are on the same floor, which one of the following must be true?
   (A) D and E are on the third floor.
   (B) D and E are on the second floor.
   (C) A is on the fourth floor.
   (D) B and C are on the first floor.
   (E) F and G are on the second floor.

5. If C's apartment is on the first floor, and A is the owner of the penthouse, which one of the following must be true?
   (A) G's apartment is on the third floor.
   (B) D's apartment is on the second floor.
   (C) E's apartment is on the second floor.
   (D) B's apartment is on the first floor.
   (E) F's apartment is on the second floor.

GO ON TO THE NEXT PAGE.

6. Which one of the following is possible?
   (A) A and C are on the same floor.
   (B) A and E are on the same floor.
   (C) A is on the first floor.
   (D) D is on the first floor.
   (E) C is on the fourth floor.

Questions 7–12

A new bank has decided to stay open only on weekends—all day Saturday and Sunday—and no other days. The bank has hired two managers (U and V), four tellers (W, X, Y, and Z), and two operations officers (S and T), for a total of exactly eight full-time employees. No part-time employees are hired. Each employee works a complete day when working.

A manager must be on duty each day.
The managers cannot work on the same day.
At least two tellers must be working on the same day.
W and X will not work on the same day.
S and Z will only work on Saturday.
No employee can work on consecutive days, but each employee must work on Saturday or Sunday.

7. Which one of the following could be false?
   (A) If U works on Saturday, then V works on Sunday.
   (B) If X works on Saturday, then W works on Sunday.
   (C) T can work either day.
   (D) If W works on Saturday and Y works on Sunday, then X works on Sunday.
   (E) If U works on Sunday, then X works on Saturday.

8. Which one of the following is an acceptable group of employees who could work on Saturday?
   (A) Z W Y S T
   (B) U V W Y Z S
   (C) V W X Z T
   (D) U Z S T
   (E) V W Z S

9. What is the greatest number of employees who can work on Saturday?
   (A) 2
   (B) 3
   (C) 4
   (D) 5
   (E) 6

10. If W works on Sunday, then which one of the following must be true?
   (A) X works on Saturday.
   (B) Y works on Saturday.
   (C) T works on Sunday.
   (D) Z works on Sunday.
   (E) U works on Saturday.

11. Which one of the following must be true?
   (A) T always works the same day as Y.
   (B) S never works the same day as U.
   (C) Z never works the same day as X.
   (D) If W works on Sunday, then Y always works on Saturday.
   (E) Only two tellers work on Saturday.

12. Which one of the following is a complete and accurate list of the employees who have the possibility of working on Sunday?
   (A) U W Y Z
   (B) U W Y S
   (C) U V W X T
   (D) U V W X Y T
   (E) U V W X Y T S

GO ON TO THE NEXT PAGE.

2 2 2 2 2

Questions 13–19

A homeowner has purchased six paintings, one each from six local artists. The artists' first names are Diego, Frank, Glenda, Rich, Tina, and Yolanda. The six paintings will be positioned in a straight row, numbered left to right as one through six. The following restrictions will apply:

Rich's painting is positioned to the right of Tina's painting.

Glenda's painting is positioned to the left of Tina's painting.

Tina's painting is positioned to the right of Frank's painting.

Diego's painting is positioned to the left of both Frank's painting and Yolanda's painting.

13. If Glenda's painting is hanging in position #4, then each of the following could be true EXCEPT:

(A) Diego's painting is hanging to the left of and next to Frank's painting.
(B Glenda's painting is hanging to the right of and next to Frank's painting.
(C) Tina's painting is hanging to the left of and next to Yolanda's painting.
(D) Yolanda's painting is hanging to the right of and next to Diego's painting.
(E) Yolanda's painting is hanging to the left of and next to Frank's painting.

14. What is the maximum number of paintings that can be placed between Glenda's painting and Yolanda's painting?

(A) none
(B) one
(C) two
(D) three
(E) four

15. If Frank's painting is in position #2, then which one of the following must be true?

(A) Tina's painting is in position #5.
(B) Glenda's painting is in position #3.
(C) Rich's painting is in position #6.
(D) Diego's painting is in position #1.
(E) Yolanda's painting is in position #4.

16. If Yolanda's painting is hanging to the left of Frank's painting, then which one of the following must be true?

(A) Frank's painting is hanging to the left of and next to Glenda's painting.
(B) Glenda's painting is hanging to the left of and next to Tina's painting.
(C) Rich's painting is hanging to the right of and next to Tina's painting.
(D) Tina's painting is hanging to the right of and next to Frank's painting.
(E) Yolanda's painting is hanging to the right and next to Diego's painting.

17. Which one of the following conditions would not result in only one possible arrangement of the six paintings?

(A) Diego's painting is between and next to Yolanda's painting and Glenda's painting.
(B) Diego's painting is next to Yolanda's painting and Glenda's painting is next to Tina's painting.
(C) Frank's painting is between and next to Glenda's painting and Yolanda's painting.
(D) Tina's painting is between and next to Yolanda's painting and Glenda's painting.
(E) Yolanda's painting is next to Glenda's painting and Tina's painting is next to Glenda's painting.

18. If Glenda's painting is hanging next to Yolanda's painting, then how many possible arrangements are there for the six paintings?

(A) one
(B) two
(C) three
(D) four
(E) five

19. Which one of the following CANNOT be a true statement?

(A) Frank's painting is hanging to the left of Glenda's painting.
(B) Glenda's painting is hanging to the left of Frank's painting.
(C) Tina's painting is hanging to the left of Diego's painting.
(D) Tina's painting is hanging to the right of Yolanda's painting.
(E) Yolanda's painting is hanging to the right of Rich's painting.

<u>Questions 20–24</u>

Four teams (Red, Blue, Green, and Yellow) participate in the Junior Olympics, in which there are five events. In each event participants place either 1st, 2nd, 3rd, or 4th. First place is awarded a gold medal, 2nd place is awarded a silver medal, and 3rd place is awarded a bronze medal. There are no ties, and each team enters one contestant in each event. All contestants finish each event.

The results of the Junior Olympics are:

No team wins gold medals in two consecutive events.

No team fails to win a medal within two consecutive events.

The Blue team wins only two medals, neither of them gold.

The Red team only wins three gold medals, and no other medals.

20. If the green team wins only one gold medal, then which one of the following must be true?

(A) The yellow team wins two gold medals.
(B) The red team wins only two bronze medals.
(C) The yellow team wins only one gold medal.
(D) The yellow team wins only silver medals.
(E) The green team wins only bronze medals.

21. Which one of the following must be true?

(A) The yellow team wins only bronze and gold medals.
(B) The yellow team wins five medals.
(C) The green team cannot win a silver medal.
(D) The yellow team cannot win a bronze medal.
(E) The green team wins exactly three medals.

22. If the yellow team wins five silver medals, then the green team must win

(A) more silver than gold
(B) more gold than bronze
(C) two gold, two bronze, one silver
(D) two gold, three bronze
(E) six medals

2 2 2 2 2

23. All of the following must be true EXCEPT:

    (A) The green team wins five medals.
    (B) The yellow team wins five medals.
    (C) If the green team wins one gold medal, the yellow team wins one gold medal.
    (D) If the green team wins only one silver medal, the yellow team wins only one silver medal.
    (E) If the yellow team wins only silver medals, the green team cannot win a silver medal.

24. If a fifth team, Orange, enters all events and wins only three consecutive silver medals, which one of the following must be true?

    (A) If green wins a gold in the 2nd event, it also wins a bronze in the 3rd event.
    (B) If green wins a gold in the 2nd event, it also wins a silver in the 4th event.
    (C) If yellow wins a gold in the 2nd event, green wins a bronze in the 3rd event.
    (D) If yellow wins a gold in the 2nd event, blue wins a silver in the 3rd event.
    (E) If red wins a gold in the 1st event, orange wins a silver in the last event.

STOP

IF YOU FINISH BEFORE TIME IS CALLED,
YOU MAY CHECK YOUR WORK ON THIS SECTION ONLY.
DO NOT WORK ON ANY OTHER SECTION IN THE TEST.

3 3 3 3 3

SECTION III

Time—35 minutes
26 Questions

Directions: In this section you will be given brief statements or passages and will be required to evaluate the reasoning involved. In some instances, more than one choice will appear to be a possible answer. You are to choose the best answer. Use common sense and reasonableness in making your selection; then mark the proper space on the answer sheet.

1. Though the benefits of the hot tub and the Jacuzzis have been well publicized by their manufacturers, there are also some less widely known dangers. Young children, of course, cannot be left unattended near a hot tub, and even adults have fallen asleep and drowned. Warm water can cause the blood vessels to dilate and the resulting drop in blood pressure can make people liable to fainting, especially when they stand up quickly to get out. Improperly maintained water can promote the growth of bacteria that can cause folliculitis.

   The main point of this passage is that

   (A) the benefits of the hot tub and the Jacuzzi have been overrated
   (B) the dangers of the hot tub and Jacuzzi outweigh their potential publicized benefits
   (C) users of hot tubs and Jacuzzis should be aware of the dangers connected with their use
   (D) the hot tub and Jacuzzi are dangerous only when improperly maintained
   (E) the hot tub is potentially beneficial in the treatment of high blood pressure

2. *Chariots of Fire* may have caught some professional critics off guard in 1982 as the Motion Picture Academy's choice for an Oscar as the year's best film, but it won wide audience approval as superb entertainment.

   Refreshingly, *Chariots of Fire* features an exciting story, enchanting English and Scottish scenery, a beautiful musical score, and appropriate costumes.

   All of these attractions are added to a theme that extols traditional religious values—without a shred of offensive sex, violence, or profanity.

   Too good to be true? See *Chariots of Fire* and judge for yourself.

   Those who condemn the motion picture industry for producing so many objectionable films can do their part by patronizing wholesome ones, thereby encouraging future Academy Award judges to recognize and reward decency.

   Which one of the following is a basic assumption underlying the final sentence of the passage?

   (A) Academy judges are not decent people.
   (B) The popularity of a film influences academy judges.
   (C) Future academy judges will be better than past ones.
   (D) There are those who condemn the motion picture industry.
   (E) *Chariots of Fire* is a patronizing film.

GO ON TO THE NEXT PAGE.

3 3 3 3 3

3. *Andy*: All teachers are mean.

Bob: That is not true. I know some doctors who are mean, too.

Bob's answer demonstrates that he thought Andy to mean that

(A) all teachers are mean
(B) some teachers are mean
(C) doctors are meaner than teachers
(D) teachers are meaner than doctors
(E) only teachers are mean

4. Theodore Roosevelt was a great hunter. He was the mighty Nimrod of his generation. He had the physical aptitude and adventurous spirit of the true frontiersman. "There is delight," he said, "in the hardy life of the open; in long rides, rifle in hand; in the thrill of the fight with dangerous game." But he was more than a marksman and tracker of beasts, for he brought to his sport the intellectual curiosity and patient observation of the natural scientist.

Which one of the following would most weaken the author's concluding contention?

(A) Theodore Roosevelt never studied natural science.
(B) Actually, Theodore Roosevelt's sharpshooting prowess was highly exaggerated.
(C) Theodore Roosevelt always used native guides when tracking game.
(D) Theodore Roosevelt was known to leave safaris if their first few days were unproductive.
(E) Theodore Roosevelt's powers of observation were significantly hampered by his nearsightedness.

5. The following is an excerpt from a letter sent to a law school applicant:

"Thank you for considering our school to further your education. Your application for admission was received well before the deadline and was processed with your admission test score and undergraduate grade report.

"We regret to inform you that you cannot be admitted for the fall semester. We have had to refuse admission to many outstanding candidates because of the recent cut in state funding of our program.

"Thank you for your interest in our school, and we wish you success in your future endeavors."

Which one of the following can be deduced from the above letter?

(A) The recipient of the letter did not have a sufficiently high grade point average to warrant admission to this graduate program.
(B) The recipient of the letter was being seriously considered for a place in the evening class.
(C) The law school sending the letter could not fill all the places in its entering class due to a funding problem.
(D) Criteria other than test scores and grade reports were used in determining the size of the entering class.
(E) The school sending the letter is suffering severe financial difficulties.

Model Test 2

GO ON TO THE NEXT PAGE.

Questions 6–7

At birth we have no self-image. We cannot distinguish anything from the confusion of light and sound around us. From this beginning of no-dimension, we gradually begin to differentiate our body from our environment and develop a sense of identity, with the realization that we are a separate and independent human being. We then begin to develop a conscience, the sense of right and wrong. Further, we develop social consciousness, where we become aware that we live with other people. Finally, we develop a sense of values, which is our overall estimation of our worth in the world.

6. Which one of the following would be the best completion of this passage?
   (A) The sum total of all these developments we call the self-image or the self-concept.
   (B) This estimation of worth is only relative to our value system.
   (C) Therefore, our social consciousness is dependent on our sense of values.
   (D) Therefore, our conscience keeps our sense of values in perspective.
   (E) The sum total of living with other people and developing a sense of values makes us a total person.

7. The author of this passage would most likely agree with which one of the following?
   (A) Children have no self-dimension.
   (B) Having a conscience necessitates the ability to differentiate between right and wrong.
   (C) Social consciousness is our most important awareness.
   (D) Heredity is predominant over environment in development.
   (E) The ability to tell the difference between moral issues depends on the overall dimension of self-development.

8. *Editorial*: A previously undisclosed transcript has revealed that Richard Nixon's secret White House slush fund that was used to silence the Watergate burglars came from illegally donated campaign money. After Nixon resigned, his successor, Gerald Ford, pardoned him. The same Gerald Ford has joined Presidents Carter and Bush in urging campaign funding reforms. Recent hearings have shown all too clearly that both parties have been guilty of highly questionable fund-raising practices. Unless the laws are changed, the shoddy practices of the last thirty years will undoubtedly continue.

   Which one of the following most accurately states the main point of the argument?
   (A) It is hypocritical of Gerald Ford to urge campaign reform after his pardon of Richard Nixon.
   (B) Both the Democrats and the Republicans have been guilty of unethical campaign fund-raising practices.
   (C) The laws governing campaign fund-raising must be reformed.
   (D) Reform of campaign fund-raising has been supported by former presidents of both parties.
   (E) We cannot expect that those who benefit from a problem will wish to take steps to solve it.

GO ON TO THE NEXT PAGE.

3 3 3 3 3

Questions 9–10

In a report released last week, a government-funded institute concluded that there is "overwhelming" evidence that violence on television leads to criminal behavior by children and teenagers.

The report, based on an extensive review of several hundred research studies conducted during the 1970s, is an update of a 1972 Surgeon General's report that came to similar conclusions.

9. Which one of the following is the most convincing statement in support of the argument in the first paragraph above?

(A) A 50-state survey of the viewing habits of prison inmates concluded that every inmate watches at least 2 hours of violent programming each day.
(B) A 50-state survey of the viewing habits of convicted adolescents shows that each of them had watched at least 2 hours of violent programming daily since the age of 5.
(C) One juvenile committed a murder that closely resembled a crime portrayed on a network series.
(D) The 1972 Surgeon General's report was not nearly as extensive as this more recent study.
(E) Ghetto residents who are burglarized most often report the theft of a television set.

10. The argument above is most weakened by its vague use of the word

(A) violence
(B) government
(C) extensive
(D) update
(E) overwhelming

Questions 11–12

Violence against racial and religious minority groups increased sharply throughout the county last year, despite a slight decline in statewide figures. Compiling incidents from police departments and private watchdog groups, the County Human Relations Committee reported almost 500 hate crimes in the year, up from only 200 last year. It was the first increase since the committee began to report a yearly figure six years ago. The lower statewide figures are probably in error due to underreporting in other counties; underreporting is the major problem that state surveyors face each year.

11. All of the following, if true, would support the conclusion or the explanation of the discrepancy in the state and county figures EXCEPT:

(A) The number of hate crimes and those resulting in fatalities has increased in neighboring states.
(B) Anti-immigration sentiment was fanned this year by an anti-immigration ballot referendum.
(C) Funding for police departments throughout the state has decreased.
(D) Many law-abiding members of minority groups are fearful or distrustful of the police.
(E) All of the counties in the state have active private watchdog groups that carefully monitor hate crimes.

12. The author of this passage makes his case by
    (A) establishing the likelihood of an event by ruling out several other possibilities
    (B) combining several pieces of apparently unrelated evidence to build support for a conclusion
    (C) contrasting a single certain case with several others with less evidence in their support
    (D) assuming that what is only probable is certain
    (E) using a general rule to explain a specific case

13. The study of village communities has become one of the fundamental methods of discussing the ancient history of institutions. It would be out of the question here to range over the whole field of human society in search for communal arrangements of rural life. It will be sufficient to confine the present inquiry to the varieties presented by nations of Aryan race, not because greater importance is to be attached to these nations than to other branches of humankind, although this view might also be reasonably urged, but principally because the Aryan race in its history has gone through all sorts of experiences, and the data gathered from its historical life can be tolerably well ascertained. Should the road be sufficiently cleared in this particular direction, it will not be difficult to connect the results with similar researches in other racial surroundings.

    Which one of the following, if true, most weakens the author's conclusion?

    (A) Information about the Aryan race is no more conclusive than information about any other ethnic group.
    (B) The experiences and lifestyle of Aryans are uniquely different from those of other cultures.
    (C) The Aryan race is no more important than any other race.
    (D) The historical life of the Aryans dates back only 12 centuries.
    (E) Aryans lived predominantly in villages, while today 90 percent of the world population live predominantly in or around major cities.

3 3 3 3 3

14. Although any reasonable modern citizen of the world must abhor war and condemn senseless killing, we must also agree that honor is more valuable than life. Life, after all, is transient, but honor is ___________ .

Which one of the following most logically completes the passage above?

(A) sensible
(B) real
(C) eternal
(D) of present value
(E) priceless

Questions 15–16

Bill said, "All dogs bark. This animal does not bark. Therefore it is not a dog."

15. Which one of the following most closely parallels the logic of this statement?

(A) All rocks are hard. This lump is hard. Therefore, it may be a rock.
(B) All foreign-language tests are difficult. This is not a foreign language test. Therefore, it is not difficult.
(C) All Blunder automobiles are poorly built. Every auto sold by Joe was poorly built. Therefore, Joe sells Blunder automobiles.
(D) Rocks beat scissors, scissors beat paper, and paper beats rocks. Therefore, it is best to choose paper.
(E) All paint smells. This liquid does not smell. Therefore, it is not paint.

16. Which one of the following would weaken Bill's argument the most?

(A) Animals other than dogs bark.
(B) Some dogs cannot bark.
(C) Dogs bark more than cockatiels.
(D) You can train a dog not to bark.
(E) You can train birds to bark.

17. In the last three years the number of arrests for burglary and robbery in Sandy Beach has declined by more than 30 percent. At the same time, the city has reduced the size of its police force by 25 percent.

Which one of the following helps to resolve an apparent discrepancy in the information above?

(A) Neighborhood Watch programs have always been active in Sandy Beach.
(B) The number of reported burglaries and robberies in Sandy Beach has increased in the last three years.
(C) Compared to other cities in the state, Sandy Beach has one of the lowest crime rates.
(D) By using motorcycles rather than foot patrols, the police are able to cover larger areas of the city using fewer officers.
(E) Many of the residents of Sandy Beach have installed expensive security systems in their homes.

Model Test 2

GO ON TO THE NEXT PAGE.

3 3 3 3 3

Questions 18–19

California and Nevada officials have questioned the impartiality of the board of scientists from the National Academy of Science who assess the safety of proposed nuclear dumping sites. They claim that the panels are heavily weighted in favor of the nuclear power companies that have been lobbying for the creation of nuclear dump sites in the deserts of the Southwest. At least ten members of the panels are or have been employees of the Department of Energy, but none is associated with any environmental organization. Environmentalists fear that long-lived nuclear wastes may leach into the groundwater and ultimately into the waters of the Colorado River. They also point out that 90 percent of the budget of the National Academy's Radioactive Waste Management Board is provided by the Department of Energy. The inventory of radioactive waste has been growing larger and larger in temporary storage places, but so far there has been virtually no agreement about a permanent dump site.

18. The officials who question the impartiality of the Management Board assume that the Department of Energy
    (A) supports the activities of the nuclear power industry
    (B) supports the activities of environmental groups
    (C) wishes to delay the selection of permanent nuclear waste dumping sites for as long as possible
    (D) is indifferent to the growing mass of nuclear wastes in temporary storage sites
    (E) has declined to take a stand for or against the use of nuclear power

19. The Nuclear Waste Management Board could best allay doubt of its impartiality if it were to
    (A) publish the results of its studies of the feasibility of locating nuclear waste dumps in the deserts of the Southwest
    (B) add one or two environmentalists to the panels that assess locations for nuclear dump sites
    (C) make public the sources of all its funding
    (D) recommend desert sites at a greater distance from the Colorado River
    (E) base decisions on feasibility studies by scientists with no connection to the National Academy

20. The law of parsimony urges a strict economy upon us; it requires that we can never make a guess with two or three assumptions in it if we can make sense with one.

    Which one of the following is the main point of the author's statement?
    (A) Complications arise from economy.
    (B) Simplify terminology whenever possible.
    (C) Don't complicate a simple issue.
    (D) Assumptions are necessarily simple in nature.
    (E) Excess assumptions never clarify the situation.

GO ON TO THE NEXT PAGE.

3 3 3 3 3

21. You can use a bottle opener to open the new beer bottles. You do not need to use a bottle opener to open the new beer bottles.

Which one of the following most closely parallels the logic of these statements?

(A) You must turn on the switch to light the lamp. If you turn on the switch, the lamp may not light.
(B) A cornered rattlesnake will strike, so do not corner a rattlesnake.
(C) If you do not study you will fail the test. If you do study, you may fail the test.
(D) Every candidate I voted for in the election lost his race. I must learn to vote better.
(E) I can move the sofa with my brother's help. If my brother is not available, I'll get a neighbor to help me.

22. To be admitted to Bigshot University, you must have a 3.5 grade-point average (GPA) and a score of 800 on the admissions test, a 3.0 GPA and a score of 1,000 on the admissions test, or a 2.5 GPA and a score of 1,200 on the admissions test. A sliding scale exists for other scores and GPAs.

Which one of the following is inconsistent with the above?

(A) The higher the GPA, the lower the admissions test score needed for admission.
(B) Joe was admitted with a 2.7 GPA and a score of 1,100 on the admissions test.
(C) No student with a score of less than 800 on the admissions test and a 3.4 GPA will be admitted.
(D) More applicants had a GPA of 3.5 than had a GPA of 2.5.
(E) Some students with a score of less than 1,200 on the admissions test and a GPA of less than 2.5 were admitted.

23. The Census Bureau's family portrait of America may remind us of the problems we face as a nation, but it also gives us reason to take heart in our ability to solve them in an enlightened way. The 1980 census was the first in history to show that the majority of the population in every state has completed high school. And the percentage of our people with at least 4 years of college rose from 11 percent in 1970 to 16.3 percent in 1980. That's progress—where it really counts.

Which one of the following assumptions underlies the author's conclusion in the above passage?

(A) Greater numbers of high-school and college degrees coincide with other firsts in the 1980 census.
(B) Greater numbers of high-school and college degrees coincide with greater numbers of well-educated people.
(C) Greater numbers of high-school and college degrees coincide with a great commitment to social progress.
(D) Greater numbers of high-school and college degrees coincide with a better chance to avoid national catastrophe.
(E) Greater numbers of high-school and college degrees coincide with the 1980 census.

24. *Advertisement:* Add No-NOCK to your car and watch its performance soar. No-NOCK will give it more get-up-and-go and keep it running longer. Ask for No-NOCK when you want better mileage!

According to the advertisement above, No-NOCK claims to do everything EXCEPT:

(A) improve your car's performance
(B) increase your car's life
(C) improve your car's miles per gallon
(D) cause fewer breakdowns
(E) stop the engine from knocking

GO ON TO THE NEXT PAGE.

3 **3** **3** **3** **3**

25. So many arrogant and ill-tempered young men have dominated the tennis courts of late that we have begun to fear that those characteristics were prerequisites for championship tennis.

Tennis used to be a gentleman's game. What is sad is not just that the game has changed. With so much importance placed on success, it may be that something has gone out of the American character—such things as gentleness and graciousness.

Which one of the following statements, if true, would most weaken the above argument?

(A) The American character is a result of American goals.
(B) Tennis has only recently become a professional sport.
(C) Some ill-tempered tennis players are unsuccessful.
(D) The "gentlemen" of early tennis often dueled to the death off the court.
(E) Some even-tempered tennis players are successful.

26. *Dolores*: To preserve the peace, we must be prepared to go to war with any nation at any time, using either conventional or nuclear weapons.

Fran: Which shall it be, conventional weapons or nuclear weapons?

Fran mistakenly concludes that the "either . . . or" phrase in Dolores's statement indicates

(A) fear
(B) indecision
(C) a choice
(D) a question
(E) a refusal

Model Test 2

STOP

IF YOU FINISH BEFORE TIME IS CALLED,
YOU MAY CHECK YOUR WORK ON THIS SECTION ONLY.
DO NOT WORK ON ANY OTHER SECTION IN THE TEST.

4 4 4 4 4

SECTION IV

Time—35 minutes

24 Questions

Directions: In this section you will be given groups of questions based on different sets of conditions. Drawing a simple diagram may be helpful in answering some of the questions. You are to choose the best answer and mark the corresponding space on your answer sheet.

Questions 1–6

A group of tourists is planning to visit a cluster of islands—U, V, W, X, Y, and Z, connected by bridges. The tourists must stay on each island visited for exactly three days and three nights. Each bridge takes one hour to cross, may be crossed in either direction, and can be crossed only in the morning to give the tourists a full day on the island.

The islands are connected by bridges only as indicated below:

U is connected to W, X, and Y
V is connected to Y and Z
X is connected to Z and W
Y is connected to X and Z

1. If the group visits island W first, eight days later it could NOT be at which one of the following islands?

(A) U
(B) V
(C) X
(D) Y
(E) Z

2. If the group stays on island X for three nights, it CANNOT spend the next three days and nights on island

(A) U
(B) V
(C) W
(D) Y
(E) Z

3. Which one of the following is a possible order of islands visited in 12 days and nights?

(A) U W Y Z
(B) U V Y Z
(C) U Y V X
(D) U X Z V
(E) U W Y X

4. If the group visits island W first and can visit an island more than once, but does not use a bridge more than once, what is the greatest number of visits it can make?

(A) 5
(B) 6
(C) 7
(D) 8
(E) 9

5. Assume the group visits island X first, and does not use a bridge more than once. Assume also that the group does stay at island Y twice. What is the greatest number of different islands the group can visit?

(A) 3
(B) 4
(C) 5
(D) 6
(E) 7

Model Test 2

GO ON TO THE NEXT PAGE.

6. Assume another island, T, is added to the tour. Assume also that T is connected only to U. Which one of the following statements must be true?

   (A) On the eighth day of a tour, starting its visit at island T, the group could be on island V.
   (B) On the fifth day of a tour, starting its visit at island T, the group could be on island X.
   (C) On the seventh day of a tour, starting its visit at island T, the group could be on island U.
   (D) On the eighth day of a tour, starting its visit at island V, the group could be on island T.
   (E) On the tenth day of a tour, starting its visit at island Z, the tour group could be on island T.

Questions 7–13

On the sixth floor of an office building there are eight offices in a row, numbered from 1 to 8. Five custodians are employed to clean these eight offices. They are Alisa, Bart, Clyde, Drew, and Ethel. The maximum number of offices that can be cleaned by one custodian is two. Each office is cleaned by only one custodian. The following conditions govern the cleaning assignments:

Bart and Clyde are the only two custodians assigned to clean only one office each.
Alisa does not clean the office at either end of the row of offices.
One of the offices cleaned by Ethel is adjacent to both of the offices cleaned by Alisa.
The lower numbered office cleaned by Ethel is numbered higher than the office cleaned by Bart.
Office 7 has been assigned to Ethel.

7. If Drew cleans office 2, which one of the following CANNOT be true?

   (A) Bart cleans office 1.
   (B) Clyde cleans office 3.
   (C) Alisa cleans office 6.
   (D) Ethel cleans office 4.
   (E) Drew cleans office 4.

8. Which one of the following is true about the cleaning assignment for office 4?

   (A) The office is not cleaned by Alisa or Clyde.
   (B) The office is not cleaned by Clyde or Ethel.
   (C) The office is not cleaned by Bart or Drew.
   (D) The office is not cleaned by Alisa or Drew.
   (E) The office is not cleaned by Drew or Ethel.

9. Which one of the following represents a complete and accurate list of the offices that could be cleaned by Drew?

   (A) 1, 2, 3, 5, 6
   (B) 1, 2, 3, 5, 6, 8
   (C) 1, 2, 4, 8
   (D) 1, 2, 4, 6, 8
   (E) 2, 3, 4, 5, 6, 8

4 4 4 4 4

10. If Drew cleans office 8 and Drew and Alisa clean consecutive offices, then how many different cleaning assignments are possible?
    (A) three
    (B) four
    (C) five
    (D) six
    (E) seven

11. Consecutive offices could be cleaned by which one of the following custodians?
    (A) Alisa
    (B) Bart
    (C) Clyde
    (D) Drew
    (E) Ethel

12. Which one of the following represents a complete and accurate list of custodians who could clean office 6?
    (A) Alisa, Clyde, Drew
    (B) Bart, Clyde, Ethel
    (C) Alisa, Bart, Clyde, Ethel
    (D) Clyde, Drew, Ethel
    (E) Alisa, Clyde, Drew, Ethel

13. If both end offices are cleaned by Drew, and Alisa and Clyde clean consecutive offices, which one of the following must be true?
    (A) Alisa cleans office 6.
    (B) Bart and Clyde clean consecutive offices.
    (C) Clyde cleans an even-numbered office.
    (D) Both of Alisa's offices are numbered lower than Clyde's.
    (E) Bart cleans office 2.

Questions 14–18

Eight busts of American Presidents are to be arranged on two shelves, left to right. Each shelf accommodates exactly four busts. One shelf is directly above the other shelf. The busts are of John Adams, George Washington, Abraham Lincoln, Thomas Jefferson, James Monroe, John Kennedy, Theodore Roosevelt and Franklin Delano Roosevelt.

The Roosevelt busts may not be directly one above the other.

The bust of Kennedy must be adjacent to the bust of a Roosevelt.

The bust of Jefferson must be directly above the bust of John Adams.

The busts of Monroe, Adams, Kennedy and Franklin Delano Roosevelt must be on the bottom shelf.

The bust of Monroe must be third from the left.

14. If the bust of Theodore Roosevelt is second from the left on one shelf, which one of the following must be true?
    (A) The bust of Adams must be first on a shelf.
    (B) The bust of Adams must be third on a shelf.
    (C) The bust of Kennedy must be first on a shelf.
    (D) The bust of Kennedy must be second on a shelf.
    (E) The bust of Kennedy must be third on a shelf.

15. Which one of the following must be true about the bust of Monroe?
    (A) It is next to the bust of Adams.
    (B) It is next to the bust of Kennedy.
    (C) It is next to the bust of Franklin Delano Roosevelt.
    (D) It is directly under the bust of Lincoln.
    (E) It is directly under the bust of Theodore Roosevelt.

GO ON TO THE NEXT PAGE.

4 4 4 4 4

16. If the bust of Washington is first, directly above Kennedy's, all of the following must be true EXCEPT:
    (A) the bust of Jefferson is fourth
    (B) the bust of Theodore Roosevelt is third
    (C) the bust of Franklin Delano Roosevelt is second
    (D) the bust of Lincoln is third
    (E) the bust of Adams is fourth

17. Which one of the following is not a possible order for the busts on either shelf?
    (A) Washington, Lincoln, Theodore Roosevelt, Jefferson
    (B) Franklin Delano Roosevelt, Kennedy, Monroe, Adams
    (C) Theodore Roosevelt, Lincoln, Washington, Jefferson
    (D) Lincoln, Theodore Roosevelt, Washington, Jefferson
    (E) Kennedy, Adams, Monroe, Franklin Delano Roosevelt

18. If the bust of Lincoln is next to the bust of Jefferson, all of the following are true EXCEPT:
    (A) If the bust of Kennedy is first, the bust of Theodore Roosevelt is also first.
    (B) If the bust of Washington is first, the bust of Franklin Delano Roosevelt is also first.
    (C) If the bust of Washington is second, the bust of Kennedy is also second.
    (D) If the bust of Kennedy is second, the bust of Theodore Roosevelt is also second.
    (E) If the bust of Washington is second, the bust of Franklin Delano Roosevelt is also second.

Questions 19–24

Six houses are numbered from 1 to 6 in order from left to right. Each house is to be painted a different color. Each house is to be painted by a different painter. Each painter paints using only colors he or she likes. No two painters use the same color.

The first house is painted by a painter who likes only orange, white, and yellow.

The second house is painted by a painter who likes only blue, green, and yellow.

The third and fourth houses are painted by painters who each like only red and yellow.

The fifth house is painted by a painter who likes only blue, green, red, and yellow.

The sixth house is painted by a painter who likes only red, orange, violet, and white.

19. Which one of the following could be true?
    (A) The first house is painted yellow.
    (B) The second house is painted red.
    (C) The fifth house is painted red.
    (D) The fifth house is painted yellow.
    (E) The sixth house is painted orange.

20. What is the maximum number of possible color combinations for the six houses if orange is not used?
    (A) four
    (B) five
    (C) six
    (D) seven
    (E) eight

GO ON TO THE NEXT PAGE.

4 4 4 4 4

21. Which one of the following would provide sufficient information to determine the color of each of the six houses?
    (A) The houses that are painted blue, white, and yellow.
    (B) The houses that are painted blue, red, violet, and yellow.
    (C) The houses that are painted green, orange, red, and white.
    (D) The houses that are painted blue, green, red, and yellow.
    (E) The houses that are painted blue, green, orange, and white.

22. If the primary colors are red, blue, and yellow, and the secondary colors are green, orange, and violet, which one of the following could be true?
    (A) The second and fifth houses are painted primary colors.
    (B) The third and sixth houses are painted primary colors.
    (C) The second and fifth houses are painted secondary colors.
    (D) The first and fourth houses are painted secondary colors.
    (E) The second and sixth houses are painted secondary colors.

23. If the violet house is next to the green house and the blue house is next to the yellow house, then which one of the following must be true?
    (A) The first house is white.
    (B) The first house is orange.
    (C) The third house is red.
    (D) The fourth house is red.
    (E) The fifth house is blue.

24. Suppose that the painter of the third house also likes the color pink. If all the other conditions remain the same, then each of the following could be true EXCEPT:
    (A) The fourth house is yellow and the sixth house is red.
    (B) The second house is green and the sixth house is white.
    (C) The second house is yellow and the third house is red.
    (D) The first house is yellow and the fifth house is blue.
    (E) The first house is white and the second house is yellow.

STOP

IF YOU FINISH BEFORE TIME IS CALLED, YOU MAY CHECK YOUR WORK ON THIS SECTION ONLY. DO NOT WORK ON ANY OTHER SECTION IN THE TEST.

5 ⟨5⟩ ⟨5⟩ ⟨5⟩ 5

SECTION V

Time—35 minutes
25 Questions

Directions: In this section you will be given brief statements or passages and will be required to evaluate the reasoning involved. In some instances, more than one choice will appear to be a possible answer. You are to choose the best answer. Use common sense and reasonableness in making your selection; then mark the proper space on the answer sheet.

1. Chrysanthemums that have not been fertilized in July will normally not blossom in October. In October, the chrysanthemums did not blossom.

   With the premises given above, which one of the following would logically complete an argument?

   (A) Therefore, the chrysanthemums were not fertilized in July.
   (B) Therefore, the chrysanthemums may not have been fertilized in July.
   (C) Therefore, the chrysanthemums may blossom later in the fall.
   (D) Therefore, the chrysanthemums will blossom in the fall.
   (E) Therefore, the chrysanthemums will not blossom later in the fall.

2. When asked about the danger to public health from the spraying of pesticides by helicopters throughout the county, the County Supervisor replied, "The real danger to the public is the possibility of an infestation of harmful fruit-flies, which this spraying will prevent. Such an infestation would drive up the cost of fruits and vegetables by 15 percent."

   Which one of the following is the most serious weakness in the Supervisor's reply to the question?

   (A) He depends upon the ambiguity in the word "danger."
   (B) His response contains a self-contradiction.
   (C) He fails to support his argument concretely.
   (D) He fails to answer the question that has been asked.
   (E) His chief concern is the economic consequences of spraying.

5 ◇5◇ ◇5◇ ◇5◇ 5

3. So far this year researchers have reported the following:

Heavy coffee consumption can increase the risk of heart attacks.

Drinking a cup of coffee in the morning increases feelings of well-being and alertness.

Boiled coffee increases blood cholesterol levels.

Coffee may protect against cancer of the colon.

If all these statements are true, which one of the following conclusions can be drawn from this information?

(A) Reducing coffee consumption will make people healthier.
(B) Reducing coffee consumption will make people feel better.
(C) People at risk for heart attack should limit their coffee drinking.
(D) Percolated coffee will not affect cholesterol levels.
(E) People at risk for cancer should reduce their coffee consumption.

4. *Governor:* Compared with children in other states, infants born in California weigh more, survive the first years in greater numbers, and live longer. The hysteria about the danger of pesticides in California has attracted attention simply because a few Hollywood stars have appeared on television talk shows. Pesticides are the responsibility of the California Department of Food and Agriculture, and we can be sure its members are doing their job.

The governor's argument would be weakened if all of the following were shown to be true EXCEPT:

(A) rates of melanoma and some forms of leukemia in California are above national norms
(B) the three highest positions at the California Department of Food and Agriculture are held by farm owners
(C) synthetic pesticide residues in food cause more cancer than do "natural pesticides" that the plants themselves produce
(D) more Californians suffer the consequences of air pollution than do the citizens in any other state
(E) children of farm workers are three times more likely to suffer childhood cancers than children of urban parents

5 ◇5◇ ◇5◇ ◇5◇ 5

5. Should we allow the Fire Department to continue to underpay its women officers by using policies of promotion that favor men?

   The question above most closely resembles which one of the following in terms of its logical features?

   (A) Should the excessive tax on cigarettes, liquor, and luxury goods be unfairly increased again this year?
   (B) Should corrupt politicians be subject to the same sentencing laws as blue-collar felons?
   (C) Should the police chief be chosen by examination score regardless of gender or seniority?
   (D) Should the religious right be allowed to determine the censorship laws for all of society?
   (E) Are liberal political values an appropriate basis for all of the social values in this state?

6. If airline fares have risen, then either the cost of fuel has risen or there are no fare wars among competing companies. If there are no fare wars among competing companies, the number of airline passengers is larger than it was last year.

   According to the passage above, if there has been a rise in airline fares this month, which one of the following CANNOT be true?

   (A) There are no fare wars among competing airlines.
   (B) The cost of fuel has risen, and the number of passengers is the same as last year.
   (C) The cost of fuel has risen, there are no fare wars, and the number of passengers is larger than it was last year.
   (D) There are no fare wars, and the number of passengers is larger than it was last year.
   (E) The cost of fuel has risen, there are no fare wars, and the number of passengers is smaller than it was last year.

7. Only 75 years ago, the best fishing in the world was the Grand Banks of the North Atlantic. But now overfishing and man's pollution have decimated the area. There will be no fishing industry in the Americas in a very few years. The waters off Newfoundland now yield less than half the catch of five years ago, and less than one quarter of the total of ten years ago. The cod has almost disappeared. The numbers of fishermen in Newfoundland and New England have declined, and their yearly earnings are now at an all-time low. Yet radar has made fishing methods more efficient than ever.

   Which one of the following identifies most clearly a faulty assumption in the reasoning of this passage?

   (A) Ten years is too short a time period to use to draw conclusions about the natural world.
   (B) The argument assumes that the waters off Newfoundland are representative of all the American oceans.
   (C) The pollution of the sea may have been caused by natural as well as by human forces.
   (D) The argument does not allow for the possibility that the catch may increase in size in the next five years.
   (E) The argument fails to consider that the decline in the catch may be due to factors other than pollution.

GO ON TO THE NEXT PAGE.

5 ◇5◇ ◇5◇ ◇5◇ **5**

8. A cigarette advertisement in a magazine asks, "What do gremlins, the Loch Ness monster, and a filter cigarette claiming 'great taste' have in common?" The answer is "You've heard of all of them, but don't really believe they exist." The advertisement contains no pictures and no additional text except the words Gold Star Cigarettes and the Surgeon General's warning in a box in the lower corner.

   Which one of the following conclusions can be drawn from the information given above?

   (A) Cigarette advertising depends upon visual appeal to create images for specific brands.
   (B) All cigarette advertising depends on praising a specific brand.
   (C) Gold Star Cigarettes are non-filters.
   (D) The writers of this advertisement do not believe in advertising.
   (E) The writers of this advertisement do not believe the Surgeon General's warning is true.

9. The traffic on the Imperial Highway has always been slowed by the dangerous curves in the road. It was built when cars were much smaller and less powerful, and very few drivers traveled between Imperial City and Fremont. All this has changed. The cost of widening and straightening the road would now be many times greater than building the proposed new toll road on the borders of the Imperial Wetlands reserve. Environmentalists fear the construction noise and waste will harm the wildlife in the reserve, and have urged that the toll road not be constructed.

   Which one of the following, if true, would most strengthen the case of the environmentalists?

   (A) None of the animals living in the Imperial Wetlands is on the list of endangered species.
   (B) The traffic congestion on the Imperial Highway increases each year.
   (C) The cost of building the new road will be amortized in ten years by the tolls collected.
   (D) There are several less direct routes the toll road could take between Fremont and Imperial City.
   (E) The environmentalists threaten to bring a lawsuit in federal court to halt construction of the road.

Model Test 2

GO ON TO THE NEXT PAGE.

10. Despite the very large increase in the federal tax on luxury items, the value of the stock of Harry Evans, Inc., seller of the world's most expensive jewelry, continues to rise. Six months after the introduction of the tax, Evans's stock is at an all-time high. Moreover, sales in the United States continue to increase. In other countries, where Evans does 30 percent of its business, there have been no rises in excise taxes and the company will open new stores in Tokyo, Monte Carlo, and Singapore. According to a company spokesperson, ____________.

    Which one of the following most logically completes this paragraph?

    (A) American customers who can afford to shop at Evans are not likely to be deterred by a rise in luxury taxes
    (B) American customers are expected to spend far less at Evans because of the tax rise
    (C) American sales are not significant enough to affect the overall profits of the firm
    (D) the company will probably be forced to close most of its stores in America
    (E) state taxes are more likely to influence jewelry sales than federal taxes

11. *Speaker:* A recent study of cigarette smokers has shown that, of cancer patients who are heavy smokers of unfiltered cigarettes, 40 percent will die of the disease. For cancer patients who are light smokers of filter cigarettes, the percentage is 25 percent.

    Which one of the following conclusions can be drawn from the information above?

    (A) There are more heavy smokers of unfiltered cigarettes than light smokers of filter cigarettes.
    (B) More heavy smokers of unfiltered cigarettes die of cancer than light smokers of filter cigarettes.
    (C) A heavy smoker of unfiltered cigarettes who has cancer is more likely to die than a light smoker of unfiltered cigarettes.
    (D) A heavy smoker of unfiltered cigarettes who has cancer may be more likely to die than a light smoker of unfiltered cigarettes.
    (E) A heavy smoker of unfiltered cigarettes who has cancer is more likely to die than a light smoker of filtered cigarettes who has cancer.

GO ON TO THE NEXT PAGE.

5 5 5 5 5

Questions 12–13

Archeologists have come to the support of Arctic anthropologists. A small minority of anthropologists assert that Stone Age tribes of the Arctic domesticated wolves and trained them to haul sleds. Excavations have recently found evidence to support this claim. Archeologists have found wolf bones near the site of a Stone Age village. They have also found walrus bones that might have been used on primitive sleds. The small minority of anthropologists believe that their theories have been proved.

12. Which one of the following is true of the evidence cited in the paragraph above?
    (A) It is not relevant to the anthropologists' conclusions.
    (B) It conclusively contradicts the anthropologists' conclusions.
    (C) It neither supports nor refutes the anthropologists' conclusions positively.
    (D) It supports the anthropologists' conclusions authoritatively.
    (E) It conclusively supports only a part of the anthropologists' conclusions.

13. Which one of the following, if true, would best support the theory of the anthropologists?
    (A) Wolves are known to have fed upon the garbage of villages in northern Europe.
    (B) Wolves as a species are easily domesticated and trained.
    (C) Almost all Stone Age Arctic tools were made of walrus bone.
    (D) Stone Age villages were located on the migration routes of the caribou herds upon which wolves preyed.
    (E) The earliest sled part found in the Arctic was made one thousand years after the Stone Age.

Questions 14–15

The following criticism of a self-portrait by Vincent van Gogh appeared in a magazine in 1917:

"Here we have a work of art which is so self-evidently a degenerate work by a degenerate artist that we need not say anything about the inept creation. It is safe to say that if we were to meet in our dreams such a villainous looking jailbird with such a deformed Neanderthal skull, degenerate ears, hobo beard and insane glare, it would certainly give us a nightmare."

14. The author of this passage makes his point by using
    (A) invective
    (B) analogy
    (C) citation of authority
    (D) paradox
    (E) example

15. In relation to the first sentence of the quotation, the second sentence is
    (A) an example of an effect following a cause
    (B) a specific derived from a general principle
    (C) a logical conclusion
    (D) a contradiction
    (E) a personal experience in support of a generalization

Model Test 2

GO ON TO THE NEXT PAGE.

16. A company called Popcorn Packaging is promoting the use of popcorn as a cushioning material in packing. Unlike the commonly used Styrofoam beads or chips, popcorn can be recycled as a food for birds or squirrels and can serve as a garden mulch. Used out of doors, popcorn disappears almost overnight, while the Styrofoam beads may be in the environment for centuries. Even before we became ecology conscious, popcorn was used in packing in the 1940s. Since it now costs less to produce than Styrofoam, there is every reason to return to wide-scale use of packaging by popcorn.

    Which one of the following, if true, would most seriously weaken the author's argument?

    (A) A package using popcorn as a cushioning material will weigh less than a package using Styrofoam beads.
    (B) Popcorn may attract rodents and insects.
    (C) A large number of squirrels can damage a garden by consuming flowering bulbs.
    (D) Less than 1 percent of the material now used for package cushioning is recycled.
    (E) Styrofoam replaced popcorn in the early 1950s because it was cheaper to produce.

17. This produce stand sells fruits and vegetables. All fruits are delicious, and all vegetables are rich in vitamins. Every food that is vitamin-rich is delicious, so everything sold at this stand is delicious.

    Which one of the following assumptions is necessary to make the conclusion in the argument above logically correct?

    (A) The stand sells many fruits and vegetables.
    (B) This produce stand sells only fruits and vegetables.
    (C) Something cannot be both vitamin-rich and delicious.
    (D) Some stands sell fruits that are not delicious.
    (E) Some vegetables are delicious.

GO ON TO THE NEXT PAGE.

5 5 5 5 5

18. Voter turnout in primary elections has declined steadily from 1982 to 1990. In 1990, more than 80 percent of the Americans eligible to vote failed to do so. Only 11.9 percent of the Democrats and 7.7 percent of the Republicans went to the polls. The largest number of voters turned out for elections in the District of Columbia (28 percent) and in Massachusetts, where the 32 percent total was the highest since 1962. In each of the twenty-four other states holding elections, the number of voters was smaller than it had been in 1986 and 1982.

    Based on the information in this passage, which one of the following must be true?

    (A) The turnout in the District of Columbia was affected by favorable weather conditions.
    (B) Fewer than 20 percent of the eligible major-party voters voted in the 24 states other than Massachusetts.
    (C) The voter turnout in Massachusetts is always higher than the turnouts in other states.
    (D) The voter turnout decline is a signal of a nationwide voter rebellion.
    (E) More voters cast their votes in general elections than in primary elections.

19. Each year the number of schools that no longer allow smoking on school property grows larger. Four states, New Jersey, Kansas, Utah, and New Hampshire, now require tobacco-free schools. The Tobacco Institute has fought against regulations restricting smoking everywhere from airlines to restaurants on the grounds that they trample on the rights of smokers, but is conspicuously absent from school board lobbyists. Tobacco industry spokesmen have denounced the rules treating teachers like children but have said they will not go on record to defend policies that affect children.

    Which one of the following, if true, best accounts for the Tobacco Institute's behavior?

    (A) The tobacco industry is presently fighting the charge that it attempts to recruit new smokers among minors.
    (B) The tobacco industry can depend on continued high profits from overseas operations, where restrictions do not exist.
    (C) Most tobacco companies are highly diversified corporations whose profits no longer depend wholly on tobacco products.
    (D) The tobacco industry believes the rights of children to be equal to the rights of adults.
    (E) The tobacco industry agrees with the schools that have rules against tobacco.

Model Test 2

GO ON TO THE NEXT PAGE.

Questions 20–21

A number of lawsuits have been brought against popular singing groups charging that suicidal themes in their songs have led to teenage suicides. So far, the courts have found that the lyrics are protected by the First Amendment. But what if this should change, and a court decides that suicidal themes in popular songs are dangerous? In fact, the songs that have been charged so far are antisuicide; they present sardonically the self-destructive behavior of drinking, drugs, and escape by death. They describe a pitiful state of mind, but they do not endorse it.

Blaming suicide on the arts is nothing new. In the late eighteenth century, Goethe's popular novel Werther was said to be the cause of a rash of suicides in imitation of the novel's hero. If we begin to hold suicide in books or music responsible for suicides in real life, the operas of Verdi and Puccini will have to go, and Romeo and Juliet and Julius Caesar will disappear from high school reading lists.

20. The author of this passage argues by

(A) providing examples to support two opposing positions
(B) using an observation to undermine a theoretical principle
(C) disputing an interpretation of evidence cited by those with an opposing view
(D) predicting personal experience from a general principle
(E) accusing the opposing side of using inaccurate statistical information

21. Which one of the following is an assumption necessary to the author's argument?

(A) A lyric presenting suicide in a favorable light should not have First Amendment protection.
(B) Literature or music cannot directly influence human behavior.
(C) Many record albums already carry labels warning purchasers of their dangerous contents.
(D) The audience, not the performer, is responsible for the audience's actions.
(E) Freedom of speech is the most threatened of our personal freedoms.

22. Haven't you at some time had a favorite song or book or film that was not well known but later became popular? And didn't you feel somehow betrayed and resentful when what you had thought was unique became commonplace? On a larger scale, the same thing happens to novelists or film makers who have enjoyed critical esteem without popular success. Let them become public sensations, and the critics who praised their work will attack them virulently.

This paragraph most likely introduces an article on a film maker who has made a

(A) series of commercially successful films
(B) series of commercially unsuccessful films
(C) single film, a commercial success
(D) single film, a commercial failure
(E) critical success and a commercial success

GO ON TO THE NEXT PAGE.

23. Studies of the effects of drinking four or more cups of coffee per day have shown that coffee consumption increases work efficiency by improving the ability to process information. People who drink two cups of coffee in the morning are more alert and feel better than those who do not. But there are other factors to be considered.

Which one of the following sentences would provide the most logical continuation of this paragraph?

(A) Contrary to popular belief, drinking coffee cannot erase the effect of alcohol.
(B) Some studies suggest that coffee drinking will protect against cancer of the colon.
(C) Combined with the stress of heavy exercise, coffee drinking may be the cause of higher blood pressure.
(D) Drinking two or more cups of coffee per day increases the risk of heart attacks in men.
(E) Many people cannot distinguish between the taste of decaffeinated and that of regular coffee.

24. All of the members of the chorus will sing in the performance of the oratorio *Messiah*. Some of these are highly trained professionals, some are gifted amateurs, and some are singers of mediocre ability.

If the statements above are true, which one of the following must also be true?

(A) *Messiah* will be performed by highly trained professionals, gifted amateurs, and some singers of mediocre ability.
(B) Some of the members of the chorus are not highly trained professionals, gifted amateurs, or singers of mediocre ability.
(C) *Messiah* will be performed by some highly trained professionals, but not all of them are in the chorus.
(D) Not all of those in the chorus who are gifted amateurs will perform in the oratorio.
(E) All of those who will perform *Messiah* are members of the chorus.

25. *Politician*: The passage of laws that limit elected officials to one or two terms in office is an admission that voters are civic fools, unable to tell good lawmakers from bad ones. To ban all the politicians when the real intention is to get rid of the corrupt ones is to burn the house down to get rid of the vermin.

The author of this passage makes his point chiefly by

(A) defining a key term
(B) exposing a self-contradiction
(C) drawing an analogy
(D) questioning the evidence of his opponents
(E) citing an example

STOP

IF YOU FINISH BEFORE TIME IS CALLED,
YOU MAY CHECK YOUR WORK ON THIS SECTION ONLY.
DO NOT WORK ON ANY OTHER SECTION IN THE TEST.

Writing Sample

Directions: You have 35 minutes to write an essay in response to a given topic. Take a few minutes to plan your work before you begin writing. DO NOT WRITE ON A TOPIC OF YOUR OWN CHOICE. ESSAYS THAT DO NOT ADDRESS THE GIVEN TOPIC ARE UNACCEPTABLE.

The quality of your writing is more important than the length of your response or the content. Pay attention to organization, appropriate diction, and correct usage. You will not be expected to display any specialized knowledge in your response, nor will you be expected to write a "perfect" essay; law schools understand that you are writing under a time constraint, and will allow for the minor lapses in writing ability that might occur under this circumstance.

Only the lined area on your response sheets will be reproduced for the law schools, so do not write outside this space. Make sure your handwriting is legible.

Scratch Paper

Do not write your essay in this space

Sample Topic

Read the following descriptions of Jackson and Brown. *Then, in the space provided, write an argument for deciding which of the two should be assigned the responsibility of hiring teachers for the Hapsville School System.* The following criteria are relevant to your decision:

- The taxpayers want educators who can instill in students the desire to learn and an excitement for knowledge, something that has been lacking in their schools.
- A majority of students' parents believe that their children should be equipped, upon graduation, to earn a living, and thus favor a more trade-oriented (rather than academic) approach to schooling.

JACKSON was appointed as Superintendent of Schools by the Hapsville School Board, which was elected by the community's taxpayers. As a 30-year resident of Hapsville (population 45,000), Jackson is unique in that he holds not only a doctorate in administration, but also a master's degree in education. He taught in the Hapsville schools for 16 years until he served on the state Commission on Education. He has always favored a progressive approach to education, although it may not always have been popular with the town's population. Through the years he has brought many fine teachers to the faculty, because of his willingness to encourage new classroom techniques.

BROWN is a 52-year resident of Hapsville, having been born in the same house in which he now lives. He was elected to the School Board 13 years ago, and continues to win nearly unanimous reelection every two years. As the foremost developer in the Four Counties area, Mr. Brown has had the opportunity to build hundreds of new homes in the six housing developments he's planned and actualized, and, in the interim, has employed hundreds of Hapsville residents as carpenters, electricians, plumbers, architects, landscapers, groundskeepers, etc. As such, he is held in high esteem by most of the town, not only for his providing livelihoods for many, but also for his fair and realistic outlook on life. Mr. Brown feels strongly that the key to life is having a marketable skill.

Scratch Paper

Do not write your essay in this space

Answer Key

Section I: Reading Comprehension

1. E	6. A	11. C	16. E	21. B	26. D
2. C	7. A	12. B	17. A	22. D	27. A
3. D	8. C	13. C	18. B	23. A	28. B
4. A	9. D	14. A	19. E	24. E	
5. B	10. E	15. C	20. D	25. B	

Section II: Analytical Reasoning

1. C	5. D	9. D	13. C	17. C	21. B
2. A	6. B	10. A	14. E	18. D	22. D
3. E	7. E	11. E	15. D	19. C	23. D
4. C	8. E	12. D	16. C	20. C	24. C

Section III: Logical Reasoning

1. C	6. A	11. E	16. B	21. E	26. B
2. B	7. B	12. C	17. B	22. E	
3. E	8. C	13. B	18. A	23. B	
4. D	9. B	14. C	19. E	24. E	
5. D	10. E	15. E	20. C	25. D	

Section IV: Analytical Reasoning

1. B	5. D	9. B	13. E	17. E	21. C
2. B	6. E	10. D	14. D	18. C	22. E
3. D	7. E	11. D	15. A	19. E	23. D
4. E	8. C	12. A	16. D	20. A	24. C

Section V: Logical Reasoning

1. B	6. E	11. E	16. B	21. D
2. D	7. B	12. C	17. B	22. E
3. C	8. C	13. B	18. B	23. D
4. D	9. D	14. A	19. A	24. A
5. A	10. A	15. D	20. C	25. C

Model Test Analysis

Doing model exams and understanding the explanations afterwards are, of course, important in acquainting you with typical LSAT question types and successful approaches to the questions. However, another benefit of carefully analyzing these model tests is to understand the kinds of errors you are making and thus work to minimize them. For instance, if a very high percentage of your incorrect answers is due to "careless error" or "misread problem" then perhaps you are working much too fast and should slow your pace accordingly. If your incorrect answers are due primarily to "lack of knowledge," then a careful rereading and reworking of the appropriate question-type chapter may be in order. Or, if you find that you aren't completing a large number of questions because of lack of time, you may need to either increase your speed or learn to use the "one-check, two-check" technique more effectively.

This kind of analysis of the model tests will enable you to identify your particular weaknesses and thus remedy them.

MODEL TEST TWO ANALYSIS

Section	Total Number of Questions	Number Correct	Number Incorrect	Number Unanswered*
I. Reading Comprehension	28			
II. Analytical Reasoning	24			
III. Logical Reasoning	26			
IV. Analytical Reasoning	24			
V. Logical Reasoning	25			
Writing Sample				
TOTALS:	127			

*At this stage in your preparation, you should not be leaving any blank answer spaces. At least fill in a guess, as there is no penalty for a wrong answer.

REASONS FOR INCORRECT ANSWERS

You may wish to evaluate the explanations before completing this chart.

Section	Total Number Incorrect	Lack of Knowledge	Misread Problem	Careless Error	Unanswered or Wrong Guess
I. Reading Comprehension					
II. Analytical Reasoning					
III. Logical Reasoning					
IV. Analytical Reasoning					
V. Logical Reasoning					
TOTALS:					

Answers Explained

Section I

Passage 1

1. **(E)** Each of the first four cases is public or quasi-public land. The last is private, not likely to be open to the general public and therefore the owner may deny free speech on the property.

2. **(C)** In this instance, the property is clearly private; in the other cases, it is not always clear whether the property is public or private.

3. **(D)** The nature or character of the owner of the property is not a factor mentioned by the passage. All of the four other options are alluded to in the opening paragraphs of the passage.

4. **(A)** The author approvingly quotes the words of a mall chairman in support of this position. Choice (E) may not be true if the charity seekers are offensive.

5. **(B)** The passage cites Lord Chief Justice Hale's remarks of 1675. (C) and (D) are false and the passage does not discuss current practice in Canada and Great Britain (E).

6. **(A)** The passage concludes with Justice Black's remarks on the "preferred position" of First Amendment freedoms.

Passage 2

7. **(A)** Both passages agree that a lack of copyright laws on the Internet means less profit for creators, and therefore (A) is the best answer. This fact is a main point in Passage A, while the author of Passage B believes profit shouldn't be the "sole consideration" (lines 63–64). The passages do not agree on the statements in any of the other choices. Both passages see that there are problems with current copyright laws on the Internet, but Passage A sees these problems as a matter of enforcement, not limiting the free flow of information.

8. **(C)** Choice (C) best summarizes the main idea in each passage. The argument throughout Passage A is that using material on the Internet without regard to copyright laws is stealing and will therefore discourage creators of original material, while the author of Passage B focuses on the Internet as a "powerful new force" for passing on ideas, and therefore it shouldn't be subject to barriers. (E) may seem like a good answer, but the author of Passage B isn't opposed to copy-

right laws because they may favor business; rather, the passage says that financial motives shouldn't be primary.

9. **(D)** The author of Passage B would be most likely to identify (D) as the basis of the arguments in Passage A. The author of Passage A in lines 13–15, 22–23, and 27–29 indicates that copyright laws ensure profits for creators. (A) is the second-best answer, since Passage A in lines 10–11 cites the fact that for over 200 years copyright laws have protected intellectual property. But it isn't this "tradition" that the author is using as a basis of argument but rather the financial considerations concerning copyright. (C) is too broad, and (B) and (E) are irrelevant.

10. **(E)** Choice (E) is the best answer. This is the only specific provision of the Act that is covered in Passage A (lines 23–25). (B) is contradicted in both passages, and although AOL and Earthlink are mentioned, the passage states they are exempted by the Act from copyright violations on their networks.

11. **(C)** The best meaning for "cached" here is (C). "Cached" is a commonly used term in the computer world. It is also, in context, the meaning that makes most sense.

12. **(B)** The best meaning for *inimical* in this context is (B). The author's point throughout the passage is that the Internet encourages the free flow of information, and the concept of exclusive ownership is "unfriendly" to such a technology. One dictionary definition of inimical is "reflecting or indicating hostility." This clearly rules out (D) and (E), and neither (A) nor (B) makes sense in context.

13. **(C)** Choice (C) is the best answer (lines 105–110). Although Google undoubtedly had many objections, it is the virtually impossible task of compliance that is cited in the submission. Beyond the issue of compliance, Google stated that the law would condemn Australia to a "pre-Internet era," but this is not one of the choices given.

Passage 3

14. **(A)** The author is obviously most concerned with the work of historians and the current state of written history, which is what prompts his discussion of fiction in relation to history. See lines 4–6, 14–16, 44–49, 54–59. Literature and literary concerns (C) are secondary.

15. **(C)** See lines 57–58: ". . . their abandonment of the narrative style. . . ." A decline in the writing ability of historians (E) is not implied. And although the author does mention the movies and television, he does not attribute the growth of fictional history to an increase in their audiences (B).

16. **(E)** This attitude is clearly stated in lines 41–44. (B) may seem correct, but the author does not say that fictional history on its own has won the audience away from traditional history. On the contrary, he suggests that professional historians themselves may be partly responsible for the growth of fictional history (lines 54–57).

17. **(A)** This book would most clearly fit the definition of fictional history given in lines 29–33. According to the author, it is fictional history that causes the greatest confusion (lines 41–44). (B) and (C) would be classified as historical fiction according to the author's definitions, and (D) and (E) as nonfiction.

18. **(B)** The second paragraph is devoted to defining and contrasting the two terms. (D) might be considered a possible answer but is less clear and specific. The other answers are simply inaccurate.

19. **(E)** Nothing in the passage suggests a judgment of history taught in the schools. The other statements are all supported in the passage: (A)—lines 14–16; (B)—lines 54–58; (C)—lines 44–49; (D)—lines 10–14.

20. **(D)** Throughout the passage the author is most concerned with the growth of fictional history and its effects. None of the other answers presents his attitude as clearly, though (C) does define fictional history.

21. **(B)** The author is obviously concerned with the "mischief" that the mixture of history with fiction can cause. However, he presents his concern in a moderate fashion. He is not hostile, he does not preach, he is not pedantic, and he does not display irony. (E) suggests an elevated tone not present in the passage.

Passage 4

22. **(D)** The author simply presents facts, both historical and modern, concerning faith healing and doesn't necessarily suggest that it is effective, only that some aspects of it now appear in modern medical practice. All of the other choices suggest opinions not given by the author or facts not in evidence in the passage.
23. **(A)** "Charlatans" are mentioned in the passage only in the context of what "most of modern society is convinced" of, but the author does not indicate that it is true or proven that faith healing is practiced by charlatans. Choice (C) is suggested by the passage; the term *holistic* is used in the discussion of modern medicine. Note that it would be incorrect if it said "*only* a modern term," which is not suggested.
24. **(E)** The final paragraph discusses the modern medical world and its inclusion of certain elements of faith healing. It doesn't deal with historical attitudes at all, choices (A) and (C), or with scientific objections (D). Although it mentions spirituality and faith (B), that choice is too narrow to best describe the purpose of the entire paragraph.
25. **(B)** In the last paragraph, the author writes that "certain medicinal herbs used by ancient healers, 'medicines' once ridiculed, have now been found to have curative powers previously unknown and unappreciated." In mentioning that fact, it is likely that the author would appreciate open-minded behavior on the part of scientists and their not dismissing a drug or procedure simply because it has not yet been fully tested.
26. **(D)** Because holistic medicine practitioners attempt to treat the "whole" person, they are likely to investigate not only the physical condition of their patients but also the psychological condition. The fact that an individual being treated might disagree with the importance of the "will to live" would not logically be likely to keep practitioners from conducting that investigation in some manner in order to do their job as they feel appropriate. We have no information from the passage that holistic practitioners are necessarily aware of the lost opportunities in finding medicines (A); that trained psychological personnel would be involved (B), although one could assume they *might* be; or that patients would be referred to faith healers (C). Holistic practitioners and ancient faith healers *do* have something in common (E)—they are both concerned with the affect of the mind on the state of the body.
27. **(A)** Faith healers would be unlikely to rely solely on physical intervention in a disease. From the passage, it is clear that modern practitioners of faith healing "*most* often promote a combination of spirituality . . . and science," so they might well refer a patient for long-term physical care (E), but it is *not* clear that *all* of them involve science in their treatment, so it is likely that some would engage in the activities of (B) and (D). Given the information, it's likely that *all* such practitioners would engage in (C), creating a comfortable psychological atmosphere so as to understand the patient's state of mind in order to improve it.
28. **(B)** The author's tone is factual, presenting information for the reader about faith healing practices and the place in modern medicine that some of them might have. The author isn't promoting a particular point of view concerning faith healing, (C) and (D), or particularly addressing readers looking for medical alternatives (E). Although there is some comparison of past practices with modern ones, in that modern practices often accept hard science as well, choice (A), this choice is too narrow to be the best answer.

Section II

Answers 1–6

From the information given, you could have made the following diagram:

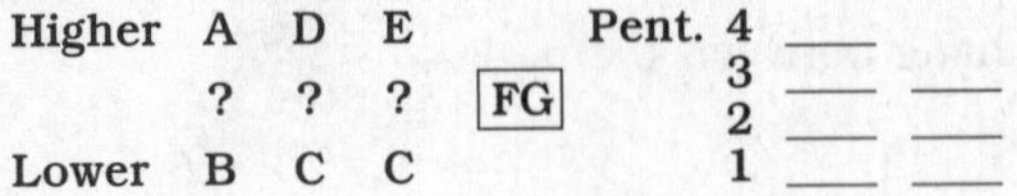

1. (C) Since F and G are on the same floor, they can't be on 4. Since B and C are below A or D/E, they can't be on 4; therefore only A, D, or E can be on 4.
2. (A) If F's apartment is on 2, so is G's. For B and C to be below A, D, and E, B and C must be on 1 and A, D, and E on 3 and 4, but we don't know exactly where on 3/4.
3. (E) If D is on 4, G (and F) can be on 3, 2, or 1.

D	D	D
FG	AE	AE
AE	FG	BC
BC	BC	FG

4. (C) If D and E are on the same floor, A must be on 4. All the other answers are possible but not certain.
5. (D) If A is on 4 or C on 1, the arrangement must be either

A		A
FG	or	DE
DE		FG
BC		BC

6. (B) A and E can be on the same floor if D is on 4.

D		D
AE	or	AE
FG		BC
BC		FG

Answers 7–12

From the information given, you may have constructed a simple grouping display of information similar to this:

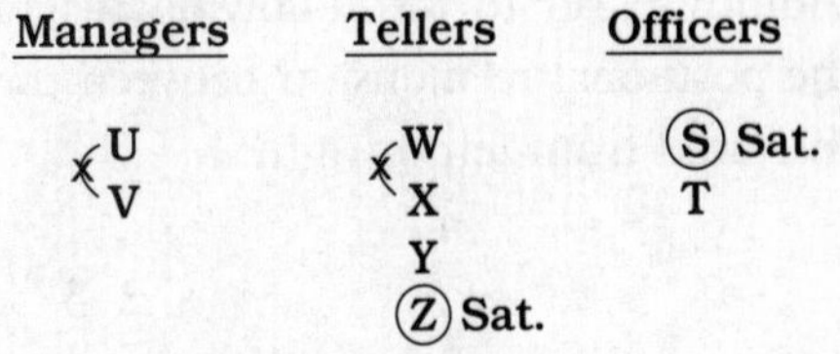

Another possible display might look like this:

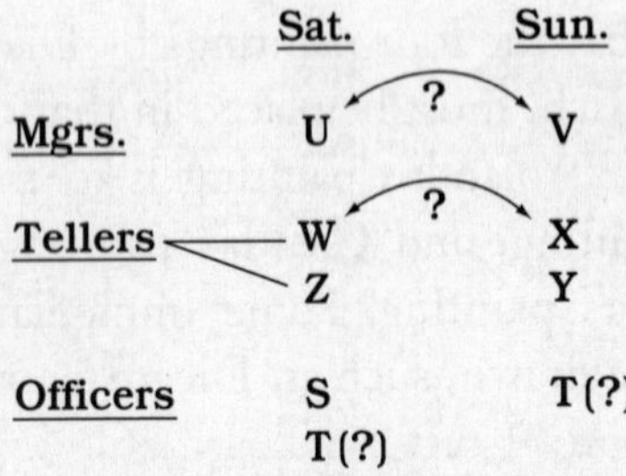

7. (E) From the original information, a manager must be on duty each day and the managers cannot work on the same day. Therefore (A) must be true. (E) does not have to be true, since U's schedule has no bearing on X's schedule. Since W and X will not work on the same day, (B) must also be true. There is no restriction placed on T.
8. (E) V, W, Z, S can work on Saturday without breaking any of the conditions given. Choice (A) is missing a manager. Choice (B) has two managers working on the same day. Choices (C) and (D) have W and X working on the same day.
9. (D) Five employees, U or V, X or W, Z, S, and T are the greatest number to work on Saturday.
10. (A) Since W and X will not work on the same day, (A) must be true. (B) is false since Y must work on Sunday. (C) could be true. Since W's schedule has no effect on Z and U, (D) and (E) may be true or false.
11. (E) Since no employee can work on consecutive days, and there are four tellers, then two must work on Saturday.

12. **(D)** U, V, W, X, Y, Z, and T have the possibility of working on Sunday; S and Z do not.

Answers 13–19

The conditions lead to the following diagram that shows the positional relationship between the paintings, illustrated from left to right.

```
|—Y→                    1 2 3 4 5 6
D   F    T    R
←G—|
```

It is clear that the four paintings by Diego, Frank, Tina, and Rich, must be placed in that order from left to right. Yolanda's painting is to the right of Diego's painting, and Glenda's painting is to the left of Tina's painting. Some immediate conclusions can be drawn, such as, Diego's painting must be in position #1 or #2.

Although you probably wouldn't have the time to do a complete analysis at the beginning of the set, some other conclusions that you could draw include: Tina's painting must be in position #4 (if Yolanda's painting is to the right of Tina's painting) or #5 (if only Rich's painting is to its right). Yolanda's painting could be in positions #2–#6, and Glenda's painting could be in positions #1–#4.

13. **(C)** (C) cannot be true since there are only two positions to the right of Glenda's position, positions #5 and #6, and they must be occupied by Tina's and Rich's paintings. There is no room for Yolanda's painting. The other four choice are possible as shown below:

	1	2	3	4	5	6	
(A)	D	F	Y	G	T	R	
(B)	D	Y	F	G	T	R	
(C)				G	T	R	Y?
(D)	D	Y	F	G	T	R	
(E)	D	Y	F	G	T	R	

14. **(E)** Glenda's painting must hang to the left of Tina's painting, and Yolanda's painting must hang to the right of Diego's painting. Therefore, Glenda's painting could be in position #1, and Yolanda's painting could be in position #6. Therefore, four paintings could hang between them.

1	2	3	4	5	6
G	D	F	T	R	Y

15. **(D)** Diego's painting must hang to the left of Frank's painting. Since Frank's painting is in position #2, Diego's painting must be in position #1. At this point you should scan the answers looking for Diego. (D) is correct. Go on to the next question. But for your information, (A) is not correct, since Tina's painting could be in position #4 with Yolanda's painting in position #5. (B) is not correct, since Glenda's painting could be in position #4. (C) is not correct, since Rich's painting could be in position #5 with Yolanda's painting in position #6. (E) is not correct, since Yolanda's painting could be in positions #3–#6.

16. **(C)** If Yolanda's painting is hanging to the left of Frank's painting, then there are four paintings to the left of Tina's painting. This implies that Tina's painting must be in position #5 and Rich's painting must be in position #6. Therefore, (C) is correct. Since Glenda's painting can be positioned anywhere to the left of Tina's painting, it could be between any of the other pairs. Thus, (A), (B), (D), and (E), could be true, but they do not have to be true. For your information, the following four possibilities exist:

1	2	3	4	5	6
G	D	F	Y	T	R
D	G	F	Y	T	R
D	F	G	Y	T	R
D	F	Y	G	T	R

17. **(C)** Choice C results in two possible arrangements. Choices A, B, D, and E, result in only one possible arrangement.

	1	2	3	4	5	6
(A)	G	D	Y	F	T	R
(B)	D	Y	F	G	T	R
(C)	D	Y	F	G	T	R
(C)	D	G	F	Y	T	R
(D)	D	F	G	T	Y	R
(E)	D	F	Y	G	T	R

18. **(D)** Since Glenda's painting is hanging to the left of Tina's painting, and Yolanda's painting is hanging to the right of Diego's painting, there are four possible arrangements:

1	2	3	4	5	6
D	F	Y	G	T	R
D	F	G	Y	T	R
D	Y	G	F	T	R
D	G	Y	F	T	R

19. **(C)** (C) cannot be true since the only painting that can hang to the left of Diego's painting is Glenda's painting. The other choices are possible as illustrated.

	1	2	3	4	5	6
(A)	D	Y	F	G	T	R
(B)	D	Y	G	F	T	R
(D)	D	G	F	Y	T	R
(E)	D	G	F	T	R	Y

Answers 20–24

Drawing a diagram, below, will help answer the questions.

	EVENTS				
	1	2	3	4	5
RED	G	—	G	—	G
BLUE	—	B/S	—	B/S	—
GREEN					
YELLOW					

Since the red team wins only 3 gold medals, it must win gold medals in events 1, 3, and 5, since no team wins gold medals in consecutive events. Also, note that since blue wins only two medals (neither of them gold), it must have won medals in events 2 and 4, so that it didn't fail to win a medal within two consecutive events. Be aware then that green and yellow, therefore, must each have won medals in all five events.

20. **(C)** If the green team wins only one gold medal, there remains only one gold medal, which the yellow team must win.

21. **(B)** Since three medals are given for each event, and, according to our diagram from the facts, red and blue already account for their total awards with one medal in each event, the other two medals in each event must go to yellow and green. Thus, yellow and green will each be awarded five medals.

22. **(D)** By completing the chart such that the yellow team wins five silver medals, we can see that green must win two gold and three bronze medals.

	1	2	3	4	5
RED	G	—	G	—	G
BLUE	—	B/S	—	B/S	—
GREEN					
YELLOW	S	S	S	S	S

23. **(D)** We know choices (A) and (B) are both true: Both the green and yellow teams each must win five medals. Therefore, (E) is also true. Choice (C) is true because three of the gold medals are already won by the red team; since blue doesn't win gold, if green wins one gold, yellow wins the remaining gold medal. Choice (D) is not true: if the green team wins only one silver medal, the yellow team must win at least two silver medals.

Model Test 2

24. (C) If a fifth team enters all events and wins only three consecutive silver medals, it must win the silver in events 2, 3, and 4, so that it does not fail to win a medal within two consecutive events. Therefore, our diagram would look like this:

	1	2	3	4	5
RED	G	—	G	—	G
BLUE	—	B	—	B	—
GREEN					
YELLOW					
ORANGE	—	S	S	S	—

Therefore, if yellow wins a gold in the 2nd event, green must win a medal in the 3rd event (since no team fails to win a medal within two consecutive events). Thus, green must win a bronze in the 3rd event.

Section III

1. (C) The passage is more restrained in its criticism than (A) or (B), while (D) and (E) are only elements of the paragraph, not its main point.

2. (B) By urging moviegoers to patronize films in order to influence academy judges, the author reveals his assumption that the academy will be influenced by the number of people paying to see a movie.

3. (E) Bob's answer shows that he thinks that people other than teachers are mean. His thought was that Andy meant otherwise.

4. (D) The author's concluding contention is that Roosevelt was not only a good marksman, but also an intellectually curious and patient man. If Roosevelt was known to leave safaris which were not immediately productive, this fact would substantially weaken the author's contention about Roosevelt's "patient observation."

5. (D) The words "because of a recent cut in state funding of our program" indicate that another criterion was used in determining entering class size besides candidates' scores and grades, namely, the financial situation of the college. The words seriously in choice (B) and severe in choice (E) are not necessarily supported by the passage, and thus make those choices incorrect. Since grade point average is only one of several criteria for admission, we cannot deduce (A) with certainty.

6. (A) This sentence not only fits well stylistically but completes the thought of the passage by tying it into the opening statement.

7. (B) The author of this passage actually defines conscience as the ability to sense right and wrong.

8. (C) The main point of the paragraph is the need for campaign reform. Choice (D) supports the argument, while the other three choices are assumptions that might arise, but these are not the main point of the paragraph.

9. (B) This choice offers the most thorough and comprehensive evidence that the viewing of violent television precedes criminal behavior. (A) is not the best choice because it describes viewing habits that follow rather than precede criminal behavior.

10. (E) The use of *overwhelming* leaves the evidence unspecified, thus opening to challenge the extent and nature of the report's data.

11. (E) All of the first four statements can be used to explain the underreporting. In (D), for example, if the size of police departments has declined, they would have less manpower available to gather and report information. (E) is a reason against underreporting rather than an explanation for it.

12. (C) The argument uses the case of the county to call the state figures into question. The underreported figures are "less evidence."

13. (B) If the experiences and lifestyle of the Aryan race are uniquely different from those of other cultures, it would seriously weaken the author's conclusion that studying the Aryan race will be helpful in understanding the experiences and lifestyles of other races.

That its communal arrangements are unique would make comparison between the Aryan race and other cultures impossible.

14. **(C)** The author presents a contrast between life and honor: in particular, the final sentence suggests that life and honor have opposite qualities. Of the choices, the only opposite of *transient* is *eternal.*

15. **(E)** The logic of this statement goes from the general absolute ("all") to the specific ("this animal"), concluding with specific to specific. Symbolically, if *P* implies *Q*, then *not Q* implies not *P*. (E) goes from general absolute ("all") to specific ("this liquid"), concluding with specific to specific. Notice how and where the inverse ("not") is inserted. Using symbols, we have that, if *P* implies *Q*, then *not Q* implies *not P*.

16. **(B)** This is a close one. (B) and (D) both weaken the argument by pointing out that all dogs do not always bark, but (B) is absolute. (D) is tentative, since a dog trained not to bark might do so by accident.

17. **(B)** The apparent discrepancy in the paragraph is why should arrests decline when there are fewer policemen to arrest the criminals? One explanation is that though the number of arrests has declined, the number of crimes has risen, and because there are fewer police officers, more crimes are unsolved.

18. **(A)** The complaint about ex-employees of the Department of Energy on the board, and the financial ties of the National Academy Board to the Energy Department indicate the officials' belief that the Department of Energy supports the nuclear power industry against the views of environmentalists.

19. **(E)** Though adding one or two environmentalists might help, they would still be outnumbered by the ten panel members with ties to the Department of Energy. Of the five choices, (E) offers the best hope of impartiality.

20. **(C)** (A) contradicts the statement's urging of economy. (B) introduces an irrelevant word, *terminology*. (D) and (E) are absolute statements about assumptions, but the statement itself is relative, urging us only to simplify our assumptions if one such simplification is possible; in other words, "If an issue is simple, don't complicate it."

21. **(E)** The question demonstrates a solution and the fact that an alternative exists.

22. **(E)** (A) is obviously true. (B) also satisfies the conditions. (C) is correct, since 3.5 was required with a score of 800. (D) is correct, since we do not know anything about numbers of applicants. (E) is inconsistent, since a score of 1,200 is required with a GPA of 2.5. (E) specifies a score less than 1,200. Therefore, a GPA greater than (not less than) 2.5 would be required for admittance.

23. **(B)** To speak in positive terms about the increase in school degrees, the author must assume that the degrees indicate what they are supposed to indicate, that is, well-educated individuals. (A) and (E) are empty statements; (C) and (D) are altogether unsubstantiated by either expressed or implied information.

24. **(E)** Although the brand name is No-NOCK, the advertisement makes no claim to stop the engine from knocking. All the other claims are contained in the advertisement.

25. **(D)** The choice repudiates the suggestion that gentleness and graciousness were once part of the American character. (B), another choice worth considering, is not best because it does not address the temperament of tennis players as directly as does (D).

26. **(B)** By asking Dolores to choose between conventional and nuclear weapons, Fran has concluded that Dolores's statement calls for a decision. (C), worth considering, is not best because Fran supposes that Dolores has not made a choice—hence her question.

Section IV

Answers 1–6

From the information given, you should have constructed a diagram similar to this:

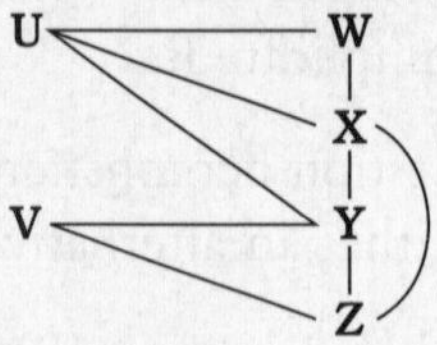

1. (B) From the diagram, if the group begins on island W, it could not reach island V in the eight days. Remember, three days would have to be spent on W and three on X.
2. (B) From the diagram, if the group stays on island X for three nights, then the group cannot get to island V on the next visit.
3. (D) To answer this question, you must try each answer choice and eliminate the ones that do not connect. From the diagram, the only possible order listed would be U X Z V.
4. (E) From the diagram, if the group visits island W first, it could go to X to Y to Z, back to X, to U back to Y, to V and back to Z. A total of 9 visits. You could work from the choices, but remember to start from the highest number.
5. (D) From the diagram, the group could go from X to W to U to Y to V to Z to Y. This would be 6 different islands.
6. (E) Adding island T to the diagram connected only to U could look like this:

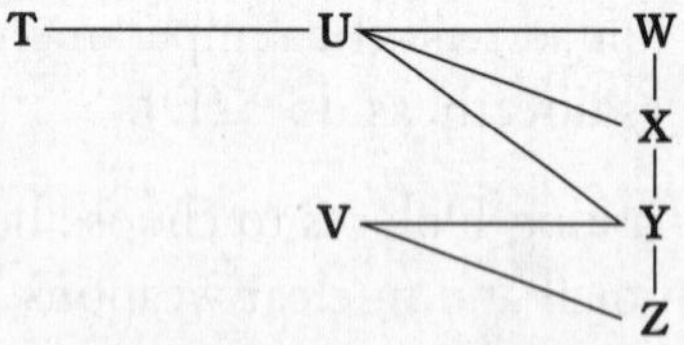

From this revised diagram, only (E) must be true. On the tenth day of a tour starting on Z, the tour group could be on island T. It would go from Z to Y to U to T or Z to X to U to T.

Answers 7–13

From the information given, you could have constructed the following display:

~~A~~					E	~~A~~	1B	2A
1	2	3	4	5	6	7	8	1C 2D
								2E

B? AEA

7. (E) Office 4 can be cleaned only by A or E. Therefore, answer choice (E) is incorrect. The other choices are possible as follows.

	1	2	3	4	5	6	7	8
(A)	B	A	E	A	D	D	E	C
(B) & (C)	B	D	C	A	E	A	E	D
(D)	B	D	A	E	A	C	E	D

8. (C) Office 4 can be cleaned only by A or E. Therefore, choice (C) is the only correct one.

9. (B) Office 4 can be cleaned only by A or E. Therefore, choices (C), (D), and (E) are incorrect. Choice (A) is incorrect because D can clean office 8, so this choice is accurate but not complete. Choice (B) is correct.

10. (D) There are six possible arrangements as follows. Thus, choice (D) is correct.

1	2	3	4	5	6	7	8
B	A	E	A	D	C	E	D
B	D	A	E	A	C	E	D
B	C	A	E	A	D	E	D
B	C	D	A	E	A	E	D
C	B	A	E	A	D	E	D
C	B	D	A	E	A	E	D

11. (D) Choices (B) and (C) are incorrect since they each clean only one office. Choice (A) is incorrect since the conditions state that A's offices are separated by one of E's offices. Answer (E) is incorrect since one of E's offices is between A's offices. Only choice (D) is possible as follows.

1	2	3	4	5	6	7	8
B	A	E	A	D	D	E	C

12. **(A)** Bart cannot clean office 6 since his office must be numbered lower than E's lowest. Also, Ethel cannot clean office 6 since E must be between A's and E is already cleaning office 7.

13. **(E)** There are two possible arrangements of rooms, as follows.

1	2	3	4	5	6	7	8
D	B	A	E	A	C	E	D
D	B	C	A	E	A	E	D

Choice (A) is incorrect since A may clean office 6. Choice (B) is incorrect since B and C may clean consecutive offices. Choice (C) is incorrect since C may or may not clean an even-numbered office. Choice (D) is incorrect since this may or may not be true. The only one that *must* be true is choice (E), Bart cleans office 2.

Answers 14–18

Drawing a simple diagram, like the one below, will help answer the questions.

```
                                         TR
                                          *
                          J              FDR
M, A, K, FDR → ___ ___ ___ ___      
               ___ ___ _M_ _A_      K – FDR or
                                    FDR – K
```

Note that, once Madison is placed in position 3 on the bottom, Adams must go in position 4 in order to leave spots for Kennedy to be adjacent to Franklin Delano Roosevelt.

14. **(D)** If Theodore Roosevelt is second from the left (on top), then Franklin Delano Roosevelt must be first on the bottom since one Roosevelt may not be above the other. Therefore, Kennedy must be second on the bottom.

15. **(A)** Adams must go to the far right on the bottom to allow Kennedy to be adjacent to Franklin Delano Roosevelt.

16. **(A)** If Washington and Kennedy are both first on their shelves, then Franklin Delano Roosevelt must be second on the lower shelf. Therefore, Theodore Roosevelt cannot be second on the top shelf and therefore must be third. Thus, statement (D) cannot be true.

17. **(E)** Since Adams must be on the right in the second row, only (E) is not possible.

18. **(C)** If Lincoln is next to Jefferson, that leaves Theodore Roosevelt and Washington for the first two positions on the top shelf. All of the choices are therefore true except (C) because that choice would place one Roosevelt above the other, which is not permitted.

Answers 19–24

The following display can be drawn from the information given:

1	2	3	4	5	6
O	B	R	R	B	R
W	G	Y	Y	G	O
Y	Y			R	V
				Y	W

19. **(E)** The only two color choices for houses 3 and 4 are R and Y. Therefore, houses 3 and 4 must be the two houses painted R and Y. Therefore, no other house is painted R or Y. Thus, choice (A) is incorrect. Choices (B), (C), and (D) are incorrect for the same reason.

20. **(A)** If orange is not used, the color choices reduce to the following possibilities:

1	2	3	4	5	6
W	B	R	R	B	W
	G	Y	Y	G	V

There is one way to paint houses 1 and 6. Since house 1 must be W, house 6 must be V. There are two ways to paint houses 2 and 5: BG or GB. There are two ways to paint houses 3 and 4: RY or YR. Therefore, there are $1 \times 2 \times 2$ ways, or 4 ways to paint the houses.

21. (C) Since houses 3 and 4 are the R and Y houses, the possible color combinations reduce to the following:

1	2	3	4	5	6
O	B	R	R	B	O
W	G	Y	Y	G	V
					W

Choice (A) is incorrect since, if house 1 is painted W, we still do not know the color of house 6. Choice (B) is incorrect since, if house 6 is painted V, we still do not know the color of house 1. Choice (D) is incorrect since we do not know the colors of houses 1 or 6. Choice (E) is incorrect since we do not know the colors of houses 3 and 4. Choice (C) is correct since all colors are determined. If you know G you know B, if you know R you know Y, and if you know W you know O.

22. (E) Since houses 3 and 4 are the R and Y houses, the possible color combinations reduce to the following (p = primary, s = secondary):

1	2	3	4	5	6
Os	Bp	Rp	Rp	Bp	Os
W	Gs	Yp	Yp	Gs	Vs
					W

Choice (A) is incorrect since it is not possible for both the second and sixth house to be Bp. Choice (B) is incorrect since the sixth house cannot be painted a primary color. Choice (C) is incorrect since it is not possible for both the second and fifth house to be Gs. Choice (D) is incorrect since the fourth house must be painted a primary color. Choice (E) is the only possible combination.

23. (D) Since houses 3 and 4 are the R and Y houses, the possible color combinations reduce to the following:

1	2	3	4	5	6
O	B	R	R	B	O
W	G	Y	Y	G	V
					W

If the V house is next to the G house, the possible combinations reduce to the following:

1	2	3	4	5	6
O	B	R	R	G	V
W		Y	Y		

If the B house is next to the Y house, the possible combinations reduce to the following:

1	2	3	4	5	6
O	B	Y	R	G	V
W					

Choices (A) and (B) are incorrect since the first house could be either O or W. Choice (C) is incorrect since the third house is not R. Choice (E) is incorrect since the fifth house is not B. Choice (D) is correct.

24. (C) If the painter of the third house also likes pink, then the possible color combinations are as follows:

1	2	3	4	5	6
O	B	R	R	B	R
W	G	Y	Y	G	O
Y	Y	P		R	V
				Y	W

Choices (A), (B), (D), and (E) are possible as follows:

1	2	3	4	5	6	
O	B	P	Y	G	R	(A)
O	G	R	Y	B	W	(B)
Y	G	P	R	B	W	(D)
W	Y	P	R	G	V	(E)

Choice (C) is correct, since if the second house is yellow, the fourth house, not the third house, must be red.

Section V

1. (B) The correct answer must use both premises. The first qualifies the assertion with "normally," so (A) will not follow, but (B) (with the qualifier "may") will. (C) may or may not be true, but it is not a logical con-clu-sion based on the two premises. (D) and (E), like (A), do not use both premises.

2. **(D)** The question asked concerns the danger to public health, but the reply does not deal with this issue at all. It changes the subject.

3. **(C)** Reducing coffee consumption in general will not guarantee a healthier population (A) if "heavy" consumers do not reduce their coffee intake. Reducing coffee consumption would make those who drink a morning cup of coffee feel less well (B). (C) is a logical conclusion since heavy consumption increases heart attack risk. There is no information in the passage to justify the assertion about percolated coffee (D). If coffee may protect against colon cancer, (E) is not true.

4. **(D)** The issue of the danger of pesticides is addressed by (A), (C), and (E), while (B) calls into question the objectivity of the Food and Agriculture Department. But (D) deals with a different issue: air pollution. And if air pollution is a cause of illness, pesticides may be less to blame.

5. **(A)** The question contains its own prior judgment (underpay, unfair promotion policies) on what it asks, regardless of a "yes" or "no" answer. Similarly, the adjective "excessive" and the adverb "unfairly" prejudge any answer in choice (A).

6. **(E)** Since fares have risen, the cost of fuel has risen or there are no fare wars. And if there are no fare wars, the number of passengers is larger. Only (E) cannot be true. (B) is possible if fuel costs have risen, and there are fare wars.

7. **(B)** Though the argument for a decline in fishing off Newfoundland is convincing, the generalization that the "fishing industry in the Americas" will disappear is here based only on information about the Atlantic waters off Canada. It is possible that other areas have not been so affected.

8. **(C)** The advertisement asserts filter cigarettes cannot have great taste. A reasonable inference is that Gold Star is not a filter cigarette. (A) is contradicted by this ad without visual appeal. (B) is contradicted by this ad, which does not specifically praise a brand. (D) is illogical given the existence of this ad. Nothing in the ad supports (E).

9. **(D)** Choices (A), (B), and (C) strengthen the case for building the toll road. The environmentalists may be able to make their case for one of the other possible routes that, if less direct, would not disturb the reserve. With the information we have, the value of (E) is indeterminable.

10. **(A)** There is nothing in the paragraph to support (E), and there are details that contradict (B), (C), and (D). That "sales in the United States continue to increase" supports (A).

11. **(E)** The passage does not give the information that would lead to the conclusion in (A), (B), or (C). (E) is a better answer than (D), the odds against the heavy smoker being 40 in 100 as compared to 25 in 100 for the light smoker.

12. **(C)** The presence of wolf bones and walrus bones near a village is not evidence that wolves were trained to haul sleds; it does not disprove the theory, however.

13. **(B)** Choices (A), (C), (D), and (E) would undermine the theory. But if wolves were easily domesticated and trained, it would make the theory of their domestication by Stone Age tribes more plausible.

14. **(A)** The author makes his point by invective, an abrasive verbal attack.

15. **(D)** The first sentence asserts the needlessness of commenting on the picture; the second nonetheless makes a detailed criticism.

16. **(B)** If popcorn attracts rodents and insects, warehouses where packages using popcorn are stored would have vermin problems.

17. **(B)** Only (B) is a necessary assumption. It must be assumed that no other items (for example, dressings, recipes, or spices) are sold at the stand in order to conclude definitively that everything sold there is delicious.

18. **(B)** Though (E) is probably true, it is not a conclusion based on the information in the passage. But the passage does assert that only 19.67 percent (11.9 plus 7.7) of the eligible voters in the Democratic and Republican parties went to the polls.

19. **(A)** Choices (B) and (C), although true, are not relevant, while (D) and (E) are probably untrue. That it is only in the schools that the tobacco spokesmen are silent supports the inference of (A).

20. **(C)** In both paragraphs, the author disputes the interpretations of his opponents.

21. **(D)** The author assumes that an audience is able to evaluate a work and determine its own course of action.

22. **(E)** The opening lines describe esteem without popularity, later followed by popular success.

23. **(D)** The "But" introducing the last sentence suggests that a contrast, a disadvantage of coffee, is to follow. Either (C) or (D) is possible, but since exercise has not been an issue, (D) is the better choice.

24. **(A)** Only choice (A) must be true. There may be other performers as well as the chorus members (the orchestra, for example) in the performance, so (E) is incorrect.

25. **(C)** The passage draws an analogy comparing corrupt politicians to vermin.

Model Test Three

This chapter contains full-length Model Test Three. It is geared to the format of the LSAT, and it is complete with answers and explanations. It is equivalent to the LSAT in question structure, number of questions, level of difficulty, and time allotments. (The questions used are not taken directly from the LSAT, as those questions are copyrighted and may not be reproduced.)

Model Test Three should be taken under strict test conditions. The test ends with a 35-minute Writing Sample, which is not scored.

Model Test Three

Section	Description	Number of Questions	Time Allowed
I.	Logical Reasoning	26	35 minutes
II.	Reading Comprehension	28	35 minutes
III.	Analytical Reasoning	24	35 minutes
IV.	Logical Reasoning	26	35 minutes
V.	Reading Comprehension	28	35 minutes
	Writing Sample		35 minutes
TOTALS:		132	3 hours 30 minutes

Now please turn to the next page, remove your answer sheet, and begin Model Test Three.

Remove answer sheet by cutting on dotted line

Answer Sheet

MODEL TEST THREE

Section I	Section II	Section III	Section IV	Section V
1 Ⓐ Ⓑ Ⓒ Ⓓ Ⓔ	1 Ⓐ Ⓑ Ⓒ Ⓓ Ⓔ	1 Ⓐ Ⓑ Ⓒ Ⓓ Ⓔ	1 Ⓐ Ⓑ Ⓒ Ⓓ Ⓔ	1 Ⓐ Ⓑ Ⓒ Ⓓ Ⓔ
2 Ⓐ Ⓑ Ⓒ Ⓓ Ⓔ	2 Ⓐ Ⓑ Ⓒ Ⓓ Ⓔ	2 Ⓐ Ⓑ Ⓒ Ⓓ Ⓔ	2 Ⓐ Ⓑ Ⓒ Ⓓ Ⓔ	2 Ⓐ Ⓑ Ⓒ Ⓓ Ⓔ
3 Ⓐ Ⓑ Ⓒ Ⓓ Ⓔ	3 Ⓐ Ⓑ Ⓒ Ⓓ Ⓔ	3 Ⓐ Ⓑ Ⓒ Ⓓ Ⓔ	3 Ⓐ Ⓑ Ⓒ Ⓓ Ⓔ	3 Ⓐ Ⓑ Ⓒ Ⓓ Ⓔ
4 Ⓐ Ⓑ Ⓒ Ⓓ Ⓔ	4 Ⓐ Ⓑ Ⓒ Ⓓ Ⓔ	4 Ⓐ Ⓑ Ⓒ Ⓓ Ⓔ	4 Ⓐ Ⓑ Ⓒ Ⓓ Ⓔ	4 Ⓐ Ⓑ Ⓒ Ⓓ Ⓔ
5 Ⓐ Ⓑ Ⓒ Ⓓ Ⓔ	5 Ⓐ Ⓑ Ⓒ Ⓓ Ⓔ	5 Ⓐ Ⓑ Ⓒ Ⓓ Ⓔ	5 Ⓐ Ⓑ Ⓒ Ⓓ Ⓔ	5 Ⓐ Ⓑ Ⓒ Ⓓ Ⓔ
6 Ⓐ Ⓑ Ⓒ Ⓓ Ⓔ	6 Ⓐ Ⓑ Ⓒ Ⓓ Ⓔ	6 Ⓐ Ⓑ Ⓒ Ⓓ Ⓔ	6 Ⓐ Ⓑ Ⓒ Ⓓ Ⓔ	6 Ⓐ Ⓑ Ⓒ Ⓓ Ⓔ
7 Ⓐ Ⓑ Ⓒ Ⓓ Ⓔ	7 Ⓐ Ⓑ Ⓒ Ⓓ Ⓔ	7 Ⓐ Ⓑ Ⓒ Ⓓ Ⓔ	7 Ⓐ Ⓑ Ⓒ Ⓓ Ⓔ	7 Ⓐ Ⓑ Ⓒ Ⓓ Ⓔ
8 Ⓐ Ⓑ Ⓒ Ⓓ Ⓔ	8 Ⓐ Ⓑ Ⓒ Ⓓ Ⓔ	8 Ⓐ Ⓑ Ⓒ Ⓓ Ⓔ	8 Ⓐ Ⓑ Ⓒ Ⓓ Ⓔ	8 Ⓐ Ⓑ Ⓒ Ⓓ Ⓔ
9 Ⓐ Ⓑ Ⓒ Ⓓ Ⓔ	9 Ⓐ Ⓑ Ⓒ Ⓓ Ⓔ	9 Ⓐ Ⓑ Ⓒ Ⓓ Ⓔ	9 Ⓐ Ⓑ Ⓒ Ⓓ Ⓔ	9 Ⓐ Ⓑ Ⓒ Ⓓ Ⓔ
10 Ⓐ Ⓑ Ⓒ Ⓓ Ⓔ	10 Ⓐ Ⓑ Ⓒ Ⓓ Ⓔ	10 Ⓐ Ⓑ Ⓒ Ⓓ Ⓔ	10 Ⓐ Ⓑ Ⓒ Ⓓ Ⓔ	10 Ⓐ Ⓑ Ⓒ Ⓓ Ⓔ
11 Ⓐ Ⓑ Ⓒ Ⓓ Ⓔ	11 Ⓐ Ⓑ Ⓒ Ⓓ Ⓔ	11 Ⓐ Ⓑ Ⓒ Ⓓ Ⓔ	11 Ⓐ Ⓑ Ⓒ Ⓓ Ⓔ	11 Ⓐ Ⓑ Ⓒ Ⓓ Ⓔ
12 Ⓐ Ⓑ Ⓒ Ⓓ Ⓔ	12 Ⓐ Ⓑ Ⓒ Ⓓ Ⓔ	12 Ⓐ Ⓑ Ⓒ Ⓓ Ⓔ	12 Ⓐ Ⓑ Ⓒ Ⓓ Ⓔ	12 Ⓐ Ⓑ Ⓒ Ⓓ Ⓔ
13 Ⓐ Ⓑ Ⓒ Ⓓ Ⓔ	13 Ⓐ Ⓑ Ⓒ Ⓓ Ⓔ	13 Ⓐ Ⓑ Ⓒ Ⓓ Ⓔ	13 Ⓐ Ⓑ Ⓒ Ⓓ Ⓔ	13 Ⓐ Ⓑ Ⓒ Ⓓ Ⓔ
14 Ⓐ Ⓑ Ⓒ Ⓓ Ⓔ	14 Ⓐ Ⓑ Ⓒ Ⓓ Ⓔ	14 Ⓐ Ⓑ Ⓒ Ⓓ Ⓔ	14 Ⓐ Ⓑ Ⓒ Ⓓ Ⓔ	14 Ⓐ Ⓑ Ⓒ Ⓓ Ⓔ
15 Ⓐ Ⓑ Ⓒ Ⓓ Ⓔ	15 Ⓐ Ⓑ Ⓒ Ⓓ Ⓔ	15 Ⓐ Ⓑ Ⓒ Ⓓ Ⓔ	15 Ⓐ Ⓑ Ⓒ Ⓓ Ⓔ	15 Ⓐ Ⓑ Ⓒ Ⓓ Ⓔ
16 Ⓐ Ⓑ Ⓒ Ⓓ Ⓔ	16 Ⓐ Ⓑ Ⓒ Ⓓ Ⓔ	16 Ⓐ Ⓑ Ⓒ Ⓓ Ⓔ	16 Ⓐ Ⓑ Ⓒ Ⓓ Ⓔ	16 Ⓐ Ⓑ Ⓒ Ⓓ Ⓔ
17 Ⓐ Ⓑ Ⓒ Ⓓ Ⓔ	17 Ⓐ Ⓑ Ⓒ Ⓓ Ⓔ	17 Ⓐ Ⓑ Ⓒ Ⓓ Ⓔ	17 Ⓐ Ⓑ Ⓒ Ⓓ Ⓔ	17 Ⓐ Ⓑ Ⓒ Ⓓ Ⓔ
18 Ⓐ Ⓑ Ⓒ Ⓓ Ⓔ	18 Ⓐ Ⓑ Ⓒ Ⓓ Ⓔ	18 Ⓐ Ⓑ Ⓒ Ⓓ Ⓔ	18 Ⓐ Ⓑ Ⓒ Ⓓ Ⓔ	18 Ⓐ Ⓑ Ⓒ Ⓓ Ⓔ
19 Ⓐ Ⓑ Ⓒ Ⓓ Ⓔ	19 Ⓐ Ⓑ Ⓒ Ⓓ Ⓔ	19 Ⓐ Ⓑ Ⓒ Ⓓ Ⓔ	19 Ⓐ Ⓑ Ⓒ Ⓓ Ⓔ	19 Ⓐ Ⓑ Ⓒ Ⓓ Ⓔ
20 Ⓐ Ⓑ Ⓒ Ⓓ Ⓔ	20 Ⓐ Ⓑ Ⓒ Ⓓ Ⓔ	20 Ⓐ Ⓑ Ⓒ Ⓓ Ⓔ	20 Ⓐ Ⓑ Ⓒ Ⓓ Ⓔ	20 Ⓐ Ⓑ Ⓒ Ⓓ Ⓔ
21 Ⓐ Ⓑ Ⓒ Ⓓ Ⓔ	21 Ⓐ Ⓑ Ⓒ Ⓓ Ⓔ	21 Ⓐ Ⓑ Ⓒ Ⓓ Ⓔ	21 Ⓐ Ⓑ Ⓒ Ⓓ Ⓔ	21 Ⓐ Ⓑ Ⓒ Ⓓ Ⓔ
22 Ⓐ Ⓑ Ⓒ Ⓓ Ⓔ	22 Ⓐ Ⓑ Ⓒ Ⓓ Ⓔ	22 Ⓐ Ⓑ Ⓒ Ⓓ Ⓔ	22 Ⓐ Ⓑ Ⓒ Ⓓ Ⓔ	22 Ⓐ Ⓑ Ⓒ Ⓓ Ⓔ
23 Ⓐ Ⓑ Ⓒ Ⓓ Ⓔ	23 Ⓐ Ⓑ Ⓒ Ⓓ Ⓔ	23 Ⓐ Ⓑ Ⓒ Ⓓ Ⓔ	23 Ⓐ Ⓑ Ⓒ Ⓓ Ⓔ	23 Ⓐ Ⓑ Ⓒ Ⓓ Ⓔ
24 Ⓐ Ⓑ Ⓒ Ⓓ Ⓔ	24 Ⓐ Ⓑ Ⓒ Ⓓ Ⓔ	24 Ⓐ Ⓑ Ⓒ Ⓓ Ⓔ	24 Ⓐ Ⓑ Ⓒ Ⓓ Ⓔ	24 Ⓐ Ⓑ Ⓒ Ⓓ Ⓔ
25 Ⓐ Ⓑ Ⓒ Ⓓ Ⓔ	25 Ⓐ Ⓑ Ⓒ Ⓓ Ⓔ	25 Ⓐ Ⓑ Ⓒ Ⓓ Ⓔ	25 Ⓐ Ⓑ Ⓒ Ⓓ Ⓔ	25 Ⓐ Ⓑ Ⓒ Ⓓ Ⓔ
26 Ⓐ Ⓑ Ⓒ Ⓓ Ⓔ	26 Ⓐ Ⓑ Ⓒ Ⓓ Ⓔ	26 Ⓐ Ⓑ Ⓒ Ⓓ Ⓔ	26 Ⓐ Ⓑ Ⓒ Ⓓ Ⓔ	26 Ⓐ Ⓑ Ⓒ Ⓓ Ⓔ
27 Ⓐ Ⓑ Ⓒ Ⓓ Ⓔ	27 Ⓐ Ⓑ Ⓒ Ⓓ Ⓔ	27 Ⓐ Ⓑ Ⓒ Ⓓ Ⓔ	27 Ⓐ Ⓑ Ⓒ Ⓓ Ⓔ	27 Ⓐ Ⓑ Ⓒ Ⓓ Ⓔ
28 Ⓐ Ⓑ Ⓒ Ⓓ Ⓔ	28 Ⓐ Ⓑ Ⓒ Ⓓ Ⓔ	28 Ⓐ Ⓑ Ⓒ Ⓓ Ⓔ	28 Ⓐ Ⓑ Ⓒ Ⓓ Ⓔ	28 Ⓐ Ⓑ Ⓒ Ⓓ Ⓔ
29 Ⓐ Ⓑ Ⓒ Ⓓ Ⓔ	29 Ⓐ Ⓑ Ⓒ Ⓓ Ⓔ	29 Ⓐ Ⓑ Ⓒ Ⓓ Ⓔ	29 Ⓐ Ⓑ Ⓒ Ⓓ Ⓔ	29 Ⓐ Ⓑ Ⓒ Ⓓ Ⓔ
30 Ⓐ Ⓑ Ⓒ Ⓓ Ⓔ	30 Ⓐ Ⓑ Ⓒ Ⓓ Ⓔ	30 Ⓐ Ⓑ Ⓒ Ⓓ Ⓔ	30 Ⓐ Ⓑ Ⓒ Ⓓ Ⓔ	30 Ⓐ Ⓑ Ⓒ Ⓓ Ⓔ

SECTION I

Time—35 minutes
26 Questions

Directions: In this section you will be given brief statements or passages and will be required to evaluate the reasoning involved. In some instances, more than one choice will appear to be a possible answer. You are to choose the *best* answer. Use common sense and reasonableness in making your selection; then mark the proper space on the answer sheet.

Questions 1–2

Professor: Probability is a curiously unstable concept. Semantically speaking, it is an assumption, a pure artifice, a concept that may or may not be true, but nevertheless facilitates a logical process. It is not a hypothesis because, by its very nature, it cannot be proved. Suppose we flip a coin that has a distinguishable head and tail. In our ignorance of the coming result we say that the coin has one chance in two of falling heads up, or that the probability of a head turning up is one-to-two. Here it must be understood that the one-to-two is not "true" but is merely a species of the genus probability.

1. The professor assumes that

(A) nothing about our coin influences its fall in favor of either side or that all influences are counterbalanced by equal and opposite influences
(B) probability can be dealt with or without the use of logic
(C) an assumption must be plausible
(D) the probability of the coin's landing on an edge is counterbalanced by the probability of its not landing on an edge
(E) probability can be precisely calculated

2. The last sentence implies that

(A) probability is not absolute
(B) one-to-two is merely a guess
(C) one-to-two is a worthless ratio
(D) truth is not important
(E) genus is a category of species

3. Self-confidence is a big factor in success. The person who thinks he can, will master most of the things he attempts. The person who thinks he can't, may not try.

The author of these statements would agree that

(A) nothing is impossible
(B) no task is too large
(C) success relies on effort
(D) self-confidence is of utmost importance
(E) trying is half the battle

GO ON TO THE NEXT PAGE.

1 1 1 1 1

4. People who risk riding on roller coasters are more likely to take risks in other areas of their lives than those who avoid roller coasters. So roller coaster riders are more likely than others to be successful in situations in which taking risks can result in benefit to them.

   If the above comments are true, they most strongly support which one of the following statements?

   (A) No roller coaster riders avoid taking risks in other areas of their lives, but some may take more risks than others.
   (B) Risk taking in life decisions is important not only because of the possible financial gain but because of the psychological benefits produced.
   (C) Some people who are not roller coaster riders may take more risks in other areas of their lives than do roller coaster riders.
   (D) Mountain climbing is riskier than riding on roller coasters, so people who climb mountains will be more successful in other areas of their lives than are roller coaster riders.
   (E) Risk taking in one type of activity indicates a likelihood of risk taking in other types of activities.

5. *Anthropologist:* For many years, anthropologists believed that the longevity of the men of the island of Zobu was the result of their active lives and their eating only fish from the lagoon and fruits and vegetables grown on the island. However, recent studies of the inhabitants of nearby Luku, where the way of life and diet are virtually identical with Zobu's, have revealed that the men there rarely survive beyond early middle age.

   If the information in this paragraph is correct, it best supports which one of the following ?

   (A) There are important differences in the lagoons of the two islands of which scientists are unaware.
   (B) The inhabitants of Luku and Zobu probably have many ancestors in common.
   (C) The longevity of the natives of Zobu is not due simply to their diet and way of life.
   (D) Some, though not all, of the residents of Luku live as long as some of the residents of Zobu.
   (E) Since longevity depends on so many different factors, it is useless to compare longevity in one area with that in another.

1 1 1 1 1

Questions 6–7

Because college-educated men and women as a group earn more than those without college educations, and because in Eastern Europe and Latin America, 105 women are enrolled in colleges for every 100 men, the total earnings of college women in these areas should be equal to, if not greater than, the earnings of college men. But college women in Eastern Europe and in Latin America earn only 65 percent of what college men in these countries earn.

6. Which one of the following, if true, is most useful in explaining this discrepancy?

(A) The earning power of both men and women rises sharply in accord with their level of education.
(B) In some countries of Western Europe, the earning power of college-educated women is higher than that of men in Eastern Europe and Latin America.
(C) In Eastern Europe, more men than women who enter college fail to complete their educations.
(D) The largest percentage of women in Eastern European and Latin American universities study to become teachers; the largest percentage of men study engineering.
(E) In Eastern Europe and Latin America, about 60 percent of the total workforce is college educated.

7. Which one of the following is a faulty assumption based on the statistics of the passage?

(A) The passage assumes that all of the college women enter the workforce.
(B) The passage assumes conditions in Eastern Europe and in Latin America are the same.
(C) The passage assumes that men and women should be paid equally.
(D) The passage assumes that college-educated women outnumber women who have not attended college in Eastern Europe and Latin America.
(E) The passage assumes that all college-educated workers will be paid more than workers who do not have college educations.

GO ON TO THE NEXT PAGE.

1 1 1 1 1

8. *Economist:* When consumers are in a buying mood, and the cost of money is low, a shrewd retailer with a popular product will reduce prices of items that are selling slowly and will make up for any loss by raising prices on the product or products that are popular.

In which one of the following situations are these recommendations observed?

(A) At Easter, John's Markets offered one dozen eggs at half their usual price and hams and turkeys at a 40 percent discount, but because of heavy rains, they raised the price of many green vegetables.
(B) This Christmas, Arrow Clothiers is offering six-month interest-free charge accounts to any customers who purchase $50 or more of merchandise from their stock of discontinued summer wear and the fashionable new op-art neck wear.
(C) Since interest rates have reached a yearly low, the price of tax-free bonds is near an all-time high. Discount Brokerage has launched a campaign to sell off all of its holding in precious metals mutual funds that are now at their lowest price in years.
(D) Angus Jewelry is offering special savings for customers who make purchases in May. With graduations coming soon, they are offering engraved gold Swiss watches, as well as lower prices on heart-shaped jewelry items that were featured on Valentine's Day.
(E) Travel agents in Orlando are capitalizing on the lowered air-fares to lure tourists by offering special rates on hotel accommodations and discounted admission tickets to two of the large theme parks in the area.

9. While some cities impose tough, clear restrictions on demolitions of older buildings, our city has no protection for cultural landmarks. Designation as a landmark by the Cultural Heritage Commission can delay a demolition for only one year. This delay can be avoided easily by an owner's demonstrating an economic hardship. Developers who simply ignore designations and tear down buildings receive only small fines. Therefore, ...

Which one of the following best completes the passage above?

(A) the number of buildings protected by Cultural Heritage Commission designation must be increased
(B) developers must be encouraged to help preserve our older buildings
(C) the designation as landmark must be changed to delay demolition for more than one year
(D) developers who ignore designations to protect buildings must be subject to higher fines
(E) if our older buildings are to be saved, we need clearer and more rigorously enforced laws

1 1 1 1 1

10. In ballet schools throughout the country, 95 percent of the students and teachers are female, and 5 percent are male, but professional dance companies need at least 45 percent male dancers.

Which one of the following, if true, would help to explain these statistics?

(A) The social acceptance of dancing as a profession is much higher for females than for males.
(B) Modern choreographers can create dances that can be performed by companies with more female than male dancers.
(C) There are fewer dances than songs in most films and stage musicals.
(D) Men who have classical ballet training develop the same muscles as are used in track events such as the hurdles and the high jump.
(E) Women's bodies are more likely to mature at an earlier age than men's.

Questions 11–12

Sixty percent of the American people, according to the latest polls, now believe that inflation is the nation's most important problem. This problem of inflation is closely related to rising prices. The inflation rate has been 10 percent or more most of this year. Undoubtedly, our gluttonous appetite for high-priced foreign oil has been a major factor. We have been shipping billions of dollars overseas, more than foreigners can spend or invest here. Dollars are selling cheaply and this has forced the value of the dollar down. Government programs now being inaugurated to slow this trend are at best weak, but deserve our support, as they appear to be the best our government can produce. Hopefully, they won't fail as they have in the past.

11. The author of this passage implies that

(A) inflation cannot be stopped or slowed, because of a weak government
(B) the fear of inflation is not only unwarranted, but also detrimental
(C) 40 percent of non-Americans believe inflation is not the most important problem
(D) foreign oil is the sole reason for the sudden increase in inflation
(E) the present programs will probably not slow inflation

12. Which one of the following contradicts something in the preceding passage?

(A) Foreign oil is actually underpriced.
(B) The inflation rate has not risen for most of this year.
(C) Overseas investors are few and far between.
(D) Our government is trying a new approach to end inflation.
(E) The weakness of the programs stems from lack of support.

1 1 1 1 1

13. Sales of new homes in Arizona fell almost 20 percent in the month of February, compared to last year. Analysts attribute the decline to several factors. Record rainfalls kept both builders and buyers indoors for most of the month. The rise in the interest rates have brought mortgage rates to a ten-month high. Both the sales of new homes and housing starts have reached new lows. With every indication that mortgage rates will remain high for the rest of the year, Arizona home-builders foresee a very grim year ahead.

Which one of the following would add support to the conclusion of this passage?

(A) Last year's sales increased in the second half of the year, despite some increase in interest rates.
(B) Last year's sales were accelerated by good weather in January and February.
(C) Widespread advertising and incentives to attract buyers this February were ineffective.
(D) Rain in Arizona usually ends late in February.
(E) Home sales and building starts throughout the country are about the same this year as last year.

14. No one reads *Weight-Off* magazine unless he is fat. Everyone reads *Weight-Off* magazine unless he eats chocolate.

Which one of the following is inconsistent with the above?

(A) No one is fat and only some people eat chocolate.
(B) Some people are fat and no one eats chocolate.
(C) Everyone is fat.
(D) No one is fat and no one reads *Weight-Off*.
(E) No one who is fat eats chocolate.

15. *Jerry:* Every meal my wife cooks is fantastic.

Dave: I disagree. Most of my wife's meals are fantastic, too.

Dave's response shows that he understood Jerry to mean that

(A) Dave's wife does not cook fantastic meals
(B) only Jerry's wife cooks fantastic meals
(C) every one of Jerry's wife's meals is fantastic
(D) not every one of Jerry's wife's meals is fantastic
(E) no one cooks fantastic meals all the time

GO ON TO THE NEXT PAGE.

1 1 1 1 1

Questions 16–17

Commentators and politicians are given to enlisting the rest of America as allies, sprinkling such phrases as "Americans believe" or "Americans will simply not put up with" into their pronouncements on whatever issue currently claims their attentions. They cite polls showing 60 or 80 or 90 percent support for their views. There may (or may not) have been such polls, but even if the polls are real, their finer points will not be reported because they usually contradict the speaker's point. The alleged 80 percent support for a balanced budget amendment, for example, plummets to less than 30 percent if the pollster so much as mentions an entitlement program like social security. People do have opinions, but they are rarely so specific or so unequivocal as your news broadcaster or your senator would lead you to believe.

16. The argument of this passage would be less convincing if it could be shown that

(A) In a recent poll, 80 percent of the Americans responding supported a balanced budget amendment.
(B) Most polls used by television commentators are conducted by telephone calls lasting less than 35 seconds.
(C) Far more Americans are indifferent to or badly informed about current affairs than are well informed.
(D) The polls' predictions of who will be elected president have been correct about every presidential election since Truman defeated Dewey.
(E) Many polls are based on samples that do not accurately represent the demographics of an area.

17. The argument of this passage proceeds by using all of the following EXCEPT:

(A) supporting a general point with a specific example
(B) questioning the honesty of politicians and commentators
(C) reinterpreting evidence presented as supporting a position being rejected
(D) pointing out inherent inconsistencies in the claims of the politicians and commentators
(E) exposing the limitations of arguments based on statistics

18. The most often heard complaint about flights on Scorpio Airlines is that there is insufficient room in the cabin of the plane to accommodate all of the passengers' carry-on baggage. The number of passengers who carry on all of their luggage rather than checking it at the ticket counter has increased so much that on more than half of the flights on Scorpio Airlines passengers have difficulty finding space for their bags in the cabin of the plane. The company is considering ways to alleviate this problem.

All of the following are plausible ways of dealing with the problem EXCEPT:

(A) reducing the allowable size of carry-on luggage
(B) charging passengers who carry on more than one bag a fee
(C) increasing the fares of flights on lightly traveled routes
(D) reducing the seating capacity of the cabins to provide more space for luggage
(E) offering a price reduction to ticket buyers who check their bags

1 1 1 1 1

19. *X*: "We discover new knowledge by the syllogistic process when we say, for example, 'All men are mortal; Socrates is a man; therefore Socrates is mortal.'"

Y: "Yes, but the fact is that if all men are mortal we cannot tell whether Socrates is a man until we have determined his mortality—in other words, until we find him dead. Of course, it's a great convenience to assume that Socrates is a man because he looks like one, but that's just a deduction. If we examine its formulation—'Objects that resemble men in most respects are men; Socrates resembles men in most respects; therefore Socrates is a man'—it's obvious that if he is a man, he resembles men in *all* necessary respects. So it's obvious we're right back where we started."

X: "Yes, we must know all the characteristics of men, and that Socrates has all of them, before we can be sure."

Which one of the following best expresses X's concluding observation?

(A) In deductive thinking we are simply reminding ourselves of the implications of our generalizations.
(B) It is often too convenient to arrive at conclusions simply by deduction instead of induction.
(C) Socrates' mortality is not the issue; the issue is critical thinking.
(D) Socrates' characteristics do not necessarily define his mortality.
(E) The key to the syllogistic process is using theoretical, rather than practical, issues of logic.

20. It takes a good telescope to see the moons of Neptune. I can't see the moons of Neptune with my telescope. Therefore, I do not have a good telescope.

Which one of the following most closely parallels the logic of this statement?

(A) It takes two to tango. You are doing the tango. Therefore, you have a partner.
(B) If you have a surfboard, you can surf. You do not have a surfboard. Therefore, you cannot surf.
(C) You need gin and vermouth to make a martini. You do not have any gin. Therefore, you cannot make a martini.
(D) If you know the area of a circle, you can find its circumference. You cannot figure out the circumference. Therefore, you do not know the area.
(E) You can write a letter to your friend with a pencil. You do not have a pencil. Therefore, you cannot write the letter.

GO ON TO THE NEXT PAGE.

1 1 1 1 1

Questions 21–22

Over 90 percent of our waking life depends on habits which for the most part we are unconscious of, from brushing our teeth in the morning to the time and manner in which we go to sleep at night. Habits are tools which serve the important function of relieving the conscious mind for more important activities. Habits are stored patterns of behavior which are found to serve the needs of the individual who has them and are formed from what once was conscious behavior which over years of repetition can become an automatic behavior pattern of the unconscious mind.

21. It can be inferred that the author bases his beliefs on
    (A) the testimony of a controlled group of students
    (B) biblical passages referring to the unconscious state
    (C) an intense psychological research
    (D) extensive psychological research
    (E) recent findings of clinical psychologists

22. The last sentence implies that
    (A) all repetitious patterns become unconscious behavior
    (B) conscious behavior eventually becomes habit
    (C) the unconscious mind causes repetitive behavior
    (D) automatic behavior patterns of the conscious mind are not possible
    (E) habits can be good or bad

Questions 23–24

It should be emphasized that only one person in a thousand who is bitten by a disease-carrying mosquito develops symptoms that require hospitalization, according to Dr. Reeves. But it is a potentially serious disease that requires close collaboration by citizens and local government to prevent it from reaching epidemic proportions.

Citizens should fill or drain puddles where mosquitoes breed. They should repair leaking swamp coolers and be sure swimming pools have a good circulating system. Make sure drain gutters aren't clogged and holding rainwater. Keep barrels and other water-storage containers tightly covered. Use good window screens.

23. Which one of the following statements, if true, would most strengthen the advice given in the second paragraph above?
    (A) Leaking swamp coolers are the primary cause of mosquito infestation.
    (B) It is possible to completely eliminate mosquitoes from a neighborhood.
    (C) No one can completely protect herself from being bitten by a mosquito.
    (D) Tightly covered water containers do not ensure the purity of the water in all cases.
    (E) Window screens seldom need to be replaced.

24. What additional information would strengthen the clarity of the second sentence above?
    (A) The names of some local governments that have fought against disease.
    (B) The name of the disease under discussion.
    (C) The names of those bitten by disease-carrying mosquitoes.
    (D) The full name of Dr. Reeves.
    (E) A description of the symptoms that a bitten person might develop.

GO ON TO THE NEXT PAGE.

1 1 1 1 1

25. That which is rare is always more valuable than that which is abundant. And so we are continually frustrated in our attempts to teach young people how to use time wisely; they have too much of it to appreciate its value.

Which one of the following statements, if true, would most weaken the argument above?

(A) Appreciation is not the same as obedience.
(B) "Abundant" is a term whose definition varies widely.
(C) Currency that is based on rare metals is more valuable than currency that is not.
(D) Many young people possess an intuitive knowledge of what time is, a knowledge they lose around middle age.
(E) The leisure time of people aged 18–24 has decreased by 80 percent over the last 10 years.

26. Many theorists now believe that people cannot learn to write if they are constantly worrying about whether their prose is correct or not. When a would-be writer worries about correctness, his ability to be fluent is frozen.

With which one of the following statements would the author of the above passage probably agree?

(A) Writing theorists are probably wrong.
(B) Writing prose is different from writing poetry.
(C) Literacy is a function of relaxation.
(D) Fear blocks action.
(E) Most good writers are careless.

STOP

IF YOU FINISH BEFORE TIME IS CALLED,
YOU MAY CHECK YOUR WORK ON THIS SECTION ONLY.
DO NOT WORK ON ANY OTHER SECTION IN THE TEST.

2 2 2 2 2

SECTION II

Time—35 minutes
28 Questions

Directions: Read the passages and answer the questions following each passage by blackening the appropriate space on the answer sheet. You may refer back to the passages when answering the questions. Answer all questions on the basis of what is stated or implied.

The Sixth Amendment's right to the "assistance of counsel" has been the subject of considerable litigation in twentieth-century American courts. The emphasis has traditionally centered on the degree to which a criminal defendant can demand the assistance of counsel in various courts and at different hierarchical stages of the criminal proceeding. Although past courts have alluded to the idea that a defendant has a converse right to proceed without counsel, the issue had not been squarely addressed by the United States Supreme Court until late in its 1974–75 term. At that time, the Court held that within the Sixth Amendment rests an implied right of self-representation.

As early as 1964, Justice Hugo Black wrote that "the Sixth Amendment withholds from federal courts, in all criminal proceedings, the power and authority to deprive an accused of his life or liberty unless he has or waives the assistance of counsel." However, recognizing that the Sixth Amendment does not require representation by counsel, it is quite another thing to say that the defendant has a constitutional right to reject professional assistance and proceed on his own. Notwithstanding such a logical and legal fallacy, the Court has, by way of opinion, spoken of a Sixth Amendment "correlative right" to dispense with a lawyer's help. Many lower federal courts have seized upon this and supported their holdings on it, in whole or in part.

The basic motivation behind this proffered right of self-representation is that "respect for individual autonomy requires that (the defendant) be allowed to go to jail under his own banner if he so desires" and that he should not be forced to accept counsel in whom he has no confidence. Courts have ruled that neither due process nor progressive standards of criminal justice require that the defendant be represented at trial by counsel. The Supreme Court, in its 1975 decision, held that a defendant in a state criminal trial has a constitutional right to waive counsel and carry on his own case *in propria persona.* In raising this obscure privilege to a constitutional level, the Court stated that, so long as the defendant is made aware of the dangers and disadvantages of self-representation, his lack of technical legal knowledge will not deprive him of the right to defend himself personally.

The Court conceded that the long line of right to counsel cases have alluded to the idea that the assistance of counsel is a prerequisite to the realization of a fair trial. However, the Court noted that the presence of counsel is of minor significance when a stubborn, self-reliant defendant prohibits the lawyer from employing his knowledge and skills. This line of reasoning is concluded

Model Test 3

GO ON TO THE NEXT PAGE.

with the observation that "the defendant and not his lawyer or the state, will bear the personal consequences of a conviction." The logical extension of this premise brings the Court to its decision that, recognizing the traditional American respect for the individual, the defendant "must be free personally to decide whether in his particular case counsel is to his advantage."

1. According to the passage, the chief purpose of the Sixth Amendment is to

    (A) assure a defendant the assistance of counsel in capital cases
    (B) assure a defendant the assistance of counsel in civil cases
    (C) assure a defendant the assistance of counsel in criminal cases
    (D) allow a defendant to represent himself in a criminal trial
    (E) allow a defendant to represent himself in a civil trial

2. The "logical and legal fallacy" referred to in lines 28–29 is probably

    (A) the ability to waive a right does not automatically give rise to a replacement of that right
    (B) the right to reject implies a correlative right to refuse to reject
    (C) the right to dispense with a lawyer's help
    (D) the right to legal assistance
    (E) the defendant who chooses to go to jail is free to do so

3. From the passage, the phrase *"in propria persona"* in lines 48–49 means

    (A) in his own person
    (B) by an appropriate person
    (C) in place of another person
    (D) improperly
    (E) by using a stand-in

4. In allowing a defendant to refuse counsel, the Supreme Court may have reasoned all of the following EXCEPT:

    (A) A defendant who objected to a court-appointed attorney would prevent the lawyer from defending him effectively.
    (B) The assistance of counsel is necessary to the realization of a fair trial.
    (C) In the event of an unfavorable verdict, the defendant will suffer the consequences.
    (D) American tradition recognizes the individual's freedom to make decisions that will affect him.
    (E) It is possible that a defendant might defend himself more effectively than a court-appointed lawyer.

GO ON TO THE NEXT PAGE.

2 2 2 2 2

5. A defendant who is acting as counsel in his own defense must be

(A) given additional legal assistance
(B) allowed to give up his own defense if he chooses to do so before the trial has concluded
(C) warned of the disadvantages of self-representation
(D) assisted by the judge in areas where the defendant's lack of knowledge of technical legal terms is deficient
(E) tried before a jury

6. All of the following are objections that might be raised to self-representation EXCEPT:

(A) By accepting the right to self-representation, a defendant must waive his right to assistance of counsel.
(B) A defendant determined to convict himself can do so more easily.
(C) If the right to self-representation is not asserted before the trial begins, it is lost.
(D) Self-representation has a tradition in American law that dates back to the colonial period.
(E) A self-representation defendant may be unruly or disruptive.

African art could have been observed and collected by Europeans no earlier than the second half of the fifteenth century. Before that time Europe knew of Africa only through the writing of classical authors such as Pliny and Herodotus and the reports of a few Arabic travelers. Unfortunately, until the latter years of the nineteenth century Europe was little interested in the arts of Africa except as curiosities and souvenirs of exotic peoples. Indeed, with the growth of the slave trade, colonial exploitation, and Christian missionizing the arts were presented as evidence of the low state of heathen savagery of the African, justifying both exploitation and missionary zeal. Even with the early growth of the discipline of anthropology the assumption was that Africa was a continent of savages, low on the scale of evolutionary development, and that these savages, because they were "preliterate," could, by definition, have no history and no government worth notice.

In recent years the development of critical studies of oral traditions, of accounts by Islamic travelers of the great Sudanese kingdoms, of the descriptions of the coast by early European travelers, and—above all—of the concept of cultural relativism, has led to a far more realistic assessment of the African, his culture, history, and arts.

Cultural relativism is, in essence, the attitude whereby cultures other than one's own are viewed in *their* terms and on *their* merits. As an alternative to the prejudgment of missionaries and colonials it allows us to view the cultures and arts of the African without the necessity of judging his beliefs and actions against a Judeo-Christian moralistic base, or his art against a Greco-Renaissance yardstick.

Model Test 3

GO ON TO THE NEXT PAGE.

2 2 2 2 2

Curiously, the "discovery" and enthusiasm for African art early in this century was not based on an objective, scientific assessment but rather resulted from an excess of romantic rebellion at the end of the last century against the Classical and Naturalist roots of western art. Unfortunately this uncritical adulation swept aside many rational concerns to focus upon African sculpture as if it were the product of a romantic, rebellious, *fin de siècle,* European movement. Obviously, African art is neither anti-classical nor anti-naturalistic: to be either it would have had to have had its roots in Classicism or in Naturalism, both European in origin. Nor was the concept of rebellion a part of the heritage of art in sub-Saharan Africa; rather, as we shall see, it was an art conservative in impulse and stable in concept.

We may admire these sculptures from a purely twentieth-century aesthetic, but if we so limit our admiration we will most certainly fail to understand them in the context of their appearance as documents of African thought and action.

In sharp contrast to the arts of the recent past in the Western world, by far the greatest part, in fact nearly all of the art of the history of the world, including traditional Africa, was positive in its orientation; that is, it conformed in style and meaning to the expectations—the norms—of its patrons and audience. Those norms were shared by nearly all members of the society; thus, the arts were conservative and conformist. However, it must be stressed that they were not merely passive reflections, for they contributed actively to the sense of well-being of the parent culture. Indeed, the perishable nature of wood—the dominant medium for sculpture—ensured that each generation reaffirmed its faith by re-creating its arts.

7. According to the passage, before the latter part of the nineteenth century, Europeans viewed African art as

(A) simple and direct
(B) odd but beautifully crafted
(C) savage and of little value
(D) ugly and of grotesque proportions
(E) warlike and lacking in beauty

8. According to the passage, which one of the following contributed to the initial dismissal of African art by Europeans?

(A) Europeans valued color and sophisticated techniques, both of which were absent in African arts.
(B) It was easier to justify exploitation of Africans if their art was dismissed as heathen.
(C) Europeans were made uncomfortable by the Africans' tendency to depict coarse acts and vulgar positions.
(D) It was important to reject African art because it was dangerous to a stable European society.
(E) It was believed that an influx of African art could seriously disrupt the market for European art.

9. According to the passage, all of the following contributed to a change in the European view of African art EXCEPT:

(A) the writings of Pliny
(B) cultural relativism
(C) Islamic travel accounts
(D) descriptions by early European travelers
(E) studies of oral traditions

GO ON TO THE NEXT PAGE.

2 2 2 2 2

10. Which one of the following most accurately represents the concept of cultural relativism as defined in the passage?
(A) The words "good" and "bad" are irrelevant when judging between works of art.
(B) One cannot enjoy a work of art without a complete understanding of the culture from which it came.
(C) The best art will always be art that is positive in its orientation.
(D) If an artist goes outside his own tradition in creating a work of art, that work of art will be inferior.
(E) To determine the success of a work of art, it should be judged against the values of its own culture.

11. According to the passage, the early twentieth-century European view of African art was inadequate because it
(A) was based on a limited number of objects available to the Western world
(B) was a result of a romantic rebellion against traditions in Western art
(C) did not take into account the importance of oral traditions
(D) was dependent on classical rather than naturalistic standards
(E) was dictated by the judgments of Christian missionaries

12. Which one of the following best describes the author's point about the relationship between twentieth-century Western art and African art?
(A) African art and twentieth-century Western art both have their roots in a desire to escape tradition and rediscover man's primitive state.
(B) The techniques used in African sculpture are remarkably similar to the techniques used in twentieth-century Western sculpture.
(C) It isn't possible to enjoy African art if we judge it by twentieth-century European aesthetic standards.
(D) Compared to twentieth-century Western art, African art is conservative and conformist, in that it is in keeping with the expectations of its society.
(E) Because it was produced by artists unschooled in technique, African art does not display the sophistication and ingenuity of twentieth-century Western art.

GO ON TO THE NEXT PAGE.

2 2 2 2 2

13. According to the author, the use of wood in African art is especially significant because
    (A) it is a simpler, more available medium than marble
    (B) unlike the hardness of stone, its relative softness allows intricate carvings representing African beliefs
    (C) it represents a rebellion from the media used in Western sculpture and a return to African roots
    (D) it is unique to primitive cultures uncorrupted by the Western world.
    (E) its impermanence ensures that each generation creates new art reaffirming the beliefs of the culture

14. In this passage, one of the principal methods the author uses to develop his subject is
    (A) discussion and explanation of reactions to African art in the Western world
    (B) examination and analysis of several specific African works of art
    (C) criticism and refutation of Western traditions such as Classicism and Naturalism
    (D) description and explanation of African religious and social beliefs
    (E) discussion and analysis of the aesthetic principles at the foundation of African art

In the competitive model—the economy of many sellers each with a small share of the total market—the restraint on the private exercise of economic power was provided by other firms on the same side of the market. It was the eagerness of competitors to sell, not the complaints of buyers, that saved the latter from spoliation. It was assumed, no doubt accurately, that the nineteenth-century textile manufacturer who overcharged for his product would promptly lose his market to another manufacturer who did not. If all manufacturers found themselves in a position where they could exploit a strong demand, and mark up their prices accordingly, there would soon be an inflow of new competitors. The resulting increase in supply would bring prices and profits back to normal.

As with the seller who was tempted to use his economic power against the customer, so with the buyer who was tempted to use it against his labor or suppliers. The man who paid less than the prevailing wage would lose his labor force to those who paid the worker his full (marginal) contribution to the earnings of the firm. In all cases the incentive to socially desirable behavior was provided by the competitor. It was to the same side of the market—the restraint of sellers by other sellers and of buyers by other buyers, in other words to competition—that economists came to look for the self-regulatory mechanisms of the economy.

They also came to look to competition exclusively and in formal theory still do. The notion that there might be another regulatory mechanism in the economy had been almost completely excluded from economic thought. Thus, with the widespread disappearance of competition in its classical form and its replacement by the small group of firms if not in overt, at least in conventional or tacit, collusion, it was easy to suppose that since

GO ON TO THE NEXT PAGE.

2 2 2 2 2

competition had disappeared, all effective restraint on private power had disappeared. Indeed, this conclusion was all but inevitable if no search was made for other restraints, and so complete was the preoccupation with competition that none was made.

In fact, new restraints on private power did appear to replace competition. They were nurtured by the same process of concentration which impaired or destroyed competition. But they appeared not on the same side of the market but on the opposite side, not with competitors but with customers or suppliers. It will be convenient to have a name for this counterpart of competition and I shall call it countervailing power.

To begin with a broad and somewhat too dogmatically stated proposition, private economic power is held in check by the countervailing power of those who are subject to it. The first begets the second. The long trend toward concentration of industrial enterprise in the hands of a relatively few firms has brought into existence not only strong sellers, as economists have supposed, but also strong buyers, a fact they have failed to see. The two develop together, not in precise step, but in such manner that there can be no doubt that the one is in response to the other.

15. Which one of the following would be the best title for this passage?
(A) Capitalism and the Competitive Model
(B) Competition and the Concept of "Countervailing Power"
(C) Problems in American Capitalism
(D) The Importance of Economic Regulatory Mechanisms
(E) The Failure of the Classic Competition Model

16. In the classic competition model, when competitive manufacturers marked up prices because of strong demand, a return to normal was provided by
(A) new manufacturers entering the market
(B) refusal to buy on the part of customers
(C) governmental intervention in the form of regulation
(D) repositioning of the labor force
(E) failure of weaker manufacturers

17. In the classic competition model, the incentive for manufacturers to behave in a socially desirable way toward workers was provided by
(A) competition for the labor supply
(B) competition for the customer
(C) imbalance between supply and demand
(D) self-regulation among competitors
(E) humanistic economic theory

18. According to the author, which one of the following statements is true?
(A) The classic model of competition was inadequate because it ignored the role of labor and rewarded individual greed.
(B) The classic model of competition provided self-regulation prior to, but not after, the Industrial Revolution.
(C) The classic model of competition was undermined by the "restraint of sellers by other sellers and of buyers by other buyers."
(D) The classic model of competition was replaced by concentration of industrial enterprise and collusion among manufacturers.
(E) The classic model of competition was destroyed by the growth of "countervailing power."

GO ON TO THE NEXT PAGE.

2 2 2 2 2

19. Examples of "countervailing power" in the regulation of the economic power of manufacturers could include all of the following EXCEPT:

(A) organized customer boycotts
(B) cooperative buying organizations
(C) large retail chains
(D) retailers developing their own sources of supply
(E) organizations that network manufacturers

20. According to the author, a weakness of economic thought has been

(A) a preoccupation with competition
(B) a failure to recognize the need for reasonable government regulation
(C) a belief in the "trickle-down" theory
(D) a failure to recognize concentration of industrial enterprise
(E) a bias toward unregulated capitalism

21. Which one of the following best describes the structure of this passage?

(A) The first three paragraphs describe the strengths of economic competition and the fourth and fifth paragraphs describe its weaknesses.
(B) The first paragraph presents the historical perspective on competition, the second and third present examples of its effect on the economy, and the fourth and fifth paragraphs set forth the idea of "countervailing power."
(C) The first two paragraphs describe how competition is thought to work, the third paragraph provides a transition, and the fourth and fifth paragraphs describe "countervailing power."
(D) The first three paragraphs describe the classic model of competition, while the fourth and fifth paragraphs describe "countervailing power."
(E) The first three paragraphs present a view of competition in opposition to the author's, while the fourth and fifth paragraphs present the author's view.

GO ON TO THE NEXT PAGE.

2 2 2 2 2

Passage A

Antoine-Laurent Lavoisier (1743–1794) can justly be called the father of modern chemistry, not because of earth-shaking discoveries or experiments but because he introduced a new approach to the understanding of chemical reactions. Some of his conclusions were later called into question or improved upon, but his relentless pursuit of knowledge and logical reasoning led to hundreds of experiments, all of which challenged the preconceived scientific notions of his day.

Lavoisier at twenty-five was elected to France's Academy of Sciences, in large part because of his work in geology, not chemistry. In 1775, he was appointed to the Royal Gunpowder and Saltpeter Administration, and in his laboratory he produced better gunpowder, in part by focusing on the purity of its ingredients and improved methods of granulating the powder.

An important aspect of Lavoisier's work was his determination of the weights of reagents and products, including gaseous components, involved in chemical reactions. He believed that matter, identified by weight, would always be conserved through these reactions. Lavoisier's methods led to, among other things, his definitive proof that water was made up of oxygen and hydrogen.

His methods also led him to challenge the phlogistic theory of combustion, which initially had been proposed by the German alchemist Johann Joachim Becher in the late 1600s and which was still widely accepted well into the eighteenth century. According to that theory, something called "phlogiston," named by Georg Ernst Stahl, existed in all materials and was released during combustion, the resulting ash being the remaining material, but "dephlogisticated." Since phlogiston wasn't—according to its proponents—a material substance, it was unweighable and without color or odor. Also according to the theory, acids produced by combustion were elementary substances, not the products of a chemical reaction. Lavoisier, through his experiments, came to recognize that a chemical reaction with oxygen, not a vague principle called phlogiston, caused combustion.

At first, Lavoisier referred to oxygen as "air in its purest form," but he later called it oxygen, from the Greek words *oxus*, meaning sharp, acidic, and *ginomai*, meaning to become or cause to be. He believed that oxygen caused the acids produced by combustion. Later, however, Sir Humphry Davy, Louis Joseph Gay-Lussac, and Louis-Jacques Thenard showed in their experiments with hydrochloric acid, chlorine, and hydrocyanic acid that acid could be produced without oxygen.

But Lavoisier, even though some of his ideas were later proved wrong, succeeded in turning away from alchemy and the theory of phlogiston. In the words of Justus von Liebig, Lavoisier's immortal glory "consists in this—that he infused into the body of the science a new spirit."

Passage B

Among the definitions of *theory* is "the analysis of a set of facts in their relation to one another." That definition doesn't take us very far, however, because almost any set of facts can be analyzed in a dozen or more ways. In science, theories are set forth and later discarded, or modified, all the time.

For example, in the seventeenth century, heat was erroneously explained through theories of combustion. Johann Joachim Becher and George Ernst Stahl introduced the theory that phlogiston, present in all matter, was released during combustion. It was thought to be the source of heat. Phlogiston couldn't

GO ON TO THE NEXT PAGE.

be weighed and, in fact, wasn't considered a material at all but rather a principle. Such notable scientists as Joseph Priestley (1733–1804), who conducted extensive research on the nature and property of gases, interpreted his results in terms of phlogiston. Priestley's experiments isolated and characterized eight gases, including oxygen, which he described as "dephlogisticated air."

Antoine Lavoisier, a French scientist who rightly explained combustion in terms of oxygen and not the principle of phlogiston, introduced another theory of heat. In his *Reflexions sur le phlogistique* (1783), he argued that the phlogiston theory was inconsistent with his experimental results. Ironically, however, Lavoisier proposed a substance called *caloric* (which he considered an "element"—one of 33 substances that couldn't be broken down into simpler entities) as the source of heat. Like phlogiston, caloric couldn't be weighed, and Lavoisier called it "a subtle fluid." The quantity of caloric, according to Lavoisier, was constant throughout the universe and flowed from warmer to colder bodies.

Not surprisingly, observable facts could be explained by the caloric theory. For instance, a hot bowl of soup cools at room temperature. Why? Because caloric slowly flows from regions dense with it (the hot soup) to regions less dense with it (the cooler air in the room). Another example is that air expands when heated. According to the caloric theory, this would be because caloric is absorbed by air molecules, thereby increasing the volume of the air.

Ultimately, the caloric theory as posited by Lavoisier was discarded. The calorists' principle of the conservation of heat was replaced by a principle of conservation of energy.

Modern thermodynamics defines heat not as a result of a "subtle fluid" but as a result of the kinetic energy of molecules.

22. Which of the following characterizes the main difference between Passage A and Passage B?

(A) Passage A praises Antoine Lavoisier, whereas Passage B discredits him.
(B) The focus in Passage A is on a scientist's work, while the focus in Passage B is on a particular theory.
(C) Passage A explains the phlogiston theory, whereas Passage B does not.
(D) In Passage A, the emphasis is on chemical reactions, while in Passage B the emphasis is on the scientific method.
(E) The author of Passage A is objective toward science, while the author of Passage B is skeptical.

23. The author of Passage B uses the term "ironically" in line 52 to

(A) emphasize how fallible scientists can be in interpreting their own results and the results of their predecessors
(B) undermine Lavoisier's designation as the "father of modern chemistry"
(C) note that while Lavoisier proved that phlogiston didn't exist, he introduced another nonexistent substance
(D) suggest the absurdity of scientific debates
(E) lighten the tone of the passage as a whole

24. According to Passage A, among Lavoisier's accomplishments was

(A) proving the chemical composition of water
(B) explaining the cause of heat
(C) changing the composition of gunpowder
(D) identifying caloric as a fluid
(E) isolating and characterizing eight gases

GO ON TO THE NEXT PAGE.

2 2 2 2 2

25. Which of the following best illustrates that facts can be explained by more than one theory (paragraph one of Passage B)?
    - (A) Hydrochloric acid cannot be produced without oxygen.
    - (B) The agent of combustion is weightless and odorless.
    - (C) Boiling water will cool at room temperature.
    - (D) Combustion results in ash made up of "dephlogisticated" material.
    - (E) Acids produced by combustion are elementary substances.

26. The author of Passage B would most likely agree with which of the following statements?
    - (A) Alchemy contributed nothing to science.
    - (B) Joseph Priestley was not as important as Antoine Lavoisier in the study of gases.
    - (C) Thermodynamics is an inexact science.
    - (D) A theory is a possible, but not necessarily the only, explanation of facts.
    - (E) The scientific method is seriously flawed and cannot be counted on to prove a fact.

27. According to information in Passage A and Passage B, Lavoisier believed that
    - (A) matter was not destroyed during a chemical reaction
    - (B) the acids produced during combustion were elementary substances
    - (C) molecular movement was responsible for the production of heat
    - (D) matter was converted to energy in chemical reactions
    - (E) a fluid called "caloric" caused combustion

28. In Passage B, Joseph Priestley is used as an example of
    - (A) a scientist who relied heavily on alchemy
    - (B) the importance of an open exchange of ideas between scientists
    - (C) a scientist who made a major discovery, as distinguished from Lavoisier
    - (D) a precursor to Lavoisier's experiments with gases
    - (E) the persistence of the phlogistic theory well into the eighteenth century

STOP

IF YOU FINISH BEFORE TIME IS CALLED,
YOU MAY CHECK YOUR WORK ON THIS SECTION ONLY.
DO NOT WORK ON ANY OTHER SECTION IN THE TEST.

SECTION III

Time—35 minutes
24 Questions

Directions: In this section you will be given groups of questions based on different sets of conditions. Drawing a simple diagram may be helpful in answering some of the questions. You are to choose the best answer and mark the corresponding space on your answer sheet.

Questions 1–6

There are five flagpoles lined up next to each other in a straight row in front of a school. Each flagpole flies one flag (red, white, or blue) and one pennant (green, white, or blue). The following are conditions that affect the placement of flags and pennants on the poles:

On a given flagpole, the pennant and the flag cannot be the same color.

Two adjacent flagpoles cannot fly the same color flags.

Two adjacent flagpoles cannot fly the same color pennants.

No more than two of any color flag or pennant may fly at one time.

1. If the 2nd and 5th pennants are blue, the 2nd and 5th flags are red, and the 3rd flag is white, then which one of the following must be true?

   (A) Two of the flags are white.
   (B) Two of the pennants are white.
   (C) The 4th pennant is green.
   (D) If the 1st pennant is green, then the 1st flag is blue.
   (E) If the 1st flag is white, then the 1st pennant is green.

2. If the 1st flag is red and the 2nd pennant is blue, then which one of the following is NOT necessarily true?

   (A) The 2nd flag is white.
   (B) If the 5th flag is red, then the 3rd flag is blue.
   (C) If the 4th pennant is green, then the 1st pennant is white.
   (D) If the 1st and 5th flags are the same color, then the 3rd flag is blue.
   (E) If the 4th pennant is green and the 5th pennant is white, then the 1st and 3rd pennants are different colors.

3. If the 1st and 3rd flags are white and the 2nd and 4th pennants are blue, then which one of the following is false?

   (A) The 4th flag is red.
   (B) The 1st pennant is green.
   (C) The 3rd pennant is not red.
   (D) The 5th pennant is green.
   (E) There is one blue flag.

GO ON TO THE NEXT PAGE.

3 3 3 3 3

4. If the 1st and 4th flags are blue, and the 3rd pennant is white, then which one of the following must be true?

(A) If the 1st pennant is green, then the 5th pennant is white.
(B) If the 5th pennant is white, then the 1st pennant is green.
(C) The 2nd flag is red.
(D) The 5th flag is red.
(E) The 1st pennant is green.

5. If the 2nd flag is red and the 3rd flag is white, and the 4th pennant is blue, then which one of the following must be true?

(A) If the 5th flag is white, then two of the pennants are blue.
(B) If the 1st flag is white, then the 2nd flag is white.
(C) If the 1st pennant is blue, then the 5th pennant is green.
(D) If the 1st pennant is green, then the 5th flag is not blue.
(E) If the 1st and 5th flags are the same color, then the 1st and 5th pennants are not the same color.

6. If the 1st flag and the 2nd pennant are the same color, the 2nd flag and the 3rd pennant are the same color, the 3rd flag and the 4th pennant are the same color, and the 4th flag and the 5th pennant are the same color, then which one of the following must be true?

(A) The 1st pennant is white.
(B) The 2nd flag is not white.
(C) The 5th flag is red.
(D) The 3rd pennant is blue.
(E) The 4th flag is white.

Questions 7–13

In the Norfolk Library returned book section there are ten books standing next to each other on a shelf. There are two math books, two science books, three English books, and three poetry books. The books are arranged as follows:

There is a math book on one end and an English book on the other end.
The two math books are never next to each other.
The two science books are always next to each other.
The three English books are always next to each other.

7. If the 8th book is a math book, then which one of the following must be true?

(A) The 5th book is a science book.
(B) The 7th book is an English book.
(C) The 6th book is not a poetry book.
(D) The 4th book is next to an English book.
(E) The 9th book is a science book.

8. If the 9th book is an English book and the 5th and 6th books are poetry books, then which one of the following must be true?

(A) There is a math book next to a poetry book.
(B) The 2nd book is a science book.
(C) The 3 poetry books are all next to one another.
(D) The 7th book is a math book.
(E) The 4th book is not a poetry book.

GO ON TO THE NEXT PAGE.

3 3 3 3 3

9. If the 1st book is a math book and the 7th book is a science book, then which one of the following could be false?

(A) Both math books are next to poetry books.
(B) All three poetry books are next to each other.
(C) The 2nd book is a poetry book.
(D) The 10th book is an English book.
(E) The 6th book is a science book.

10. If the 4th book is a math book and the 5th book is a science book, then which one of the following must be true?

(A) An English book is next to a science book.
(B) If the 7th book is a poetry book, then the 3rd book is an English book.
(C) If the 8th book is an English book, then the 2nd book is a poetry book.
(D) If the 10th book is a math book, then a poetry book is next to an English book.
(E) The three poetry books are next to each other.

11. If no two poetry books are next to each other, then which one of the following must be true?

(A) A science book is next to a math book.
(B) The 7th book is a poetry book.
(C) The 8th book is an English book.
(D) An English book is next to a science book.
(E) A poetry book is next to an English book.

12. If a science book is next to an English book, but not next to a poetry book, then which one of the following must be true?

(A) The 7th book is a poetry book.
(B) The 3rd book is an English book or a math book.
(C) The 5th or the 6th book is a math book.
(D) The 3 poetry books are not next to each other.
(E) The 7th or the 10th book is a math book.

13. If the 7th and 8th books are poetry books, how many different arrangements are there for the 10 books?

(A) 1
(B) 2
(C) 3
(D) 4
(E) 5

GO ON TO THE NEXT PAGE.

3 3 3 3 3

Questions 14–19

Seven friends—Paul, Ron, Sam, Tom, Victor, Willard, and Zack—are having dinner together. Each orders one of two possible starters, soup or salad, but not both. The following conditions must be satisfied:

If Tom orders salad, then Willard orders soup.
If Tom orders soup, then Ron orders salad.
If Zack orders soup, then Paul orders salad.
If Paul orders salad, then Willard orders salad.
If Victor orders salad, then Willard orders soup.
If Sam orders soup, then Tom orders soup.
If Zack orders soup, then Victor orders salad.
If Victor orders salad, then Ron orders soup.

14. If Paul and Willard make different choices for their starters, then which one of the following must be true?

(A) Sam orders soup.
(B) Paul orders salad.
(C) Victor orders soup.
(D) Tom orders salad.
(E) Zack orders soup.

15. If Victor orders salad, then which one of the following must be true?

(A) Willard orders salad.
(B) Sam orders soup.
(C) Zack orders soup.
(D) Paul orders salad.
(E) Tom orders salad.

16. If Paul and Tom have the same starter, each of the following could be true EXCEPT:

(A) Zack and Victor order different starters.
(B) Victor and Willard order different starters.
(C) Tom and Victor order different starters.
(D) Willard and Sam order different starters.
(E) Sam and Ron order different starters.

17. Which of the following pairs of friends together must order at least one soup?

(A) Sam and Tom
(B) Paul and Victor
(C) Tom and Zack
(D) Sam and Ron
(E) Paul and Willard

18. If Ron orders soup, then which of the following must be true?

(A) Tom orders soup.
(B) Victor orders salad.
(C) Zack orders soup.
(D) Paul orders soup.
(E) Willard orders salad.

19. What is the maximum number of friends who could order soup?

(A) two
(B) three
(C) four
(D) five
(E) six

Model Test 3

GO ON TO THE NEXT PAGE.

3 3 3 3 3

Questions 20–24

Seven track and field coaches, A, B, C, D, E, F, and G, are each assigned to coach exactly one of four activities—sprints, distance, jumpers, and throwers. Coaching assignments are made subject to the following conditions:

Each sport is coached by one or two of the seven coaches.
B coaches jumpers.
Neither E nor F is a distance coach.
If C coaches sprints, F and G coach throwers.
If D coaches distance or throwers, A and G do not coach either distance or throwers.

20. If C and E coach sprints, which one of the following must be true?

(A) Distance has two coaches.
(B) G coaches jumping.
(C) A coaches jumping or throwing.
(D) D coaches jumping.
(E) Jumping has one coach.

21. If G coaches jumping and A coaches distance, which one of the following must be true?

(A) D coaches sprints.
(B) F coaches throwing.
(C) E coaches sprints.
(D) C coaches distance.
(E) F coaches sprints.

22. If D coaches throwing, which one of the following CANNOT be true?

(A) G coaches sprints.
(B) A coaches jumping.
(C) E coaches sprints.
(D) F coaches throwing.
(E) C coaches jumping.

23. If G is the only throwing coach, which one of the following could be true?

(A) D coaches distance.
(B) If F coaches sprints, D coaches sprints.
(C) A coaches jumping.
(D) If F coaches jumping, D coaches jumping.
(E) C and D coach the same sport.

24. If A does not coach sprints and D coaches distance, which one of the following CANNOT be true?

(A) C coaches distance.
(B) E coaches throwing.
(C) G coaches jumping.
(D) F coaches sprints.
(E) E coaches sprints.

Model Test 3

STOP

IF YOU FINISH BEFORE TIME IS CALLED,
YOU MAY CHECK YOUR WORK ON THIS SECTION ONLY.
DO NOT WORK ON ANY OTHER SECTION IN THE TEST.

SECTION IV

Time—35 minutes
26 Questions

Directions: In this section you will be given brief statements or passages and will be required to evaluate the reasoning involved. In some instances, more than one choice will appear to be a possible answer. You are to choose the *best* answer. Use common sense and reasonableness in making your selection; then mark the proper space on the answer sheet.

Questions 1–2

The spate of bills in the legislature dealing with utility regulation shows that our lawmakers recognize a good political issue when they see one. Among the least worthy is a proposal to establish a new "Consumers Utility Board" to fight proposed increases in gas and electric rates.

It is hardly a novel idea that consumers need representation when rates are set for utilities which operate as monopolies in their communities. That's exactly why we have a state Public Utilities Commission.

Supporters of the proposed consumer board point out that utility companies have the benefit of lawyers and accountants on their payrolls to argue the case for rate increases before the PUC. That's true. Well, the PUC has the benefit of a $40 million annual budget and a staff of 900—all paid at taxpayer expense—to find fault with these rate proposals if there is fault to be found.

1. Which one of the following is the best example to offer in support of this argument against a Consumers Utility Board?

(A) the percentage of taxpayer dollars supporting the PUC
(B) the number of lawyers working for the Consumers Utility Board
(C) the number of concerned consumers
(D) a PUC readjustment of rates downward
(E) the voting record of lawmakers supporting the board

2. Which one of the following would most seriously weaken the above argument?

(A) Private firms are taking an increasing share of the energy business.
(B) Water rates are also increasing.
(C) The PUC budget will be cut slightly, along with other state agencies.
(D) Half of the PUC lawyers and accountants are also retained by utilities.
(E) More tax money goes to education than to the PUC.

Model Test 3

GO ON TO THE NEXT PAGE.

4 4 4 4 4

3. Most of those who enjoy music play a musical instrument; therefore, if Maria enjoys music, she probably plays a musical instrument.

Which one of the following most closely parallels the reasoning in the statement above?

(A) The majority of those who voted for Smith in the last election oppose abortion; therefore, if the residents of University City all voted for Smith, they probably oppose abortion.
(B) If you appreciate portrait painting you are probably a painter yourself; therefore, your own experience is probably the cause of your appreciation.
(C) Most of those who join the army are male; therefore, if Jones did not join the army, Jones is probably female.
(D) Over 50 percent of the high-school students polled admitted hating homework; therefore, a majority of high-school students do not like homework.
(E) If most workers drive to work, and Sam drives to work, then Sam must be a worker.

4. *Mayor:* There must be no official or unofficial meeting of two or more members of the City Council that is not open to the public or a matter of public record. Though certain subjects can only be discussed in private, the danger of elected officials pursuing a private agenda, rather than what most benefits the public, is a serious concern in an age when politicians are too often willing to promote their private interests behind closed doors.

On which one of the following grounds is this argument especially subject to criticism?

(A) It treats popular opinion as if it were conclusive evidence.
(B) It misleadingly generalizes from the actions of a few to the actions of an entire group.
(C) It concedes the point that effectively undermines its argument.
(D) It uses an ambiguous term without making clear which meaning of the term applies here.
(E) It reaches a conclusion based on limited evidence chosen only because that evidence supports the argument.

GO ON TO THE NEXT PAGE.

4 4 4 4 4

5. "Good personnel relations of an organization depend upon mutual confidence, trust, and goodwill. The basis of confidence is understanding. Most troubles start with people who do not understand each other. When the organization's intentions or motives are misunderstood, or when reasons for actions, practices, or policies are misconstrued, complete cooperation from individuals is not forthcoming. If management expects full cooperation from employees, it has a responsibility of sharing with them the information which is the foundation of proper understanding, confidence, and trust. Personnel management has long since outgrown the days when it was the vogue to 'treat them rough and tell them nothing.' Up-to-date personnel management provides all possible information about the activities, aims, and purposes of the organization. It seems altogether creditable that a desire should exist among employees for such information which the best-intentioned executive might think would not interest them and which the worst-intentioned would think was none of their business."

The above paragraph implies that one of the causes of the difficulty that an organization might have with its personnel relations is that its employees

(A) have not expressed interest in the activities, aims, and purposes of the organization
(B) do not believe in the good faith of the organization
(C) have not been able to give full cooperation to the organization
(D) do not recommend improvements in the practices and policies of the organization
(E) can afford little time to establish good relations with their organization

6. Of all psychiatric disorders, depression is the most common; yet, research on its causes and cures is still far from complete. As a matter of fact, very few facilities offer assistance to those suffering from this disorder.

The author would probably agree that

(A) depression needs further study
(B) further research will make possible further assistance to those suffering from depression
(C) most facilities are staffed by psychiatrists whose specialty is not depression
(D) those suffering from depression need to know its causes and cures
(E) depression and ignorance go hand in hand

7. *Editorial:* The politicians who wish to see the schools run like businesses will have some trouble establishing a standard of accountability. In the business world, profits provide a clear standard, measurable in numbers. But in public education, standards are culturally derived, and differ very widely among age, ethnic, and political groups. We can evaluate a school's record keeping or its facilities, but there is no way to use the standards of quality control that are used to judge the profitability of a business and apply them to the academic performance of students throughout a public school system.

To which one of the following is the writer of this passage objecting?

(A) the assumption that a school and a business are analogous
(B) the belief that profitability is a universal standard
(C) the assumption that schools, like businesses, can show a financial profit
(D) the belief that school vouchers are undemocratic
(E) the assumption that record keeping and facilities are adequate gauges of business success

GO ON TO THE NEXT PAGE.

4 4 4 4 4

8. *Ivan:* What the Church says is true because the Church is an authority.
Mike: What grounds do you have for holding that the Church is a genuine authority?
Ivan: The authority of the Church is implied in the Bible.
Mike: And why do you hold that the Bible is true?
Ivan: Because the Church holds that it is true.

Which one of the following is the best description of the reasoning involved in the argument presented in the foregoing dialogue?

(A) deductive
(B) inductive
(C) vague
(D) pointed
(E) circular

9. *Mary:* All Italians are great lovers.
Kathy: That is not so. I have met some Spaniards who were magnificent lovers.

Kathy's reply to Mary indicates that she has misunderstood Mary's remark to mean that

(A) every great lover is an Italian
(B) Italians are best at the art of love
(C) Spaniards are inferior to Italians
(D) Italians are more likely to be great lovers than are Spaniards
(E) there is a relationship between nationality and love

<u>Questions 10–11</u>

Mr. Dimple: Mrs. Wilson's qualifications are ideal for the position. She is intelligent, forceful, determined, and trustworthy. I suggest we hire her immediately.

10. Which one of the following, if true, would most weaken Mr. Dimple's statement?

(A) Mrs. Wilson is not interested in being hired.
(B) There are two other applicants whose qualifications are identical to Mrs. Wilson's.
(C) Mrs. Wilson is currently working for a rival company.
(D) Mr. Dimple is not speaking directly to the hiring committee.
(E) Mrs. Wilson is older than many of the other applicants.

11. Which one of the following, if true, offers the strongest support of Mr. Dimple's statement?

(A) All the members of the hiring committee have agreed that intelligence, trustworthiness, determination, and forcefulness are important qualifications for the job.
(B) Mr. Dimple holds exclusive responsibility for hiring new employees.
(C) Mr. Dimple has known Mrs. Wilson longer than he has known any of the other applicants.
(D) Mrs. Wilson is a member of Mr. Dimple's family.
(E) Mrs. Dimple is intelligent, forceful, determined, and trustworthy.

GO ON TO THE NEXT PAGE.

4 4 4 4 4

12. All of the candidates for the spring track team must have participated in fall cross-country and winter track. Some runners, however, find cross-country tedious, and refuse to run in the fall. Thus, some winter track runners who would like to be members of the spring track teams are not permitted to try out.

In which one of the following is the reasoning most like that of this passage?

(A) Mice become aggressive if confined in close quarters for an extended period of time, or if they are deprived of protein-rich foods. Therefore, highly aggressive mice have been closely confined and denied high-protein foods.
(B) Roses grown in full sun are less susceptible to mildew than roses grown in partial shade. Roses grown in partial shade are also more susceptible to black spot. Thus, roses should be grown in full sun.
(C) To qualify for the June primary, a candidate for office must reside in the district for six months and gather 500 signatures of district residents who support the candidate. Thus, a longtime district resident would not qualify for the June primary if she gathered only 300 signatures.
(D) A convenience store sells three chocolate bars for a dollar, and a large soft drink for 50 cents. A competitor sells four chocolate bars for a dollar, and a medium-size soft drink for 50 cents. Therefore, neither of the two stores offers more for the same price.
(E) The City Council has passed an ordinance that allows cyclists to use the city bike paths only if they are over 12 years old and are wearing bicycle helmets. Thus, parents with children under 12 will be unable to cycle with their families on the city bike paths unless they wear helmets.

13. When a dental hygienist cleans your teeth, you may not see much evidence that she is supervised by a dentist. Hygienists often work pretty much on their own, even though they are employed by dentists. Then why can't hygienists practice independently, perhaps saving patients a lot of money in the process? The patients would not have to pay the steep profit that many dentists make on the hygienists' labors.

Which one of the following statements weakens the argument above?

(A) Some patients might get their teeth cleaned more often if it costs less.
(B) Some dentists do not employ dental hygienists.
(C) Hygienists must be certified by state examinations.
(D) A dentist should be on hand to inspect a hygienist's work to make sure the patient has no problems that the hygienist is unable to detect.
(E) In some states, there are more female hygienists than male.

14. There are those of us who, determined to be happy, are discouraged repeatedly by social and economic forces that cause us nothing but trouble. And there are those of us who are blessed with health and wealth and still grumble and complain about almost everything.

To which one of the following points can the author be leading?

(A) Happiness is both a state of mind and a state of affairs.
(B) Both personal and public conditions can make happiness difficult to attain.
(C) Happiness may be influenced by economic forces and by health considerations.
(D) No one can be truly happy.
(E) Exterior forces and personal views determine happiness.

GO ON TO THE NEXT PAGE.

4 4 4 4 4

15. "Keep true, never be ashamed of doing right; decide on what you think is right and stick to it."—*George Eliot*

If one were to follow Eliot's advice, one
(A) would never change one's mind
(B) would do what is right
(C) might never know what is right
(D) would never be tempted to do wrong
(E) would not discriminate between right and wrong

16. To paraphrase Oliver Wendell Holmes, taxes keep us civilized. Just look around you, at well-paved superhighways, air-conditioned schools, and modernized prisons, and you cannot help but agree with Holmes.

Which one of the following is the strongest criticism of the statement above?

(A) The author never actually met Holmes.
(B) The author does not acknowledge those of us who do not live near highways, schools, and prisons.
(C) The author does not assure us that he has been in a modernized prison.
(D) The author does not offer a biographical sketch of Holmes.
(E) The author does not define "civilized."

Questions 17–18

Information that is published is part of the public record. But information that a reporter collects, and sources that he contacts, must be protected in order for our free press to function free of fear.

17. The above argument is most severely weakened by which one of the following statements?

(A) Public information is usually reliable.
(B) Undocumented evidence may be used to convict an innocent person.
(C) Members of the press act ethically in most cases.
(D) The sources that a reporter contacts are usually willing to divulge their identity.
(E) Our press has never been altogether free.

18. Which one of the following statements is consistent with the argument above?

(A) Privileged information has long been an important and necessary aspect of investigative reporting.
(B) Not all the information a reporter collects becomes part of the public record.
(C) Tape-recorded information is not always reliable.
(D) The victim of a crime must be protected at all costs.
(E) The perpetrator of a crime must be protected at all costs.

GO ON TO THE NEXT PAGE.

4 4 4 4 4

Questions 19–21

A federal court ruling that San Diego County can't sue the government for the cost of medical care of illegal aliens is based upon a legal technicality that ducks the larger moral question. But the U.S. Supreme Court's refusal to review this decision has closed the last avenue of legal appeal.

The medical expenses of indigent citizens or legally resident aliens are covered by state and federal assistance programs. The question of who is to pay when an undocumented alien falls ill remains unresolved, however, leaving California counties to bear this unfair and growing burden.

19. The author implies that
    - (A) the U.S. Supreme Court has refused to review the federal court ruling
    - (B) the burden of medical expenses for aliens is growing
    - (C) the larger moral question involves no legal technicalities
    - (D) San Diego should find another avenue of appeal
    - (E) the federal government is dodging the moral issue

20. Which one of the following arguments, if true, would most seriously weaken the argument above?
    - (A) There are many cases of undocumented aliens being denied medical aid at state hospitals.
    - (B) A private philanthropic organization has funded medical aid programs that have so far provided adequate assistance to illegal aliens nationwide.
    - (C) Illegal aliens do not wish federal or state aid, because those accepting aid risk detection of their illegal status and deportation.
    - (D) Undocumented aliens stay in California only a short time before moving east.
    - (E) Judges on the Supreme Court have pledged privately to assist illegal aliens with a favorable ruling once immigration laws are strengthened.

21. Which one of the following changes in the above passage could strengthen the author's argument?
    - (A) adding interviews with illegal aliens
    - (B) a description of the stages that led to a rejection by the Supreme Court
    - (C) a clarification with numbers of the rate at which the burden of medical expenses is growing
    - (D) the naming of those state and federal assistance programs that aid indigent citizens
    - (E) the naming of those California counties that do not participate in medical aid to illegal aliens

GO ON TO THE NEXT PAGE.

22. *Historian:* History is strewn with the wreckage of experiments in communal living, often organized around farms and inspired by religious or philosophical ideals. To the more noble failures can now be added Mao Tse-Tung's notorious Chinese communes. The current rulers of China, still undoing the mistakes of the late Chairman, are quietly allowing their agricultural communes to . . . .

    Which one of the following is the most logical completion of the passage above?

    (A) evolve
    (B) increase
    (C) recycle
    (D) disintegrate
    (E) organize

23. *Sal:* Herb is my financial planner.
    Keith: I'm sure he's good; he's my cousin.

    Which one of the following facts is Keith ignoring in his response?

    (A) Financial planning is a professional, not a personal, matter.
    (B) Sal is probably flattering Keith.
    (C) Professional competence is not necessarily a family trait.
    (D) "Good" is a term with many meanings.
    (E) Sal's financial planner is no one's cousin.

24. Many very effective prescription drugs are available to patients on a "one time only" basis. Suspicious of drug abuse, physicians will not renew a prescription for a medicine that has worked effectively for a patient. This practice denies a patient her right to health.

    Which one of the following is a basic assumption made by the author?

    (A) A new type of medicine is likely to be more expensive.
    (B) Physicians are not concerned with a patient's health.
    (C) Most of the patients who need prescription renewals are female.
    (D) Most physicians prescribe inadequate amounts of medicine.
    (E) Patients are liable to suffer the same ailment repeatedly.

GO ON TO THE NEXT PAGE.

4 4 4 4 4

Questions 25–26

Forty years ago, hardly anybody thought about going to court to sue somebody. A person could bump a pedestrian with his Chrysler Airflow, and the victim would say something like "No harm done" and walk away. Ipso facto. No filing of codicils, taking of depositions, or polling the jury. Attorneys need not apply.

25. Which one of the following sentences most logically continues the above passage?

(A) The Chrysler Airflow is no longer the harmless machine it used to be.
(B) Fortunately, this is still the case.
(C) Unfortunately, times have changed.
(D) New legislation affecting the necessity for codicils is a sign of the times.
(E) But now, as we know, law schools are full of eager young people.

26. Which one of the following details, if true, would most strengthen the above statement?

(A) There were fewer courthouses then than now.
(B) The marked increase in pedestrian accidents is a relatively recent occurrence.
(C) Most citizens of 40 years ago were not familiar with their legal rights.
(D) The number of lawsuits filed during World War II was extremely low.
(E) Most young attorneys were in the armed forces 40 years ago.

STOP

IF YOU FINISH BEFORE TIME IS CALLED,
YOU MAY CHECK YOUR WORK ON THIS SECTION ONLY.
DO NOT WORK ON ANY OTHER SECTION IN THE TEST.

5 5 5 5 5

SECTION V

Time—35 minutes
28 Questions

Directions: Read the passages and answer the questions following each passage by blackening the appropriate space on the answer sheet. You may refer back to the passages when answering the questions. Answer all questions on the basis of what is stated or implied.

In the negotiation of tax treaties, developing nations, as a group, share two objectives somewhat at odds with those of developed-nation treaty partners. One such goal, attracting foreign investment, is in the broader context of foreign policy objectives. In the narrower realm of tax policy a common developing-country objective is to maximize the public capture of revenues from foreign investment activities.

Unfortunately for potential Third World treaty partners, this latter goal can conflict directly with the desires of both First World governments and individual investors. The preference of First World authorities for restricted source-based taxation is due to considerations of administrative feasibility. Such restrictions, though formally reciprocal, only produce equitable revenue effects when investment flows between treaty partners are relatively equal. However, when investment flows primarily in one direction, as it generally does from industrial to developing countries, the seemingly reciprocal source-based restrictions produce revenue sacrifices primarily by the state receiving most of the foreign investment and producing most of the income—namely, the developing country partner. The benefit is captured either by the taxpayer in the form of reduced excess credits, or by the treasury of the residence (First World) state as the taxpayer's domestically creditable foreign tax liabilities decrease. The potential public revenue gain to the residence state further bolsters the industrial nations' preference for restrictions on source-based taxation—at the direct expense of the treaty partner's revenue goals.

The facilitation of foreign investment by tax treaties, whereas potentially serving the tax-policy goal of maximizing public revenue, also (or even instead) may serve broader economic objectives of developing countries. Foreign investments may be seen as essential sources of technical and managerial knowledge, capital, jobs, and foreign exchange. As such, the significance of foreign investments as an immediate source of public revenue could pale next to their longer-term "ripple effect" on development. In the negotiation of tax treaties, then, a developing country might be expected to ignore revenue goals and accept substantial limitations on source-based taxation, at least insofar as such limitations could be expected to encourage investment.

Frequently, however, Third World nations take a considerably more aggressive approach, seeking treaty terms that, in effect, provide subsidies to private investors at the expense of First World treaty partners. The United States traditionally has followed a strict policy of "capital export neutrality," providing no tax incentives for investment in the Third World through either the Internal Revenue Code or tax treaty provisions.

GO ON TO THE NEXT PAGE.

5 5 5 5 5

1. Normally, a developing country will negotiate a tax treaty for the purpose of

(A) attracting foreign workers
(B) decreasing tax revenues
(C) attracting international investment and reducing tax revenues
(D) attracting foreign investment and increasing tax revenues
(E) decreasing dependence on special interest local investors

2. We can infer that a reciprocal source-based taxation treaty between a First World and a developing nation will produce

(A) greater revenues for the First World nation
(B) greater revenues for the developing nation
(C) equal revenues for each country
(D) no revenues for either country
(E) losses to the economy of the First World nation

3. In negotiated treaties with developing countries, a First World country is likely to prefer

(A) unrestricted source-based taxation
(B) reciprocal restricted source-based taxation
(C) nonreciprocal source-based taxation
(D) equal investment flow between the partners
(E) limited investment flow between the partners

4. In a treaty with a developing country that generates an excess of foreign tax credits, all of the following are likely EXCEPT:

(A) the treaty will require some reduction of at-source taxation
(B) the treaty will discourage private investors
(C) the treaty will not produce what is perceived as the optimal revenue-producing balance
(D) the treaty will require some expansion of at-source taxation
(E) the excess of tax credits will be larger if the source country reserves more taxing jurisdiction

5. According to the passage, all of the following are potential advantages of foreign investment to developing countries EXCEPT:

(A) increased managerial expertise
(B) increased capital
(C) increased availability of new materials
(D) increased foreign exchange
(E) increased employment

6. A developing country that did not insist upon immediate higher public revenues might be expected to

(A) deter foreign investment
(B) increase foreign investment
(C) avoid the "ripple effect"
(D) decrease employment
(E) decrease the availability of raw materials

GO ON TO THE NEXT PAGE.

5 ◇5◇ ◇5◇ ◇5◇ 5

How buildings are depicted indicates how they are perceived. To the serious travelers of the eighteenth century, like James Stuart and Nicholas Revett who took it upon themselves to record the legendary remains of Greece for the first time since antiquity, there are two modes of perception: the topical and the archaeological. To introduce each monument, they resorted to the picturesque tableau. They show the Parthenon at the time of their visit in 1751, when Athens was a sleepy provincial town within the Ottoman Empire and the Akropolis served as the headquarters for the Turkish governor. The temple stands in a random cluster of modest houses; in it we can see a Turk on horseback and, through the colonnade, the vaulted forms of the small Byzantine church that rose within the body of the temple during the Middle Ages. This is what the Parthenon looks like today, the authors are saying; and this depiction carries at once the quaint appeal of an exotic land and that sense of the vanity of things which comes over us at the sight of the sad dilapidation of one-time splendors.

But when they turn from romance to archaeology, the task of showing the Parthenon not as it is now but as it was then, Stuart and Revett restrict themselves to the measured drawing. They re-create, in immaculate engravings of sharp clear lines, the original design of the temple in suitably reduced scale and with a careful tally of dimensions. We are confronted again with the traditional abstractions of the architect's trade. Indeed, those architects who, in subsequent decades, wished to imitate the Parthenon as a venerable form of rich associational value could do so readily from these precise plates of Stuart and Revett, without once having seen Athens for themselves. In nineteenth-century Philadelphia, for example, the disembodied facade of the Parthenon is reconstructed as the Second Bank of the United States in an urban milieu that is completely alien to the setting of the prototype.

Against the engravings of Stuart and Revett, we might pit two pencil sketches of the Akropolis made by Le Corbusier during his apprenticeship travels in the early years of this century. The close-up view is neither picturesque nor archaeological. It does not show us the ubiquitous tourists scrambling over the site, for example, nor any other transient feature of local relevance. Nor is the sketch a reproducible paradigm of the essential design of the Parthenon. Instead, we see the temple the way Le Corbusier experienced it, climbing toward it up the steep west slope of this natural citadel, and catching sight of it at a dynamic angle through the inner colonnade of the Propylaia, the ceremonial gate of the Akropolis. The long view shows the building in relation to the larger shapes of nature that complement its form: the pedestal of the Akropolis spur that lifts it up like a piece of sculpture and the Attic mountain chain on the horizon which echoes its mass. And when Le Corbusier draws on this experience later in his own work, it is the memory of the building as a foil to nature that guides his vision.

7. From paragraph one, which one of the following best describes Stuart and Revett's pictures of the remains of ancient Greece?

(A) They show the grandeur of the Akropolis and depict the surrounding mountain ranges.
(B) They emphasize the original design and dimensions of the building.
(C) They show the antiquities as they appeared at the time of the pictures, not as they appeared in ancient Greece.
(D) Human figures and modest houses dominate the scenes that are shown in the pictures, whereas the natural surroundings are missing entirely.
(E) They are designed to contrast classical Grecian architecture with Byzantine architecture from the Middle Ages.

GO ON TO THE NEXT PAGE.

5 5 5 5 5

8. Which one of the following best summarizes the author's point about Stuart and Revett's first set of pictures (paragraph one)?
   (A) Although the pictures are from 1751, they capture the way the Greek monuments looked to the average Greek citizen at the time they were constructed.
   (B) By mixing grand monuments such as the Akropolis with modest houses, Stuart and Revett are making an ironic comment about architecture.
   (C) Stuart and Revett's intention was to give as exact a picture as possible of the dimensions, scale, and grandeur of the original Greek antiquities.
   (D) The pictures have a quaint appeal but they also convey a sense of the vanity of human efforts by showing the effects of time on the Greek antiquities.
   (E) The pictures capture not just the beauty and grandeur of the Greek antiquities but also suggest the positive spirit possessed by the people who created them.

9. In paragraph two, Stuart and Revett's engravings that depict the Parthenon are best described as
   (A) exact and measured
   (B) romantic and abstract
   (C) topical and picturesque
   (D) exotic and quaint
   (E) uninteresting and pedantic

10. In paragraph two, the author mentions the Second Bank of the United States (line 44) in order to
   (A) show how Stuart and Revett's archaeological plates were exact enough to allow the Parthenon to be copied without an architect ever seeing the original building
   (B) emphasize that classical architecture was so timeless that a building such as the Parthenon could be copied in an entirely alien environment and still retain its beauty
   (C) indict Stuart and Revett for allowing inferior copies of Greek antiquities to be made, thereby detracting from the splendor of the original structures
   (D) show the difference in the way that architecture was depicted in nineteenth-century America from the way it was depicted in eighteenth-century England as illustrated in Stuart and Revett's plates
   (E) contrast the inferiority of imitative nineteenth-century architecture with the greatness of classical Greek architecture

11. According to the author, Le Corbusier's sketches of the Akropolis primarily show its
   (A) beauty and importance as a monument
   (B) relationship to its natural surroundings
   (C) importance as a citadel in Athens
   (D) connection to the common man in ancient Greece
   (E) role as a model for other monuments

GO ON TO THE NEXT PAGE.

12. Which one of the following can be inferred from information in the passage?

    (A) Classical Greek architecture, although often imitated, has never been surpassed.
    (B) The engraving process is the most effective way to create accurate architectural drawings.
    (C) The same building, depending on how it is depicted, may elicit various responses from a viewer.
    (D) Romantic depictions of structures are generally superior to strictly archaeological drawings.
    (E) Stuart and Revett were superior to Le Corbusier in depicting architecture in various ways.

13. Which one of the following does the author primarily use to make his point about architectural depiction?

    (A) anecdote and allusion
    (B) irony and understatement
    (C) metaphor and personification
    (D) logical argument and persuasion
    (E) description and contrast

War and change—political and economic foremost, but social and cultural not far behind—have been linked in America from the beginning. War was the necessary factor in the birth of the new American republic, as it has been in the birth of every political state known to us in history. War, chiefly the Civil War, in U.S. history has been a vital force in the rise of industrial capitalism, in the change of America from a predominantly agrarian and pastoral country to one chiefly manufacturing in nature. War, in focusing the mind of a country, stimulates inventions, discoveries, and fresh adaptations. Despite its manifest illth*, war, by the simple fact of the intellectual and social changes it instigates, yields results which are tonics to advancement.

By all odds, the most important war in U.S. history, the war that released the greatest number and diversity of changes in American life, was the Great War, the war that began in Europe in August 1914 and engulfed the United States in April 1917. Great changes in America were immediate.

In large measure these changes reflected a release from the sense of isolation, insularity, and exceptionalism that had suffused so much of the American mind during the nineteenth century. The early Puritans had seen their new land as a "city upon a hill" with the eyes of the world on it. It was not proper for the New World to go to the Old for its edification; what was proper was for the Old World, grown feeble and hidebound, to come to America for inspiration. A great deal of that state of mind entered into what Tocqueville called the "American Religion," a religion compounded of Puritanism and ecstatic nationalism.

*illth = ill effects (word coined by the author earlier in the full selection)

GO ON TO THE NEXT PAGE.

5 5 5 5 5

What we think of today as modernity—in manners and morals as well as ideas and mechanical things—came into full-blown existence in Europe in the final part of the nineteenth century, its centers such cities as London, Paris, and Vienna. In contrast America was a "closed" society, one steeped in conventionality and also in a struggle for identity. This was how many Europeans saw America and it was emphatically how certain somewhat more sophisticated Americans saw themselves. The grand tour was a veritable obligation of better-off, ambitious, and educated Americans—the tour being, of course, of Europe.

Possibly the passage of American values, ideas, and styles from "closed" to "open," from the isolated to the cosmopolitan society, would have taken place, albeit more slowly, had there been no transatlantic war of 1914–1918. We can't be sure. What we do know is that the war, and America's entrance into it, gave dynamic impact to the processes of secularization, individualization, and other kinds of social-psychological change which so drastically changed this country from the America of the turn of the century to the America of the 1920s.

14. In the passage the author makes all of the following points about war EXCEPT:
    (A) war increases the pace of changes that might occur anyway
    (B) war stimulates new inventions and discoveries
    (C) war causes social and intellectual changes
    (D) war in a capitalistic society is inevitable
    (E) war sometimes stimulates a closed society toward greater openness

15. If true, which of the following best illustrates the author's point about the effects of war on American society?
    (A) During World War II, the Germans developed a variety of lethal nerve gas to use in the field.
    (B) The development of radioactive isotopes used in treating cancer grew out of research to build the atomic bomb used in World War II.
    (C) The American influenza epidemic of 1919 in all likelihood was a result of the return of infected soldiers from the battlefields of World War I.
    (D) After the Civil War and the abolition of slavery in the South, racial intolerance across America grew in bitterness.
    (E) A significant drain on America's material resources was a result of relaxed immigration policies occurring after World War II.

16. According to the author, World War I was the most important war in U.S. history because it
    (A) ended the notion of a war to end all wars
    (B) resulted in a weakened Germany that in turn led to Hitler's appeal
    (C) changed America from a dominantly agrarian country to a manufacturing country
    (D) led to more changes and a wider diversity of changes than any other American war
    (E) made Americans more aware of advances made in European centers such as London, Paris, and Vienna

GO ON TO THE NEXT PAGE.

5 ◇5◇ ◇5◇ ◇5◇ 5

17. The main purpose of paragraph three is to

(A) characterize the American mind in the nineteenth century
(B) define Tocqueville's concept of American religion
(C) indicate the main cause of America's entrance into World War I
(D) contrast Civil War America with World War I America
(E) indicate the areas of America's strength at the start of World War I

18. According to the author, which one of the following contributed to America's insularity before World War I?

(A) The inability of all but the most wealthy, educated Americans to travel abroad
(B) The nationalistic view that the New World (America) shouldn't turn to the Old World (Europe) for ideas
(C) The emphasis on agrarian pursuits as opposed to belief in industry and technology
(D) The puritanical idea that traveling widely in the world exposed one to sin and corruption
(E) The superiority of the New World (America) to a feeble, decadent Old World (Europe)

19. Which one of the following best describes the main subject of this passage?

(A) a comparison of wars in America
(B) the benefits of war to society
(C) the importance of World War I to changes in America
(D) the contrast between the New World (America) and the Old World (Europe)
(E) secularization and individualization in American society

20. The relationship of paragraph one to the rest of the passage is best described by which one of the following?

(A) It presents a popular view that is proved inadequate by the rest of the passage.
(B) It introduces a philosophical question that is then answered in the rest of the passage.
(C) It outlines the contents of each of the other four paragraphs in the passage.
(D) It sets up the first of four examples developed in the rest of the passage.
(E) It presents a general idea that introduces the specific topic developed in the rest of the passage.

21. According to information in the passage, all of the following inferences can be made EXCEPT:

(A) Well-to-do nineteenth-century American parents would be more likely to send their son to Europe than to California.
(B) European "ecstatic nationalism" would be greater after World War I than before it.
(C) Religious influence in the daily workings of American society would be less evident in 1920 than 1900.
(D) A census in America 20 years after the Civil War would indicate more manufacturing operations than before the war.
(E) In the nineteenth century, avant garde movements in art and literature would be more likely to originate in Europe than in the U.S.

GO ON TO THE NEXT PAGE.

5 5 5 5 5

The theory of natural selection cites the fact that every organism produces more gametes and/or organisms than can possibly survive. If every gamete produced by a given species united in fertilization and developed into offspring, the world would become so overcrowded in a short period of time that there would be no room for successive generations. This does not happen. There is a balance that is maintained in the reproduction of all species and therefore natural populations remain fairly stable, unless upset by a change in conditions. In the struggle for existence, some organisms die and the more hardy survive.

The differences that exist between organisms of the same species, making one more fit to survive than another, can be explained in terms of variations. Variations exist in every species and in every trait in members of a species. Therefore some organisms can compete more successfully than others for the available food or space in which to grow, or they can elude their enemies better. These variations are said to add survival value to an organism. Survival value traits are passed on to the offspring by those individuals that live long enough to reproduce. As time goes on, these special adaptations for survival are perpetuated and new species evolve from a common ancestral species. The environment is the selecting agent in natural selection because it determines which variations are satisfactory for survival and which are not.

The major weakness in Darwin's theory of natural selection is that he did not explain the source, or genetic basis, for variations. He did not distinguish between variations that are hereditary and those that are nonhereditary, making the assumption that all variations that have survival value are passed on to the progeny. Like Jean Baptiste Lamarck, Darwin believed in the inheritance of even acquired characteristics.

Hugo De Vries (1845–1935), a Dutch botanist, explained variations in terms of mutations. His study of 50,000 plants belonging to the evening primrose species enabled him to identify changes in the plants that were passed on from parent to offspring. In 1901 De Vries offered his mutation theory to explain organic evolution. Today, we know that mutations are changes in genes that can come about spontaneously or can be induced by some mutagenic agent. Spontaneous mutation rates are very low, and mutations alone do not affect major changes in the frequencies of alleles, which are alternative forms of genes that occupy a given place on a chromosone.

An important cause of variation within species is genetic recombination that results from sexual reproduction. The genes of two individuals are sorted out and recombined into a new combination, producing new traits—and thus variation.

Gene flow is also responsible for the development of variations. It is the movement of new genes into a population. Gene flow often acts against the effects of natural selection. Genetic drift is a change in a gene pool that takes place in a population as a result of chance. If a mutation occurs in a gene of one person, and that person does not reproduce, the gene is lost to the population. Sometimes a small population breaks off from a larger one. Within that population is a mutant gene, and because the mating within the small population is very close, the frequencies of the mutant gene will increase. In the Amish population, for example, where there is little or no outbreeding, an increase in the homozygosity of the genes in the gene pool is evinced in the high frequencies of genetic dwarfism and polydactyly (six fingers). The isolated smaller population has a different gene frequency than the larger population from which it came. This is known as the

GO ON TO THE NEXT PAGE.

"founder principle." Genetic drift and the random mutations that increase or decrease as the result of genetic drift are known as non-Darwinian evolution.

Another cause of variation is speciation, or the forming of new species from a species already in existence. This can happen when a population becomes geographically divided and part of the original species continues life in a new habitat. The separated populations cannot interbreed. Over evolutionary time, different environments present different selective pressures, and the change in gene pools will eventually produce new species.

22. The passage supports which one of the following statements?
    - (A) Spontaneous mutations cause the most significant evolutionary changes.
    - (B) Darwin's theory of evolution depends on rejecting the idea that acquired characteristics can be inherited.
    - (C) Variations among individual members of a species occur only when new genes move into an established population of that species.
    - (D) It is possible for a survival value trait to be eliminated from a species.
    - (E) New species are generally the result of genetic recombination.

23. Which one of the following, if true, would support the idea that acquired characteristics can be inherited?
    - (A) A spontaneous mutation causes some members of a rodent population to develop webbed feet. This segment of the population becomes isolated and is unable to breed with the original group. An exceptionally high frequency of webbed feet occurs in the successive generations of the isolated segment.
    - (B) A gene from a virus is experimentally transmitted to a fruit fly, making it vulnerable to carbon dioxide poison. This vulnerability is then passed on to the fruit fly's offspring.
    - (C) Antelopes raised in captivity are released into the wild. They run significantly more slowly than the wild antelope. After a year, the released antelopes' speed equals that of the wild antelopes.
    - (D) A population of long-haired dogs is shaved and bred with a population of hairless dogs. Their offspring include more hairless than long-haired pups.
    - (E) Fourteen different species of finches live on the Galapagos Islands. It is determined that all descended from a single species of finch found on mainland Peru.

24. The passage provides explanations for each of the following EXCEPT:
    - (A) genetic drift
    - (B) the founder principle
    - (C) survival value
    - (D) speciation
    - (E) homozygosity

GO ON TO THE NEXT PAGE.

5 5 5 5 5

25. Random mutations are known as non-Darwinian evolution because they

(A) are not necessarily related to the survival value of an organism
(B) are more infrequent than spontaneous mutations
(C) tend to refute Darwin's theories about the formation of species
(D) occur only in small populations that have been isolated
(E) were first described by Hugo De Vries, not Charles Darwin

26. The founder principle

(A) accounts for genetic dwarfism
(B) supports the importance of "weeding out" non-adaptive organisms
(C) explains the concept of homozygosity
(D) relates to gene frequencies in isolated populations
(E) refutes Darwin's theory of natural selection

27. Based on the passage, which one of the following can be inferred about Charles Darwin?

(A) Darwin did not believe the theory of genetic inheritance.
(B) Darwin did not believe that genetic theories were relevant to evolution.
(C) Darwin's work was more concerned with the survival value of traits than with the mechanics of how they were inherited.
(D) Darwin's theories did not include a recognition that variation within members of a species was crucial to evolution.
(E) Darwin was more interested in traits that were acquired and passed on than he was in genetically inherited traits.

28. In the passage, the author's primary concern is to

(A) address briefly the history of evolutionary theory
(B) provide a brief overview of the concept of variation
(C) expose the weakness inherent in Darwin's evolutionary theory
(D) differentiate between genetic and evolutionary theories
(E) describe one of the ways in which non-adaptive traits can be inherited

STOP

IF YOU FINISH BEFORE TIME IS CALLED,
YOU MAY CHECK YOUR WORK ON THIS SECTION ONLY.
DO NOT WORK ON ANY OTHER SECTION IN THE TEST.

Writing Sample

Directions: You have 35 minutes to write an essay in response to a given topic. Take a few minutes to plan your work before you begin writing. DO NOT WRITE ON A TOPIC OF YOUR OWN CHOICE. ESSAYS THAT DO NOT ADDRESS THE GIVEN TOPIC ARE UNACCEPTABLE.

The quality of your writing is more important than the length of your response or the content. Pay attention to organization, appropriate diction, and correct usage. You will not be expected to display any specialized knowledge in your response, nor will you be expected to write a "perfect" essay; law schools understand that you are writing under a time constraint, and will allow for the minor lapses in writing ability that might occur under this circumstance.

Only the lined area on your response sheets will be reproduced for the law schools, so do not write outside this space. Make sure your handwriting is legible.

Scratch Paper

Do not write your essay in this space

Sample Topic

Read the following descriptions of Thomas and Peters, candidates for the position of head coach of the Ventura Vultures professional football team. *Then, in the space provided, write an argument for appointing one candidate over the other.* Use the information in this description and assume that the two general policies below equally guide the Vultures' decision on the appointment:

- The head coach should possess the ability to work with players and coaching staff toward achieving a championship season.
- The head coach should successfully manage the behind-the-scenes activities of recruiting, analyzing scouting reports, and handling the media and fans in order to enhance the public relations and image of the team.

THOMAS has been General Manager of the Vultures for the past ten years. A physical education major with a master's in psychology, he knows the player personnel as well as anyone, including the coaching staff. His on-target assessment of player skills and weaknesses has been instrumental in building a more balanced team over the past decade through his skillful trading and recruitment of college athletes. As the chief managing officer, he has also enhanced the team's image by his careful press relationship and understated approach when negotiations with star players reached an impasse. He rarely alienates players, coaches, press, or fans with his even-handed (though sometimes unemotional) attitude, and the Vultures' owners feel fortunate that they were able to entice him away from his high-school coaching position, which he left 10 years ago. He has never played either pro or college ball.

PETERS is presently a wide receiver and defensive end for the Vultures. A one-time star, Peters has played both offense and defense for the Vultures since their inception in the league 14 years ago, a remarkable feat equaled by few in the game. He was elected captain of the team the past five years because of his charisma, although he occasionally angers management and fellow players with his strong comments about his philosophy of the game. His only experience in the front office was leading a player charity benefit for the Vultures, which raised more than $2,000,000 for abused Ventura County children. Although a high school dropout, Peters is a self-made man who firmly believes the key to life is having a strong educational background, even though he sometimes feels uncomfortable around college-educated athletes. The Vulture owners believe Peters may provide the emotional charge the team needs at its helm to win its first championship.

Scratch Paper

Do not write your essay in this space

Answer Key

Section I: Logical Reasoning

1. A	6. D	11. E	16. D	21. D	26. D
2. A	7. A	12. D	17. D	22. B	
3. D	8. B	13. C	18. C	23. B	
4. E	9. E	14. A	19. A	24. B	
5. C	10. A	15. B	20. D	25. E	

Section II: Reading Comprehension

1. C	6. D	11. B	16. A	21. C	26. D
2. A	7. C	12. D	17. A	22. B	27. A
3. A	8. B	13. E	18. D	23. C	28. E
4. B	9. A	14. A	19. E	24. A	
5. C	10. E	15. B	20. A	25. C	

Section III: Analytical Reasoning

1. E	5. A	9. B	13. B	17. B	21. A
2. C	6. C	10. C	14. C	18. D	22. E
3. D	7. D	11. E	15. E	19. D	23. B
4. B	8. A	12. C	16. C	20. D	24. C

Section IV: Logical Reasoning

1. D	6. B	11. A	16. E	21. C	26. D
2. D	7. A	12. C	17. B	22. D	
3. A	8. E	13. D	18. A	23. C	
4. C	9. A	14. D	19. E	24. E	
5. B	10. B	15. B	20. B	25. C	

Section V: Reading Comprehension

1. D	6. B	11. B	16. D	21. B	26. D
2. A	7. C	12. C	17. A	22. D	27. C
3. B	8. D	13. E	18. B	23. B	28. B
4. D	9. A	14. D	19. C	24. E	
5. C	10. A	15. B	20. E	25. A	

Model Test Analysis

Doing model exams and understanding the explanations afterwards are, of course, important in acquainting you with typical LSAT question types and successful approaches to the questions. However, another benefit of carefully analyzing these model tests is to understand the kinds of errors you are making and thus work to minimize them. For instance, if a very high percentage of your incorrect answers is due to "careless error" or "misread problem" then perhaps you are working much too fast and should slow your pace accordingly. If your incorrect answers are due primarily to "lack of knowledge," then a careful rereading and reworking of the appropriate question-type chapter may be in order. Or, if you find that you aren't completing a large number of questions because of lack of time, you may need to either increase your speed or learn to use the "one-check, two-check" technique more effectively.

This kind of analysis of the model tests will enable you to identify your particular weaknesses and thus remedy them.

MODEL TEST THREE ANALYSIS

Section	Total Number of Questions	Number Correct	Number Incorrect	Number Unanswered*
I. Logical Reasoning	26			
II. Reading Comprehension	28			
III. Analytical Reasoning	24			
IV. Logical Reasoning	26			
V. Reading Comprehension	28			
Writing Sample				
TOTALS:	132			

*At this stage in your preparation, you should not be leaving any blank answer spaces. At least fill in a guess, as there is no penalty for a wrong answer.

REASONS FOR INCORRECT ANSWERS

You may wish to evaluate the explanations before completing this chart.

Section	Total Number Incorrect	Lack of Knowledge	Misread Problem	Careless Error	Unanswered or Wrong Guess
I. Reading Comprehension					
II. Analytical Reasoning					
III. Logical Reasoning					
IV. Analytical Reasoning					
V. Logical Reasoning					
TOTALS:					

Answers Explained

Section I

1. **(A)** The author must assume that "nothing about our coin influences its fall in favor of either side or that all influences are counterbalanced by equal and opposite influences"; otherwise "our ignorance of the coming result" is untrue. Also, he mentions that the chances are one out of two that the coin will fall heads up; this could not be correct if the coin had been weighted or tampered with.

2. **(A)** (A) is implied by the author's statement that one-to-two is not "true." (B), (C), (D), and (E) are not implied and would not follow from the passage.

3. **(D)** The author is actually pointing out that self-confidence is of most importance. (C) and (E) focus on behavior, while the author is focusing on mental attitude.

4. **(E)** Only choice (E) is supported by these comments. The comments suggest that riding on roller coasters is taking a risk and that this risk translates to a proclivity to taking other risks in life. The passage doesn't suggest, however, that *no* roller coaster riders avoid taking risks elswhere (A), nor does it have any bearing on the importance of taking risks (B). Choice (C) is a difficult one to eliminate because the passage certainly doesn't rule out this possibility (the passage says "than other," not "than *all* others")—but it doesn't directly support it, either. The comments have nothing to do with varying levels or types of risk taking (D).

5. **(C)** If the diet and way of life of the men of the two islands are alike, but the life expectancies are very different, the cause of the difference is probably something other than diet and the way of life. Some of the other answers are reasonable inferences, but they do not follow so clearly from the paragraph as (C).

6. **(D)** None of the other four choices offer information that explains the discrepancy. If the women in college are preparing for a profession that pays less (teaching) than the profession the men will enter (engineering), the discrepancy is explained.

7. **(A)** To conclude that the women should earn as much as or more than the men, the passage must assume that all of the men and all of the women, or at least an equal number, enter the workforce. It also assumes that all of

them, or at least an equal number, graduate from college, though the passage says only "are enrolled."

8. **(B)** The six-month interest-free charge is the money at a low cost; the stock of discontinued summer wear is the slow selling product, and the fashionable new neck wear is the popular product. None of the other choices covers all three conditions.

9. **(E)** Though all of the choices are plausible, (E) deals with all three of the problems mentioned in the paragraph. Each of the other choices deals only with one.

10. **(A)** The statistics present the very small percentage of male dance students. Of the five statements, (A) does throw light on the figures. If dancing is not a socially accepted career for men, it is not surprising that there are few students. The other four statements have no real relevance to the statistics.

11. **(E)** The author states that the present programs are at best weak and hopefully won't fail as they have in the past.

12. **(D)** The statement that "Hopefully, they won't fail as they have in the past" tells us that our government is not trying a new approach to end inflation. (A) is close, but the passage states that foreign oil is "high-priced," not "overpriced." "High-priced" tells us the relative cost, not the actual comparative value.

13. **(C)** The conclusion is the prediction of a grim year for home-builders. Choices (A), (B), (D), and (E) do not point to continued bad sales, but (C), revealing that sales fell even with advertising and incentives, supports the prediction of a bad year ahead.

14. **(A)** Three possibilities exist:
(a) You read *Weight-Off* magazine, are fat, and do not eat chocolate.
(b) You are fat, eat chocolate, but do not read *Weight-Off* magazine.
(c) You eat chocolate, are not fat, and do not read *Weight-Off* magazine.
Thus, (A) is inconsistent by (a) and (b). (B) is not inconsistent if (b) and (c) are void of people. (C) is not inconsistent if (c) is void of people. (D) and (E) are not inconsistent by (c) and (a).

15. **(B)** Dave felt that Jerry implied that no one except Jerry's wife cooks fantastic meals.

16. **(D)** Only (D) offers an instance of success in the polls. (A) simply repeats a point of the passage without including the qualification that comes later. Choices (B), (C), and (E) would support rather than undermine the viewpoint of the passage.

17. **(D)** The passage does not point out inherent inconsistencies. It does support a point with a specific example (the two figures on the balanced budget poll), question the honesty of politicians (the phrase "or may not"), reinterprets the 80 percent support figure, and shows how statistics can be used to mislead.

18. **(C)** Decreasing the fares on lightly traveled routes might attract some passengers away from the overcrowded, more popular flights, but increasing the fares would not help to solve the luggage problem. The four other suggestions are plausible ways of dealing with the lack of space.

19. **(A)** X's new realization is expressed in his final sentence: "We must know all the characteristics of men, and that Socrates has all of them, before we can be sure." The "characteristics of men" are what is implied by the generalization "man," in "Socrates is a man." Therefore, deductive thinking is simply reminding ourselves of the particular specifics implied by generalizations.

20. **(D)** Symbolically, A is necessary to have B (a good telescope to see moons of Neptune). You do not have B (can't see moons with my telescope). Therefore, you cannot have A (a good telescope). (D) is the only choice that follows this line of reasoning. Symbolically, A is necessary to have B (knowing area of circle to find circumference). You do not have B (can't figure out circumference). Therefore, you cannot have A (area of circle).

21. (D) Extensive psychological research would most likely give the information that the author discusses. (E) limits the research to clinical psychologists and to recent findings.

22. (B) "Conscious behavior eventually becomes habit" is indirectly stated in the last sentence. (A) is a close answer, but that absolute word "all" is inconsistent with the words "can become" in the last sentence. This does not imply that they *must* become unconscious behavior.

23. (B) The given advice would be strengthened by the assurance that such measures are effective. Each of the other choices either weakens the advice, or addresses only a portion of the paragraph.

24. (B) The disease under discussion is termed "it," and thus its identity is unclear. The other choices either are not applicable to the second sentence or refer to terms that require no further definition.

25. (E) (E) weakens the argument that young people have abundant time. The other choices are only tangentially relevant to the argument.

26. (D) The passage says that worrying about writing unfortunately keeps one from writing at all; (D) summarizes this viewpoint. (B) and (C) are irrelevant notions; (A) contradicts the author's implied support for writing theorists; and (E) is an unreasonable, unsupported conclusion.

Section II

Passage 1

1. (C) The chief purpose of the Sixth Amendment was to ensure the assistance of counsel in criminal cases. The guarantee to the right of self-representation was not the chief purpose of the amendment although the amendment has been used to support it.

2. (A) The phrase refers to the end of the second paragraph. The author regards the waiving of the right to counsel as a choice, which should not be seen as a guarantee of the right of self-representation.

3. (A) The phrase "*in propria persona*" means "in his own person," "by himself," or "by herself."

4. (B) If the Court had believed a fair trial was impossible without the assistance of counsel, it would not have allowed self-representation.

5. (C) The passage emphasizes the importance of warning a defendant of the risks of self-representation.

6. (D) Though true, the tradition of self-representation is not a valid objection to the practice. In fact, it might be cited as an argument in favor of self-representing defendants.

Passage 2

7. (C) The passage states that African arts were curiosities and were presented as evidence of the "low state of heathen savagery of the African." The implication of lines 16–22 is that the arts, like the government and history, were not worth notice. (D) and (E) are incorrect; nothing is implied concerning the proportions or the subjects of African art. (A) and (B) both suggest a positive reaction to the art; this reaction is not supported by the passage.

8. (B) See lines 11–16. (C), whether true or not, is not supported by the passage. (D) is incorrect; Africa wasn't a threat to European society. In fact, Africans were exploited or made objects of missionary zeal. (A) and (E) are clearly irrelevant or incorrect.

9. (A) The writings of Pliny are cited as one of the early sources of knowledge about Africa—not one of the factors contributing to a change in the European view. See lines 23–30 for support of (B), (C), (D), and (E).

10. (E) Lines 31–33 make it clear that cultural relativism refers to viewing a culture in its own terms and on its own merits rather than judging it by the standards of one's own culture. (E) most clearly defines this point of view in relation to art. (A) is incorrect; the passage does not suggest that value judgments about works of art cannot be made, as long as

the works are judged against the values of their own culture. (B) and (C) are irrelevant to the idea of cultural relativism. (D) is also irrelevant, and its judgment is not supported by any statements in the passage.

11. **(B)** See lines 41–47. The author states that when the attitude toward African art did change, it changed as a result of an "excess of romantic rebellion" against Classicism and Naturalism, not as a result of an objective assessment. No point is made in the passage about the availability of African art (A). (C) is unclear, and (D) is clearly inaccurate. The judgments of missionaries (E) were irrelevant to the twentieth-century European assessment of African art.

12. **(D)** See lines 66–75. One of the author's main points is that African art was very much in tune with its audience, unlike modern European art, which represented a rebellion against European traditions. (A) is the opposite of the point the author makes about African art. (B) and (E) are irrelevant and not supported by information in the passage. (C) is incorrect because although the author says we cannot have full understanding of African art if we judge it by twentieth-century Western aesthetic standards, we can still "admire" the works in a limited way. See lines 60–65.

13. **(E)** See lines 79–82. The author states that the works of art, while conservative and conformist, were not "passive reflections" of the culture; the perishable nature of wood ensured that every generation reaffirmed its faith. No comparison between wood and stone is made (with the exception of the implied comparison of impermanence and permanence). Therefore, (A) and (B) are incorrect. Also, no point is made about Western art or the Western world (C), (D).

14. **(A)** Throughout the passage the author talks about European or Western reactions to African art, from the earliest knowledge of Africa in Europe until the twentieth-century reassessment of African art. No specific works are analyzed (B), nor is any information included about African religious and social beliefs (D) or African aesthetic principles (E).

Passage 3

15. **(B)** (B) is the best choice because the passage first describes the classic model of competition and then introduces what the author refers to as the concept of "countervailing power." Although the ideas in (D) and (E) are both present in the passage, these titles are too restrictive. (A) is incomplete, and (C) is clearly wrong, in that the passage doesn't specifically address "American capitalism."

16. **(A)** (A) is directly from the passage (lines 15–18). Although (B) and (C) might occur, these are not part of the classic competition model described by the author. (E) would certainly not provide a return to normal prices; although it might offer a change in *supply*, it would not alter *demand*. Answer (D) is simply unclear.

17. **(A)** (A) is the best choice. See lines 22–28. (D) and (E) are clearly wrong. (C) is unclear. The second-best answer is (B), since the behavior of manufacturers is ultimately related to competition for the customer. However, (A) is the more specific answer provided by the passage.

18. **(D)** (D) is the best choice. See lines 39–46. (A) is incorrect because the classic model of competition does *not* ignore the role of labor (lines 22–26). Also, although the author might agree that greed undermined the classic model, this is not an issue addressed in the passage. (B) is incorrect because the author does not relate change in self-regulation of competition to any particular event, nor does he place it in a specific time frame. (C) is clearly the opposite of the point made in the passage. The restraint of "sellers by other sellers and buyers by other buyers" is part of the classic model of competition. (E) is incorrect because, according to the author, "countervailing power" did not destroy competition but grew as a result of a change in the classic model, i.e., the reduction of the number of

competitors and resulting concentration of power among a small group of firms.

19. (E) Organizations that network manufacturers would not provide a customer- or supplier-generated restraint on them, which is the way the author defines "countervailing power." All of the other choices are possible wielders of "countervailing power."

20. (A) In lines 28–38 and lines 47–50, the author makes it clear that economists have almost exclusively focused on the classic model of competition in considering restraints on manufacturers. (B) is incorrect because the author does not discuss government regulation or the lack of it as part of economic theory. Similarly, (C) is incorrect; the "trickle-down" theory (i.e., that what is good for those at the top will ultimately benefit those at the bottom) is also not mentioned in the passage. (D) is contradicted in the passage; according to the author, economists did recognize the trend toward concentration (lines 39–46, 65–71). Finally, although the author might agree with (E), the passage suggests that economists have been preoccupied with the classic model of competition (including its built-in restraints) rather than biased toward "unregulated" capitalism. The preoccupation with the classic models led them to ignore other types of restraint in the economy.

21. (C) The passage sets up the classic model of competition in paragraphs one and two. Paragraph three is a shift in the discussion to the idea that there might be a restraining mechanism exclusive of the competitive model that economists haven't recognized. Paragraphs four and five describe this restraining mechanism. The second-best answer is (D); however, paragraph three does provide a transition, which makes (C) the better choice.

Passage 4

22. (B) Although Passage B includes Lavoisier, its focus is on the caloric theory of heat, while Passage A covers other aspects of the scientist, not just one theory. Passage B, while showing how Lavoisier's theory of heat was later disproved, does not "discredit" him (A). (E) is also inaccurate; while showing how theories can be supplanted by new theories, the author's tone toward science is not skeptical.

23. (C) The use of the term follows the statement that Lavoisier disproved the theory of phlogiston, a nonexistent substance (or "flammability principle"). It is ironic that he then posits another substance, caloric, that cannot be weighed or measured.

24. (A) In lines 29–31, the passage states that Lavoisier's methods led to his proof that oxygen and hydrogen made up water, and therefore (A) is the best answer. Lavoisier's caloric theory was incorrect in explaining heat (B) and (D), and it was Priestley (mentioned in Passage B), not Lavoisier, who isolated eight gases (E). Although Passage A says that Lavoisier produced better gunpowder, there is no indication that he changed its composition (C).

25. (C) (C) is the best example of the author's point in the first paragraph. In lines 117–125, two specific examples are given of how observable facts can be explained by Lavoisier's caloric theory, a theory that was later proved wrong. None of the other choices are observable facts explained by the caloric theory.

26. (D) The best answer is (D), a point the author makes in the first paragraph. The passage doesn't imply either that alchemy "contributed nothing to science" (A) or that thermodynamics is an inexact science (C). Although (E) may seem like a possible answer, the author doesn't criticize the scientific method but merely suggests that theories can be disproved or modified in time.

27. (A) (A) is the best answer (lines 27–29). Although Lavoisier did believe in a fluid called caloric, he thought it caused heat, not combustion (E). (B) was part of the phlogiston theory, not Lavoisier's theory, and (C) and (D) are related to theories after Lavoisier.

28. (E) Passage B refers to Priestley as an important eighteenth century scientist who firmly believed in the phlogiston theory, making (E) the best answer.

Section III

Answers 1–6

UPPER-case letters denote colors given in the problem, and lower-case letters denote deduced colors.

1. (E)

1	2	3	4	5	
b/w	R	W	b	R	(flag)
w/g	B	g	w	B	(pennant)

The 3rd pennant cannot be blue or white, so therefore it is green. The 4th flag cannot be white or red, so it must be blue. The 4th pennant cannot be green or blue, so it must be white. The 1st flag cannot be red, so it is either blue or white. The 1st pennant cannot be blue, so it must be green or white.

2. (C)

1	2	3	4	5	
R	w	r/b			(flag)
g/w	B	g/w			(pennant)

(A) is clearly true. If the 5th flag is red, then the 3rd flag cannot be, since the 1st flag is red and we can have only two of any one color. Thus, (B) is true. If the 4th pennant is green, then the 3rd pennant must be white. But that does not determine the color of the 1st pennant. Thus, (C) is not necessarily true. (D) is the same as (A) and is also true. If the 4th pennant is green, this implies that the 3rd pennant must be white. If the 5th pennant is white, then the 1st pennant cannot be. Therefore, (E) is true.

3. (D)

1	2	3	4	5	
W	r	W	r	b	(flag)
g	B	g	B	w	(pennant)

The facts in this problem determine the complete configuration of flags and pennants. (D) is the one statement that is false.

4. (B)

1	2	3	4	5	
B	w	r	B		(flag)
		W	g		(pennant)

Statement (B) is true since the 1st pennant cannot be blue or white. Statement (A) is false since the 5th pennant could be blue or white. Statement (C) is false since it is white. Statements (D) and (E) are false since they could be white.

5. (A)

1	2	3	4	5	
	R		W	r	(flag)
		g		B	(pennant)

If the 5th flag is white, then the 5th pennant must be green. Thus, the 1st and 2nd pennants cannot be green and cannot be the same color, so one of them is blue. Therefore, (A) is true. All the other statements are false.

6. (C)

1	2	3	4	5	
W	B	W	B	r	(flag)
g	W	B	W	B	(pennant)

1	2	3	4	5	
B	W	B	W	r	(flag)
g	B	W	B	W	(pennant)

Since blue and white are the two common colors between flags and pennants, the above are the only two arrangements possible. In both cases, the 5th flag is red and the 1st pennant is green.

Answers 7–13

7. (D)

1	2	3	4	5	6	7	8	9	10
E	E	E					M		M

If the 8th book is a math book, then the three English books must be in positions 1, 2, and 3, since they cannot be in positions 8, 9, and 10. Thus, the other math book is in position 10. The 4th book must be next to the English book in position 3.

8. (A)

1	2	3	4	5	6	7	8	9	10
M				P	P		E	E	E

If the 9th book is an English book, then so are the 8th and 10th books. Thus there is a math book in position 1. The science books must be in positions 2 and 3 *or* 3 and 4. This leaves only positions 4 and 7 for the other math book. Thus (A) is always true. (C) could be true, but does not have to be true. The 3rd poetry book could be in position 2.

Model Test 3

9. (B)

1	2	3	4	5	6	7	8	9	10
M					S	S	E	E	E

If the 1st book is a math book, then the 8th, 9th, and 10th books must be the English books. If the 7th book is a science book, so must be the 6th book. This means that the other math book must be either the 3rd, the 4th, or the 5th book. The remainder of the books are poetry books, including the 2nd book.

10. (C)

1	2	3	4	5	6	7	8	9	10
M	P	P	M	S	S	P	E	E	E

or

1	2	3	4	5	6	7	8	9	10
E	E	E	M	S	S	P	P	P	M

If the 4th book is a math book and the 5th book is a science book, then the 6th book is also a science book. This leaves two possible arrangements for the remaining books, as shown above. Statement (C) is the only correct one.

11. (E)

1	2	3	4	5	6	7	8	9	10
E	E	E	P					P	M

or

1	2	3	4	5	6	7	8	9	10
M	P					P	E	E	E

The poetry books must be in positions 4 and 9 *or* 2 and 7, depending on whether the math book is in position 1 or 10. See diagrams above. For example, let us assume that the math book is the 10th book. In order for no two poetry books to be next to each other, the 4th and 9th books must be poetry books, with the 3rd poetry book in either position 6 or 7, depending on the positions of the science books. The same argument holds if the 1st book is a math book.

12. (C)

1	2	3	4	5	6	7	8	9	10
E	E	E	S	S	M	P	P	P	M

and

1	2	3	4	5	6	7	8	9	10
M	P	P	P	M	S	S	E	E	E

These are the two possible arrangements. We see that (A) is false, (B) could be false, (D) is false, and (E) could be false. Only (C) is always true.

13. (B)

1	2	3	4	5	6	7	8	9	10
E	E	E	M	S	S	P	P	P	M

and

1	2	3	4	5	6	7	8	9	10
E	E	E	S	S	M	P	P	P	M

These are the only two possible combinations; thus, (B) is the correct answer.

Answers 14–19

The following display can be constructed from the conditions:

Soup **Salad**

W ←—— T
T ——→ R
Z ——→ P, V
P → W
S → T
R, W ←—— V

14. (C) If Paul orders salad, so must Willard. Therefore, Paul must order soup (eliminate (B)) and Willard orders salad. Since Willard orders salad, Tom must order soup (eliminate (D)). Thus, Ron must order salad. Zack must order salad. He cannot order soup (eliminate (E)). If Zack orders soup, then Paul must order salad and Paul can't order the same as Willard. The correct choice is (C). Victor must order soup, since, if he orders salad, that would force Ron and Willard to order soup (and Willard can't order the same as Paul). Sam can order either soup or salad (eliminate (A)).

Soup	Salad
P	W
T	R
V	Z

← S →

15. (E) If Victor orders salad, then the following ordering arrangement results:

Soup	Salad
R	V
W	T
P	Z
	S

If Victor orders salad, then both Ron and Willard order soup. Since Ron orders soup, Tom must order salad. We know that Zack must order salad; otherwise, Paul, Victor, and Willard would have to order salad. Since Tom orders salad, so must Sam, Since Willard orders soup, so must Paul. From this diagram, it is clear that choice (E) is the correct choice.

16. **(C)** If Paul and Tom have the same starter, it must be soup. It cannot be salad because if Paul has salad, so must Willard, and if Tom has salad, Willard must have soup. This is a contradiction. Thus, Paul and Tom have soup. Ron has salad since Tom has soup. Victor must have soup since Ron has salad. From the following diagram we can see that Zack and Victor do have different starters, Victor and Willard could have different starters, Willard and Sam could have different starters, and Sam and Ron could have different starters. Only choice (C) is not true.

Soup	Salad
P	Z
T	R
V	

← W →

← S →

17. **(B)** The correct answer choice is (B). If Victor orders salad, then Willard orders soup. If Paul orders salad, then Willard orders salad. Willard cannot order both soup and salad. Each of the other choices is possible, as seen in the following two possible arrangements:

Soup	Salad	Soup	Salad
	Z	T	R
W	T	V	W
P	V		S
R	S		P
			Z

18. **(D)** If Ron orders soup, then Tom must order salad. If Tom orders salad, then Willard must order soup. Paul must order soup since Willard ordered soup. Sam must order salad since Tom ordered salad. Only Victor has a choice. Choice (A) is incorrect since Tom orders salad. Choice (B) is incorrect since Victor may or may not order salad. Choice (C) is incorrect since Zack must order salad. Choice (E) is incorrect since Willard orders soup.

Soup	Salad
R	T
W	Z
P	S

← V →

19. **(D)** The following arrangement results in a maximum of five friends ordering soup:

Soup	Salad
T	R
V	Z
P	
W	
S	

Answers 20–24

From the information given, you could have constructed the following display:

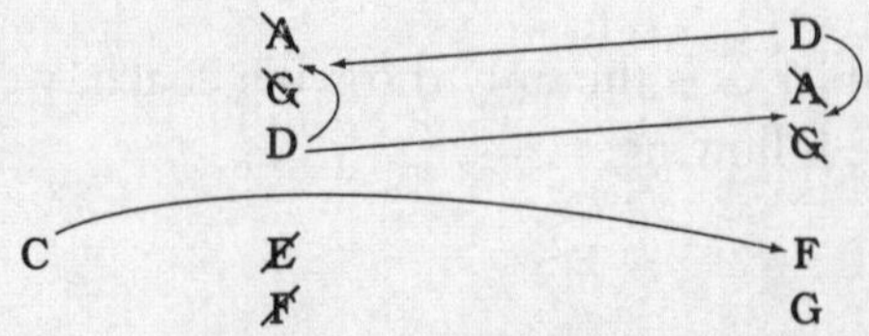

Sprints	Distance	Jumping	Throwing
____	____	B	____
?____	?____	?____	?____

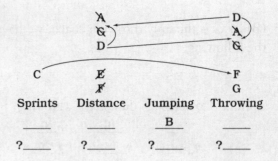

20. **(D)** If C and E are both sprint coaches, then from the original conditions, F and G coach throwers. Since G coaches throwers, D cannot coach distance, so D must coach jumping.

Sprints	Distance	Jumping	Throwing
C	____	B	F
? E	?____	? D	? G

21. **(A)** If G coaches jumping and A coaches distance we have:

Sprints	Distance	Jumping	Throwing
____	A	B	____
?____	?____	? G	?____

If D coaches distance or throwing, A must coach sprints or jumping. Since A coaches distance, D cannot coach distance or throwing. This means D must coach sprints. The other choices are possible, but not necessarily true.

Sprints	Distance	Jumping	Throwing
D	A	B	___
?___	?___	? G	?___

22. (E) If D coaches throwing, A and G cannot coach distance or throwing. This leaves only C to be the distance coach. So C CANNOT coach jumping.

Sprints	Distance	Jumping	Throwing
	~~E~~ ~~F~~		
___	C	B	D
?___	?___	?___	?___
	~~A~~ ~~G~~		~~A~~ ~~G~~

23. (B) If G is the only throwing coach, we have the following:

Sprints	Distance	Jumping	Throwing
	~~E~~ ~~F~~		
___	___	B	G
?___	?___	?___	? X

If D coaches distance or throwers, G must coach sprints or jumping. Since G coaches throwing, D does not coach distance or throwers. Thus, A and C must coach distance giving the following arrangement:

Sprints	Distance	Jumping	Throwing
	~~E~~ ~~F~~		
___	A	B	G
?___	? C	?___	? X
	~~D~~		~~D~~

Choice (A) is incorrect since D doesn't coach distance.
Choice (C) is incorrect since A coaches distance.
Choice (D) is incorrect since, if F coaches jumping, D and E must coach sprints.
Choice (E) is incorrect since C and D coach different sports.

24. (C) If D coaches distance, A and G do not coach distance or throwing.

Sprints	Distance	Jumping	Throwing
	~~E~~ ~~F~~		
~~A~~	D	B	___
?___	?___	?___	?___
	~~A~~ ~~G~~		~~A~~ ~~G~~

Since A does not coach sprints, then A must coach jumping. So A and B coach jumping; therefore, G CANNOT coach jumping.

Sprints	Distance	Jumping	Throwing
	~~E~~ ~~F~~		
~~A~~	D	B	___
?___	?___	? A	?___
	~~A~~ ~~G~~		~~A~~ ~~G~~

Section IV

1. (D) This choice provides the most direct evidence of the effectiveness of the PUC consumer action. Each of the other choices is only tangentially related to the argument.
2. (D) This choice most seriously weakens the author's contention that the PUC acts in the public interest. (C) is a weaker choice, especially because "slightly" softens the statement.
3. (A) This choice parallels both the reasoning and the structure of the original. The original reasoning may be summarized as follows: most $X \rightarrow Y$; therefore $X \rightarrow Y$ (probably).
4. (C) By conceding that certain subjects can only be discussed in private, the argument self-destructs. Several of the other choices are tempting, but none is as much to the point as choice (C).

5. **(B)** Since good personnel relations of an organization, according to the passage, rely upon "mutual confidence, trust and goodwill," one of the causes of personnel difficulties would most certainly be the employees' not believing in the good faith of the organization.

6. **(B)** In the second sentence, the author implies that the lack of facilities is related to the lack of research mentioned in the first sentence. In any case, the passage reveals the author's concern with both research and assistance, and therefore agrees more fully with (B) than with (A), which mentions research only.

7. **(A)** The "But" that begins the third sentence marks a contrast between the business world and the schools. The writer's point is that they are not alike and therefore cannot be run using the same standards of judgment.

8. **(E)** The correct answer is "circular." The argument that what the Church says is true is ultimately based upon this same assertion.

9. **(A)** Kathy believes Mary to have meant that only Italians are great lovers. Therefore, Kathy takes issue with this and points out in her reply that there are non-Italians who are great lovers. (A), if replaced for Mary's statement, would make Kathy's reply a reasonable one.

10. **(B)** Only (B) addresses Dimple's assumption that Mrs. Wilson is the only applicant whose qualifications are ideal. Other choices are irrelevant to the argument, although some may be relevant to the implied situation.

11. **(A)** Only (A) addresses the substance of Dimple's argument.

12. **(C)** The passage offers a pattern in which failure to meet one of two specific requirements results in a failure to qualify for something. In (C), the fall and winter track seasons become the residence requirement and the collecting of signatures. Failure to complete both leads to disqualification (for the spring team, for the June primary).

13. **(D)** The author of the argument avoids the issue of quality. The statement that stresses the incompleteness of the pro-hygienist position weakens it. (B) and (E) are irrelevant.

14. **(D)** The passage describes two types of obstacles to happiness: exterior forces and personal attitude. Both these factors are mentioned in (A), (B), (C), and (E). (D) requires the assumption that the two categories discussed by the author are the only categories.

15. **(B)** (A) may be eliminated because changing one's mind need not involve issues of right and wrong (in the moral sense that Eliot implies). (C) and (E) may be eliminated because they refute the underlying assumption of Eliot's words, that one can tell what is right. The passage does not address the issue of temptation (D).

16. **(E)** Without an implied or explicit definition of "civilized," the relevance of the examples is vague, at best. (A) and (D) are irrelevant considerations, and (B) and (C), although possibly relevant, do not address the most apparent weakness of the passage.

17. **(B)** (A) and (C) strengthen the argument. Although (D) and (E) partially weaken certain aspects of the argument, only (B) introduces a situation which suggests that freedom of the press may have harmful consequences.

18. **(A)** (B) and (C) are irrelevant to the argument. (D) and (E) contradict the implied assertion that a free press must be protected at all costs. Only (A) offers a statement both favorable to the concept of a free press and directly relevant to the subject discussed: the use of privileged information.

19. **(E)** By stating that "a legal technicality . . . ducks the . . . moral question," the author is implying that the federal government, which benefits from the technicality, is associated with dodging the issue. (A) and (B) restate explicit information; (C) is implausible; and (D) contradicts information in the passage.

20. (B) Private medical aid would render the author's argument unnecessary. (C), a choice worth considering, is not the best one because the author's focus is less on the aliens' needs than on the monetary burden borne by the counties.

21. (C) By documenting the rate at which the medical expense burden grows, the author could strengthen the argument that the situation he describes is indeed a burden.

22. (D) The passage talks about communes as failures. Therefore, the most logical completion must be a negative term consistent with failure. The only negative choice is (D).

23. (C) By linking Herb's ability with his "cousinhood," Herb is assuming that the latter determines the former; therefore, he is ignoring (C). (B) is irrelevant. (A) is too vague to be the best answer. (D) is inapplicable, because Keith uses "good" in a context that makes its meaning clear. Finally, (E) refers to contradictory information.

24. (E) In order to argue for the value of renewable prescriptions, the author must first assume that more medicine may be necessary, or, in other words, that the patient may suffer a relapse. Without the possibility of relapse, a call for more medicine that has already effected a cure ("worked effectively") is illogical.

25. (C) The passage consistently implies a difference between the past and the present, and (C) makes this contrast explicit. (B) contradicts the implication of the passage, while (A) and (D) narrow the focus unnecessarily, and (E) is irrelevant.

26. (D) This fact would strengthen the merely impressionistic evidence that lawsuits were less prevalent 40 years ago. It is the only choice dealing directly with the implied subject of the passage—lawsuits.

Section V

Passage 1

1. (D) According to the first paragraph, a developing country hopes to attract foreign investment and increase its revenues from taxation ("maximize the public capture of revenues").

2. (A) Unless the investment flow is equal in each direction, the First World nation from which the greater revenue is likely to come is more likely to benefit.

3. (B) According to the second paragraph, reciprocal source-based taxation produces revenue sacrifices by the state receiving most of the foreign investment, that is, the developing country.

4. (D) Excess foreign tax credits are a disincentive to private investors. If the at-source taxation is reduced, there will be fewer excess foreign credits.

5. (C) The passage makes no reference to the availability of raw materials. The four other options are cited.

6. (B) A country that reduced its revenue expectations would be expected to increase foreign investment.

Passage 2

7. (C) See lines 8–12. The point of the paragraph is to show how Stuart and Revett depicted the way the antiquities looked at the time of their visit in 1751. (A) is incorrect; not only is grandeur not shown but it is also undermined by the modest houses, Turkish influences, and sleepy atmosphere. (B) is also incorrect; these drawings are described in paragraph two. (D) is incorrect because the description does not say that the human figures and houses "dominate" the scenes. (E) is incorrect; although the Byzantine church is briefly mentioned, the paragraph does not contrast its architecture with the Grecian architecture.

8. (D) See lines 19–25. The author describes Stuart and Revett's topical drawings as being picturesque and conveying a sense of "the vanity of things." (A) is incorrect; the point is clearly made that the drawings do not show the monuments as they originally looked. (B) is also incorrect; although the contrast is shown, there is no implication that Stuart and Revett are making an ironic comment. (C) is

true for the depictions described in the second paragraph, not the first. (E) is not supported by any information in the passage.

9. **(A)** See lines 26–33. The engravings are described by the author as archaeological; they re-create the original design and provide a "careful tally of dimensions." (C) and (D) describe the drawings discussed in paragraph one. The term *romantic*, used in answer (B), also describes the drawings discussed in paragraph one. (E) is not supported by the passage; "traditional abstractions of the architect's trade" do not necessarily equal "uninteresting and pedantic" drawings.

10. **(A)** See lines 35–46. (B) and (E) are incorrect; no judgment is made as to the success of the Philadelphia building. (C) is also incorrect because no criticism of Stuart and Revett is suggested. (D) is inaccurate because the Philadelphia building is not a "depiction," as are the Stuart and Revett plates.

11. **(B)** The focus of the Le Corbusier sketches, according to the author, is on the way they show the Akropolis in relation to its natural surroundings. See lines 63–71. (A), (C), (D), and (E) are not supported by information in the passage.

12. **(C)** This inference is suggested by the point of the entire passage—that buildings are depicted according to how they are perceived. If they are depicted in various ways, it is implied that a viewer will have different responses, depending on the depiction. None of the other answers is supported by information in the passage. Nothing implies that classical architecture is superior to all other architecture (A) or that engraving is a superior process for depicting architecture (B). Also, there is not sufficient information to rank Stuart and Revett as superior to Le Corbusier (E) or to see romantic depiction as superior to archaeological drawings (D). In fact, the passage indicates that there are different ways to depict architecture, not that one way is superior to another.

13. **(E)** The author describes the three methods of depiction (topical, archaeological, in relation to nature) and contrasts them. The passage does not employ anecdote or allusion (A), irony or understatement (B), personification (C), or logical argument and persuasion (D).

Passage 3

14. **(D)** The author says that war and change have been inevitably linked in America, and that war has been a vital force in the rise of capitalism, but he does not say that war is inevitable. All of the other answers are supported by the passage: (A)—lines 57–69; (B)—lines 12–14; (C)—lines 15–17; (E)—lines 57–62.

15. **(B)** See lines 11–14. Radioactive isotopes used in treating cancer are an example of a positive advance caused by preparations for war. On the other hand, lethal nerve gases (A), in addition to being a German and not an American development, did not lead to positive peacetime uses. (C), (D), and (E), while possibly effects of wars that have changed America, did not "yield results which are tonics to advancement."

16. **(D)** See lines 20–24. (C) is incorrect; the author states that this is a result of the Civil War. (E) is a statement supported by the passage, but is not the primary reason for World War I's importance. (A) and (B) are not supported by information in the passage.

17. **(A)** In this paragraph the author paints a picture of, and indicates some of the reasons for, the "isolation, insularity, and exceptionalism" of America before World War I. The paragraph does define "American Religion" (B), but this is too limited an answer to describe the paragraph's main point. (C) and (E) are not covered in this paragraph. There is no contrast drawn between Civil War America and World War I America (D).

18. **(B)** See lines 30–39. (A) is incorrect; the grand tour is cited as an example that sophisticated Americans saw a trip to Europe as necessary to overcome insularity and complete an education. No social comment is made about its availability only to the rich. (D) is also

incorrect; Puritanism is cited in paragraph four, but not in the context indicated in this answer, i.e., the sin and corruption of the world. (E) might seem correct at first, but the passage does not state that America was in fact superior to Europe; it comments on the view that Americans had of their country. (C) is irrelevant; this point is not made in relation to America's insularity.

19. **(C)** After the first paragraph introduces the idea of war as a force of change, the passage is devoted to the importance of World War I in changing American society. (B) is incorrect; paragraph one concerns some of the benefits of war, but this is not the main topic of the passage; it is an underlying idea. (A) is also incorrect; the passage mentions the Civil War briefly but is mostly concerned with World War I. (D) and (E) are points touched on in the passage, but neither is the main subject.

20. **(E)** War as a force for change (the topic of paragraph one) is a general idea that introduces the passage's main subject of World War I. It is not a "popular view" that is refuted in the passage (A), nor does the passage ask a question (B). The first paragraph doesn't outline the contents of the passage (C), nor does it set up the first of four examples (D).

21. **(B)** "Ecstatic nationalism" is part of what Tocqueville called "American Religion." It would not increase in Europe after World War I. (A) can be inferred because Europe was seen as a necessity in a young man's education. (California would have been considered the Wild West.) The inference in (C) is supported by lines 62–69; (D), by lines 7–111; (E), by lines 42–50.

Passage 4

22. **(D)** In lines 71–75, the passage describes genetic drift, a change in the gene pool that occurs by chance. If an organism with a survival trait gene doesn't reproduce, the gene is lost. (A) is incorrect; the passage does not indicate which mutations are most "significant." (B) is contrary to fact; see lines 42–44. (C) is contradicted by several examples in the passage of the ways variations occur, and genetic recombination (E) is not cited as the cause of the formation of new species.

23. **(B)** The vulnerability to carbon dioxide was a trait from a gene that was transmitted to the fruit fly by an outside agent; it is therefore an acquired characteristic. That the fruit fly's offspring exhibit the same vulnerability supports the theory that acquired characteristics can be inherited. In (A), the webbed feet are not an acquired characteristic but a result of mutation and were perpetuated by inbreeding. (C) has no relevance to the question of inheritance, and in (D), the shaving of the dogs has nothing to do with the number of hairless offspring; genetic inheritance (dominant and recessive genes) account for that. (E) does not address the issue of how characteristics were transmitted.

24. **(E)** (A), (B), (C), and (D) are all explained (however briefly) in the passage. Although (E) is mentioned in line 83, it is not defined or explained.

25. **(A)** By definition, random mutations occur by chance and are therefore not necessarily related to any survival trait. Darwin's theory states that natural selection accounts for the perpetuation of traits. (B) is incorrect; although spontaneous mutations are said to be infrequent, the frequency of random mutations is not addressed. That random mutations occur doesn't refute or replace Darwin's evolutionary concept; it is simply another possibility for explaining the inheritance of certain traits (C). Both (D) and (E) are factually incorrect.

26. **(D)** The founder principle (lines 88–89) is that a smaller, isolated population has a gene frequency different from the larger population from which it came. (A) is incorrect because although the passage states that more genetic dwarfism occurs in the Amish population as a result of the founder principle, it does not state that the founder principle explains all genetic dwarfism. The principle doesn't refute the theory of natural selection (E), nor does it explain homozygosity (C), although the term is related. (B) is incorrect; nothing intrinsic in

the principle supports the importance of "weeding out" non-adaptative organisms.

27. **(C)** Darwin was more concerned with why certain traits were passed on (survival of the fittest) than with the mechanics of inheritance. (A) and (B) are incorrect; the passage doesn't imply that Darwin had any opinion about genetics. (In fact, the concept of the gene was developed after Darwin's work.) (D) is incorrect because Darwin recognized that variation among members of a species was central to the idea of natural selection. Although the passage states that he believed acquired characteristics could be inherited, it does not imply that he felt acquired traits were more important than hereditary ones (E).

28. **(B)** Most of the passage deals briefly with how variation occurs, not with the history of a theory (A) or the differences between genetic and evolutionary theories (D). (C) may seem to be a good answer because the author mentions that Darwin's failure to address the source of variations is "a major weakness." "Expose," however, is too strong a word; the passage is focused not on Darwin's weakness but rather on brief explanations of variation. (E) is a minor, not the primary, concern of the passage.

Model Test Four

This chapter contains full-length Model Test Four. It is geared to the format of the LSAT, and it is complete with answers and explanations. It is equivalent to the LSAT in question structure, number of questions, level of difficulty, and time allotments. (The questions used are not taken directly from the LSAT, as those questions are copyrighted and may not be reproduced.)

Model Test Four should be taken under strict test conditions. The test ends with a 35-minute Writing Sample, which is not scored.

Model Test Four

Section	Description	Number of Questions	Time Allowed
I.	Reading Comprehension	28	35 minutes
II.	Analytical Reasoning	24	35 minutes
III.	Logical Reasoning	26	35 minutes
IV.	Reading Comprehension	28	35 minutes
V.	Logical Reasoning	25	35 minutes
	Writing Sample		35 minutes
TOTALS:		131	3 hours 30 minutes

Now please turn to the next page, remove your answer sheet, and begin Model Test Four.

Answer Sheet

MODEL TEST FOUR

	Section I	Section II	Section III	Section IV	Section V
1	Ⓐ Ⓑ Ⓒ Ⓓ Ⓔ	Ⓐ Ⓑ Ⓒ Ⓓ Ⓔ	Ⓐ Ⓑ Ⓒ Ⓓ Ⓔ	Ⓐ Ⓑ Ⓒ Ⓓ Ⓔ	Ⓐ Ⓑ Ⓒ Ⓓ Ⓔ
2	Ⓐ Ⓑ Ⓒ Ⓓ Ⓔ	Ⓐ Ⓑ Ⓒ Ⓓ Ⓔ	Ⓐ Ⓑ Ⓒ Ⓓ Ⓔ	Ⓐ Ⓑ Ⓒ Ⓓ Ⓔ	Ⓐ Ⓑ Ⓒ Ⓓ Ⓔ
3	Ⓐ Ⓑ Ⓒ Ⓓ Ⓔ	Ⓐ Ⓑ Ⓒ Ⓓ Ⓔ	Ⓐ Ⓑ Ⓒ Ⓓ Ⓔ	Ⓐ Ⓑ Ⓒ Ⓓ Ⓔ	Ⓐ Ⓑ Ⓒ Ⓓ Ⓔ
4	Ⓐ Ⓑ Ⓒ Ⓓ Ⓔ	Ⓐ Ⓑ Ⓒ Ⓓ Ⓔ	Ⓐ Ⓑ Ⓒ Ⓓ Ⓔ	Ⓐ Ⓑ Ⓒ Ⓓ Ⓔ	Ⓐ Ⓑ Ⓒ Ⓓ Ⓔ
5	Ⓐ Ⓑ Ⓒ Ⓓ Ⓔ	Ⓐ Ⓑ Ⓒ Ⓓ Ⓔ	Ⓐ Ⓑ Ⓒ Ⓓ Ⓔ	Ⓐ Ⓑ Ⓒ Ⓓ Ⓔ	Ⓐ Ⓑ Ⓒ Ⓓ Ⓔ
6	Ⓐ Ⓑ Ⓒ Ⓓ Ⓔ	Ⓐ Ⓑ Ⓒ Ⓓ Ⓔ	Ⓐ Ⓑ Ⓒ Ⓓ Ⓔ	Ⓐ Ⓑ Ⓒ Ⓓ Ⓔ	Ⓐ Ⓑ Ⓒ Ⓓ Ⓔ
7	Ⓐ Ⓑ Ⓒ Ⓓ Ⓔ	Ⓐ Ⓑ Ⓒ Ⓓ Ⓔ	Ⓐ Ⓑ Ⓒ Ⓓ Ⓔ	Ⓐ Ⓑ Ⓒ Ⓓ Ⓔ	Ⓐ Ⓑ Ⓒ Ⓓ Ⓔ
8	Ⓐ Ⓑ Ⓒ Ⓓ Ⓔ	Ⓐ Ⓑ Ⓒ Ⓓ Ⓔ	Ⓐ Ⓑ Ⓒ Ⓓ Ⓔ	Ⓐ Ⓑ Ⓒ Ⓓ Ⓔ	Ⓐ Ⓑ Ⓒ Ⓓ Ⓔ
9	Ⓐ Ⓑ Ⓒ Ⓓ Ⓔ	Ⓐ Ⓑ Ⓒ Ⓓ Ⓔ	Ⓐ Ⓑ Ⓒ Ⓓ Ⓔ	Ⓐ Ⓑ Ⓒ Ⓓ Ⓔ	Ⓐ Ⓑ Ⓒ Ⓓ Ⓔ
10	Ⓐ Ⓑ Ⓒ Ⓓ Ⓔ	Ⓐ Ⓑ Ⓒ Ⓓ Ⓔ	Ⓐ Ⓑ Ⓒ Ⓓ Ⓔ	Ⓐ Ⓑ Ⓒ Ⓓ Ⓔ	Ⓐ Ⓑ Ⓒ Ⓓ Ⓔ
11	Ⓐ Ⓑ Ⓒ Ⓓ Ⓔ	Ⓐ Ⓑ Ⓒ Ⓓ Ⓔ	Ⓐ Ⓑ Ⓒ Ⓓ Ⓔ	Ⓐ Ⓑ Ⓒ Ⓓ Ⓔ	Ⓐ Ⓑ Ⓒ Ⓓ Ⓔ
12	Ⓐ Ⓑ Ⓒ Ⓓ Ⓔ	Ⓐ Ⓑ Ⓒ Ⓓ Ⓔ	Ⓐ Ⓑ Ⓒ Ⓓ Ⓔ	Ⓐ Ⓑ Ⓒ Ⓓ Ⓔ	Ⓐ Ⓑ Ⓒ Ⓓ Ⓔ
13	Ⓐ Ⓑ Ⓒ Ⓓ Ⓔ	Ⓐ Ⓑ Ⓒ Ⓓ Ⓔ	Ⓐ Ⓑ Ⓒ Ⓓ Ⓔ	Ⓐ Ⓑ Ⓒ Ⓓ Ⓔ	Ⓐ Ⓑ Ⓒ Ⓓ Ⓔ
14	Ⓐ Ⓑ Ⓒ Ⓓ Ⓔ	Ⓐ Ⓑ Ⓒ Ⓓ Ⓔ	Ⓐ Ⓑ Ⓒ Ⓓ Ⓔ	Ⓐ Ⓑ Ⓒ Ⓓ Ⓔ	Ⓐ Ⓑ Ⓒ Ⓓ Ⓔ
15	Ⓐ Ⓑ Ⓒ Ⓓ Ⓔ	Ⓐ Ⓑ Ⓒ Ⓓ Ⓔ	Ⓐ Ⓑ Ⓒ Ⓓ Ⓔ	Ⓐ Ⓑ Ⓒ Ⓓ Ⓔ	Ⓐ Ⓑ Ⓒ Ⓓ Ⓔ
16	Ⓐ Ⓑ Ⓒ Ⓓ Ⓔ	Ⓐ Ⓑ Ⓒ Ⓓ Ⓔ	Ⓐ Ⓑ Ⓒ Ⓓ Ⓔ	Ⓐ Ⓑ Ⓒ Ⓓ Ⓔ	Ⓐ Ⓑ Ⓒ Ⓓ Ⓔ
17	Ⓐ Ⓑ Ⓒ Ⓓ Ⓔ	Ⓐ Ⓑ Ⓒ Ⓓ Ⓔ	Ⓐ Ⓑ Ⓒ Ⓓ Ⓔ	Ⓐ Ⓑ Ⓒ Ⓓ Ⓔ	Ⓐ Ⓑ Ⓒ Ⓓ Ⓔ
18	Ⓐ Ⓑ Ⓒ Ⓓ Ⓔ	Ⓐ Ⓑ Ⓒ Ⓓ Ⓔ	Ⓐ Ⓑ Ⓒ Ⓓ Ⓔ	Ⓐ Ⓑ Ⓒ Ⓓ Ⓔ	Ⓐ Ⓑ Ⓒ Ⓓ Ⓔ
19	Ⓐ Ⓑ Ⓒ Ⓓ Ⓔ	Ⓐ Ⓑ Ⓒ Ⓓ Ⓔ	Ⓐ Ⓑ Ⓒ Ⓓ Ⓔ	Ⓐ Ⓑ Ⓒ Ⓓ Ⓔ	Ⓐ Ⓑ Ⓒ Ⓓ Ⓔ
20	Ⓐ Ⓑ Ⓒ Ⓓ Ⓔ	Ⓐ Ⓑ Ⓒ Ⓓ Ⓔ	Ⓐ Ⓑ Ⓒ Ⓓ Ⓔ	Ⓐ Ⓑ Ⓒ Ⓓ Ⓔ	Ⓐ Ⓑ Ⓒ Ⓓ Ⓔ
21	Ⓐ Ⓑ Ⓒ Ⓓ Ⓔ	Ⓐ Ⓑ Ⓒ Ⓓ Ⓔ	Ⓐ Ⓑ Ⓒ Ⓓ Ⓔ	Ⓐ Ⓑ Ⓒ Ⓓ Ⓔ	Ⓐ Ⓑ Ⓒ Ⓓ Ⓔ
22	Ⓐ Ⓑ Ⓒ Ⓓ Ⓔ	Ⓐ Ⓑ Ⓒ Ⓓ Ⓔ	Ⓐ Ⓑ Ⓒ Ⓓ Ⓔ	Ⓐ Ⓑ Ⓒ Ⓓ Ⓔ	Ⓐ Ⓑ Ⓒ Ⓓ Ⓔ
23	Ⓐ Ⓑ Ⓒ Ⓓ Ⓔ	Ⓐ Ⓑ Ⓒ Ⓓ Ⓔ	Ⓐ Ⓑ Ⓒ Ⓓ Ⓔ	Ⓐ Ⓑ Ⓒ Ⓓ Ⓔ	Ⓐ Ⓑ Ⓒ Ⓓ Ⓔ
24	Ⓐ Ⓑ Ⓒ Ⓓ Ⓔ	Ⓐ Ⓑ Ⓒ Ⓓ Ⓔ	Ⓐ Ⓑ Ⓒ Ⓓ Ⓔ	Ⓐ Ⓑ Ⓒ Ⓓ Ⓔ	Ⓐ Ⓑ Ⓒ Ⓓ Ⓔ
25	Ⓐ Ⓑ Ⓒ Ⓓ Ⓔ	Ⓐ Ⓑ Ⓒ Ⓓ Ⓔ	Ⓐ Ⓑ Ⓒ Ⓓ Ⓔ	Ⓐ Ⓑ Ⓒ Ⓓ Ⓔ	Ⓐ Ⓑ Ⓒ Ⓓ Ⓔ
26	Ⓐ Ⓑ Ⓒ Ⓓ Ⓔ	Ⓐ Ⓑ Ⓒ Ⓓ Ⓔ	Ⓐ Ⓑ Ⓒ Ⓓ Ⓔ	Ⓐ Ⓑ Ⓒ Ⓓ Ⓔ	Ⓐ Ⓑ Ⓒ Ⓓ Ⓔ
27	Ⓐ Ⓑ Ⓒ Ⓓ Ⓔ	Ⓐ Ⓑ Ⓒ Ⓓ Ⓔ	Ⓐ Ⓑ Ⓒ Ⓓ Ⓔ	Ⓐ Ⓑ Ⓒ Ⓓ Ⓔ	Ⓐ Ⓑ Ⓒ Ⓓ Ⓔ
28	Ⓐ Ⓑ Ⓒ Ⓓ Ⓔ	Ⓐ Ⓑ Ⓒ Ⓓ Ⓔ	Ⓐ Ⓑ Ⓒ Ⓓ Ⓔ	Ⓐ Ⓑ Ⓒ Ⓓ Ⓔ	Ⓐ Ⓑ Ⓒ Ⓓ Ⓔ
29	Ⓐ Ⓑ Ⓒ Ⓓ Ⓔ	Ⓐ Ⓑ Ⓒ Ⓓ Ⓔ	Ⓐ Ⓑ Ⓒ Ⓓ Ⓔ	Ⓐ Ⓑ Ⓒ Ⓓ Ⓔ	Ⓐ Ⓑ Ⓒ Ⓓ Ⓔ
30	Ⓐ Ⓑ Ⓒ Ⓓ Ⓔ	Ⓐ Ⓑ Ⓒ Ⓓ Ⓔ	Ⓐ Ⓑ Ⓒ Ⓓ Ⓔ	Ⓐ Ⓑ Ⓒ Ⓓ Ⓔ	Ⓐ Ⓑ Ⓒ Ⓓ Ⓔ

Remove answer sheet by cutting on dotted line

SECTION I

Time—35 minutes
28 Questions

Directions: Read the passages and answer the questions following each passage by blackening the appropriate space on the answer sheet. You may refer back to the passages when answering the questions. Answer all questions on the basis of what is stated or implied.

Although statutory law (a law enacted by the legislature) expressly forbids strikes by government workers, the constitutional validity of these laws as well as their interpretative applications have been under attack in various cases, the most publicized case being that of the federal government air traffic controllers.

The First Amendment to the United States Constitution guarantees the right of free speech. The constitutional issue to be resolved therefore is whether strikes are a form of "symbolic speech" or "symbolic conduct" that should be accorded the same degree of First Amendment protection as verbal communications. In a case that involved private rather than public employees, a Texas Court held that picketing as an incident to a labor dispute is a proper exercise of freedom of speech. The court went on to say that only a "clear and present danger of substantive evil will justify an abridgement of the right to picket." Later, the New Jersey state court concluded that even though picketing is protected by freedom of speech, this does not mean that statutes prohibiting strikes are constitutionally invalid. This case involved a constitutional interpretation of the New Jersey statute. The court stated that the justification of this statute is based on the ground of "clear and present danger" that would result to the state if the performance of functions of a public utility was ceased or impaired by a strike. Those in favor of no-strike clauses seem to concede that strikes are a form of symbolic speech that should be accorded the same degree of First Amendment protection as verbal speech. Their justification for upholding these clauses is the "clear and present danger" doctrine. They tend to believe that strikes by government employees automatically present a "clear and present danger of substantive evil." However, according to the U.S. Supreme Court, legislatures cannot be relied upon to make a determination of what constitutes a "clear and present danger." In effect this is what happened when President Reagan ordered the firing of the air traffic controllers, based on the antistrike clause pronounced by Congress. The Supreme Court held that courts themselves must determine what constitutes a clear and present danger. The Supreme Court went on to say that mere public inconvenience or annoyance is not enough to constitute a clear and present danger. Thus, the public inconvenience and annoyance created by the curtailment of air traffic as a result of the controllers' strike may not be sufficient to constitute such a danger. The argument that a clear and present danger resulted from the emergency staffing of control towers by military and supervisory personnel is invalidated by the fact that the airlines have run safely since the strike.

GO ON TO THE NEXT PAGE.

This is not to suggest that every employee should automatically have the right to strike. However, constitutional consideration of due process and freedom of speech should bar denying government workers, as a class, the right to strike. A close look should be taken at what actually constitutes a "clear and present danger of substantive evil." It is an evasion for courts to allow legislatures to prejudge all government services to be different for "strike" purposes than those provided by the private sector. The court itself should look at such factors as the nature of the service in determining whether particular no-strike clauses are constitutionally valid. The nature of the provider of the service (i.e., government v. private) is not a compelling justification for upholding no-strike clauses.

1. According to the passage, strikes by government workers are
   (A) constitutionally invalid
   (B) forbidden by statutory law
   (C) permissible when there is no danger of substantial evil
   (D) permissible when there is no public inconvenience or annoyance
   (E) permissible when there is no danger to national security and safety

2. If government workers as a class are denied the right to strike, it can be argued that they have been denied all of the following EXCEPT:
   (A) due process
   (B) freedom of speech
   (C) the clear and present danger doctrine
   (D) redress from abnormally dangerous working conditions
   (E) an abridgment of the right to picket

3. According to the passage, the "clear and present danger" justification of forbidding a strike has been misapplied for all of the following reasons EXCEPT:
   (A) The dangers were determined by the executive branch.
   (B) The dangers are often merely inconveniences.
   (C) The dangers were determined by the courts.
   (D) Strikes by government workers do not automatically present dangers.
   (E) The inconvenience caused by the air traffic controllers may not have been a danger.

4. The fact that there was no rise in the number of airline accidents in the first six months after the firing and replacement of the striking air traffic controllers undermines the
   (A) government's argument that a strike would present a danger to the public
   (B) argument that the no-strike clause violates First Amendment rights
   (C) argument that a strike is a form of symbolic speech
   (D) air traffic controllers' argument that they left their jobs because of dangerous working conditions
   (E) argument that no-strike clauses discourage more highly qualified individuals from applying for positions

GO ON TO THE NEXT PAGE.

5. The author of the passage objects to the current situation in which
   (A) all employees equally have the right to strike
   (B) the government regards national security as more important than an individual's freedom
   (C) the Supreme Court avoids taking a position in its dealing with regret-to-strike cases
   (D) an unfair burden of proof is placed upon workers who leave jobs they believe to have unsafe working conditions
   (E) a false distinction is made between workers doing similar jobs for the government and private employers

6. Which one of the following might the author cite to exemplify another of the harmful effects of the no-strike rule?
   (A) It deters the highly skilled from taking government jobs.
   (B) It can be used as a precedent in the private sector.
   (C) It places too much power in the hands of the judicial branch of the government.
   (D) It encourages the courts to determine whether or not particular no-strike clauses are valid.
   (E) It protects some workers from abnormally dangerous working conditions.

When completing *David Copperfield,* Dickens experienced a powerful aftereffect that left him confused about "whether to laugh or to cry . . . strangely divided . . . between sorrow and joy." He felt that he had been turned inside out, his inner life now visible, in partly disguised forms, in the shadowy world of ordinary daylight. The story he had written was so deeply personal that "no one can believe [it] in the reading, more than I have believed it in the writing." Having transformed his private memories and his emotional life into a public myth about himself, particularly his development from an abandoned child into a great popular artist surrounded by love and success, he felt the excitement both of exposure and catharsis. Exorcising the wounds of childhood and young adulthood, he also dramatized the unresolved problems of his personality and his marriage, anticipating the turmoil that was to come. Though energized by the process of writing, he was also exhausted by "heaps of Copperfieldian blots," by that "tremendous paroxysm of Copperfield." Towards the end, he felt "rigid with Copperfield . . . from head to foot." When he finally put down his pen in October 1850, he took up his "idea of wandering somewhere for a day or two." Almost inevitably, he went back "to Rochester . . . where I was a small boy."

In *David Copperfield* he re-created in mythic terms his relationship with his mother, his father, his siblings, particularly Fanny, and with his wife and his wife's sisters. The novel was more precious to him than his own children because the favorite child was himself. Soon after beginning, he confessed that he had stuck to that fictional name through the exploration of alternative titles because he had, even at the earliest stage, recognized that he was writing a book about himself.

GO ON TO THE NEXT PAGE.

His passion for names also expressed his need to pattern and control. After the birth of Katie in 1839, he assumed the right to name all his children (Catherine had "little or nothing to say" about that). The elaborate christening of Alfred D'Orsay Tennyson Dickens provides the representative example of the novelist imposing his literary constructs on other people's lives as well as his own. When it came to his family, he did not admit of any distinction. When it came to his novels, the distinction between self and other was subordinated to the dramatization of the many varieties of the single self. Changing Charles Dickens into David Copperfield had the force both of unconscious reversal and of minimal autobiographical distancing. At the heart of the novel was a partly mediated version of himself that represented his effort to claim that he had come through, that all was well with him as he approached the age of forty.

7. Which one of the following best expresses the main idea of the passage?
   - (A) The creation of *David Copperfield* was, for Dickens, a painful, wrenching experience.
   - (B) While writing *David Copperfield,* Dickens put his novel above everything else, including his children.
   - (C) In creating *David Copperfield,* Dickens transformed his memories and feelings into a public myth about himself.
   - (D) In addition to being autobiographical, *David Copperfield* is a prophetic novel.
   - (E) *David Copperfield,* in addition to being Dickens's most autobiographical novel, is also his greatest masterpiece.

8. The author's primary intention in this passage is to
   - (A) provide a psychological study of Dickens's motivations for writing *David Copperfield* and suggest a basis for evaluating the novel
   - (B) create a picture of Dickens as a writer burdened by childhood memories and contrast this with his public image
   - (C) show the connection between Dickens as a self-centered husband and father and as a literary genius
   - (D) present Dickens's reactions to writing *David Copperfield* and comment on the novel's relationship to his life and personality
   - (E) describe Dickens as he finished *David Copperfield* and show how that novel became a turning point in his career

9. The purpose of the last sentence of paragraph one (lines 30–32) is to
   - (A) show Dickens's complete exhaustion after finishing *David Copperfield*
   - (B) emphasize the connection between Dickens's writing of *David Copperfield* and his own childhood memories
   - (C) indicate Dickens's emotional response to writing *David Copperfield* and his inability to separate reality from fiction
   - (D) inform the reader of Dickens's actual origins as opposed to the fictional origins created in *David Copperfield*
   - (E) show that in finishing *David Copperfield* Dickens had finally exorcised the traumas of his childhood

GO ON TO THE NEXT PAGE.

10. Which one of the following can be inferred about Charles Dickens's life from information presented in the passage?
    (A) His marriage would end badly.
    (B) His most successful works were heavily autobiographical.
    (C) He was a distant, uncaring father.
    (D) His relationship with his sister Fanny had been significant to him.
    (E) Because of the problems in his childhood, he was a man driven by the need for public success.

11. According to the passage, the title of *David Copperfield* is most significant because
    (A) it demonstrates Dickens's view of the protagonist as a version of himself
    (B) with the unconscious reversal of initials, it shows Dickens's inability to come to terms with his life
    (C) it demonstrates Dickens's need to pattern and control his experience
    (D) it is a prime example of Dickens's passion for names
    (E) it represents both Dickens seeing the protagonist as himself and playing a game with the reader

12. The primary effect of lines 46–49—"After the birth of Katie in 1839, he assumed the right to name all his children (Catherine had 'little to say' about that)"—is to
    (A) suggest that Catherine Dickens was an inadequate mother
    (B) indicate that Dickens's creativity with names extended to his family
    (C) show that Dickens tended to confuse art with life
    (D) suggest the relationship between Dickens and Catherine
    (E) indicate that Dickens put his work over his family life

13. Which one of the following best describes the author's tone in the passage?
    (A) cool and ironic
    (B) argumentative and sarcastic
    (C) detached and condescending
    (D) intimate and persuasive
    (E) objective and analytical

14. Which one of the following best describes the structure of the passage?
    (A) Paragraph one focuses on Dickens's reactions to writing *David Copperfield,* while paragraph two includes more of the author's comments and ties in related points.
    (B) Paragraph one recounts Dickens's problems in writing *David Copperfield,* while paragraph two describes his creative solutions and his reactions to the work.
    (C) Paragraph one presents Dickens's opinions of *David Copperfield,* while paragraph two provides the author's critique and relates the book to Dickens's other works.
    (D) Paragraph one describes Dickens's relationship to his novels, while paragraph two describes his relationship to his family.
    (E) Paragraph one shows the effect of his childhood on Dickens, while paragraph two describes his later life and its effect on his novels.

GO ON TO THE NEXT PAGE.

Passage A

The Corporation for Public Broadcasting (CPB) was created by the U.S. Congress in 1967 as part of President Lyndon B. Johnson's mission to create a "Great Society." Johnson said, as he signed the bill into law, "Public television will help make our nation a replica of the old Greek marketplace, where public affairs took place in view of all citizens."

After the creation of the CPB, existing educational stations and their umbrella organization, National Educational Television, were affiliated into a membership organization, the Public Broadcasting System (PBS). To clarify, the Corporation for Public Broadcasting, as distinguished from the Public Broadcasting System, is a private corporation, funded by the federal government, that does not produce or distribute programs itself. PBS, on the other hand, is a private, nonprofit media enterprise owned and operated by member stations. Currently, there are about 350 PBS stations in the United States.

Congress appropriates funds for the CPB, which uses 95 percent of the money to strengthen PBS's technical infrastructure and develop programming. The 1967 Public Broadcasting Act called for public broadcasting to take "creative risks," "address the needs of unserved and underserved audiences," and "encourage the growth of nonbroadcast telecommunications technologies." The biggest single source of funds for PBS is individual membership (thus, the many pledge drives on PBS) and contributions by "Friends of..." groups.

The United States was actually late in establishing public broadcasting. It was already well established in other countries. In England, the British Broadcasting Corporation (BBC) took control of television in 1932. It is still supported primarily by television household license fees. Other countries, such as Denmark, France, Japan, the Netherlands, Sweden, and Switzerland support their public broadcasting similarly. In Germany, commercial broadcasters underwrite public broadcasting by paying special fees. It should be noted that federal governments in Australia, Canada, and Britain provide generous subsidies for their public broadcasting—a much greater percentage of their gross national product (GNP) than the United States provides of its GNP.

A few of the many goals of public broadcasting are programming that is available throughout the country; programming that caters to a wide variety of interests and tastes and addresses all citizens, including minorities; and programming that is free from commercialism, vested interests, and government control. In addition, quality and impartiality are prime concerns of public broadcasting.

Passage B

Public television in the U.S. is in trouble. Between 1993 and 2003, PBS memberships declined by 20 percent, and fewer members means fewer viewers. The question is "Why?" One obvious reason is that viewers have more and more choices. In the 1980s, cable television blossomed, which meant more diversified and specialized programming than had been available on the major commercial networks. Cable news networks cut into the PBS news and public affairs franchise, certain "niche" networks offered competition to PBS's cultural and performance programming, and PBS's well-received children's programming went up against competitors such as the Disney Channel, Nickelodeon, and the Cartoon Network. The public, since the advent of cable, has been flooded with viewing opportunities. According to some critics, the quality and innovation on some cable channels are noteworthy. Generally, PBS has been unable to keep up.

GO ON TO THE NEXT PAGE.

1 1 1 1 1

Part of the reason is that PBS, which receives funding from viewers but also from the federal government, has been under attack by both conservatives and liberals. In 2005, $100 million was slashed from the PBS budget. PBS's programming was deemed to be slanted to the left by many of those voting for the cut. The money was later restored, but the criticism continued. Actions by the chairman of the Corporation for Public Broadcasting then angered the liberals. The issue of PBS's neutrality, or lack of it, has become a hot button among both conservatives and liberals.

Because of funding problems and loss of members, PBS has been unable to create many new, different programs, which further erodes viewership. To avoid cuts and shortfalls, it has also been forced to accept what amount to watered-down commercials from corporate interests, and endless pledge drives that tend to feature bland programming or "specials" that have been shown too many times. According to polls, most people agree that we need public television, that it is a good thing in a free society. There is less agreement, however, on how to cure the patient without sacrificing the original noble intentions of its founders.

15. The main purpose of Passage A is to
    (A) briefly explain the government's role in U.S. public television
    (B) contrast public broadcasting in the U.S. with public broadcasting in England
    (C) emphasize the importance of public television in the U.S.
    (D) criticize the method of funding PBS
    (E) briefly explain the origin and organization of public television in the U.S.

16. The main purpose of Passage B is to
    (A) set forth some reasons for the problems facing PBS
    (B) criticize the method of funding PBS
    (C) explain why PBS is accepting commercial messages
    (D) predict the demise of public television in the U.S.
    (E) answer the arguments of politicians who criticize PBS

17. The author of Passage B would be most likely to argue that the goals for public television set forth in the last paragraph of Passage A have been most hindered by
    (A) PBS's lack of creativity
    (B) programming that focuses on children more than adults
    (C) the effect of political controversy on funding
    (D) limited distribution of programs
    (E) management issues at the Corporation for Public Broadcasting

18. Which of the following most accurately states the tone of Passage A and the tone of Passage B?
    (A) Passage A is generally objective, whereas Passage B includes some negative judgments.
    (B) Passage A is optimistic about public television, whereas Passage B is pessimistic.
    (C) While the author of Passage A is mildly critical, the author of Passage B is harshly critical.
    (D) Both authors are neutral and objective.
    (E) Passage A praises public television, while Passage B questions its importance.

GO ON TO THE NEXT PAGE.

19. According to Passage A, the Corporation for Public Broadcasting (CPB)

(A) is the main source of funding for PBS
(B) is based on the model of the British Broadcasting Corporation
(C) distributes programs created for PBS
(D) is funded by Congress
(E) uses 95 percent of its money to promote public broadcasting

20. In Passage B, which of the following is cited as an obvious reason for declining membership in PBS?

(A) a conservative bias
(B) a liberal bias
(C) more choices for viewers
(D) bland programming
(E) too many pledge drives

21. In line 75 of Passage B, the best definition of the word "niche" is

(A) small
(B) specialized
(C) non-profit
(D) recessed
(E) restricted

22. In Passage A, all of the following are mentioned as ways that countries fund public broadcasting EXCEPT:

(A) government subsidies
(B) government trust funds
(C) viewer membership
(D) household license fees
(E) fees from commercial broadcasters

Taxonomy, the science of classifying and ordering organisms, has an undeserved reputation as a harmless, and mindless, activity of listing, cataloguing, and describing—consider the common idea of a birdwatcher, up at 5:30 in the morning with binoculars, short pants, and "life list" of every bird he has seen. Even among scientists, taxonomy is often treated as "stamp collecting." It was not always so. During the eighteenth and early nineteenth centuries, taxonomy was in the forefront of the sciences. The greatest biologists of Europe were professional taxonomists—Linnaeus, Cuvier, Lamarck. Darwin's major activity during the twenty years separating his Malthusian insights from the publication of his evolutionary theory was a three-volume work on the taxonomy of barnacles. Thomas Jefferson took time out from the affairs of state to publish one of the great taxonomic errors in the history of paleontology—he described a giant sloth claw as a lion's three times the size of Africa's version. These heady days were marked by discovery as naturalists collected the fauna and flora of previously uncharted regions. They were also marked by the emergence of intellectual structure, as coherent classifications seemed to mirror the order of God's thought.

America played its part in this great epoch of natural history. We often forget that 150 years ago much of our continent was as unknown and potentially hazardous as any place on earth. During the eighteenth century, when most naturalists denied the possibility of extinction, explorers expected to find mammoths and other formidable fossil creatures alive in the American West. There are a number of passionate, single-minded iconoclasts who fought the hostility of the wilderness, and often of urban literary people, to disclose the rich fauna and flora of America. For the most part, they worked alone, with

GO ON TO THE NEXT PAGE.

1 1 1 1 1

small support from patrons or government. The Lewis and Clark expedition is an exception—and its primary purpose was not natural history. We may now look upon tales of frontier toughness and perseverance as the necessary mythology of a nation too young to have real legends. But there is often a residue of truth in such tales, and naturalists are among the genuine pioneers.

Alexander Wilson walked from New England to Charleston peddling subscriptions to his *American Ornithology.* Thomas Nuttall—oblivious to danger, a Parsifal under a lucky star, vanquishing every Klingsor in the woods, discovered some of the rarest, most beautiful, and most useful of American plants. J. J. Audubon drank his way across Europe selling his beautiful pictures of birds to lords and kings. John Lawson, captured by Tuscarora Indians, met the following fate according to an eyewitness: "They struck him full of fine small, splinters or torchwoods like hog's bristles and so set them gradually afire." David Douglas fell into a pit trap for wild cattle and was stomped to death by a bull.

23. According to the passage, taxonomy was considered to be an important science from about

(A) 1700 to 1800
(B) 1700 to 1830
(C) 1700 to 1950
(D) 1800 to 1930
(E) 1818 to 1918

24. As they are used in the first paragraph (lines 25–26), "flora and fauna" refer to

(A) lands and waters
(B) botanists and zoologists
(C) plants and animals
(D) cataloging and describing
(E) mythology and folklore

25. We can infer from the passage that

(A) taxonomy was favorably regarded in the sixteenth and seventeenth centuries
(B) taxonomy was invented in the eighteenth century
(C) the number of kinds of barnacles is very large
(D) Lamarck and Linnaeus were amateur scientists
(E) most of the world's plants have already been classified

26. The relation of the third paragraph to the rest of the passage may be best described as

(A) a comic contrast to the seriousness of the first two paragraphs
(B) specific examples of the pioneers mentioned in the second paragraph
(C) examples of American taxonomists to set against the exclusively European names of the first paragraph
(D) real taxonomists of the western United States as opposed to the legendary figures of the second paragraph
(E) examples of the tall tales of the frontier days

GO ON TO THE NEXT PAGE.

27. In the third paragraph, Parsifal and Klingsor were probably a

(A) hunter and his prey
(B) German taxonomist and his subject of study
(C) knight and his enemy
(D) colonizer and the colonized
(E) mythical animal and its master

28. This passage is best described as a(n)

(A) description of the modern bias against taxonomy
(B) comparison of nineteenth-century and twentieth-century scientists
(C) account of famous American naturalists
(D) history and defense of taxonomy
(E) argument for the renewed study of the classification of organisms

STOP

IF YOU FINISH BEFORE TIME IS CALLED,
YOU MAY CHECK YOUR WORK ON THIS SECTION ONLY.
DO NOT WORK ON ANY OTHER SECTION IN THE TEST.

SECTION II
Time—35 minutes
24 Questions

Directions: In this section you will be given groups of questions based on different sets of conditions. Drawing a simple diagram may be helpful in answering some of the questions. You are to choose the best answer and mark the corresponding space on your answer sheet.

Questions 1–6

A radio station will play eight songs during its "Winners" hour. Each song will be played once. The eight songs represent the following types of music: Jazz, Rock, and Country, with at least two songs of each type. The following restrictions are placed on the order and type of songs:

All the jazz songs are played consecutively.
No two rock songs are played consecutively.
No two country songs are played consecutively.
A rock song must be played before a jazz song is played.
There are more jazz songs than country songs.

1. If four jazz songs are played, and the first and last songs are of the same type, which one of the following must be true?
   (A) A jazz song is played second.
   (B) A jazz song is played third.
   (C) A rock song is played seventh.
   (D) A rock song is played eighth.
   (E) A country song is played first.

2. If three rock songs are played and a country song is played sixth, which one of the following CANNOT be true?
   (A) A jazz song is played second.
   (B) A rock song is played fifth.
   (C) A rock song is played first.
   (D) A country song is played last.
   (E) A country song is played first.

3. If a jazz song is played third, and the first and last songs are of the same type, which one of the following CANNOT be true?
   (A) A jazz song is sixth.
   (B) A country song is sixth.
   (C) A country song is first.
   (D) A rock song is second.
   (E) A rock song is seventh.

4. If all the jazz songs are played last, how many different arrangements of song types are possible?
   (A) one
   (B) two
   (C) three
   (D) four
   (E) five

5. If a country song is played first and seventh, which one of the following must be true?
   (A) A country song is sixth.
   (B) A jazz song is sixth.
   (C) A country song is third.
   (D) A jazz song is second.
   (E) A jazz song is third.

GO ON TO THE NEXT PAGE.

6. If a single classical song is added to the play list (making nine songs in all) and it is to be played fourth and a country song is to be played fifth, which one of the following must be true?

   (A) A jazz song is sixth.
   (B) A jazz song is last.
   (C) A rock song is second.
   (D) A rock song is third.
   (E) A country song is last.

Questions 7–13

Seven students—George, Hal, Ken, Jon, Neil, Lynn, and Melanie—are playing a game involving play money. The only bills used are play dollar bills. No coins are used.

Jon has more bills than Lynn, Melanie, and Neil combined.

The total of Lynn's and Melanie's bills are equal to Neil's bills.

Melanie has more bills than Ken and George combined.

Hal has fewer bills than George.

Ken and George have the same number of bills.

7. Which one of the following students has the most bills?

   (A) Ken
   (B) George
   (C) Jon
   (D) Lynn
   (E) Melanie

8. Which one of the following students has the fewest bills?

   (A) Melanie
   (B) Neil
   (C) George
   (D) Ken
   (E) Hal

9. Which one of the following must be true?

   (A) Melanie has fewer bills than Ken.
   (B) Neil has more bills than Lynn.
   (C) Lynn has fewer bills than Melanie.
   (D) Lynn has more bills than George.
   (E) George has more bills than Melanie.

10. Assume that Ken is given one bill from Hal. Assume also that Melanie has more bills than Ken, George, and Lynn combined. If none of the students has the same number of bills, which one of the following is a possible order from highest to lowest of students who have the most bills?

    (A) Jon, Melanie, Lynn, Neil, Ken, George, Hal
    (B) Jon, Neil, Melanie, Lynn, George, Ken, Hal
    (C) Neil, Jon, Melanie, George, Ken, Hal, Lynn
    (D) Jon, Neil, Ken, Melanie, George, Lynn, Hal
    (E) Jon, Neil, Melanie, Ken, George, Hal, Lynn

11. Assume that Lynn does not have the same number of bills as Ken. Which one of the following must be false?

    (A) Lynn has the same number of bills as Hal.
    (B) Neil has twice as many bills as Melanie.
    (C) George has more bills than Hal and Lynn combined.
    (D) George does not have the same number of bills as Lynn.
    (E) Jon has fewer than twice the number of Lynn's and Melanie's bills combined.

GO ON TO THE NEXT PAGE.

12. If Lynn and Melanie have the same number of bills, then which one of the following must be false?
    (A) Neil has more bills than Melanie.
    (B) Melanie has more bills than Ken, George, and Hal combined.
    (C) George has fewer bills than Hal and Ken combined.
    (D) Neil has fewer bills than Lynn, George, and Hal combined.
    (E) Jon has more bills than Lynn, Ken, George, and Hal combined.

13. Assume that Tom decides to join the game. Assume also that he is given bills from the bank. If his total number of bills are more than Ken's and fewer than Lynn's, which one of the following must be true?
    (A) Melanie has fewer bills than Tom.
    (B) Tom has fewer bills than George.
    (C) Lynn has fewer bills than Melanie.
    (D) Melanie and Lynn have the same number of bills.
    (E) Lynn has more bills than Hal.

Questions 14–20

At the snack bar at a party, Alli, Boris, Cisco, and Dan are eating cookies. There are five kinds of cookies to choose from—chocolate chip cookies, oatmeal cookies, sugar cookies, peanut butter cookies, and raisin cookies. Each of these four people eat at least two kinds of cookies. Their choices are governed by the following rules:

At most two of them eat oatmeal cookies.
At least two of them eat sugar cookies.
Alli does not eat any sugar cookies.
Boris and Cisco do not eat the same type of cookie.
Boris eats chocolate chip cookies.
Cisco eats sugar cookies.
No one eats both raisin cookies and sugar cookies.
If someone eats raisin cookies, they also eat peanut butter cookies.

14. Which one of the following must be true?
    (A) Cisco eats chocolate chip cookies.
    (B) Alli eats chocolate chip cookies.
    (C) Boris does not eat peanut butter cookies.
    (D) Dan does not eat raisin cookies.
    (E) Alli does not eat peanut butter cookies.

15. If Boris eats exactly three kinds of cookies, which one of the following must be true?
    (A) Cisco eats exactly three kinds of cookies.
    (B) Dan eats only sugar cookies.
    (C) If Alli eats oatmeal cookies, Dan eats oatmeal cookies.
    (D) Boris eats oatmeal cookies.
    (E) Cisco eats oatmeal cookies.

16. Which one of the following CANNOT be true?
    (A) No one eats raisin cookies.
    (B) Alli and Dan both eat oatmeal cookies.
    (C) Alli and Dan both eat chocolate chip cookies.
    (D) Boris and Cisco eat the same number of kinds of cookies.
    (E) Dan does not eat raisin cookies.

17. Which pair of cookie types could each be eaten by at least three different people?
    (A) chocolate chip and oatmeal
    (B) oatmeal and peanut butter
    (C) chocolate chip and peanut butter
    (D) oatmeal and sugar
    (E) sugar and raisin

18. Which pair of cookie types contains a cookie type eaten by exactly two different people?
    (A) chocolate chip and oatmeal
    (B) oatmeal and peanut butter
    (C) chocolate chip and peanut butter
    (D) oatmeal and raisin
    (E) sugar and raisin

GO ON TO THE NEXT PAGE.

2 2 2 2 2

19. If Alli does not eat chocolate chip or raisin cookies, which one of the following could be true?
    (A) Dan eats oatmeal cookies.
    (B) More people eat chocolate chip cookies than sugar cookies.
    (C) Only one person eats peanut butter cookies.
    (D) Cisco does not eat peanut butter cookies.
    (E) Boris eats sugar cookies.

20. Which cookie type could be eaten by none of the people?
    (A) chocolate chip
    (B) oatmeal
    (C) sugar
    (D) peanut butter
    (E) raisin

Questions 21–24

The National Domino League is planning to expand by adding one more team. All of the players for the new team will be chosen from the existing teams. Each team must make three players eligible to be chosen for the new team.

(1) The players eligible to be chosen from Team 1 are A, B, and C.
(2) The players eligible to be chosen from Team 2 are D, E, and F.
(3) The players eligible to be chosen from Team 3 are G, H, and K.
(4) The new team must choose two players from each of the three teams.
(5) B refuses to play with D.
(6) If C is chosen, then K must be chosen.
(7) G and H refuse to play together.

21. If A is not chosen, then how many members of the new team are determined?
    (A) 2
    (B) 3
    (C) 4
    (D) 5
    (E) 6

22. If D is chosen, then which one of the following groups of three players could NOT be chosen?
    (A) A, G, K
    (B) B, C, G
    (C) C, E, K
    (D) A, E, G
    (E) E, H, K

23. Which one of the following is (are) true?
    (A) C must be chosen.
    (B) If A is chosen, then F must be chosen.
    (C) If B is chosen, then E must be chosen.
    (D) E must be chosen.
    (E) If G is chosen, then K is not chosen.

24. In addition to facts (1), (2), (3), and (4), which of the facts lead(s) to the conclusion that K must be chosen?
    (A) (5)
    (B) (6)
    (C) (7)
    (D) (6) and (7)
    (E) (5), (6), and (7)

STOP

IF YOU FINISH BEFORE TIME IS CALLED,
YOU MAY CHECK YOUR WORK ON THIS SECTION ONLY.
DO NOT WORK ON ANY OTHER SECTION IN THE TEST.

SECTION III
Time—35 minutes
26 Questions

Directions: In this section you will be given brief statements or passages and will be required to evaluate the reasoning involved. In some instances, more than one choice will appear to be a possible answer. You are to choose the *best* answer. Use common sense and reasonableness in making your selection; then mark the proper space on the answer sheet.

1. *Mr. Kent:* Recent studies show that reduction in the maximum speed limit from 65 mph to 55 mph substantially reduces the number of highway fatalities.

   The preceding statement would be most weakened by establishing that

   (A) most fatal car accidents occur at night
   (B) most accidents occurring at speeds between 45 and 55 mph are nonfatal
   (C) few fatal accidents involve only one vehicle
   (D) prior to this reduction, 97 percent of fatal accidents occurred below 45 mph
   (E) prior to the reduction, 97 percent of fatal accidents occurred between 55 and 65 mph

2. Board member Smith will vote for the busing of students if she is reelected to the board. If the busing of students is passed by the board, then Smith was not reelected to the board. Smith was reelected to the board.

   Given the foregoing information, which one of the following can be concluded?

   (A) Smith assisted in the passage of student busing.
   (B) The passage of busing carried Smith to a reelection victory.
   (C) Smith voted against busing; however, it still passed.
   (D) Busing was defeated despite Smith's vote in favor of it.
   (E) Student busing was voted down by a majority of the board.

GO ON TO THE NEXT PAGE.

3. Daniel Webster said, "Falsehoods not only disagree with truths, but usually quarrel among themselves."

   Which one of these would follow from Webster's statement?

   (A) Quarreling is endemic to American political life.
   (B) Truth and falsehood can be distinguished from one another.
   (C) Liars often quarrel with each other.
   (D) Those who know the truth are normally silent.
   (E) Truth and falsehood are emotional, rather than intellectual, phenomena.

4. A recording industry celebrity observed: "I am not a star because all my songs are hits; all my songs are hits because I am a star."

   Which one of the following most nearly parallels this reasoning?

   (A) A college professor noted: "I am the final word in the classroom not because my judgment is always correct, but my judgment in the classroom is always correct because I am the instructor."
   (B) A nurse observed: "I am not competent in my duties because I am a nurse, but I am competent in my duties because of my training in nursing."
   (C) A dance instructor noted: "I am not the instructor because I know all there is about dance; rather I am an instructor because of my ability to teach dancing."
   (D) A recording industry celebrity observed: "I am not wealthy because I am a star; I am wealthy because so many people buy my recordings."
   (E) A recording industry celebrity observed: "I am not a star because my every song is enjoyed; I am a star because people pay to watch me perform."

5. *Economist:* As a rule, the price of gasoline at the pump increases when the oil refineries in the United States are operating at below 75 percent of capacity. If the unrest in the Middle East continues, the shipment of oil to the United States will decline, and refineries here will have to operate at 60 percent of capacity for at least six months.

   If the statements above are correct, which one of the following is the most likely conclusion?

   (A) Imports from oil producing areas other than the Middle East are likely to increase next year.
   (B) A sudden resolution of tensions in the Middle East will have little or no effect on the price of gasoline.
   (C) Oil prices decline only when refineries in the United States operate at more than 75 percent of their capacity.
   (D) The rise or fall in gasoline prices is determined by supply and demand and not by political events.
   (E) It is likely that prices of gasoline in the United States will increase in the next year.

GO ON TO THE NEXT PAGE.

6. If a speaker were highly credible, would an objectively irrelevant personal characteristic of the speaker influence the effectiveness of her communication? For example, if a Nobel Prize-winning chemist were speaking on inorganic chemistry, would she induce a lesser change in the opinions of an audience if she were known to be a poor cook? Would the speaker's effectiveness be different if she were obese rather than trim, sloppy rather than neat, ugly rather than attractive?

By failing to consider irrelevant aspects of communicator credibility, studies in communication science have unknowingly implied that audiences are composed of individuals who are responsive only to objectively relevant aspects of a speaker.

Which one of the following represent(s) assumptions upon which the foregoing passage is based?

(A) Audiences are composed of people who are responsive only to objectively relevant aspects of a communicator.
(B) Objectively irrelevant personal characteristics have a bearing on a speaker's effectiveness.
(C) Some characteristics of a communicator are of greater relevance than others.
(D) A trim speaker is likely to be more persuasive than an obese one.
(E) Irrelevant aspects of a communication have more effect on an audience than the content of a speech.

<u>Questions 7–8</u>

I read with interest the statements of eminent archaeologists that the presence of a crude snare in an early Neolithic grave indicates that man of this period subsisted by snaring small mammals. I find this assertion open to question. How do I know the companions of the deceased did not toss the snare into the grave with the corpse because it had proved to be totally useless?

7. The author employs which one of the following as a method of questioning the archaeologists' claims?

(A) evidence that contradicts the conclusion drawn by the archaeologists
(B) a doubtful tone about the motives of the archaeologists
(C) a body of knowledge inconsistent with that employed by the archaeologists
(D) an alternative to the conclusion drawn by the archaeologists
(E) the suggestion that archaeological studies are of little use

8. Which one of the following best expresses the author's criticism of the archaeologists whose statements he questions?

(A) They have not subjected their conclusions to scientific verification.
(B) They have stressed one explanation and ignored others.
(C) They have drawn a conclusion that does not fit the evidence upon which it was based.
(D) They have failed to employ proper scientific methods in arriving at their conclusion.
(E) They have based their conclusion on behaviors exhibited by more modern humans.

9. Semanticists point out that words and phrases often acquire connotations tinged with emotions. Such significances are attached because of the context, the history of the usage of the expression, or the background of the person reading or listening. Thus, "the hills of home" may evoke a feeling of nostalgia or a pleasant sensation; but "Bolshevik" may arouse derision or disgust in the minds of many people.

The term "progressive education" has gone through several stages in the connotative process. At one time progressive education was hailed as the harbinger of all that was wise and wholesome in classroom practice, such as the recognition of individual differences and the revolution against formalized dictatorial procedures. However, partly because of abuses on the fanatical fringe of the movement, many people began to associate progressive schools with frills, fads, and follies. What had been discovered and developed by Froebel in Germany, by Pestalozzi in Switzerland, by Montessori in Italy, and by men like Parker and Dewey in the United States was muddled in a melange of mockery and misunderstanding and submerged in satirical quips. As a result, many educators have recently avoided the expression and have chosen to call present educational practices "new" or "modern" rather than "progressive."

Which one of the following would most seriously weaken the author's argument?

(A) In a recent poll of American voters, 76 percent responded that they would certainly not vote for the Progressive Labor Party.
(B) Open classrooms have recently fallen out of the educational limelight.
(C) New techniques in teaching cognitive skills, called "progressive learning," have recently met with widespread approval in middle class public schools.
(D) Parker and Dewey were well respected by academicians and educational theorists.
(E) Every new advance in education is first denounced as a "fad."

10. *Bill:* Professor Smith has been late for class almost every morning.
Dave: That can't be true; he was on time yesterday.

Dave apparently believes that Bill has said which one of the following?

(A) Professor Smith is seldom late.
(B) Professor Smith does not enjoy teaching.
(C) Professor Smith has been late every day without exception.
(D) Professor Smith was late yesterday.
(E) Professor Smith informs Bill of his whereabouts.

11. Sunbathers do not usually spend much time in the shade. Shade prevails during most of June in La Jolla. It is June 14.

Which one of the following conclusions would be logically defensible, based upon the foregoing premises?

(A) La Jolla is the site of frequent sunbathing.
(B) The sun is not shining today.
(C) There are sunbathers in La Jolla today.
(D) There may be sunbathers in La Jolla today.
(E) There are more sunbathers in La Jolla in July than in June.

GO ON TO THE NEXT PAGE.

3 3 3 3 3

12. *Political Theorist:* Although American politicians disagree about many things, none of them disagrees with Wendell Wilkie's assertion that "the Constitution does not provide for first- and second-class citizens."

    Wilkie's statement implies that

    (A) the Constitution provides for third- and fourth-class citizens
    (B) first-class citizens don't need to be provided for
    (C) there is no such thing as a second-class citizen
    (D) the Constitution makes no class distinctions
    (E) no citizens can be first and second class simultaneously

13. There are 500 students in the school. In the fall semester, 30 were in the glee club, 30 were members of the debating society, and 40 were on the staff of the school newspaper. In the spring semester, all three of these activities had twice as many participants. Thus, in the course of the school year, all but 200 of the 500 students in the school participated in these extracurricular activities.

    All of the following can be used to question the conclusion of this passage EXCEPT:

    (A) Some students participated in more than one activity in the fall semester.
    (B) Some students participated in an activity in more than one semester.
    (C) Some students participated in activities in only the fall semester.
    (D) Some students never participated in activities.
    (E) Some students participated in more than one activity in both semesters.

14. Nothing can come of nothing; nothing can go back to nothing.

    Which one of the following follows most logically from the above statement?

    (A) Something can come out of something; something can go back to something.
    (B) Something can come out of nothing; something can go back to nothing.
    (C) Nothing can come out of something; nothing can go back to something.
    (D) Something must come out of something; something must go back to something.
    (E) Something must come out of something; nothing can go back to nothing.

GO ON TO THE NEXT PAGE.

15. The president has vowed in speeches across the country that there will be no increase in taxes and no reduction in defense; he has repeatedly challenged Congress to narrow the deficit through deeper spending cuts. Congressional critics have responded with labored comparisons between a bloated Pentagon and the nation's poor being lacerated by merciless budget cutters. In Democratic cloakrooms, laments about the "intolerable deficit" are code words for higher taxes.

Which one of the following additions to the passage would make clear the author's position on the budget issue?

(A) Everyone agrees that the president's budget deficit of around $100 billion is highly undesirable, to say the least.
(B) Everyone agrees that the president's budget deficit is both undesirable and unavoidable.
(C) Everyone agrees that this will be a summer of hot debate in Congress over the president's budget proposal.
(D) Everyone agrees that the partisan disagreement over the president's budget proposal will be won by those who create the most persuasive terminology.
(E) Everyone agrees that the president's budget proposal is a product of careful, honest, but sometimes misguided analysis.

16. *The average wage in this plant comes to exactly $7.87 per working day.* In this statement *average* has the strict mathematical sense. It is the quotient obtained by dividing the sum of all wages for a given period by the product of the number of workers and the number of days in the period.

Which one of the following is the most logical implication of the passage above?

(A) More workers in the plant earn $7.87 per day than those who do not earn $7.87 per day.
(B) Any particular worker in the plant receives $7.87 per day.
(C) There must be workers in the plant who earn far more than $7.87 per day.
(D) If some workers in the plant earn more than $7.87 per day, there must be others in the plant who earn less than $7.87 per day.
(E) There must be workers in the plant who earn exactly $7.87 per day.

17. *Magazine article:* Davy "Sugar" Jinkins is one of the finest boxers to have ever fought. Last week Davy announced his retirement from the ring, but not from the sport. Davy will continue in boxing as the trainer of "Boom Boom" Jones. With Jinkins handling him, we are sure that Boom Boom will become a title contender in no time.

The foregoing article is based upon all of the following assumptions EXCEPT:

(A) Boxers who have a good trainer can do well.
(B) Those who were good boxers can be fine trainers.
(C) Jones is capable of being trained.
(D) Title contenders should be well trained.
(E) Jinkins did well as a boxer.

GO ON TO THE NEXT PAGE.

3 3 3 3 3

Model Test 4

18. You can solve a problem. You cannot solve a dilemma, for it requires a choice between two disagreeable alternatives.

All of the following exemplify a dilemma EXCEPT:

(A) Amleth must avenge his father's death by killing his assassins. He must also protect his mother who was one of the murderers.
(B) The zoo has one vacant enclosure that is suitable for the exhibition of hyenas or lesser kudus. Hyenas prey upon kudus. The zoo will lose a federal grant if it fails to exhibit both kinds of animals.
(C) Ames must relocate his business in Belmont or Arlington. Office rentals are much more expensive in Belmont; office locations in Arlington are inconvenient for customers.
(D) To have enough meat to feed the four guests I must buy two pounds of beef. But one pound of beef costs two dollars and I have only three dollars.
(E) I must park my car on Ash or Maple Street and go to the market. If I park on Ash Street, I will probably get a parking ticket; if I park on Maple Street, my radio will probably be stolen.

19. The stores are always crowded on holidays. The stores are not crowded; therefore, it must not be a holiday.

Which one of the following most closely parallels the kind of reasoning used in the above sentences?

(A) The stores are always crowded on Christmas. The stores are crowded; therefore, it must be Christmas.
(B) Reptiles are present on a hot day in the desert. Reptiles are absent in this desert area; therefore, this cannot be a hot desert day.
(C) There is a causal relationship between the occurrence of holidays and the number of people in stores.
(D) The voting places are empty; therefore, it is not an election day.
(E) The stores are always empty on Tuesdays. It is Tuesday; therefore, the stores will be empty.

Questions 20–21

For one to be assured of success in politics, one must have a sound experiential background, be a polished orator, and possess great wealth. Should an individual lack any one of these attributes, he most certainly will be considered a dark horse in any campaign for public office. Should an individual be without any two of these attributes, he cannot win an election. If Nelson Nerd is to win the presidency, he must greatly improve his ability as a public speaker. His extraordinary wealth is not enough.

20. The author of the above passage appears to believe that

(A) Nerd is the wealthiest candidate
(B) Nerd is a sufficiently experienced politician
(C) being a good public speaker alone can win one a high public office
(D) if Nerd's public speaking improves, he will win the presidency
(E) Nerd is not a dark horse now

21. Which one of the following would most weaken the speaker's claims?

(A) Nerd is not the wealthiest candidate running for president.
(B) The incumbent president had little relevant experience before coming into office and has always been a poor public speaker.
(C) Of the individuals elected to public office, 0.001 percent have lacked either oratory skill, experience, or money.
(D) Nerd failed in his last bid for the presidency.
(E) The incumbent president, who is running for reelection, is as wealthy as Nerd.

22. Tom is test driving a blue car. After driving for a short while he comes to the following conclusion: Since this car is blue, it must not accelerate quickly.

The foregoing conclusion can be properly drawn if it is also known that

(A) all red cars accelerate quickly
(B) there are some slow blue cars
(C) all blue cars may not accelerate slowly
(D) all cars that accelerate quickly are red
(E) all slow cars are red

Questions 23–24

As almost everyone is painfully aware, the federal government has butted into almost every sector of human existence in recent years. But this manic intrusiveness isn't always the government's fault. Sometimes there is a compulsion to enlist Uncle Sam as a superbusybody.

23. Which one of the following is one of the author's basic assumptions?

(A) Most of his readers have suffered government intrusion.
(B) All government intrusion is unwarranted.
(C) Government intrusion is always government-initiated.
(D) All memories of government intrusion are painful memories.
(E) At no time has the federal government practiced nonintrusiveness.

GO ON TO THE NEXT PAGE.

24. Which one of the following most nearly restates the final sentence?

    (A) Most of the time government is responsible for government intrusion.
    (B) Sometimes government does more than intrude; it compels intrusion.
    (C) Sometimes Uncle Sam himself enlists in the ranks of the intruders.
    (D) Sometimes Uncle Sam is compulsive rather than merely symbolic.
    (E) Sometimes the government itself is not responsible for government intrusion.

25. Those who dictate what we can and cannot see on television are guilty of falsely equating knowledge with action. They would have us believe that to view violent behavior is to commit it.

    On the basis of the content of the above passage, we may infer that the author would believe which one of the following?

    (A) Knowing how to manufacture nuclear weapons leads to nuclear war.
    (B) Those guilty of committing a crime were not necessarily influenced by an awareness that such crimes occurred.
    (C) Media censorship is based upon logical justification.
    (D) Know your enemy.
    (E) The truth shall set you free.

26. In 1975, the U.S. Supreme Court ruled that the federal government has exclusive rights to any oil and gas resources on the Atlantic Outer Shelf beyond the three-mile limit.

    Which one of the following must be true in order for this ruling to be logical?

    (A) The U.S. Supreme Court has met recently.
    (B) The Atlantic Outer Shelf may possibly contain oil and gas resources.
    (C) No oil and gas resources exist within the three-mile limit.
    (D) In 1977, the Court reversed this ruling.
    (E) Oil and gas on the Atlantic Shelf has not been explored for in the past three years.

STOP

IF YOU FINISH BEFORE TIME IS CALLED,
YOU MAY CHECK YOUR WORK ON THIS SECTION ONLY.
DO NOT WORK ON ANY OTHER SECTION IN THE TEST.

SECTION IV

Time—35 minutes
28 Questions

Directions: Read the passages and answer the questions following each passage by blackening the appropriate space on the answer sheet. You may refer back to the passages when answering the questions. Answer all questions on the basis of what is stated or implied.

The Constitution gives the Congress power to make the laws that determine the election of senators and representatives. At first Congress exercised its power to supervise apportionment by simply specifying in the statutes how many representatives each state was to have. From 1842 until the 1920s, it went further and required that the districts be relatively compact (not scattered areas) and relatively equal in voting population.

Major shifts in population occurred in the twentieth century: large numbers of farmers could no longer maintain small farms and moved to the cities to find employment; rapidly growing industries, organized in factory systems, attracted rural workers; and many blacks who could no longer find work in southern agriculture moved to the North to get better jobs and get away from strict Jim Crow living conditions. The rural areas of the country became more sparsely populated while the city populations swelled.

As these changes were occurring, Congress took less interest in its reapportionment power, and after 1929 did not reenact the requirements. In 1946, voters in Illinois asked the Supreme Court to remedy the serious malapportionment of their state congressional districts. Justice Frankfurter, writing for the Court, said the federal courts should stay out of "this political thicket." Reapportionment was a "political question" outside the jurisdiction of these courts. Following this holding, malapportionment grew more severe and widespread in the United States.

In the Warren Court era, voters again asked the Court to pass on issues concerning the size and shape of electoral districts, partly out of desperation because no other branch of government offered relief, and partly out of hope that the Court would reexamine old decisions in this area as it had in others, looking at basic constitutional principles in the light of modern living conditions. Once again, the Court had to work through the problem of separation of powers, which had stood in the way of court action concerning representation. In this area, too, the Court's rulings were greeted by some as shockingly radical departures from "the American way," while others saw them as a reversion to the democratic processes established by the Constitution, applied to an urbanized setting.

1. The primary purpose of the passage is to
   (A) criticize public apathy concerning apportionment
   (B) describe in general the history of political apportionment
   (C) argue for the power of the Supreme Court
   (D) describe the role of the Warren Court in political apportionment
   (E) stress that reapportionment is essentially a congressional concern

GO ON TO THE NEXT PAGE.

4 4 4 4 4

Model Test 4

2. The author implies which one of the following opinions about federal supervision of apportionment?
   (A) Federal supervision is unnecessary.
   (B) Federal supervision is necessary.
   (C) Apportionment should be regulated by the Court.
   (D) Apportionment should be regulated by Congress.
   (E) Court rulings on apportionment violate "the American way."

3. In the third paragraph, "malapportionment" refers to the
   (A) influx of farmers into the city
   (B) Jim Crow phenomenon
   (C) shift from rural to urban populations
   (D) distribution of voters in Illinois
   (E) unfair size and shape of congressional districts

4. We may infer that during the Warren Court era
   (A) the most dissatisfied voters lived in cities
   (B) the constituency was dissatisfied
   (C) the separation of powers became important for the first time
   (D) the public turned its attention away from issues of apportionment
   (E) a ballot issue concerning electoral apportionment passed

5. The passage answers which one of the following questions?
   (A) Does the Constitution delegate authority for supervising apportionment?
   (B) Do population shifts intensify racism?
   (C) Should the Constitution still be consulted, even though times have changed?
   (D) Why did the Warren Court agree to undertake the issue of representation?
   (E) How did the Warren Court rule on the separation of powers issue?

6. We may conclude that Justice Frankfurter was
   (A) a member of the Warren Court
   (B) not a member of the Warren Court
   (C) opposed to reapportionment
   (D) skeptical about the separation of powers
   (E) too attached to outmoded interpretations of the Constitution

7. In the passage the author is primarily concerned with
   (A) summarizing history
   (B) provoking a controversy
   (C) suggesting a new attitude
   (D) reevaluating old decisions
   (E) challenging constitutional principles

GO ON TO THE NEXT PAGE.

Under very early common law, all felonies were punishable by death. The perpetrators of the felony were hanged whether or not a homicide had been committed during the felony. Later, however, most felonies were declared to be noncapital offenses. The common law courts, in need of a deterrent to the use of deadly force in the course of these noncapital felonies, developed the "felony-murder" rule. The first formal statement of the rule stated: "Any killing by one in the commission of a felony is guilty of murder." The killing was a murder whether intentional or unintentional, accidental or mistaken. The usual requirement of malice was eliminated and the only criminal intent necessary was the intent to commit the particular underlying felony. All participants in the felony were guilty of murder—actual killer and nonkiller confederates.

Proponents of the rule argued that it was justified because the felon demonstrated a lack of concern for human life by the commission of a violent and dangerous felony and that the crime was murder either because of a conclusive presumption of malice or simply by force of statutory definition.

Opponents of the rule describe it as a highly artificial concept and "an enigma wrapped in a riddle." They are quick to point out that the rule has been abandoned in England where it originated, abolished in India, severely restricted in Canada and a number of other commonwealth countries, is unknown in continental Europe, and abandoned in Michigan. In reality, the real strength of the opponents' criticism stems from the bizarre and oft times unfair results achieved when the felony-murder rule is applied mechanically. Defendants have been convicted under the rule where the killing was purely accidental, or the killing took place after the felony during the later flight from the scene; or a third party killed another (police officer killed a citizen or vice versa; or a victim died of a heart attack 15–20 minutes after the robbery was over; or the person killed was an accomplice in the felony).

Attacks on the rule have come from all directions with basically the same demand—reevaluate and abandon the archaic legal fiction; restrict and limit vicarious criminal liability; prosecute killers for murder, not nonkillers; increase punishment for the underlying felony as a real deterrent; and initiate legislative modifications. With the unstable history of the felony-murder rule, including its abandonment by many jurisdictions in this country, the felony-murder rule is dying a slow but certain death.

8. Which one of the following best states the central idea of the passage?
   - (A) The felony-murder rule should be abolished.
   - (B) Some jurisdictions are about to abandon the felony-murder rule.
   - (C) The felony-murder rule can be unfair.
   - (D) The felony-murder rule should be abolished by the Supreme Court of the United States.
   - (E) There are strong arguments to be made both for and against the felony-murder rule.

9. The felony-murder rule was developed in order to
   - (A) deter felonies
   - (B) deter murders
   - (C) deter deadly force in felonies
   - (D) return death for death
   - (E) extend the definition of murder to any malicious act resulting in death

GO ON TO THE NEXT PAGE.

10. Arguments in favor of the felony-murder rule may include all of the following EXCEPT:
    (A) We can infer that anyone undertaking a violent felony does so maliciously.
    (B) We can infer that anyone undertaking a dangerous felony demonstrates an indifference to human life.
    (C) If the punishment for the use of deadly force whether intended or not is the same, criminals will be less likely to use deadly force.
    (D) Because a life has been taken, the crime is murder by force of statutory definition.
    (E) The victim of murder may be an accomplice of the felon.

11. According to the passage, opponents of the felony-murder rule have raised all of the following objections to the statute EXCEPT:
    (A) The felony-murder rule results in murder prosecutions of defendants who have not committed murder.
    (B) The felony-murder rule is an archaic law based upon a legal fiction.
    (C) The felony-murder rule is based upon a presumption of malice even if the death is wholly accidental.
    (D) The felony-murder rule deters the use of deadly force in noncapital felonies.
    (E) The felony-murder rule assigns a criminal liability vicariously.

12. In which one of the following situations would the defendant NOT be liable to the charge of murder under the felony-murder rule?
    (A) In escaping from an unsuccessful attempt to rob a bank, the defendant crashes his car, killing an innocent pedestrian in another city.
    (B) A bank security officer, pursuing the defendant after a robbery, falls down a flight of stairs and suffers serious permanent brain and spinal cord injuries.
    (C) The driver of the escape car, who has not entered the bank, crashes the car, killing the armed gunman who committed the robbery.
    (D) A bank teller, locked safely in the bank vault by the robber, has a stroke and dies.
    (E) The driver of a stolen car forces another car off the road, killing a passenger.

13. According to the passage, the decline of support for the felony-murder rule is indicated by the abandoning of the rule in all of the following locations EXCEPT:
    (A) continental Europe
    (B) Michigan
    (C) India
    (D) England
    (E) Canada

14. The author believes that the felony-murder rule is
    (A) unconstitutional
    (B) bizarre and unfair
    (C) supported by several hundred years of sound legal tradition
    (D) an unfair equating of intent to commit a felony and intent to commit murder
    (E) a serviceable rule unfairly attacked by the "intelligentsia"

GO ON TO THE NEXT PAGE.

4 4 4 4 4

The paganism of the Greeks and Romans, though a religion without salvation or afterlife, was not necessarily indifferent to man's moral behavior. What has misled some historians is that this religion, without theology or church, was, if I may put it this way, more an à la carte religion than a religion with a fixed menu. If an established church is a "one-party state," then paganism was "free enterprise." Each man was free to found his own temple and preach whatever god he liked, just as he might open a new inn or peddle a new product. And each man made himself the client of whichever god he chose, not necessarily his city's favorite deity: The choice was free.

Such freedom was possible because between what the pagans meant by "god" and what Jews, Christians, and Moslems mean, there is little in common but the name. For the three religions of the Book, God is infinitely greater than the world which he created. He exists solely as an actor in a cosmic drama in which the salvation of humankind is played out. The pagan gods, by contrast, live their lives and are not confined to a metaphysical role. They are part of this world, one of three races that populate the earth: animals, which are neither immortal nor gifted with reason; humans, who are mortal but reasonable; and gods, who are immortal and reasonable. So true is it that the divine race is an animal genus that every god is either male or female. From this it follows that the gods of all peoples are true gods. Other nations might worship gods unknown to the Greeks and Romans, or they might worship the same gods under different names. Jupiter was Jupiter the world over, just as a lion is a lion, but he happened to be called Zeus in Greek, Taranis in Gallic, and Yao in Hebrew. The names of the gods could be translated from one language to another, just like the names of planets and other material things. Belief in alien gods foundered only where it was the product of an absurd superstition, something that smacked of a fantastic bestiary. The Romans laughed at the gods with animal bodies worshiped by the Egyptians. In the ancient world religious people were as tolerant of one another as are Hindu sects. To take a special interest in one god was not to deny the others.

This fact was not without consequence for man's idea of his own place in the natural order. Imagine a circle, which represents the world according to the religions of the Book. Given man's importance in the cosmic drama, he occupies at least half the circle. What about God? He is so exalted, so awesome, that he remains far above the circle. To represent Him, draw an arrow, pointing upward from the center of the circle and mark it with the sign of infinity. Now consider the pagan world. Imagine a sort of staircase with three steps. On the lowest step stand the animals; on the next step, humans; and on the third step, the gods. In order to become a god, one did not need to rise very far. The gods stood just above humans, so that it often makes sense to translate the Latin and Greek words for "divine" as "superhuman."

15. Which one of the following best expresses the main idea of the passage?
    (A) Under Greek and Roman paganism, people were not bound by a set theology or teachings from a sacred book.
    (B) In Greek and Roman paganism, humans differed from animals in that they possessed reason.
    (C) Greek and Roman paganism was not, as some historians have claimed, indifferent to man's morality.
    (D) Central to Greek and Roman paganism was the belief that the gods were of this world, not above it.
    (E) Greek and Roman paganism cannot accurately be called a "religion" because of its concept of the gods.

GO ON TO THE NEXT PAGE.

4 4 4 4 4

16. In the first paragraph, the effect of the metaphors "à la carte/fixed menu" and "free enterprise/one-party state" is to
   (A) suggest the immorality of the gods
   (B) indicate the origins of the gods
   (C) suggest the earthbound quality of the gods
   (D) suggest the selfishness and pettiness of the gods
   (E) indicate the economic role of the gods

17. The central contrast between an "à la carte" religion and a "fixed menu" religion is best expressed as
   (A) choice among many gods vs. obedience to one true god
   (B) belief in female gods vs. belief in male gods
   (C) choice among holy books vs. adherence to one holy book
   (D) belief in life on earth vs. belief in life in heaven
   (E) choice among varieties of worship vs. acceptance of one liturgy

18. To develop his points, the author uses all of the following methods EXCEPT:
   (A) contrast
   (B) example
   (C) figurative language
   (D) irony
   (E) explanation

19. From information in the passage, we can infer which one of the following would be true under Greek and Roman paganism?
   (A) People would be happier and more fulfilled.
   (B) Religious wars would be less likely.
   (C) Family life would be less significant.
   (D) The arts would flourish.
   (E) People would behave immorally.

20. According to the author, why have some historians assumed that the Greeks and Romans were indifferent to man's moral behavior?
   (A) Their gods had no significant power.
   (B) They laughed at the religious practices of others.
   (C) Their religion did not include salvation.
   (D) Their gods were immoral role models.
   (E) They viewed gods and animals as the same.

21. The passage attributes the religious tolerance under paganism to the fact that
   (A) human reason was valued over faith
   (B) no one god was seen as the "true god"
   (C) religion was not at the center of human activity
   (D) the same gods were worshiped by different nations
   (E) gods were not taken seriously

22. The purpose of the third paragraph of the passage is to
   (A) summarize and evaluate the contrasts between paganism and religions of the Book
   (B) show the connection between the concepts of the "divine" and the "superhuman"
   (C) contrast the place of man in relation to God under paganism and under religions of the Book
   (D) explain the conflicts between the concept of monotheism and the concept of polytheism
   (E) simplify the points made in paragraphs one and two so that they will be more understandable to the reader

GO ON TO THE NEXT PAGE.

In contrast to the planets, the stars seem to be motionless, or fixed to their spots on the celestial sphere. But it only looks that way because they are so far away from us—distances that are measured in light-years. In reality, the fixed stars also move in the sky, but they do so at such a slow pace that their motion (called "proper" motion) becomes visually apparent only over thousands of years and otherwise can be proven to exist only through precision measurements.

The fixed stars shine with their own light. They are suns like our Sun, that is, spheres of incandescent gases (called plasma by scientists). In the interior of these spheres, energy is produced through thermonuclear reactions. The number of suns in the universe is vast beyond guessing. The unaided eye can detect about 4,000 stars on a very clear night; a telescope reveals many millions in the region of the Milky Way alone.

The stars are so far removed from Earth that their distance is difficult to measure. Distances up to about 70 light-years can be established with relative accuracy by using a method similar to triangulation, which is used by surveyors. Greater stellar distances are determined indirectly. Because a star (like any other luminous body) appears fainter the farther away it is, scientists try to calculate a star's magnitude theoretically by applying methods based on physics. They then compare the results with the actual magnitude observed. However, this method is less accurate, and the distances given by different astronomers vary considerably, diverging sometimes as much as 100 percent, especially for very remote stars.

Many stars do not always exhibit the same brightness. Instead, they change their magnitude in cycles anywhere from several hours to several years in length, but most commonly with so-called periods of up to 100 days. In many of these variable stars the magnitudinal fluctuations occur with considerable regularity, whereas in others they follow no clearly recognizable pattern. There are two reasons for the fluctuations in brightness. Either the physical characteristics of the star change—it may be growing larger or smaller or its surface temperature may rise and drop—or the star is concealed by another star that stands in our direct line of vision—as the Sun is hidden by the Moon in a solar eclipse—and blocks the light of the star behind it from our view for a certain period.

One of the most fascinating areas of research in modern astronomy is the study of the life history of stars. Stars are formed from huge interstellar gas clouds in whose interior gases and particles of matter gradually concentrate. A star is born when, at the core of this concentrated mass, energy is first produced through the conversion of hydrogen, the most prevalent element in space, into helium. The star then goes on to spend the main part of its life in a stable state, shining with a steady light.

But at some point all the hydrogen is used up and the star enters its next life stage. It tries to find alternate sources of energy by transforming the helium it has produced. But this is accomplished only with difficulty. The interior parts of the star contract while the outer ones expand. The star swells up in size and becomes a red giant. Eventually, when all sources of energy are exhausted, the star's life comes to an end. The star goes through a final, cataclysmic reaction and then either dies in a spectacular supernova explosion or simply ceases to emit light. The outer layers go hurling into space as gas nebulas, and what remains is either a star corpse whose glow gradually fades away—a white dwarf—or a neutron star. Conditions in such a neutron star are beyond anything imaginable: The mass of the entire Sun can be compressed into a ball 6 to 12 miles in diameter, and one cubic centimeter of matter

GO ON TO THE NEXT PAGE.

4 4 4 4 4

weighs 10 million to 1 billion tons. The life span of a star depends largely on its initial mass. Heavy stars with more than five times the mass of our Sun live a relatively short time, about 100 to 200 million years, whereas stars like our Sun have a life span of 7 to 10 billion years.

23. Which one of the following is the most likely reason astronomers vary in their calculations of a distant star's magnitude?

(A) Distance measurements of remote stars can be made only indirectly using theoretical methods.
(B) Triangulation is a surveyor's, not an astronomer's, method and is therefore imprecise in measuring star distances.
(C) Astronomers do not agree on the concept of light-years and therefore their calculations have different bases.
(D) Some astronomers use sophisticated and precise measuring instruments, whereas others rely on theoretical methods.
(E) Fluctuations in the brightness of remote stars cause magnitude measurements to be estimates at best.

24. Based on the passage, all of the following statements about stars are true EXCEPT:

(A) The accuracy of distance determinations for remote stars is open to question.
(B) No one knows the number of stars in the universe.
(C) Stars are composed of both gases and particles of matter.
(D) Heavy stars have a shorter life span than stars of smaller mass.
(E) A star's life span depends on the types of incandescent gases in its core.

25. Which one of the following inferences can be made about the cycle of stars?

(A) If a star uses up its hydrogen, it becomes a "white dwarf."
(B) A neutron star remaining after a supernova explosion is highly concentrated.
(C) Supernova explosions occur only when stars are created.
(D) The brightest stars will most likely have the longest life.
(E) The sun is able to transform hydrogen into helium, which means that its life span is longer than that of most stars.

26. Which one of the following best describes the organization of the passage?

(A) The first paragraph introduces the subject of stars. Paragraphs 2, 3, 4, and 5 enumerate the difficulties inherent in studying the stars. Paragraph 6 draws a conclusion.
(B) The first four paragraphs describe qualities of stars. Paragraphs 5 and 6 explain a star's cycle.
(C) The first three paragraphs make general statements about stars. Paragraphs 4, 5, and 6 provide concrete examples.
(D) The first paragraph includes a thesis statement about stars. Paragraphs 2 through 4 present arguments supporting the thesis. Paragraphs 5 and 6 develop a subtopic.
(E) Each of the six paragraphs of the passage discusses a different aspect of star formation and destruction.

GO ON TO THE NEXT PAGE.

27. The author of the passage would agree with all of the following statements EXCEPT:

(A) A star's energy is produced by the conversion of helium to hydrogen.
(B) A star may change in brightness because it is blocked by another star.
(C) The surface temperature of a star can fluctuate.
(D) Before a star dies, its outer parts expand.
(E) A neutron star may remain after the death of a star.

28. Which one of the following best describes the purpose of the passage?

(A) to summarize the life span of stars
(B) to contrast stars and planets
(C) to encourage the study of astronomy
(D) to describe the difficulties inherent in the study of stars
(E) to provide general information about stars

STOP

IF YOU FINISH BEFORE TIME IS CALLED,
YOU MAY CHECK YOUR WORK ON THIS SECTION ONLY.
DO NOT WORK ON ANY OTHER SECTION IN THE TEST.

SECTION V

Time—35 minutes
25 Questions

Directions: In this section you will be given brief statements or passages and will be required to evaluate the reasoning involved. In some instances, more than one choice will appear to be a possible answer. You are to choose the best answer. Use common sense and reasonableness in making your selection; then mark the proper space on the answer sheet.

Questions 1–2

By passing more and more regulations allegedly to protect the environment, the state is driving the manufacturing industry away. And when the employers leave, the workers will follow. The number of new no-growth or environmental rules passed each year is increasing by leaps and bounds. Rich environmentalists who think they are sympathetic to workers have no real sympathy for the blue-collar employees who are injured by their activities. One major manufacturer has been fined for failing to establish a car pool plan. Another is accused of polluting the air with industrial emissions, although everyone knows that two thirds of the pollutants come from cars and trucks. No wonder the large manufacturers are moving to states with fewer restrictive laws. And as the manufacturers go, unemployment and the number of workers leaving the state will rise more rapidly than ever before.

1. The author's argument that strict environmental laws will eventually lead to loss of workers in the state will be most weakened if it can be shown that
   (A) so far, the number of manufacturers who have left the state is small
   (B) the unemployment rate has climbed steadily in the last three years
   (C) most workers who leave the state give as their reason for leaving the poor environmental quality
   (D) several other manufacturing states have strict environmental laws
   (E) rich environmentalists are more powerful in many other states

2. Which one of the following is NOT an argument of this passage?
   (A) Environmentalists are responsible for depriving workers of their jobs.
   (B) When workers leave a state, it is a sign that manufacturers will follow.
   (C) A car pool law should not be enforced, as cars and trucks are responsible for most air pollution.
   (D) Large manufacturers prefer states with fewer restrictions.
   (E) A rise in unemployment will lead to an increase in workers leaving the state.

GO ON TO THE NEXT PAGE.

3. *Dick:* There will be a disastrous rise in the temperatures on Earth unless we are able to reduce the carbon dioxide content of the atmosphere to the levels of the 1980s. The only way to do this is to reduce drastically our use of carboniferous fuels.
Harry: The fear of too much carbon dioxide in the atmosphere is unwarranted. Throughout geological time, the oceans have absorbed carbon dioxide from the atmosphere and precipitated it as limestone. Since the ocean waters are alkaline and contain large amounts of calcium and magnesium, they can control any excessive carbon dioxide in the atmosphere.

In replying to Dick, Harry does which one of the following?

(A) questions Dick's assumption that reducing the use of carboniferous fuels will reduce the amount of carbon dioxide in the atmosphere
(B) denies that the reduction of the use of carbon-producing fuel will reduce the likelihood of global warming
(C) asserts that the reduction of carbon dioxide in the atmosphere is not the only way to avoid global warming
(D) suggests that reducing the use of fuels that produce carbon dioxide is economically unfeasible
(E) challenges Dick's belief that the increasing amounts of carbon dioxide in the atmosphere are dangerous

4. Unlike most graduates of American high schools, all graduates of high schools in Bermuda have completed four years of advanced mathematics.

Which one of the following, if true, would best explain the situation described above?

(A) Math anxiety is higher in the United States than in Bermuda.
(B) There are far more high schools and high school students in the United States than in Bermuda.
(C) More students in America take full-time jobs without completing high school.
(D) Math programs in American high schools are frequently understaffed.
(E) High schools in Bermuda require four years of advanced mathematics for graduation.

5. Psychological novels are superior to novels of adventure. Immature readers prefer novels of adventure to novels with less action and greater psychological depth. The immature reader, who prefers James Bond's exploits to the subtleties of Henry James, can be identified easily by his choice of inferior reading matter.

A criticism of the logic of this argument would be likely to find fault with the author's

(A) presupposing the conclusion he wishes to prove
(B) failure to define "adventure" clearly
(C) failure to cite possible exceptions to this rule
(D) hasty generalization on the basis of a limited specific case
(E) inaccurate definitions of key terms

GO ON TO THE NEXT PAGE.

6. *Literary critic:* A good mystery novel should have three strengths: an interesting location, complex and engaging characters, and a plot that is unpredictable but observes probability. If two of the three are especially good, the book may please many readers. In Kate Rudman's latest mystery story, the detective and the suspects are original and entertaining, and the plot is full of surprises, but the book will probably disappoint most readers.

   If the above is true, we can infer that

   (A) it is too easy for a reader to solve the mystery before the detective can do so
   (B) the setting is unrealized and the events of the book are hard to believe
   (C) the solution depends on information that is unfairly concealed from the reader, and the setting is the same as that of Rudman's last novel
   (D) the language of the book is unsuitable for children and, at the end, evil wins out over good
   (E) most mystery readers are satisfied if a story has an interesting detective and a plot that is full of surprises

7. In professional athletics, the small number of record-setting performers in each thirty-year span is remarkably consistent. In hockey, for example, 5 percent of all the professional players were responsible for more than half of the new records, and 95 percent of the new records were set by only 8 percent of the players. Similar percentages were found in baseball, football, and basketball records, where the numbers of participants are much higher.

   If the statements above are true, which one of the following conclusions may be most reasonably inferred?

   (A) An increase in the number of athletic teams playing hockey, football, or baseball would significantly increase the number of record-setting performances.
   (B) Reducing the number of athletic teams playing hockey, football, or baseball would not necessarily cause a decrease in the number of record-setting performances.
   (C) Record-setting performances would increase if the number of amateur teams were increased.
   (D) Many record-setting performances are not recorded by statisticians.
   (E) As records become higher with the passage of time, fewer and fewer records will be broken.

GO ON TO THE NEXT PAGE.

8. By refusing to ban smoking in restaurants, the city council has put the financial well-being of restaurant owners above the health of the citizens of this city. No doubt, the council would support the restaurateurs if they decided to use asbestos tablecloths and to barbecue using radioactivity. These devices would be no more risky.

   The author of this paragraph makes her case by arguing

   (A) from experience
   (B) from example
   (C) by authority
   (D) from observation
   (E) from analogy

9. The GOP's attempt to win the South has, however indirectly, played on the racial anxiety of white voters. It has produced a vocabulary of civility to conceal their opposition to school integration ("forced busing") and affirmative action ("quotas"). And, to the horror of regular Republicans, the party's candidate for senator in Louisiana is a neo-Nazi and Ku Klux Klan alumnus. The ease with which this candidate has merged his bigotry with a respectable conservative social agenda is frightening. There is, however, a ray of hope. The candidate is supported by about 30 percent of the voters.

   The passage above is structured to lead to which one of the following conclusions?

   (A) If the candidate disavows his views, he will lose his support; but if he does not disavow them, he cannot gain any new supporters.
   (B) And that 30 percent has grown from only 15 percent three weeks ago.
   (C) We cannot predict now whether that percentage will increase or decrease before the election.
   (D) Two opponents also have about 30 percent of voters with another 10 percent undecided.
   (E) There is still a possibility that Louisiana, with its unmatched history of corrupt, demagogic, and ineffectual state politics, will support his candidacy.

GO ON TO THE NEXT PAGE.

5 ⟨5⟩ ⟨5⟩ ⟨5⟩ 5

Questions 10–11

The gill-net is used to catch halibut and sea bass, but up to 72 percent of what it ensnares is not marketable and is thrown back dead. Gill-nets are often called "walls of death" because they entangle and painfully kill mammals such as dolphins, whales, and sea otters. To use the gill-net at sea is like strip mining or clear-cutting on land.

Powerful lobbyists representing the commercial fishing industry have prevented the legislature from passing a ban on the use of gill-nets within the three-mile limit. They claim that the banning of gill-nets will raise the price of fish. They also charge that the law would benefit rich sport fishermen who want the ocean for their yachts.

10. In the first paragraph, the case against gill-nets is made by using
    (A) statistical analysis
    (B) ambiguity and indirection
    (C) biased definitions
    (D) simile and metaphor
    (E) understatement

11. Which one of the following, if true, would support the argument in favor of a ban on gill-nets within the three-mile limit?
    (A) Less than one percent of the fish sold in this country is imported from abroad.
    (B) Gill-net users catch all but two percent of their fish within the three-mile limit.
    (C) The halibut population has fallen to a near extinction level.
    (D) There is a serious overpopulation of the coastal sea otter.
    (E) Coastal sea otters have nearly destroyed the abalone beds along the coast.

12. According to the Supreme Court, the First Amendment does not protect "obscene" speech. To be "obscene," the Court explained, speech must appeal to a "prurient" interest, describe conduct in a way "patently offensive to contemporary community standards," and lack serious literary, artistic or scientific value.

    All of the following arguments can be used to question the validity of the Court's definition of "obscene" EXCEPT:
    (A) There is no certain way of knowing just what an "appeal" to "prurient interest" is.
    (B) The phrase "patently offensive" is impossible to define precisely.
    (C) No two communities are likely to have the same standards of decency.
    (D) Most juries are incapable of determining what is "serious" artistic or literary value.
    (E) There is no writing that is without some "scientific value."

13. There are no edible fish in the streams of this county because there are no pesticide controls.

    Which one of the following assumptions must be made before the conclusion above can be reached?
    (A) Edible fish cannot be found in areas where there are no pesticide controls.
    (B) If there are pesticide controls, there will be many edible fish.
    (C) Without adequate pesticide controls, the fish population will rapidly decline.
    (D) If there are pesticide controls, there will be some edible fish.
    (E) With pesticide controls, the fish population will rapidly increase.

GO ON TO THE NEXT PAGE.

5 ⟨5⟩ ⟨5⟩ ⟨5⟩ 5

14. For eighteen years, a state has had three conservative congressmen, all representing the agricultural counties in the northern parts of the state. It also has three liberal congressmen from the large capital city in the south. One of the two senators is a liberal from the south, and the other is a conservative from the north.

Which one of the following can be inferred from this passage?

(A) Voters in the southern parts of the state will always vote liberal.
(B) Voters in the northern part of the state are likely to vote liberal in the next election.
(C) Voters in the state are influenced more by a candidate's political leanings than by where the candidate lives.
(D) The population of the three northern counties is about equal to the population of the capital city.
(E) The governor of the state is probably a liberal.

15. In the United States, people can get their medications. Those who say they can't are being vocal about it just to get another free ride. HMOs offer drug coverage at only a minimal copay; other private policies have many drug options; state programs offer discounted prescriptions for low-income families; and drug companies make free medications available to those who cannot afford them.

All of the following, if true, would weaken the argument above EXCEPT:

(A) Drug companies change the types of medications they offer free from month to month.
(B) Incomes may vary considerably from month to month and year to year.
(C) The definition of what is a "minimal" copay varies depending on the income of the individual paying it.
(D) Private insurers set rates based on previous prescription usage of an individual.
(E) Drug companies sell drugs in other countries for less than they do in the United States, so people are forced to order their medications by mail from those countries or go there to purchase them.

GO ON TO THE NEXT PAGE.

16. *Political Analyst:* Over the last three decades, the President's party has lost an average of 22 House of Representatives seats and two Senate seats in the midterm elections. This year, with a popular Republican President in the White House, GOP strategists had hoped to pick up seats in the House and the Senate. But the polls show these expectations are unrealistic. This should be an election with results much like those of the recent past.

According to information in this passage, the election should

(A) produce large Republican gains in the House and the Senate
(B) produce about 25 new House and Senate seats for the Democrats
(C) result in virtually no change in the balance of Republican and Democratic members of the House
(D) produce small Republican gains in the House and even smaller gains in the Senate
(E) produce two new Republican seats in the Senate

17. Ten percent of the state lottery winners interviewed by researchers of the paranormal have reported that they had visions or other signs instructing them to select the winning numbers. On the basis of these results, the researchers claim to have proved the existence of paranormal gifts.

Which one of the following pieces of additional information would be most relevant in assessing the logical validity of the researcher's claim?

(A) the total sum of money these men and women win on the lottery
(B) the percentage of lottery players who win money
(C) the percentage of contestants interviewed who were not lottery winners
(D) the percentage of lottery players who had visions or signs but did not win money
(E) the amount of money the lottery winners spend each year on lottery tickets

18. By spraying with pesticides like malathion, we can eradicate dangerous pests like the fruit-fly. But malathion spraying also destroys the ladybug, the best natural predator of aphids. Areas that have been sprayed with malathion are now free of the fruit-fly, but infested with aphids. This is the price we must pay to protect our citrus crop.

    The argument above assumes all of the following EXCEPT:

    (A) Pesticide spraying is the only way to eradicate the fruit-fly.
    (B) The aphid infestation is caused by the lack of ladybugs.
    (C) A pesticide that would kill fruit-flies and spare ladybugs cannot be made.
    (D) The use of pesticides has disadvantages.
    (E) The aphid infestation could be prevented by introducing a natural predator other than the ladybug.

19. The Superintendent of Education complains that the share of the total state budget for education has decreased in each of the last four years; he blames the fall-off on the steady rise in the cost of law enforcement. Organizations opposing increased spending on education point out that the amount of money the state has spent on education has increased by at least three million dollars in each of the last four years.

    Which one of the following, if true, best resolves the apparent contradiction in the passage above?

    (A) The total state budget has increased more rapidly than the expenditure for education.
    (B) Both the pro- and con-educational-spending spokesmen have failed to take inflation into account.
    (C) Law-enforcement costs have not risen as rapidly as the superintendent claims.
    (D) Some educational expenses are not included in the state budget, but are paid by local taxes.
    (E) School construction is paid for by funds from bonds, not by funds from the state budget.

GO ON TO THE NEXT PAGE.

5 5 5 5 5

20. How can I write any of the essays when there are so many essays to be written?

    In terms of its logical structure, the remark above most closely resembles which one of the following?

    (A) How can he buy a new car when he is already deeply in debt?
    (B) How can she increase her collection of books when it is already so large?
    (C) How can he iron any of his shirts when he has so many shirts that need ironing?
    (D) How can she visit London and Paris when she has not yet visited New York and Washington?
    (E) How can they raise horses when they already raise so many cows?

21. Great playwrights do not develop in countries where there is no freedom of opinion. Repressive countries are likely to produce great satiric writers.

    If both of these statements are true, which of the following is the most logical continuation?

    (A) Therefore, countries with no restrictions on expression will produce great satiric playwrights.
    (B) Therefore, great satirists in repressive countries will use forms other than the play.
    (C) Therefore, playwrights in repressive countries will not write satire.
    (D) Therefore, great satiric writers will not develop in countries where there is freedom of speech.
    (E) Therefore, no great satire is likely to be written in dramatic forms.

22. Contrary to the expectations of the Canadian government, a majority of the Mohawk population in Quebec is calling for native sovereignty. The Mohawk separatists cite a written agreement from colonial times in which Great Britain recognized the Mohawks' separateness from Canada. Unfortunately, the various Mohawk factions, each with its own agenda, have made it difficult to reach lasting agreements. What satisfies one group displeases another. The bleak outlook is for .

    Which one of the following most logically concludes this paragraph?

    (A) continued struggle within the tribe and between the tribe and the Canadian government
    (B) some kind of compromise which recognizes the rights of both the Indians and the government of Canada
    (C) some sort of agreement among the divided groups within the Mohawk tribe
    (D) the establishment of a separate Mohawk state with its sovereignty recognized by the Canadian government
    (E) a decline in Mohawk militarism and a series of fence-mending conferences

GO ON TO THE NEXT PAGE.

23. A new law will require labels giving consumers more nutritional information on all prepackaged foods manufactured in the United States. Food sold by restaurants or grocers with annual sales of less than $500,000 will be exempt. The required labels will reveal the number of servings, the serving size, the number of calories per serving, and the amount of fat, cholesterol, sodium, and dietary fiber.

    The effectiveness of the new labels in improving overall U.S. nutrition could be seriously questioned if which one of the following were shown to be true?

    (A) More than 80 percent of the food sold in this country is not prepackaged.
    (B) More than 80 percent of the prepackaged food sold in this country is marketed by the eight major food corporations.
    (C) The amount of money Americans spend on prepackaged foods for microwaving has more than tripled every year for the last five years, and the trend is expected to continue.
    (D) An increasingly large number of consumers now read the nutritional information on food packages.
    (E) Small retailers who manufacture packaged foods sell to only a tiny percentage of American food buyers.

24. A year ago the presidential science advisor announced prematurely that the United States would reveal its plan for combating global warming at the World Climate Conference in Geneva, Switzerland. Five European countries have already announced plans to make reductions in carbon dioxide emissions, and five others have committed themselves to goals of stabilizing their emissions. But the United States is still unprepared to announce targets or a schedule for reducing carbon dioxide emissions.

    Which one of the following sentences would provide the most logical continuation of this paragraph?

    (A) The Geneva Conference will be the last international meeting before negotiations on a global-warming convention begin next year.
    (B) The United States accounts for about 22 percent of the carbon dioxide pumped into the atmosphere, while the former Soviet Union accounts for 18 percent.
    (C) By adopting renewable energy strategies that would permit stabilization of carbon dioxide emissions, the United States could save millions of dollars.
    (D) The British Prime Minister and top environmental officials of many nations will attend the conference in Geneva.
    (E) Anticipating a debate in which the Europeans will criticize the United States for failing to act, the administration is downplaying the importance of the conference.

GO ON TO THE NEXT PAGE.

25. There is increasing reason to believe that Americans are talking themselves into a recession. Consumers are becoming more and more pessimistic, and the index of consumer confidence has plunged to its lowest level in years. What bothers analysts is fear that consumer pessimism about the economy will lead to spending cuts and become a self-fulfilling prophecy, speeding the onset of a recession.

    Widespread predictions in the media of a coming recession may be one reason for the pessimistic attitudes of consumers. They may be bracing for a recession by cutting back on spending plans for new cars, vacations, and restaurant meals—the very behavior pattern that analysts say will intensify the slump. Real estate values have been in decline for a year and a half, and the stock market has declined for four months in a row. When the economy is on the ropes, waning consumer confidence can deliver the knock-out punch.

    The argument in the passage above would be weakened if it were shown that

    (A) in the 1955 recession, the widespread concern over the President's health precipitated an economic downturn
    (B) although consumer spending in the last fiscal quarter was the same as last year's, most of that strength stemmed from unusual government military spending
    (C) the steady rise in car sales has continued, despite the phasing out of discount prices and low-interest car loans
    (D) the predicted recession after the steep fall in stock prices two years ago did not lead to recession
    (E) some consumers are more eager than ever to maintain the living standards they have enjoyed for the last two years

STOP

IF YOU FINISH BEFORE TIME IS CALLED,
YOU MAY CHECK YOUR WORK ON THIS SECTION ONLY.
DO NOT WORK ON ANY OTHER SECTION IN THE TEST.

Writing Sample

Directions: You have 35 minutes to write an essay in response to a given topic. Take a few minutes to plan your work before you begin writing. DO NOT WRITE ON A TOPIC OF YOUR OWN CHOICE. ESSAYS THAT DO NOT ADDRESS THE GIVEN TOPIC ARE UNACCEPTABLE.

The quality of your writing is more important than the length of your response or the content. Pay attention to organization, appropriate diction, and correct usage. You will not be expected to display any specialized knowledge in your response, nor will you be expected to write a "perfect" essay; law schools understand that you are writing under a time constraint, and will allow for the minor lapses in writing ability that might occur under this circumstance.

Only the lined area on your response sheets will be reproduced for the law schools, so do not write outside this space. Make sure your handwriting is legible.

Scratch Paper

Do not write your essay in this space

Sample Topic

The State Legislature has appropriated funds to build a new maximum-security prison somewhere in Metropolis County. The prison is to house one hundred prisoners convicted of serious crimes and also the two hundred prisoners awaiting trial or being tried in Metropolis City. These prisoners are now held at the overcrowded and antiquated Metropolis City Jail. Two locations have been proposed.

As an aide to the state senator who represents Metropolis County, you have been asked to write an argument to be presented to the Legislature in support of one of the sites over the other. Two considerations guide your decision:

- The state funds for building and maintaining the prison and for transporting the prisoners to the courts are limited.
- The senator is eager to increase his popular support in anticipation of the upcoming election.

The Metropolis City site is located ten minutes from the court buildings near the downtown district. This area of the city is densely populated and has a high, slowly declining crime rate. Residents of the district strongly oppose the building of the prison in their neighborhood, especially since a number of prisoners have recently escaped from the old Metropolis City Jail. Art-preservation groups also oppose the proposed location, since it would require the destruction of two buildings with unique architectural features. The estimated cost for the land and the construction of the prison on the Metropolis City site is eight million dollars.

The Deer Valley site is located in the sparsely populated Metropolis County, seventy-five miles from the court buildings. Deer Valley is a small town in a depressed rural area. Many of the residents of Deer Valley favor the construction of the prison, since they believe it will bring new jobs to the area. The roads between Deer Valley and Metropolis are narrow, and in a winter when the rains or snows are heavy, they may be impassable. The cost of utilities in Deer Valley is about twice the cost of utilities in Metropolis City. The estimated building cost in Deer Valley is seven million dollars.

Scratch Paper

Do not write your essay in this space

Answer Key

Section I: Reading Comprehension

1. B
2. C
3. A
4. A
5. E
6. A
7. C
8. D
9. B
10. D
11. A
12. D
13. E
14. A
15. E
16. A
17. C
18. A
19. D
20. C
21. B
22. B
23. B
24. C
25. C
26. B
27. C
28. D

Section II: Analytical Reasoning

1. B
2. E
3. B
4. C
5. E
6. D
7. C
8. E
9. B
10. E
11. E
12. D
13. E
14. D
15. E
16. B
17. C
18. E
19. D
20. E
21. D
22. B
23. C
24. C

Section III: Logical Reasoning

1. D
2. D
3. C
4. A
5. E
6. C
7. D
8. B
9. C
10. C
11. D
12. D
13. D
14. D
15. A
16. D
17. E
18. D
19. B
20. B
21. B
22. D
23. A
24. E
25. B
26. B

Section IV: Reading Comprehension

1. B
2. B
3. E
4. E
5. A
6. B
7. A
8. A
9. C
10. E
11. D
12. B
13. E
14. D
15. D
16. C
17. A
18. D
19. B
20. C
21. B
22. C
23. A
24. E
25. B
26. B
27. A
28. E

Section V: Logical Reasoning

1. C
2. B
3. E
4. E
5. A
6. B
7. B
8. E
9. A
10. D
11. C
12. E
13. A
14. D
15. E
16. B
17. D
18. E
19. A
20. C
21. B
22. A
23. A
24. E
25. C

Model Test Analysis

Doing model exams and understanding the explanations afterwards are, of course, important in acquainting you with typical LSAT question types and successful approaches to the questions. However, another benefit of carefully analyzing these model tests is to understand the kinds of errors you are making and thus work to minimize them. For instance, if a very high percentage of your incorrect answers is due to "careless error" or "misread problem" then perhaps you are working much too fast and should slow your pace accordingly. If your incorrect answers are due primarily to "lack of knowledge," then a careful rereading and reworking of the appropriate question-type chapter may be in order. Or, if you find that you aren't completing a large number of questions because of lack of time, you may need to either increase your speed or learn to use the "one-check, two-check" technique more effectively.

This kind of analysis of the model tests will enable you to identify your particular weaknesses and thus remedy them.

MODEL TEST FOUR ANALYSIS

Section	Total Number of Questions	Number Correct	Number Incorrect	Number Unanswered*
I. Reading Comprehension	28			
II. Analytical Reasoning	24			
III. Logical Reasoning	26			
IV. Reading Comprehension	28			
V. Logical Reasoning	25			
Writing Sample				
TOTALS:	131			

*At this stage in your preparation, you should not be leaving any blank answer spaces. At least fill in a guess, as there is no penalty for a wrong answer.

REASONS FOR INCORRECT ANSWERS

You may wish to evaluate the explanations before completing this chart.

Section	Total Number Incorrect	Lack of Knowledge	Misread Problem	Careless Error	Unanswered or Wrong Guess
I. Reading Comprehension					
II. Analytical Reasoning					
III. Logical Reasoning					
IV. Analytical Reasoning					
V. Logical Reasoning					
TOTALS:					

Answers Explained

Section I

Passage 1

1. (B) The first sentence of the passage makes it clear that government workers are forbidden by statutory law to strike.

2. (C) If strikes are a form of symbolic speech, the denial of the right to strike is arguably a denial of free speech. It also can be argued that it denies due process, the right to picket, and the right to avoid abnormally dangerous working conditions.

3. (A) The courts, not the legislative or the executive branches, must determine the "clear and present danger," according to the Supreme Court decision described in the second paragraph.

4. (A) Because the firing of the controllers had the same effect as a strike, it appears that there was no danger to the public.

5. (E) The author points out that workers in government who do the same job as workers in private industry cannot strike. The passage argues that the nature of the service should determine the right to strike, not the employer.

6. (A) It is possible that the "highly qualified" may seek employment outside of government, because of the no-strike clause. Choices (B), (C), (D), (E) are not plausible weaknesses of the no-strike rule.

Passage 2

7. (C) This is the best answer because the passage recounts both Dickens's realization that the novel, based on his memories, was deeply personal and also his recognition that he was creating a "mediated version" of himself. See lines 12–18, 59–66. (A) covers only paragraph one of the passage; (B) is a secondary point, not the main idea. The novel can hardly be called prophetic (C), although one line suggests it "anticipated" turmoil in his marriage. However, this is not a main idea. (E) is an opinion not presented or suggested in the passage.

8. (D) This answer is supported by the main points in both paragraphs one and two. The author does not present a "psychological study of motivations" (A) nor does he primarily contrast two aspects of Dickens (B), (C). (E) is inaccurate; the passage does not show that the novel became a turning point in his life.

9. **(B)** The line indicates that writing the book has called up his childhood memories and therefore "almost inevitably" led him back to the place where he was a small boy. The line does not indicate complete exhaustion (A) nor does it suggest that he was unable to separate reality and fiction (C). (D) is simply inaccurate. It is too far a leap to infer that because he returns to Rochester, he has overcome the trauma of his childhood (E), particularly because of the inclusion of the words "almost inevitably."

10. **(D)** This is the best of the answers because Fanny's significance is clearly suggested in lines 33–37. Although (A) might seem correct because future turmoil in his marriage is indicated (lines 19–22), an end to the marriage is not implied. (C) is incorrect because although it is suggested that he sometimes put his work and his own ego above his family, coolness and distance are not implied. (B) and (E) are not supported by information in the passage.

11. **(A)** Although (C) and (D) are accurate statements, they are not the most significant reasons for Dickens's choice of the name. Lines 59–66 suggest that (A) is the correct answer. (B) and (E) are not supported by information in the passage.

12. **(D)** This is the best answer because the parenthetical phrase concerning Catherine indicates her reaction to her husband's assumption of the right to name the children, which in turn suggests something about their relationship. Failing to insist on naming her children does not indicate that she is an inadequate mother (A). (B), (C), and (E) are simply not suggested in this line.

13. **(E)** The author is primarily objective and analytical in the passage. (A) is incorrect because although there is perhaps some irony (e.g., lines 40–42), it is minor. (B), (C), and (D) are simply incorrect; the author is neither argumentative, condescending, nor persuasive, for example.

14. **(A)** The first paragraph includes an account of Dickens's reactions to writing the novel, using many of his own quotations. The second paragraph relies on more commentary from the author, and also introduces related points, such as Dickens's choice of the novel's title and his interest in names. (E) is incorrect because paragraph one doesn't show the effect of Dickens's childhood on him, nor does the second paragraph connect his later life with his novels. Similarly, (B), (C), and (D) all include inadequate (or inaccurate) descriptions of the two paragraphs of the passage.

Passage 3

15. **(E)** Choice (E) best describes the purpose of Passage A. Although the passage does briefly explain the government's role (A), that is only part of its main idea.

16. **(A)** In Passage B, line 68, the author asks a question ("Why has public broadcasting declined in the U.S.?") and then proceeds in the rest of the passage to cite some reasons, making (A) the best answer. (B) may be implied in the passage, but criticism of funding is not its main purpose, and (C) is a secondary point.

17. **(C)** Choice (C) is the best answer. The last paragraph of Passage B cites funding issues as being responsible for many of PBS's problems, and the federal government's role in funding is emphasized in the second paragraph. The author of Passage B states that because of the lack of sufficient funding, PBS has been unable to create many new, different programs, but he/she does not imply that PBS "lacks creativity" (A).

18. **(A)** Both passages are generally neutral (D), but Passage B includes mild criticism (i.e., "endless pledge drives that tend to feature bland programming or 'specials' that have been shown too many times," "watered-down commercials"). This makes (A) the best answer. Although perhaps Passage B is somewhat pessimistic, Passage A is neither pessimistic nor optimistic (B). (C) and (E) are too extreme: Passage B isn't "harshly" critical, nor does Passage A "praise" public television.

19. **(D)** Choice (D) is the best answer. PBS's primary funding comes from viewers (lines 33–36), but CPB is directly funded by Congress (line 18). (E) is not accurate; CPB uses 95 percent of its funds to "strengthen PBS's technical infrastructure and develop programming," but it does use funds to promote PBS.
20. **(C)** In lines 69–70, the author of Passage B cites one "obvious reason" for fewer PBS viewers: more choices since the advent of cable.(C) is therefore correct. (A), (B), (D), and (E) may also be responsible for the decline in viewership, but they are not the "obvious reason."
21. **(B)** One of the definitions of "niche" is "a specialized market," making (B) the best answer in this context. (The Disney Channel, Nickelodeon, and the Cartoon Network are networks that specialize in children's programming.)
22. **(B)** Choice (B) is the correct answer. Government subsidies (line 51), viewer membership (line 34), household license fees (line 43), and fees from commercial broadcasters (line 47) are all mentioned.

Passage 4

23. **(B)** The first paragraph states that taxonomy was "in the forefront of the sciences" in "the eighteenth and early nineteenth centuries."
24. **(C)** The terms refer to plants and animals.
25. **(C)** The passage gives us no information to support (A), (B), or (E). (D) is untrue (they were among the "greatest biologists of Europe"). That Darwin spent many years and wrote three volumes about the taxonomy of barnacles suggest that there are a large number of kinds to describe.
26. **(B)** The third paragraph gives examples of the "genuine pioneers" mentioned at the end of the second paragraph. The scientists of the first paragraph are not "exclusively European," (Jefferson).
27. **(C)** Parsifal was a naive knight of German legend, and Klingsor was his enemy, a magician with an enchanted garden. The reference to Parsifal's bravery and the use of the word "vanquished" should suggest this answer.
28. **(D)** Though the passage does include (A), (B), and (C), the best choice here is (D), which describes all three paragraphs in the passage.

Section II

Answers 1–6

From the information given you should pull out information and list the two possibilities:

1 2 3 4 5 6 7 8

JJJJ or JJJ
~~RR~~
~~CC~~

R ? J

Two Possibilities:

JJJJ		JJJ
R R	or	R R R
C C		C C

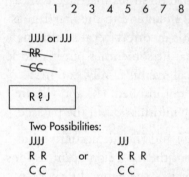

1. **(B)** If four jazz songs are played, and the first and last song are of the same type, there are two possible arrangements. Remember, at least two of each type of song are required. Start by placing the first and last song; for example, two rock songs. It is apparent that there is only one place for the four jazz songs, since, other than jazz, no two songs of the same type can be consecutive.

R	C	J	J	J	J	C	R
C	R	J	J	J	J	R	C

In both arrangements a jazz song is played third. For each of the other answer choices, there are two types of songs played.

2. **(E)** If three rock songs are played, the remaining five songs must be made up of two country songs and three jazz songs, since there must be more jazz songs than country songs. Since a rock song must precede the first jazz

song, there is only one arrangement where a country song is played sixth.

R	J	J	J	R	C	R	C

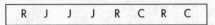

3. (B) There are four possible arrangements where a jazz song is played third and the first and last songs are of the same type.

R	J	J	J	C	R	C	R
R	C	J	J	J	R	C	R
R	C	J	J	J	J	C	R
C	R	J	J	J	J	R	C

In none of the arrangements is the sixth song a country song.

4. (C) There is only one arrangement containing three jazz songs where all three jazz songs are last. There are two arrangements containing four jazz songs. The songs at the beginning of the play list must alternate.

R	C	R	C	R	J	J	J
R	C	R	C	J	J	J	J
C	R	C	R	J	J	J	J

5. (E) If a country song is played first and seventh, there is only one possible arrangement using three jazz songs and one arrangement using four jazz songs. In both cases, a jazz song is being played third.

C	R	J	J	J	R	C	R
C	R	J	J	J	J	C	R

6. (D) Since a country song was fifth, the first three songs must be rock-country-rock. This leaves only three arrangements for the remaining songs.

R	C	R	K	C	J	J	J	J
R	C	R	K	C	J	J	J	R
R	C	R	K	C	R	J	J	J

In all three arrangements, there is a rock song played third.

Answers 7–13

From the information given, you could have made the following relationships:

$$J > L + M + N$$
$$N = L + M$$
$$M > K + G$$
$$G > H$$
$$K = G$$

7. (C) From the diagram above, since Jon has more bills than Lynn, Melanie, and Neil combined and since Melanie has more bills than Ken and George combined, then Jon has the most bills.

8. (E) Since Hal has fewer bills than George, and George has fewer bills than Melanie, and Melanie has fewer bills than Neil, and Neil has fewer bills than Jon, then Hal has the fewest number of bills. At this point you may have deduced most of the order of students:

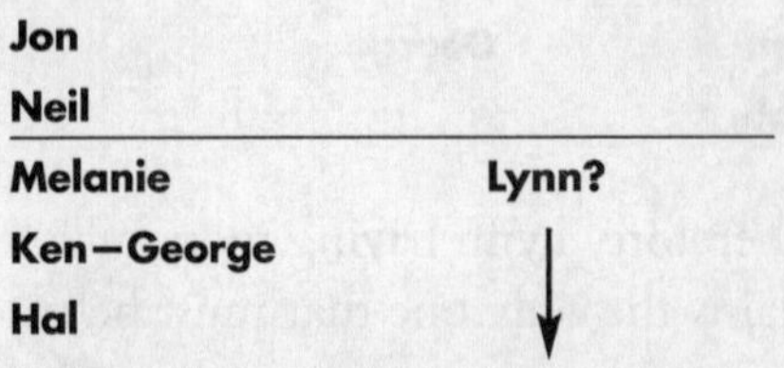

If you realized these relationships immediately from the initial conditions, you should have made this part of your first diagram.

9. (B) From the chart for the previous problem, we see that only choice (B) must be true.

10. (E) Using this new information with the order chart, we have the following chart:

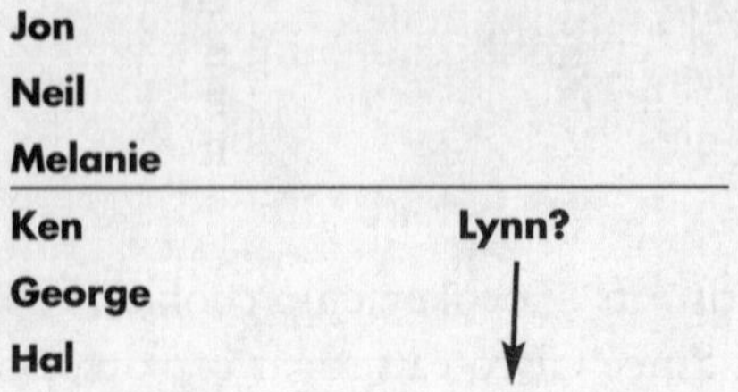

You may have approached this problem by eliminating the incorrect choices.

11. (E) Since Neil has the same number of bills as Lynn and Melanie combined, and Jon has more bills than Lynn, Melanie, and Neil combined, therefore Jon has more bills than twice the number of Lynn's and Melanie's bills. (E) is false.

12. (D) If Lynn and Melanie have the same number of bills, then Lynn has more bills than Ken and George combined. Since George has more bills than Hal and since Neil has the same number of bills as Lynn and Melanie combined, then Neil has more bills than Lynn, George, and Hal combined.

13. (E) If Tom has more bills than Ken and fewer than Lynn, the order of students would now be as follows:

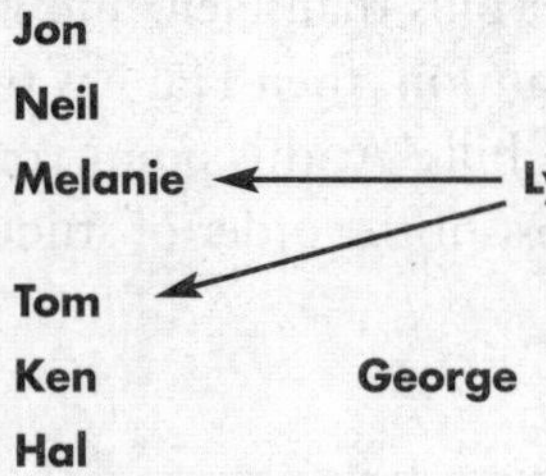

Therefore, Lynn having more bills than Hal is the only one that must be true.

Answers 14–20

From the information given, you may have set up the following display:

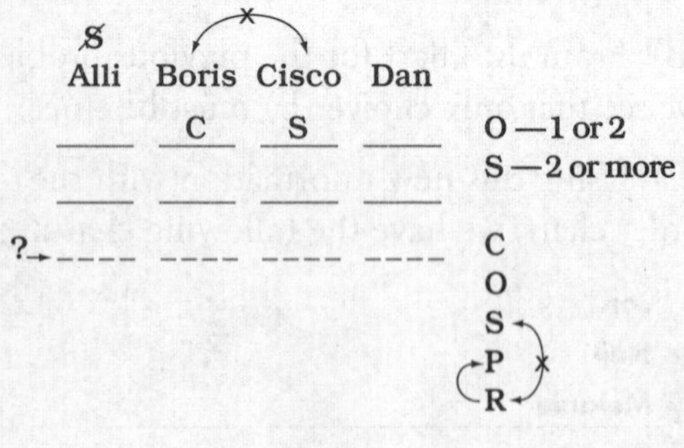

Since Boris eats chocolate chip cookies, Cisco does not. Since Cisco eats sugar cookies, Boris does not. We are given that Alli does not eat sugar cookies and at least two people must eat sugar cookies, so Dan must eat sugar cookies. Anyone who eats sugar cookies does not eat raisin cookies; thus, Dan does not eat raisin cookies. Your display should now look like this:

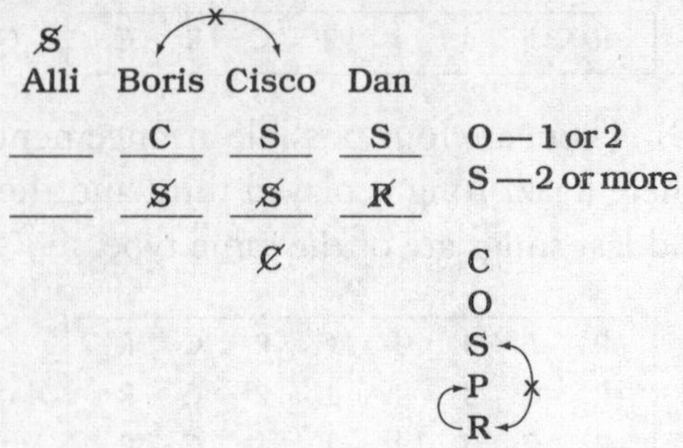

14. (D) From the display above you can see that Dan does not eat raisin cookies.

15. (E) If Boris eats exactly three kinds of cookies, they must be chocolate chip, peanut butter, and raisin. Since Boris eats chocolate chip cookies but does not eat sugar cookies, he must eat two of the remaining three—peanut butter, raisin, oatmeal. If Boris eats raisin, then he must eat peanut butter. If Boris does not eat raisin, then he eats oatmeal and peanut butter. Therefore, Cisco doesn't eat chocolate chip, peanut butter, or raisin, so he must eat oatmeal. The display should look like this:

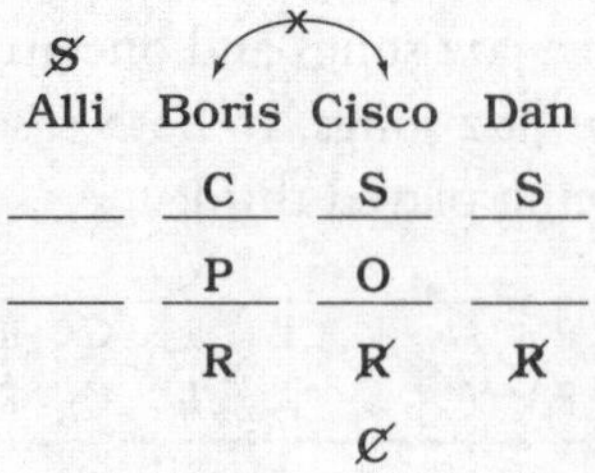

16. (B) At most, two people eat oatmeal cookies; thus, if Alli and Dan eat oatmeal cookies, Boris and Cisco cannot. Thus, Boris must eat at least one more type of cookie. Either Boris eats peanut butter cookies, or raisin and peanut butter cookies. Either way, Boris eats peanut butter cookies. Thus, Cisco cannot eat peanut butter cookies. This is not a possible arrangement since Cisco must eat at least two types of cookies. The display would look like this:

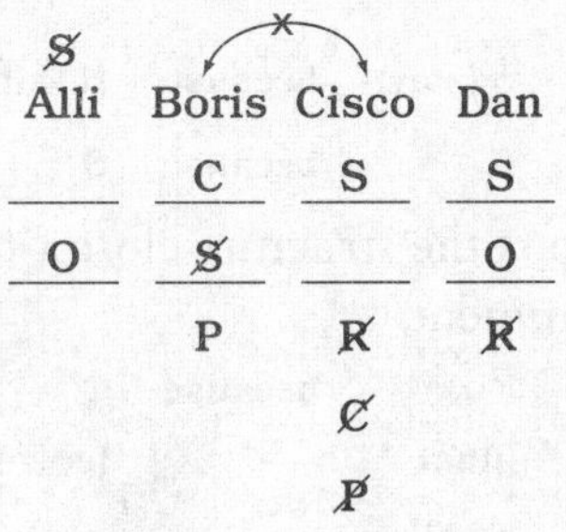

17. (C) The general conditions state that oatmeal cookies can only be eaten by a maximum of two people; thus, choices (A), (B), and (D) are incorrect. (E) can be eliminated, since Alli cannot eat sugar cookies, and Boris does not eat them either. Therefore, by process of elimination, choice (C) must be correct.

18. (E) This problem follows directly from the given conditions. Sugar cookies are the only cookie type that must be eaten by exactly two different people.

19. (D) If Alli does not eat chocolate chip or raisin cookies (or sugar cookies), she must eat oatmeal and peanut butter cookies, since those are the only ones left.

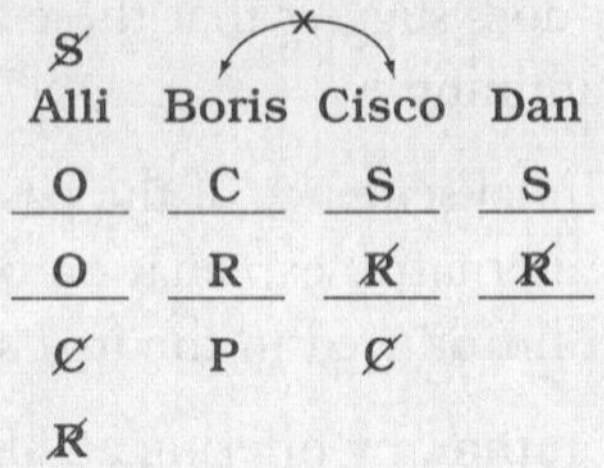

It is possible for Boris to eat raisin and peanut butter cookies, which would preclude Cisco from eating peanut butter cookies.
(A) is not possible. If Dan eats oatmeal cookies, Boris and Cisco cannot, since at most two people eat oatmeal cookies. In order for Cisco to eat two kinds of cookies, he must eat peanut butter cookies. If Cisco eats peanut butter cookies, Boris cannot. But this is not possible, since Boris needs to eat two types of cookies, too, and he cannot eat raisin cookies without peanut butter cookies.
(B) is incorrect, since two people eat sugar cookies and at most two can eat chocolate chip cookies.
(C) is incorrect. If only Alli eats peanut butter cookies, Boris does not eat peanut butter or raisin cookies. Thus Boris would have to eat oatmeal cookies in order to eat two types. But Cisco would also have to eat oatmeal cookies in order to eat two types. Boris and Cisco cannot both eat oatmeal cookies. (E) is incorrect because the initial conditions state that Cisco eats sugar cookies, so Boris could not.

20. (E) Raisin cookies cannot be eaten by Cisco and Dan, and they do not have to be eaten by Alli or Boris. We can also eliminate the other choices. From initial conditions, chocolate chip cookies are eaten by at least one person and sugar cookies are eaten by two people. This eliminates (A) and (C). If no one eats peanut butter cookies, no one can eat raisin cookies either. This would force Boris and Cisco to eat oatmeal cookies, but they can't eat the same cookie. This eliminates (D). If no one eats oatmeal cookies, Cisco must eat peanut butter cookies, since he must eat two kinds of cookies. Boris must eat raisin cookies in order to eat at least two kinds of cookies, but if he eats raisin cookies, he must eat peanut butter cookies as well. This is not possible, since Cisco is already eating peanut butter cookies. This eliminates (B).

Answers 21–24

From the information given, it would be helpful to construct the following chart to answer the questions:

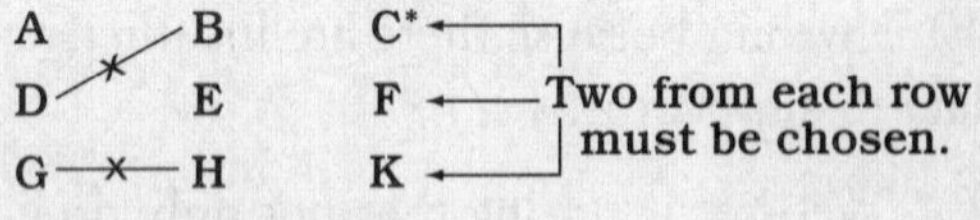

*If C, then also K.

21. (D) If A is not chosen, then B and C are chosen. Since C is chosen, K is chosen too. Since B is chosen, D is not chosen. Thus, E and F are chosen. So, if A is not chosen, B, C, E, F, and K must be chosen.

22. (B) If D is chosen, then B is not chosen. Therefore, (B) could NOT be chosen. Also, A and C must be chosen. If C is chosen, then so is K. E or F is chosen. G or H is chosen.

23. (C) If B is chosen, then D is not chosen. Thus, E and F are chosen. Notice that statement 6 is not two-directional.

24. (C) Since G and H do not play together, only one will be chosen. Thus, K must be chosen.

Section III

1. (D) If 97 percent of fatalities occurred *below* 45 mph, then a reduction in the maximum speed from 65 to 55 mph would have little impact, no more than a 3 percent reduction (if we assume that all other fatalities occurred between 55 and 65 mph). (A) and (C) are not relevant, (B) provides no conclusive data, and (E) *strengthens* the argument.

2. (D) The information states:
   1. If busing passes, then Smith was not reelected.
   2. Smith was reelected.

   Therefore, busing failed.

   3. If Smith is reelected she will vote for busing.
   4. Smith was reelected.

   Therefore, Smith voted for busing.

   (A) and (B) are wrong, because busing failed. (C) is wrong because Smith voted for busing. (E) is wrong because there are insufficient data to support it.

3. (C) Webster is stating that not only do lies disagree with truth, but they usually also disagree with other lies. Thus, it would follow that liars often quarrel with other liars.

4. (A) The given argument can be reduced to:

is not	**S (star)**	**because**	**H (hit)**
is	**H**	**because**	**S**

(A) exhibits the structure closest to that of the given argument:

is not	**F (final word)**	**because**	**C (correct)**
is	**C (correct)**	**because**	**F ("Instructor" is the final word.)**

5. (E) The logic here is straightforward. If the refineries are operating at 60 percent of their capacity, not 75 percent, then oil prices will probably rise.

6. (C) The discussion points out that (A) is an implication (rather than an assumption) of the studies. (B) is also not an assumption but is a restatement of the discussion's central issue. In order to consider speaker characteristics as either relevant or irrelevant, the author must assume that such a distinction exists; that assumption is expressed by (C). The passage does not assume a trim speaker will be "more persuasive" (D) or that irrelevant aspects are more influential than content (E), though it does suggest that these are issues worth examining.

7. (D) The final sentence of the passage offers an alternative explanation of the phenomenon introduced in the first sentence.

8. (B) The author, by offering an alternative explanation, stresses the scientists' unwillingness to consider such alternatives. (A), a choice worth considering, should be eliminated because the alternative suggested by the author is no more verifiable than the assertion he criticizes.

9. (C) The author argues that the term "progressive" is avoided by educators because of abuses in the progressive education movement, and that therefore, recently new, educational practices have avoided being tagged with the name "progressive." If (C) were true—that "progressive learning" has recently met with approval in middle class public schools—it would con-

tradict the author's statement about the connotation of the word "progressive" and seriously weaken his argument.

10. **(C)** The misunderstanding arises from Dave's assumption that Bill has said *every* morning, not *almost* every morning. (D), although worth considering, is not best because it does not address the scope of Bill's remark.

11. **(D)** Because the first two statements are not absolute, we may conclude that sunbathing is unlikely but still possible. There is no information in the passage to support (A), (B), (C), or (E).

12. **(D)** (A) and (B) are, by commonsense standards, implausible. (C) might be a valid statement, but it is not implied by Wilkie's assertion, which makes no distinction between first- and second-class citizens, and so implies (D).

13. **(D)** Since the passage does not say that the 200 students in spring activities were all different and all different from the 100 in fall activities, the total number of students could be much lower than 300. A single student could participate in all three activities in both semesters. (C) could apply if there were more than one activity, but (D) is a correct assumption in any case.

14. **(D)** If *nothing* produces only nothing, then the production of something *must* require something. (A) makes the production of something from something a possibility; however, the original statement implies that the something/something relationship is imperative.

15. **(A)** Only (A) makes an unqualified negative assessment; each of the other choices is either a neutral statement or one that attempts to balance positive and negative terms.

16. **(D)** The term "average" in the passage implies that if some workers earned more than $7.87 per day, others must have earned less. In (C) the words "far more than" make that choice not necessarily true.

17. **(E)** The magazine is sure that Jones will be a contender soon, and all that is offered to support this is the fact that Jinkins will train him. Therefore, (A) and (B) are the assumptions motivating the passage. (E) is not an assumption but rather a statement made explicitly in the article.

18. **(D)** All the other examples are dilemmas. Amleth must choose between failure to avenge or failure to protect his mother; the zoo must choose between the loss of the grant and the loss of a kudu. Ames must choose between higher rent and customer inconvenience. The driver must choose between a parking ticket and losing a radio. In (D), there is no choice between disagreeable alternatives. If you don't have enough money, you can't buy enough meat.

19. **(B)** The structure of question 19 may be simplified as follows:

C (crowded) whenever H (holiday)
Not C; therefore, not H

(B) is most nearly parallel to the relationships presented in the question:

R (reptiles) whenever D (hot desert day)
Not R (absent); therefore, not D.

20. **(B)** (A) is not a strong choice; the author indicates only that Nerd is *very* wealthy. The author does not compare Nerd's wealth to that of the other candidates. (C) contradicts the third sentence of the author's statement. Since the author tells us that Nerd has the necessary wealth and should acquire skill as a speaker, the author must believe that the third attribute (experience) is not an issue. In other words, the author believes that Nerd has satisfactory experience. The passage does not assert that an improvement in Nerd's public speaking will guarantee a win (D). Since Nerd has wealth and experience but inadequate speaking skills, he is a dark horse (E).

21. **(B)** (A) would not weaken the argument, since being wealthy, but not necessarily wealthiest, is all that is called for. (D) and (E) are consistent with the expressed or implied

information in the argument. Although (C) is a possible answer choice, (B) is superior; it directly contradicts the author's assertions.

22. **(D)** The given statement tells us only that the car is blue. For us to be *assured* that it is slow, we must know either that every blue car is slow *or* that no blue car accelerates quickly. (D) restricts quick acceleration to red cars.

23. **(A)** The argument obviously avoids absolute terms, relying instead on words such as "almost" and "sometimes." Therefore, it would seem consistent that a basic assumption would also avoid absolute terms; only (A) does so. In addition, (A) makes explicit the assumption underlying the first sentence of the passage.

24. **(E)** The second sentence diminishes the government's "fault," and the final sentence continues this idea; the only restatement that takes into account extragovernmental responsibility for intrusion is (E).

25. **(B)** The key phrase in the author's remarks is "*falsely* equating knowledge [viewing] with action [crime]." (A) is poor because it links knowledge with action. (C) is poor because the author indicates that those who dictate what we see (in other words, the censors) are guilty of drawing false (illogical) relationships. (D) and (E) are not relevant to the author's argument. (B) is consistent with the author's position that knowledge and action do not necessarily go hand in hand.

26. **(B)** A ruling on resources must at least presume the possibility that such resources exist; otherwise it is absurd. All other choices are irrelevant to the ruling.

Section IV

Passage 1

1. **(B)** Each of the other choices is too specific and/or not indicative of the *neutral*, rather than *argumentative*, tone of the passage.

2. **(B)** In the fourth paragraph, the author notes that after Congress had stopped enacting its reapportionment power, "serious malapportionment" problems ensued; the author thus implies that federal supervision is necessary. (C), (D), and (E) are issues on which the author does not imply an opinion.

3. **(E)** A clue to this answer occurs in paragraph 5, in which "malapportionment" is replaced by "the size and shape of electoral districts." Each of the other choices may contribute to malapportionment, but each is too specific to be the best choice.

4. **(E)** In the fifth paragraph we learn that the voters asked the Warren Court to rule on apportionment issues; therefore, we must assume that a ballot was taken that expressed the voters' opinions.

5. **(A)** Question 1 is answered in the first paragraph. The other questions, although they may be implied as issues in the passage, are not answered.

6. **(B)** Justice Frankfurter did not declare his opinion about reapportionment per se, but did declare that the Supreme Court should not address the issue; the Warren Court, on the other hand, did deliberate over the reapportionment issue. Therefore, we may conclude that Frankfurter was not a member of the Warren Court.

7. **(A)** The passage is a summary of events that occurred through the century, relative to apportionment. Each of the other choices has the author writing a passage calculated to persuade rather than inform.

Passage 2

8. **(A)** The passage makes the author's support of the abandonment of the felony-murder rule. (B) and (C) are true but are not the central idea of the passage. The passage makes no recommendations on Supreme Court actions.

9. **(C)** The best answer here is to deter the use of deadly force in felonies.

10. **(E)** Each of choices (A), (B), (C), and (D) can be cited to support the felony-murder rule.

11. **(D)** All of the arguments except (D), which supports the rule, have been made against the felony-murder rule.

12. **(B)** Because death does not occur in (B), the felony-murder rule would not apply. It could be used in the other cases.

13. **(E)** Canada has "restricted" its application, but not yet wholly abandoned the rule.

14. **(D)** The author uses "bizarre and unfair" to describe the results often achieved by the law, but not to describe the law itself. In the final sentence of the next-to-last paragraph, he explicitly objects to the equating of the intent to commit murder with "the mere intent to commit the underlying felony."

Passage 3

15. **(D)** The passage is concerned with the earthly nature of the pagan gods and the implications of that earthly nature. (A), (B), and (C) are correct statements but are subtopics or minor points.

16. **(C)** Both metaphors, which involve eating out in restaurants and conducting business, suggest the earthbound nature of the gods. (A) and (D) are incorrect because they address qualities not attributed to the gods in this passage.

17. **(A)** "À la carte" means that each menu item is chosen separately (cf. choice of gods), while "fixed menu" refers to an entire meal ordered as one item (cf. one true god). It is clear in paragraph one that the choice is among deities, not among holy books (C) or varieties of worship (E).

18. **(D)** There is no irony in the passage. For examples of *contrast*, see lines 19–31; for *example*, see lines 42–52; for *figurative language*, see lines 7–15; for *explanation*, see lines 63–71.

19. **(B)** See lines 58–67. According to the passage, tolerance was an aspect of paganism, making religious wars unlikely. (A), (C), and (D) are not implied in the passage, and (E) is contradicted.

20. **(C)** Lines 1–8 imply that "morality" is sometimes erroneously linked to salvation and an afterlife, and that historians have made this error with paganism because of the nature of the religion. (A) and (D) are not suggested by information in the passage, (B) is irrelevant, and (E) is inaccurate.

21. **(B)** See lines 32–33, 48–51. (D) is a correct statement but does not explain the basis of religious tolerance. (A), (C), and (E) are not supported anywhere in the passage.

22. **(C)** Paragraph three essentially creates a diagram in words to explain man's relationship to God in both paganism and the religions of the Book. (A) and (E) might be considered correct but both are imprecise; paragraph three doesn't actually summarize or evaluate, nor does it simplify all the points in paragraphs one and two.

Passage 4

23. **(A)** See lines 22–23 and lines 30–32. Astronomers use a method ***similar*** to triangulation, but only to measure distances up to about 70 light-years; also, nothing indicates that the method is imprecise (B). Conflicting beliefs of astronomers are not addressed in the passage (C) nor is the quality of their instrumentation (D). (E) is not supported in the passage.

24. **(E)** A star's life span depends largely on its initial mass, not the types of gases at its core. See lines 82–84. All the other statements are true. (A) is supported by paragraph 3, (B) by lines 17–20, (C) by paragraph 5, and (D) by paragraph 6.

25. **(B)** Support for this inference can be found in lines 86–91. (A) is incorrect because not all stars that lose their hydrogen become white dwarfs (see lines 82–86). (C) is contradicted by lines 81–82. (D) is not supported; initial mass is the only factor cited to account for a star's life span. Although the passage states that the Sun has a long life, it does not imply that the reason is its ability to transform hydrogen into helium but rather its size (E).

26. (B) Of the choices, (B) is the best. Although (D) recognizes the difference between the first four and the last two paragraphs, it says that the first paragraph includes a thesis statement. This passage does not develop a thesis. (A), (C), and (E) do not refer to the shift in focus in paragraphs 5 and 6.

27. (A) Hydrogen is converted to helium, not helium to hydrogen. See paragraph 5, (B) and (C) are supported in paragraph 4, and (D) and (E) in paragraph 6 (lines 84–86).

28. (E) Although the author might want to encourage the study of astronomy (C), the method used to present material is informational, not motivational. (A), (B), and (D) are all aspects of the passage but too limited to describe its purpose.

Section V

1. (C) The passage argues that environmental restrictions will lead to losses of jobs and hence workers, but if workers are already leaving because the environmental quality is poor, the argument is seriously weakened.

2. (B) The passage makes no comment on workers leaving before a manufacturer. It argues that the loss of manufacturers leads to a loss of workers (E).

3. (E) Harry does not need to deal with the connection between excessive carbon dioxide and global warming, because he does not believe there is too much carbon dioxide in the atmosphere. He argues that the oceans take care of the gas, so there is no danger.

4. (E) Though choices (A), (B), (C), and (D) might contribute to increased study of math in Bermuda, (E) leaves no doubt. High schools in Bermuda require four years of advanced math for graduation; high schools in the United States do not.

5. (A) Though all of the choices are plausible here, (A) is the best choice. The first sentence asserts the conclusion ("superior"), and the second asserts a consequence ("immature . . . prefer"). The last repeats what has already been insisted upon.

6. (B) The critic requires a good mystery to have "an interesting location" and "a plot that observes probability." If the book in question is disappointing, it may well have "an unrealized setting" and events that "are hard to believe."

7. (B) The passage suggests that records are set only by rare, superior performers, and an increase or decrease in the number of participants would not significantly change the number of record-setting performances.

8. (E) The passage makes its point by analogy, comparing the dangers of smoking to the dangers of asbestos and radioactivity.

9. (A) The passage is clearly hostile to the racist candidate, and has found a "ray of hope." The conclusion should logically predict his defeat. Choice (A) also draws a conclusion related to the part of the paragraph that refers to "regular Republicans."

10. (D) The argument uses both simile ("like strip mining or clear-cutting") and metaphor ("walls of death").

11. (C) If the halibut population is endangered, the banning of gill-nets would improve the fish's chance for survival. If (A) and (B) are true, the fisheries' argument about the price rise has more merit. If (D) and (E) are true, the reduction of the sea otter population would be more defensible.

12. (E) Choices (A), (B), (C), and (D) are reasonable objections, but the argument that no writing is without some scientific value is an overstatement.

13. (A) The assumption is that where there are no pesticide controls, no edible fish can be found, not the reverse as in (B), (D), and (E).

14. (D) The results of the elections and the fact that there are three congressmen from the north and three from the south suggest that the populations are nearly equal. (A) would be a likely choice if "always" were changed to

"usually." (B) is unlikely, and the passage gives us no reason either to believe in or to disbelieve (C) and (E).

15. **(E)** The argument is that, one way or another, people can afford to buy their medications. Choice (E), in some measure, supports that argument or at the least is irrelevant to it. People who travel to buy their prescriptions or order them by mail *are*, it would seem, able to afford them somehow. All the other choices weaken the argument, with (B), (C), and (D) each suggesting reasons why people couldn't afford the drugs and (A) indicating that the type of drug needed may not be available free from the drug companies.

16. **(B)** If the results are like those of the "recent past," the total should approximate "an average of 22 House" and "2 Senate seats."

17. **(D)** The conclusion could be more reasonably assessed if we knew how often the paranormal signs had been false. The issue is not how many contestants win money or how much money they win. The issue is the paranormal aid.

18. **(E)** The words "this is the price we must pay" (that is, we must suffer aphid infestation because the rutabagas have been destroyed) indicated that the author makes all of the assumptions of (A), (B), (C), and (D). The idea of (E) may be true, but it is not an assumption of the passage.

19. **(A)** The apparent contradiction disappears if the total state budget has increased enough so that the *expenditure* on education has been raised by three million each year while at the same time the *percentage* spent on education is a smaller part of the whole budget.

20. **(C)** In each case, the verb ("iron" . . . "need ironing"; "write" . . . "to be written") is repeated, while the adjective ("many") modifies the repeated noun.

21. **(B)** The first statement asserts that great playwrights will not develop in repressive countries. Therefore, the great satirists whom repressive countries will produce (the second statement) will not write plays.

22. **(A)** The details of the paragraph and the phrase "bleak outlook" suggest that a settlement is not likely.

23. **(A)** If the new labels will appear on less than 20 percent of the food sold, they will not be very effective.

24. **(E)** As the United States is still unwilling to act, its downplaying the conference is a predictable response. Though several of the other choices are plausible, none follows so clearly from what the paragraph has already said.

25. **(C)** If there has been a steady rise in car sales, consumers cannot be "cutting back on spending plans for new cars," as the predictions assert.

Overview of ABA-Approved Law Schools

The following table provides information about the tuition, programs, and academic community at 194 schools that have been approved by the American Bar Association. This is designed to provide a quick overview of the schools.

The information on this table is self-explanatory.

In several sections of the table, a check (✔) indicates "yes" and a blank indicates "no." For example, under Calendar, the possibilities are Fall, Winter, Spring, and Summer. At any given school, you can begin your law studies only at those times indicated by a check.

Since most law schools operate on a semester basis, information about credits and required courses is given in terms of semester hours. If a school operates on the quarter system, the abbreviation *qh* is added.

Similarly, tuition is generally given for a full year. When part-time tuition is given per credit, this refers to semester courses unless the abbreviation *qh* is used.

Where a category does not apply to a school or when information was not available, the cell is left blank.

INSTITUTION	Profile Page	APPLICATIONS: Fee	APPLICATIONS: Deadline	APPLICATIONS: Deadline Financial Aid	TUITION: In State Full Time (Part Time)	TUITION: Out of State Full Time (Part Time)	CALENDAR: Fall	CALENDAR: Winter	CALENDAR: Spring	CALENDAR: Summer	PROGRAMS: Day	PROGRAMS: Evening	PROGRAMS: Credits for JD	PROGRAMS: Required Creits for Courses	PROGRAMS: Transferable Summer Courses	PROGRAMS: Joint Degree	PROGRAMS: Graduate Law Degree	ENROLLED: Full Time (Part Time)	STUDENT BODY: Average Age First Year	STUDENT BODY: % Women	STUDENT BODY: % Minority	STUDENT BODY: Attrition Rate %	FACULTY: Full Time (Part Time)	LIBRARY: Volumes	LIBRARY: Microforms
Albany Law School 80 New Scotland Avenue Albany, NY 12208 518-445-2326 Fax: 518-445-2369 *admissions@mail.als.edu*	198	$60	March 15	rolling	$32,360 ($19,540)	$32,360 ($19,540)	✓				✓		87	32	✓	✓	✓	702 (37)	26	50	15	1	49 (30)	269,633	1,673,848
American University (Washington College of Law) 4801 Massachusetts Avenue, N.W. Washington, DC 20016-8186 202-274-4101 Fax: 202-274-4107 *wcladmit@wcl.american.edu*	200	$65	March 1	March 1	$32,452 ($22,838)	$32,452 ($22,838)	✓				✓	✓	86	34	✓	✓	✓	1128 (276)	24	58	32	17	101 (180)	568,391	85,290
Appalachian School of Law P.O. Box 2825 Grundy, VA 24614 276-935-4349 Fax: 276-935-8261 *npruitt@asl.edu*	202	$50	June 1	July 1	$21,100 ($880/hr)	$21,100 ($880/hr)	✓				✓		90	69				364	26	32	7		21 (3)	96,339	99,910
Arizona State University (College of Law/Armstrong Hall) Box 877906 Tempe, AZ 85287-7906 480-965-1474 Fax: 480-727-7930 *chitra.damania@asu.edu*	204	$50	Feb 15	rolling	$12,716	$22,980	✓				✓	✓	88	37	✓	✓	✓	650	27	44	27		62 (52)	272,356	141,521
Ave Maria School of Law 3475 Plymouth Road Ann Arbor, MI 48105 734-827-8063 Fax: 734-622-0123 *info@avemarialaw.edu*	206	$50	April 1	June 1	$28,900	$28,900	✓				✓	✓	90	60				360	26	31	14	8	29	79,283	378,729
Barry University (School of Law) 6441 East Colonial Drive Orlando, FL 32807 407-275-2000, ext. 237 Fax: 407-275-2010 *lawinfo@mail.barry.edu*	208	$50	April 1		$23,600 ($17,386)	$23,600 ($17,386)	✓				✓	✓	90	53 to 55	✓			131 (180)	28	44	39	3	24	78,715	92,839
Baylor University (School of Law) P.O. Box 97288 Waco, TX 76798-7288 254-710-1911 Fax: 254-710-2316 *becky-beck@baylor.edu*	210	$40	March 1	May 1	$26,796	$26,796	✓		✓	✓	✓		126	79	✓	✓		435	24	45	13	7	23 (33)	224,929	121,106
Boston College (Law School) 885 Centre Street Newton, MA 02459 617-552-4351 Fax: 617-552-2917 *bclawadm@bc.edu*	212	$75	March 1	March 15	$33,110	$33,110	✓				✓		85	38		✓		807 (2)	24	49	25	1	55 (71)	450,833	216,341

INSTITUTION		APPLICATIONS			TUITION		CALENDAR				PROGRAMS							ENROLLED	STUDENT BODY				FACULTY	LIBRARY	
	Profile Page	Fee	Deadline	Deadline Financial Aid	In State Full Time (Part Time)	Out of State Full Time (Part Time)	Fall	Winter	Spring	Summer	Day	Evening	Credits for JD	Required Creits for Courses	Transferable Summer Courses	Joint Degree	Graduate Law Degree	Full Time (Part Time)	Average Age First Year	% Women	% Minority	Attrition Rate %	Full Time (Part Time)	Volumes	Microforms
Boston University (School of Law) 765 Commonwealth Avenue Boston, MA 02215 617-353-3100 *bulawadm@bu.edu*	214	$60	March 1	March 1	$28,712	$28,712	✓				✓	✓	84	33		✓	✓	807	23	48	23	4	63 (25)	643,045	299,282
Brigham Young University (J. Reuben Clark Law School) 342 JRCB Brigham Young University Provo, UT 84602 801-422-4277 Fax: 801-422-0389 *kucharg@lawgate.byu.edu*	216	$50	Feb 1	March 1	$7,450	$11,176	✓				✓		90	36		✓	✓	472	26	38	18	1	38 (32)	469,905	148,156
Brooklyn Law School 250 Joralemon Street Brooklyn, NY 11201 718-780-7906 Fax: 718-780-0395 *admitq@brooklaw.edu*	218	$65	April 1	April 30	$34,650 ($25,987)	$34,650 ($25,987)	✓				✓	✓	86 sem.	31	✓	✓	✓	1134 (359)	25	49	25	5	80 (121)	544,380	1,323,747
California Western School of Law 225 Cedar Street San Diego, CA 92101-3046 619-525-1401 Fax: 619-615-1401 *admissions@cwsl.edu*	220	$45	April 1	March 10	$26,200 ($18,500)	$26,200 ($18,500)	✓		✓		✓		89	43	✓	✓	✓	848 (103)	27	53	31	18	42 (56)	306,682	786,070
Campbell University (Norman Adrian Wiggins School of Law) P.O. Box 158 Buies Creek, NC 27506 910-893-1754 Fax: 910-893-1780 *admissions@ian.campbell.edu*	222	$50	open	open	$23,000	$23,000	✓				✓	✓	90 sem.	67		✓		339	26	45	9	9	18 (23)	104,501	82,077
Capital University (Law School) 303 East Broad Street Columbus, OH 43215-3200 614-236-6500 Fax: 614-236-6972 *admissions@law.capital.edu*	224	$40	May 1	April 1	$24,795 ($16,245)	$24,795 ($16,245)	✓				✓	✓	86 sem.	46	✓	✓	✓	457 (273)	27	46	11	11	39 (83)	267,746	51,111
Case Western Reserve University (Case School of Law) 11075 East Boulevard Cleveland, OH 44106 216-368-3600 Fax: 216-368-1042 *lawadmissions@case.edu*	226	$40	April 1	May 1	$31,800 ($1,230/hr)	$31,800 ($1,230/hr)	✓				✓	✓	88	35	✓	✓	✓	667 (25)	25	38	14	3	59 (148)	302,504	100,174
Catholic University of America (Columbus School of Law) Cardinal Station Washington, DC 20064 (202) 319-5151 Fax: (202) 319-6285 *admissions@law.edu*	228	$60	March 1	July 15	$30,230 ($1,105/hr)	$30,230 ($1,105/hr)	✓				✓	✓	84	33	✓	✓	✓	689 (261)	26	50	18	10	49 (87)	203,232	199,613

Chapman University (School of Law) One University Drive Orange, CA 92866 714-628-2500 Fax: 714-628-2501 *heyer@chapman.edu*	230	$60	open	March 2	$25,350 ($17,420)	$25,350 ($17,420)	✓				✓		88	51 to 52	✓	✓	✓	352 (97)	24	51	27	12	25 (31)	265,500	190,381
City University of New York (School of Law at Queens College) 65-21 Main Street Flushing, NY 11367-1300 718-340-4210 Fax: 718-340-4435 *mail.law.cuny.edu*	232	$50	March 15	May 1	$8,900	$14,800	✓				✓	✓	91	61	✓			434	27	67	33	1	41 (18)	278,498	1,054,146
Cleveland State University (Cleveland-Marshall College of Law) 2121 Euclid Avenue LB138 Cleveland, OH 44115-2214 216-687-2304 Fax: 216-687-6881 *melody.stewart@law.csuohio.edu*	234	$35	May 1	May 1	$13,988 ($10,760)	$19,209 ($14,776)	✓				✓	✓	90	41	✓	✓	✓	494 (253)	26	45	14	12	47 (26)	519,563	298,337
College of William & Mary (William & Mary Law School) P.O. Box 8795 Williamsburg, VA 23187-8795 757-221-3785 Fax: 757-221-3261 *lawadm@.wm.edu*	236	$50	March 1	Feb 15	$15,300	$25,500	✓				✓		86	35	✓	✓	✓	603	24	45	15	1	43 (68)	386,618	880,396
Columbia University (School of Law) 435 West 116th Street New York, NY 10027 212-854-2670 Fax: 212-854-1109 *admissions@law.columbia.edu*	238	$70	Feb 15	March 1	$38,120		✓				✓		83	35		✓	✓	1242	24	45	30		98 (69)	1,092,534	235,424
Cornell University (Law School) Myron Taylor Hall Ithaca, NY 14853-4901 607-255-5141 Fax: 607-255-7193 *lawadmit@postoffice.law.cornell.edu*	240	$70	Feb 1	March 15	$37,750	$37,750	✓				✓		84	36	✓	✓	✓	580	23	48	30		33 (3)	670,000	5,500
Creighton University (School of Law) 2500 California Plaza Omaha, NE 68178 402-280-2872 Fax: 402-280-5564 *lawadmit@creighton.edu*	242	$45	May 1	March 1	$22,604 ($750/hr)	$22,604 ($750/hr)	✓				✓	✓	94	57	✓	✓		451 (18)	24	46	11		29 (34)	345,458	153,513
De Paul University (College of Law) 25 East Jackson Boulevard Chicago, IL 60604 312-362-6831 Fax: 312-362-5280 *lawinfo@depaul.edu*	244	$60	March 1	March 1	$28,660 ($18,600)	$28,660 ($18,600)	✓				✓	✓	86	43	✓	✓	✓	822 (343)	24	50	20	3	55 (103)	378,000	178,266
Drake University (Law School) 2507 University Avenue Des Moines, IA 50311 515-271-2782 Fax: 515-271-1990 *lawadmit@drake.edu*	246	$40	April 1	March 1	$23,900 ($830/hr)	$23,900 ($830/hr)	✓			✓	✓		90	41	✓	✓		462 (9)	24	51	10	6	29 (33)	320,000	110,000
Duke University (Duke University School of Law) Science Drive and Towerview Road, Box 90362 Durham, NC 27708-0362 919-613-7020 Fax: 919-613-7257 *admissions@law.duke.edu*	248	$70	Jan 1	March 15	$35,870	$35,870	✓			✓	✓		84	32		✓	✓	617 (31)	25	46	23	1	55 (67)	622,400	78,067

INSTITUTION		APPLICATIONS			TUITION		CALENDAR				PROGRAMS							ENROLLED	STUDENT BODY				FACULTY	LIBRARY	
	Profile Page	Fee	Deadline	Deadline Financial Aid	In State Full Time (Part Time)	Out of State Full Time (Part Time)	Fall	Winter	Spring	Summer	Day	Evening	Credits for JD	Required Creits for Courses	Transferable Summer Courses	Joint Degree	Graduate Law Degree	Full Time (Part Time)	Average Age First Year	% Women	% Minority	Attrition Rate %	Full Time (Part Time)	Volumes	Microforms
Duquesne University (School of Law) 900 Locust Street, Hanley Hall Pittsburgh, PA 15282 412-396-6296 Fax: 412-396-1073 *campion@duq.edu*	250	$60	April 1	May 31	$23,759 ($18,258)	$23,759 ($18,258)	✓				✓	✓	86	56	✓	✓		420 (143)	22	44	4	2	26 (45)	221,483	72,625
Emory University (School of Law) Gambrell Hall Atlanta, GA 30322 404-727-6801 Fax: 404-727-2477 *Sfleming@law.emory.edu*	252	$70	March 1	April 1	$34,700	$34,700	✓				✓	✓	90	47		✓	✓	680	24	50	26	2	63 (28)	296,381	104,548
Florida Agricultural and Mechanical University (Florida A & M University College of Law) 201 N. Beggs Avenue Orlando, FL 32801 407-254-3268 *ruth.witherspoon@famu.edu*	254	$20	May 1	March 1	$6,441 ($4,723)	$23,144 ($16,973)	✓				✓	✓	90	62				231 (162)	31	59	60	3		303,000	25,000
Florida Coastal (School of Law) 7555 Beach Boulevard Jacksonville, FL 32216 904-680-7710 Fax: 904-680-7776 *admissions@fcsl.edu*	256	$50	open		$23,970 ($19,160)	$23,970 ($19,160)	✓		✓		✓	✓	87	56	✓			834 (214)	27	46	18	8	30 (27)	220,091	469,002
Florida International University (College of Law) FIU College of Law, 6L 475 Miami, FL 33199 (305) 348-8006 Fax: (305) 348-2965 *miroa@fiu.edu*	258	$20	May 1	March 1	$8,292 ($5,617)	$22,535 ($15,266)	✓				✓	✓	90	31	✓	✓		176 (156)	28	47	54	24	28 (9)	190,000	66,000
Florida State University (College of Law) 425 W. Jefferson St. Tallahassee, FL 32306-1601 850-644-3787 Fax: 850-644-7284 *admissions@law.fsu.edu*	260	$30	Feb 15	April 1	$9,001	$27,580	✓				✓	✓	88	35	✓	✓	✓	773	24	46	20	2	45 (36)	447,041	1,017,140
Fordham University (School of Law) 140 West 62nd Street New York, NY 10023 212-636-6810 Fax: 212-636-7984 *lawadmissions@law.fordham.edu*	262	$65	March 1	May 15	$34,675 ($26,000)	$34,675 ($26,000)	✓				✓	✓	83	39	✓	✓	✓	1222 (391)	24	50	26	2	73 (117)	384,966	241,265
Franklin Pierce Law Center 2 White Street Concord, NH 03301 603-228-9217 Fax: 603-228-1074 *admissions@piercelaw.edu*	264	$55	April 1	open	$27,250	$27,250	✓				✓	✓	84	39	✓	✓	✓	437 (3)	27	40	12	8	24 (38)	260,165	545,214

George Mason University (School of Law) 3301 Fairfax Drive Arlington, VA 22201 703-993-8010 Fax: 703-993-8088 *arichar5@gmu.edu*	266	$35	April 1		$12,936 ($10,626)	$24,500 ($20,125)	✓				✓	✓	84	43	✓	✓	✓	414 (303)	26	38	17	2	36 (113)	447,746	201,818
George Washington University (Law School) 2000 H Street, N.W. Washington, DC 20052 202-994-7230 Fax: 202-994-3597 *jd@law.gwu.edu*	268	$80	March 1		$34,500 ($24,260)	$34,500 ($24,260)	✓				✓	✓	84	34	✓	✓	✓	1366 (270)	24	45		1	96 (243)	591,863	38,373
Georgetown University (Georgetown University Law Center) 600 New Jersey Avenue, N.W. Washington, DC 20001 202-662-9010 Fax: 202-662-9439 *admis@law.georgetown.edu*	270	$75	Feb 1	March 1	$35,080 ($28,270)	$35,080 ($28,270)	✓				✓	✓	84	32	✓	✓	✓	1582 (358)	25	44	24		108 (107)	540,626	582,573
Georgia State University (College of Law) P.O. Box 4037 Atlanta, GA 30302-4037 404-651-2048 Fax: 404-651-2048 *cjjackson@gsu.edu*	272	$50	March 15	April 1	$5,544 ($231/hr)	$20,704 ($863/hr)	✓				✓	✓	90	43	✓	✓		494 (191)	27	48	20	11	42 (28)	163,100	786,955
Golden Gate University (School of Law) 536 Mission Street San Francisco, CA 94105-2968 415-442-6630 *lawadmit@ggu.edu*	274	$60	March 1	rolling	$29,100 ($20,370)	$29,100 ($20,370)	✓		✓		✓	✓	88	54	✓	✓	✓	669 (182)	26	57	32	23	36 (62)	133,568	219,911
Gonzaga University (School of Law) Box 3528 Spokane, WA 99220-3528 509-323-5532 Fax: 509-323-3697 *admissions@lawschool.gonzaga.edu*	276	$50	Feb 1	Feb 1	$26,250	$26,250	✓				✓		90	44	✓	✓		556 (22)	26	45	12	14	41 (50)	156,920	127,079
Hamline University (School of Law) 1536 Hewitt Avenue St. Paul, MN 55104-1284 651-523-2461 Fax: 651-523-3064 *lawadm@gw.hamline.edu*	278	$40	April 1	open	$25,245 ($18,180)	$25,245 ($18,180)	✓				✓	✓	88	33	✓	✓	✓	516 (194)	24	54	13	2	42 (74)	145,878	122,131
Harvard University (Harvard Law School) Cambridge, MA 02138 617-495-3179 *jdadmiss@law.harvard.edu*	280	$75	Feb 1		$35,100	$35,100	✓				✓		82	30		✓	✓	1666	24	45	33	1	132 (71)	1,723,645	1,973,552
Hofstra University (School of Law) 121 Hofstra University Hempstead, NY 11549 516-463-5916 Fax: 516-463-6264 *lawadmissions@hofstra.edu*	282	$60	April 15	April 1	$33,534 ($24,360)	$33,534 ($24,360)	✓				✓		87	39	✓	✓	✓	828 (197)	24	47	26	11	40 (59)	550,765	1,823,120
Howard University (Howard University) 2900 Van Ness Street, N.W. Washington, DC 20008 202-806-8008 Fax: 202-806-8162 *admissions@law.howard.edu*	284	$60	march 31	April 1	$12,950	$13,595	✓		✓		✓	✓	88	n/av	✓	✓	✓	412 (3)	25	60	94	5	33 (23)	428,494	54,000

INSTITUTION	Profile Page	APPLICATIONS: Fee	APPLICATIONS: Deadline	APPLICATIONS: Deadline Financial Aid	TUITION: In State Full Time (Part Time)	TUITION: Out of State Full Time (Part Time)	CALENDAR: Fall	CALENDAR: Winter	CALENDAR: Spring	CALENDAR: Summer	PROGRAMS: Day	PROGRAMS: Evening	PROGRAMS: Credits for JD	PROGRAMS: Required Creits for Courses	PROGRAMS: Transferable Summer Courses	PROGRAMS: Joint Degree	PROGRAMS: Graduate Law Degree	ENROLLED: Full Time (Part Time)	STUDENT BODY: Average Age First Year	STUDENT BODY: % Women	STUDENT BODY: % Minority	STUDENT BODY: Attrition Rate %	FACULTY: Full Time (Part Time)	LIBRARY: Volumes	LIBRARY: Microforms
Illinois Institute of Technology (Chicago-Kent College of Law) 565 West Adams Street Chicago, IL 60661 312-906-5020 Fax: 312-906-5274 *admit@kentlaw.edu*	286	$60	March 1	March 15	$29,950 ($21,976)	$29,950 ($21,976)	✓				✓	✓	87	42	✓	✓	✓	806 (241)	25	45	22	8	67 (143)	547,378	143,432
Indiana University at Bloomington (School of Law) 211 S. Indiana Avenue Bloomington, IN 47405-1001 812-855-4765 Fax: 812-855-0555 *Lawadmis@indiana.edu*	288	$35	open	March 1	$14,349	$28,398	✓				✓		86	36	✓	✓	✓	662 (1)	24	43	19	1	53 (31)	448,644	290,614
Indiana University-Purdue University at Indianapolis (Indiana University School of Law-Indianapolis) 530 West New York Street Indianapolis, IN 46202-3225 317-274-2459 Fax: 317-278-4780 *khmiller@iupui.edu*	290	$50	March 1	March 1	$11,648 ($7,515)	$25,742 ($16,608)	✓				✓	✓	90	39	✓	✓	✓	642 (271)	26	49	15	4	47 (33)	590,230	63,793
Inter American University of Puerto Rico (School of Law) P.O. Box 70351 San Juan, PR 00936-8351 809-751-1912, ext. 2013	292		March		$12,710 ($10,250)	$12,710 ($10,250)	✓				✓	✓	92	62				451 (331)	24	57		8	20 (16)	160,098	139,963
John Marshall Law School 315 South Plymouth Court Chicago, IL 60604 312-987-1406 Fax: 312-427-5136 *admission@jmls.edu*	294	$60	March 1	June 1	$29,400 ($980)	$29,400 ($980)	✓		✓		✓	✓	90	48	✓	✓	✓	1133 (362)	25	43	16	5	62 (122)	353,737	55,710
John Marshall Law School - Atlanta (John Marshall Law School) 1422 W. Peachtree St., NW Atlanta, GA 30309 404-872-3593 Fax: 404-873-3802 *admissions@johnmarshall.edu*	296	$50	open	open	$11,700 ($9,360)	$11,700 ($9,360)	✓				✓	✓	88	63	✓			152 (14)	30	47	24	10	1 (18)	61,421	766,392
Lewis and Clark College (Lewis and Clark Law School) 10015 Southwest Terwilliger Boulevard Portland, OR 97219 503-768-6613 Fax: 503-768-6793 *lawadmss@lclark.edu*	298	$50	March 1	March 1	$26,348 ($19,764)	$26,348 ($19,764)	✓				✓	✓	86	28-35			✓	499 (199)	27	53	18	11	44 (47)	199,342	277,946
Liberty University (School of Law) 1971 University Blvd. Lynchburg, VA 24502 434-592-5300 Fax: 434-592-0202 *law@liberty.edu*	300	$50	June 1	March 1	$22,000		✓				✓		90	75			✓	103	26	37	14	10	12	58,000	155,000

Louisiana State University **(Paul M. Hebert Law Center)** Baton Rouge, LA 70803 225-578-8646 Fax: 225-578-8647 *eeden@lsu.edu*	302	$25	Feb 1	April 1	$12,022	$21,118	✓				✓		97	70	✓	✓	✓	637	25	50	10	6	48 (50)	443,507	2,153,035
Loyola Marymount University **(Loyola Law School)** 919 S. Albany Street Los Angeles, CA 90015 213-736-1180 *admissions@lls.edu*	304	$50	Feb 2	March 2	$31,176 ($20,852)	$31,176 ($20,852)	✓				✓	✓	87	41	✓	✓	✓	1000 (360)	23	47			73 (54)	576,330	115,072
Loyola University of Chicago **(School of Law)** One East Pearson Street Chicago, IL 60611 312-915-7170 Fax: 312-915-7906 *law-admissions@luc.edu*	306	$50	April 1	March 1	$29,900 ($22,430)	$29,900 ($22,430)	✓				✓	✓	86	46	✓	✓	✓	602 (241)	24	53	21	4	45 (93)	408,900	223,404
Loyola University of New Orleans **(School of Law)** 7214 St. Charles Avenue New Orleans, LA 70118 504-861-5575 Fax: 504-861-5772 *ladmit@loyno.edu*	308	$40			$28,000 ($19,000)	$28,000 ($19,000)	✓						90	53	✓	✓		661 (187)	25	53	20	12	32 (57)	330,000	132,186
Marquette University **(Law School)** Office of Admissions, Sensenbrenner Hall, P.O. Box 1881 Milwaukee, WI 53201-1881 414-288-6767 Fax: 414-288-0676 *law.admission@marquette.edu*	310	$50	April 1	March 1	$26,176 ($16,720)	$26,176 ($16,720)	✓				✓	✓	90	38	✓	✓		568 (146)	25	43	9	2	39 (71)	325,048	145,569
Mercer University **(Walter F. George School of Law)** 1021 Georgia Ave. Macon, GA 31207 478-301-2605 Fax: 478-301-2989 *Sutton_me@mercer.edu*	312	$50	March 15	April 1	$27,600	$27,600	✓				✓		91	56	✓	✓		407 (1)	23	45	14	4	26 (31)	190,538	143,120
Michigan State University **(College of Law)** 230 Law College Bldg. East Lansing, MI 48824-1300 517-432-0222 Fax: 517-432-0098 *andrea.campbell@law.msu.edu*	314	$60	March 1	April 1	$25,897 ($19,646)	$25,897 ($19,646)	✓				✓	✓	88	44	✓	✓	✓	848 (219)	25	44	16	6	38 (45)	133,882	147,637
Mississippi College **(School of Law)** 151 E. Griffith Street Jackson, MS 39201 601-925-7150 *pevans@mc.edu*	316	$40	May 1		$18,000	$18,000	✓				✓		90	36	✓	✓		400	26	44	10	7	18 (18)	253,000	540,000
New England School of Law 154 Stuart Street Boston, MA 02116 617-422-7210 Fax: 617-457-3033 *admit@admin.nesl.edu*	318	$65	March 15	April 20	$24,010 ($18,010)	$24,010 ($18,010)	✓				✓	✓	86	43	✓		✓	705 (390)	27	53	11	13	33 (74)	351,612	759,092
New York Law School 57 Worth Street New York, NY 10013-2960 212-431-2888 Fax: 212-966-1522 *admissions@nyls.edu*	320	$60	April 1	April 15	$38,600 ($29,680)	$38,600 ($29,680)	✓				✓	✓	86	38	✓	✓	✓	1106 (374)	25	54	25	3	58 (83)	513,597	263,585

INSTITUTION	Profile Page	APPLICATIONS: Fee	APPLICATIONS: Deadline	APPLICATIONS: Deadline Financial Aid	TUITION: In State Full Time (Part Time)	TUITION: Out of State Full Time (Part Time)	CALENDAR: Fall	CALENDAR: Winter	CALENDAR: Spring	CALENDAR: Summer	PROGRAMS: Day	PROGRAMS: Evening	PROGRAMS: Credits for JD	PROGRAMS: Required Creits for Courses	PROGRAMS: Transferable Summer Courses	PROGRAMS: Joint Degree	PROGRAMS: Graduate Law Degree	ENROLLED: Full Time (Part Time)	STUDENT BODY: Average Age First Year	STUDENT BODY: % Women	STUDENT BODY: % Minority	STUDENT BODY: Attrition Rate %	FACULTY: Full Time (Part Time)	LIBRARY: Volumes	LIBRARY: Microforms
New York University **(School of Law)** 161 Avenue of the Americas. 5th Floor New York, NY 10012 212-998-6060 Fax: 212-995-4527 *law.moreinfo.nyu*	322	$85	Feb 1	April 15	$37,150	$37,150	✓				✓	✓	83	45		✓	✓	1424	26	46	25	1	101 (56)	1,082,282	145,960
North Carolina Central University **(School of Law)** 1512 S. Alston Avenue Durham, NC 27707 919-560-6333 Fax: 919-560-6339 *jfaucett@wpo.nccu.edu*	324	$30	April 15	Feb 1	$3,000 ($3,000)	$12,000 ($12,000)	✓				✓	✓	88	65	✓	✓		255 (107)		56	53		23 (9)	284,115	639,314
Northeastern University **(School of Law)** 400 Huntington Avenue Boston, MA 02115 617-373-2395 Fax: 617-373-8865 *m.knoll@neu.edu*	326	$65	March 1	Feb 15	$32,700	$32,700	✓				✓		103	53	✓	✓		623	25	61	29	2	31 (27)	275,908	126,403
Northern Illinois University **(College of Law)** Swen Parson Hall, Room 151 De Kalb, IL 60115-2890 815-753-1420 Fax: 815-753-4501 *lawadm@niu.edu*	328	$50	May 15	March 1	$8,910	$17,820	✓				✓		90	37	✓	✓		320 (14)	26	51	23	10	24 (8)	242,270	503,357
Northern Kentucky University **(Salmon P. Chase College of Law)** Louie B. Nunn Hall Highland Heights, KY 41099 859-572-6476 Fax: 859-572-6081 *brayg@nku.edu*	330	$30	March 1	March 1	$10,128 ($7,593)	$22,104 ($16,578)	✓				✓	✓	90	52	✓	✓		301 (287)	26	46	9	13	31 (28)	317,855	170,911
Northwestern University **(School of Law)** 357 East Chicago Avenue Chicago, IL 60611 312-503-8465 Fax: 312-503-0178	332	$80	Feb 15	Feb 1	$38,122	$38,122	✓				✓		86	29		✓	✓	773	26	47	33	1	99 (58)	733,026	170,425
Nova Southeastern University **(Shepard Broad Law Center)** 3305 College Avenue Fort Lauderdale, FL 33314-7721 954-262-6117 Fax: 954-262-3844 *admission@nsu.law.nova.edu*	334	$50	March 1	March 1	$25,280 ($18,960)	$25,280 ($18,960)	✓				✓	✓	90	57	✓	✓		744 (199)	25	51	28	17	59 (69)	359,673	143,355
Ohio Northern University **(Claude W. Pettit College of Law)** 525 South Main Street Ada, OH 45810 419-772-2211 Fax: 419-772-3042 *l-english@onu.edu*	336	$40	open	April 3	$22,000	$22,000	✓			✓	✓		87	45	✓			292	25	45	11	3	18 (7)	222,422	115,944

Ohio State University (Michael E. Moritz College of Law) 55 West 12th Avenue, John Deaver Drinko Hall Columbus, OH 43210-1391 614-292-8810 Fax: 614-292-1383 *lawadmit@osu.edu*	338		March 1		$15,909	$29,511	✓				✓		88	37	✓	✓	✓	727	22	48	22	1	50 (41)	560,969	228,646
Oklahoma City University (School of Law) 2501 North Blackwelder Oklahoma City, OK 73106-1493 405-521-5354 Fax: 405-208-5814 *lawadmit@okcu.edu*	340	$50	April 1	March 1	$24,750 ($16,500)	$24,750 ($16,500)	✓				✓	✓	90	57	✓	✓		541 (139)	25	40	20	5	36 (20)	311,643	142,146
Pace University (School of Law) 78 North Broadway White Plains, NY 10603 914-422-4210 Fax: 914-989-8714 *calexander@law.pace.edu*	342	$65	March 1	Feb 1	$33,650 ($25,240)	$33,650 ($25,240)	✓				✓	✓	84	36	✓	✓	✓	495 (248)	25	57	16	6	44 (62)	367,541	62,148
Pennsylvania State University (Dickinson School of Law) 150 South College Street Carlisle, PA 17013 717-240-5207 Fax: 717-241-3503 *dsladmit@psu.edu*	344	$60	March 1	March 1	$25,000	$25,000	✓				✓	✓	88	40	✓	✓	✓	638 (1)	24	48	15		38 (33)	482,938	1,055,000
Pepperdine University (School of Law) 24255 Pacific Coast Highway Malibu, CA 90263 310-506-4631 Fax: 310-506-7668 *soladmis@pepperdine.edu*	346	$50	March 1	April 1	$29,000	$29,000	✓				✓		88	57	✓	✓	✓	680	23	51	17	5	30	342,450	87,000
Pontifical Catholic University of Puerto Rico (School of Law) Avenida Las Americas-Station 6 Ponce, PR 00732 787-841-2000, ext. 1836 Fax: 787-840-4620 *derecho@pucpr.edu*	348		n/av	Check			✓				✓	✓	94	82		✓	✓	220 (220)	24	50		11	14 (18)	135,000	15,000
Quinnipiac University (School of Law) 275 Mt. Carmel Avenue Hamden, CT 06518-1948 203-582-3400 Fax: 203-582-3339 *ladm@quinnipiac.edu*	350	$40	rolling		$31,400 ($21,900)	$31,400 ($21,900)	✓				✓	✓	86	32 - 33	✓	✓		395 (152)	26	51	17	6	38 (63)	177,775	223,730
Regent University (School of Law) 1000 Regent University Drive Virginia Beach, VA 23464-9800 757-226-4584 Fax: 757-226-4139 *lawschool@regent.edu*	352	$40	June 1	April 1	$23,870 ($17,710)	$23,870 ($17,710)	✓				✓		90	59		✓	✓	444 (45)	26	48	12	12	27 (25)	132,734	258,386
Roger Williams University (Ralph R. Papitto School of Law) Ten Metacom Avenue Bristol, RI 02809-5171 401-254-4555 Fax: 401-254-4516 *Admissions@rwu.edu*	354	$60	April 15	March 15	$26,390	$26,390	✓				✓	✓	90	48	✓	✓		510 (98)	25	50	12		34 (33)	288,500	1,023,600

INSTITUTION		APPLICATIONS			TUITION		CALENDAR				PROGRAMS							ENROLLED	STUDENT BODY				FACULTY	LIBRARY	
	Profile Page	Fee	Deadline	Deadline Financial Aid	In State Full Time (Part Time)	Out of State Full Time (Part Time)	Fall	Winter	Spring	Summer	Day	Evening	Credits for JD	Required Creits for Courses	Transferable Summer Courses	Joint Degree	Graduate Law Degree	Full Time (Part Time)	Average Age First Year	% Women	% Minority	Attrition Rate %	Full Time (Part Time)	Volumes	Microforms
Rutgers University/Camden (School of Law) Fifth and Penn Streets Camden, NJ 08102 856-225-6102 Fax: 856-225-6537	356	$50	April 1	March 1	$16,213 ($671/hr)	$23,806 ($991/hr)	✓				✓	✓	84	32	✓	✓		571 (216)	25	40	23	3	35 (47)	440,000	127,000
Rutgers University/Newark (School of Law) Center for Law and Justice, 123 Washington St. Newark, NJ 07102 973-353-5557/5554 Fax: 973-353-3459 *nwklaw@rci.rutgers.edu*	358	$50	March 15	March 1	$16,213 ($13,430)	$23,806 ($19,832)	✓				✓	✓	84	34 to 35	✓	✓		571 (241)	27	43	38	2	55 (31)	353,600	163,600
Saint John's University (School of Law) 8000 Utopia Parkway Queens, NY 11439 718-990-6474 Fax: 718-990-2526 *lawinfo@stjohns.edu*	360	$60	April 1	March 1	$32,700 ($24,525)	$32,700 ($24,525)	✓				✓	✓	86	58	✓	✓	✓	756 (196)	23	47	25		53 (72)	221,808	265,456
Saint Louis University (School of Law) 3700 Lindell Boulevard St. Louis, MO 63108 314-977-2800 Fax: 314-977-1464 *admissions@law.slu.edu*	362	$50	March 1	March 1	$28,610 ($20,880)	$28,610 ($20,880)	✓				✓	✓	91	37	✓	✓	✓	668 (217)	25	51	10	9	37 (36)	639,517	255,354
Saint Mary's University (School of Law) One Camino Santa Maria San Antonio, TX 78228-8601 210-436-3523 Fax: 210-431-4202 *wwilsoncstmary.edu*	364	$55	March 1	April 1	$20,910	$20,910	✓				✓		90	46	✓	✓	✓	761		42	30	16	36 (53)	320,000	633,117
Saint Thomas University (School of Law) 16400 N.W. 32nd Avenue Miami, FL 33054 305-623-2310 *lamy@stu.edu*	366	$40	n/av	May 1	$25,000	$25,000	✓		✓		✓	✓	87	62	✓	✓	✓	466 (1)	27	48	46	32	26 (21)	301,971	1,032,585
Samford University (Cumberland School of Law) 800 Lakeshore Drive Birmingham, AL 35229 205-726-2702 Fax: 205-726-2057 *law.admissions@samford.edu*	368	$50	Feb 28	March 1	$24,708 ($14,832)	$24,708 ($14,832)	✓				✓		90	51	✓	✓	✓	527 (5)	23	39	11	2	26 (4)	194,413	96,541
Santa Clara University (School of Law) 500 El Camino Real Santa Clara, CA 95053 408-554-4800 Fax: 408-554-7897 *lawadmissions@scu.edu*	370	$75	Feb 1	Feb 1	$31,980 ($22,386)	$31,980 ($22,386)	✓				✓	✓	86	45	✓	✓	✓	721 (234)	26	49	42	12	40 (34)	351,098	1,060,751

Seattle University (School of Law) 901 12th Ave, Sullivan Hall PO Box 222000 Seattle, WA 98122-4340 206-398-4200 Fax: 206-398-4058 *lawadmis@seattleu.edu*	372	$50	April 1	March 1	$25,980 ($21,650)	$25,980 ($21,650)	✓			✓	✓	✓	90	44	✓	✓	✓	875 (234)	28	56	25	2	50 (51)	356,028	198,641
Seton Hall University (School of Law) One Newark Center Newark, NJ 07102-5210 973-642-8747 Fax: 973-642-8876 *admitme@shu.edu*	374	$65	April 1	April 1	$32,430 ($23,782)	$32,430 ($23,782)	✓				✓	✓	85	44	✓	✓	✓	770 (444)	25	41	18	2	61 (96)	443,681	498,403
South Texas College of Law 1303 San Jacinto Street Houston, TX 77002-7000 713-646-1810 Fax: 713-646-2906 *admissions@stcl.edu*	376	$50	Feb 15	May 1	$20,250 ($13,500)	$20,250 ($13,500)	✓		✓		✓	✓	90	46	✓			959 (303)	27	46	21	11	59 (50)	238,545	266,111
Southern Illinois University (School of Law) Lesar Law Building, Mail Code 6804 Carbondale, IL 62901 618-453-8858 Fax: 618-453-8921 *lawadmit@siu.edu*	378	$50	March 1	April 1	$8,190	$24,570	✓				✓		90	48	✓	✓	✓	377 (2)	25	38	8	12	28 (22)	393,131	185,639
Southern Methodist University (Dedman School of Law) Office of Admissions, P.O. Box 750110 Dallas, TX 75275-0110 214-768-2550 Fax: 214-768-2549 *lawadmit@smu.edu*	380	$60	Feb 15	June 1	$31,238 ($23,946)	$31,238 ($23,946)	✓				✓	✓	87	37		✓	✓	660 (231)	26	47	20	3	41 (31)	601,946	132,114
Southern University and A & M College (Law Center) Post Office Box 9294 Baton Rouge, LA 70813-9294 225-771-5340 Fax: 225-771-2121 *vwilkerson@sulc.edu*	382	$25	Feb 28	April 15	$5,000 ($2,000)	$10,000 ($7,000)	✓				✓		96	75	✓	✓		413 (20)	27	48	69	10	28 (24)	453,396	206,603
Southwestern University (School of Law) 675 South Westmoreland Avenue Los Angeles, CA 90005-3992 213-738-6717 Fax: 213-383-1688 *admissions@swlaw.edu*	384	$50	June 30	June 1	$28,000 ($18,000)	$28,000 ($18,000)	✓				✓	✓	87	52	✓		✓	693 (286)	27	51	37	16	50 (25)	448,140	60,438
Stanford University (Stanford Law School) Crown Quadrangle, 559 Nathan Abbott Way Stanford, CA 94305-8610 650-723-4985 Fax: 650-723-0838 *admissions@law.stanford.edu*	386	$70	Feb 1	March 15	$35,400	$35,400	✓				✓		86	27		✓	✓	527	24	45	30		43	539,300	87,167
State University of New York (University at Buffalo Law School) 309 O'Brian Hall Buffalo, NY 14260 716-645-2907 Fax: 716-645-6676 *lwiley@buffalo.edu*	388	$50	March 15	March 1	$12,170	$18,270	✓				✓	✓	90	33	✓	✓	✓	749	25	55	16	2	55 (133)	290,583	259,758

INSTITUTION		APPLICATIONS			TUITION		CALENDAR				PROGRAMS							ENROLLED	STUDENT BODY				FACULTY	LIBRARY	
	Profile Page	Fee	Deadline	Deadline Financial Aid	In State Full Time (Part Time)	Out of State Full Time (Part Time)	Fall	Winter	Spring	Summer	Day	Evening	Credits for JD	Required Creits for Courses	Transferable Summer Courses	Joint Degree	Graduate Law Degree	Full Time (Part Time)	Average Age First Year	% Women	% Minority	Attrition Rate %	Full Time (Part Time)	Volumes	Microforms
Stetson University (Stetson University College of Law) 1401 61st Street South Gulfport, FL 33707 727-562-7802 Fax: 727-343-0136 *lawadmit@hermes.law.stetson.edu*	390	$55	March 1	open	$26,100 ($18,020)	$26,100 ($18,020)	✓		✓	✓	✓	✓	88	52	✓	✓	✓	757 (234)	24	53	24	3	57 (40)	403,644	49,879
Suffolk University (Law School) 120 Tremont Street Boston, MA 02108-4977 617-573-8144 Fax: 617-523-1367	392	$60	March 1	March 1	$31,694 ($23,770)	$31,694 ($23,770)	✓				✓	✓	84	58	✓	✓	✓	1039 (629)	26	50	14	8	60 (114)	318,000	801,693
Syracuse University (College of Law) Office of Admissions and Financial Aid Syracuse, NY 13244-1030 315-443-1962 Fax: 315-443-9568	394	$60	April 1	Feb 15	$32,820	$32,820	✓				✓		87	40	✓	✓		749 (7)	24	46	21	4	51 (56)	440,000	440,000
Temple University (James E. Beasley School of Law) 1719 N. Broad Street Philadelphia, PA 19122 215-204-5949 Fax: 215-204-1185 *lawadmis@temple.edu*	396	$60	March 1	March 1	$13,570 ($10,856)	$23,628 ($18,902)	✓				✓	✓	87	40	✓	✓	✓	796 (248)	26	48	24	3	59 (212)	573,568	179,200
Texas Southern University (Thurgood Marshall School of Law) 3100 Cleburne Avenue Houston, TX 77004 713-313-7114 Fax: 713-313-1049 *cgardner@tsulaw.edu*	398		April 1	Check	$10,000	$12,500	✓				✓		90	70	✓			632	27	46	80	35	34 (19)	229,464	100,536
Texas Tech University (School of Law) 1802 Hartford Avenue Lubbock, TX 79409 806-742-3990, ext. 273 Fax: 806-742-4617 *donna.williams@ttu.edu*	400	$50	Feb 1		$10,020	$17,400	✓				✓		90	55	✓	✓		701	24	49	18	5	36 (17)	190,764	638,844
Texas Wesleyan University (School of Law) 1515 Commerce Street Fort Worth, TX 76102 817-212-4040 Fax: 817-212-4002 *lawadmissions@law.txwes.edu*	402	$55	March 31	Check	$21,060 ($15,030)	$21,060 ($15,030)	✓				✓	✓	90	50	✓			429 (266)	25	48	21	15	21 (24)	204,000	83,490
Thomas Jefferson School of Law 2121 San Diego Avenue San Diego, CA 92110 619-297-9700 Fax: 619-294-4713 *adm@tjsl.edu*	404	$35	open	Feb 15	$25,000 ($16,000)	$25,000 ($16,000)	✓		✓		✓	✓	88	55	✓			611 (225)	24	41	20		32 (28)	247,764	127,842

Thomas M. Cooley Law School 300 South Capitol Avenue Lansing, MI 48901 517-371-5140 Fax: 517-334-5718 *admissions@cooley.edu*	406		rolling	Rolling	$22,000 ($14,000)	$22,000 ($14,000)	✓	✓		✓			90	63	✓	✓	✓	422 (1881)	29	49	33	30	81 (100)	486,348	267,637
Touro College (Jacob D. Fuchsberg Law Center) 300 Nassau Road Huntington, NY 11743 631-421-2244 ext. 314 Fax: 631-421-9708 *lindab@tourolaw.edu*	408	$50	rolling	April 15	$24,240 ($18,800)	$24,240 ($18,800)	✓				✓	✓	87	51 to 52	✓	✓	✓	432 (287)	26	45	23	5	31 (41)	429,683	225,964
Tulane University (Law School) Weinmann Hall, 6329 Freret Street New Orleans, LA 70118 504-865-5930 Fax: 504-865-6710 *admissions@law.tulane.edu*	410	$60	May 1	Feb 15	$30,350	$30,350	✓				✓		88	31	✓	✓	✓	853 (3)	24	48	24	5	48 (33)	500,000	500,000
University of Akron (School of Law) 150 University Avenue Akron, OH 44325-2901 330-972-7331 Fax: 330-258-2343 *lfile@uakron.edu*	412	$35	March 1	May 1	$11,910 ($9,528)	$19,904 ($15,923)	✓				✓	✓	88	44	✓	✓	✓	309 (216)	24	40	10	2	30 (27)	288,287	416,266
University of Alabama (School of Law) Box 870382 Tuscaloosa, AL 35487-0382 205-348-5440 Fax: 205-348-3917 *admissions@law.ua.edu*	414	$35	March 1	March 1	$8,660	$18,038	✓				✓		90	36		✓	✓	555	25	39	9	4	45 (55)	438,444	143,115
University of Arizona (James E. Rogers College of Law) 120 E. Speedway P.O. Box 210176 Tucson, AZ 85721-0176 520-621-3477 Fax: 520-621-9140 *admissions@law.arizona.edu*	416	$50		March 1	$11,000	$20,000	✓				✓		85	39	✓	✓	✓	475	25	50	29	1	30 (55)	410,000	426,000
University of Arkansas (School of Law) Robert A. Leflar Law Center, Waterman Hall Fayetteville, AR 72701 479-575-3102 Fax: 479-575-3937 *jkmiller@uark.edu*	418		April 1	April 1	$9,210	$18,510	✓				✓		90	43	✓	✓	✓	440	25	44	23		34 (13)	305,052	43,584
University of Arkansas at Little Rock (UALR William H. Bowen School of Law) 1201 McMath Avenue Little Rock, AR 72202-5142 501-324-9439 Fax: 501-324-9433 *lawadm@ualr.edu*	420		Aug 1	March 1	$8,220 ($5,480)	$17,670 ($11,780)	✓						90	45	✓	✓		212 (160)	27	50	10	1	28 (29)	181,979	108,014
University of Baltimore (School of Law) 1420 North Charles Street Baltimore, MD 21201-5779 410-837-4459 Fax: 410-837-4450 *lwadmiss@ubmail.ubalt.edu; mkbell@ubalt.edu*	422	$60	April 1	March 1	$7,989 ($662/hr)	$14,256 ($1,115/hr)	✓				✓	✓	90	39	✓	✓	✓	674 (312)	28	49	21	7	46 (79)	320,526	561,053

INSTITUTION		APPLICATIONS			TUITION		CALENDAR				PROGRAMS							ENROLLED	STUDENT BODY				FACULTY	LIBRARY	
	Profile Page	Fee	Deadline	Deadline Financial Aid	In State Full Time (Part Time)	Out of State Full Time (Part Time)	Fall	Winter	Spring	Summer	Day	Evening	Credits for JD	Required Creits for Courses	Transferable Summer Courses	Joint Degree	Graduate Law Degree	Full Time (Part Time)	Average Age First Year	% Women	% Minority	Attrition Rate %	Full Time (Part Time)	Volumes	Microforms
University of California (Hastings College of the Law) 200 McAllister Street San Francisco, CA 94102 415-565-4623 Fax: 415-581-8946 *admiss@uchastings.edu*	424	$75	March 1	March 1	$19,725	$30,950	✓				✓		86	34		✓	✓	1286	24	55	32	5	48 (87)	672,273	71,498
University of California at Berkeley (School of Law) 215 Boalt Hall Berkeley, CA 94720 510-642-2274 Fax: 510-643-6222 *adissions@law.berkeley.edu*	426	$75		March 2	$17,000	$29,000	✓				✓		85	32		✓	✓	924	24	61	43	1	68 (60)	678,371	179,821
University of California at Davis (School of Law) Martin Luther King, Jr. Hall - 400 Mrak Hall Drive Davis, CA 95616-5201 530-752-6477 *lawadmissions@ucdavis.edu*	428	$75	Feb 1	March 2	$23,524	$35,769	✓				✓		88	33		✓	✓	571	25	60	37	5	35 (18)	287,968	733,271
University of California at Los Angeles (School of Law) P.O. Box 951445 Los Angeles, CA 90095-1445 310-825-2080 Fax: 310-825-9450 *admissions@law.ucla.edu*	430	$75		March 2	$18,000	$18,000	✓				✓		87	35		✓	✓	962	25	48	31	2	91 (38)	534,030	388,760
University of Chicago (Law School) 1111 East 60th Street Chicago, IL 60637 773-702-9484 Fax: 773-834-0942 *admissions@law.uchicago.edu*	432	$65	n/av	March 1	$30,500	$30,500	✓				✓		105	40			✓	649	24	40	23	1	50 (21)	651,822	64,007
University of Cincinnati (College of Law) P.O. Box 210040 Cincinnati, OH 45221-0040 513-556-6805 Fax: 513-556-2391 *admissions@law.uc.edu*	434	$35	April 1	April 1	$16,210	$29,284	✓				✓		90	36	✓	✓		397	24	50	17	1	26	421,870	859,290
University of Colorado (School of Law) 403 UCB Boulder, CO 80309-0403 303-492-7203 Fax: 303-492-2542	436	$65	Feb 15	March 1	$13,546	$28,450	✓				✓		89	40	✓	✓		495	25	52	22	3	45 (37)	525,000	864,769
University of Connecticut (School of Law) 55 Elizabeth Street Hartford, CT 06105 860-570-5159 Fax: 860-570-5153 *admit@law.uconn.edu*	438	$30	March 1	March 1	$15,648 ($10,920)	$33,024 ($23,040)	✓				✓	✓	86	36	✓	✓	✓	514 (231)	25	52	22	1	45 (64)	527,337	213,416

University of Dayton **(School of Law)** 300 College Park Dayton, OH 45469-2760 937-229-3555 Fax: 937-229-4194 *lawinfo@notes.udayton.edu*	440	$20	May 1	March 1	$24,000	$24,000	✓				✓	✓	87	36	✓	✓		481	25	43	13	4	28 (32)	295,590	713,783
University of Denver **(Sturm College of Law)** 2255 E. Evans Avenue Denver, CO 80208 303-871-6135 Fax: 303-871-6992 *khigganb@law.du.edu*	442	$60	March 1	Feb 15	$29,388 ($18,900)	$29,388 ($18,900)	✓				✓	✓	90	44	✓	✓	✓	814 (418)	27	46	22	5	61 (83)	216,273	142,191
University of Detroit Mercy **(School of Law)** 651 East Jefferson Avenue Detroit, MI 48226 313-596-0264 Fax: 313-596-0280 *udmlawao@udmercy.edu*	444	$50	April 15	April 1	$23,000	$23,000	✓				✓	✓	90	51	✓	✓		353 (189)	28	50	11	10	27 (26)	199,047	105,707
University of Florida **(Fredric G. Levin College of Law)** 209 Bruton-Geer Hall P.O. Box 117622 Gainesville, FL 32611-7622 352-273-0890 Fax: 352-392-4087 *patrick@law.ufl.edu*	446	$30	Jan 15	April 1	$8,833	$27,753	✓				✓		88	34	✓	✓	✓	1322	25	44	22	3	79	620,792	304,024
University of Georgia **(School of Law)** Hirsch Hall, 225 Herty Drive Athens, GA 30602-6012 706-542-7060 Fax: 706-542-5556 *gkennedy@uga.edu*	448	$30	Feb 1		$9,126	$27,102	✓				✓		88	33	✓	✓	✓	694	24	51	20	5	46 (35)	370,000	504,653
University of Hawaii at Manoa **(William S. Richardson School of Law)** 2515 Dole Street Honolulu, HI 96822 808-956-7966 Fax: 808-956-3813 *lawadm@hawaii.educ*	450	$60	March 1	March 1	$11,000	$18,600	✓				✓		89	42	✓	✓	✓	311	26	48	60	5	22 (17)	248,838	875,305
University of Houston **(Law Center)** 100 Law Center Houston, TX 77204-6060 713-743-2280 Fax: 713-743-2194 *lawadmissions@uh.edu*	452	$70	Feb 15	April 1	$5,205 ($2,429)	$8,670 ($4,046)	✓				✓		90	34	✓	✓	✓	838 (199)	25	46	25	3	61 (75)	488,931	268,297
University of Idaho **(College of Law)** P.O. Box 442321 Moscow, ID 83844-2321 208-885-2300 Fax: 208-885-5709 *sperez@uidaho.edu*	454	$50	Feb 15	Feb 15	$8,908	$17,678	✓				✓		88	37		✓		295	27	41	10	4	17 (7)	204,375	321,816
University of Illinois **(College of Law)** 504 East Pennsylvania Avenue Champaign, IL 61820 217-244-6415 Fax: 217-244-1478 *admissions@law.uiuc.edu*	456	$40	March 15	March 15	$13,740	$26,644	✓				✓		90	36		✓	✓	640	24	39	33	2	44 (50)	596,969	850,296
University of Iowa **(College of Law)** 320 Melrose Avenue Iowa City, IA 52242 319-335-9095 Fax: 319-335-9646 *law-admissions@uiowa.edu*	458	$50	March 1	open	$12,320	$27,098	✓			✓	✓		90	37	✓	✓	✓	657	25	46	16	4	55 (30)	762,886	391,863

INSTITUTION	Profile Page	APPLICATIONS			TUITION		CALENDAR				PROGRAMS							ENROLLED	STUDENT BODY				FACULTY	LIBRARY	
		Fee	Deadline	Deadline Financial Aid	In State Full Time (Part Time)	Out of State Full Time (Part Time)	Fall	Winter	Spring	Summer	Day	Evening	Credits for JD	Required Creits for Courses	Transferable Summer Courses	Joint Degree	Graduate Law Degree	Full Time (Part Time)	Average Age First Year	% Women	% Minority	Attrition Rate %	Full Time (Part Time)	Volumes	Microforms
University of Kansas (School of Law) 205 Green Hall Lawrence, KS 66045 785-864-4378 Fax: 785-864-5054 *cenglish@ku.edu*	460	$50	March 15	March 1	$9,889	$18,858	✓			✓	✓		90	43 to 45	✓	✓	✓	497	24	43	18	3	39 (26)	315,196	96,902
University of Kentucky (College of Law) 209 Law Building Lexington, KY 40506-0048 606-257-7938 Fax: (859) 323-1061 *dbakert@email.uky.edu*	462	$50	March 1	April 1	$10,890	$20,592	✓				✓		90	34	✓	✓		453	23	42	8	5	30 (29)	465,187	212,722
University of La Verne (College of Law) 320 East D Street Ontario, CA 91764 909-460-2001 Fax: 909-460-2082 *lawadm@ulv.edu*	464	$60	March 31	June 15	$30,600 ($23,150)		✓				✓	✓	88	60		✓	✓	172 (84)	27	46	30	23	18 (11)	85,937	202,711
University of Louisville (Louis D. Brandeis School of Law) University of Louisville Belknap Campus-Wilson W. Wyatt Hall Louisville, KY 40292 502-852-6364 Fax: 502-852-8971 *lawadmissions@louisville.edu*	466	$50	March 1	June 1	$10,098 ($9,262)	$22,220 ($20,372)	✓				✓	✓	90	44	✓	✓		312 (104)	27	48	8	15	29 (6)	415,986	184,030
University of Maine (School of Law) 246 Deering Avenue Portland, ME 04102 207-780-4341 Fax: 207-780-4239 *mainelaw@usm.maine.edu*	468	$50	March 1	Feb 15	$15,750	$25,050	✓				✓		90	56	✓	✓		251 (7)	27	53	6	3	18 (7)	330,999	132,739
University of Maryland (School of Law) 500 West Baltimore Street Baltimore, MD 21201 410-706-3492 Fax: 410-706-1793 *admissions@law.umaryland.edu*	470	$60	March 1	March 1	$17,014 ($12,723)	$28,293 ($21,183)	✓				✓	✓	85	36 to 37	✓	✓		670 (145)	26	57	32	1	55 (95)	331,927	136,393
University of Memphis (Cecil C. Humphreys School of Law) 207 Humphreys Law School Memphis, TN 38152-3140 901-678-5403 Fax: 901-678-5210 *lawadmissions@mail.law.memphis.edu*	472	$25	March 1	April 1	$9,264 ($3,984)	$26,126 ($21,808)	✓				✓		90	56	✓	✓		368 (32)	25	45	16	9	28 (17)	268,179	103,687
University of Miami (School of Law) P.O. Box 248087, 1311 Miller Drive Coral Gables, FL 33124-8087 305-284-2523 *admissions@law.miami.edu*	474	$60	Feb 6	March 1	$30,641 ($22,980)	$30,641 ($22,980)	✓				✓	✓	88	73	✓	✓	✓	1009 (52)	24	44	25	2	57 (109)	402,514	1,162,368

University of Michigan (Law School) 625 South State Street Ann Arbor, MI 48109-1215 734-764-0537 Fax: 734-647-3218 *law.jd.admissions@umich.edu*	476	$60	Feb 15	rolling	$32,730	$35,730	✓			✓	✓		82	32		✓	✓	1179	24	46	26		75 (41)	965,069	1,556,779
University of Minnesota (Law School) 229 19th Avenue S. Minneapolis, MN 55455 612-625-3487 Fax: 612-626-1874	478	$65	March 1	May 15	$17,059	$27,443	✓				✓		88	33	✓	✓	✓	848	25	44	16	3	67 (115)	1,020,040	343,282
University of Mississippi (L.Q.C. Lamar Hall) P.O. Box 1848 Lamar Law Center University, MS 38677 601-915-6910 Fax: 601-915-1289 *bvinson@olemiss.edu*	480	$40	March 1	March 1	$7,720	$14,360	✓			✓	✓		90	36 to 37	✓	✓		568 (1)	23	45	11	9	32 (17)	328,134	168,070
University of Missouri-Columbia (School of Law) 103 Hulston Hall Columbia, MO 65211 573-882-6042 Fax: 573-882-9625 *CatheyA@missouri.edu*	482	$50	March 1	March 1	$14,048	$28,100	✓				✓		89	45	✓	✓	✓	446	25	39	10	3	28 (12)	363,074	191,121
University of Missouri-Kansas City (School of Law) 500 East 52nd Street Kansas City, MO 64110-2499 816-235-1644 Fax: 816-235-5276 *brooks@umkc.edu*	484	$50			$12,803 ($9,214)	$24,504 ($17,572)	✓				✓	✓	91	52	✓	✓	✓	513 (49)	23	44	10	11	36 (42)	208,625	116,719
University of Montana (School of Law) Missoula, MT 59812 406-243-2698 Fax: 406-243-2576 *heidi.fanslow@umontana.edu*	486	$60	March 1	March 1	$9,113	$18,677	✓				✓		90	56	✓	✓		237	27	51	7		22 (21)	123,661	134,480
University of Nebraska (College of Law) P.O. Box 830902 Lincoln, NE 68583-0902 402-472-2161 Fax: 402-472-5185 *lawadm@unl.edu*	488	$25	March 1	March 1	$6,468	$18,134	✓				✓		96	45	✓	✓	✓	389 (5)	23	46	10	5	29 (30)	232,564	169,181
University of Nevada, Las Vegas (William S. Boyd School of Law) 4505 Maryland Parkway, Box 451003 Las Vegas, NV 89154-1003 702-895-2440 Fax: 702-895-2414 *request@law.unlv.edu*	490	$50	March 15	Feb 1	$8,900 ($317/hr)	$17,800 ($635/hr)	✓				✓	✓	89	41	✓	✓		322 (157)	27	49	25		36 (15)	285,000	165,000
University of New Mexico (School of Law) MSCII-6070, University of New Mexico Albuquerque, NM 87131-0001 505-277-0958 Fax: 505-277-9958 *witherrington@law.unm.edu*	492	$50	Feb 15	March 1	$8,816	$21,394	✓				✓		86	41		✓		360	29	51	41		34 (30)	425,093	35,390
University of North Carolina at Chapel Hill (School of Law) Campus Box 3380, Van Hecke-Wettach Hall Chapel Hill, NC 27599-3380 919-962-5109 Fax: 919-843-7939 *law_admission@unc.edu*	494	$70	Feb 1	Dec 31	$11,981	$24,199	✓				✓		86	33		✓		707	23	53	24	3	44 (35)	447,320	11,302

INSTITUTION	Profile Page	APPLICATIONS: Fee	APPLICATIONS: Deadline	APPLICATIONS: Deadline Financial Aid	TUITION: In State Full Time (Part Time)	TUITION: Out of State Full Time (Part Time)	CALENDAR: Fall	CALENDAR: Winter	CALENDAR: Spring	CALENDAR: Summer	PROGRAMS: Day	PROGRAMS: Evening	PROGRAMS: Credits for JD	PROGRAMS: Required Creits for Courses	PROGRAMS: Transferable Summer Courses	PROGRAMS: Joint Degree	PROGRAMS: Graduate Law Degree	ENROLLED: Full Time (Part Time)	STUDENT BODY: Average Age First Year	STUDENT BODY: % Women	STUDENT BODY: % Minority	STUDENT BODY: Attrition Rate %	FACULTY: Full Time (Part Time)	LIBRARY: Volumes	LIBRARY: Microforms
University of North Dakota (School of Law) Box 9003 Grand Forks, ND 58202 701-777-2104 Fax: 701-777-2217 *linda.kohoutek@thor.law.und.nodak.edu*	496	$35		Check	$6,000	$13,000	✓				✓		90	34	✓	✓		200	26	52	11	6	11 (16)	251,320	129,554
University of Notre Dame (Notre Dame Law School) P.O. Box 780 Notre Dame, IN 46556-0780 574-631-6626 Fax: 574-631-5474 *lawadmit@nd.edu*	498	$55	March 1	Feb 15	$31,820	$31,820	✓				✓		90	42	✓	✓	✓	538 (1)	24	42	22	1	50 (35)	634,905	1,673,220
University of Oklahoma (College of Law) Andrew M. Coats Hall, 300 Timberdell Roa Norman, OK 73019 405-325-4728 Fax: 405-325-0502 *kmadden@ou.edu*	500	$50	March 15	March 1	$8,946	$18,875	✓				✓		90	42	✓	✓		516	24	45	21	4	34 (20)	345,394	90,657
University of Oregon (School of Law, William W. Knight Law Center) 1515 Agate Street Eugene, OR 97403-1221 541-346-1553 Fax: 541-346-3984 *admissions@law.uoregon.edu*	502	$50	n/av	Check	$15,500	$19,500	✓				✓		85	37	✓	✓		535	25	48	16	2	32 (11)	177,409	169,187
University of Pennsylvania (Law School) 3400 Chestnut Street Philadelphia, PA 19104-6204 215-898-7400 *admissions@law.upenn.edu*	504	$70	March 1	March 1	$34,920	$34,920	✓				✓	✓	89	28		✓	✓	777	24	45	30	1	64 (75)	826,096	124,068
University of Pittsburgh (School of Law) 3900 Forbes Avenue Pittsburgh, PA 15260 412-648-1413 Fax: 412-648-1318 *Mccall@law.pitt.edu*	506	$55	March 1	March 1	$19,602	$28,210	✓				✓		88	34		✓	✓	691	24	45	16	2	51 (90)	440,116	225,426
University of Puerto Rico (School of Law) P.O. Box 23349, UPR Station Rio Piedras, PR 00931-3349 787-999-9551 Fax: 787-764-4360 *wandi_perez@hotmail.com*	508	$15		May 1	$3,300 ($2,100)	$7,000	✓				✓	✓	92	46		✓	✓	475 (239)	23			5	37 (28)	228,985	158,503
University of Richmond (School Of Law) 28 Westhampton Way University of Richmond, VA 23173 804-289-8189 Fax: 804-287-6516 *lawadmissions@richmond.edu*	510	$35	Jan 15	Feb 25	$27,060 ($1,350/hr)	$27,060 ($1,350/hr)	✓			✓	✓		86	38	✓	✓		484 (2)	24	43	209	1	35 (76)	382,741	206,412

University of Saint Thomas (School of Law) 1000 LaSalle Ave. Minneapolis, MN 55403 651-962-4895 Fax: 651-962-4876 *lawschool@stthomas.edu*	512	$50	July 1	July 1	$25,404	$25,404	✓				✓	✓	88	51	✓	✓		418	26	52	15	3	27 (53)	165,537	536,070
University of San Diego (School of Law) 5998 Alcala Park San Diego, CA 92110 619-260-4528 Fax: 619-260-2218 *jdinfo@sandiego.edu*	514	$50	Feb 1	March 2	$33,740 ($23,960)	$33,740 ($23,960)	✓				✓	✓	85	35	✓	✓	✓	817 (343)	24	47	30	2	60 (46)	511,215	1,800,000
University of San Francisco (School of Law) 2130 Fulton Street San Francisco, CA 94117-1080 415-422-6586 Fax: 415-422-6433 *lawschool@usfca.edu*	516	$60	Feb 1	Feb 15	$30,570 ($21,900)	$30,570 ($21,900)	✓				✓		86	48	✓	✓	✓	598 (128)	26	52	32	9	29 (64)	147,053	207,796
University of South Carolina (School of Law) 701 South Main Street Columbia, SC 29208 803-777-6605 Fax: 803-777-7751 *usclaw@law.law.sc.edu*	518	$60	March 31	April 15	$14,824	$29,960	✓				✓		90	46	✓	✓		739	23	45	9	3	42 (55)	330,000	2,718
University of South Dakota (School of Law) 414 East Clark Street Vermillion, SD 57069-2390 605-677-5443 Fax: 605-677-5417 *lawreq@usd.edu*	520	$35	March 1		$4,196 ($2,098)	$12,161 ($6,081)	✓				✓		90	43	✓	✓		247 (3)	26	43	6	4	18 (1)	205,506	45,916
University of Southern California (Gould School of Law) Los Angeles, CA 90089-0074 213-740-2523	522	$70	Feb 1	Feb 15	$36,025	$36,025	✓				✓		88	33		✓	✓	628	24	48	37	1	42 (97)	482,896	100,686
University of Tennessee (College of Law) 1505 W. Cumberland Avenue Knoxville, TN 37996-1810 865-974-4131 Fax: 865-974-1572 *lawadmit@libra.law.utk.edu*	524	$15	March 1	March 1	$8,790	$23,134	✓				✓		89	38	✓	✓		457	25	51	15	1	41 (67)	324,442	233,820
University of Texas at Austin (School of Law) 727 East Dean Keeton Street Austin, TX 78705 512-232-1200 Fax: 512-471-2765 *admissions@mail.law.utexas.edu*	526	$70	Feb 1	March 31	$18,236	$31,363	✓				✓		86	38	✓	✓	✓	1441	25	43	31	3	87 (93)	1,026,598	1,142,419
University of the District of Columbia (David A. Clarke School of Law) 4200 Connecticut Avenue, N.W. Washington, DC 20008 202-274-7341 Fax: 202-274-5583 *vcanty@udc.edu; l* *aw addmission@udc.edu*	528	$35	March 15	March 31	$7,000	$14,000	✓				✓	✓	90	75	✓			232	29	62	47	1	17 (12)	250,000	110,647
University of the Pacific (McGeorge School of Law) 3200 Fifth Avenue Sacramento, CA 95817 916-739-7105 Fax: 916-739-7134 *admissionsmcgeorge@uop.edu*	530	$50		open	$28,000 ($19,000)	$28,000 ($19,000)	✓				✓	✓	88	58	✓	✓	✓	754 (356)	24	49	20	26	48 (50)	454,775	1,189,824

INSTITUTION	Profile Page	APPLICATIONS: Fee	APPLICATIONS: Deadline	APPLICATIONS: Deadline Financial Aid	TUITION: In State Full Time (Part Time)	TUITION: Out of State Full Time (Part Time)	CALENDAR: Fall	CALENDAR: Winter	CALENDAR: Spring	CALENDAR: Summer	PROGRAMS: Day	PROGRAMS: Evening	PROGRAMS: Credits for JD	PROGRAMS: Required Creits for Courses	PROGRAMS: Transferable Summer Courses	PROGRAMS: Joint Degree	PROGRAMS: Graduate Law Degree	ENROLLED: Full Time (Part Time)	STUDENT BODY: Average Age First Year	STUDENT BODY: % Women	STUDENT BODY: % Minority	STUDENT BODY: Attrition Rate %	FACULTY: Full Time (Part Time)	LIBRARY: Volumes	LIBRARY: Microforms
University of Toledo (College of Law) 2801 West Bancroft Street Toledo, OH 43606-3390 419-530-4131 Fax: 419-530-4345 *law.utoledo.edu*	532	$40	July 1	July 1	$12,432 ($9,842)	$22,675 ($17,951)	✓						89	42	✓	✓		351 (159)	28	41	7	7	33 (34)	344,863	134,529
University of Tulsa (College of Law) 3120 East Fourth Place Tulsa, OK 74104-2499 918-631-2406 Fax: 918-631-3630 *george-justice@utulsa.edu*	534	$30	open	open	$23,392 ($16,378)	$23,392 ($16,378)	✓		✓		✓	✓	88	44-45	✓	✓	✓	506 (85)	28	37	13	2	40 (27)	385,167	1,027,037
University of Utah (S.J. Quinney College of Law) 332 South 1400 East Room 101 Salt Lake City, UT 84112 801-581-7479 Fax: 801-581-6897 *aguilarr@law.utah.edu*	536	$50	Feb 1	March 15	$11,289	$24,071	✓				✓		88	40	✓	✓	✓	406	28	40	13	2	39 (28)	322,320	98,000
University of Virginia (School of Law) 580 Massie Road Charlottesville, VA 22903-1789 434-924-7351 Fax: 434-982-2128 *lawadmit@virginia.edu*	538	$70	Jan 15	Feb 15	$28,300	$33,300	✓				✓		86 quar-ter	29		✓	✓	1118	24	41	17		75 (117)	882,770	1,308,144
University of Washington (School of Law) 1100 Northeast Campus Parkway Seattle, WA 98105-6617 206-543-4078 *admissions@law.washington.edu*	540	$50	n/av	Feb 28	$7,500	$18,500	✓				✓		135 quarter		✓	✓	✓	485	25	51	27	2	43	539,771	163,030
University of Wisconsin (Law School) 975 Bascom Mall Madison, WI 53706 608-262-5914 Fax: 608-262-5485 *admissions@law.wisc.edu*	542	$45	Feb 1	Feb 1	$11,658 ($488/hr)	$28,870 ($1,205/hr)	✓				✓	✓	90	40 to 45	✓	✓	✓	794 (45)	25	47	21		70 (58)	395,634	450,178
University of Wyoming (College of Law) Dept. 3035, 1000 East University Avenue Laramie, WY 82071 307-766-6416 Fax: 307-766-6417 *dbourke@uwyo.edu*	544	$50	March 1	March 1	$5,859	$13,139	✓				✓		88	51	✓			227	26	44	10	2	17 (10)	285,827	142,825
Valparaiso University (School of Law) Wesemann Hall, 656 S. Greenwich Street Valparaiso, IN 46383-6493 219-465-7829 Fax: 219-465-7808 *tony.credit@valpo.edu*	546	$50	April 1	March 1	$26,400 ($965/hr)	$26,400 ($965/hr)	✓				✓	✓	90	57	✓	✓	✓	479 (47)	25	46	12	14	37 (40)	319,604	906,834

Vanderbilt University (Law School) 131 21st Avenue South Nashville, TN 37203 615-322-6452 Fax: 615-322-1531 *admissions@law.vanderbilt.edu*	548	$50	March 15	Feb 15	$33,700	$33,700	✓				✓		88	37		✓	✓	640	23	46	20	1	45 (58)	588,413	466,693
Vermont Law School P.O. Box 96, Chelsea Street South Royalton, VT 05068-0096 802-831-1239 Fax: 802-763-7071 *admiss@vermontlaw.edu*	550	$50	March 1	March 1	$28,114	$28,114	✓				✓		84	44	✓	✓	✓	653	27	49	14	8	45 (40)	234,929	116,681
Villanova University (School of Law) Garey Hall Villanova, PA 19085 610-519-7010 Fax: 610-519-6291 *admissions@law.villanova.edu*	552	$75	March 1	March 1	$27,640	$27,640	✓						88	44		✓	✓		24	49	17	1	40 (67)	519,795	1,024,280
Wake Forest University (School of Law) P.O. Box 7206, Reynolda Station Winston-Salem, NC 27109 336-758-5437 Fax: 336-758-4632 *admissions@law.wfu.edu*	554	$60	March 1	May 1	$27,900	$27,900	✓				✓		89	41	✓	✓	✓	468 (20)	24	45	10	3	39 (32)	432,306	1,248,754
Washburn University (School of Law) 1700 College Topeka, KS 66621 785-670-1185 Fax: 785-670-1120 *admissions@washburnlaw.edu*	556	$40	April 1	April 1	$13,020	$21,421	✓		✓		✓	✓	90	43	✓			452	26	43	15	6	29 (25)	379,815	151,070
Washington and Lee University (School of Law) Lewis Hall Lexington, VA 24450 540-458-8503 Fax: 540-458-8586 *lawadm@wlu.edu*	558	$50	Feb 1	Feb 15	$27,230	$27,230	✓				✓		85	38		✓	✓	391	23	43	19	1	34 (21)	427,978	944,085
Washington University in St. Louis (School of Law) Box 1120, One Brookings Drive St. Louis, MO 63130 314-935-4525 Fax: 314-935-8778 *admiss@wulaw.wustl.edu*	560	$70	March 1	March 1	$34,300	$34,300	✓				✓		85	35	✓	✓	✓	828 (39)	23	41	21	6	54 (107)	660,000	1,389,966
Wayne State University (Law School) 471 W. Palmer Detroit, MI 48202 313-577-3937 Fax: 313-577-6000 *linda.sims@wayne.edu*	562	$20	n/av	April 30	$10,500 ($7,500)	$20,500 ($15,500)	✓				✓	✓	86	36	✓	✓	✓	503 (244)	26	47		11	33 (48)	388,390	199,607
West Virginia University (College of Law) P.O. Box 6130 Morgantown, WV 26506 304-293-5304 Fax: 304-293-6891 *wvulaw.Admissions@mail.wvu.edu*	564	$50	Feb 1	March 1	$4,582 ($460/hr)	$13,282 ($650/hr)	✓				✓		91	37	✓			469 (4)	26	44	8	1	19 (21)	347,393	550,200
Western New England College (School of Law) 1215 Wilbraham Road Springfield, MA 01119 413-782-1406 Fax: 413-796-2067 *lawadmis@wnec.edu*	566	$50	open	rolling	$27,814 ($20,860)	$27,814 ($20,860)	✓				✓	✓	88	46	✓	✓	✓	416 (160)	27	46	11	9	34 (33)	490,000	185,000

INSTITUTION		APPLICATIONS			TUITION		CALENDAR				PROGRAMS							ENROLLED	STUDENT BODY				FACULTY	LIBRARY	
	Profile Page	Fee	Deadline	Deadline Financial Aid	In State Full Time (Part Time)	Out of State Full Time (Part Time)	Fall	Winter	Spring	Summer	Day	Evening	Credits for JD	Required Creits for Courses	Transferable Summer Courses	Joint Degree	Graduate Law Degree	Full Time (Part Time)	Average Age First Year	% Women	% Minority	Attrition Rate %	Full Time (Part Time)	Volumes	Microforms
Western State University (College of Law) 1111 North State College Blvd Fullerton, CA 92831 714-459-1101 Fax: 714-441-1748 *adm@wsulaw.edu*	568	$50	April 1	March 2	$25,920 ($17,440)	$25,920 ($17,440)	✓				✓		88 units units	60	✓			323 (166)	26	51	35		21 (33)	195,934	95,228
Whittier College (Whittier Law School) 3333 Harbor Blvd. Costa Mesa, CA 92626 714-444-4141, ext. 121 Fax: 714-444-0250 *info@law.whittier.edu*	570	$50	March 15	May 1	$29,230 ($19,500)	$29,230 ($19,500)	✓		✓		✓	✓	87	40	✓		✓	503 (385)	28	52	42	31	28 (41)	421,678	133,552
Widener University (Widener University School of Law) 3800 Vartan Way, P.O. Box 69381 Harrisburg, PA 17106-9381 717-541-3903 Fax: 717-541-3999 *law.admissions@law.widener.edu*	572	$60	May 15	open	$28,270 ($21,170)	$28,270 ($21,170)	✓				✓	✓	87	67	✓	✓		338 (161)	27	43	8	11	22 (40)	281,873	307,706
Widener University (Widener University School of Law) 4601 Concord Pike, P.O. Box 7474 Wilmington, DE 19803-0474 302-477-2162 Fax: 302-477-2224 *law.admissions@law.widener.edu*	574	$60	May 15	open	$28,270 ($21,170)	$28,270 ($21,170)	✓				✓	✓	87	57	✓	✓	✓	659 (415)	27	47	15	21	57 (82)	281,873	307,706
Willamette University (College of Law) 245 Winter Street S.E. Salem, OR 97301 503-370-6282 Fax: 503-370-6087 *law-admission@willamette.edu*	576	$50	April 1	March 1	$24,400	$24,400	✓				✓		90	40	✓	✓	✓	439 (5)	26	44	9	8	28 (13)	288,204	898,195
William Mitchell College of Law (William Mitchelle College of Law) 875 Summit Avenue St. Paul, MN 55105-3076 651-290-6476 Fax: 651-290-6414 *admissions@wmitchell.edu*	578	$50	May 1	March 15	$25,950 ($18,780)	$25,950 ($18,780)	✓				✓	✓	86	46	✓	✓		735 (382)	25	52	11	12	34 (186)	521,968	1,021,604
Yale University (Yale Law School) P.O. Box 208329 New Haven, CT 06520-8329 203-432-4995 *admissions.law@yale.edu*	580	$70	Feb 1	March 15	$38,800	$38,800	✓				✓		83	19		✓	✓	586	25	44	32		66 (42)	857,353	40,781
Yeshiva University (Benjamin N. Cardozo School of Law) 55 Fifth Avenue New York, NY 10003 212-790-0274 Fax: 212-790-0482 *lawinfo@yu.edu*	582	$65	April 1	April 15	$34,500	$34,500	✓		✓	✓	✓		84	36		✓	✓	931 (115)	25	48	19	4	52 (67)	515,715	1,193,832

Your Chances of Law School Admission

A Profile of Recent First-Year Law Students

The table in this section provides basic admissions statistics for the law schools that have been approved by the American Bar Association. All these schools offer the J.D. degree. The information has been compiled from the most recent available information received from schools. If you compare your own GPA and your LSAT percentile with those of students recently admitted, and if you note the number of students who applied and the number who were accepted, you will be able to get an idea of your chances of admission to any given law school.

Bear in mind that many law schools take into account factors other than strictly academic qualifications.

A blank cell on the chart means that information was not available.

LAW SCHOOL	ACADEMIC STATISTICS				ADMISSION STATISTICS		
	Median LSAT Percentile of Enrolled	Median LSAT Score of Enrolled	Lowest LSAT Percentile of Accepted	Median GPA (4.0 scale) of Enrolled	Total Applicants	Applicants Accepted	Applicants Enrolled
Albany Law School 80 New Scotland Avenue Albany, NY 12208 518-445-2326; Fax: 518-445-2369 *admissions@mail.als.edu*	*63*	*155*		*3.22*	*2175*	*876*	*247*
American University (Washington College of Law) 4801 Massachusetts Avenue, N.W. Washington, DC 20016-8186 202-274-4101; Fax: 202-274-4107 *wcladmit@wcl.american.edu*	*79*	*161*	*32*	*3.42*	*8864*	*2066*	*464*
Appalachian School of Law P.O. Box 2825 Grundy, VA 24614 276-935-4349; Fax: 276-935-8261 *npruitt@asl.edu*	*41*	*149*	*13*	*2.96*	*1302*	*527*	*149*
Arizona State University (College of Law/Armstrong Hall) Box 877906 Tempe, AZ 85287-7906 480-965-1474; Fax: 480-727-7930 *chitra.damania@asu.edu*	*78*	*159*	*8*	*3.44*	*3040*	*832*	*256*
Ave Maria School of Law 3475 Plymouth Road Ann Arbor, MI 48105 734-827-8063; Fax: 734-622-0123 *info@avemarialaw.edu*	*59*	*155*	*20*	*3.2*	*906*	*610*	*147*
Barry University (School of Law) 6441 East Colonial Drive Orlando, FL 32807 407-275-2000, ext. 237; Fax: 407-275-2010 *lawinfo@mail.barry.edu*		*148*		*3*	*863*	*459*	*174*
Baylor University (School of Law) P.O. Box 97288 Waco, TX 76798-7288 254-710-1911; Fax: 254-710-2316 *becky-beck@baylor.edu*		*160*	*158*	*3.63*	*4357*	*822*	*180*
Boston College (Law School) 885 Centre Street Newton, MA 02459 617-552-4351; Fax: 617-552-2917 *bclawadm@bc.edu*	*88*	*164*		*3.62*	*6927*	*1372*	*275*
Boston University (School of Law) 765 Commonwealth Avenue Boston, MA 02215 617-353-3100 *bulawadm@bu.edu*	*92*	*164*	*42*	*3.52*	*7246*	*1396*	*268*
Brigham Young University (J. Reuben Clark Law School) 342 JRCB Brigham Young University Provo, UT 84602 801-422-4277; Fax: 801-422-0389 *kucharg@lawgate.byu.edu*	*86*	*164*	*24*	*3.72*	*940*	*254*	*153*
Brooklyn Law School 250 Joralemon Street Brooklyn, NY 11201 718-780-7906; Fax: 718-780-0395 *admitq@brooklaw.edu*	*90*	*163*		*3.43*	*4813*	*1340*	*496*
California Western School of Law 225 Cedar Street San Diego, CA 92101-3046 619-525-1401; Fax: 619-615-1401 *admissions@cwsl.edu*		*153*	*25*	*3.09*	*3110*	*1220*	*335*

LAW SCHOOL	ACADEMIC STATISTICS				ADMISSION STATISTICS		
	Median LSAT Percentile of Enrolled	Median LSAT Score of Enrolled	Lowest LSAT Percentile of Accepted	Median GPA (4.0 scale) of Enrolled	Total Applicants	Applicants Accepted	Applicants Enrolled
Campbell University (Norman Adrian Wiggins School of Law) P.O. Box 158 Buies Creek, NC 27506 910-893-1754; Fax: 910-893-1780 *admissions@ian.campbell.edu*	*50*	*156*		*3.5*	*1118*	*229*	*119*
Capital University (Law School) 303 East Broad Street Columbus, OH 43215-3200 614-236-6500; Fax: 614-236-6972 *admissions@law.capital.edu*	*58*	*153*	*15*	*3.2*	*1587*	*621*	*255*
Case Western Reserve University (Case School of Law) 11075 East Boulevard Cleveland, OH 44106 216-368-3600; Fax: 216-368-1042 *lawadmissions@case.edu*		*159*		*3.37*	*2793*	*724*	*225*
Catholic University of America (Columbus School of Law) Cardinal Station Washington, DC 20064 (202) 319-5151; Fax: (202) 319-6285 *admissions@law.edu*		*158*		*3.32*	*3502*	*1060*	*329*
Chapman University (School of Law) One University Drive Orange, CA 92866 714-628-2500; Fax: 714-628-2501 *heyer@chapman.edu*	*69*	*156*	*34*	*3.2*	*1732*	*491*	*185*
City University of New York (School of Law at Queens College) 65-21 Main Street Flushing, NY 11367-1300 718-340-4210; Fax: 718-340-4435 *mail.law.cuny.edu*	*50*	*151*	*26*	*3.22*	*2663*	*497*	*166*
Cleveland State University (Cleveland-Marshall College of Law) 2121 Euclid Avenue LB138 Cleveland, OH 44115-2214 216-687-2304; Fax: 216-687-6881 *melody.stewart@law.csuohio.edu*	*55*	*154*	*20*	*3.41*	*1796*	*541*	*236*
College of William & Mary (William & Mary Law School) P.O. Box 8795 Williamsburg, VA 23187-8795 757-221-3785; Fax: 757-221-3261 *lawadm@.wm.edu*	*91*	*164*	*20*	*3.63*	*4116*	*924*	*205*
Columbia University (School of Law) 435 West 116th Street New York, NY 10027 212-854-2670; Fax: 212-854-1109 *admissions@law.columbia.edu*	*99*	*171*	*50*	*3.67*	*8020*	*1143*	*378*
Cornell University (Law School) Myron Taylor Hall Ithaca, NY 14853-4901 607-255-5141; Fax: 607-255-7193 *lawadmit@postoffice.law.cornell.edu*	*97*	*167*		*3.67*	*4177*		*193*
Creighton University (School of Law) 2500 California Plaza Omaha, NE 68178 402-280-2872; Fax: 402-280-5564 *lawadmit@creighton.edu*	*57*	*153*	*24*	*3.53*	*1470*	*520*	*161*
De Paul University (College of Law) 25 East Jackson Boulevard Chicago, IL 60604 312-362-6831; Fax: 312-362-5280 *lawinfo@depaul.edu*	*84*	*160*	*18*	*3.43*	*5028*	*1411*	*330*

LAW SCHOOL	ACADEMIC STATISTICS				ADMISSION STATISTICS		
	Median LSAT Percentile of Enrolled	Median LSAT Score of Enrolled	Lowest LSAT Percentile of Accepted	Median GPA (4.0 scale) of Enrolled	Total Applicants	Applicants Accepted	Applicants Enrolled
Drake University (Law School) 2507 University Avenue Des Moines, IA 50311 515-271-2782; Fax: 515-271-1990 *lawadmit@drake.edu*	61	154		3.43	1162	491	144
Duke University (Duke University School of Law) Science Drive and Towerview Road, Box 90362 Durham, NC 27708-0362 919-613-7020; Fax: 919-613-7257 *admissions@law.duke.edu*	96	168		3.72	4486		199
Duquesne University (School of Law) 900 Locust Street, Hanley Hall Pittsburgh, PA 15282 412-396-6296; Fax: 412-396-1073 *campion@duq.edu*	66	156		3.5			192
Emory University (School of Law) Gambrell Hall Atlanta, GA 30322 404-727-6801; Fax: 404-727-2477 *Sfleming@law.emory.edu*	91	163		3.47	3659	1064	235
Florida Agricultural and Mechanical University (Florida A & M University College of Law) 201 N. Beggs Avenue Orlando, FL 32801 407-254-3268 *ruth.witherspoon@famu.edu*	50	146		3.01	1037	295	172
Florida Coastal (School of Law) 7555 Beach Boulevard Jacksonville, FL 32216 904-680-7710; Fax: 904-680-7776 *admissions@fcsl.edu*	50	152	25	3.22	4719	1755	449
Florida International University (College of Law) FIU College of Law, 6L 475 Miami, FL 33199 (305) 348-8006; Fax: (305) 348-2965 *miroa@fiu.edu*			152	3.31	1496	238	127
Florida State University (College of Law) 425 W. Jefferson St. Tallahassee, FL 32306-1601 850-644-3787; Fax: 850-644-7284 *admissions@law.fsu.edu*	79	159		3.44	3750	821	272
Fordham University (School of Law) 140 West 62nd Street New York, NY 10023 212-636-6810; Fax: 212-636-7984 *lawadmissions@law.fordham.edu*	93	165	62	3.56	6866	1493	483
Franklin Pierce Law Center 2 White Street Concord, NH 03301 603-228-9217; Fax: 603-228-1074 *admissions@piercelaw.edu*	61	154	13	3.2	1536	576	142
George Mason University (School of Law) 3301 Fairfax Drive Arlington, VA 22201 703-993-8010; Fax: 703-993-8088 *arichar5@gmu.edu*	90	163		3.49	5950	914	216
George Washington University (Law School) 2000 H Street, N.W. Washington, DC 20052 202-994-7230; Fax: 202-994-3597 *jd@law.gwu.edu*	93	165	41	3.57	11072	2113	535

LAW SCHOOL	ACADEMIC STATISTICS				ADMISSION STATISTICS		
	Median LSAT Percentile of Enrolled	Median LSAT Score of Enrolled	Lowest LSAT Percentile of Accepted	Median GPA (4.0 scale) of Enrolled	Total Applicants	Applicants Accepted	Applicants Enrolled
Georgetown University (Georgetown University Law Center) 600 New Jersey Avenue, N.W. Washington, DC 20001 202-662-9010; Fax: 202-662-9439 *admis@law.georgetown.edu*	*97*	*169*	*49*	*3.68*	*11702*	*2235*	*584*
Georgia State University (College of Law) P.O. Box 4037 Atlanta, GA 30302-4037 404-651-2048; Fax: 404-651-2048 *cjjackson@gsu.edu*	*80*	*159*	*40*	*3.36*	*3308*	*586*	*219*
Golden Gate University (School of Law) 536 Mission Street San Francisco, CA 94105-2968 415-442-6630 *lawadmit@ggu.edu*	*57*	*153*	*23*	*3.2*	*3298*	*1184*	*321*
Gonzaga University (School of Law) Box 3528 Spokane, WA 99220-3528 509-323-5532; Fax: 509-323-3697 *admissions@lawschool.gonzaga.edu*	*61*	*154*	*34*	*3.34*	*1485*	*546*	*192*
Hamline University (School of Law) 1536 Hewitt Avenue St. Paul, MN 55104-1284 651-523-2461; Fax: 651-523-3064 *lawadm@gw.hamline.edu*	*66*	*155*	*18*	*3.35*	*1610*	*688*	*226*
Harvard University (Harvard Law School) Cambridge, MA 02138 617-495-3179 *jdadmiss@law.harvard.edu*	*99*	*173*		*3.81*	*7127*	*811*	*557*
Hofstra University (School of Law) 121 Hofstra University Hempstead, NY 11549 516-463-5916; Fax: 516-463-6264 *lawadmissions@hofstra.edu*	*71*	*157*	*8*	*3.3*	*5232*	*1991*	*386*
Howard University 2900 Van Ness Street, N.W. Washington, DC 20008 202-806-8008; Fax: 202-806-8162 *admissions@law.howard.edu*	*50*	*152*		*3.2*			
Illinois Institute of Technology (Chicago-Kent College of Law) 565 West Adams Street Chicago, IL 60661 312-906-5020; Fax: 312-906-5274 *admit@kentlaw.edu*	*82*	*160*		*3.46*	*3926*	*1040*	*335*
Indiana University at Bloomington (School of Law) 211 S. Indiana Avenue Bloomington, IN 47405-1001 812-855-4765; Fax: 812-855-0555 *Lawadmis@indiana.edu*	*89*	*163*	*13*	*3.46*	*2405*	*916*	*228*
Indiana University-Purdue University at Indianapolis (Indiana University School of Law-Indianapolis) 530 West New York Street Indianapolis, IN 46202-3225 317-274-2459; Fax: 317-278-4780 *khmiller@iupui.edu*	*65*	*155*	*6*	*3.51*	*1938*	*598*	*277*
Inter American University of Puerto Rico (School of Law) P.O. Box 70351 San Juan, PR 00936-8351 809-751-1912, ext. 2013		*140*	*2*	*3.1*			
John Marshall Law School 315 South Plymouth Court Chicago, IL 60604 312-987-1406; Fax: 312-427-5136 *admission@jmls.edu*		*154*		*3.2*	*3208*	*1158*	*391*

LAW SCHOOL	ACADEMIC STATISTICS				ADMISSION STATISTICS		
	Median LSAT Percentile of Enrolled	Median LSAT Score of Enrolled	Lowest LSAT Percentile of Accepted	Median GPA (4.0 scale) of Enrolled	Total Applicants	Applicants Accepted	Applicants Enrolled
John Marshall Law School - Atlanta (John Marshall Law School) 1422 W. Peachtree St., NW Atlanta, GA 30309 404-872-3593; Fax: 404-873-3802 *admissions@johnmarshall.edu*		151	25	3.04	883	277	158
Lewis and Clark College (Lewis and Clark Law School) 10015 Southwest Terwilliger Boulevard Portland, OR 97219 503-768-6613; Fax: 503-768-6793 *lawadmss@lclark.edu*		161	14	3.37	2394	909	232
Liberty University (School of Law) 1971 University Blvd. Lynchburg, VA 24502 434-592-5300; Fax: 434-592-0202 *law@liberty.edu*	53	152	15	3.26	221	84	50
Louisiana State University (Paul M. Hebert Law Center) Baton Rouge, LA 70803 225-578-8646; Fax: 225-578-8647 *eeden@lsu.edu*	68	156	15	3.49	1682	467	216
Loyola Marymount University (Loyola Law School) 919 S. Albany Street Los Angeles, CA 90015 213-736-1180 *admissions@lls.edu*		161		3.28	4835	1105	410
Loyola University of Chicago (School of Law) One East Pearson Street Chicago, IL 60611 312-915-7170; Fax: 312-915-7906 *law-admissions@luc.edu*	85	161	37	3.43	2675	692	261
Loyola University of New Orleans (School of Law) 7214 St. Charles Avenue New Orleans, LA 70118 504-861-5575; Fax: 504-861-5772 *ladmit@loyno.edu*	58	153	24	3.27	2233	662	264
Marquette University (Law School) Office of Admissions, Sensenbrenner Hall, P.O. Box 1881 Milwaukee, WI 53201-1881 414-288-6767; Fax: 414-288-0676 *law.admission@marquette.edu*	73	157		3.41	1913	719	215
Mercer University (Walter F. George School of Law) 1021 Georgia Ave. Macon, GA 31207 478-301-2605; Fax: 478-301-2989 *Sutton_me@mercer.edu*		156		3.42	1538	450	155
Michigan State University (College of Law) 230 Law College Bldg. East Lansing, MI 48824-1300 517-432-0222; Fax: 517-432-0098 *andrea.campbell@law.msu.edu*	70	158	38	3.36	2724	995	375
Mississippi College (School of Law) 151 E. Griffith Street Jackson, MS 39201 601-925-7150 *pevans@mc.edu*	50	150		3.13	909	404	165
New England School of Law 154 Stuart Street Boston, MA 02116 617-422-7210; Fax: 617-457-3033 *admit@admin.nesl.edu*	49	151	9	3.27	3383	1305	382
New York Law School 57 Worth Street New York, NY 10013-2960 212-431-2888; Fax: 212-966-1522 *admissions@nyls.edu*		156		3.4	5845	2042	545

LAW SCHOOL	ACADEMIC STATISTICS				ADMISSION STATISTICS		
	Median LSAT Percentile of Enrolled	Median LSAT Score of Enrolled	Lowest LSAT Percentile of Accepted	Median GPA (4.0 scale) of Enrolled	Total Applicants	Applicants Accepted	Applicants Enrolled
New York University (School of Law) 161 Avenue of the Americas. 5th Floor New York, NY 10012 212-998-6060; Fax: 212-995-4527 *law.moreinfo.nyu*		*170*			*7872*	*1566*	*448*
North Carolina Central University (School of Law) 1512 S. Alston Avenue Durham, NC 27707 919-560-6333; Fax: 919-560-6339 *jfaucett@wpo.nccu.edu*	*50*	*148*	*143*	*3.1*	*1080*	*258*	*116*
Northeastern University (School of Law) 400 Huntington Avenue Boston, MA 02115 617-373-2395; Fax: 617-373-8865 *m.knoll@neu.edu*	*79*	*161*	*23*	*3.36*	*3708*	*986*	*212*
Northern Illinois University (College of Law) Swen Parson Hall, Room 151 De Kalb, IL 60115-2890 815-753-1420; Fax: 815-753-4501 *lawadm@niu.edu*	*68*	*156*	*15*	*3.39*	*1480*	*514*	*132*
Northern Kentucky University (Salmon P. Chase College of Law) Louie B. Nunn Hall Highland Heights, KY 41099 859-572-6476; Fax: 859-572-6081 *brayg@nku.edu*	*57*	*153*	*3*	*3.3*	*1045*	*313*	*190*
Northwestern University (School of Law) 357 East Chicago Avenue Chicago, IL 60611 312-503-8465; Fax: 312-503-0178	*98*	*169*	*20*	*3.7*	*4678*	*781*	*243*
Nova Southeastern University (Shepard Broad Law Center) 3305 College Avenue Fort Lauderdale, FL 33314-7721 954-262-6117; Fax: 954-262-3844 *admission@nsu.law.nova.edu*	*37*	*150*	*8*	*3.01*	*2813*	*775*	*336*
Ohio Northern University (Claude W. Pettit College of Law) 525 South Main Street Ada, OH 45810 419-772-2211; Fax: 419-772-3042 *l-english@onu.edu*	*50*	*151*	*14*	*3.32*	*1260*	*423*	*130*
Ohio State University (Michael E. Moritz College of Law) 55 West 12th Avenue, John Deaver Drinko Hall Columbus, OH 43210-1391 614-292-8810; Fax: 614-292-1383 *lawadmit@osu.edu*	*80*	*161*		*3.5*	*2282*	*629*	*217*
Oklahoma City University (School of Law) 2501 North Blackwelder Oklahoma City, OK 73106-1493 405-521-5354; Fax: 405-208-5814 *lawadmit@okcu.edu*	*36*	*149*	*4*	*3.09*	*1377*	*566*	*217*
Pace University (School of Law) 78 North Broadway White Plains, NY 10603 914-422-4210; Fax: 914-989-8714 *calexander@law.pace.edu*	*62*	*154*	*30*	*3.3*	*3270*	*1050*	*260*
Pennsylvania State University (Dickinson School of Law) 150 South College Street Carlisle, PA 17013 717-240-5207; Fax: 717-241-3503 *dsladmit@psu.edu*		*155*		*3.3*	*2421*	*724*	*225*

LAW SCHOOL	ACADEMIC STATISTICS				ADMISSION STATISTICS		
	Median LSAT Percentile of Enrolled	Median LSAT Score of Enrolled	Lowest LSAT Percentile of Accepted	Median GPA (4.0 scale) of Enrolled	Total Applicants	Applicants Accepted	Applicants Enrolled
Pepperdine University (School of Law) 24255 Pacific Coast Highway Malibu, CA 90263 310-506-4631; Fax: 310-506-7668 *soladmis@pepperdine.edu*	*77*	*158*		*3.3*	*3450*	*909*	*273*
Pontifical Catholic University of Puerto Rico (School of Law) Avenida Las Americas-Station 6 Ponce, PR 00732 787-841-2000, ext. 1836; Fax: 787-840-4620 *derecho@pucpr.edu*	*13*			*2.9*			
Quinnipiac University (School of Law) 275 Mt. Carmel Avenue Hamden, CT 06518-1948 203-582-3400; Fax: 203-582-3339 *ladm@quinnipiac.edu*	*61*	*156*	*25*	*3.26*	*2557*	*603*	*132*
Regent University (School of Law) 1000 Regent University Drive Virginia Beach, VA 23464-9800 757-226-4584; Fax: 757-226-4139 *lawschool@regent.edu*		*153*		*3.3*	*752*	*333*	*164*
Roger Williams University (Ralph R. Papitto School of Law) Ten Metacom Avenue Bristol, RI 02809-5171 401-254-4555; Fax: 401-254-4516 *Admissions@rwu.edu*		*152*		*3.29*	*1743*	*716*	*198*
Rutgers University/Camden (School of Law) Fifth and Penn Streets Camden, NJ 08102 856-225-6102; Fax: 856-225-6537	*85*	*161*	*45*	*3.45*	*2481*	*575*	*259*
Rutgers University/Newark (School of Law) Center for Law and Justice, 123 Washington St. Newark, NJ 07102 973-353-5557/5554; Fax: 973-353-3459 *nwklaw@rci.rutgers.edu*		*158*		*3.32*	*3492*	*811*	*249*
Saint John's University (School of Law) 8000 Utopia Parkway Queens, NY 11439 718-990-6474; Fax: 718-990-2526 *lawinfo@stjohns.edu*		*160*		*3.45*	*4070*	*1284*	*325*
Saint Louis University (School of Law) 3700 Lindell Boulevard St. Louis, MO 63108 314-977-2800; Fax: 314-977-1464 *admissions@law.slu.edu*	*73*	*157*	*17*	*3.55*	*2095*	*840*	*300*
Saint Mary's University (School of Law) One Camino Santa Maria San Antonio, TX 78228-8601 210-436-3523; Fax: 210-431-4202 *wwilsoncstmary.edu*	*62*	*154*	*25*	*3.15*	*2069*	*749*	*267*
Saint Thomas University (School of Law) 16400 N.W. 32nd Avenue Miami, FL 33054 305-623-2310 *lamy@stu.edu*	*35*	*147*	*16*	*2.8*	*1466*	*853*	*186*
Samford University (Cumberland School of Law) 800 Lakeshore Drive Birmingham, AL 35229 205-726-2702; Fax: 205-726-2057 *law.admissions@samford.edu*	*63*	*156*	*23*	*3.23*	*1425*	*455*	*175*

LAW SCHOOL	ACADEMIC STATISTICS				ADMISSION STATISTICS		
	Median LSAT Percentile of Enrolled	Median LSAT Score of Enrolled	Lowest LSAT Percentile of Accepted	Median GPA (4.0 scale) of Enrolled	Total Applicants	Applicants Accepted	Applicants Enrolled
Santa Clara University (School of Law) 500 El Camino Real Santa Clara, CA 95053 408-554-4800; Fax: 408-554-7897 *lawadmissions@scu.edu*	78	159	49	3.37	4487	1665	310
Seattle University (School of Law) 901 12th Ave, Sullivan Hall PO Box 222000 Seattle, WA 98122-4340 206-398-4200; Fax: 206-398-4058 *lawadmis@seattleu.edu*	65	157	13	3.43	3124	845	365
Seton Hall University (School of Law) One Newark Center Newark, NJ 07102-5210 973-642-8747; Fax: 973-642-8876 *admitme@shu.edu*	82	160	44	3.36	3080	984	367
South Texas College of Law 1303 San Jacinto Street Houston, TX 77002-7000 713-646-1810; Fax: 713-646-2906 *admissions@stcl.edu*		153		3.21	2952	1086	453
Southern Illinois University (School of Law) Lesar Law Building, Mail Code 6804 Carbondale, IL 62901 618-453-8858; Fax: 618-453-8921 *lawadmit@siu.edu*	61	154	13	3.43	713	262	122
Southern Methodist University (Dedman School of Law) Office of Admissions, P.O. Box 750110 Dallas, TX 75275-0110 214-768-2550; Fax: 214-768-2549 *lawadmit@smu.edu*	87	162		3.73	3002	714	290
Southern University and A & M College (Law Center) Post Office Box 9294 Baton Rouge, LA 70813-9294 225-771-5340; Fax: 225-771-2121 *vwilkerson@sulc.edu*		146		2.8	1002	249	177
Southwestern University (School of Law) 675 South Westmoreland Avenue Los Angeles, CA 90005-3992 213-738-6717; Fax: 213-383-1688 *admissions@swlaw.edu*				3	3823	967	364
Stanford University (Stanford Law School) Crown Quadrangle, 559 Nathan Abbott Way Stanford, CA 94305-8610 650-723-4985; Fax: 650-723-0838 *admissions@law.stanford.edu*		169		3.87	4938	399	173
State University of New York (University at Buffalo Law School) 309 O'Brian Hall Buffalo, NY 14260 716-645-2907; Fax: 716-645-6676 *lwiley@buffalo.edu*	66	155	33	3.42	1544	560	247
Stetson University (Stetson University College of Law) 1401 61st Street South Gulfport, FL 33707 727-562-7802; Fax: 727-343-0136 *lawadmit@hermes.law.stetson.edu*		154		3.49	3600	839	345
Suffolk University (Law School) 120 Tremont Street Boston, MA 02108-4977 617-573-8144; Fax: 617-523-1367	73	157	61	3.3	3195		540
Syracuse University (College of Law) Office of Admissions and Financial Aid Syracuse, NY 13244-1030 315-443-1962; Fax: 315-443-9568	61	154		3.32	7265		266

LAW SCHOOL	ACADEMIC STATISTICS				ADMISSION STATISTICS		
	Median LSAT Percentile of Enrolled	Median LSAT Score of Enrolled	Lowest LSAT Percentile of Accepted	Median GPA (4.0 scale) of Enrolled	Total Applicants	Applicants Accepted	Applicants Enrolled
Temple University (James E. Beasley School of Law) 1719 N. Broad Street Philadelphia, PA 19122 215-204-5949; Fax: 215-204-1185 *lawadmis@temple.edu*	84	161	20	3.35	5243	1544	323
Texas Southern University (Thurgood Marshall School of Law) 3100 Cleburne Avenue Houston, TX 77004 713-313-7114; Fax: 713-313-1049 *cgardner@tsulaw.edu*		142		2.7	952	417	322
Texas Tech University (School of Law) 1802 Hartford Avenue Lubbock, TX 79409 806-742-3990, ext. 273; Fax: 806-742-4617 *donna.williams@ttu.edu*	61	154	13	3.5	1834	636	270
Texas Wesleyan University (School of Law) 1515 Commerce Street Fort Worth, TX 76102 817-212-4040; Fax: 817-212-4002 *lawadmissions@law.txwes.edu*	66	155		3.2	2373	932	365
Thomas Jefferson School of Law 2121 San Diego Avenue San Diego, CA 92110 619-297-9700; Fax: 619-294-4713 *adm@tjsl.edu*		150	20	3.02	3204	1166	288
Thomas M. Cooley Law School 300 South Capitol Avenue Lansing, MI 48901 517-371-5140; Fax: 517-334-5718 *admissions@cooley.edu*		146	138	2.95	4646	2829	1173
Touro College (Jacob D. Fuchsberg Law Center) 300 Nassau Road Huntington, NY 11743 631-421-2244 ext. 314; Fax: 631-421-9708 *lindab@tourolaw.edu*		149	15	3.04	2075	711	286
Tulane University (Law School) Weinmann Hall, 6329 Freret Street New Orleans, LA 70118 504-865-5930; Fax: 504-865-6710 *admissions@law.tulane.edu*	85	161	25	3.56	3651	1070	314
University of Akron (School of Law) 150 University Avenue Akron, OH 44325-2901 330-972-7331; Fax: 330-258-2343 *lfile@uakron.edu*	75	158		3.42	1964	642	183
University of Alabama (School of Law) Box 870382 Tuscaloosa, AL 35487-0382 205-348-5440; Fax: 205-348-3917 *admissions@law.ua.edu*	90	163		3.47	1071	283	157
University of Arizona (James E. Rogers College of Law) 120 E. Speedway P.O. Box 210176 Tucson, AZ 85721-0176 520-621-3477; Fax: 520-621-9140 *admissions@law.arizona.edu*	89	162		3.5	2589	455	153
University of Arkansas (School of Law) Robert A. Leflar Law Center, Waterman Hall Fayetteville, AR 72701 479-575-3102; Fax: 479-575-3937 *jkmiller@uark.edu*		155		3.41	1449	354	143
University of Arkansas at Little Rock (UALR William H. Bowen School of Law) 1201 McMath Avenue Little Rock, AR 72202-5142 501-324-9439; Fax: 501-324-9433 *lawadm@ualr.edu*	57	153	25	3.37	1077	233	143

LAW SCHOOL	ACADEMIC STATISTICS				ADMISSION STATISTICS		
	Median LSAT Percentile of Enrolled	Median LSAT Score of Enrolled	Lowest LSAT Percentile of Accepted	Median GPA (4.0 scale) of Enrolled	Total Applicants	Applicants Accepted	Applicants Enrolled
University of Baltimore (School of Law) 1420 North Charles Street Baltimore, MD 21201-5779 410-837-4459; Fax: 410-837-4450 *lwadmiss@ubmail.ubalt.edu;* *mkbell@ubalt.edu*	61	154	23	3.23	3094	841	325
University of California (Hastings College of the Law) 200 McAllister Street San Francisco, CA 94102 415-565-4623; Fax: 415-581-8946 *admiss@uchastings.edu*	88	163	23	3.5	6337	1470	419
University of California at Berkeley (School of Law) 215 Boalt Hall Berkeley, CA 94720 510-642-2274; Fax: 510-643-6222 *adissions@law.berkeley.edu*		169	35	3.83	7503	769	286
University of California at Davis (School of Law) Martin Luther King, Jr. Hall - 400 Mrak Hall Drive Davis, CA 95616-5201 530-752-6477 *lawadmissions@ucdavis.edu*	84	161	27	3.63	3768	877	194
University of California at Los Angeles (School of Law) P.O. Box 951445 Los Angeles, CA 90095-1445 310-825-2080; Fax: 310-825-9450 *admissions@law.ucla.edu*	95	166	46	3.68	7286	965	305
University of Chicago (Law School) 1111 East 60th Street Chicago, IL 60637 773-702-9484; Fax: 773-834-0942 *admissions@law.uchicago.edu*	97	169		3.62	3859	749	195
University of Cincinnati (College of Law) P.O. Box 210040 Cincinnati, OH 45221-0040 513-556-6805; Fax: 513-556-2391 *admissions@law.uc.edu*	82	160	13	3.66	1186	435	133
University of Colorado (School of Law) 403 UCB Boulder, CO 80309-0403 303-492-7203; Fax: 303-492-2542	88	162	37	3.66	2537	646	168
University of Connecticut (School of Law) 55 Elizabeth Street Hartford, CT 06105 860-570-5159; Fax: 860-570-5153 *admit@law.uconn.edu*	90	161		3.41	3472	637	200
University of Dayton (School of Law) 300 College Park Dayton, OH 45469-2760 937-229-3555; Fax: 937-229-4194 *lawinfo@notes.udayton.edu*	51	151	28	3.03	1685	775	183
University of Denver (Sturm College of Law) 2255 E. Evans Avenue Denver, CO 80208 303-871-6135; Fax: 303-871-6992 *khigganb@law.du.edu*	79	159	33	3.3	3386	862	350
University of Detroit Mercy (School of Law) 651 East Jefferson Avenue Detroit, MI 48226 313-596-0264; Fax: 313-596-0280 *udmlawao@udmercy.edu*	39	149	12	3.2	1234	527	233

LAW SCHOOL	ACADEMIC STATISTICS				ADMISSION STATISTICS		
	Median LSAT Percentile of Enrolled	Median LSAT Score of Enrolled	Lowest LSAT Percentile of Accepted	Median GPA (4.0 scale) of Enrolled	Total Applicants	Applicants Accepted	Applicants Enrolled
University of Florida (Endric G. Levin College of Law) 209 Bruton-Geer Hall P.O. Box 117622 Gainesville, FL 32611-7622 352-273-0890; Fax: 352-392-4087 *patrick@law.ufl.edu*		*161*		*3.67*	*2989*	*704*	*300*
University of Georgia (School of Law) Hirsch Hall, 225 Herty Drive Athens, GA 30602-6012 706-542-7060; Fax: 706-542-5556 *gkennedy@uga.edu*	*90*	*163*	*40*	*3.55*	*2754*	*599*	*210*
University of Hawaii at Manoa (William S. Richardson School of Law) 2515 Dole Street Honolulu, HI 96822 808-956-7966; Fax: 808-956-3813 *lawadm@hawaii.educ*	*74*	*158*	*23*	*3.43*	*1091*	*203*	*96*
University of Houston (Law Center) 100 Law Center Houston, TX 77204-6060 713-743-2280; Fax: 713-743-2194 *lawadmissions@uh.edu*	*81*	*160*	*20*	*3.49*	*3672*	*896*	*318*
University of Idaho (College of Law) P.O. Box 442321 Moscow, ID 83844-2321 208-885-2300; Fax: 208-885-5709 *sperez@uidaho.edu*	*69*	*156*	*18*	*3.39*	*946*	*270*	*105*
University of Illinois (College of Law) 504 East Pennsylvania Avenue Champaign, IL 61820 217-244-6415; Fax: 217-244-1478 *admissions@law.uiuc.edu*	*96*	*166*	*25*	*3.4*	*2993*	*446*	*188*
University of Iowa (College of Law) 320 Melrose Avenue Iowa City, IA 52242 319-335-9095; Fax: 319-335-9646 *law-admissions@uiowa.edu*	*84*	*161*	*41*	*3.59*	*1339*	*519*	*225*
University of Kansas (School of Law) 205 Green Hall Lawrence, KS 66045 785-864-4378; Fax: 785-864-5054 *cenglish@ku.edu*	*77*	*158*	*11*	*3.57*	*1200*	*303*	*157*
University of Kentucky (College of Law) 209 Law Building Lexington, KY 40506-0048 606-257-7938; Fax: (859) 323-1061 *dbakert@email.uky.edu*	*82*	*160*	*30*	*3.5*	*1208*	*419*	*172*
University of La Verne (College of Law) 320 East D Street Ontario, CA 91764 909-460-2001; Fax: 909-460-2082 *lawadm@ulv.edu*	*37*	*148*	*26*	*2.91*	*542*	*281*	*84*
University of Louisville (Louis D. Brandeis School of Law) University of Louisville Belknap Campus-Wilson W. Wyatt Hall Louisville, KY 40292 502-852-6364; Fax: 502-852-8971 *lawadmissions@louisville.edu*		*157*	*16*	*3.39*	*1237*	*379*	*137*
University of Maine (School of Law) 246 Deering Avenue Portland, ME 04102 207-780-4341; Fax: 207-780-4239 *mainelaw@usm.maine.edu*	*65*	*156*	*15*	*3.31*	*694*	*280*	*75*

LAW SCHOOL	ACADEMIC STATISTICS				ADMISSION STATISTICS		
	Median LSAT Percentile of Enrolled	Median LSAT Score of Enrolled	Lowest LSAT Percentile of Accepted	Median GPA (4.0 scale) of Enrolled	Total Applicants	Applicants Accepted	Applicants Enrolled
University of Maryland (School of Law) 500 West Baltimore Street Baltimore, MD 21201 410-706-3492; Fax: 410-706-1793 *admissions@law.umaryland.edu*	*84*	*161*	*23*	*3.54*	*4114*	*638*	*258*
University of Memphis (Cecil C. Humphreys School of Law) 207 Humphreys Law School Memphis, TN 38152-3140 901-678-5403; Fax: 901-678-5210 *lawadmissions@mail.law.memphis.edu*	*69*	*156*	*11*	*3.35*	*1208*	*286*	*141*
University of Miami (School of Law) P.O. Box 248087, 1311 Miller Drive Coral Gables, FL 33124-8087 305-284-2523 *admissions@law.miami.edu*	*73*	*157*	*26*	*3.42*	*5061*	*1811*	*413*
University of Michigan (Law School) 625 South State Street Ann Arbor, MI 48109-1215 734-764-0537; Fax: 734-647-3218 *law.jd.admissions@umich.edu*	*97*	*168*		*3.64*	*5771*	*1125*	*366*
University of Minnesota (Law School) 229 19th Avenue S. Minneapolis, MN 55455 612-625-3487; Fax: 612-626-1874	*90*	*164*		*3.54*	*3068*	*866*	*273*
University of Mississippi (L.Q.C. Lamar Hall) P.O. Box 1848 Lamar Law Center University, MS 38677 601-915-6910; Fax: 601-915-1289 *bvinson@olemiss.edu*	*66*	*155*	*9*	*3.51*	*1678*	*456*	*189*
University of Missouri-Columbia (School of Law) 103 Hulston Hall Columbia, MO 65211 573-882-6042; Fax: 573-882-9625 *CatheyA@missouri.edu*	*77*	*158*	*33*	*3.51*	*977*	*314*	*153*
University of Missouri-Kansas City (School of Law) 500 East 52nd Street Kansas City, MO 64110-2499 816-235-1644; Fax: 816-235-5276 *brooks@umkc.edu*	*62*	*154*	*37*	*3.42*	*1254*	*475*	*178*
University of Montana (School of Law) Missoula, MT 59812 406-243-2698; Fax: 406-243-2576 *heidi.fanslow@umontana.edu*	*60*	*154*	*9*	*3.41*	*458*	*172*	*85*
University of Nebraska (College of Law) P.O. Box 830902 Lincoln, NE 68583-0902 402-472-2161; Fax: 402-472-5185 *lawadm@unl.edu*	*69*	*156*	*13*	*3.65*	*865*	*352*	*136*
University of Nevada, Las Vegas (William S. Boyd School of Law) 4505 Maryland Parkway, Box 451003 Las Vegas, NV 89154-1003 702-895-2440; Fax: 702-895-2414 *request@law.unlv.edu*	*73*	*157*		*3.5*	*2456*	*317*	*151*
University of New Mexico (School of Law) MSCII-6070, University of New Mexico Albuquerque, NM 87131-0001 505-277-0958; Fax: 505-277-9958 *witherrington@law.unm.edu*	*66*	*155*		*3.44*	*1162*	*242*	*119*
University of North Carolina at Chapel Hill (School of Law) Campus Box 3380, Van Hecke-Wettach Hall Chapel Hill, NC 27599-3380 919-962-5109; Fax: 919-843-7939 *law_admission@unc.edu*	*100*	*161*	*24*	*3.71*	*3735*	*594*	*231*

LAW SCHOOL	ACADEMIC STATISTICS				ADMISSION STATISTICS		
	Median LSAT Percentile of Enrolled	Median LSAT Score of Enrolled	Lowest LSAT Percentile of Accepted	Median GPA (4.0 scale) of Enrolled	Total Applicants	Applicants Accepted	Applicants Enrolled
University of North Dakota (School of Law) Box 9003 Grand Forks, ND 58202 701-777-2104; Fax: 701-777-2217 *linda.kohoutek@thor.law.und.nodak.edu*		151		3.57	382	153	69
University of Notre Dame (Notre Dame Law School) P.O. Box 780 Notre Dame, IN 46556-0780 574-631-6626; Fax: 574-631-5474 *lawadmit@nd.edu*		165		3.54	3507	637	175
University of Oklahoma (College of Law) Andrew M. Coats Hall, 300 Timberdell Road Norman, OK 73019 405-325-4728; Fax: 405-325-0502 *kmadden@ou.edu*	73	157	62	3.51	1278	336	174
University of Oregon (School of Law, William W. Knight Law Center) 1515 Agate Street Eugene, OR 97403-1221 541-346-1553; Fax: 541-346-3984 *admissions@law.uoregon.edu*		157	17	3.5	1400	600	171
University of Pennsylvania (Law School) 3400 Chestnut Street Philadelphia, PA 19104-6204 215-898-7400 *admissions@law.upenn.edu*	93	169	50	3.68	6396	801	243
University of Pittsburgh (School of Law) 3900 Forbes Avenue Pittsburgh, PA 15260 412-648-1413; Fax: 412-648-1318 *Mccall@law.pitt.edu*		159		3.4	2349	671	243
University of Puerto Rico (School of Law) P.O. Box 23349, UPR Station Rio Piedras, PR 00931-3349 787-999-9551; Fax: 787-764-4360 *wandi_perez@hotmail.com*		147	4	3.5	739	217	192
University of Richmond (School Of Law) 28 Westhampton Way University of Richmond, VA 23173 804-289-8189; Fax: 804-287-6516 *lawadmissions@richmond.edu*	85	161	37	3.3	2203	581	171
University of Saint Thomas (School of Law) 1000 LaSalle Ave. Minneapolis, MN 55403 651-962-4895; Fax: 651-962-4876 *lawschool@stthomas.edu*	68	154	19	3.27	1039	469	148
University of San Diego (School of Law) 5998 Alcala Park San Diego, CA 92110 619-260-4528; Fax: 619-260-2218 *jdinfo@sandiego.edu*	87	162		3.34	5343		365
University of San Francisco (School of Law) 2130 Fulton Street San Francisco, CA 94117-1080 415-422-6586; Fax: 415-422-6433 *lawschool@usfca.edu*	79	159		3.34	4154	1265	259
University of South Carolina (School of Law) 701 South Main Street Columbia, SC 29208 803-777-6605; Fax: 803-777-7751 *usclaw@law.law.sc.edu*		157		3.38	1505	484	240

LAW SCHOOL	ACADEMIC STATISTICS				ADMISSION STATISTICS		
	Median LSAT Percentile of Enrolled	Median LSAT Score of Enrolled	Lowest LSAT Percentile of Accepted	Median GPA (4.0 scale) of Enrolled	Total Applicants	Applicants Accepted	Applicants Enrolled
University of South Dakota (School of Law) 414 East Clark Street Vermillion, SD 57069-2390 605-677-5443; Fax: 605-677-5417 *lawreq@usd.edu*	57	153	8	3.31	519	181	89
University of Southern California (Gould School of Law) Los Angeles, CA 90089-0074 213-740-2523	95	166		3.65	7075	1438	207
University of Tennessee (College of Law) 1505 W. Cumberland Avenue Knoxville, TN 37996-1810 865-974-4131; Fax: 865-974-1572 *lawadmit@libra.law.utk.edu*	82	160	15	3.63	1622	322	158
University of Texas at Austin (School of Law) 727 East Dean Keeton Street Austin, TX 78705 512-232-1200; Fax: 512-471-2765 *admissions@mail.law.utexas.edu*	94	166	35	3.63	5442	992	442
University of the District of Columbia (David A. Clarke School of Law) 4200 Connecticut Avenue, N.W. Washington, DC 20008 202-274-7341; Fax: 202-274-5583 *vcanty@udc.edu; law addmission@udc.edu*	43	151	23	3	1373	320	82
University of the Pacific (McGeorge School of Law) 3200 Fifth Avenue Sacramento, CA 95817 916-739-7105; Fax: 916-739-7134 *admissionsmcgeorge@uop.edu*	70	156		3.15	2672	960	409
University of Toledo (College of Law) 2801 West Bancroft Street Toledo, OH 43606-3390 419-530-4131; Fax: 419-530-4345 *law.utoledo.edu*	78	157	45	3.61	1500	342	174
University of Tulsa (College of Law) 3120 East Fourth Place Tulsa, OK 74104-2499 918-631-2406; Fax: 918-631-3630 *george-justice@utulsa.edu*	57	153	34	3.18	1596	541	208
University of Utah (S.J. Quinney College of Law) 332 South 1400 East Room 101 Salt Lake City, UT 84112 801-581-7479; Fax: 801-581-6897 *aguilarr@law.utah.edu*	83	160	18	3.67	1176	360	127
University of Virginia (School of Law) 580 Massie Road Charlottesville, VA 22903-1789 434-924-7351; Fax: 434-982-2128 *lawadmit@virginia.edu*	97	169	35	3.67	5495	1111	374
University of Washington (School of Law) 1100 Northeast Campus Parkway Seattle, WA 98105-6617 206-543-4078 *admissions@law.washington.edu*	88	162	138	3.62	1954	468	177
University of Wisconsin (Law School) 975 Bascom Mall Madison, WI 53706 608-262-5914; Fax: 608-262-5485 *admissions@law.wisc.edu*	85	161	11	3.57	3202	743	271
University of Wyoming (College of Law) Dept. 3035, 1000 East University Avenue Laramie, WY 82071 307-766-6416; Fax: 307-766-6417 *dbourke@uwyo.edu*	58	153	16	3.33	715	188	79

LAW SCHOOL	ACADEMIC STATISTICS				ADMISSION STATISTICS		
	Median LSAT Percentile of Enrolled	Median LSAT Score of Enrolled	Lowest LSAT Percentile of Accepted	Median GPA (4.0 scale) of Enrolled	Total Applicants	Applicants Accepted	Applicants Enrolled
Valparaiso University (School of Law) Wesemann Hall, 656 S. Greenwich Street Valparaiso, IN 46383-6493 219-465-7829; Fax: 219-465-7808 *tony.credit@valpo.edu*	*52*	*153*	*17*	*3.3*	*3225*	*682*	*199*
Vanderbilt University (Law School) 131 21st Avenue South Nashville, TN 37203 615-322-6452; Fax: 615-322-1531 *admissions@law.vanderbilt.edu*	*93*	*165*		*3.69*	*3437*	*791*	*200*
Vermont Law School P.O. Box 96, Chelsea Street South Royalton, VT 05068-0096 802-831-1239; Fax: 802-763-7071 *admiss@vermontlaw.edu*	*62*	*154*		*3.12*	*1116*	*565*	*196*
Villanova University (School of Law) Garey Hall Villanova, PA 19085 610-519-7010; Fax: 610-519-6291 *admissions@law.villanova.edu*	*80*	*162*	*57*	*3.51*	*2991*	*945*	*245*
Wake Forest University (School of Law) P.O. Box 7206, Reynolda Station Winston-Salem, NC 27109 336-758-5437; Fax: 336-758-4632 *admissions@law.wfu.edu*	*91*	*164*	*28*	*3.44*	*2418*	*571*	*154*
Washburn University (School of Law) 1700 College Topeka, KS 66621 785-670-1185; Fax: 785-670-1120 *admissions@washburnlaw.edu*		*153*		*3.34*	*1105*	*397*	*152*
Washington and Lee University (School of Law) Lewis Hall Lexington, VA 24450 540-458-8503; Fax: 540-458-8586 *lawadm@wlu.edu*	*94*	*166*	*49*	*3.57*	*4007*	*847*	*136*
Washington University in St. Louis (School of Law) Box 1120, One Brookings Drive St. Louis, MO 63130 314-935-4525; Fax: 314-935-8778 *admiss@wulaw.wustl.edu*		*166*	*50*	*3.6*	*3770*	*954*	*222*
Wayne State University (Law School) 471 W. Palmer Detroit, MI 48202 313-577-3937; Fax: 313-577-6000 *linda.sims@wayne.edu*	*64*	*154*	*20*	*3.33*	*1049*	*531*	*250*
West Virginia University (College of Law) P.O. Box 6130 Morgantown, WV 26506 304-293-5304; Fax: 304-293-6891 *wvulaw.Admissions@mail.wvu.edu*	*81*	*151*	*9*	*3.51*	*831*	*326*	*152*
Western New England College (School of Law) 1215 Wilbraham Road Springfield, MA 01119 413-782-1406; Fax: 413-796-2067 *lawadmis@wnec.edu*	*62*	*154*	*32*	*3.05*	*1849*	*795*	*192*
Western State University (College of Law) 1111 North State College Blvd Fullerton, CA 92831 714-459-1101; Fax: 714-441-1748 *adm@wsulaw.edu*	*16*	*149*	*3*	*3.06*	*1005*	*378*	*155*

LAW SCHOOL	ACADEMIC STATISTICS				ADMISSION STATISTICS		
	Median LSAT Percentile of Enrolled	Median LSAT Score of Enrolled	Lowest LSAT Percentile of Accepted	Median GPA (4.0 scale) of Enrolled	Total Applicants	Applicants Accepted	Applicants Enrolled
Whittier College (Whittier Law School) 3333 Harbor Blvd. Costa Mesa, CA 92626 714-444-4141, ext. 121; Fax: 714-444-0250 *info@law.whittier.edu*	*61*	*154*	*23*	*3.1*	*3144*	*982*	*273*
Widener University (Widener University School of Law) 3800 Vartan Way, P.O. Box 69381 Harrisburg, PA 17106-9381 717-541-3903; Fax: 717-541-3999 *law.admissions@law.widener.edu*	*49*	*151*	*11*	*3.11*	*1173*	*446*	*190*
Widener University (Widener University School of Law) 4601 Concord Pike, P.O. Box 7474 Wilmington, DE 19803-0474 302-477-2162; Fax: 302-477-2224 *law.admissions@law.widener.edu*	*53*	*152*	*17*	*3.14*	*2761*	*924*	*360*
Willamette University (College of Law) 245 Winter Street S.E. Salem, OR 97301 503-370-6282; Fax: 503-370-6087 *law-admission@willamette.edu*	*65*	*155*		*3.42*	*1554*	*546*	*145*
William Mitchell College of Law (William Mitchelle College of Law) 875 Summit Avenue St. Paul, MN 55105-3076 651-290-6476; Fax: 651-290-6414 *admissions@wmitchell.edu*		*153*		*3.39*	*1591*	*835*	*375*
Yale University (Yale Law School) P.O. Box 208329 New Haven, CT 06520-8329 203-432-4995 *admissions.law@yale.edu*	*99*	*172*	*80*	*3.89*	*3778*	*235*	*199*
Yeshiva University (Benjamin N. Cardozo School of Law) 55 Fifth Avenue New York, NY 10003 212-790-0274; Fax: 212-790-0482 *lawinfo@yu.edu*	*91*	*164*		*3.5*	*5212*	*1308*	*364*